# SCHAUM'S
# OUTLINE OF

# BEGINNING
# FINITE
# MATHEMATICS

SCHAUM'S
OUTLINE OF

# Theory and Problems of
# BEGINNING
# FINITE
# MATHEMATICS

**SEYMOUR LIPSCHUTZ, Ph.D.**
*Professor of Mathematics*
*Temple University*

**JOHN J. SCHILLER, Ph.D.**
*Associate Professor of Mathematics*
*Temple University*

**R. ALU SRINIVASAN, Ph.D.**
*Professor of Mathematics*
*Temple University*

**Schaum's Outline Series**

**McGRAW-HILL**
New York    Chicago    San Fransisco    Lisbon
London    Madrid    Mexico City    Milan    New Delhi
San Juan    Seoul    Singapore    Sydney    Toronto

**SEYMOUR LIPSCHUTZ** is a Professor of Mathematics at Temple University. He formerly taught at Polytechnic Institute of Brooklyn and was a visiting professor at the Computer Science Department of Brooklyn College. He received his Ph.D. in 1960 from the Courant Institute of Mathematical Sciences of New York University. Some of his other books are *Schaum's Outline of Discrete Mathematics*, 2nd ed.; *Schaum's Outline of Probability*; and *Schaum's Outline of Linear Algebra*, 3rd ed.

**JOHN J. SCHILLER** is an Associate Professor of Mathematics at Temple University. He received his Ph.D. from the University of Pennsylvania and has published research papers in the areas of Riemann surfaces, discrete mathematics, and mathematical biology. He has coauthored texts in precalculus and calculus, and the *Schaum's Outline of Finite Mathematics* and *Schaum's Outline of Probability and Statistics,* 2nd ed.

**R. ALU SRINIVASAN** is a Professor of Mathematics at Temple University. He received his Ph.D. from Wayne State University and has published extensively in probability and statistics. He is also a coauthor of *Schaum's Outline of Probability and Statistics*, 2nd ed.

Schaum's Outline of Theory and Problems of
BEGINNING FINITE MATHEMATICS

1  2  3  4  5  6  7  8  9  10  11  12  13  14  15  16  VFM  VFM  0  9  8  7  6  5  4

ISBN 0-07-138897-4

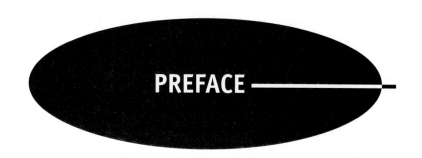

# PREFACE

Since the pioneering text *Introduction to Finite Mathematics*, by Kemeny, Snell, and Thompson appeared in 1957, finite mathematics has established deep roots in the undergraduate mathematics curriculum. In fact, courses in finite mathematics are offered by most colleges and universities, and hundreds of texts on the subject have been written. Over the years, the emphasis in some of the standard material has shifted, and new topics have been added. A major change from classical to modern applied topics occurred with the introduction of the text *For All Practical Purposes* in 1988. FAPP included such topics as Euler and Hamiltonian circuits, planning and scheduling, voting systems, fair division and apportionment, and statistical inference. Clones of FAPP soon appeared, and for a time two distinct types of texts – classical and modern – were in use. In our experience, students with relatively strong math backgrounds felt more comfortable with the classical, more formal, texts, and those with weaker backgrounds have preferred the modern, less formal, approach. Also, many instructors have shown strong preferences for one type of text over the other. Recently, texts have appeared that blend the classical and modern topics, and this type now seems to be the trend. Our book, *Beginning Finite Mathematics*, follows this trend Major topics covered include linear and exponential growth (including financial mathematics), probability, descriptive and inferential statistics, graphs and networks, voting systems, geometry, and linear programming. The coverage of geometry varies considerably in today's texts, but since many students now entering college do not have a firm grasp of basic notions regarding shape and measurement, due in large part to a de-emphasis of classical Euclidean geometry in the schools, we develop geometric topics in a traditional manner, emphasizing moderately rigorous proofs along with straight-edge and compass constructions.

The positive qualities that distinguish Schaum's Outline Series have been incorporated in *Beginning Finite Mathematics*. Each chapter begins with a clear statement of pertinent definitions, principles, and theorems, together with illustrative and other descriptive material. This is followed by graded sets of solved and supplementary problems. The solved problems serve to illustrate and amplify the theory, bring into sharp focus the fine points whose understanding is needed to build confidence, and provide the emphasis on basic principles vital to effective learning. Proofs of theorems and derivations of basic results are included among the solved problems. The supplementary problems serve as a complete review of the material in each chapter.

More material has been included than can be covered in most first courses. This has been done to make the book more flexible, to provide a more useful book of reference, and to stimulate further interest in the topics.

We wish to thank Maureen Walker of McGraw Hill for her considerable help at every stage in preparing this *Schaum's Outline*.

*Use of Calculators and Computer Software.* The computations in the text can be done with a basic scientific or business calculator, along with the help of Appendix A. More computing power can be had with a graphing calculator, which, in addition to having graphing capability, can do combinatorial, statistical, and financial computations. Also, it can be programmed to carry out specialized instructions. Of course, there are quite a few computer software packages that can also be used. In particular, *Geometer's Sketchpad* is ideal for use in the Chapter 11.

SEYMOUR LIPSCHUTZ
JOHN J. SCHILLER
R. ALU SRINIVASAN

# CONTENTS

# CHAPTER 1

# Linear Equations and Linear Growth

## 1.1 INTRODUCTION; REAL LINE R

This chapter will mainly investigate the notion of linear growth, which is closely related to linear equations in two unknowns. (Such equations are pictured as lines in the plane.) We begin with a review of the real number system **R**, the Cartesian plane $\mathbf{R}^2$, and linear equations in one unknown.

### Real Line R

The notation **R** will be used to denote the real numbers. These are the numbers one uses in basic algebra, and unless otherwise stated or implied, all our numbers (constants) will be real numbers.

The real numbers include the *integers* (signed whole numbers), such as 5, 21, and $-12$, and the *rational numbers*, which are ratios of integers, such as $\frac{2}{3}$ and $-\frac{3}{4}$. Those real numbers that are not rational numbers, such as $\pi$ and $\sqrt{2}$, i.e., real numbers that cannot be represented as ratios of integers, are called *irrational numbers*. The integer 0 is also a real number. Furthermore, for each positive real number, there is a corresponding negative real number.

One of the most important properties of the real numbers is that they can be represented graphically by the points on a straight line. Specifically, as shown in Fig. 1-1, a point, called the *origin*, is chosen to represent 0, and another point, usually to the right of 0, is chosen to represent 1. The direction from 0 to 1 is the *positive direction* and is usually indicated by an arrowhead at the end of the line. The distance between 0 and 1 is the *unit length*. Now there is a natural way to pair off the points on the line and the real numbers, that is, where each point on the line corresponds to a unique real number and vice versa. The positive numbers are those to the right of 0 (on the same side as 1), and the negative numbers are to the left of 0. The points representing the rational numbers $\frac{5}{4}$ and $-\frac{3}{2}$ are indicated in Fig. 1-1. We refer to such a line as the *real line* or the *real line* **R**.

Real numbers can also be represented by *decimals*. The decimal expansion of a rational number will either stop, as in $\frac{3}{4} = 0.75$, or will have a pattern that repeats indefinitely, such as $\frac{17}{11} = 1.545454\ldots$. The decimal expansion of an irrational number never stops nor does it have a repeating pattern. The points representing the decimals 2.5 and 4.75 are indicated in Fig. 1-1.

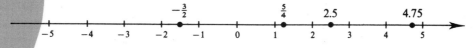

**Fig. 1-1**   Real line **R**.

1

## Inequalities

The relation *a is less than b*, written $a < b$, may be described geometrically as $a$ is to the left of $b$ on the real line **R**. (See Fig. 1-2.)   Algebraically, $a < b$ whenever $b - a$ is positive.   The following notation is also used:

$$a > b, \text{ read } a \text{ is greater than } b, \text{ means } b < a$$
$$a \le b, \text{ read } a \text{ is less than or equal to } b, \text{ means } a < b \text{ or } a = b$$
$$a \ge b, \text{ read } a \text{ is greater than or equal to } b, \text{ means } b \le a$$

We refer to the relations $<$, $>$, $\le$, and $\ge$ as inequalities.

**Fig. 1-2**   $a < b$.

We note that $a > 0$ or $a < 0$ according as $a$ is positive or $a$ is negative.   Also, for any nonzero $a$, its square $a^2$ is always positive.

## EXAMPLE 1.1

(a)   $5 < 9$,  $-6 < 2$,  $2 \le 2$,  $3 > -8$,  $-4 < 0$.

(b)   Sorting the numbers $4, -7, 9, -2, 6, 0, -11, 3, 10, -1, -5$ in increasing order, we obtain:

$$-11, -7, -5, -2, -1, 0, 3, 4, 6, 9, 10$$

(c)   The notation $2 < x < 5$ means $2 < x$ and $x < 5$; hence, $x$ will lie between 2 and 5 on the real line.

## Absolute Value, Distance

The *absolute value* of a real number $a$, denoted by $|a|$, may be described geometrically as the distance between $a$ and the origin 0 on the real line **R**.   Algebraically, $|a| = a$ or $-a$ according as $a$ is positive or negative, and $|0| = 0$.   Thus, $|a|$ is always positive when $a \ne 0$.   Intuitively, $|a|$ may be viewed as the magnitude of $a$ without regard to sign.

The *distance d* between two points (real numbers) $a$ and $b$ is denoted and obtained from the formula

$$d = d(a, b) = |a - b| = |b - a|$$

Alternatively:

$$d = \begin{cases} |a| + |b| & \text{if } a \text{ and } b \text{ have different signs} \\ |a| - |b| & \text{if } a \text{ and } b \text{ have the same sign and } |a| \ge |b| \end{cases}$$

That is:

(a)   If $a$ and $b$ are on different sides of the origin (different signs), then add their "numerical parts."   For example:

$$d(2, -5) = 7, \quad d(-3, 5) = 8, \quad d(6, -1) = 7, \quad d(-3, 2) = 5$$

(b)   If $a$ and $b$ are on the same sides of the origin (same signs), then subtract their "numerical parts."   For example:

$$d(2, 5) = 3, \quad d(-3, -5) = 2, \quad d(-6, -1) = 5, \quad d(3, 2) = 1$$

(Here "numerical part" of a number means its distance to the origin or, equivalently, its absolute value.)    These two cases are pictured in Fig. 1-3.

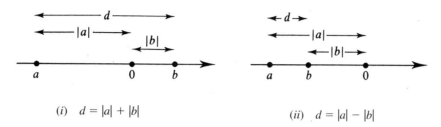

$(i)\quad d = |a| + |b|$ $(ii)\quad d = |a| - |b|$

**Fig. 1-3**

## EXAMPLE 1.2

(a)    $|15| = 15,\quad |-8| = 8,\quad |3.25| = 3.25,\quad |0| = 0,\quad |-0.75| = 0.75.$

(b)    Using Fig. 1-3,    $d(-3, 8) = 3 + 8 = 11,\quad d(4, 6) = 6 - 4 = 2,\quad d(5, -9) = 5 + 9 = 14.$

## 1.2   CARTESIAN PLANE $\mathbf{R}^2$

The notation $\mathbf{R}^2$ is used to denote the collection of all ordered pairs $(a, b)$ of real numbers.    [By definition, $(a, b) = (c, d)$ if and only if $a = c$ and $b = d$.] Just as we can identify $\mathbf{R}$ with points on the line, so can we identify $\mathbf{R}^2$ with points in the plane.    This identification, discussed below, was initiated by the French mathematician René Descartes (1596–1650); hence, such an identification is called the *cartesian plane* or *coordinate plane* or simply the *plane* $\mathbf{R}^2$.

Two perpendicular lines $L_1$ and $L_2$ are chosen in the plane; the first line $L_1$ is pictured horizontally and the second line $L_2$ is pictured vertically.    The point of intersection of the lines is called the *origin* and is denoted by 0.    These lines, called *axes*, are now viewed as number lines each with zero at the common origin and with the positive direction to the right on $L_1$ and upward on $L_2$.    Also, $L_1$ is usually called the *x axis* and $L_2$ the *y axis*.    [See Fig. 1-4(a)].    Normally, we choose the same unit length on both axes, but this is not an absolute requirement.

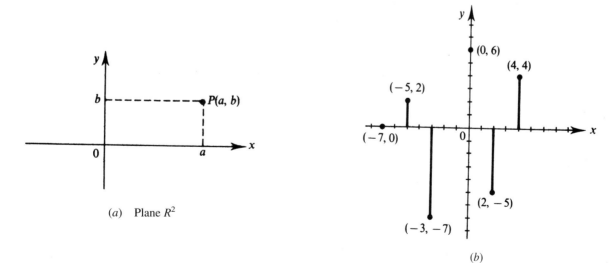

(a)   Plane $R^2$

(b)

**Fig. 1-4**

Now each point $P$ in the plane corresponds to a pair of real numbers $(a, b)$, called the *coordinates of P*, as pictured in Fig. 1-4($a$), that is, where the vertical line through $P$ intersects the $x$ axis at $a$ and where the horizontal line through $P$ intersects the $y$ axis at $b$.  [We will frequently write $P(a, b)$ when we want to indicate a point $P$ and its coordinates $a$ and $b$.] Note that this correspondence is one-to-one, i.e., each point $P$ corresponds to a unique ordered pair $(a, b)$, and vice versa.  Thus, in this context, the terms point and ordered pair of real numbers are used interchangeably.

**EXAMPLE 1.3**   Locate the following points in the plane $\mathbf{R}^2$: $(2, -5)$, $(-5, 2)$, $(-3, -7)$ $(4, 4)$, $(0, 6)$, $(-7, 0)$.

To locate the point $(x, y)$, start at the origin, go $x$ directed units along the $x$ axis and then $y$ directed units parallel to the $y$ axis.  The endpoint has the coordinates $(x, y)$, as pictured in Fig. 1-4($b$).

### Quadrants

The two axes partition the plane into four regions, called *quadrants* and usually numbered using the Roman numerals I, II, III, and IV, as pictured in Fig. 1-5.  That is:

Quadrant I:   Both coordinates are positive, $(+, +)$.

Quadrant II:   First coordinate negative, second positive $(-, +)$.

Quadrant III:   Both coordinates are negative, $(-, -)$.

Quadrant IV:   First coordinate positive, second negative, $(+, -)$.

Thus, the quadrants are numbered counterclockwise from the upper right-hand position.

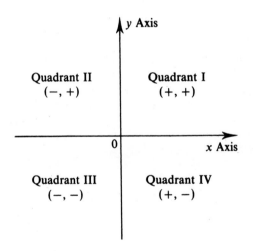

**Fig. 1-5**   Quadrants.

### Distance between Points; Midpoint

Suppose $P(x_1, y_1)$ and $Q(x_2, y_2)$ are two points in the plane $\mathbf{R}^2$.  The distance $d$ between $P$ and $Q$, denoted by $d(P, Q)$ or $|PQ|$, is given by the formula

$$d = d(P, Q) = \sqrt{(x_2 - x_1)^2 + (y_2 - y_1)^2} = \sqrt{d_x^2 + d_y^2} \tag{1.1}$$

where
$d_x^2 = (x_2 - x_1)^2 = |x_2 - x_1|^2$ is the distance between the $x$ values squared
$d_y^2 = (y_2 - y_1)^2 = |y_2 - y_1|^2$ is the distance between the $y$ values squared
This formula for $d$ is obtained using the Pythagorean theorem, as pictured in Fig. 1-6($a$).

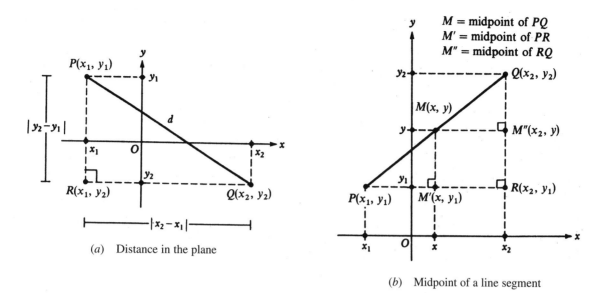

(a)   Distance in the plane

(b)   Midpoint of a line segment

**Fig. 1-6**

The midpoint $M=M(x, y)$ of the line segment joining $P(x_1, y_1)$ and $Q(x_2, y_2)$ is given by

$$M = M\left(\frac{x_1 + x_2}{2}, \frac{y_1 + y_2}{2}\right) \qquad (1.2)$$

Note that the two coordinates of $M$ are the average of the $x$ values and the average of the $y$ values, respectively.   [See Fig. 1-6($b$).]

**EXAMPLE 1.4**   Find the distance $d$ and midpoint $M$ between the points:

$\qquad$ ($a$)   $A(2, -5)$ and $B(8, 3)$, $\qquad$ ($b$)   $A(6, 1)$ and $B(-4, -8)$.

Use formulas ($1.1$) and ($1.2$) to obtain

($a$)   $d = \sqrt{36 + 64} = \sqrt{100} = 10$ and $M = (\frac{10}{2}, \frac{-2}{2}) = (5, -1)$.

($b$)   $d = \sqrt{100 + 81} = \sqrt{181} \approx 13.5$ and $M = (\frac{2}{2}, \frac{-7}{2}) = (1, -3.5)$

## 1.3   LINEAR EQUATIONS IN ONE UNKNOWN

A linear equation in one unknown $x$ can always be expressed in the *standard form* $ax = b$, where $a$ and $b$ are constants.   If $a \neq 0$, this equation has the unique solution

$$x = \frac{b}{a} \qquad (1.3)$$

**EXAMPLE 1.5**   Consider the equations   ($a$) $5x = 10$,   ($b$) $2x = -5$,   ($c$) $4x = 15$.

The solutions are as follows:   ($a$) $x = \frac{10}{5} = 2$,   ($b$) $x = \frac{-5}{2} = -2.5$,   ($c$) $x = \frac{15}{4} = 3.75$.

**Remark:**   The equation $ax = b$ is said to be *degenerate* when $a = 0$.   There are two cases:

($i$)   Suppose $a = 0$ but $b \neq 0$.   Then $0x = b$ has no solution.
($ii$)   Suppose $a = 0$ and $b = 0$.   Then every number is a solution to $0x = 0$.

Thus, generally, $ax = b$ has a unique solution, no solution, or an infinite number of solutions.

## 1.4   LINEAR EQUATIONS IN TWO UNKNOWNS AND THEIR GRAPHS

A linear equation in two unknowns, $x$ and $y$, can be put in the *standard form*

$$Ax + By = C \qquad\qquad (1.4)$$

where $A$, $B$, and $C$ are real numbers. We also assume that the equation is *nondegenerate*, that is, that $A$ and $B$ are not both zero. A *solution* of the equation consists of a pair of numbers $(x_1, y_1)$ which satisfies the equation, that is, such that

$$Ax_1 + By_1 = C$$

Solutions of the equation can be found by assigning arbitrary values to $x$ and solving for $y$ (or vice versa).

**EXAMPLE 1.6**   Consider the equation

$$2x + y = 4$$

If we substitute $x = -2$ in the equation, we obtain

$$2(-2) + y = 4 \qquad \text{or} \qquad -4 + y = 4 \qquad \text{or} \qquad y = 8$$

Hence, $(-2, 8)$ is a solution. If we substitute $x = 3$ in the equation, we obtain

$$2(3) + y = 4 \qquad \text{or} \qquad 6 + y = 4 \qquad \text{or} \qquad y = -2$$

Hence, $(3, -2)$ is a solution. The following table lists six possible values for $x$ and the corresponding values for $y$.

| $x$ | $-2$ | $-1$ | $0$ | $1$ | $2$ | $3$ |
|-----|------|------|-----|-----|-----|-----|
| $y$ | $8$ | $6$ | $4$ | $2$ | $0$ | $-2$ |

That is, the above table gives six solutions of the equation.

### Graph of a Linear Equation; Intercepts

The *graph* of the linear equation $Ax + By = C$ consists of all points $(x, y)$ in the plane $\mathbf{R}^2$ which satisfy the equation. This graph is a straight line when $A$ and $B$ are not both zero; hence, the name *linear equation*. [This fact is indicated by Fig. 1-7(a), which shows a straight line containing the six solutions of $2x + y = 4$ appearing in Example 1.6.]

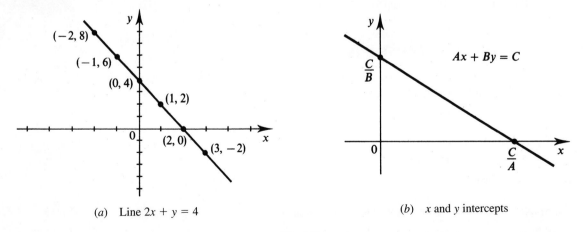

(a)   Line $2x + y = 4$                  (b)   $x$ and $y$ intercepts

**Fig. 1-7**

The *x intercept* and the *y intercept* of the linear equation $Ax + By = C$ are the points at which its graph crosses the $x$ axis and $y$ axis, respectively. Alternatively, the $x$ intercept is the $x$ value when $y = 0$, and the $y$

intercept is the $y$ value when $x = 0$. Thus, $x = C/A$ is the $x$ intercept when $A \neq 0$, and $y = C/B$ is its $y$ intercept when $B \neq 0$. [See Fig. 1-7($b$).]

Since two points determine a straight line, we can obtain the graph of Eq. (*1.4*) by first plotting *any* two points that satisfy the equation and then drawing the line through these points. In particular, if $A \neq 0$, we usually plot the $x$ intercept, and if $B \neq 0$, we usually plot the $y$ intercept.

**EXAMPLE 1.7**   Find the graph of the following lines:

$$(a)\quad 2x + 3y = 12; \qquad (b)\quad 4x - 5y = 10; \qquad (c)\quad x = 3; \qquad (d)\quad y = -1$$

The graphs appear in Fig. 1-8, which also shows the two points used to obtain each graph.

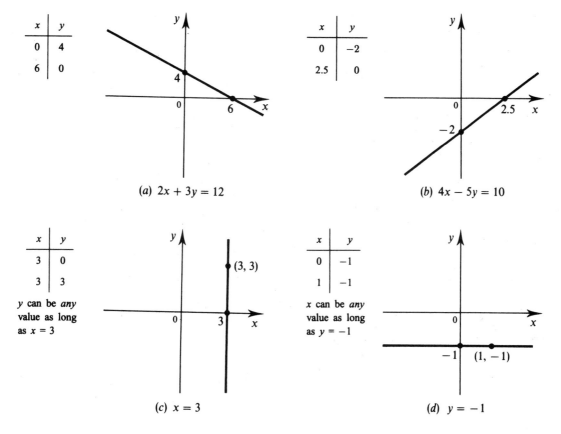

Fig. 1-8

## Horizontal and Vertical Lines

The graph of $x = a$, for any constant $a$, is a vertical line with $x$ intercept $a$; and the graph of $y = b$, for any constant $b$, is a horizontal line with $y$ intercept $b$. This fact is illustrated in Fig. 1-8($c$) for the equation $x = 3$ and Fig. 1-8($d$) for the equation $y = -1$.

## 1.5   SLOPE OF A LINE

Suppose $P_1(x_1, y_1)$ and $P_2(x_2, y_2)$ are any two points on a nonvertical line $L$ in the plane $\mathbf{R}^2$. [See Fig. 1-9($a$).] The *slope m* of the line is defined as the ratio of the change in $y$ to the change in $x$, that is,

$$m = \frac{\text{Change in } y}{\text{Change in } x} = \frac{y_2 - y_1}{x_2 - x_1} \qquad (x_2 \neq x_1) \tag{1.5}$$

The slope of a vertical line, i.e., a line for which $x_2 = x_1$, is not defined.  One can easily show by geometry that the slope does not depend on the particular two points $P_1$ and $P_2$ that are chosen.

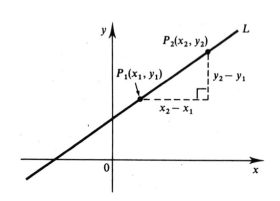

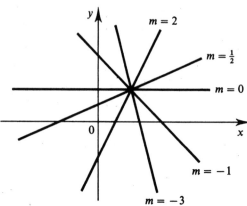

(a)   $P_1$ and $P_2$ are any two points on $L$.          (b)   Slope measures steepness and direction.

**Fig. 1-9**

The slope measures the steepness and the direction of a line.  Specifically, as shown in Fig. 1-9(b), lines with positive slope rise (from left to right), lines with negative slope fall (from left to right), and lines with zero slope are horizontal.  Also, the larger the magnitude (absolute value) of the slope, the steeper is the line.

**EXAMPLE 1.8**   Find, if possible, the slope m of the line through the points $P$ and $Q$ where:

   (a)   $P(0, 1)$, $Q(2, 5)$;     (b)   $P(-2, 3)$, $Q(5, 3)$;     (c)   $P(4, -1)$, $Q(4, 6)$;     (d)   $P(4, -1)$, $Q(1, 1)$

Use formula ($1.5$) to obtain

(a)   $m = \dfrac{5 - 1}{2 - 0} = 2,$          (c)   $m = \dfrac{6 - (-1)}{4 - 4} = \dfrac{7}{0}$, which is undefined,

(b)   $m = \dfrac{3 - 3}{5 - (-2)} = 0,$          (d)   $m = \dfrac{1 - (-1)}{1 - 4} = -\dfrac{2}{3}.$

## PARALLEL AND PERPENDICULAR LINES

Slopes also tell us when two nonvertical lines are parallel or perpendicular.  Specifically, suppose lines $L_1$ and $L_2$ have slopes $m_1$ and $m_2$, respectively.  Then

   (i)    If the slopes are equal, i.e., if $m_2 = m_1$, then $L_2$ is parallel to $L_1$.  [See Fig. 1–10(a).]
   (ii)   If one slope is the negative reciprocal of the other, i.e., if $m_2 = -1/m_1$ (or $m_1 m_2 = -1$), then $L_2$ is perpendicular to $L_1$.  [See Fig. 1–10(b).]

Otherwise, the lines are neither parallel nor perpendicular.

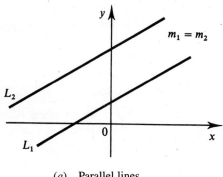

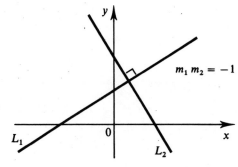

(a)   Parallel lines                    (b)   Perpendicular lines

**Fig. 1-10**

**EXAMPLE 1.9**  Suppose distinct lines $L_1, L_2, L_3, L_4, L_5,$ and $L_6$ have, respectively, the following slopes:

$$m_1 = \tfrac{2}{3} \qquad m_2 = -4 \qquad m_3 = -\tfrac{2}{3} \qquad m_4 = \tfrac{1}{4} \qquad m_5 = -\tfrac{3}{2} \qquad m_6 = -4$$

Since $m_6 = m_2$, lines $L_2$ and $L_6$ are parallel.  Since $m_5 = -1/m_1$, $L_5$ is perpendicular to $L_1$.  Similarly, $L_4$ is perpendicular to both $L_2$ and $L_6$.  Line $L_3$ is neither parallel nor perpendicular to any of the other lines.

**Remark:**  Suppose line $L$ is given by an equation $Ax + By = C$, which is in standard form.  The collection of all lines parallel to $L$ can be represented by the equation

$$Ax + By = k \tag{1.6}$$

where $k$ is any real number except $C$; that is, every value for $k$ determines a line parallel to $L$ and every line parallel to $L$ is of the above form for some $k$.  (We call $k$ a *parameter*.)  Similarly, the collection of all lines perpendicular to $L$ can be represented by the equation

$$Bx - Ay = k \qquad \text{or} \qquad -Bx + Ay = k \tag{1.7}$$

Again, $k$ is a parameter.  (See Problem 1.21.)

## 1.6  LINEAR FUNCTIONS AND LINEAR GROWTH

A variable $y$ is said to be a *linear function* of a variable $x$ when $x$ and $y$ are related by an equation of the form

$$y = mx + b \tag{1.8}$$

where $m$ and $b$ are constants.  In such a case, $x$ is called an *independent variable* and $y$ is called the *dependent variable*.

The equation (1-8) is a linear equation in the two unknowns $x$ and $y$; hence, it can be represented by a line $L$ in the plane $\mathbf{R}^2$.  The coefficient $m$ of $x$ in $(1-8)$ turns out to be the slope of the line $L$ (Problem 1.20), and the constant $b$ in (1-8) is the $y$ intercept of the line $L$ since it is the value of $y$ when $x = 0$.

If $y$ is related to $x$ by an equation of the form $(1-8)$, then the constant $m$ is also called the *rate of change* or *rate of growth* of $y$ as a function of $x$.  In such a case, we say that $y$ *grows linearly* with respect to $x$.

Frequently, the independent variable is time denoted by the letter $t$.  In such a case, the linear functional equation has the form

$$y = mt + b \qquad \text{or} \qquad y = b + mt$$

Whenever time $t \geq 0$, the constant $b$ is then called the *initial value* of $y$ since it is the value of $y$ when $t = 0$.

**EXAMPLE 1.10**  A poker player, Marc, begins with $N = 20$ chips, and wins 6 chips every hour.  Marc begins playing at 5:00 P.M. and leaves the game at midnight.

(*a*)  Express his number $N$ of chips as a function of the number $t$ of hours that he plays poker.

(*b*)  Find the number $N$ of his chips after 3 hours.

(*c*)  At what time will Marc have 50 chips?

(*d*)  How many chips $N$ will he have when he stops playing.

(*a*)  Here $N = 20 + 6t$, since the initial value (when $t = 0$) is 20, and his rate of increase is 6 chips per hour.

(*b*)  He wins 6 chips per hour, so after 3 hours he wins $3 \cdot 6 = 18$ chips.  Thus, after 3 hours, he will have $N = 20 + 18 = 38$ chips.  Alternately, substituting $t = 3$ in the equation for $N$ yields

$$N = 20 + 6\,(3) = 20 + 18 = 38$$

(*c*)  Substitute $N = 50$ in the equation for $N$ obtaining:

$$50 = 20 + 6t \qquad \text{or} \qquad 30 = 6t \qquad \text{or} \qquad t = 5$$

Thus, he will have 50 chips after 5 hours.  Since he began at 5:00 P.M., the time after 5 hours is 10:00 P.M.

(*d*)  Marc stops playing at midnight, which is 7 hours after 5:00 P.M.  Thus, when he stops playing, he will have

$$N = 20 + 6(7) = 20 + 42 = 62 \text{ chips.}$$

(His winnings are only 42 chips, since he began with 20 chips.)

**EXAMPLE 1.11**   The population $P$ of a town, Yardsville, in 1998 is 4000.   Suppose the population $P$ increases 200 people each year.

($a$)   Write $P$ as a linear function of the number $t$ of years after 1998.

($b$)   Find the population $P$ in 2001.

($a$)   The population increases 200 per year beginning with 4000 in 1998.   Thus, $P$ can be obtained from the formula

$$P = 4000 + 200t$$

($b$)   2001 is $t = 3$ years after 1998, so the population $P$ in 2001 follows:

$$P = 4000 + 200\,(3) = 4000 + 600 = 4600$$

**Remark:**   Suppose in Example 1.11 the population $P$ increases 5 percent each year, not 200.

(1)   The increase and population $P$ in the first year follows:

$$\text{Increase: } 5\% \, (4000) = 200; \text{ hence, } P = 4000 + 200 = 4200$$

(2)   The increase and population $P$ in the second year follows:

$$\text{Increase: } 5\% \, (4200) = 210; \text{ hence, } P = 4200 + 210 = 4410$$

(3)   The increase and population $P$ in the third year follows:

$$\text{Increase: } 5\% \, (4410) = 221; \text{ hence, } P = 4410 + 221 = 4631$$

Here the population $P$ is not a linear function of the time $t$.   (This type of "geometric" growth will be studied in Chapter 2.)

## Linear Equations as Linear Functions

Consider again the standard form of a linear equation, $Ax + By = C$.   Suppose $B \neq 0$.   Then we can solve for $y$ in terms of $x$ to obtain the equation:

$$y = -\frac{A}{B}x + \frac{C}{B}$$

Thus, we may view $y$ as a linear function of $x$.   In particular, we have:

$$\text{Slope:} \quad m = -A/B, \qquad y \text{ intercept:} \quad b = C/B$$

**EXAMPLE 1.12**   Find the slope $m$ and $y$ intercept $b$ for each of the following linear equations:

($a$)   $y = 5x - 10$,       ($b$)   $9x + 2y = 18$,       ($c$)   $2x - y = 7$,       ($d$)   $6x - 4y = 8$

Rewrite the equation in the form $y = mx + b$.

($a$)   Here we directly obtain $m = 5$ and $b = -10$.

($b$)   Solve for $y$ in terms of $x$ to get

$$2y = -9x + 18 \qquad \text{or} \qquad y = -4.5x + 9$$

Thus, $m = -4.5$ and $b = 9$.

($c$)   Solve for $y$ in terms of $x$ to get $y = 2x - 7$. Thus $m, = 2$ and $b = -7$.

($d$)   Solve for $y$ in terms of $x$ to get

$$-4y = -6x + 8 \qquad \text{or} \qquad y = 1.5x - 2$$

Thus, $m = 1.5$ and $b = -2$.

## 1.7   LINES AND THEIR EQUATIONS; POINT-SLOPE FORMULA

This section discusses how to find the equation of a given line with certain properties.   Frequently, we use the following formula, which gives the equation of a line $L$ through a given point $P(x_1, y_1)$ with a given direction (slope) $m$:

$$y - y_1 = m(x - x_1) \qquad (1.9)$$

(Here a subscript with $x$ and $y$ denotes a given value of $x$ and $y$.)   The proceeding is called the *point-slope formula* for a line. (See Fig. 1-11.)   We emphasize that a line $L$ through a point $P$ with a given slope $m$ is unique.

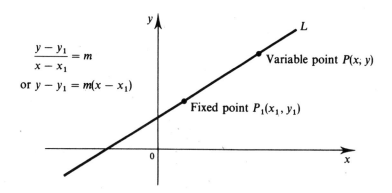

**Fig. 1-11**   Point-slope formula.

**EXAMPLE 1.13**   Find the equation of the line with slope $m = 3$ and passing through the point $P(5, -2)$.

We do this problem two ways.

   (*i*)   Substitute in the preceeding formula (*1.9*) to obtain

$$y + 2 = 3\,(x - 5) \qquad \text{or} \qquad y + 2 = 3x - 15 \qquad \text{or} \qquad y = 3x - 17$$

   (*ii*)   Since the slope $m = 3$, the equation has the form

$$y = 3x + b \qquad (1.10)$$

We need to find the $y$ intercept $b$.   Since $P(5, -2)$ lies on the line, we substitute $x = 5$, $y = -2$ in (*1.10*) to get

$$-2 = 3(5) + b \qquad \text{or} \qquad -2 = 15 + b \qquad \text{or} \qquad b = -17$$

Substitute $b = -17$ in (*1.10*) to finally obtain the desired equation

$$y = 3x - 17$$

**EXAMPLE 1.14**   Find the equation of the line $L$ with the given properties:

(*a*)   Passes through the points $P(3, 2)$ and $Q(5, -6)$.

(*b*)   Parallel to the line $2x - 5y = 7$ and passes through $P(3, 4)$.

(*c*)   Perpendicular to $y = 3x + 4$ and passes through $P(6, -1)$.

(a)  First find the slope $m$ of the line $L$:

$$m = \frac{y_2 - y_1}{x_2 - x_1} = \frac{-6 - 2}{5 - 3} = -4$$

Thus, using formula ($1.9$), the equation of $L$ is

$$y - 2 = -4\,(x - 3) \qquad \text{or} \qquad y - 2 = -4x + 12 \qquad \text{or} \qquad y = -4x + 14$$

(b)  Using Eq. ($1.6$), we see that the line $L$ belongs to the collection

$$2x - 5y = k \tag{1.11}$$

We seek the value of $k$, which gives the equation of $L$.  Since $P(3, 4)$ lies on $L$, we substitute $x = 3$, $y = 4$ in ($1.11$) to get

$$2(3) - 5(4) = k \qquad \text{or} \qquad 6 - 20 = k \qquad \text{or} \qquad k = -14$$

Substitute $k = -14$ into ($1.11$) to finally obtain the desired equation

$$2x - 5y = -14$$

(c)  The slope of the given line is $m' = 3$.  Thus, the slope of $L$ is the negative reciprocal of $m'$, which is $m = -1/3$.  Using the point $P(6, -1)$ and the point-slope formula ($1.9$), the equation of $L$ follows:

$$y + 1 = -\frac{1}{3}(x - 6) \qquad \text{or} \qquad y + 1 = -\frac{1}{3}x + 2 \qquad \text{or} \qquad y = -\frac{1}{3}x + 1$$

**Remark**   Usually, unless otherwise stated, we leave an equation of a line $L$ in either the slope intercept form $y = mx + b$ (which is unique) or in standrad form $Ax + By = C$ (which is unique up to multiples).

## 1.8   GENERAL EQUATIONS AND CURVES; FUNCTIONS

Many applications of mathematics involve relationships that can be expressed as an equation $E$ in two variables $x$ and $y$.   Some examples of such equations follow:

$$y = x^2 + x - 6 \qquad 2x - 5y = 10 \qquad x^2 + y^2 = 25$$

Each such equation in $x$ and $y$ determines a collection $C$ of points in the plane $\mathbf{R}^2$.   Namely, a point $(a, b)$ belongs to $C$ if it satisfies the equation.   This collection $C$ of points normally forms a curve in the plane, and the pictoral representation of this curve is called the *graph* of the equation.   The process of drawing the graph is called *sketching* or *plotting*.

The main method for sketching the graph of an equation is as follows:

(a)  Find a table of points that satisfy the equation.

(b)  Plot these points in the plane $\mathbf{R}^2$.

(c)  Draw a smooth continuous curve through the points.

It is also helpful to know the type of the curve, e.g., whether the graph is a circle, straight line, parabola, or some other well-known figure.   Moreover, we note that, in part ($c$), the graph may actually consist of more than one continuous curve through the points.   For example, the graph of $y = 1/x$, obtained in Problem 1.26, consists of two such curves.

Frequently, a relationship between variables $x$ and $y$ has the property that each value of $x$ yields a unique value of $y$.   We then say that $y$ is a *function of $x$*, and we call $x$ the *independent variable* and $y$ the *dependent variable*.   Sometimes such a function is given or can be expressed in the form

$$y = f(x)$$

where $f(x)$ is an expression involving only $x$.   In such a case, where $y$ is given explicitly as a function of $x$, we find a table of points for the graph of the equation by choosing various values for the independent variable $x$ and then solving for the corresponding values of $y$.

**EXAMPLE 1.15** (**Parabola**) Sketch the graph of $y = x^2 + 2x - 3$.

Here $y$ is expressed explicitly in terms of the variable $x$. Thus, first set up a table consisting of values of $x$, say, the integral values from $-3$ to $3$, as follows:

| $x$ | $-3$ | $-2$ | $-1$ | $0$ | $1$ | $2$ | $3$ |
|-----|------|------|------|-----|-----|-----|-----|
| $y$ |      |      |      |     |     |     |     |

Next, fill in the table by finding the corresponding value of $y$ for each value of $x$. For example:

$$x = -3 \text{ yields } y = (-3)^2 + 2(-3) - 3 = 9 - 6 - 3 = 0$$
$$x = -2 \text{ yields } y = (-2)^2 + 2(-2) - 3 = 4 - 4 - 3 = -3$$
$$x = -1 \text{ yields } y = (-1)^2 + 2(-1) - 3 = 1 - 2 - 3 = -4$$

And so on. The completed table follows:

| $x$ | $-3$ | $-2$ | $-1$ | $0$ | $1$ | $2$ | $3$ |
|-----|------|------|------|-----|-----|-----|-----|
| $y$ | $0$  | $-3$ | $-4$ | $-3$ | $0$ | $5$ | $12$ |

(Frequently, the table is written vertically instead of horizontally.) Now plot the points in the plane $\mathbf{R}^2$, and then draw a smooth continuous curve through the points, as in Fig. 1-12($a$).

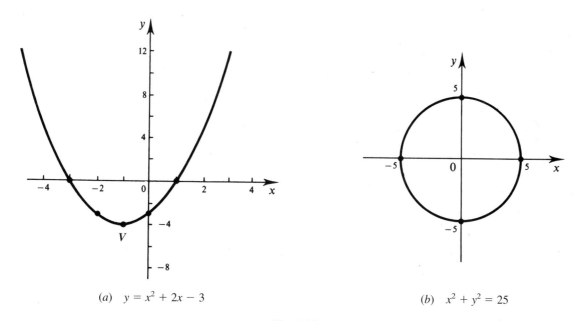

(a)  $y = x^2 + 2x - 3$          (b)  $x^2 + y^2 = 25$

**Fig. 1-12**

**Remark 1.** The graph in Fig. 1-12($a$) is called a *parabola*. The point $V(-1, -4)$ is called the *vertex* of the parabola. In general, the graph of the equation

$$y = ax^2 + bx + c \qquad (a \neq 0) \tag{1.12}$$

is such a parabola. [The parabola opens upward when $a$ is positive, as in Fig. 1-12($a$), and it opens downward when $a$ is negative.] The vertex of the parabola can be found by using $x = -b/2a$ as its $x$ value.

**Remark 2.**   The points at which a graph intersects the $x$- axis are called the $x$ *intercepts*, and the points at which the graph intersects the $y$ axis are called the $y$ *intercepts*.   Thus, in Fig. 1-12($a$), the $x$ intercepts of the graph are $-3$ and $1$, and the $y$ intercept is $-3$.

**EXAMPLE 1.16**   (**Circle**)  Sketch the graph of the equation $x^2 + y^2 = 25$.

This is the equation of a circle whose center is the origin and whose radius $r = \sqrt{25} = 5$, as shown in Fig. 1-12($b$). Note that the $x$ intercepts are $\pm\, 5$ and the $y$ intercept are also $\pm\, 5$. (Here the notation $\pm\, 5$ is short for $x = 5$ and $x = -5$.)

**Remark:**   In general, the equation of a circle with center $C$ $(h,\, k)$ and radius $r$ follows:

$$(x - h)^2 + (y - k)^2 = r^2 \qquad\qquad (1.13)$$

[See Problem 1.26.] Example 1.16 is a special case of (*1.13*) where the center is the origin.

**EXAMPLE 1.17**   (**Polymonial***)*   Sketch the graph of the equation $y = x^3 - 3x^2 - x + 3$.

Set up a table of values for $x$, and then find the corresponding values for $y$, say, as follows:

| $x$ | $-2$ | $-1$ | $0$ | $1$ | $2$ | $3$ | $4$ |
|---|---|---|---|---|---|---|---|
| $y$ | $-15$ | $0$ | $3$ | $0$ | $-3$ | $0$ | $15$ |

Next, plot the points in the coordinate plane $\mathbf{R}^2$, and then draw a smooth continuous curve through the points, as in Fig. 1-13($a$).   Observe that the $x$ intercepts of the curve are $-1$, $1$, $3$; and it has only one $y$ intercept, which is $-3$. Observe that different unit lengths are used for the $x$ axis and the $y$ axis.

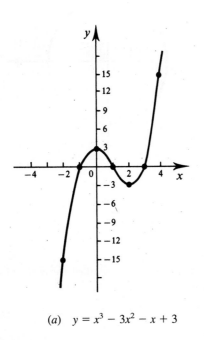

(*a*)   $y = x^3 - 3x^2 - x + 3$

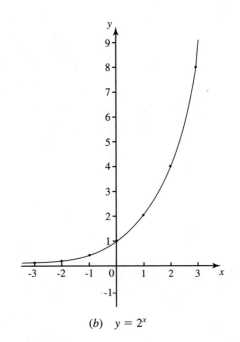

(*b*)   $y = 2^x$

**Fig. 1-13**

**Remark:**   Generally speaking, a *polynomial function of degree n* is given by an equation of the form

$$y = a_0 x^n + a_1 x^{n-1} + \dots + a_{n-1}x + a_n \qquad (a_0 \neq 0)$$

Example 1.17 is a typical polynomial function of degree 3.

**EXAMPLE 1.18   (Exponential Function***)***  Sketch the graph of $y = 2^x$.

Set up a table of values for $x$, and then find the corresponding values for $y$, say, as follows:

| $x$ | $-3$ | $-2$ | $-1$ | $0$ | $1$ | $2$ | $3$ |
|---|---|---|---|---|---|---|---|
| $y$ | $\frac{1}{8}$ | $\frac{1}{4}$ | $\frac{1}{2}$ | $1$ | $2$ | $4$ | $8$ |

Next, plot the points in the coordinate plane $\mathbf{R}^2$, and then draw a smooth continuous curve through the points, as in Fig. 1-13(*b*).   Observe that the curve has no $x$ intercepts, and it has only one $y$ intercept, which is 1.

**Remark:**   An *exponential function with base b*, is given by an equation of the form

$$y = b^x, \qquad b > 0, b \neq 1$$

Observe that the independent variable $x$ appears as an exponent in the functional equation.   Example 1.18 is an important example of an exponential function with base $b = 2$.

# Solved Problems

## REAL LINE R

**1.1.**   Plot the numbers   $\dfrac{5}{2}$,   3.8,   $-4.5$,   $-3.3$   on the real line **R**.

The points corresponding to the numbers are shown in Fig. 1-14.

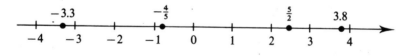

**Fig. 1-14**

**1.2.**   Evaluate  (*a*) $|-5|$,   $|7.2|$,   $|0|$,   $|-1.23|$; (*b*) $|3 - 5|$,   $|-3 + 5|$,   $|-3 - 5|$.

(*a*)   The absolute value is the magnitude of the number without regard to sign:

$$|-5| = 5 \qquad |7.2| = 7.2 \qquad |0| = 0 \qquad |-1.23| = 1.23$$

(*b*)   Evaluate inside the absolute-value sign first:

$$|3 - 5| = |-2| = 2 \qquad |-3 + 5| = |2| = 2 \qquad |-3 - 5| = |-8| = 8$$

**1.3.**   Find the distance $d$ between each pair of real numbers: (*a*) 3 and $-5$,   (*b*) $-1$ and 2, (*c*) 4 and 9,   (*d*) $-7$ and $-3$,   (*e*) 6 and $-6$,   (*f*) $-2$ and $-8$.

The distance $d$ between $a$ and $b$ is given by $d = |a - b|$.   Alternatively, $d = |a| + |b|$ when $a$ and $b$ have different signs, and $d = |a| - |b|$ when $a$ and $b$ have the same signs and $|a| \geq |b|$.   (See Fig. 1-3.)   Thus,
(*a*) $d = 3 + 5 = 8$     (*c*) $d = 9 - 4 = 5$     (*e*) $d = 6 + 6 = 12$
(*b*) $d = 1 + 2 = 3$     (*d*) $d = 7 - 3 = 4$     (*f*) $d = 8 - 2 = 6$

## CARTESIAN PLANE R²

**1.4.** Consider the following points in $\mathbf{R}^2$:

$A(1, 4)$, $B(-5, 2)$,  $C(0, -3)$, $D(4, 2)$,  $E(-3, -4)$, $F(2, 0)$,  $G(3, -2)$

(*a*) Locate the points in the plane $\mathbf{R}^2$.     (*b*) Find the quadrant where each point lies.

(*a*)  To locate the point $(x, y)$, start at the origin 0, go $x$ directed units along the $x$ axis, and then go $y$ directed units parallel to the $y$ axis.   The endpoint has coordinates $(x, y)$.   This process yields the points in Fig. 1-15.

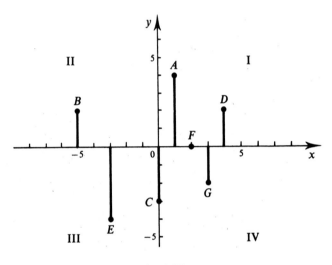

**Fig. 1-15**

(*b*)  The quadrants are numbered counterclockwise beginning in the upper right region, as indicated in Fig. 1-15.   Thus, points $A$ and $D$ lie in quadrant I, $B$ in quadrant II, $E$ in quadrant III, and $G$ in quadrant IV.   Points $C$ and $F$ lie on the axes, and hence do not lie within a quadrant but rather on the boundary between quadrants.

**1.5.** Find the distance $d$ and midpoint $M$ between the following points:
(*a*) $A(-3, 5)$ and $B(6, 4)$; (*b*) $A(5, -2)$ and $B(-1, -4)$.

Use formulas (*1.1*) and (*1.2*):

(*a*)   $d = \sqrt{9^2 + 1^2} = \sqrt{81 + 1} = \sqrt{82}$,   $M = \left( \dfrac{-3 + 6}{2}, \dfrac{5 + 4}{2} \right) = (\tfrac{3}{2}, \tfrac{9}{2})$

(*b*)   $d = \sqrt{6^2 + 2^2} = \sqrt{36 + 4} = \sqrt{40} = 2\sqrt{10}$,   $M = \left( \dfrac{5 - 1}{2}, \dfrac{-2 - 4}{2} \right) = (2, -3)$

## LINEAR EQUATIONS IN ONE UNKNOWN

**1.6.** Solve: (*a*)   $7x = 21$,      (*b*)   $2x = -12$,      (*c*)   $5x = 17$,      (*d*)   $-3x = 11$.

If $a \neq 0$, then $ax = b$ has unique solution $x = b/a$. Thus: (*a*)   $x = \frac{21}{7} = 3$, (*b*)   $x = \frac{-12}{2} = -6$, (*c*)   $x = \frac{17}{5}$, (*d*)   $x = -\frac{11}{3}$.

**1.7.** Solve: $(a)$ $\quad 3x = 5\pi$, $(b)$ $\quad 0x = 5$, $(c)$ $\quad 0x = 0$.

$(a)$ $\quad x = 5\pi/3$.

$(b)$ $\quad$ The equation has no solution.

$(c)$ $\quad$ Every number is a solution of the equation.

**1.8.** Solve: $(a)$ $\quad 6x - 8 + x + 4 = 2x + 11 - 5x$, $\qquad (b)$ $\quad 2x - \frac{2}{3} = \frac{1}{2}x + 4$, $(c)$ $\quad 3x - 4 - x = 5x + 8 - 3x - 3$.

Put each equation in the standard form $ax = b$.

$(a)$ $\quad$ Simplify each side first:

$$7x - 4 = -3x + 11 \quad \text{or} \quad 10x = 15 \quad \text{or} \quad x = \frac{15}{10} \quad \text{or} \quad x = \frac{3}{2}$$

$(b)$ $\quad$ Multiply both sides by 6 to remove fractions:

$$12x - 4 = 3x + 24 \quad \text{or} \quad 9x = 28 \quad \text{or} \quad x = \frac{28}{9}$$

$(c)$ $\quad$ Simplify each side first:

$$2x - 4 = 2x + 5 \quad \text{or} \quad 0x = 9$$

The equation has no solution.

## LINEAR EQUATIONS IN TWO UNKNOWNS; LINES

**1.9.** Plot the following lines: $\quad (a)$ $\quad 4x + 3y = 6$, $\quad (b)$ $\quad 2x - 3y = 6$.

In each case find at least two points on the line, preferably the intercepts, and as a check a third point. The line drawn through these points is the required line.

$(a)$ $\quad$ If $x = 0$, $y = 2$; if $y = 0$, $x = \frac{3}{2} = 1.5$. Also, if $y = -2$, $x = 3$. Plot the points and draw the line through the points [Fig. 1-16($a$)]

$(b)$ $\quad$ If $x = 0$, $y = -2$; if $y = 0$, $x = 3$. Also, if $y = 1$, $x = 4.5$. Plot the points and draw the line through the points [Fig. 1-16($b$)].

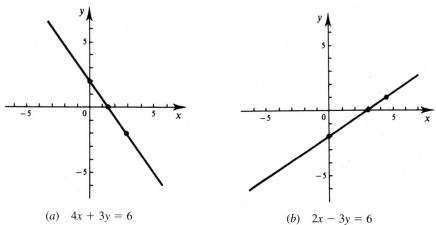

$\qquad (a)$ $\quad 4x + 3y = 6$ $\qquad\qquad\qquad (b)$ $\quad 2x - 3y = 6$

**Fig. 1-16**

**1.10.** Plot the following lines: (*a*)  $x = -4$,  $x = -1$,  $x = 3$,  $x = 5$;
(*b*)  $y = 4$,  $y = 1$,  $y = -2$,  $y = -3$.

(*a*)  Each line is vertical and meets the *x* axis at its respective value of *x* [Fig. 1-17(*a*)].

(*b*)  Each line is horizontal and meets the *y* axis at its respective value of *y* [Fig. 1-17(*b*)].

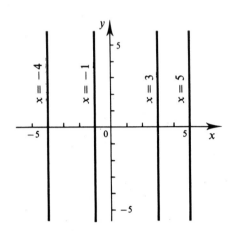

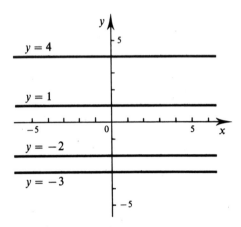

(*a*)   Vertical lines                          (*b*)   Horizontal lines

**Fig. 1-17**

**1.11.** Let *L* be the line $3x + 2y = 0$.   Plot the graph of *L*.

Find at least two points on *L*, preferably intercepts, and as a check find a third point.   If $x = 0$, then $y = 0$.   Thus, *L* passes through the origin.   If $x = 2$, $y = -3$; if $x = -4$, $y = 6$.   Thus, *L* passes through the points $(0, 0)$, $(2, -3)$, and $(4, 6)$ [Fig. 1-18(*a*)].

**1.12.** Show that the equations $y - 2 = 3x + 3$ and $6x - 2y = -10$ have the same graph.   Find their common graph.

Solve each equation for *y* in terms of *x*.   Both equations yield $y = 3x + 5$.   Hence, both equations have the same graph.   If $x = 0$, $y = 5$; and if $x = 1$, $y = 8$.   Draw the line through these points [Fig. 1-18(*b*)].   This is the common graph.

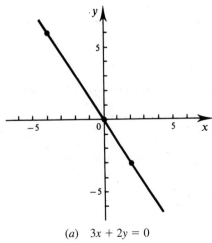

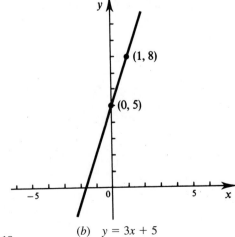

(*a*)   $3x + 2y = 0$                   **Fig. 1-18**                   (*b*)   $y = 3x + 5$

## SLOPES; EQUATIONS OF LINES

**1.13.** Find the slope $m$ of the line $L$ through
(a) $P(1, 3)$, $Q(5, 6)$;   (b) $P(1, 1)$, $Q(2, 11)$;   (c) $P(1, 6)$, $Q(5, 3)$;   (d) $P(2, 11)$, $Q(3, 1)$.

Without drawing the lines, determine which lines are rising, which lines are falling, and which are steeper.

To find the slope $m$, use the formula $m = \dfrac{y_2 - y_1}{x_2 - x_1}$:

$$(a) \quad m = \frac{6 - 3}{5 - 1} = \frac{3}{4} \qquad\qquad (c) \quad m = \frac{3 - 6}{5 - 1} = -\frac{3}{4}$$

$$(b) \quad m = \frac{11 - 1}{2 - 1} = 10 \qquad\qquad (d) \quad m = \frac{1 - 11}{3 - 2} = -10$$

Lines (a) and (b) are rising, since their slopes are positive, and (b) is steeper than (a), since the magnitude of its slope is larger.   Lines (c) and (d) are falling, since their slopes are negative, and (d) is steeper than (c), since the magnitude (absolute value) of its slope is larger.

**1.14.** Find the slope of each line:

(a) $y = 4x - 5$         (c) $3x - 4y = 6$         (e) $x = 7$

(b) $2x + 3y = 6$       (d) $y = 3$             (f) $a^2x + b^2y = c^2$

Rewrite each equation in the slope-intercept form $y = mx + b$; that is, solve for $y$ in terms of $x$.   Then the coefficient of $x$ is the slope.

(a) The equation $y = 4x - 5$ is in the desired form; so $m = 4$.

(b) Transpose $2x$ and then divide both sides by 3 to obtain

$$3y = -2x + 6 \qquad \text{and then} \qquad y = -\tfrac{2}{3}x + 2$$

Hence, $m = -\tfrac{2}{3}$.

(c) Solving for $y$ yields $-4y = -3x + 6$; then $y = \tfrac{3}{4}x - \tfrac{3}{2}$.  Thus, $m = \tfrac{3}{4}$.

(d) Here $y = 3$, short for $y = 0x + 3$, is in the desired form; hence, $m = 0$.  (Recall $y = 3$ is a horizontal line).

(e) Here $x = 7$, short for $x + 0y = 7$, cannot be solved for $y$ in terms of $x$.  That is, $x = 7$ is a vertical line and its slope is not defined.

(f) Solving for $y$ yields $y = -\dfrac{a^2}{b^2}x + \dfrac{c^2}{b^2}$ when $b \neq 0$.  Hence, $m = -\dfrac{a^2}{b^2}$ when $b \neq 0$.  The slope is not defined when $b = 0$.

**1.15.** Find the equation of the line passing through the point $P$ with slope $m$ where:

(a) $P(3, 2)$, $m = -1$;      (b) $P(-4, 1)$, $m = \dfrac{1}{2}$;      (c) $P(-2, -5)$, $m = 2$

Write each equation in the slope-intercept form $y = mx + b$ or in the standard form $Ax + By = C$.

Use the point-slope formula $y - y_1 = m(x - x_1)$, where $m$ is the slope and $P(x_1, y_1)$ is the point.

(a)   $y - 2 = -1(x - 3)$   or   $y = -x + 5$.

(b)   $y - 1 = \frac{1}{2}(x + 4)$   or   $y = \frac{1}{2}x + 3$ (or $x - 2y = -6$).

(c)   $y + 5 = 2(x + 2)$   or   $y = 2x - 1$.

**1.16.**  Find the equation of the line $L$ passing through the points: (a)   $P(1, 3)$ and $Q(4, -5)$, (b)   $P(-2, -6)$ and $Q(3, 1)$.

First find the slope $m$ of $L$ using $m = (y_2 - y_1)/(x_2 - x_1)$, and then find the equation of $L$ using the point-slope formula.

(a)   $m = \dfrac{-5 - 3}{4 - 1} = -\dfrac{8}{3}$.   The equation of the line is $y - 3 = -\frac{8}{3}(x - 1)$ or $8x + 3y = 17$.

(b)   $m = \dfrac{1 + 6}{3 + 2} = \dfrac{7}{5}$.   The equation of the line is $y - 1 = \frac{7}{5}(x - 3)$ or $7x - 5y = 16$.

**1.17.**  Find the equation of the line $L$ passing through the point $P(5, -3)$ and parallel to the line $3x + y = 8$.

*Method 1.*   First find the slope $m$ of the given line $3x + y = 8$.   Solve for $y$ to obtain $y = -3x + 8$; hence, $m = -3$.   Since $L$ is parallel to $3x + y = 8$, the slope of $L$ is also $m = -3$.   Now use the point-slope formula to obtain the equation of $L$:

$$y + 3 = -3(x - 5) \qquad \text{or} \qquad y = -3x + 12 \qquad (\text{or } 3x + y = 12)$$

*Method 2.*   The line $L$ belongs to the collection $3x + y = k$, for some value of $k$.   Substitute the point $P(5, -3)$ into the equation to obtain $3(5) - 3 = k$ or $k = 12$.   Thus, $3x + y = 12$ is the equation of $L$.

**1.18.**  Find the slope $m$ of the line $L$ perpendicular to a line $L'$ with slope:

(a)   $m' = \dfrac{1}{2}$,       (b)   $m' = -\dfrac{3}{4}$,       (c)   $m' = -3$,       (d)   $m' = 4$

The slope $m$ must be the negative reciprical of $m'$.   Thus:

(a)   $m = -2$,       (b)   $m = \dfrac{4}{3}$,       (c)   $m = \dfrac{1}{3}$,       (d)   $m = -\dfrac{1}{4}$.

**1.19.**  Find the equation of the line $L$ passing through the point $P(6, -2)$ and perpendicular to the line $3x + 2y = 4$.

*Method 1.*   To find the slope $m$ of $L$, first find the slope $m'$ of the given line.   Solve for $y$ to obtain $y = -\frac{3}{2}x + 2$.   Thus, $m' = -\frac{3}{2}$.   Therefore, $m = \frac{2}{3}$, the negative reciprocal of $m'$.   Now use the point-slope formula to obtain the equation of $L$:

$$y + 2 = \tfrac{2}{3}(x - 6) \qquad \text{or} \qquad y = \tfrac{2}{3}x - 6 \qquad (\text{or } 2x - 3y = 18)$$

*Method 2.*   The line $L$ belongs to the collection $2x - 3y = k$.   Substitute the point $P(6, -2)$ into the equation to obtain $2(6) - 3(-2) = k$ or $k = 18$.   Thus, $2x - 3y = 18$ is the equation of $L$.

**1.20.** The following is called the *slope-intercept form* of a linear equation:

$$y = mx + b \qquad (1)$$

Justify this name by showing $b$ is the $y$ intercept and that $m$ is the slope of the corresponding line $L$.

If we substitute $x = 0$ in Eq. (*1*), then we get $y = b$; hence $b$ is the $y$ intercept of $L$. We next show that $m$ is the slope of $L$. Suppose $P_1(x_1, y_1)$ and $P_2(x_2, y_2)$ are two points on $L$ and hence satisfy Eq. (*1*). Therefore,

$$y_2 = mx_2 + b \qquad \text{and} \qquad y_1 = mx_1 + b$$

By subtracting, we get

$$y_2 - y_1 = mx_2 - mx_1 = m(x_2 - x_1)$$

Therefore,

$$m = \frac{y_2 - y_1}{x_2 - x_1} \qquad (x_2 \neq x_1)$$

which is formula (*1.5*) for the slope.

**1.21.** Let $Ax + By = C$ be the equation of a (nondegenerate) line $L$. Show that the collection of lines perpendicular to $L$ has the form

$$Bx - Ay = k \qquad (2)$$

There is the special case where $B = 0$, and the special case where $A = 0$. Then there is the general case where $B \neq 0$ and $A \neq 0$.

If $B = 0$, then $L$ is vertical, and formula (2) is the equation of the collection of horizontal lines; hence, formula (2) is the collection of lines perpendicular to $L$.

On the other hand, if $A = 0$, then $L$ is horizontal and formula (2) is the equation of the collection of vertical lines; hence, formula (2) is the collection of lines perpendicular to $L$.

Lastly, suppose $B \neq 0$ and $A \neq 0$. Then the slope of $L$ is $-A/B$ and formula (2) is the equation of lines with slope $B/A$. But $(-A/B)(B/A) = -1$; hence, again, formula (2) is the collection of lines perpendicular to $L$.

## LINEAR FUNCTIONS AND LINEAR GROWTH

**1.22.** Suppose the population $P$ of a town in 2002 is 6000, and suppose the population $P$ increases 300 per year.

Write $P$ as a linear function of the number $t$ of years after 2000. Also, find the population $P$ in: (*a*) 2003, (*b*) 2004, (*c*) 2005.

The population increases 300 per year beginning with 6000 in 2002. Thus, the population $P$ in $t$ years after 2002 can be obtained from the formula

$$P = 6000 + 300t$$

(*a*) 2003 is $t = 1$ years after 2002; hence, $P = 6000 + 300(1) = 6000 + 300 = 6300$
(*b*) 2004 is $t = 2$ years after 2002; hence, $P = 6000 + 300(2) = 6000 + 600 = 6600$
(*c*) 2005 is $t = 3$ years after 2002; hence, $P = 6000 + 300(3) = 6000 + 900 = 6900$

**1.23.** Suppose the amount $A$ in a savings account in a bank in 2002 is \$6000, and suppose the bank gives 5 percent interest each year.    Find the amount $A$ in the account in:

(a)  2003,        (b)  2004,        (c)  2005.

There is a 5 percent increase each year in the amount $A$.    Thus, the increase (interest) $I$ and amount $A$ in each of the years follows:

(a)  $I = 5\% \ (6000) = 300,$   so $A = \$6000 + \$300 = \$6300.$
(b)  $I = 5\% \ (6300) = 315,$   so $A = \$6300 + \$315 = \$6615.$
(c)  $I = 5\% \ (6615) = 330.75,$   so $A = \$6615 + \$300.75 = \$6915.75.$

**Remark:**   Here the amount $A$ is not a linear function of the time $t$, since the increase changes each year.

**1.24.** Suppose a refrigerator $R$ costs \$500 and decreases in value \$50 each year.    Let $t$ be the number of years after the refrigerator $R$ is purchased.

(a)   Express the value $V$ of $R$ as a function of the time $t$.

(b)   Find the value $V$ after $t = 4$ years.

(c)   Find $t$ when the value $V = \$200$.

(d)   Express $t$ as a function of $V$.

(e)   Find $t$ when the refrigerator $R$ becomes worthless.

(a)   Here $V = 500 - 50t$, since the initial value of $R$ is 500 and the rate of decrease is 50 dollars per year.

(b)   After $t = 4$ years, the value $V$ decreases $4(50) = 200$.    Thus, after 4 years, $V = 500 - 200 = 300$ dollars.    Alternately, substituting $t = 4$ in the equation for $V$ yields:

$$V = 500 - 4(50) = 500 - 200 = 300$$

(c)   Substitute $V = 200$ in the equation for $V$, obtaining

$$200 = 500 - 50t \qquad \text{or} \qquad 50t = 300 \qquad \text{or} \qquad t = 6$$

(d)   Solve for $t$ in the equation for $V$, obtaining

$$50t = 500 - V \qquad \text{or} \qquad t = \frac{500 - V}{50} = 10 - \frac{V}{50}$$

(e)   Substitute $V = 0$ in the equation for $t$ yields $t = 10$.    Alternately, dividing the initial value $V = 500$ by the decrease 50 yields $t = 10$.

## EQUATIONS AND CURVES; FUNCTIONS

**1.25.**   Sketch the graph of   (a) $y = x^2 + x - 6$,  (b) $(x - 1)^2 + (y - 2)^2 = 16$.

(a)   This is a parabola which opens upward.   (See Example 1.15.)   Set up a table of values for $x$, and find the corresponding values of $y$, say, as follows:

| $x$ | $-4$ | $-3$ | $-2$ | $-1$ | 0 | 1 | 2 | 3 |
|-----|------|------|------|------|---|---|---|---|
| $y$ | 6 | 0 | $-4$ | $-6$ | $-6$ | $-4$ | 0 | 6 |

Plot the points in the plane $\mathbf{R}^2$, and draw a smooth continuous curve through the points, as in Fig. 1-19($a$).

(b)　This is the equation of a circle with center $C(1, 2)$ and radius $r = \sqrt{16} = 4$. 　[See Example 1.16 and Equation (1.11).] Draw the circle with the given center $C$ and radius $r = 4$, as in Fig. 1-19($b$).

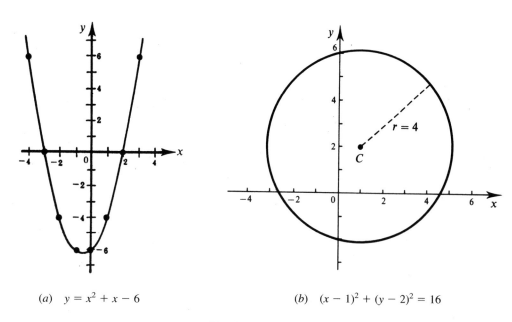

(a)　$y = x^2 + x - 6$ 　　　　　　　　　　　(b)　$(x - 1)^2 + (y - 2)^2 = 16$

**Fig. 1-19**

**1.26.**　Sketch the graph of (a)　$y = x^3 - 3x + 2$, (b)　$y = 1/x$.

(a)　This is a polynomial function. 　(See Example 1.17.) 　Set up a table of values for $x$ and find the corresponding values of $y$, say, as follows:

| $x$ | $-3$ | $-2$ | $-1$ | $0$ | $1$ | $2$ | $3$ |
|---|---|---|---|---|---|---|---|
| $y$ | $-16$ | $0$ | $4$ | $2$ | $0$ | $4$ | $20$ |

Plot the points in the plane $R^2$, and draw a smooth continuous curve through the point, as in Fig. 1-20($a$).

(Note that some of the points lie outside of the graph.)

(b)　Set up a table consisting of points in the graph, say, as follows:

| $x$ | $4$ | $2$ | $1$ | $\dfrac{1}{2}$ | $\dfrac{1}{4}$ | $0$ | $-\dfrac{1}{4}$ | $-\dfrac{1}{2}$ | $-1$ | $-2$ | $-4$ |
|---|---|---|---|---|---|---|---|---|---|---|---|
| $y$ | $\dfrac{1}{4}$ | $\dfrac{1}{2}$ | $1$ | $2$ | $4$ | $-$ | $-4$ | $-2$ | $-1$ | $-\dfrac{1}{2}$ | $-\dfrac{1}{4}$ |

Note that $y$ is not defined for $x = 0$.   Plot the points and draw smooth continuous curves through the points, as in Fig. 1-20(b).

(This graph is called a *hyperbola*.   It consists of two continuous curves.)

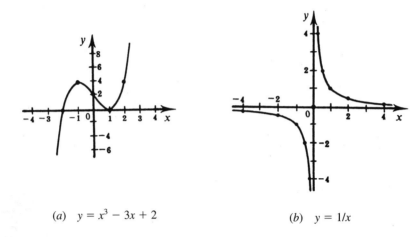

(a)   $y = x^3 - 3x + 2$          (b)   $y = 1/x$

**Fig. 1-20**

# Supplementary Poblems

**REAL LINE R**

**1.27.**   Evaluate:   (a)  $|9|$, $|-9|$, $|-3|$,    (b)  $|4 - 9|$, $|9 - 4|$, $|-2 - 7|$, $|-7 + 2|$

**1.28.**   Find the distance between each pair of points:
(a)  4 and $-6$,    (b)  $-3$ and $-7$,    (c)  $-8$ and 5.

**1.29.**   Arrange the following numbers in increasing order: $3, -4, -7, 5, 0, 2, -3$

**CARTESIAN PLANE R²**

**1.30.**   Find the quadrant where each point lies:   $A(2, -3)$,      $B(-3, -5)$,      $C(6, 1)$,      $D(-5, 7)$,
$E(8, -4)$,      $F(-2, -9)$

**1.31.**   Suppose $(s, t)$ is in Quadrant II.  Find the quadrant of:   (a)  $(-s, -t)$,    (b)  $(s, -t)$,
(c)  $(-s, t)$,    (d)  $(t, s)$

**1.32.**   Find the distance $d$ between each pair of points $P$ and $Q$ where:   (a)  $P(2, 1), Q(-2, 4)$,
(b)  $P(-4, -2), Q(1, 10)$,    (c)  $P(5, 0), Q(3, 6)$,    (d)  $P(8, -5), Q(-5, 8)$

**1.33.**   Find the midpoint $M$ between $P$ and $Q$ in Problem 1.32.

**1.34.**   Find the perimeter of the triangle $A(3,1)$, $B(-1, 4)$, $C(11, 1)$.

**1.35.**   Find $x$ and $y$ if $M$ is the midpoint between points $A$ and $B$, where:   (a)  $M(x, 4)$, $A(2, 5)$, $B(-7, y)$,
(b)  $M(2, 3)$, $A(-4, 5)$, $B(x, y)$.

**1.36.**   Audrey walks 1 km east, then 8 km north, and then $4\sqrt{2}$ km northeast.   Find the distance that Audrey is from her starting point.

## LINEAR EQUATIONS IN ONE UNKNOWN

**1.37.** Solve each equation:    (*a*)   $4x = 28$,       (*c*)   $0x = -2$,       (*e*)   $0x = 0$,
                                  (*b*)   $3x = -18$,      (*d*)   $7x = 11$,       (*f*)   $0x = 6$

**1.38.** Solve each equation:      (*a*)   $3(x + 1) = 2x + 4$,       (*b*)   $4x - 3 + 2x = 9 + 6x - 2$,
     (*c*)   $\dfrac{3}{2}x - \dfrac{8}{3} = \dfrac{x}{6}$

**1.39.** Emily has grades 78, 80, 87 in her first three tests.   Find the grade she must get on her fourth test so that her average is 84.

## LINEAR EQUATIONS IN TWO UNKNOWNS AND THEIR GRAPHS

**1.40.** Plot each equation in the plane.:     (*a*)   $3x - 2y = 6$,       (*b*)   $x + 2y = 4$,       (*c*)   $2x = 6$,
     (*d*)   $y = -3$

**1.41.** Find the slope, if possible, of the line through points $P$ and $Q$:
(*a*)  $P(4,3)$, $Q(3,4)$,       (*c*)  $P(8, 1)$, $Q(0, -3)$,       (*e*)  $P(-1, 2)$, $Q(4, -3)$,
(*b*)  $P(2, -5)$, $Q(6, -7)$,     (*d*)  $P(3, 7)$, $Q(3, 5)$,        (*f*)  $P(7, 3)$, $Q(5, 3)$,

**1.42.** Find the slope, if possible, of each line:    (*a*)   $y = -2x + 8$,    (*b*)   $2x - 5y = 14$,    (*c*)   $x = 3y - 7$,
     (*d*)   $x = -2$

**1.43.** Find the equation of the line $L$, where:
(*a*)   $L$ passes through $(2, 5)$ with slope $m = 3$.        (*c*)   $L$ passes through $(2, 6)$ and $(3, -1)$.

(*b*)   $L$ passes through $(3, -2)$ with slope $m = \dfrac{1}{4}$.      (*d*)   $L$ passes through $(-5, 0)$ and $(3, 5)$.

**1.44.** Find the equation of the line $L$, where:

(*a*)   $L$ passes through $(1, -3)$ and is parallel to $2x - 3y = 7$.
(*b*)   $L$ passes through $(2, -1)$ and is perpendicular to $3x + 4y = 6$.
(*c*)   $L$ is parallel to the $x$ axis and contains the point $(3, -4)$.
(*d*)   $L$ is parallel to the $y$ axis and contains the point $(-2, 1)$.

## LINEAR FUNCTIONS AND LINEAR GROWTH

**1.45.** The following equation gives the number $N$ of chips as a function of the time $t$ (in hours):

$$N = 15 + 3t$$

(*a*)   Find the initial number of chips (when $t = 0$).
(*b*)   Find the rate of change of $N$.
(*c*)   Solve for $t$ in terms of $N$.
(*d*)  Find $N$ when $t = 4$.
(*e*)  Find $t$ when $N = 30$.

**1.46.** The population $P$ of of Pleasantville as a function of time $t$ in years since 1995 follows:

$$P = 3000 + 75t$$

(*a*)   Find the population in 1998.
(*b*)   Find the rate of change of the population.
(*c*)   Find the time $t$ and the year $Y$ for the populaion to reach 3450 people.
(*d*)   Solve for $t$ in terms of $P$.

**1.47.** The following equation gives the monthly production cost $C$ (in dollars) of a company as a function of the number $n$ of units produced:

$$C = 9000 + 10n$$

    (*a*)   Find the overhead (when $n = 0$ units are produced).

    (*b*)   Find: (*i*) $C$ when $n = 2000$, (*ii*) $n$ when $C = 14000$.

    (*c*)   Solve for $n$ in terms of $C$.

**1.48.** A computer costs \$800 and depreciates \$160 per year. Let $V$ be the value (in dollars) of the computer as a function of the age $t$ (in years) of the computer.

    (*a*)   Find the equation relating $V$ to $t$.    (*c*)   Find $t$ when $V = 320$.

    (*b*)   Find $V$ when $t = 2$.             (*d*)   When does the computer lose all of its value?

## EQUATIONS AND CURVES

**1.49.** Sketch the graph of each equation:   (*a*)  $y = 4x - x^2$,   (*b*)  $y = x^3 - 9x$.

**1.50.** Sketch the graph of each equation: (*a*)  $(x - 1)^2 + (y + 2)^2 = 9$,   (*b*)  $y = 3^x$.

**1.51.** Find the equation $E$ of the circle:   (*a*)  with center $C(2, -1)$ and radius $r = 3$,
(*b*)  with center $C(1, 3)$ and contains the point $P(-2, 7)$.

**1.52.** Six functions are pictured in Fig. 1-21.   Match them with the following functions:

$$y = x^3, \quad y = 2^{-x}, \quad y = \sqrt{x}, \quad y = |x|, \quad y = 1/x^2, \quad y = |x|/x$$

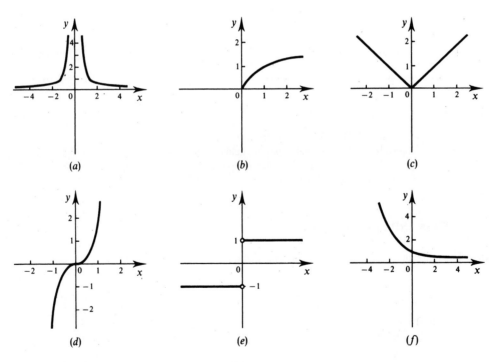

**Fig. 1.21**

# Answers to Supplementary Problems

**1.27.**  (*a*)  9, 9, 3,        (*b*)  5, 5, 9, 5

**1.28.**  10, 4, 13

**1.29.**  $-7, -4, -3, 0, 2, 3, 5$

**1.30.**  Quadrants IV, III, I, II, IV, III

**1.31.**  Quadrants IV, III, I, IV

**1.32.**  (*a*)  5,        (*b*)  13,        (*c*)  $\sqrt{40} = 2\sqrt{10}$,        (*d*)  $\sqrt{338} = 13\sqrt{2}$

**1.33.**  $M(0, 2.5)$,  $M(-1.5, 4)$,  $M(4, 3)$,  $M(1.5, 1.5)$

**1.34.**  $18 + \sqrt{153}$

**1.35.**  (*a*)  $x = -2.5,\ y = 3$,        (*b*)  $x = 8,\ y = 1$

**1.36.**  13

**1.37.**  (*a*)  7,        (*b*)  $-6$,        (*c*)  no solution,        (*d*)  11/7,        (*e*)  every number,        (*f*)  no solution.

**1.38.**  (*a*)  1,        (*b*)  no solution,        (*c*)  2

**1.39.**  91

**1.40.**  (*a*)  Fig. 1-22(*a*),        (*b*)  Fig. 1-22(*b*),        (*c*)  Vertical line through $x = 3$,
(*d*)  Horizontal line through $y = -3$ [Fig. 1-22(*c*)].

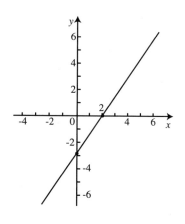

(*a*)  $3x - 2y = 6$            (*b*)  $x + 2y = 4$            (*c*)  $x = 3$ and $y = -3$

**Fig. 1-22**

**1.41.** (*a*)  $-1$,       (*b*)  $-\dfrac{1}{2}$,       (*c*)  $\dfrac{1}{2}$,       (*d*)  not defined,       (*e*)  $-1$,       (*f*)  $0$

**1.42.** (*a*)  $-2$,       (*b*)  $\dfrac{2}{5}$,       (*c*)  $\dfrac{1}{3}$,       (*d*)  not defined.

**1.43.** (*a*)  $y = 3x - 1$,       (*b*)  $x - 4y = 11$   or   $y = \dfrac{1}{4}x - \dfrac{11}{4}$,       (*c*)  $y = -7x + 20$

      (*d*)  $5x - 8y = -25$   or   $y = \dfrac{5}{8}x + \dfrac{28}{8}$

**1.44.** (*a*)  $2x - 3y = 11$,       (*b*)  $4x - 3y = 11$,       (*c*)  $y = -4$,       (*d*)  $x = -2$

**1.45.** (*a*)  $15$,       (*b*)  $3$,       (*c*)  $t = N/3 - 5$,       (*d*)  $27$,       (*e*)  $5$

**1.46.** (*a*)  $3225$,       (*b*)  $75$,       (*c*)  $t = 6, y = 2001$,       (*d*)  $t = P/75 - 40$

**1.47.** (*a*)  $\$9000$,       (*b*)  $\$29{,}000, n = 500$,       (*c*)  $n = C/10 - 900$

**1.48.** (*a*)  $V = 800 - 160t$,       (*b*)  $480$,       (*c*)  $3$,       (*d*)  $t = 5$

**1.49.** See Fig. 1-23.

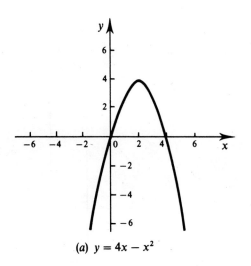

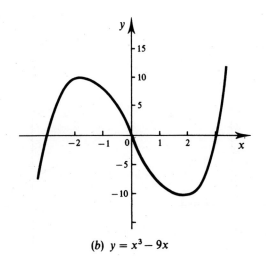

(*a*) $y = 4x - x^2$            (*b*) $y = x^3 - 9x$

**Fig. 1-23**

**1.50.** See Fig. 1-24.

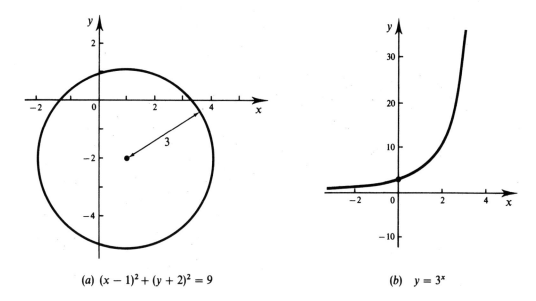

(a) $(x - 1)^2 + (y + 2)^2 = 9$          (b) $y = 3^x$

**Fig. 1-24**

**1.51.** (a) $(x - 2)^2 + (y + 1)^2 = 9$,          (b) $(x - 1)^2 + (y - 3)^2 = 25$

**1.52.** (a) $1/x^2$,     (b) $y = \sqrt{x}$     (c) $y = |x|$,     (d) $y = x^3$,
(e) $y = |x|/x$,          (f) $y = 2^{-x}$

# Exponential Growth

### 2.1  INTRODUCTION: LINEAR VS. EXPONENTIAL CHANGE

A quantity $y$ grows or declines *linearly* with time $t$ if whenever $t$ increases by one unit, $y$ changes by a constant amount, i.e., the *difference* in $y$ values is a constant.   In symbols, $y = y_0 + at$, where $y_0$ is the amount at time 0, and $a$ is the constant change in $y$ for each increase in $t$ by one unit.   Geometrically, the graph of $y = y_0 + at$ is a straight line with $y$ intercept $y_0$ and slope $a$.

For example, if the water level $y$ in a lake is originally 6 feet, and steady rain causes it to rise by 0.25 feet per hour, then in $t$ hours, $y = 6 + 0.25t$, whose graph is shown in Fig. 2-1.

| $t$ | $y$ | Difference in $y$ values |
|---|---|---|
| 0 | 6.00 | |
| 1 | 6.25 | $6.25 - 6.00 = 0.25$ |
| 2 | 6.50 | $6.50 - 6.25 = 0.25$ |
| 3 | 6.75 | $6.75 - 6.50 = 0.25$ |
| 4 | 7.00 | $7.00 - 6.75 = 0.25$ |
| 5 | 7.25 | $7.25 - 7.00 = 0.25$ |
| $\vdots$ | $\vdots$ | $\vdots$ |
| 19 | 10.75 | $10.75 - 10.50 = 0.25$ |
| 20 | 11.00 | $11.00 - 10.75 = 0.25$ |

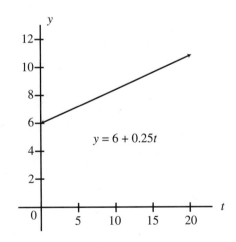

**Fig. 2-1**  $y = 6 + 0.25t$.

A quantity $y$ grows or decays *exponentially* with time $t$ if whenever $t$ increases by one unit, $y$ changes by a constant factor, i.e., the *ratio* of $y$ values is a constant.   In symbols, $y = y_0 a^t$, where $y_0$ is the amount at time 0, and $a$ is the factor by which $y$ changes for each increase in $t$ by one unit.

For example, if a bacteria population is 2000 at time $t = 0$, and the population is increasing by 8.5 percent each hour, then the population increases by a factor of 1.085 each hour, and $y = 2(1.085)^t$, where the population is measured in thousands (Fig. 2-2).

| $t$ | $y$ | Ratio of $y$ values |
|-----|-----|---------------------|
| 0 | 2.0000 | |
| 1 | 2.1700 | 2.1700/2.0000 = 1.085 |
| 2 | 2.3545 | 2.3545/2.1700 = 1.085 |
| 3 | 2.5546 | 2.5546/2.3545 = 1.085 |
| 4 | 2.7717 | 2.7717/2.5546 = 1.085 |
| 5 | 3.0073 | 3.0073/2.7717 = 1.085 |
| ⋮ | ⋮ | ⋮ |
| 19 | 9.4231 | 9.4231/8.6849 = 1.085 |
| 20 | 10.2241 | 10.2241/9.4231 = 1.085 |

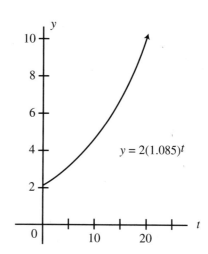

**Fig. 2-2**   $y = 2(1.085)^t$.

## 2.2   EXPONENTIAL GROWTH

The general equation representing exponential change of a quantity $y$ in terms of time $t$ is

$$y = y_0 a^t,$$

where $y_0$ is the (positive) amount of the quantity when $t = 0$, and the base $a$ is a positive quantity, unequal to 1. If $a > 1$, then $y$ increases with time, and $a$ is called the *growth factor*. The *growth rate* is $a - 1$, and the *percentage growth rate* is $100(a - 1)$ percent.

For example, suppose an investment of \$1000 is changing exponentially according to the formula $y = 1000(1.065)^t$, where $t$ is time in years after the investment. Here, $a = 1.065$, which is greater than 1, so the investment is growing. Also, $a - 1 = 0.065$, so the growth rate is $0.065 = 6.5$ percent per year. Or, we can say that the annual growth rate is 6.5 percent.

**EXAMPLE 2.1**   Suppose a population $P$, measured in millions, is growing exponentially according to the equation $P = 1.5(1.025)^t$, where time $t$ is measured in years. What is the population when $t = 0$? What is the growth factor? What is the growth rate? What is the population when $t = 5$ years? If the population continues to grow at the given rate, in how many years will it reach 1.8 million?

The population at time $t = 0$ is $1.5(1.025)^0 = 1.5$ million, and the annual growth factor is 1.025. The growth rate is $1.025 - 1 = 0.025$, or 2.5 percent per year. When $t = 5$, the population will be $1.5(1.025)^5 \approx 1.7$ million. To see when the population reaches 1.8 million, we set $P = 1.8$ and solve for $t$. That is, $1.8 = 1.5(1.025)^t$, and dividing both sides by 1.5, we get

$$1.2 = (1.025)^t.$$

Hence, $t$ is the exponent to which 1.025 must be raised in order to equal 1.2. We call this exponent the *logarithm* of the number to the given base. Here we write

$$t = \log_{1.025}(1.2),$$

which is read "$t$ is the logarithm of 1.2 to the base 1.025." We find the approximate value of $\log_{1.025}(1.2)$ in the next section.

## 2.3   LOGARITHMS

In Example 2.1, we determined that the time $t$ for the population to reach 1.8 million is equal to the logarithm of 1.2 to the base 1.025, i.e., the exponent to which 1.025 must be raised in order to equal 1.2. In symbols, $t = \log_{1.025}(1.2)$.   We normally use a scientific calculator to compute logarithms, but you will not find logarithms to the base 1.025 on a standard scientific calculator.   You will find a $\boxed{\log}$ key, which computes a logarithm to the base 10, and an $\boxed{\ln}$ key, which computes a *natural logarithm*, i.e., a logarithm to the base $e \approx 2.71828$, which is called the *natural base*.   That is, by definition, $\log(x) = \log_{10}(x)$ and $\ln(x) = \log_e(x)$. To compute a logarithm to some other base $a$, we use either of the *change-of-base* equations

$$\log_a(x) = \frac{\log(x)}{\log(a)} \qquad \text{or} \qquad \log_a(x) = \frac{\ln(x)}{\ln(a)}$$

Change-of-Base Equations

(See Problem 2.16.) With reference to Example 2.1, we find that

$$\log_{1.025}(1.2) = \frac{\log(1.2)}{\log(1.025)} = \frac{.0792}{.0107} \approx 7.4.$$

Similarly,

$$\log_{1.025}(1.2) = \frac{\ln(1.2)}{\ln(1.025)} = \frac{.1823}{.0247} \approx 7.4.$$

Hence, it will take approximately 7.4 years for the population in Example 2.1 to reach 1.8 million.

**EXAMPLE 2.2**   In each of the following cases, find the exponent $t$ to which the base $a$ must be raised in order to equal the number $x$.   State the results in terms of logarithms.

(a)   $a = 2, x = 16$        (b)   $a = 2, x = 0.125$        (c)   $a = 3.5, x = 10$

(a)   $2^t = 16$ when $t = 4$, i.e., $\log_2(16) = 4$.

(b)   $2^t = 0.125$ when $t = -3$ because $2^{-3} = \frac{1}{2^3} = \frac{1}{8} = 0.125$.   In terms of logarithms, we write $\log_2(0.125) = -3$.

(c)   $(3.5)^t = 10$ means $t = \log_{3.5}(10)$.   Using a calculator and a change-of-base equation given above, we find that

$$\log_{3.5}(10) = \frac{\log(10)}{\log(3.5)} = 1.8380.$$

**EXAMPLE 2.3**   Solve each of the following equations for $t$.

(a)   $5.24 = (1.05)^t$        (b)   $7.36 = 2(1.045)^t$

(a)   $t = \log_{1.05}(5.24) = \dfrac{\log(5.24)}{\log(1.05)} = 33.9479$

(b)   First, divide both sides of the equation by 2, obtaining $3.68 = (1.045)^t$.   Then

$$t = \log_{1.045}(3.68) = \frac{\log(3.68)}{\log(1.045)} = 29.6003.$$

## 2.4   DOUBLING TIME

The equation $y = y_0 a^t$ represents exponential growth when the base $a > 1$ (we always assume that $y_0 > 0$).   The time required for $y$ to double in value is called the *doubling time*.   By setting $y = 2y_0$, we get $2y_0 = y_0 a^t$, i.e., $2 = a^t$, which means that

$$\boxed{t = \log_a(2)}$$

Doubling Time for $y = y_0 a^t$   $(a > 1)$

or, using the change-of-base equations for computational purposes,

$$t = \frac{\log(2)}{\log(a)} \qquad \text{or} \qquad t = \frac{\ln(2)}{\ln(a)}$$

Computing Doubling Time for $y = y_0 a^t$   ($a > 1$)

For instance, the doubling time for the population in Example 2.1, in which $a = 1.025$, is

$$t = \frac{\log(2)}{\log(1.025)} \approx 28.1 \text{ years.}$$

Hence, the initial population of 1.5 million in Example 2.1 will reach 3 million in approximately 28.1 years. In the next 28.1 years, the population will double again, reaching 6 million. In fact, the population at any one time will double in 28.1 years after that time. A constant doubling time is characteristic of exponential growth.

**EXAMPLE 2.4**   A bacteria culture is growing exponentially at the rate of 5 percent per day. Initially there are 10,000 bacteria in the culture.

(*a*)   What is the equation for the number of bacteria in terms of time $t$, measured in days?

(*b*)   What is the doubling time for the culture?

(*c*)   Use part (*b*) to determine when there will be 80,000 bacteria in the culture.

(*a*)   Letting $N$ denote the number of bacteria $t$ days from the time in which there were 10,000 bacteria present, the equation is $N = 10,000(1.05)^t$.

(*b*)   The doubling time is $t = \dfrac{\log(2)}{\log(1.05)} \approx 14.2$ days.

(*c*)   To reach 80,000, the culture must double three times, i.e., from 10,000 to 20,000, then from 20,000 to 40,000, and then from 40,000 to 80,000. Therefore, the time required to reach 80,000 is $3(14.2) = 42.6$ days. This result can be verified by solving the equation $80,000 = 10,000(1.05)^t$ for $t$.

## 2.5  EXPONENTIAL DECAY

If a population $y$ is changing exponentially according to the equation $y = y_0 a^t$, where the base $a$ is between 0 and 1 ($0 < a < 1$), then the population is actually declining or decaying in time. Exponential decay is illustrated in Fig. 2-3, where $y = 5(0.75)^t$.

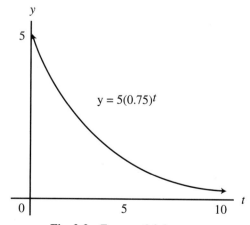

**Fig. 2-3**   Exponential decay.

If $0 < a < 1$, then $a$ is called the *decay factor*. The *decay rate* is $1 - a$, and the *percentage decay rate* is $100(1 - a)$ percent.

For example, suppose the value $y$ of an investment of \$1000 is given by the equation $y = 1000(0.95)^t$, where $t$ is time in years after the \$1000 investment. Here $a = 0.95$, which is less than 1, so the value of the investment is declining. The decay rate is $1 - 0.95 = 0.05$, which is 5 percent per year. Or, we can say that the annual decay rate is 5 percent. In Fig. 2-3, where $y = 5(0.75)^t$, the decay rate is 0.25, or 25 percent per unit of time.

## 2.6  HALF-LIFE

If a quantity is decaying exponentially, then the time for the quantity to be reduced to half of its original value is called the *half-life* of the quantity. Note that half-life of a declining quantity does not mean "half of the life" of the quantity but is the time for the quantity to change by a factor of 1/2. We can get a formula for half-life as follows. Given $y = y_0 a^t$, where $0 < a < 1$, set $y = \frac{1}{2} y_0$ and solve for $t$. That is, $\frac{1}{2} y_0 = y_0 a^t$, and after dividing both sides by $y_0$, we get $\frac{1}{2} = a^t$, which means that

$$\boxed{t = \log_a(1/2)}$$

Half-Life for $y = y_0 a^t$   $(0 < a < 1)$

By using the change-of-base equations for computational purposes, we get

$$\boxed{t = \frac{\log(1/2)}{\log(a)}} \quad \text{or} \quad \boxed{t = \frac{\ln(1/2)}{\ln(a)}}$$

Computing Half-Life for $y = y_0 a^t$   $(0 < a < 1)$

**EXAMPLE 2.5**  Radium 226, which is used in cancer radiotherapy, decays according to the equation $y = y_0(0.999573)^t$, where the amount $y$ is measured in grams and time $t$ in years.

(*a*)  What is the half-life of radium 226?

(*b*)  If 100 grams of radium 226 is stored in a laboratory, how many grams will remain after 25 years?

(*a*)  With reference to the above formulas for computing half-life,

$$t = \frac{\log(1/2)}{\log(0.999573)} \approx 1{,}623 \text{ years.}$$

(*b*)  In 25 years, there will be $100(0.999573)^{25} \approx 99.94$ grams.

The fact that many toxic radioactive materials take so long to decay is one of the major environmental problems of today's society. Scientists have yet to find a solution for radioactive pollution.

## 2.7  GROWTH AND DECAY IN TERMS OF NATURAL BASE

The growth rate or decay rate determines the base $a$ in the equation $y = y_0 a^t$ for exponential growth and decay. For example, if the growth rate is 2.5 percent, then the base is $a = 1 + 0.025 = 1.025$, and if the decay rate is 2.5 percent, then the base is $1 - 0.025 = 0.975$. As we will see in the next chapter, it is sometimes convenient to use the natural base $e \approx 2.71828$ as the base for both growth and decay. We can use natural logarithms to represent exponential change in terms of $e$ as follows.

Suppose $a = 1.025$, and let $k = \ln(1.025) = 0.0247$. Then, by the definition of natural logarithm,

$1.025 = e^k = e^{0.0247}$, and $(1.025)^t = (e^k)^t = e^{kt} = e^{0.0247t}$. Similarly, if $a = 0.975$, and $j = \ln(0.975) = -0.0253$, then $(0.975)^t = (e^j)^t = e^{jt} = e^{-0.0253t}$. In general, we have the following equation for converting from base $a$ to base $e$.

$$a^t = e^{[\ln(a)]t}$$

Converting from Base $a$ to the Natural Base $e$

**EXAMPLE 2.6**   Convert each of the following formulas to the natural base.

(a)   $y = 500(1.05)^t$          (b)   $y = 100(.095)^t$

(a)   $y = 500(1.05)^t = 500e^{[\ln(1.05)]t} = 500e^{0.0488t}$

(b)   $y = 100(0.95)^t = 100e^{[\ln(0.95)]t} = 100e^{-0.0513t}$

With reference to Example 2.6, note that in part (a) we have exponential growth and $\ln(1.05)$ is positive, while in part (b) we have exponential decay and $\ln(0.95)$ is negative. In general, we have the following equations for exponential growth and decay in terms of the natural base $e$:

$$y = y_0 e^{kt} \qquad \text{and} \qquad y = y_0 e^{-kt}$$

Exponential Growth          Exponential Decay

$(k > 0)$                   $(k > 0)$

**EXAMPLE 2.7**   The number $N$ of cells in a culture increases exponentially according to the equation $N = 5000e^{kt}$, where $t$ is time in hours.

(a)   How many cells are present at time $t = 0$?

(b)   If there are 7500 cells in 2 hours, how many are present in 5 hours?

(c)   For what value of $t$ will there be 12,500 cells?

(a)   When $t = 0$, $N = 5000e^{k(0)} = 5000$.

(b)   We first use the fact that $N = 7500$ when $t = 2$ to find the value of $k$, and then solve for $N$ when $t = 5$: $7500 = 5000e^{k(2)}$ implies $1.5 = e^{2k}$, which means that $2k = \ln(1.5)$, or $k = \dfrac{\ln(1.5)}{2} = 0.2027$. Then, when $t = 5$, $N = 5000e^{0.2027(5)} \approx 13,776$ cells.

(c)   Set $N = 12,500$ and solve for $t$: $12,500 = 5000e^{0.2027t}$ implies $2.5 = e^{0.2027t}$, which means that $0.2027t = \ln(2.5)$, or $t = \dfrac{\ln(2.5)}{0.2027} \approx 4.5$ hours.

**EXAMPLE 2.8**   A cup of coffee contains 120 mg of caffeine, and the amount $A$ of caffeine $t$ hours after drinking a full cup is given by the equation $A = 120e^{-0.15t}$

(a)   How much caffeine is in the body in 2.5 hours?

(b)   When will there be 100 milligrams of caffeine in the body?

(a)   In 2.5 hours, there are $120e^{-0.15(2.5)} \approx 82.5$ mg of caffeine in the body.

(b)   Set $A = 100$ and solve for $t$: $100 = 120e^{-0.15t}$ implies $\dfrac{10}{12} = e^{-0.15t}$, which means that $\ln(10/12) = -0.15t$, or $t = \dfrac{\ln(10/12)}{-0.15} \approx 1.2$ hours.

## 2.8    DOUBLING TIME AND HALF-LIFE IN TERMS OF NATURAL BASE

Suppose $y$ is growing exponentially according to the equation $y = y_0 e^{kt}$. To find the doubling time for $y$, we set $y = 2y_0$, and solve the equation $2y_0 = y_0 e^{kt}$ for $t$ to determine that

$$t = \frac{\ln(2)}{k}$$

Doubling Time for $y = y_0 e^{kt}$    $(k > 0)$

For instance, in Example 2.7, where $N = 5000e^{0.2027t}$, the doubling time is $\dfrac{\ln(2)}{0.2027} \approx 3.4$ hours.

On the other hand, if $y$ is decaying exponentially according to the equation $y = y_0 e^{-kt}$, we set $y = \dfrac{1}{2}y_0$ and solve the equation $\dfrac{1}{2}y_0 = y_0 e^{-kt}$ for $t$ and determine that the half-life is

$$t = \frac{\ln(1/2)}{-k}$$

Half-Life for $y = y_0 e^{-kt}$    $(k > 0)$

For instance, in Example 2.8, where $A = 120e^{-0.15t}$, the half-life for caffeine in the body is $\dfrac{\ln(1/2)}{-0.15} \approx 4.6$ hours.

## 2.9    SUMMARY

The basic facts relating to exponential growth and decay are summarized in the following tables.

| Exponential Growth | Growth Factor (Per Unit of Time) | Growth Rate (Per Unit of Time) | Doubling Time |
|---|---|---|---|
| $y = y_0 a^t \; (a > 1)$ | $a$ | $100(a - 1)\%$ | $\dfrac{\ln(2)}{\ln(a)}$ |
| $y = y_0 e^{kt} \; (k > 0)$ | $e^k$ | $100(e^k - 1)\%$ | $\dfrac{\ln(2)}{k}$ |
| Relationship between $a$ and $k$ | $a = e^k$ | | $k = \ln(a)$ |

| Exponential Decay | Decay Factor (Per Unit of Time) | Decay Rate (Per Unit of Time) | Half-Life |
|---|---|---|---|
| $y = y_0 a^t \; (0 < a < 1)$ | $a$ | $100(1 - a)\%$ | $\dfrac{\ln(1/2)}{\ln(a)}$ |
| $y = y_0 e^{-kt} \; (k > 0)$ | $e^{-k}$ | $100(1 - e^{-k})\%$ | $\dfrac{\ln(1/2)}{-k}$ |
| Relationship between $a$ and $k$ | $a = e^{-k}$ | | $-k = \ln(a)$ |

## 2.10   COMMENT ON EXACT EQUATIONS, APPROXIMATE MATHEMATICAL MODELS, AND NUMERICAL ACCURACY

In this chapter we have, for the most part, applied the notions of exponential growth and decay to populations of cells or people and to radioactive substances.   In the next chapter we discuss exponential change in a financial context: compound interest and present value.   The equations for compound interest and present value are exact in that they give the amount of an investment, to the nearest penny, at a given time.   On the other hand, exponential equations applied to populations and radioactive substances are only approximations of the exact changes taking place.   They are referred to as *mathematical models* of the phenomena under study.   In any real instances of population growth or radioactive disintegration, there are factors affecting the changes that are not accounted for in the mathematical models.   Nevertheless, the models are sufficiently accurate to enable us to draw meaningful conclusions and make useful predictions.

Aside from the question of how accurately mathematical models represent actual phenomena, there is a question of numerical accuracy obtained when computations are made with the equations representing the models.   The equations in exponential growth involve powers and roots, and the numbers generated usually have decimal expansions with an infinite number of decimal places.   For instance, $\sqrt{2} \approx 1.4142$, but the complete decimal expansion of $\sqrt{2}$ has an infinite number of digits after the decimal point.   If a number is involved in the computation of a quantity, and we round off the number to so many decimal places, we get an approximation to the exact value of the quantity.   As a rule of thumb, any number computed by means of approximate values is only as accurate as the least accurate number used in the computation.   In this chapter, most of the numbers involved in computations have been rounded off to four digits after the decimal point.   Occasionally, we point out that more places are necessary to achieve reasonable accuracy.

# Solved Problems

## LINEAR VS. EXPONENTIAL CHANGE

**2.1.**   Harry has two job offers.   Company A offers $24,000 annual salary to start and guarantees a $3000 raise at the end of each year for 7 years.   Company B offers a $24,000 annual salary and guarantees a 10% increase in salary at the end of each year for 7 years.

   (*a*)   Describe the growth in salary in each case.

   (*b*)   Give a formula for the salary after $t$ years in each case ($0 \le t \le 7$).

   (*c*)   Which job offer results in a higher annual salary at the end of the seventh year?

   (*a*)   In the case of Company A, the growth in salary is linear because the difference in salary from year to year differs by the constant amount of $3000.   In Company B, the growth is exponential since the salary each year is 10% higher than that of the previous year, i.e., the annual growth factor is 1.1.

   (*b*)   For Company A, the salary formula is $S = 24,000 + 3000t$, and for Company B, $S = 24,000(1.1)^t$.

   (*c*)   For Company A, the salary in 7 years is $S = 24,000 + 3000(7) = \$45,000$, and for Company B, $S = 24,000(1.1)^7 = \$46,769.21$, so B's is higher.

**2.2.**   Starting at 6:30 A.M., snow falls at a steady rate of 0.5 inches per hour, and continues until 7 P.M.

   (*a*)   Find a mathematical model for the height of the snow between 6:30 A.M. and 7 P.M.

   (*b*)   What is the height of the snow at 3:15 P.M. and at 7 P.M?

(a)  The height $h$ is the snow in $t$ hours is $h = 0.5t$ inches, and since there are 12.5 hours between 6:30 A.M. and 7 P.M., the model holds for $0 \le t \le 12.5$.

(b)  3:15 P.M. is 8 hours and 45 minutes after 6:30 A.M., which is a total of 8.75 hours.  Therefore, at 3:15 P.M., the height of the snow is $0.5(8.75) \approx 4.4$ inches.  By 7 P.M., the height is $0.5(12.5) = 6.25$ inches.

**2.3.**  If the snow in Problem 2.2 begins to melt, starting at noon the next day, at a rate of 0.75 inches per hour, what will be the height of the snow in $t$ hours while melting, and at what time will the snow be completely gone?

The height of the snow $t$ hours after starting to melt is $h = 6.25 - 0.75t$, which holds until $h = 0$. Solving $0 = 6.25 - 0.75t$, we find that $t = 6.25/0.75 = 8\frac{1}{3}$ hours.  Hence, the snow will be completely gone by 8:20 P.M. the next day.

**2.4.**  The annual CD sales for Company A are \$2,500,000, and the company projects an increase of \$25,000 per year for the next 5 years.  Give a mathematical model for the annual sales over the 5-year period.

In $t$ years the sales will be $S = 2,500,000 + 25,000t$ dollars, which holds for $0 \le t \le 5$.

**2.5.**  Company B (see Problem 2.4) has annual CD sales of \$2,350,000, but it projects that sales will increase by 2.5 percent per year over the next five years.  Give a mathematical model for B's projected sales over the 5-year period.

The growth rate is 2.5 percent $= 0.025$ per year, so the yearly growth factor is 1.025 and the projected sales are given by $S = 2,350,000(1.025)^t$.

**2.6.**  Construct a table for the projected sales to the nearest dollar for Companies A and B in Problems 2.4 and 2.5 over the 5-year period.  When do B's projected sales overtake A's?

As the table below indicates, by the end of the fifth year, Company B's projected annual sales will be greater than A's.

| End of Year | 1 | 2 | 3 | 4 | 5 |
|---|---|---|---|---|---|
| Company A | 2,525,000 | 2,550,000 | 2,575,000 | 2,600,000 | 2,625,000 |
| Company B | 2,408,750 | 2,468,969 | 2,530,693 | 2,593,960 | 2,658,809 |

## EXPONENTIAL GROWTH

**2.7.**  A cell culture is growing exponentially with a daily growth factor of 1.015.  If there were 1500 cells at time $t = 0$, how many cells will there be one week later?

The number of cells $t$ days later is $y = 1500(1.015)^t$, so in 7 days the number will be $1500(1.015)^7 \approx 1665$.

**2.8.** The number of bacteria cells is growing exponentially according to the mathematical model $y = y_0(1.004)^t$, where $t$ is measured in hours.   If there are 10,000 cells when $t = 8$, how many cells were there when $t = 0$ ?

We have $10,000 = y_0(1.004)^8$, so $y_0 = \dfrac{10,000}{(1.004)^8} \approx 9686$ cells.

**2.9.** A population is growing exponentially, and the growth rate is 0.25 percent per year.   If the population was 1.5 million in 2002, what will it be in 2012?

In decimal form the growth rate is 0.0025, so the growth factor is 1.0025.   If we let 2002 correspond to $t = 0$, then the population $t$ years after 2002 is $P = 1.5(1.0025)^t$.   Therefore, the population in 2012 will be $1.5(1.0025)^{10} \approx 1.54$ million.

**2.10.** A cell culture is increasing exponentially according to the mathematical model $y = y_0 a^t$, where time $t$ is measured in hours.   If originally there were 1000 cells, and 2 hours later there are 9000 cells, how many cells are present in 5 hours?

Since there were originally 1000 cells, the number of cells in $t$ hours is $y = 1000a^t$, and since $y = 9000$ when $t = 2$, we have $9000 = 1000(a^2)$, which implies $9 = a^2$, so $a = 3$.   Hence, $y = 1000(3^t)$, so when $t = 5$, $y = 1000(3^5) = 1000(243) = 243,000$ cells.

**2.11.** The population of a country is growing exponentially.   If it was 2.5 million in 1980 and 3 million in 2000, what will the population be in 2010?

Let $P$ denote the population, and let the year 1980 correspond to $t = 0$.   Then $P_0 = 2.5$ million, and $P = 2.5a^t$.   The year 2000 corresponds to $t = 20$, so $3 = 2.5a^{20}$, which implies that $a = \sqrt[20]{3/2.5} \approx 1.0092$.   The year 2010 corresponds to $t = 30$, so in 2010 the population will be $2.5(1.0092)^{30} \approx 3.29$ million.

**2.12.** Suppose the number of bacteria in a culture grows exponentially and doubles every hour.   What is the hourly growth factor? What is the hourly growth rate? If originally there were 100 bacteria, how many are there after 12 hours?

The ratio of the number at any time to the number one hour earlier is 2, so the hourly growth factor is $a = 2$.   The hourly growth rate is $a - 1 = 1$, which is 100 percent per hour.   In $t$ hours there are $100(2^t)$ bacteria, so in 12 hours, the number of bacteria is $100(2^{12}) = 100(4096) = 409,600$.

**2.13.** Suppose the number of bacteria doubles every half hour.   If originally there are 100 bacteria, how many are there in $t$ hours? How many are there in 12 hours?

We first select a unit of time.   If we take 1/2 hour to be the time unit, then the ratio of the number at any time to the number one-half hour earlier is 2, so the half-hourly growth factor is $a = 2$, and in $t$ half hours there are $100(2^t)$ bacteria.   In 12 hours there are 24 half hours, so the number of bacteria in 12 hours is $100(2^{24}) = 100(16,777,216) = 1,677,721,600$.

If we take 1 hour to be the time unit, then the ratio of the number at any time to the number one hour earlier is 4, so the hourly growth factor is $a = 4$, and in $t$ hours there are $100(4^t)$ bacteria.   In 12 hours, the number of bacteria is $100(4^{12}) = 100(16,777,216) = 1,677,721,600$, which agrees, as it should, with the result obtained with 1/2 hour as the time unit.

## LOGARITHMS

**2.14.** In each of the following equations, express the solution for $t$ in terms of a logarithm.

(a)  $6 = 2^t$                (b)  $0.28 = (0.96)^t$                (c)  $35 = 4(1.04)^t$

(a)  $t = \log_2(6)$,         (b)  $t = \log_{0.96}(0.28)$,         (c) First divide both sides by 4 to obtain $8.75 = (1.04)^t$.   Then $t = \log_{1.04}(8.75)$.

**2.15.** Use the relationship $\log_a(x) = \dfrac{\log(x)}{\log(a)}$, where log denotes logarithm to the base 10, to evaluate each of the logarithms in Problem 2.14.   (Round answers to 4 decimal places.)

(a)  $\log_2(6) = \dfrac{\log(6)}{\log(2)} = 2.5850$

(b)  $\log_{0.96}(0.28) = \dfrac{\log(0.28)}{\log(0.96)} = 31.1833$

(c)  $\log_{1.04}(8.75) = \dfrac{\log(8.75)}{\log(1.04)} = 55.3038$

Note that the same answers can be obtained by the relationship $\log_a(x) = \dfrac{\ln(x)}{\ln(a)}$, where ln denotes logarithm to the natural base $e$.

**2.16.** Prove the relationship $\log_a(x) = \dfrac{\log(x)}{\log(a)}$.

Let $u = \log_a(x)$, $v = \log(x)$, and $w = \log(a)$.   Then, by the definition of logarithm, $a^u = x$, $10^v = x$, and $10^w = a$.   Therefore, $10^v = a^u = (10^w)^u = 10^{wu}$, which means $wu = v$, or $u = \dfrac{v}{w}$, which is the desired result.

The same method can be used to prove the relationship $\log_a(x) = \dfrac{\ln(x)}{\ln(a)}$.

**2.17.** A population is growing according to the formula $y = 25,000(1.0085)^t$, where the units for time $t$ are years.   When will the population reach 30,000?

We must solve the equation $30,000 = 25,000(1.0085)^t$ for $t$.   Dividing both sides by 25,000 gives $1.2 = (1.0085)^t$, so $t = \log_{1.0085}(1.2) = \dfrac{\log(1.2)}{\log(1.0085)} \approx 21.5$ years.

**2.18.** The number of bacteria cells is increasing exponentially, with an hourly growth factor of 1.075. After 6 hours there are 2000 cells.   When will there be 3000 cells?

The number of cells in $t$ hours is $y = y_0(1.075)^t$, and we are given that $2000 = y_0(1.075)^6$. Therefore, $y_0 = \dfrac{2000}{(1.075)^6} \approx 1296$, so $y = 1296(1.075)^t$. To find when there are 3000 cells, we solve $3000 = 1296(1.075)^t$ for $t$. Since $\dfrac{3000}{1296} = 2.3148$, it follows that $t = \log_{1.075}(2.3148) = \dfrac{\log(2.3148)}{\log(1.075)} \approx 11.6$ hours.

**2.19.** A cell culture is increasing in number by 2.5 percent per day. If originally there were 12,000 cells, when will there be 25,000 cells?

The daily growth rate is 2.5 percent $= 0.025$, so the daily growth factor is 1.025, and the number of cells in $t$ days is $y = 12{,}000(1.025)^t$. We must therefore solve the equation $25{,}000 = 12{,}000(1.025)^t$ for $t$. Dividing both sides by 12,000 gives $2.0833 = (1.025)^t$, so $t = \log_{1.025}(2.0833) = \dfrac{\log(2.0833)}{\log(1.025)} \approx 29.7$ days.

**2.20.** The population of a small country is growing exponentially and doubled in 10 years. When will the population triple?

Let $P$ denote the population, and let time $t$ be measured in years. Then $P = P_0 a^t$, and $2P_0 = P_0 a^{10}$, so $a = \sqrt[10]{2} = 1.0718$. Hence, $P = P_0(1.0718)^t$. To find when the population triples, we set $P = 3P_0$ and solve for $t$:

$$3P_0 = P_0(1.0718)^t \text{ implies } 3 = (1.0718)^t, \text{ so } t = \log_{1.0718}(3) = \dfrac{\log(3)}{\log(1.0718)} \approx 15.8 \text{ years.}$$

## DOUBLING TIME

**2.21.** A population is growing exponentially, with a growth factor of 1.045. What is the doubling time for the population?

The doubling time is $t = \log_{1.045}(2) = \dfrac{\log(2)}{\log(1.045)} \approx 15.75$ time units.

**2.22.** A population is growing exponentially at 7.5 percent per year. What is the doubling time for the population?

The growth rate in decimal form is 0.075, so the yearly growth factor is 1.075. The doubling time is $t = \log_{1.075}(2) = \dfrac{\log(2)}{\log(1.075)} \approx 9.6$ years.

**2.23.** A population is growing exponentially at 8 percent every 10 years. What is the doubling time?

Taking 10 years as the time unit, the doubling time is $t = \log_{1.08}(2) = \dfrac{\log(2)}{\log(1.08)} \approx 9$. Therefore, the population doubles in 90 years.

**2.24.** With reference to Problem 2.23, in which the population is growing at 8 percent every 10 years, does it grow at 0.8 percent every year?

No.   If a population grows at 0.8 percent per year, then in 10 years the population has increased by a factor of $(1.008)^{10} \approx 1.083$.   The population in Problem 2.23 grows by a factor of 1.08 every 10 years.

**2.25.** With reference to Problem 2.23, in which the population grows by 8 percent every 10 years, what is the growth rate per year?

Let $a$ denote the yearly growth factor.   If $P_0$ is the population at time 0, then the population in 10 years is $(1.08)P_0$.   Therefore, $(1.08)P_0 = P_0 a^{10}$, which means that $a^{10} = 1.08$, or $a = \sqrt[10]{1.08} \approx 1.0077$, so the annual growth rate is approximately $0.0077 = 0.77$ percent.

**2.26.** If the doubling time for a population is 5 years, will the population quadruple in 10 years?

Yes.   If $2P_0 = P_0 a^5$, then $2 = a^5$, so $4 = a^5 \cdot a^5 = a^{10}$   i.e., $4 P_0 = P_0 a^{10}$.

## EXPONENTIAL DECAY, HALF-LIFE

**2.27.** An antibiotic causes bacteria cells to die off at the rate of 20 percent per day.   If originally there were 15,000 cells present, (a) how many cells will be present in 7 days, and (b) how many days will it take for there to be fewer than 500 cells present?

The decay rate is 20 percent $= 0.2$, so the daily decay factor is $1 - 0.2 = 0.8$, and there are $15,000(0.8)^t$ bacteria cells $t$ days after administering the antibiotic.

(a)   In 7 days there are $15,000(0.8)^7 \approx 3146$ cells.

(b)   We solve $500 = 15,000(0.8)^t$ for $t$: $t = \log_{0.8}(500/15,000) = \log_{0.8}(1/30) = \dfrac{\log(1/30)}{\log(0.8)} \approx 15.24$, so sometime after the 15th day there will be fewer than 500 cells present.

**2.28.** A substance is decaying exponentially.   If originally there were 1000 grams of the substance and three months later 700 grams were left, how many grams will be left in six months?

The number of grams in $t$ months is $y = 1000a^t$, where $a$ is the monthly decay factor.   We are given that $700 = 1000a^3$, or $0.7 = a^3$, so $a = \sqrt[3]{0.7} = 0.8879$.   Then, when $t = 6$, the number of grams is $1000(0.8879)^6 \approx 490$.   Alternatively, we can say $a^6 = a^3 a^3 = 0.7(0.7) = 0.49$, so in 6 months $y = 1000a^6 = 1000(0.49) = 490$ grams.

**2.29.** If a substance that is decaying exponentially decays to 40 percent of its original value in 5 years, will it decay to 40 percent of its 5-year value in the next 5 years?

Yes.   Let $y = y_0 a^t$ be the formula for the amount of the quantity in $t$ years.   When $t = 5$, $y = 0.4y_0$, so $0.4y_0 = y_0 a^5$, which means $0.4 = a^5$.   Now 40 percent of the 5-year value is $0.4(0.4y_0) = a^5(a^5 y_0) = y_0 a^{10}$.   Hence, in 10 years, $y$ is 40 percent of its 5-year value, which is 16 percent of its original value.

**2.30.** What is the half-life of the bacteria in Problem 2.27?

The daily decay factor is 0.8, so the half-life is

$$\log_{0.8}(1/2) = \frac{\log(1/2)}{\log(0.8)} \approx 3.1 \text{ days.}$$

**2.31.** If a radioactive substance decays at the rate of 0.5 percent per year, what is its half-life?

Since the annual decay rate is 0.5 percent $= 0.005$, the annual decay factor is $1 - 0.005 = 0.995$. Therefore, the half-life of the substance is

$$\log_{0.995}(1/2) = \frac{\log(1/2)}{\log(0.995)} \approx 138.3 \text{ years.}$$

**2.32.** The half-life of a radioactive substance is 125 years. If originally there were 150 grams of the substance, how many grams will there be in 30 years?

The number of grams in $t$ years is $y = 150a^t$, where $a$ is the yearly decay factor. Since $y = 75$ when $t = 125$, we have $75 = 150(a^{125})$, or $0.5 = a^{125}$, so $a = \sqrt[125]{0.5} = 0.9945$. Therefore, in 30 years there will be $150(0.9945)^{30} \approx 127$ grams.

**2.33.** The half-life of radioactive polonium is 140 days. In how many days will there be 75 percent of the original amount left?

The amount of polonium in $t$ days is $y = y_0 a^t$, where $y_0$ is the original amount and $a$ is the daily decay factor. In 140 days, $y = \frac{1}{2}y_0$, so $\frac{1}{2}y_0 = y_0 a^{140}$, or $0.5 = a^{140}$, which means that $a = \sqrt[140]{0.5} = 0.9951$. We now solve the equation $0.75y_0 = y_0(0.9951)^t$ for $t$: $t = \log_{0.9951}(0.75) = \frac{\log(0.75)}{\log(0.9951)} \approx 58.6$ days. Note, because of the round-off of the decimal representation of $\sqrt[140]{0.5}$ to four decimal places, our answer is only approximate. We can get a possibly better approximation by leaving $a$ in the form $\sqrt[140]{0.5}$ and solving $0.75y_0 = y_0\left(\sqrt[140]{0.5}\right)^t$ for $t$. We get $t = \frac{\log(0.75)}{\log\left(\sqrt[140]{0.5}\right)} \approx 58.1$ days.

## GROWTH AND DECAY IN TERMS OF NATURAL BASE

**2.34.** Use the relationship $a^t = e^{[\ln(a)]t}$ to convert each of the following equations to the natural base.

(a) $y = 1200(1.025)^t$              (b) $y = 2500(0.75)^t$

(a) $y = 1200e^{[\ln(1.025)]t} = e^{0.0247t}$,       (b) $y = 2500e^{[\ln(0.75)]t} = e^{-0.2877t}$

**2.35.** Use the property $e^{kt} = (e^k)^t$ to convert each of the following equations to the form $y = y_0 a^t$.

(a) $y = 400e^{0.785t}$      (b) $y = 600e^{-0.25t}$

(a) $y = 400e^{0.785t} = 400(e^{0.785})^t = 400(2.1924)^t$

(b) $y = 600e^{-0.25t} = 600(e^{-0.25})^t = 600(0.7788)^t$

**2.36.** The number of bacteria in a colony increases exponentially and is modeled by $y = y_0 e^{kt}$, where $t$ is measured in hours. At time $t = 0$, there are 12,000 bacteria, and four hours later there are 50,000 bacteria. To the nearest 1000 bacteria, how many are present 10 hours after time 0?

Since there are 12,000 bacteria at time 0, we know that the number in $t$ hours is $y = 12,000e^{kt}$. To find the value of $k$, we solve $50,000 = 12,000e^{k(4)}$, or $4.1667 = e^{4k}$ for $k$. By definition, $4k = \ln(4.1667)$, so $k = \frac{\ln(4.1667)}{4} = 0.3568$. Therefore, the number present in 10 hours is $y = 12,000e^{0.3568(10)} \approx 425,000$, to the nearest 1000.

**2.37.** Check the result in Problem 2.36 by solving the problem using the growth model $y = y_0 a^t$.

Since there are 12,000 bacteria at time 0, we know that the number in $t$ hours is $y = 12,000a^t$, where $a$ is the hourly growth factor.   To find the value of $a$, we solve $50,000 = 12,000a^4$, obtaining $a = \sqrt[4]{4.1667} = 1.4287$.   Then the number of bacteria in 10 hours, to the nearest 1000, is $12,000(1.4287)^{10} \approx 425,000$, as in Problem 2.36.

**2.38.** Find the doubling time for the number of bacteria in Problem 2.36.

In the growth model for Problem 2.36, the number of bacteria in $t$ hours is $y = 12,000e^{0.3568t}$, so the doubling time is $t = \dfrac{\ln(2)}{0.3568} \approx 1.94$ hours.

# Supplementary Problems

## LINEAR VS. EXPONENTIAL CHANGE, LOGARITHMS

**2.39.** The median price of a house for Builder $A$ and Builder $B$ was \$150,000 in 1996.   The median price for $A$ went up \$5500 per year and that for $B$ went up 3.5 percent per year for the next 7 years (until 2003).   (*a*)   Find the median price for each builder in 2003.      (*b*)   Find the year that the median price for $B$ is greater than that for $A$.

**2.40.** Company $A$ and Company $B$ have \$200,000 sales in 2004.   Company $A$ expects to increase its sales \$12,000 per year and company $B$ expects to increase its sales 5 percent each year.      (*a*)   Find each projected sale in 2010.      (*b*)   Find the year that B expects to sell more than A.

**2.41.** The population of a town grew linearly between 1995 and 2002.   Suppose the population was 20,350 in 1997 and 21,000 in 2000.   Find the population in:      (*a*)   1995,      (*b*)   2002.

**2.42.** Find the exponents to which $a$ must be raised to equal $x$ where:      (*a*)   $a = 3, x = 81$,   (*b*)   $a = 64, x = 4$,      (*c*)   $a = 0.1, x = 100$.

**2.43.** Solve for $t$ in each exponential equation:      (*a*)   $72 = (4.5)^t$,      (*b*)   $1200 = 45(1.25)^t$,   (*c*)   $250 = 1500(0.95)^t$.

## EXPONENTIAL GROWTH, DOUBLING

**2.44.** A quantity grows exponentially at the rate of 4 percent per month.   Initially there were 100 units of the quantity.      (*a*)   Find the number of units (to the nearest integer) in one year.      (*b*)   Find the growth rate over a two-month period.

**2.45.** A population of 115,000 grows exponentially at the rate of 2.5 percent for 5 years and at 1.5 percent for the next 5 years.   Find (to the nearest integer) the size of the population after 10 years.

**2.46.** A population grows exponentially at the rate of 5 percent per year.   After 6 years, the population is 225,000.   Find (to the nearest integer) the original size of the population.

**2.47.** Suppose the doubling time for a bacteria culture is 1/2 hour.   Find the hourly growth rate.

**2.48.** The "*Rule of 72*" says: If the annual growth rate is $r$ percent, then the doubling time is approximately $72/r$ years. Starting with an initial amount of \$5000, find the amount after $72/r$ years where: (*a*) $r = 3$ percent, (*b*) $r = 6$ percent, (*c*) $r = 12$ percent.

### EXPONENTIAL DECAY, HALF-LIFE

**2.49.** Initially there are 1000 units of a substance which decays at the rate of 25 percent per day. (*a*) Find the number of units after 4 days, (*b*) Find the number of days for 90 percent of the substance to decay.

**2.50.** A substance is decaying exponentially. After 5 months there are 500 grams, and after eight months there are 400 grams. Find the original number of grams.

**2.51.** A radioactive substance has a half-life of 1500 years. How long will it take for one/fourth of it to disintegrate?

**2.52.** A radioactive substance disintegrates at the rate of 15 percent every 25 years. (*a*) Find the percent of the original amount left after 100 years. (*b*) How long will will it take for 75 percent of the substance to disintegrate? (*c*) Find the yearly rate of disintegration. (*d*) Find its half-life.

**2.53.** The amount of a drug decreases exponentially and is modeled by $y = 0.5e^{-0.15t}$, where $t$ is the number of hours after administrating 0.5 ml of the drug. (*a*) Find the amount of the drug left after 3 hours. (*b*) When will there be 0.1 ml left of the drug? (*c*) Find the half-life of the drug.

**2.54.** In each living thing the ratio of the amount of radioactive carbon-14 to the amount of ordinary carbon-12 remains approximately constant. However, when a plant or animal dies, the amount of carbon-14 decays exponentially and its half-life is approximately 5700 years. (*a*) Find the yearly decay factor for carbon-14. (*b*) Find the age of a piece of charcoal if 25 percent of the original amount of carbon-14 remains. (*c*) Paintings discovered in Lascaux Caves in France were found to contain, in 1950, 15 percent of the usual amount of carbon-14 in the paint. Determine the age of the paintings in 1950 to the nearest 100 years. [Willard Libby discovered this method of carbon-14 dating in 1950, and he received a Nobel Prize in 1960.]

# Answers to Supplementary Problems

**2.39.** (*a*) \$188,500 for $A$, \$190,842 for $B$. (*b*) The fourth year (2000).

**2.40.** (*a*) \$272,000 for $A$, \$268,019 for $B$, (*b*) Ninth year (2013).

**2.41.** (*a*) 19,850, (*b*) 21,600

**2.42.** (*a*) 4, (*b*) 1/3, (*c*) −2.

**2.43.** (*a*) 2.8434, (*b*) 14.7144, (*c*) 34.9317.

**2.44.** (*a*) 160, (*b*) 8.16%

**2.45.** 140,168

**2.46.** 167,898

**2.47.** 4

**2.48.** (*a*) $10,163.97, (*b*) $10,060.98, (*c*) $98869.11.

**2.49.** (*a*) 316.4, (*b*) 9 days

**2.50.** 725.36

**2.51.** 663 years

**2.52.** (*a*) 52 percent, (*b*) 213 years, (*c*) 0.65 percent, (*d*) 106.3 years

**2.53.** (*a*) 0.32 ml, (*b*) 10.7 hours, (*c*) 4.6 hours

**2.54.** (*a*) 0.9998784, (*b*) 11,400 years, (*c*) 15,600 years.

# CHAPTER 3

# Financial Mathematics

We now turn to the mathematics of finance, in particular, interest on investments and loans. Amounts accumulated on a single investment or required to pay off a loan in a single payment are covered in this chapter. Later in the chapter, we deal with amounts accumulated by a series of regular investments or required to pay off a loan in a series of regular payments.

A business or scientific calculator will be very helpful for working through the examples and exercises in this chapter. Also, there are tables having five-place accuracy in Appendix A to assist with the computations. All computations in these chapters were made with a 10-place calculator, and monetary amounts have been rounded off to the nearest cent. Hence, if you use a calculator with less than 10-place accuracy or if you use the tables in Appendix A, your answers may differ slightly from those in the text.

## 3.1 SIMPLE INTEREST

In financial transactions, *interest* is an amount paid by a borrower to a lender or investor for the use of money over a period of time. Interest that is paid as a percent of the amount borrowed or invested is called *simple interest*. The formula for simple interest is the following:

---

*Simple Interest*

$$I = Prt \qquad (3.1)$$

where $I$ = interest earned (or owed)
$P$ = principal invested (or borrowed)
$r$ = annual interest rate
$t$ = time in years

---

For example, suppose $500 is invested for 2 years at 6 percent simple interest per year. Then $P = 500$, $r = 0.06$, $t = 2$, and by formula (*3.1*)

$$I = 500(0.06)\,(2) = 60$$

Hence, the simple interest earned at the end of 2 years is $60. Note that percent means "hundredths"; therefore, to convert 6 percent to its decimal equivalent, we divided 6 by 100, obtaining 0.06.

The *accumulated amount A* of an investment (or debt) is the principal plus interest. In the case of simple interest the formula for the accumulated amount is as follows:

---

*Amount in Simple Interest*

$$A = P + I = P(1 + rt) \qquad\qquad (3.2)$$

---

The accumulated amount of the investment in the above example is

$$A = 500 + 60 = 560$$

Hence, the investment of $500 is worth $560 in 2 years.

The unit of time in simple interest transactions is the year. If time is given in months, convert the number of months to years by dividing by 12. For example, 18 months $= \frac{18}{12} = 1.5$ years. If time is given in days, convert the number of days to years by dividing by 365 in the case of an *exact interest year*, or 360 in the case of an *ordinary interest year*. Banks sometimes use 365 days per year when computing interest on savings and 360 days when computing interest on loans.

**EXAMPLE 3.1**  A person borrows $2500 at 8 percent simple interest per year. Find the accumulated amount $A$ of the debt in (*i*) 90 days, assuming an ordinary interest year; (*ii*) 6 months; (*iii*) 1.5 years.

In all three cases, the principal $P$ is 2500 and the annual interest rate $r$ is 0.08. To find the accumulated amount $A$, we first express the given time in terms of years and then use formula (*3.2*).

(*i*)   $t = \frac{90}{360};$   $A = 2500[1 + 0.08(\frac{90}{360})] = 2500(1.02) = \$2550$

(*ii*)   $t = \frac{6}{12};$   $A = 2500[1 + 0.08(\frac{6}{12})] = 2500(1.04) = \$2600$

(*iii*)   $t = 1.5;$   $A = 2500[1 + 0.08(1.5)] = 2500(1.12) = \$2800$

The principal $P$ is also called the *present value*, and the accumulated amount $A$ is also called the *future value*. In the case of simple interest, the formula for the present value, obtained from formula (*3.2*), is as follows:

---

*Present Value in Simple Interest*

$$P = \frac{A}{1 + rt} \qquad\qquad (3.3)$$

---

**EXAMPLE 3.2**  It is desired that the value of an investment at 5 percent annual simple interest should be $12,000 in 4 years. What amount must be invested now?

Substitute $A = 12,000$, $r = 0.05$, and $t = 4$ in formula (*3.3*) for present value to obtain

$$P = \frac{12,000}{1 + 0.05(4)} = 10,000$$

Hence, an investment of $10,000 will yield $12,000 in 4 years.

## 3.2  SIMPLE DISCOUNT

If a lender deducts in advance the interest due on a loan, the amount deducted is called the *discount*. The formula for simple discount is the following:

---

*Simple Discount*

$$D = Sdt \qquad (3.4)$$

where $D$ = discount (amount deducted in advance by lender)
     $S$ = amount of the loan (amount paid back by the borrower at the end of the loan)
     $d$ = annual discount rate
     $t$ = time of the loan in years

---

For example from formula (*3.4*) for $D$, the discount on a loan of $500 for 2 years at 6 percent simple discount is $D = 500(0.06)(2) = 60$. Hence, the lender deducts $60 from the $500 loan. The borrower receives $440 and must pay back $500 at the end of 2 years.

Note that in the above example, the borrower receives only $440 of the $500 loan, since $60 was deducted at the outset of the loan. In general, the amount actually received by the borrower in a discounted loan is called the *proceeds* of the loan. The formula for the proceeds $P$ in simple discounting is the following:

---

*Proceeds in Simple Discount*

$$P = S - D = S(1 - dt) \qquad (3.5)$$

---

The amount $S$ of the loan, which is the amount the borrower must pay back at the end of the loan, is, from (*3.5*), as follows:

---

*Amount in Simple Discount*

$$S = \frac{P}{1 - dt} \qquad (3.6)$$

---

**EXAMPLE 3.3** A loan is discounted over 30 months at a simple discount rate of 10 percent per year. (*i*) Find the proceeds if the amount of the loan is $1500. (*ii*) Find the amount of the loan if the proceeds are $1500.

In both cases the discount rate is $d = 0.1$ and the time is $t = \frac{30}{12} = 2.5$.

(*i*) For formula (*3.5*) for the proceeds, we get

$$P = 1500[1 - 0.1(2.5)] = 1125$$

Hence, of the $1500 borrowed, the borrower receives $1125.

(*ii*) From formula (*3.6*) for the amount, we get

$$S = \frac{1500}{1 - 0.1(2.5)} = \frac{1500}{0.75} = 2000$$

Hence, to receive $1500, the borrower must request $2000.

## 3.3  COMPOUND INTEREST

Simple interest is paid on the principal only. Interest that is paid on both the principal and the accrued interest is called *compound interest*. In compound interest transactions, interest is computed over regular intervals called *conversion periods*. The interest rate per conversion period is the annual interest rate divided by the number of conversion periods per year. For example, if the conversion period is monthly and the annual interest rate is 6 percent, or $r = 0.06$, then the interest rate per conversion period is $i = 0.06/12 = 0.005$, or 0.5 percent. The formula for the accumulated amount in compound interest, which is derived in Problem 3.21, is the following:

---

*Amount in Compound Interest*

   Suppose a principal $P$ is invested at an annual interest rate $r$, compounded $k$ times per year. Then the accumulated amount $A$ in $t$ years is

$$A = P(1 + i)^n \tag{3.7}$$

where $i = r/k =$ interest rate per period
   $n = kt =$ total number of conversion periods

---

   Table A-1 in Appendix A shows values of $(1 + i)^n$ for various choices of $i$ and $n$.

**EXAMPLE 3.4**  Someone invests $2500 at an 8 percent annual rate compounded monthly. Find the accumulated amount in (*i*) 3 months, (*ii*) 6 months, and (*iii*) 1.5 years. Compare with Example 3.1.

   In all cases, $P = 2500$, $r = 0.08$, and $k = 12$. Hence, $i = 0.08/12$. We use formula (*3.7*) to find the amount $A$.

   (*i*)   In 3 months there are three conversion periods, so $n = 3$. Then
$$A = 2500(1 + 0.08/12)^3 = \$2550.33$$

   (*ii*)   In 6 months there are six conversion periods, so $n = 6$. Then
$$A = 2500(1 + 0.08/12)^6 = \$2601.68$$

   (*iii*)   In 1.5 years there are $n = 12(1.5) = 18$ conversion periods. Then
$$A = 2500(1 + 0.08/12)^{18} = \$2817.62$$

By comparing the results here with parts (*i*), (*ii*), and (*iii*) of Example 3.1, we see that compound interest results in larger amounts than simple interest, and the difference between these amounts increases with time.

   In compound interest, as in simple interest, the principal $P$ and the accumulated amount $A$ are also called the *present value* and *future value*, respectively. The following formula expresses $P$ in terms of $A$:

---

*Present Value in Compound Interest*

$$P = \frac{A}{(1 + i)^n} = A(1 + i)^{-n} \tag{3.8}$$

---

   Table A-2 in Appendix A shows values of $(1 + i)^{-n}$ for various choices of $i$ and $n$.

**EXAMPLE 3.5**  It is desired that the value of an investment at 5 percent annual rate, compounded monthly, should be $12,000 in 4 years. What amount must be invested now? Compare with Example 3.2.

   The interest rate per conversion period is $i = 0.05/12$, and the total number of conversion periods is $n = 12(4) = 48$. Substituting these values and $A = 12{,}000$ in formula (*3.8*) gives

$$P = 12{,}000(1 + 0.05/12)^{-48} = \$9828.85$$

   In Example 3.2, under 5 percent simple interest, the present value was $10,000. Hence, under compound interest, a smaller present value will yield the same future value.

## 3.4  CONTINUOUS INTEREST

Compound interest for a given annual rate increases as the number of conversion periods per year increases. There is no limit to the number of annual conversion periods.   For example, interest could be compounded by the month, day, hour, minute, or second.   However, there is a limit to the amount of interest that can be obtained by increasing the number of annual conversion periods.   Suppose $r$ is the annual rate and there are $k$ conversions per year.   Then as $k$ increases without bound, the accumulated amount

$$A = P \left( 1 + \frac{r}{k} \right)^{kt}$$

approaches the following value (see Problem 3.23):

---

*Amount in Continuous Interest*

$$A_c = Pe^{rt} \qquad\qquad (3.9)$$

---

In this formula, $e$ is a number called the *natural base* (for exponential and logarithmic expressions).   The value of $e$ is approximately 2.718281828, and powers of $e$ can be obtained on a scientific calculator. In addition, Table A-3 in Appendix A shows values of $e^x$ for various choices of $x$.

The quantity $A_c$ in formula (3.9) is called the *amount obtained by continuous compounding*.   The word *continuous* is used to reflect that as $k$ gets larger and larger, the time length of each conversion period gets smaller and smaller, which ultimately results in instantaneous or continuous compounding.

**EXAMPLE 3.6**   Find the amount obtained in one year if $10,000 is invested at a 6 percent annual interest rate, and interest is compounded (*a*) monthly, (*b*) daily, (*c*) by the hour, or (*d*) continuously.

In parts (*a*), (*b*), and (*c*), we apply the formula $A = P(1 + r/k)^{kt}$, and in part (*c*), we use $A_c = Pe^{rt}$.   In all parts, $P = 10,000$.   $r = 0.06$, and $t = 1$.

(*a*)   $k = 12$;   $A = 10{,}000(1 + 0.06/12)^{12} = \$10{,}616.78$

(*b*)   $k = 365$;   $A = 10{,}000(1 + 0.06/365)^{365} = \$10{,}618.31$

(*c*)   $k = 365(24) = 8760$;   $A = 10{,}000(1 + 0.06/8760)^{8760} = \$10{,}618.36$

(*d*)   $A_c = 10{,}000e^{0.06} = \$10{,}618.37$

Note that there is only a 1 cent difference between the amount obtained in part (*c*), where there are 8760 conversions per year, and the amount obtained in part (*d*), where interest is compounded continuously.   Even if interest were computed every tenth of a second, for a total of 315,360,000 conversions, the accumulated amount would not exceed $10,618.37 for the year.

**EXAMPLE 3.7**   Find the amount obtained by continuous compounding when $1000 is invested at a 10 percent annual interest rate for (*a*) 5 years, (*b*) 10 years, and (*c*) 20 years.

In all parts, apply the formula $A_c = Pe^{rt}$, where $P = 1000$ and $r = 0.1$.

(*a*)   $rt = 0.1(5) = 0.5$;   $A_c = 1000e^{0.5} = \$1648.72$

(*b*)   $rt = 0.1(10) = 1$;   $A_c = 1000e^1 = \$2718.28$

(*c*)   $rt = 0.1(20) = 2$;   $A_c = 1000e^2 = \$7389.06$

In continuous interest, as in simple and compound interest, the principal $P$ is called the *present value* and the amount $A_c$ is called the *future value*.   The present value $P$ can be expressed in terms of $A_c$ by means of the following formula, obtained from formula (3.9):

*Present Value in Continuous Interest*

$$P = \frac{A_c}{e^{rt}} = A_c e^{-rt} \qquad\qquad (3.10)$$

Table A-3 in Appendix A shows values of $e^{-x}$ for various choices of $x$.

**EXAMPLE 3.8**   What is the present value of an investment whose value in 12 years will be $20,000 if interest is compounded continuously at an annual rate of 9 percent?

By formula (*3.10*), the present value is

$$P = 20,000e^{-0.09(12)} = 20,000e^{-1.08} = 20,000 \times 0.3395955 = \$6791.91$$

Hence, $6791.91 invested now will have a value of $20,000 in 12 years.

## 3.5   EFFECTIVE RATE OF INTEREST

In supermarkets, unit pricing is used to help the consumer compare the prices of different brands and different amounts of a given item.   Similarly, in financial transactions, the *effective annual rate of interest* can be used to compare future amounts of a given principal under different interest rates and conversion periods.

By definition, the effective annual rate of interest for a given transaction is the simple interest rate that will yield the same amount in 1 year.   For example, suppose $100 is invested at 8 percent annual interest, compounded monthly.   Then the amount in 1 year is

$$A = 100\left(1 + \frac{0.08}{12}\right)^{12} = \$108.30$$

The interest for the year is $108.30 − $100 = $8.30, which is 8.3 percent of $100.   Hence, the effective annual rate of interest is 8.3 percent.

The effective interest rate is also called the *annual yield*.   In contrast, the annual rate of compound or continuous interest is called the *nominal rate*.   These rates are related by the following formulas, which are derived in Problems 3.27 and 3.28:

*Effective Rate in Compound Interest*

In compound interest transactions, the effective annual interest rate $R$, or the annual yield, is

$$R = \left(1 + \frac{r}{k}\right)^k - 1 \qquad\qquad (3.11)$$

where $r$ is the nominal interest rate and $k$ is the number of conversions per year.

In the above example $100 was invested at an annual rate of 8 percent, compounded monthly, and we determined that the effective annual interest rate was 8.3 percent.   Formula (*3.11*) for $R$ gives

$$R = \left(1 + \frac{0.08}{12)}\right)^{12} - 1 = 0.083$$

Since 0.083 is the decimal equivalent of 8.3 percent, the formula agrees with our previous computation.

For continuous interest, we have the following, which is derived in Problem 3.28:

*Effective Rate in Continuous Interest*

In continuous interest transactions, the effective annual interest rate $R$, or the annual yield, is

$$R = e^r - 1 \qquad\qquad (3.12)$$

where $r$ is the nominal interest rate.

**EXAMPLE 3.9**  Find the annual yield equivalent to (a) 12 percent annual interest, compounded every 3 months, and (b) 11.8 percent annual interest, compounded continuously.

(a)   $r = 0.12$ and $k = 4$; by formula (3.11), the annual yield is

$$R = \left(1 + \frac{0.12}{4}\right)^4 - 1 \approx 0.1255 \text{ or } 12.55\%$$

(b)   $r = 0.118$; by formula (3.12), the annual yield is

$$R = e^{0.118} - 1 \approx 0.1252 \text{ or } 12.52\%$$

In comparing parts (a) and (b), we see that the terms in part (a) will yield a slightly larger return than those in part (b).

**EXAMPLE 3.10**  Which terms offer the best investment for 1 year?   (a) 10 percent simple interest, (b) 9.6 percent compounded monthly, or (c) 9.5 percent continuous interest.

The effective annual interest rates are as follows: (a) 10 percent; (b) $(1 + 0.096/12)^{12} - 1 \approx 0.1003$, or 10.03 percent; (c) $e^{0.095} - 1 \approx 0.0997$, or 9.97 percent.

Hence, 9.6 percent, compounded monthly, is slightly better than 10 percent simple interest, which in turn is slightly better than 9.5 percent continuous interest.

## 3.6   INTRODUCTION TO ANNUITIES

An *annuity* is a series of equal payments made at fixed intervals over a period of time.   For example, after the birth of a child, parents may start regular payments to meet the child's future college expenses.   A company may decide to set aside a certain amount each year for the purchase of new equipment 10 years from now.   These annuities are examples of *sinking funds* in which periodic payments are made to meet some *future* obligation.

Another type of annuity involves *amortization* of debts or assets.   Here periodic payments are made to dispose of a *present* obligation or holding.   For example, a home mortgage or automobile loan may be assumed, in which the debt is paid in a number of equal monthly payments.   Lottery winnings may be received in the form of an annual annuity over a period of years.   Retirement plans usually start with a sinking fund into which regular payments are made, and upon retirement the amount of the fund may be amortized in the form of monthly income.   Sinking funds are covered in Sec. 3.7 and amortization in Sec. 3.8.

The time interval for each payment in an annuity is called the *payment period*.   If the payments are made at the end of each payment period, the annuity is called an *ordinary annuity*.   Also, the conversion period for compound interest in an annuity is the same as the payment period.

## 3.7   SINKING FUNDS AND FUTURE VALUE

The amount, or future value, of an ordinary annuity in the form of a sinking fund is given by the following formula, which is derived in Problem 3.37:

---

*Future Value of an Ordinary Annuity*

Suppose a payment $R$ is made at the end of each payment period and the interest rate per period is $i$. Then the amount of the annuity after $n$ periods is

$$S = R\frac{(1 + i)^n - 1}{i} = Rs_{\overline{n}|i} \qquad\qquad (3.13)$$

---

Table A-4 in Appendix A gives values of the quantity $[(1 + i)^n - 1]/i = s_{\overline{n}|i}$ (read "$s$ sub $n$ angle $i$") to five decimal places.

**EXAMPLE 3.11**   To meet college expenses for their newborn child, the parents decide to invest $600 every 6 months in an ordinary annuity that pays 8 percent annual interest, compounded semi-annually.   What is the value of the annuity in 18 years?

The interest rate per period is $i = (\frac{1}{2})8$ percent $= 4$ percent $= 0.04$, and the number of payments is $n = 2(18) = 36$.   By formula ($3.13$), the amount of the annuity in 18 years is

$$S = 600 \; \frac{(1 + 0.04)^{36} - 1}{0.04}$$

$$= 600 s_{\overline{36}|0.04} = 600(77.59831385) = \$46{,}558.99$$

Hence, in 18 years the parents will have $46,559 for their child's college education.

The periodic payment $R$ into a sinking fund that will result in the future amount $S$ given in formula ($3.13$) is as follows:

---

*Periodic Payment into a Sinking Fund*

To obtain a future value $S$ in an ordinary annuity of $n$ payments at an interest rate $i$ per period, the periodic payment is

$$R = \frac{S}{s_{\overline{n}|i}} \qquad\qquad (3.14)$$

---

Table A-5 in Appendix A gives values of $1/s_{\overline{n}|i}$ to five decimal places.

**EXAMPLE 3.12**   A company wants to have $1,500,000 to replace old equipment in 10 years.   How much must be set aside annually in an ordinary annuity at 7 percent annual interest?

Here $i = 0.07$ and $n = 10$.   By formula ($3.14$), the annual payment is

$$R = \frac{1{,}500{,}000}{s_{\overline{10}|0.07}} = 1{,}500{,}000(0.072\ 377\ 50) = \$108{,}566.25$$

Hence, the company must set aside $108,566.25 at the end of each year for 10 years.

## 3.8   AMORTIZATION AND PRESENT VALUE

In Sec. 3.7, we discussed annuities in which periodic payments are made to accumulate a desired amount in the future.   Here we discuss a present investment that will provide income at regular time intervals, or, equivalently, a present debt that can be amortized (killed off) by a series of regular payments.   Both the present investment and the present debt are called the *present value* of an annuity which is given by the following formula, derived in Problem 3.38:

---

*Present Value of an Ordinary Annuity*

The present value $A$ of an ordinary annuity is

$$A = R \left[ \frac{1 - (1 + i)^{-n}}{i} \right] = R\, a_{\overline{n}|i} \qquad\qquad (3.15)$$

where $R =$ periodic payment
$\quad\ i =$ interest rate per period
$\quad\ n =$ the number of payment periods

---

Table A-6 in Appendix A gives values of the quantity $[1 - (1 + i)^{-n}]/i = a_{\overline{n}|i}$ (read "$a$ sub $n$ angle $i$") to five decimal places.

**EXAMPLE 3.13**   The winner of a $1 million lottery will be paid $50,000 at the end of each year for 20 years.   What is the present value of the lottery at 7 percent compounded annually?

We have $R = 50,000$, $i = 0.07$, and $n = 20$.   By formula (*3.15*), the present value is

$$A = 50,000 \, a_{\overline{20}|0.07} = 50,000 \,(10.594 \, 014 \, 25) = \$529,700.71$$

Hence, an investment of $529,700.71 now will result in annual payments totaling $1 million over a 20-year period.

The periodic payment $R$ for amortizing a present value $A$, be it a debt or a holding, can be obtained from formula (*3.15*) as follows:

---

*Periodic Payment in Amortization*

The periodic payment for amortizing a present value $A$ in an ordinary annuity is

$$R = \frac{A}{a_{\overline{n}|i}} \qquad\qquad (3.16)$$

where $n$ = number of payments
        $i$ = interest rate per payment period

---

Table A-7 in Appendix A gives values of $1/a_{\overline{n}|i}$ to five decimal places.

**EXAMPLE 3.14**   A car costing $10,000 is to be paid off by monthly payments over 4 years at 12 percent annual interest.   What is the monthly payment?

Here $A = 10,000$, $n = 12(4) = 48$, and $i = (\frac{1}{12})12$ percent $= 1$ percent $= 0.01$.   By formula (*3.16*), the monthly payment is

$$R = \frac{10,000}{a_{\overline{48}|0.01}} = 10,000(0.026 \, 333 \, 84) = \$263.34$$

Hence, 48 monthly payments of $263.34 will pay for the car.

**EXAMPLE 3.15**   The present value of a retirement fund is $500,000.   What annual income can be obtained over a 15-year period at 8 percent annual interest?

We have $A = 500,000$, $n = 15$, and $i = 0.08$.   By formula (*3.16*), the annual income is

$$R = \frac{500,000}{a_{\overline{15}|0.08}} = 500,000(0.116 \, 829 \, 54) = \$58,414.77$$

Hence, the retirement fund will yield $58,414.77 per year for 15 years.

# Solved Problems

Note that monetary values are rounded to the nearest cent.

## SIMPLE INTEREST

**3.1.**   A person borrows $1000 at 9.5 percent simple interest per year.   Find the interest owed in (*a*) 30 days, (*b*) 10 months, (*c*) 36 months, (*d*) 4.5 years.

First convert the given time to years; then use formula (3.1), where $P = 1000$ and $r = 0.095$.

(a)  Assuming an ordinary interest year, $t = \frac{30}{360}$, and $I = 1000(0.095)(\frac{30}{360}) = \$7.92$.   Assuming an exact interest year, $t = \frac{30}{365}$, and $I = 1000(0.095)(\frac{30}{365}) = \$7.81$.

(b)  $t = \frac{10}{12}$;  $I = 1000(0.095)(\frac{10}{12}) = \$79.17$.

(c)  $t = \frac{36}{12} = 3$;  $I = 1000(0.095)(3) = \$285$.

(d)  $I = 1000(0.095)(4.5) = \$427.50$.

**3.2.**  Someone invests \$1500 at 7 percent interest per year.   Find the amount of the investment in: (a) 60 days, (b) 6 months, and (c) 6 years.

First convert the given time to years; then use formula (3.2), where $P = 1500$ and $r = \frac{7}{100} = 0.07$.

(a)  Assuming an ordinary interest year, $t = \frac{60}{360}$, and $A = 1500[1 + 0.07(\frac{60}{360})] = \$1517.50$.   Assuming an exact interest year, $t = \frac{60}{365}$, and $A = 1500[1 + 0.07(\frac{60}{365})] = \$1517.26$.

(b)  $t = \frac{6}{12}$; $A = 1500[1 = 0.07(\frac{6}{12})] = \$1552.50$.

(c)  $A = 1500[1 + 0.07(6)] = \$2130$.

**3.3.**  It is desired that an investment amount to \$5000 at a simple annual interest rate $r$ in $t$ years.   Find the principal that must be invested now if (a) $r = 6$ percent, $t = 3$, (b) $r = 8$ percent, $t = 5$.

Use formula (3.3), where $A = 5000$.

(a)  $P = \dfrac{5000}{1 + 0.06(3)} = \$4237.29$

(b)  $P = \dfrac{5000}{1 + 0.08(5)} = \$3571.43$

## SIMPLE DISCOUNT

**3.4.**  Find the simple discount on a \$2500 loan for 2 years at an annual rate of (a) 10 percent, (b) 7.5 percent, (c) 12.3 percent.

Apply formula (3.4) to find the discount $D$, where $S = 2500$ and $t = 5$.

(a)  $d = 0.1$; $D = 2500(0.1)(2) = \$500$

(b)  $d = 0.075$; $D = 2500(0.075)(2) = \$375$

(c)  $d = 0.123$; $D = 2500(0.123)(2) = \$615$

**3.5.**  Find the proceeds from the loan in Problem 3.4.

Apply formula $P = S - D$ for the proceeds $P$, using the value of $D$ obtained in Problem 3.4.

(a)  $P = 2500 - 500 = \$2000$

(b)  $P = 2500 - 375 = \$2125$

(c)  $P = 2500 - 615 = \$1885$

**3.6.**  In Problem 3.5, the proceeds $P$ represent the amount actually received by the borrower, whereas the borrower must pay back \$2500 in 2 years.   Hence, the borrower in effect is paying simple interest on $P$ amounting to $I = 2500 - P = D$.   Determine the corresponding simple annual interest rate $r$ and compare $r$ with the discount rate $d$ in Problem 3.4.   Use the formula $I = Prt$ for simple interest; hence, $r = I/Pt$, where $t = 2$.

(a)   $I = 500$;   $r = 500/[2000(2)] = 0.125$,   or   12.5% compared to 10% simple discount

(b)   $I = 375$;   $r = 375/[2125(2)] \approx 0.088$,   or   8.8% compared to 7.5% simple discount

(c)   $I = 615$;   $r = 615/[1885(2)] \approx 0.163$,   or   16.3% compared to 12.3% simple discount

**3.7.**   What amount must be borrowed at 12 percent simple discount for 1.5 years in order to receive:
(a)   \$1000,          (b)   \$2800,          (c)   \$12,500?

Apply formula (3.6) for the amount $S$, where $d = 0.12$ and $t = 1.5$; hence,

$$1 - dt = 1 - 0.12(1.5) = 0.82.$$

(a)   $S = \dfrac{1000}{0.82} = \$1219.51$

(b)   $S = \dfrac{2800}{0.82} = \$3414.63$

(c)   $s = \dfrac{12{,}500}{0.82} = \$15{,}243.90$

## COMPOUND INTEREST

**3.8.**   A person invests \$10,000 for 40 months, and interest is compounded monthly.   Find the accumulated amount if the annual interest rate is (a)   5 percent, (b)   7.5 percent, (c)   10 percent.

Apply formula (3.7), where $P = 10{,}000$ and $n = 40$.

(a)   $i = \dfrac{0.05}{12}$;   $A = 10{,}000\left(1 + \dfrac{0.05}{12}\right)^{40} = \$11{,}809.51$

(b)   $i = \dfrac{0.075}{12}$;   $A = 10{,}000\left(1 + \dfrac{0.075}{12}\right)^{40} = \$12{,}830.27$

(c)   $i = \dfrac{0.1}{12}$;   $A = 10{,}000\left(1 + \dfrac{0.1}{12}\right)^{40} = \$13{,}936.86$

**3.9.**   What present value will amount to \$20,000 at 8 percent annual interest, compounded daily, in (a)   1 year, (b)   2 years, (c)   3 years?   Assume an exact interest year.

Apply formula (3.8), where $A = 20{,}000$ and $i = 0.08/365$.

(a)   $n = 365$;   $P = \dfrac{20{,}000}{(1 + 0.08/365)^{365}} = \$18{,}462.49$

(b)   $n = 365(2) = 730$;   $P = \dfrac{20{,}000}{(1 + 0.08/365)^{730}} = \$17{,}043.17$

(c)   $n = 365(3) = 1095$;   $P = \dfrac{20{,}000}{(1 + 0.08/365)^{1095}} = \$15{,}732.97$

**3.10.**   Find the future value of \$2500 in 30 months at     (a)   9 percent simple interest,     (b)   9 percent interest, compounded monthly, and     (c)   9 percent interest, compounded annually.

(a)  Using formula (*3.2*), where $t = \frac{30}{12} = 2.5$, we get $A = 2500[1 + 0.09(2.5)] = \$3062.50$.

(b)  Using formula (*3.7*), where $i = 0.09/12$ and $n = 30$, we get $A = 2500(1 + 0.09/12)^{30} = \$3128.18$.

(c)  Using formula (*3.7*), where $i = 0.09$ and $n = \frac{30}{12} = 2.5$, we get $A = 2500(1 + 0.09)^{2.5} = \$3101.03$.

## CONTINUOUS INTEREST

**3.11.**  Find the future value of $5000 at 10 percent annual interest under continuous compounding for (a)   2 years, (b)   6 months, (c)   90 days.

   We apply formula (*3.9*), where $P = 5000$ and $r = 0.1$.

(a)  $t = 2$, $rt = 0.1(2) = 0.2$, and $A_c = 5000e^{0.2} = \$6107.01$.

(b)  $t = 0.5$, $rt = 0.1(0.5) = 0.05$, and $A_c = 5000e^{0.05} = \$5256.36$.

(c)  Assuming an ordinary interest year, $t = \frac{90}{360} = 0.25$, $rt = 0.1(0.25) = 0.025$, and $A_c = 5000e^{0.025} = \$5126.58$.   Assuming an exact interest year, $t = \frac{90}{365}$, $rt = 0.1(\frac{90}{365}) = \frac{9}{365}$, and $A_c = 5000e^{(9/365)} = \$5124.82$.

**3.12.**  What principal will amount to $7000 in 5 years under continuous interest at an annual rate of (a)   4 percent, (b)   8 percent, (c)   12.5 percent?

   Apply formula (*3.10*), where $A_c = 7000$ and $t = 5$.

(a)  $rt = 0.04(5) - 0.2$; $P = 7000e^{-0.2} = \$5731.12$

(b)  $rt = 0.08(5) = 0.4$; $P = 7000e^{-0.4} = \$4692.24$

(c)  $rt = 0.125(5) = 0.625$; $P = 7000e^{-0.625} = \$3746.83$

**3.13.**  Which investment has the largest future value in 5 years: (a)  $4000 at 7 percent simple interest per year; (b) $4000 at 6.5 percent annual interest, compounded annually; or (c) $4000 at 6 percent annual interest, compounded continuously?

   We use formula (*3.1*) for (a), formula (*3.7*) for (b), and formula (*3.9*) for (c).

(a)  $A = 4000[1 + 0.07(5)] = \$5400$

(b)  $A = 4000(1 + 0.065)^5 = \$5480.35$

(c)  $rt = 0.06(5) = 0.3$;   $A_c = 4000e^{0.3} = \$5399.44$

   Hence, the investment at 6.5 percent, compounded annually, yields the largest amount.

## EFFECTIVE RATE OF INTEREST

**3.14.**  Find the annual yield $R$ for 12 percent nominal interest compounded (a) annually, (b) quarterly, (c) monthly, (d) daily, (e) continuously.

   We use formula (*3.11*) for (a) through (d), and (*3.12*) for (e).

(a)  $k = 1$; $R = (1 + 0.12/1)^1 - 1 \approx 0.12$, or 12%.

(b)  $k = 4$; $R = (1 + 0.12/4)^4 - 1 \approx 0.1255$, or 12.55%.

(c)  $k = 12$; $R = (1 + 0.12/12)^{12} - 1 \approx 0.1268$, or 12.68%.

(d)  Assuming an ordinary interest year, $k = 360$ and $R = (1 + 0.12/360)^{360} - 1 \approx 0.1275$, or 12.75%. Assuming an exact interest year, $k = 365$ and $R = (1 + 0.12/365)^{365} - 1 \approx 0.1275$, or 12.75%.

(e)  $R = e^{0.12} - 1 \approx 0.1275$, or 12.75%.

**3.15.** Which nominal interest has the highest effective interest: (*a*) 11.5 percent, compounded continuously; (*b*) 11.6 percent, compounded monthly; or (*c*) 11.8 percent compounded semiannually?

(*a*)   $R = e^{0.115} - 1 \approx 0.1219,$   or   12.19%

(*b*)   $R = (1 + 0.116/12)^{12} - 1 \approx 0.1224,$   or   12.24%

(*c*)   $R = (1 + 0.118/2)^2 - 1 \approx 0.1215,$   or   12.15%

Hence, 11.6 percent, compounded monthly, has the highest effective interest.

## MISCELLANEOUS INTEREST PROBLEMS

**3.16.** Solve formula (*3.2*) for *r* in terms of *A, P,* and *t*.

$$A = P(1 + rt) \qquad \text{[formula (3.2)]}$$
$$= P + Prt \qquad \text{(applying the distributive rule)}$$
$$A - P = Prt \qquad \text{(subtracting } P \text{ from both sides)}$$
$$r = \frac{A - P}{Pt} \qquad \text{(dividing both sides by } Pt)$$

**3.17.** Use the result of Problem 3.16 to find the simple annual interest rate *r* when (*a*)   $A = \$1980,$ $P = \$1500,$ $t = 2$ years; (*b*)   $A = \$2150,$ $P = \$2000,$ $t = 6$ months; (*c*)   $A = \$5000,$ $P = \$4800,$ $t = 90$ days (ordinary interest year).

(*a*)   $r = \dfrac{1980 - 1500}{1500(2)} = \dfrac{480}{3000} = 0.16,$ or 16%

(*b*)   $t = \frac{6}{12} = 0.5;$   $r = \dfrac{2150 - 2000}{2000(0.5)} = \dfrac{150}{1000} = 0.15,$ or 15%

(*c*)   $t = \frac{90}{360} = 0.25;$   $r = \dfrac{5000 - 4800}{4000(0.25)} = \dfrac{200}{1000} = 0.2,$ or 20%

**3.18.** Show that a simple discount rate *d* on a loan for *t* years is equivalent to a simple interest rate *r*, where $r = d/(1 - dt)$.

We set *I* from formula (*3.1*) equal to *D* from (*3.4*) and solve for *r*, assuming that the proceeds *P* in simple discount are equal to principal *P* in simple interest.

$$Prt = Sdt \qquad \text{(simple interest } I = \text{simple discount } D)$$
$$r = \frac{Sd}{P} \qquad \text{(canceling } t \text{ and solving for } r)$$
$$= \frac{Sd}{S - Sdt} \qquad \text{(proceeds } P = S - D = S - Sdt)$$
$$= \frac{d}{1 - dt} \qquad \text{(factor out } S \text{ in denominator and cancel)}$$

**3.19.** Find the simple interest rate equivalent to a simple discount rate *d* on a loan for *t* years, where
(*a*)   $d = 15$ percent, $t = 1;$     (*b*)   $d = 8$ percent, $t = 3.$

We use the formula for *r* derived in Problem 3.18.

(a)   $r = \dfrac{0.15}{1 - 0.15} \approx 0.1765$, or 17.65%

(b)   $r = \dfrac{0.08}{1 - 0.08(3)} \approx 0.1053$, or 10.53%

**3.20.**   Show that $P(1 + i)^m + P(1 + i)^m i = P(1 + i)^{m+1}$.   (This result will be useful in Problem 3.21.)

Since each term on the left in the above equation has $P(1 + i)^m$ as a factor, factor out $P(1 + i)^m$ to obtain

$$P(1 + i)^m + P(1 + i)^m i = P(1 + i)^m (1 + i) = P(1 + i)^{m+1}$$

which is the desired result.

**3.21.**   Derive the compound interest formula (*3.7*).

The desired result follows from the pattern in the listing below, where the last entry in each row is the amount at the end of the conversion period for that row (see Problem 3.20).   This amount is the principal for the next conversion period.

| Conversion Period | Principal | + Interest | = Amount |
|---|---|---|---|
| 1 | $P$ | $+ Pi$ | $= P(1 + i)$ |
| 2 | $P(1 + i)$ | $+ P(1 + i)i$ | $= P(1 + i)^2$ |
| 3 | $P(1 + i)^2$ | $+ P(1 + i)^2 i$ | $= P(1 + i)^3$ |
| 4 | $P(1 + i)^3$ | $+ P(1 + i)^3 i$ | $= P(1 + i)^4$ |
| $\vdots$ | | | |
| $n$ | $P(1 + i)^{n-1}$ | $+ P(1 + i)^{n-1} i$ | $= P(1 + i)^n$ |

**3.22.**   Use a calculator to compute values of $(1 + 1/n)^n$ for $n = 10, 100, 1000, 10,000, 100,000,$ and 1,000,000.   The values should approach the natural base $e$, which is an irrational number but whose value to 10 significant digits is 2.718 281 828.

The values, computed on a 10-place calculator, are shown in the following table.

| $n$ | $\left(1 + \dfrac{1}{n}\right)^n$ |
|---|---|
| 10 | 2.593 742 460 |
| 100 | 2.704 813 829 |
| 1,000 | 2.716 923 932 |
| 10,000 | 2.718 145 927 |
| 100,000 | 2.718 268 237 |
| 1,000,000 | 2.718 280 469 |

**3.23.** Suppose interest is compounded $k$ times a year for $t$ years at an annual rate $r$.   Show that as $k$ increases without bound, the compound amount $A = P(1 + r/k)^{kt}$ approaches the continuous amount $A_c = Pe^{rt}$, where $e$ is the natural base (see Problem 3.22).

Using algebraic rules for exponents, we write

$$P\left(1 + \frac{r}{k}\right)^{kt} = P\left(1 + \frac{r}{k}\right)^{(k/r)rt} \qquad \left(kt = \frac{k}{r}rt\right)$$

$$= P\left[\left(1 + \frac{r}{k}\right)^{k/r}\right]^{rt} \qquad [x^{pq} = (x^p)^q]$$

$$= P\left[\left(1 + \frac{1}{n}\right)^{n}\right]^{rt} \qquad \left(\text{substituting } n = \frac{k}{r}\right)$$

As $k$ increases without bound, so does $n = k/r$, and as illustrated in Problem 3.22, the value of $[1 + (1/n)]^n$ approaches $e$, the natural base.   It can then be shown that the last expression above approaches $Pe^{rt}$, as stated.

**3.24.** Suppose an amount $P$ is invested at an annual rate $r$, and interest is compounded continuously. Show that $P$ will double in $t = (\ln 2)/r$ years, where $\ln 2$ is the natural logarithm (base $e$) of 2.

We set $A_c$ equal to $2P$ in the formula $A_c = Pe^{rt}$ and solve for $t$.

$$2P = Pe^{rt} \qquad \text{(setting } A_c = 2P)$$

$$2 = e^{rt} \qquad \text{(canceling } P)$$

$$\ln 2 = \ln e^{rt} \qquad \text{(taking natural logarithms on both sides)}$$

$$\ln 2 = rt \qquad \text{(using properties of logarithms)}$$

$$\frac{\ln 2}{r} = t \qquad \text{(dividing both sides by } r)$$

Of course, the above algebraic steps required that neither $P$ nor $r$ is zero.

**3.25.** Use the result in Problem 3.24 to find the doubling time for a principal $P$ under continuous compounding when the annual interest rate is (a) 6 percent, (b) 8 percent, (c) 12 percent.

We apply the formula $t = (\ln 2)/r$ in each case.   The value of $\ln 2$ can be obtained from the appendix or a calculator.

(a)   $r = 0.06;$   $t = (\ln 2)/0.06 \approx 11.6$ years

(b)   $r = 0.08;$   $t = (\ln 2)/0.08 \approx 8.7$ years

(c)   $r = 0.12;$   $t = (\ln 2)/0.12 \approx 5.8$ years

**3.26.** The *rule of 72* says the doubling time under compound or continuous interest is approximately $72/100r$, where $r$ is the annual interest rate in decimal form.   Compute the actual doubling times when interest is compounded annually at (a) 6 percent, (b) 8 percent, and (c) 12 percent. Compare these times with those obtained by the rule of 72 and also with those obtained in Problem 3.25 under continuous compounding.

When interest is compounded annually, the compound interest formula (*3.7*) becomes $A = P(1 + r)^t$, where $r$ is the annual interest rate in decimal form and $t$ is the number of years.   Setting $A = 2P$, and proceeding as in Problem 3.24 to solve for the doubling time $t$, we get

$$2P = P(1 + r)^t$$
$$2 = (1 + r)^t$$
$$\ln 2 = t \ln(1 + r)$$
$$\frac{\ln 2}{\ln(1 + r)} = t$$

This formula, the rule of 72, and the results of Problem 3.25 can be used to construct the following doubling-time table:

| Rate | Annual compounding | Rule of 72 | Continuous compounding |
|------|--------------------|------------|------------------------|
| 6%   | 11.9 years         | 12 years   | 11.6 years             |
| 8%   | 9.0 years          | 9 years    | 8.7 years              |
| 12%  | 6.1 years          | 6 years    | 5.8 years              |

**3.27.** Derive formula (*3.11*) for the effective rate (annual yield) $R$ corresponding to an annual interest rate $r$, compounded $k$ times a year.

We set the amount $A$ in formula (*3.2*), where $t = 1$ and $r = R$, equal to the amount $A$ in formula (*3.7*), where $n = k(1) = k$, and solve for $R$.

$$P(1 + R) = P\left(1 + \frac{r}{k}\right)^k$$

$$1 + R = \left(1 + \frac{r}{k}\right)^k$$

$$R = \left(1 + \frac{r}{k}\right)^k - 1$$

**3.28.** Derive formula (*3.12*) for the effective rate (annual yield) $R$ corresponding to an annual interest rate $r$, compounded continuously.

Set the amount $A$ in formula (*3.2*), where $t = 1$ and $r = R$, equal to the amount $A_c$ in formula (*3.9*), where $t = 1$, and solve for $R$:

$$P(1 + R) = Pe^r$$

$$1 + R = e^r$$

$$R = e^r - 1$$

## SINKING FUNDS

**3.29.** A couple saves \$500 a month in an ordinary annuity paying 9 percent annual interest. What is its value in (*a*) 3 years, (*b*) 5 years, (*c*) 8 years?

We use formula (*3.13*), where $R = 500$ and $i = (\frac{1}{12})9\% = 0.75\% = 0.0075$.

(*a*)  $n = 12(3) = 36$;  $S = 500s_{\overline{36}|0.0075} = 500(41.152\ 716\ 12) = \$20{,}576.36$

(b)  $n = 12(5) = 60;$   $S = 500s_{\overline{60}|0.0075} = 500(75.424\ 136\ 93) = \$37,712.07$

(c)  $n = 12(8) = 96;$   $S = 500s_{\overline{96}|0.0075} = 500(139.856\ 163\ 8) = \$69,928.08$

**3.30.**  A debt of \$50,000 is due in 10 years.  How much must be set aside every 3 months in an ordinary annuity paying an annual interest rate of (a) 6 percent, (b) 8 percent, (c) 10 percent?

Use formula (3.14), where $S = 50,000$, $n = 4(10) = 40$.

(a)  $i = (\frac{1}{4})6\% = 1.5\% = 0.015$

$R = 50,000/s_{\overline{40}|0.015} = 50,000(0.018\ 427\ 10) = \$921.36$

(b)  $i = (\frac{1}{4})8\% = 2\% = 0.02$

$R = 50,000/s_{\overline{40}|0.02} = 50,000(0.016\ 555\ 75) = \$827.79$

(c)  $i = (\frac{1}{4})10\% = 2.5\% = 0.025$

$R = 50,000/s_{\overline{40}|0.025} = 50,000(0.014\ 836\ 23) = \$741.81$

**3.31.**  Find the future value of the following ordinary annuities: (a) \$100 a month for 7 years at 12 percent annual interest, (b) \$200 every 4 months for 15 years at 9 percent annual interest, (c) \$1000 annually for 20 years at 8 percent annual interest.

We use formula (3.13) for the value $S$ in each case.

(a)  $R = 100, n = 12(7) = 84, i = (\frac{1}{12})12\% = 1\% = 0.01$

$S = 100s_{\overline{84}|0.01} = 100(130.672\ 274\ 40) = \$13,067.23$

(b)  $R = 200, n = 3(15) = 45, i = (\frac{1}{3})9\% = 3\% = 0.03$

$S = 200s_{\overline{45}|0.03} = 200(92.719\ 861\ 39) = \$18,543.97$

(c)  $R = 1000, n = 20, i = 0.08$

$S = 1000s_{\overline{20}|0.08} = 1000(45.761\ 964\ 30) = \$45,761.96$

**3.32.**  Find the periodic payment for the following sinking funds: (a) monthly payments to accumulate to \$100,000 in 30 years at 9 percent annual interest, (b) semiannual payments to accumulate to \$250,000 in 25 years at 10 percent annual interest.

We use formula (3.14) to find $R$ in each case.

(a)  $n = 12(30) = 360, i = (\frac{1}{12})9\% = 0.75\% = 0.0075$

$R = 100,000/s_{\overline{360}|0.0075} = 100,000(0.000\ 546\ 23) = \$54.62$

(b)  $n = 2(25) = 50, i = (\frac{1}{2})10\% = 5\% = 0.05$

$R = 250,000/s_{\overline{50}|0.05} = 250,000(0.004\ 776\ 74) = \$1194.18$

## AMORTIZATION

**3.33.**  What amount invested at 8 percent annual interest in an ordinary annuity will yield an annual income of \$40,000 for (a) 15 years, (b) 20 years?

Use formula (3.15), where $R = 40,000$ and $i = 0.08$.

(a)  $n = 15;$   $A = 40,000a_{\overline{15}|0.08} = 40,000(8.559\ 478\ 69) = \$342,379.15$

(b)  $n = 20;$   $A = 40,000a_{\overline{20}|0.08} = 40,000(9.818\ 147\ 41) = \$392,725.90$

**3.34.** A credit card purchase of $500 is to be paid off in monthly installments at 18 percent annual interest. What are the payments if the installments are for (*a*) 1 year, (*b*) 2 years, (*c*) 3 years?

We use formula (*3.16*), where $A = 500$ and $i = (\frac{1}{12})18\% = 1.5\% = 0.015$.

(*a*)   $n = 12;$   $R = \dfrac{500}{a_{\overline{12}|\,0.015}} = 500(0.091\ 679\ 99) = \$45.84$

(*b*)   $n = 12(2) = 24;$   $R = \dfrac{500}{a_{\overline{24}|\,0.015}} = 500(0.049\ 924\ 10) = \$24.96$

(*c*)   $n = 12(3) = 36;$   $R = \dfrac{500}{a_{\overline{36}|\,0.015}} = 500(0.036\ 152\ 40) = \$18.08$

**3.35.** A house costing $150,000 is to be paid off in monthly payments at 9 percent annual interest. What are the payments if the mortgage is for (*a*) 15 years or (*b*) 30 years?

Use formula (*3.16*), where $A = 150{,}000$ and $i = (\frac{1}{12})9\% = 0.75\% = 0.0075$.

(*a*)   $n = 12(15) = 180;$   $R = \dfrac{150{,}000}{a_{\overline{180}|\,0.0075}} = 150{,}000(0.010\ 142\ 67) = \$1521.40$

(*b*)   $n = 12(30) = 360;$   $R = \dfrac{150{,}000}{a_{\overline{360}|\,0.0075}} = 150{,}000(0.008\ 046\ 23) = \$1206.93$

## MISCELLANEOUS ANNUITY PROBLEMS

**3.36.** The *n* terms $a, ar, ar^2, ar^3, \dots, ar^{n-1}$, where $a \neq 0$ and $r$ is called the common ratio, are said to form a *geometric progression*. Their sum $S$ is called a *geometric series*. If $r \neq 1$, it can be shown that

$$S = a + ar + ar^2 + ar^3 + \dots + ar^{n-1} = \frac{a(r^n - 1)}{r - 1}$$

(This formula will be useful below and in Problem 3.37.) Find the sum of the following geometric series:

(*a*)   $1 + 2 + 2^2 + 2^3 + 2^4 + 2^5 + 2^6$

(*b*)   $3 + 3(2) + 3(2^2) + 3(2^3) + \dots + 3(2^{10})$

(*c*)   $2 + 2(1.1) + 2(1.1)^2 + 2(1.1)^3 + \dots + 2(1.1)^{n-1}$

We apply the above formula for $S$ in each case.

(*a*)   $a = 1, r = 2,$ and $n = 7; S = \dfrac{2^7 - 1}{2 - 1} = 127$

(*b*)   $a = 3, r = 2,$ and $n = 11; S = \dfrac{3(2^{11} - 1)}{2 - 1} = 6141$

(*c*)   $a = 2, r = 1.1; S = \dfrac{2[(1.1)^n - 1]}{1.1 - 1} = 20[(1.1)^n - 1]$

**3.37.** Derive formula (*3.13*) for the future value of an ordinary annuity.

Suppose a payment $R$ is made at the end of each period and the interest rate per period is $i$. The following table gives the amount of each payment at the end of $n$ payment periods:

| Payment | Conversion periods | Amount |
|:-------:|:------------------:|:------:|
| 1 | $n - 1$ | $R(1 + i)^{n - 1}$ |
| 2 | $n - 2$ | $R(1 + i)^{n - 2}$ |
| $\vdots$ | $\vdots$ | $\vdots$ |
| $n - 2$ | 2 | $R(1 + i)^2$ |
| $n - 1$ | 1 | $R(1 + i)$ |
| $n$ | 0 | $R$ |

The future value of the annuity is the sum of the amounts in the last column of the table. Adding from bottom to top, we get a geometric series of $n$ terms, where $a = R$ and $r = 1 + i$. By the formula in Problem 3.36, the sum of the series is

$$S = \frac{R[(1 + i)^n - 1]}{i} = R\frac{(1 + i)^n - 1}{i}$$

which is the desired result.

**3.38.** Derive formula (*3.15*) for the present value of an ordinary annuity.

Suppose a lender loans an amount $A$ to be repaid by the borrower in the form of an ordinary annuity consisting of $n$ payments $R$ at an interest rate $i$ per payment period. The value of the annuity after $n$ payments should be the same as the amount the lender could obtain by investing $A$ now at compound interest for $n$ periods at the rate $i$ per period. That is, by formulas (*3.7*) and (*3.13*),

$$A(1 + i)^n = R\frac{(1 + i)^n - 1}{i}$$

By multiplying both sides of the above equation by $(1 + i)^{-n}$, and applying algebraic rules for exponents, we get the desired result:

$$A = R\frac{1 - (1 + i)^{-n}}{i}$$

**3.39.** When amortizing a debt $A$ by means of an ordinary annuity, for example, when paying off a home mortgage, part of each payment $R$ goes toward interest and the remaining part goes toward the reduction of the outstanding principal. The part that goes toward interest is $i$ times the outstanding principal, where $i$ is the periodic rate. That is, suppose $I_j$ is the part of the $j$th payment that goes toward interest and $P_j$ is the part that goes toward reduction of principal. Then

$$I_1 = iA \qquad\qquad\qquad P_1 = R - I_1$$

$$I_2 = i(A - P_1) \qquad\qquad P_2 = R - I_2$$

$$I_3 = i(A - P_1 - P_2) \qquad\quad P_3 = R - I_3$$

$$\vdots$$

$$I_n = i(A - P_1 - P_2 - \ldots - P_{n-1}) \qquad P_n = R - I_n$$

Use the above formulas to fill in the amortization schedule below for an ordinary annuity consisting of six semiannual payments over 3 years to pay off a loan of $2,000 at 15 percent.

We have $A = 2000$, $n = 6$, $i = \left(\frac{1}{2}\right)15\% = 7.5\% = 0.075$, and $R = 2{,}000/a_{\overline{6}|0.075} = 426.09$. These values substituted into the above formulas give the values in the table below:

Amortization Schedule[*]

| Payment number | Outstanding principal, $ | Payment to interest, $ | Payment to principal, $ | Remaining principal, $ |
|---|---|---|---|---|
| 1 | 2000.00 | 150.00 | 276.09 | 1723.91 |
| 2 | 1723.91 | 129.29 | 296.80 | 1427.11 |
| 3 | 1427.11 | 107.03 | 319.06 | 1108.05 |
| 4 | 1108.05 | 83.10 | 342.99 | 765.06 |
| 5 | 765.06 | 57.38 | 368.71 | 396.35 |
| 6 | 396.35 | 29.73 | 396.35[†] | 0 |

[*] Interest rate per period = 0.075; payment = $426.09.
[†] −0.01 adjustment on final payment.

# Supplementary Problems

## SIMPLE INTEREST

**3.40.** Find the simple interest on $1000 and the accumulated amount in (a) 30 days at 12 percent per year, (b) 8 months at 15 percent per year, and (c) 3.5 years at 15 percent per year.

**3.41.** At 8 percent simple interest per year, find (a) the value in 2 years of $1200 and (b) the principal amounting to $1200 in 2 years.

**3.42.** At what simple interest rate per year will $2000 amount to $3000 in (a) 2 years, (b) 5 years? (See Problems 3.16 and 3.17.)

## SIMPLE DISCOUNT

**3.43.** Find the discount on a $1500 loan and the proceeds at (a) 10 percent simple discount per year for 1 year, (b) 9.5 percent simple discount per year for 1.5 years.

**3.44.** What amount must be borrowed for 3 years at 10 percent simple discount per year in order to receive (a) $2000, (b) $2500?

**3.45.** Find the simple interest rate per year on the proceeds in each part of Problem 3.43 (see Problems 3.6 and 3.18).

## COMPOUND INTEREST

**3.46.** Find the future amount and total interest on $1000 invested for (a) 30 days at 12 percent annual interest, compounded daily; (b) 8 months at 15 percent annual interest, compounded monthly; (c) 3.5 years at 15 percent annual interest, compounded annually. Compare the results with those in Problem 3.40.

**3.47.** How much must be invested now in order to obtain $5000 in 2 years at (a) 6 percent interest, compounded monthly; (b) 12 percent annual interest, compounded monthly?

**3.48.** Which investment will amount to more in 4 years: (a) $2000 at 20 percent simple interest per year or (b) $1800 at 18 percent annual interest, compounded monthly?

## CONTINUOUS INTEREST

**3.49.** Find the future amount and total interest on $1000 invested under continuous compounding for (a) 30 days at 12 percent annual interest, (b) 8 months at 15 percent annual interest, (c) 3.5 years at 15 percent annual interest. Compare with Problem 3.46.

**3.50.** How much must be invested at 8 percent annual interest, compounded continuously, to obtain (a) $5000 in 3 years, (b) $10,000 in 6 years, (c) $7500 in 2.5 years?

**3.51.** At what annual rate $r$, compounded continuously, will a given amount double in $t$ years (see Problem 3.24)? Use this formula to find $r$ when $t$ equals (a) 6 years, (b) 8 years, (c) 10 years.

## EFFECTIVE RATE OF INTEREST

**3.52.** A bank offers certificates of deposit (CDs) at the following terms under monthly compounding: (a) 6 months at 7 percent nominal interest, (b) 18 months at 7.5 percent nominal interest, (c) 2 years at 7.75 percent nominal interest. Find the annual yield in each case.

**3.53.** A bank offers CDs at the following terms under continuous compounding: (a) 1 year at 8 percent nominal interest, (b) 3 years at 8.5 percent nominal interest, (c) 5 years at 8.8 percent nominal interest. Find the annual yield in each case.

**3.54.** What nominal rate $r$ will result in an annual yield $R$ if interest is compounded continuously (see Problem 3.28)? Apply this formula to find $r$ when (a) $R = 6$ percent, (b) $R = 9$ percent, (c) $R = 12$ percent.

## SINKING FUNDS

**3.55.** If $100 is deposited in a savings account at the end of each month, what is the amount in 5 years if the monthly interest rate is (a) $\frac{1}{2}$ percent, (b) $\frac{3}{4}$ percent, (c) 1 percent?

**3.56.** Find the future value of an ordinary annuity in 20 years at 8 percent per year if the annual payment is (a) $600, (b) $1200.

**3.57.** Computer equipment estimated to cost $10,000 will be needed to replace old equipment in 5 years. What amount must be put into a sinking fund every 6 months if the semiannual interest rate is (a) 3.5 percent, (b) 4 percent, (c) 4.5 percent?

## AMORTIZATION

**3.58.** What present value can be amortized by monthly payments of $50 for 2 years at an annual interest rate of (a) 12 percent, (b) 15 percent, (c) 18 percent?

**3.59.** An auto costing $12,500 is amortized by monthly payments at a 12 percent annual interest rate. What are the payments if the term of the annuity is (a) 3 years, (b) 4 years, (c) 5 years?

**3.60.** Construct an amortization schedule for a $5000 loan at 16 percent annual interest for 2 years, payments to be made quarterly.

# Answers to Supplementary Problems

**3.40.** (*a*)  For an ordinary interest year, $I = \$10$, $A = \$1010$; for an exact interest year, $I = \$9.86$, $A = \$1009.86$;
(*b*)  $I = \$100$, $A = \$1100$;        (*c*)  $I = \$525$, $A = \$1525$.

**3.41.** (*a*)  \$1392,        (*b*)  \$1034.48

**3.42.** (*a*)  25 percent,        (*b*)  10 percent

**3.43.** (*a*)  $D = \$150$, $P = \$1350$;        (*b*)  $D = \$213.75$, $P = \$1286.25$

**3.44.** (*a*)  \$2857.14,        (*b*)  \$3571.43

**3.45.** (*a*)  11.11 percent,        (*b*)  11.08 percent

**3.46.** (*a*)  For an ordinary interest year, $A = \$1010.05$, $I = \$10.05$; for an exact interest year, $A = \$1009.91$,
$I = \$9.91$;        (*b*)  $A = \$1104.49$, $I = \$104.49$        (*c*)  $A = \$1630.96$, $I = \$630.96$.

**3.47.** (*a*)  \$4435.93,        (*b*)  \$3937.83

**3.48.**  Investment (*b*) pays \$78.26 more than investment (*a*).

**3.49.** (*a*)  For an ordinary interest year, $A_c = \$1010.05$, $I = \$10.05$; for an exact interest year, $A_c = \$1009.91$,
$I = \$9.91$;        (*b*)  $A_c = \$1105.17$, $I = \$105.17$;        (*c*)  $= \$1690.46$, $I = \$690.46$.

**3.50.** (*a*)  \$3933.14,        (*b*)  \$6187.83,        (*c*)  \$6140.48

**3.51.**  $r = (\ln 2)/t$;        (*a*)  11.55 percent,        (*b*)  8.66 percent percent,        (*c*)  6.93 percent

**3.52.** (*a*)  7.23 percent,        (*b*)  7.76 percent,        (*c*)  8.03 percent

**3.53.** (*a*)  8.33 percent,        (*b*)  8.87 percent,        (*c*)  9.20 percent

**3.54.**  $r = \ln(R + 1)$;        (*a*)  5.83 percent,        (*b*)  8.62 percent,        (*c*)  11.33 percent

**3.55.** (*a*)  \$6977.00,        (*b*)  \$7542.51,        (*c*)  \$8166.97

**3.56.** (*a*)  \$27,457.18,        (*b*)  \$54,914.36

**3.57.** (*a*)  \$852.41,        (*b*)  \$832.91,        (*c*)  \$813.79

**3.58.** (*a*)  \$1062.17,        (*b*)  \$1031.21,        (*c*)  \$1001.52

**3.59.** (*a*)  \$415.18,        (*b*)  \$329.17,        (*c*)  \$278.06

**3.60.**

Amortization Schedule[*]

| Payment number | Outstanding principal, $ | Payment to interest, $ | Payment to principal, $ | Remaining principal, $ |
|---|---|---|---|---|
| 1 | 5000.00 | 200.00 | 542.64 | 4457.36 |
| 2 | 4457.36 | 178.29 | 564.35 | 3893.01 |
| 3 | 3893.01 | 155.72 | 586.92 | 3306.09 |
| 4 | 3306.09 | 132.24 | 610.40 | 2695.69 |
| 5 | 2695.69 | 107.83 | 634.81 | 2060.88 |
| 6 | 2060.88 | 82.44 | 660.20 | 1400.68 |
| 7 | 1400.68 | 56.03 | 686.61 | 714.07 |
| 8 | 714.07 | 28.56 | 714.07[†] | 0 |

[*] Interest rate per period = 0.004; payment = $742.64.
[†] −0.01 adjustment on final payment.

# CHAPTER 4

# Set Theory

## 4.1  INTRODUCTION

This chapter treats some of the elementary ideas and concepts of set theory which are necessary for many topics in finite mathematics.

## 4.2  SETS AND ELEMENTS; SUBSETS

A set may be viewed as any well-defined collection of objects, called the *elements* or *members* of the set. We usually use capital letters, $A$, $B$, $X$, $Y$, ..., to denote sets, and lowercase letters, $a$, $b$, $x$, $y$, ..., to denote elements of sets.   Synonyms for set are *class*, *collection*, and *family*.

Membership in a set is denoted as follows:

$a \in S$ denotes that element $a$ belongs to a set $S$.

$a$, $b \in S$ denotes that elements $a$ and $b$ belong to a set $S$.

(Here $\in$ is symbol meaning "is an element of.")

Suppose every element of a set $A$ also belongs to a set $B$.   Then $A$ is called a *subset* of $B$, or $A$ is said to be *contained* in $B$, written

$$A \subseteq B \text{ or } B \supseteq A$$

Sets $A$ and $B$ are equal if they both have the same elements or, equivalently, if each is contained in the other. That is:

$$\boxed{A = B \text{ if and only if } A \subseteq B \text{ and } B \subseteq A.}$$

The negations of $a \in A$, $A \subseteq B$, and $A = B$ are written $a \notin A$, $A \nsubseteq B$, and $A \neq B$, respectively.

**Remark 1.**   One usually puts a vertical line "|" or slanted line "/" through a symbol to indicate the opposite or negative meaning of the symbol, as above.

**Remark 2.**   The statement $A \subseteq B$ does not exclude the possibility that $A = B$.   However, if $A \subseteq B$ and $A \neq B$, then we say that $A$ is a *proper subset* of $A$ (sometimes written $A \subset B$).

### Specifying Sets

There are essentially two ways to specify a particular set. One way, if possible, is to list its elements. A second way is to state those properties which characterize the elements in the set. Examples illustrating these two ways follow:

$$A = \{1, 3, 5, 7, 9\} \text{ and } B = \{x : x \text{ is an even integer, } x > 0\}$$

That is, the first set $A$ consists of the numbers 1, 3, 5, 7, 9. The second set $B$ consists of the positive even integers. Note that a letter, usually $x$, is used to denote a typical member of the set; the colon is read as "such that"; and the comma as "and."

### EXAMPLE 4.1

(a) The above set $A$ can also be written as

$$A = \{x : x \text{ is an odd positive integer, } x < 10\}$$

We cannot list all the elements of the above set $B$, but we frequently specify the set by writing

$$B = \{2, 4, 6, \ldots\}$$

where we assume everyone knows what we mean. Observe that $9 \in A$ but $9 \notin B$. Also $6 \in B$, but $6 \notin A$.

(b) Consider the sets

$$A = \{1, 3, 5, 7, 9\}, \qquad B = \{1, 2, 3, 4, 5\}, \qquad C = \{3, 5\}$$

Then $C \subseteq A$ and $C \subseteq B$, since 3 and 5, the elements $C$, are also elements of $A$ and $B$. On the other hand, $A \nsubseteq B$, since $7 \in A$ but $7 \notin B$, and $B \nsubseteq A$, since $2 \in B$ but $2 \notin A$.

# Special Symbols

Some sets occur very often in mathematics, and so we use special symbols for them. Some such symbols follow:

**N** = The *natural numbers* or positive integers = $\{1, 2, 3, \ldots\}$

**Z** = All integers, positive, negative, and zero = $\{\ldots, -2, -1, 0, 1, 2, \ldots\}$

**R** = The real numbers.

Thus, we have $\mathbf{N} \subseteq \mathbf{Z} \subseteq \mathbf{R}$.

### Universal Set, Empty Set

All sets under investigation in any application of set theory are assumed to be contained in some large fixed set called the *universal set* or *universe of discourse*, which we denote by

$$\mathbf{U}$$

unless otherwise stated or implied.

Given a universal set **U** and a property $P$, there may be no elements in **U** which have the property $P$. Such a set with no elements is called the *empty set* or *null set*, and is denoted by

$$\emptyset$$

(that is, the Greek letter phi). The empty set $\emptyset$ is also regarded as a subset of every other set.

Accordingly, we have the following simple result, which we state formally:

**Theorem 4.1:** For any set A, we have $\emptyset \subseteq A \subseteq \mathbf{U}$.

**Disjoint Sets**

Two sets $A$ and $B$ are said to be *disjoint* if they have no elements in common.    Consider, for example, the sets

$$A = \{1, 2\}, \qquad B = \{2, 4, 6\}, \qquad C = \{4, 5, 6, 7\}$$

Observe that $A$ and $B$ are not disjoint, since each contains the element 2, and $B$ and $C$ are not disjoint, since each contains the element 4, among others.    On the other hand, $A$ and $C$ are disjoint, since they have no element in common.    We note that if $A$ and $B$ are disjoint, then neither is a subset of the other (unless one is the empty set).

## 4.3  VENN DIAGRAMS

A Venn diagram is a pictoral representation of sets using enclosed areas in the plane.    The universal set **U** is represented by the points in a rectangle, and the other sets are represented by disks lying within the rectangle.    Figure 4-1(a) pictures sets $A$ and $B$ such that $A \subseteq B$.    Figure 4-1(b) pictures sets $A$ and $B$, which are disjoint.

On the other hand, suppose $A$ and $B$ are two arbitrary sets.    Then it is possible that some elements are in $A$ but not $B$, some elements are in $B$ but not $A$, some are in both $A$ and $B$, and some are in neither $A$ nor $B$. Accordingly, in general, we represent $A$ and $B$ as in Fig. 4-1(c).

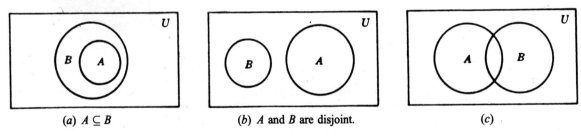

(a) $A \subseteq B$            (b) $A$ and $B$ are disjoint.            (c)

**Fig. 4-1**

## 4.4  SET OPERATIONS

This section defines a number of set operations, including the basic operations of union, intersection, and complement.

**Union and Intersection**

The *union* of two sets $A$ and $B$, denoted by $A \cup B$, is the set of all elements which belong to $A$ or to $B$.    That is:

$$A \cup B = \{x : x \in A \text{ or } x \in B\}$$

Here "or" is used in the sense of and/or.    Figure 4-2(a) is a Venn diagram in which $A \cup B$ is shaded.

The *intersection* of two sets $A$ and $B$, denoted by $A \cap B$, is the set of all elements which belong to both $A$ and $B$.    Namely:

$$A \cap B = \{x : x \in A \text{ and } x \in B\}$$

Figure 4-2(b) is a Venn diagram in which $A \cap B$ is shaded.

Recall that sets $A$ and $B$ are said to be disjoint if they have no elements in common.    Accordingly, using the definition of intersection, $A$ and $B$ are disjoint if $A \cap B = \emptyset$, the empty set.    On the other hand, if

$$S = A \cup B \text{ and } A \cap B = \emptyset,$$

then $S$ is called the *disjoint union* of $A$ and $B$.

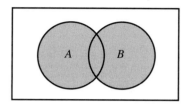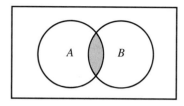

        (*a*)  $A \cup B$ is shaded.                      (*b*)  $A \cap B$ is shaded.

**Fig. 4-2**

### EXAMPLE 4.2

(*a*)   Let $A = \{1, 2, 3, 4\}$, $B = \{3, 4, 5, 6, 7\}$, $C = \{2, 3, 8, 9\}$.    Then:
$A \cup B = \{1, 2, 3, 4, 5, 6, 7\}$, $A \cup C = \{1, 2, 3, 4, 8, 9\}$,
$B \cup C = \{3, 4, 5, 6, 7, 8, 9\}$, $A \cap B = \{3, 4\}$, $A \cap C = \{2, 3,\}$, $B \cap C = \{3\}$

(*b*)   Let **U** be the set of students at a university, and let $M$ and $F$ denote, respectively, the sets of male and female students. Then **U** is the disjoint union of $M$ and $F$; that is,

$$\mathbf{U} = M \cup F \quad \text{and} \quad M \cap F = \emptyset$$

This comes from the fact that every student is in $M$ or in $F$, and clearly no student belongs to both $M$ and $F$.

### Complements, Differences

Recall first that all sets under consideration at a particular time are subsets of a fixed universal set **U**.    The *absolute complement* or, simply, *complement* of a set $A$, denoted by $A^c$, is the set of elements which belong to **U** but which do not belong to $A$.    That is:

$$A^c = \{x : x \in \mathbf{U}, \quad x \notin A\}$$

Some texts denote the complement of $A$ by $A'$ or $\bar{A}$.    Figure 4-3(*a*) is a Venn diagram in which $A^c$ is shaded.

The *relative complement* of a set $B$ with respect to a set $A$ or, simply, the *difference* of $A$ and $B$, denoted by $A \backslash B$, is the set of elements which belong to $A$ but which do not belong to $B$.    That is:

$$A \backslash B = \{x : x \in A, \quad x \notin B\}$$

The set $A \backslash B$ is read "$A$ minus $B$." Some texts denote $A \backslash B$ by $A - B$ or $A \sim B$.    Figure 4-3(*b*) is a Venn diagram in which $A \backslash B$ is shaded.

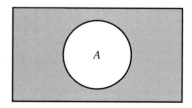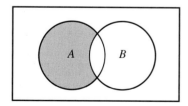

        (*a*)   $A^c$ is shaded.                     (*b*)   $A \backslash B$ is shaded.

**Fig. 4-3**

**EXAMPLE 4.3**   Let $\mathbf{U} = \mathbf{N} = \{1, 2, 3, \ldots\}$ be the universal set, and let

$$A = \{1, 2, 3, 4\}, \quad B = \{3, 4, 5, 6, 7\}, \quad E = \{2, 4, 6, 8, \ldots\}$$

(Here $E$ is the set of even positive integers.) Then:

$$A^c = \{5, 6, 7, 8, \ldots\}, \quad B^c = \{1, 2, 8, 9, 10, 11, \ldots\}, \quad E^c = \{1, 3, 5, 7, \ldots\}$$

That is, $E^c$ is the set of odd positive integers.   Also:

$$A\backslash B = \{1, 2\}, \qquad A\backslash E = \{1, 3\}, \qquad B\backslash E = \{3, 5, 7\}$$
$$B\backslash A = \{5, 6, 7\}, \qquad E\backslash A = \{6, 8, 10, \ldots\}, \qquad E\backslash B = \{2, 8.10, 12, \ldots\}$$

### Algebra of Sets

Sets under the operations of union, intersection, and complement satisfy various laws (identities) which are listed in Table 4-1.   In fact, we formally state:

**Theorem 4.2:**   Sets satisfy the laws in Table 4-1.

**Remark:**   Each law in Table 4-1 follows from an equivalent logical law.   Consider, for example, the proof of DeMorgan's law:

$$(A \cup B)^c = \{x : x \notin (A \text{ or } B)\} = \{x : x \notin A \text{ and } x \notin B\} = A^c \cap B^c$$

Here we use the equivalent (DeMorgan's) logical law:

$$\neg(p \vee q) \equiv \neg p \wedge \neg q$$

where $\neg$ means "not," $\vee$ means "or," and $\wedge$ means "and."

(Sometimes Venn diagrams are used to illustrate the laws in Table 4-1, as in Problem 4.11.)

### Table 4-1   Laws of the Algebra of Sets

| Idempotent laws | |
|---|---|
| (1a)   $A \cup A = A$ | (1b)   $A \cap A = A$ |
| **Associative laws** | |
| (2a)   $(A \cup B) \cup C = A \cup (B \cup C)$ | (2b)   $(A \cap B) \cap C = A \cap (B \cap C)$ |
| **Commutative laws** | |
| (3a)   $A \cup B = B \cup A$ | (3b)   $A \cap B = B \cap A$ |
| **Distributive laws** | |
| (4a)   $A \cup (B \cap C) = (A \cup B) \cap (A \cup C)$ | (4b)   $A \cap (B \cup C) = (A \cap B) \cup (A \cap C)$ |
| **Identity laws** | |
| (5a)   $A \cup \emptyset = A$ | (5b)   $A \cap \mathbf{U} = A$ |
| (6a)   $A \cup \mathbf{U} = \mathbf{U}$ | (6b)   $A \cap \emptyset = \emptyset$ |
| **Involution law** | |
| (7)   $(A^c)^c = A$ | |
| **Complement laws** | |
| (8a)   $A \cup A^c = \mathbf{U}$ | (8b)   $A \cap A^c = \emptyset$ |
| (9a)   $\mathbf{U}^c = \emptyset$ | (9b)   $\emptyset^c = \mathbf{U}$ |
| **DeMorgan's laws** | |
| (10a)   $(A \cup B)^c = A^c \cap B^c$ | (10b)   $(A \cap B)^c = A^c \cup B^c$ |

## 4.5    FINITE SETS; COUNTING PRINCIPLE

Sets can be finite or infinite.    A set $S$ is *finite* if $S$ is empty or if $S$ consists of exactly $m$ elements, where $m$ is a positive integer; otherwise, $S$ is infinite.

The notation $n(S)$ or $|S|$ will denote the number of elements in a finite set $S$.    Note first that $n\emptyset = 0$, since the empty set has no elements.

### EXAMPLE 4.4

(*a*)    Let $A$ denote the letters in the English alphabet, and let $D$ denote the days of the week; that is, let

$$A = \{a, b, c, \ldots, y, z\} \quad \text{and} \quad D = \{\text{Monday, Tuesday, \ldots, Sunday}\}$$

Then $A$ and $D$ are finite sets.    In particular:

$$n(A) = 26 \quad \text{and} \quad n(D) = 7$$

(*b*)    Let $E$ be the set of positive integers, and let $I$ be the *unit interval*; that is, let

$$E = \{2, 4, 6, \ldots\} \quad \text{and} \quad I = [0, 1] = \{x : 0 \leq x \leq 1\}$$

Then both $E$ and $I$ are infinite sets.

### Counting the Number of Elements in a Set

First we begin with a special case.

**Lemma 4.3:**    Suppose $A$ and $B$ are finite disjoint sets.    Then $A \cup B$ is finite and

$$n(A \cup B) = n(A) + n(B)$$

This lemma may be stated equivalently as follows:

**Lemma 4.3:**    Suppose $S$ is the disjoint union of finite sets $A$ and $B$.    Then $S$ is finite and

$$n(S) = n(A) + n(B).$$

For example, suppose a class $S$ contains 12 male sudents and 15 female students.    Clearly, $S$ contains $12 + 15 = 27$ students.    This follows from the fact that the sets of male and female students are disjoint.

**Proof of Lemma 4.3:**    In counting the elements of $A \cup B$, first count the elements of $A$.    There are $n(A)$ of these. The only other elements in $A \cup B$ are those that are in $B$ but not in $A$.    Since $A$ and $B$ are disjont, no element of $B$ is in $A$. Thus, there are $n(B)$ elements which are in $B$ but not in $A$.    Accordingly, $n(A \cup B) = n(A) + n(B)$.

### Special Cases of Disjoint Unions

Lemma 4.3 gives the following two special cases of disjoint unions.

**Theorem 4.4:**    Suppose $A$ is a subset of a finite universal set **U**.    Then:

$$n(A^c) = n(\mathbf{U}) - n(A)$$

**Theorem 4.5:**    Let $A$ and $B$ be finite sets.    Then

$$n(A \backslash B) = n(A) - n(A \cap B)$$

That is, the number of elements in $A$ but not $B$ is the number of elements in $A$ minus the number of elements in both $A$ and $B$.

**EXAMPLE 4.5**

(a)  A class **U** of 30 students has 16 full-time students.   Then clearly (Theorem 4.4) there are

$$30 - 16 = 14$$

part-time students in the class.

(b)  An art class $A$ has 20 students and 8 of the students are also taking a biology class $B$.   Then clearly (Theorem 4.5) there are

$$20 - 8 = 12$$

students in the class $A$ which are not in the class $B$.

### Inclusion-Exclusion Principle

There is also a forumula for $n(A \cup B)$ even when they are not disjoint, called the *inclusion-exclusion principle*.   Namely:

**Theorem (Inclusion-exclusion Principle) 4.6:**   Suppose $A$ and $B$ are finite sets.   Then $A \cap B$ and $A \cup B$ are finite and

$$n(A \cup B) = n(A) + n(B) - n(A \cap B)$$

That is, we find the number of elements in $A$ or $B$ (or both) by first adding $n(A)$ and $n(B)$ (inclusion) and then subtracting $n(A \cap B)$ (exclusion), since its elements were counted twice.

We can apply this result to get a similar result for three sets.

**Corollary 4.7:**   Suppose $A$, $B$, $C$ are finite sets.   Then $A \cup B \cup C$ is finite and

$$n(A \cup B \cup C) = n(A) + n(B) + n(C) - n(A \cap B) - n(A \cap C) - n(B \cap C) + n(A \cap B \cap C)$$

One may further generalize this result to any finite number of finite sets.

**EXAMPLE 4.6**   Consider the following data among students in a college dormatory:

> 30 students are on a list $A$ (taking Art 101).
> 35 students are on a list $B$ (taking Biology 101).
> 20 students are on both lists.

Find the number of students:   (a) only on list $A$,     (b) only on list B,     (c) on list $A$ or $B$ (or both)

(a)  List $A$ contains 30 names and 20 of them are on list $B$; hence, $30 - 20 = 10$ names are only on list $A$.   That is, by Theorem 4.5:

$$n(A \backslash B) = n(A) - n(A \cap B) = 30 - 20 = 10$$

(b)  Similarly, there are $35 - 20 = 15$ names only on list $B$.   That is,

$$n(B \backslash A) = n(B) - n(A \cap B) = 35 - 20 = 15$$

(c)  We seek $n(A \cup B)$.   Note that we are given that $n(A \cap B) = 20$.
By the inclusion-exclusion principle (Theorem 4.6):

$$n(A \cup B) = n(A) + n(B) - n(A \cap B) = 30 + 35 - 20 = 45$$

In other words, we combine the two lists and then cross out the 20 names which appear twice.

## 4.6   PRODUCT SETS

Let $A$ and $B$ be any two sets.   The set of all ordered pairs $(a, b)$ where $a \in A$ and $b \in B$ is called the *product*, or *cartesian product*, of $A$ and $B$.   A short designaion of this product is $A \times B$, which is read "$A$ cross $B$." One also frequently writes $A^2$ for $A \times A$.

We emphaize that two ordered pairs $(a, b)$ and $(c, d)$ are equal if and only if their first elements $a$ and $c$ are equal and their second elements $b$ and $d$ are equal.    That is:

$$(a, b) = (c, d) \text{ if and only if } a = c \text{ and } b = d.$$

**EXAMPLE 4.7**

(a)   **R** denotes the set of real numbers, and so $\mathbf{R}^2 = \mathbf{R} \times \mathbf{R}$ is the set of ordered pairs of real numbers.   [The reader is familiar with the geometrical representation of $\mathbf{R}^2$ as points in the plane as pictured in Fig. 1-4.] We note that $\mathbf{R}^2$ is frequently called the *cartesian plane*.

(b)   Let $A = \{1, 2\}$ and $B = \{x, y, z\}$.   Then:

$$A \times B = \{(1, x), (1, y), (1, z), (2, x), (2, y), (2, z)\}$$

$$B \times A = \{(x, 1), (y, 1), (z, 1), (x, 2), (y, 2), (z, 2)\}$$

$$\text{Also,} \quad A^2 = A \times A = \{(1, 1), (1, 2), (2, 1), (2, 2)\}$$

There are two things worth noting in the above example.   First of all, $A \times B \neq B \times A$, so the order in which the sets are considered is important.   Second:

$$n(A \times B) = 6 = 2 \cdot 3 = n(A) \cdot n(B)$$

In fact, this is true for any finite sets $A$ and $B$.   We state this result formally.

**Theorem 4.7:**   Suppose $A$ and $B$ are finite.   Then $A \times B$ is finite and

$$n(A \times B) = n(A) \cdot n(B)$$

The concept of a product of sets can be extended to any finite number of finite sets in a natural way.   For example:

$$A \times B \times C = \{(a, b, c) : a \in A, b \in B, c \in C\}$$

Also, just as we write $A^2$ for $A \times A$, so we write $A^m$ for $A \times A \times \ldots \times A$, where there are $m$ factors.

## 4.7   CLASSES OF SETS; POWER SETS AND PARTITIONS

Let $S$ be a given set.   We may wish to talk about some of its subsets.   Thus, we would be considering a "set of sets." Whenever such a situation arises, to avoid confusion, we will speak of a *class* of sets or a *collection* of sets.   The words *subclass* and *subcollection* have meanings analogous to subset.

**EXAMPLE 4.8**   Suppose $S = \{1, 2, 3, 4\}$.   Let $A$ be the class of subsets of $S$ which contain exactly three elements of $S$.   Then

$$A = [\{1, 2, 3\}, \{1, 2, 4\}, \{1, 3, 4\}, \{2, 3, 4\}]$$

The elements of $A$ are the sets $\{1, 2, 3\}$, $\{1, 2, 4\}$, $\{1, 3, 4\}$, and $\{2, 3, 4\}$.
    Let $B$ be the class of subsets of $S$ which contain 2 and two other elements of S.   Then

$$B = [\{1, 2, 3\}, \{1, 2, 4\}, \{2, 3, 4\}]$$

The elements of $B$ are $\{1, 2, 3\}$, $\{1, 2, 4\}$, and $\{2, 3, 4\}$.   Thus, $B$ is a subclass of $A$.   (To avoid confusion, we will usually enclose the sets of a class in brackets instead of braces.)

## Power Sets

Let $S$ be a given set. We may consider the class of all subsets of $S$. This class is called the *power set* of $S$, and it will be denoted by $\mathcal{P}(S)$. For example, suppose $S = \{1, 2, 3\}$. Then:

$$\mathcal{P}(S) = [\emptyset, \{1\}, \{2\}, \{3\}, \{1, 2\}, \{1, 3\}, \{2, 3\}, S]$$

We emphasize that $S$ and the empty set $\emptyset$ belong to $\mathcal{P}(S)$, since they are subsets of $S$.

If $S$ is finite, then so is $\mathcal{P}(S)$. In fact, the number of elements in $\mathcal{P}(S)$ is 2 raised to the power of $S$; that is;

$$n(\mathcal{P}(S)) = 2^{n(S)}$$

(For this reason, the power set of $S$ is sometimes denoted by $2^S$.) This formula is seen to hold in the above example. Namely, when $S$ has 3 elements, its power set $\mathcal{P}(S)$ has $2^3 = 8$ elements.

## Partitions

Let $S$ be a nonempty set. A *partition* of $S$ is a subdivision of $S$ into nonoverlapping, nonempty subsets. That is, a partition of $S$ is a collection $\{A_i\}$ of nonempty subsets of $S$ such that:

(*i*)   Each $a \in S$ belongs to one of the $A_i$.

(*ii*)  Any pair of distinct sets $A_i$ and $A_j$ are disjoint.

The subsets in a partition are called *cells*. Figure 4-4 is a Venn diagram of a partition of the rectangular set $S$ of points into five cells: $A_1, A_2, A_3, A_4, A_5$.

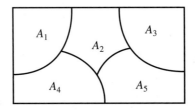

**Fig. 4-4**

**EXAMPLE 4.9**   Consider the following collections of subsets of $S = \{1, 2, 3, \ldots, 8, 9\}$:

(*a*)   $[\{1, 3, 5\}, \ \{2, 6\}, \ \{4, 8, 9\}]$,

(*b*)   $[\{1, 3, 5\}, \ \{2, 4, \ 6, 8\}, \ \{5, 7, 9\}]$

(*c*)   $[\{1, 3, 5\}, \ \{2, 4, 6, 8\}, \ \{7, 9\}]$

Then (*a*) is not a partition of $S$, since 7 in $S$ does not belong to any of the subsets. Furthermore, (*b*) is not a partition of $S$, since $\{1, 3, 5\}$ and $\{5, 7, 9\}$ are not disjoint. On the other hand, (*c*) is a partition of $S$.

## 4.8   MATHEMATICAL INDUCTION (OPTIONAL)

An essential property of the set $\mathbf{N} = \{1, 2, 3, \ldots\}$ of positive integers which is used in many proofs follows

**Principle of Mathematical Induction I:**   Let $A(n)$ be an assertion about the set $\mathbf{N}$ of positive integers, i.e., $A(n)$ is true or false for each integer $n \geq 1$. Suppose $A(n)$ has the following two properties:

(*i*)   $A(1)$ is true.

(*ii*)  $A(k + 1)$ is true whenever $A(k)$ is true.

Then $A(n)$ is true for every positive integer.

We shall not prove this principle.    In fact, this principle is usually given as one of the axioms when **N** is developed axiomatically.

**EXAMPLE 4.10**    Let $A(n)$ be the assertion that the sum of the first $n$ odd numbers is $n^2$; that is:

$$A(n) : 1 + 3 + 5 + \ldots + (2n-1) = n^2$$

(The $k$-th odd number is $2k - 1$, and the next odd number is $2k + 1$.) Observe that $A(n)$ is true for $n = 1$, since

$$A(1) : 1 = 1^2$$

Assuming $A(k)$ is true, we add $2k + 1$ to both sides of $A(k)$, obtaining

$$1 + 3 + 5 + \ldots + (2k - 1) + (2k + 1) = k^2 + (2k + 1) = (k + 1)^2$$

However, this is A($k + 1$).    That is, A($k + 1$) is true assuming A($k$) is true.    By the principle of mathematical induction, $A(n)$ is true for all $n \geq 1$.

There is another form of the principle of mathematical induction which is sometimes more convenient to use.    Although it appears different, it is really equivalent to the above principle of induction.

**Principle of Mathematical Induction II:**    Let $A(n)$ be an assertion about the set **N** of positive integers with the following two properties:

   (*i*)    $A(1)$ is true.

   (*ii*)    $A(k)$ is true whenever $A(j)$ is true for $1 \leq j < k$.    Then $A(n)$ is true for every positive integer.

   **Remark:**    Sometimes one wants to prove that an assertion $A$ is true for a set of integers of the form

$$\{a, a + 1, a + 2, \ldots\}$$

where $a$ is any integer, possibly 0.    This can be done by simply replacing 1 by $a$ in either of the above principles of mathematical induction.

## 4.9   ARGUMENTS AND VENN DIAGRAMS (OPTIONAL)

Many verbal statements can be translated into equivalent statements about sets which can be described by Venn diagrams.    Hence, Venn diagrams are frequntly used to determine the validity of an argument.    This is illustrated in the following example.

**EXAMPLE 4.11**    Show that the following argument is valid:

$S_1$:    My saucepans are the only things I have that are made of tin.

$S_2$:    I find all your presents to be very useful.

$S_3$:    None of my saucepans is of the slightest use.

S:    Your presents to me are not made of tin.

Here the statements $S_1$, $S_2$, $S_3$ above the horizontal line denote the assumptions, and the statement $S$ below the horizontal line denotes the conclusion.    (This argument is adopted from a book on logic by Lewis Carroll, author of *Alice in Wonderland*.) The argument is valid if the conclusion $S$ follows logically from the assumptions $S_1$, $S_2$, $S_3$.

By $S_1$ the tin objects are contained in the set of saucepans, and by $S_3$ the set of saucepans and the set of useful things are disjoint.    Thus, draw the Venn diagram, Fig. 4-5(*a*).

By $S_2$ the set of "your presents" is a subset of the useful things.    Thus, we can add the set "your presents" to Fig. 4-5(*a*) to obtain Fig. 4-5(*b*).

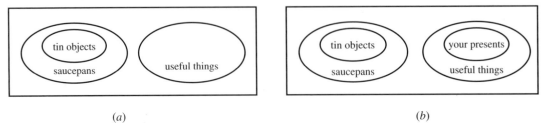

(*a*)                                                                                    (*b*)

**Fig. 4-5**

The Venn diagram in Fig. 4-5(*b*) shows that the conclusion is clearly valid.    Namely, the Venn diagram shows that the set of "your presents" is disjoint from the set of tin objects.

# Solved Problems

## SETS, ELEMENTS, SUBSETS

**4.1.**    Which of these sets are equal: $\{r, s, t\}, \{t, s, r\}, \{s, r, t\}, \{t, r, s\}$?

They are all equal.    Order does not change a set.

**4.2.**    List the elements of the following sets; here $\mathbf{N} = \{1, 2, 3, \ldots\}$.

(*a*)    $A = \{x : x \in \mathbf{N}, 2 < x < 9\}$,                      (*c*)    $c = \{x : x \in \mathbf{N}, x + 5 = 2\}$,

(*b*)    $B = \{x : x \in \mathbf{N}, x \text{ is even}, x \le 15\}$,                      (*d*)    $D = \{x ; x \in \mathbf{N}, x \text{ is a multiple of } 5\}$

(*a*)    $A$ consists of the positive integers between 2 and 9; hence, $A = \{3, 4, 5, 6, 7, 8, 9\}$.

(*b*)    $B$ consists of the even positive integers less than or equal to 15; hence, $B = \{2, 4, 6, 8, 10, 12, 14\}$.

(*c*)    There are no positive integers which satisfy the condition $x + 5 = 2$; hence, $C$ contains no elements. In other words, $C = \emptyset$, the empty set.

(*d*)    $D$ is infinite, so we cannot list all its elements.    However, sometimes we write $D = \{5, 10, 15, 20, \ldots\}$ assuming everyone understands that we mean the multiples of 5.

**4.3.**    Describe in words how you would prove each of the following:

(*a*)    $A$ is equal to $B$.              (*c*)    $A$ is a proper subset of $B$.

(*b*)    $A$ is a subset of $B$.          (*d*)    $A$ is not a subset of $B$.

(*a*)    Show that each element of $A$ also belongs to $B$, and then show that each element of $B$ also belongs to $A$.

(*b*)    Show that each element of $A$ also belongs to $B$.

(*c*)    Show that each element of $A$ also belongs to $B$, and then show that at least one element of $B$ is not in $A$.    (Note that it is not necessary to show that more than one element of $B$ is not in $A$.)

(*d*)    Show that one element of $A$ is not in $B$.

**4.4.** Show that $A = \{2, 3, 4, 5\}$ is not a subset of $B = \{x : x \in \mathbf{N},\ x \text{ is even}\}$.

It is necessary to show that at least one element in $A$ does not belong to $B$. Now $3 \in A$, but $3 \notin B$, since $B$ only consists of even integers. Hence, $A$ is not a subset of $B$.

**4.5.** Show that $A = \{3, 4, 5, 6\}$ is a proper subset of $C = \{1, 2, 3, \ldots, 8, 9\}$.

Each element of $A$ belongs to $C$; hence, $A \subseteq C$. On the other hand, $1 \in C$ but $1 \notin A$; hence, $A \neq C$. Therefore, $A$ is a proper subset of $C$.

**4.6.** Consider the following sets where $\mathbf{U} = \{1, 2, 3, \ldots, 8, 9\}$:

$$\emptyset,\ A = \{1, 3\}, \qquad B = \{1, 5, 9\}, \qquad C = \{1, 2, 3, 4, 5\}, \qquad D = \{1, 3, 5, 7, 9\}$$

Insert the correct symbol $\subseteq$ or $\nsubseteq$ between each pair of sets:

(a)  $\emptyset, A$      (b)  $A, B$      (c)  $A, C$      (d) $B, C$      (e)  $B, D$      (f)  $D, \mathbf{U}$

(a)  $\emptyset \subseteq A$, since $\emptyset$ is a subset of every set.
(b)  $A \nsubseteq B$, since $3 \in A$ but $3 \notin B$.
(c)  $A \subseteq C$, since the elements, 1 and 3, of $A$ also belong to $C$.
(d)  $B \nsubseteq C$, since $9 \in B$ but $9 \notin C$.
(e)  $B \subseteq D$, since the elements of $B$ also belong to $D$.
(f)  $D \subseteq \mathbf{U}$, since the elements of $D$ also belong to $\mathbf{U}$. (In fact, every set is a subset of the universal set $\mathbf{U}$.)

**4.7.** A pair of die are tossed and the sum of the faces are recorded. Find the smallest set $S$ which includes all possible outcomes.

The faces of a single die are the numbers 1 to 6. Thus, for a pair of die, no sum can be less than 2 nor greater than 12. Also, every number between 2 and 12 could occur as a sum. Thus:

$$S = \{2, 3, 4, 5, 6, 7, 8, 9, 10, 11, 12\}$$

## SET OPERATIONS

**4.8.** Let $\mathbf{U} = \{1, 2, \ldots, 9\}$ be the universal set, and let
$A = \{1, 2, 3, 4, 5\}, \qquad B = \{4, 5, 6, 7\},$
$C = \{1, 2, 6, 7, 8, 9\}, \qquad D = \{1, 3, 5, 7, 9\}.$

Find: (a)  $A \cup B$ and $A \cap B$,      (b)  $B \cup D$ and $B \cap D$,
        (c)  $A \cup C$ and $A \cap C$,      (d)  $C \cup D$ and $C \cap D$

Recall that the union $X \cup Y$ consists of those elements in either $X$ or in $Y$ (or both), and the intersection $X \cap Y$ consists of those elements in both $X$ and $Y$.

(a)  $A \cup B = \{1, 2, 3, 4, 5, 6, 7\}$,          $A \cap B = \{4, 5\}$
(b)  $B \cup D = \{1, 3, 4, 5, 6, 7, 9\}$,        $B \cap D = \{5, 7\}$
(c)  $A \cup C = \{1, 2, 3, 4, 5, 6, 7, 8, 9\} = \mathbf{U}$     $A \cap C = \{1, 2\}$
(d)  $C \cup D = \{1, 2, 3, 5, 6, 7, 8, 9\}$,      $C \cap D = \{1, 7, 9\}$

**4.9.** Consider the sets in the preceding Problem 4.8 Find:

(a)  $A^c, B^c, C^c, D^c$;      (b)  $A \backslash B, B \backslash A, B \backslash C, C \backslash D$.

(a)  The complement $X^c$ consists of those elements in the universal set $\mathbf{U}$ which do not belong to $X$. Hence:

$$A^c = \{6, 7, 8, 9\}, \qquad B^c = \{1, 2, 3, 8, 9\}, \qquad C^c = \{3, 4, 5\}, \qquad D^c = \{2, 4, 6, 8\}$$

(b)   The difference $X \backslash Y$ consists of the elements in $X$ which do not belong to $Y$.   Therefore:

$$A \backslash B = \{1, 2, 3\}, \quad B \backslash A = \{6, 7\}, \qquad B \backslash C = \{4, 5\}, \quad C \backslash D = \{2, 6, 8\}$$

**4.10.**   Prove: $B \backslash A = B \cap A^c$.   Thus, the set operation of difference can be written in terms of the operations of intersection and complement.

$$B \backslash A = \{x : x \in B, x \notin A\} = \{x : x \in B, x \in A^c\} = B \cap A^c$$

## VENN DIAGRAMS, ALGEBRA OF SETS

**4.11.**   Use Venn diagrams to illustrate DeMorgans's law $(A \cup B)^c = A^c \cap B^c$ (proved in Section 4.4).

Shade the area outside $A \cup B$ in a Venn diagram of sets $A$ and $B$.   This is shown in Fig. 4-6(a); hence, the shaded area represents $(A \cup B)^c$.   Now shade the area outside $A$ in a Venn diagram of $A$ and $B$ with strokes in one direction (///), and then shade the area outside $B$ with strokes in another direction (\\\\\).   This is shown in Fig. 4-6(b); hence, the cross-hatched area (where both lines are present) represents $A^c \cap B^c$, the intersection of $A^c$ and $B^c$.   Both $(A \cup B)^c$ and $A^c \cap B^c$ are represented by the same area; thus, the Venn diagrams indicate $(A \cup B)^c = A^c \cap B^c$.   (We emphasize that a Venn diagram is not a formal proof, but it can indicate relationships between sets.)

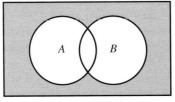     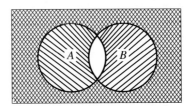

(a)  $(A \cup B)^c$ is shaded.           (b)  $A^c$ is shaded with ///.
                                               $B^c$ is shaded with \\\\.

**Fig. 4-6**

**4.12.**   Prove the Distributive law: $A \cap (B \cup C) = (A \cap B) \cup (A \cap C)$ [which appears in Table 4-1].

By definition of union and intersection:

$$A \cap (B \cup C) = \{x : x \in A, x \in B \cup C\}$$
$$= \{x : x \in A, x \in B \text{ or } x \in A, x \in C\} = (A \cap B) \cup (A \cap C).$$

Here we use the analagous logical law $p \wedge (q \vee r) \equiv (p \wedge q) \vee (p \wedge r)$, where $\wedge$ denotes "and" and $\vee$ denotes "or".

## FINITE SETS, COUNTING PRINCIPLE [INCLUSION-EXCLUSION]

**4.13.**   Determine which of the following sets are finite:

(a)   $A = \{$seasons in the year$\}$           (d)   $D = \{$odd integers$\}$

(b)   $B = \{$states in the United States$\}$        (e)   $E = \{$positive integral divisors of 12$\}$

(c)   $C = \{$Positive integers less than 1$\}$       (f)   $F = \{$cats living in the United States$\}$

(a)   *A* is finite since there are four seasons in the year, i.e., $n(A) = 4$.

(b)   *B* is finite, since there are 50 states, i.e., $n(B) = 50$.

(c)   There are no positive integers less than 1; hence, *C* is empty.   Thus, *C* is finite and $n(C) = 0$.

(d)   *D* is infinite.

(e)   The positive divisors of 12 are 1, 2, 3, 4, 6, 12.   Hence, *E* is finite and $n(E) = 6$.

(f)   Although it may be difficult to find the number of cats living in the United States, there is still a finite number of them at any point in time.   Thus, *F* is finite.

**4.14.**   A class has 40 students.

(a)   If 15 students are commuting to school, find the number *r* who are not commuting to school.

(b)   If 28 of them drive a car, find the number *s* who do not drive a car.

Clearly, $n(A^c) = n(\mathbf{U}) - n(A)$ (Theorem 4.4).   Thus:

(a)   r = 40 − 15 = 25.

(b)   s = 40 − 28 = 12.

**4.15.**   Suppose 50 science students are polled to see whether or not they have studied French (*F*) or German (*G*), yielding the following data:

25 studied French,  20 studied German,  5 studied both.

Find the number of the students who studied: (*a*) only French, (*b*) French or German, and (*c*) neither language.

(a)   Here 25 studied French, and 5 of them also studied German; hence, $25 - 5 = 20$ students only studied French.   That is, by Theorem 4.5:

$$n(F \backslash G) = n(F) - n(F \cap G) = 25 - 5 = 20.$$

(b)   By the Inclusion-Exclusion Principle Theorem 6.6,

$$n(F \cup G) = n(F) + n(G) - n(F \cap G) = 25 + 20 - 5 = 40$$

(c)   Since 40 studied French or German, $50 - 40 = 10$ studied neither language.

**4.16.**   Prove Theorem (Inclusion-Exclusion Principle) 4.6.   Suppose *A* and *B* are finite sets.   Then $A \cup B$ and $A \cap B$ are finite and $n(A \cup B) = n(A) + n(B) - n(A \cap B)$.

Since A and B are finite, clearly both $A \cup B$ and $A \cap B$ are finite.   Now suppose we count the elements of *A* and then count the elements of *B*.   Then every element in $A \cap B$ would be counted twice, once in *A* and once in *B*.   Hence, $n(A \cup B) = n(A) + n(B) - n(A \cap B)$.

## ORDERED PAIRS, PRODUCT SETS

**4.17.**   Explain the main difference between an ordered pair $(a, b)$ and the set $\{a, b\}$ of two elements.

The order of the elements in $(a, b)$ does make a difference; here *a* is designated as the first element and *b* as the second element.   Thus, $(a, b) \neq (b, a)$ unless $a = b$.   On the other hand, there is no difference between $\{a, b\}$ and $\{b, a\}$; they represent the same set.

**4.18.** Find $x$ and $y$ given that $(2x, x - 3y) = (6, -9)$.

Two ordered pairs are equal if and only if the corresponding entries are equal. This leads to the equations

$$2x = 6 \qquad \text{and} \qquad x - 3y = -9$$

Solving the equations yields $x = 3$, $y = 4$.

**4.19.** Given $A = \{1, 2, 3\}$ and $B = \{a, b\}$. Find:     $(a)\ A \times B$,      $(b)\ B \times A$,      $(c)\ B \times B$.

(a)    $A \times B$ consists of all ordered pairs $(x, y)$ where $x \in A$ and $y \in B$. Thus:

$$A \times B = \{(1, a), (1, b), (1, c), (2, a), (2, b), (2, c)\}$$

(b)    $B \times A$ consists of all ordered pairs $(x, y)$ where $x \in B$ and $y \in A$. Thus:

$$B \times A = \{(a, 1), (a, 2), (a, 3), (b, 1), (b, 2), (b, 3)\}$$

(c)    $B \times B$ consists of all ordered pairs $(x, y)$ where $x, y \in B$. Thus:

$$B \times B = \{(a, a), (a, b), (b, a), b, b)\}$$

Note that, as expected from Theorem 4.7, $n(A \times B) = 6$, $n(B \times A) = 6$, $n(B \times B) = 4$. That is, the number of elements in a product set is equal to the product of the numbers of elements in the factor sets.

**4.20.** Given $A = \{1, 2\}$, $B = \{x, y, z\}$, $C = \{3, 4\}$. Find $A \times B \times C$.

$A \times B \times C$ consists of all ordered triples $(a, b, c)$ where $a \in A$, $b \in B$, $c \in C$. These elements of $A \times B \times C$ can be systematically obtained by a so-called "tree diagram," as in Fig. 4-7. The elements of $A \times B \times C$ are precisely the 12 ordered triplets to the right of the diagram.

Observe that $n(A) = 2$, $n(B) = 3$, $n(C) = 2$ and, as expected:

$$n(A \times B \times C) = 12 = n(A) \cdot n(B) \cdot n(C)$$

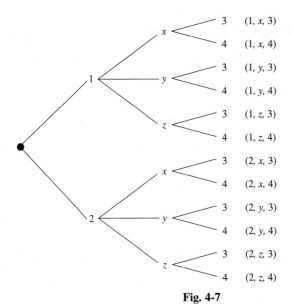

**Fig. 4-7**

**4.21.** Each toss of a coin will yield either a head or a tail. Let $C = \{H, T\}$ denote the set of outcomes. Find $C^3$, $n(C^3)$, and explain what $C^3$ represents.

Since $n(C) = 2$, we have $n(C^3) = 2^3 = 8$. Omitting certain commas and parentheses for notational convenience,

$C^3 = \{HHH, HHT, HTH, HTT, THH, THT, TTH, TTT\}$

$C^3$ represents all possible sequences of outcomes of three tosses of the coin.

## CLASSES OF SETS, PARTITIONS

**4.22.** Consider the set $A = [\{1, 2, 3\}, \{4, 5\}, \{6, 7, 8\}]$.        (a) Find the elements of $A$. (b) Find $n(A)$.

(a) $A$ is a collection of sets; its elements are the sets $\{1, 2, 3\}$, $\{4, 5\}$, and $\{6, 7, 8\}$.

(b) $A$ has only three elements; hence, $n(A) = 3$.

**4.23.** List the elements of the power set $\mathscr{P}(A)$ of $A = \{a, b, c, d\}$.

The elements of $\mathscr{P}(A)$ are the subsets of $A$. Thus:

$$\mathscr{P}(A) = [A, \{a, b, c\}, \{a, b, d\}, \{a, c, d\}, \{b, c, d\}, \{a, b\}, \{a, c\},$$
$$\{a, d\}, \{b, c\}, \{b, d\}, \{c, d\}, \{a\}, \{b\}, \{c\}, \{d\}, \varnothing]$$

As expected, $\mathscr{P}(A)$ has $2^4 = 16$ elements.

**4.24.** Let $S = \{a, b, c, d, e, f, g\}$. Determine which of the following are partitions of $S$:

(a) $P_1 = [\{a, c, e\}, \{b\}, \{d, g\}]$,        (c) $P_3 = [\{a, b, e, g\}, \{c\}, \{d, f\}]$,

(b) $P_2 = [\{a, e, g\}, \{c, d\}, \{b, e, f\}]$,        (d) $P_4 = [\{a, b, c, d, e, f, g\}]$.

(a) $P_1$ is not a partition of $S$, since $f \in S$ does not belong to any of the cells.

(b) $P_2$ is not a partition of $S$, since $e \in S$ belongs to two of the cells.

(c) $P_3$ is a partition of $S$, since each element in $S$ belongs to exactly one cell.

(d) $P_4$ is a partition of $S$ into one cell, $S$ itself.

**4.25.** Find all partitions of $S = \{a, b, c, d\}$.

Note first that each partition of $S$ contains either one, two, three, or four distinct cells. The partitions are as follows:

(1)  $[S] = [abcd]$

(2a)  $[a, bcd], [b, acd], [c, abd], [d, abc]$;

(2b)  $[ab, cd], [ac, bd], [ad, bc]$

(3)  $[a, b, cd], [a, c, bd], [a, d, bc], [b, c, ad], [b, d, ac], [c, d, ab]$

(4)  $[a, b, c, d]$

(For notational convenience, we have omitted certain commas and braces, e.g., $[a, b, cd]$ denotes $[\{a\}, \{b\}, \{c, d\}]$.)

Note that (2a) refers to partitions with one-element and three-element cells, whereas (2b) refers to partitions with two two-element cells. There are $1 + 4 + 3 + 6 + 1 = 15$ different partitions of $S$.

## MATHEMATICAL INDUCTION

**4.26.** Prove the assertion $A(n)$ that the sum of the first $n$ positive integers is $\frac{1}{2}n(n+1)$. That is, prove

$$A(n) : 1 + 2 + 3 + \ldots + n = \frac{1}{2}n(n+1)$$

The assertion holds for $n = 1$, since

$$A(1) : 1 = \frac{1}{2}(1)(1+1)$$

Assuming $A(k)$ is true, we add $k + 1$ to both sides of $A(k)$, obtaining

$$[1 + 2 + 3 + \ldots + k] + (k+1) = [\frac{1}{2}k(k+1)] + (k+1)$$

$$= \frac{1}{2}[k(k+1) + 2(k+1)]$$

$$= \frac{1}{2}[(k+1)(k+2)]$$

This is $A(k+1)$. That is, $A(k+1)$ is true whenever $A(k)$ is true. By the Principle of Induction, $A(n)$ is true for all $n$.

**4.27.** Prove the following assertion (for $n \geq 0$):

$$A(n) : 1 + 2 + 2^2 + 2^3 + \ldots + 2^n = 2^{n+1} - 1$$

$A(0)$ is true, since $1 = 2^1 - 1$. Assuming $A(k)$ is true, we add $2^{k+1}$ to both sides of $A(k)$, obtaining

$$[1 + 2 + 2^2 + 2^3 + \ldots + 2^k] + 2^{k+1} = [2^{k+1} - 1] + 2^{k+1}$$

$$= 2(2^{k+1}) - 1$$

$$= 2^{k+2} - 1$$

This is $A(k+1)$. Thus, $A(k+1)$ is true whenever $A(k)$ is true. By the Principle of Induction, $A(n)$ is true for all $n \geq 0$.

## ARGUMENTS AND VENN DIAGRAMS

**4.28.** Use Venn diagrams to show that the following argument is valid:

$S_1$: All my friends are musicians.

$S_2$: John is my friend.

$S_3$: None of my neighbors are musicians.

_____

$S$: John is not my neighbor.

The premises $S_1$ and $S_3$ lead to the Venn diagram in Fig. 4-8(a). By $S_2$, John belongs to the set of friends which is disjoint from the set of neighbors. Thus, $S$ is a valid conclusion and the argument is valid.

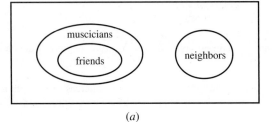
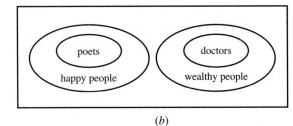

(a)                                                                      (b)

**Fig. 4-8**

**4.29.** Consider the following premises:

$S_1$: Poets are happy people.

$S_2$: Every doctor is wealthy.

$S_3$: No happy person is wealthy

Use Venn diagrams to determine the validity of each of the following conclusions:

(a)   No poet is wealthy.                              (b)   Doctors are happy people.

(c)   No person can be both a poet and a doctor.

The three premises lead to the Venn diagram Fig. 4-8(b).   From the diagram, it follows that (a) and (c) are valid conclusions, whereas (b) is not valid.

# Supplementary Problems

## SETS, ELEMENTS, SUBSETS

**4.30.** Which of the following sets are equal?

$A = \{x : x^2 - 4x + 3 = 0\}$,        $C = \{x : x \in N, x < 3\}$,        $E = \{1, 2\}$,        $G = \{3, 1\}$,

$B = \{x : x^2 - 3x + 2 = 0\}$,        $D = \{x : x \in N, x \text{ is odd}, x < 5\}$,        $F = \{1, 2, 1\}$,        $H = \{1, 1, 3\}$

**4.31.** List the elements of the following sets if the universal set is the English alphabet $\mathbf{U} = \{a, b, c, ..., y, z\}$.

Furthermore, identify which of the sets are equal.

$A = \{x : x \text{ is a vowel}\}$,                              $C = \{x : x \text{ precedes } f \text{ in the alphabet}\}$,

$B = \{x : x \text{ is a letter in the word "}little\text{"}\}$,        $D = \{x : x \text{ is a letter in the word "}title\text{"}\}$,

**4.32.** Let $A = \{1, 2, ..., 8, 9\}$,        $B = \{2, 4, 6, 8\}$,        $C = \{1, 3, 5, 7, 9\}$,        $D = \{3, 4, 5\}$,
$E = \{3, 5\}$.

Name each of the above sets which can equal set $X$ where $X$ has the following properties:

(a)   $X$ and $B$ are disjoint.        (c)   $X \subseteq A$ but $X \nsubseteq C$.

(b)   $X \subseteq D$ but $X \nsubseteq B$.        (d)   $X \subseteq C$ but $X \nsubseteq A$.

## SET OPERATIONS

**4.33.** Given the universal set $\mathbf{U} = \{1, 2, 3, ..., 8, 9\}$ and the following sets:

$A = \{1, 2, 5, 6\}, B = \{2, 5, 7\}, C = \{1, 3, 5, 7, 9\}$

Find: (a)   $A \cap B$ and $A \cap C$,        (b)   $A \cup B$ and $B \cup C$,        (c)   $A^c$ and $C^c$.

**4.34.** For the sets in Problem 4.33, find: (a)   $A \backslash B$ and $A \backslash C$,        (b)   $(A \cup C) \backslash B$,        (c)   $(A \cup B)^c$,
(d)   $(B \cap C) \backslash A$.

**4.35.** Let $A = \{a, b, c, d, e\}, B = \{a, b, d, f, g\}, C = \{b, c, e, g, h\}, D = \{d, e, f, g, h\}$.   Find:

(a)   $A \cap (B \cup D)$,        (b)   $B \backslash (C \cup D)$,        (c)   $(A \cap D) \cup B$,        (d)   $(A \cup D) \backslash C$.

**4.36.** Let $A$ and $B$ be any sets.   Prove $A \cup B$ is the disjoint union of $A \backslash B$, $A \cap B$, and $B \backslash A$.

**4.37.** The formula $A \backslash B = A \cap B^c$ defines the difference operation in terms of the operations of intersection and complement.   Find a formula which defines the union $A \cup B$ in terms of the operations of intersection and complement.

## VENN DIAGRAMS, ALGEBRA OF SETS

**4.38.** The Venn diagram in Fig. 4.9($a$) shows sets $A$, $B$, $C$.   Shade the following sets:

(*a*)   $A \backslash (B \cup C)$,          (*b*)   $A^c \cap (B \cup C)$,          (*c*)   $(A \cup C) \cap (B \cup C)$.

**4.39.** Use the laws in Table 4-1 to prove: $(A \cap B) \cup (A \cap B^c) = A$.

## FINITE SETS AND THE COUNTING PRINCIPLE

**4.40.** Determine which of the following sets are finite:

(*a*)   Lines parallel to the $x$ axis,          (*c*)   Animals living on the earth,

(*b*)   Letters in the English alphabet,          (*d*)   Circles through the origin $(0, 0)$.

**4.41.** Given $n(\mathbf{U}) = 20$, $n(A) = 12$, $n(B) = 9$, $n(A \cap B) = 4$.   Find:

(*a*)   $n(A \cup B)$,          (*b*)   $n(A^c)$,          (*c*)   $n(B^c)$,          (*d*)   $n(A \backslash B)$,          (*e*)   $n(\emptyset)$.

**4.42.** Among 90 students in a dormatory, 35 own an automobile, 40 own a bicycle, and 10 own both an automobile and a bicycle.   Find the number of students in the dormatory who:

(*a*)   Do not have an automobile.          (*c*)   Have neither an automobile nor a bicycle.

(*b*)   Have an automobile or bicycle.          (*d*)   Have an automobile or bicycle, but not both.

**4.43.** Among 120 freshman at a college, 40 take mathematics, 50 take English, and 15 take both mathematics and English.   Find the number of the freshman who:

(*a*)   Do not take mathematics.          (*d*)   Take English, but not mathematics.

(*b*)   Take mathematics or English.          (*e*)   Take exactly one of the two subjects.

(*c*)   Take mathematics, but not English.          (*f*)   Take neither mathematics nor English.

**4.44.** A survey of the magazines read by 60 people produced the following data:

25 read *Newsweek*          9 read *Newsweek* and *Fortune*

26 read *Time*          11 read *Newsweek* and *Time*

23 read *Fortune*          8 read *Time* and *Fortune*

3 read all three magazines.

(*a*)   Figure 4-9($b$) is a Venn diagram of three sets, $N$ (*Newsweek*), $T$ (*Time*), and $F$ (*Fortune*).   Fill in the correct number of people in each of the eight regions of the Venn diagram.

(*b*)   Find the number of people who read:          (*i*)   only *Newsweek*,          (*ii*)   only *Time*,   (*iii*)   only *Fortune*,          (*iv*)   *Newsweek* and *Time*, but not *Fortune*,          (*v*)   only one of the magazines,          (*vi*)   none of the magazines.

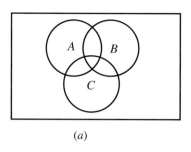
(a)

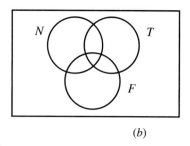
(b)

**Fig.4-9**

## PRODUCT SETS

**4.45.** Find $x$ and $y$ if: (a)  $(x + 3, 3) = (5, 3x + y)$,       (b)  $(x - 3y, 5) = (7, x - y)$.

**4.46.** Find $x, y, z$ if $(2x, x + y, x - y - 2z) = (4, -1, 3)$.

**4.47.** Let $A = \{a, b\}$ and $B = \{1, 2, 3, 4\}$.  Find: (a)  $A \times B$,       (b)  $B \times A$,       (c)  $A^2 = A \times A$.

**4.48.** Let $C = \{H, T\}$, the set of possible outcomes if a coin is tossed.  Find:
(a)  $C^2 = C \times C$,       (b)  $C^4 = C \times C \times C \times C$

**4.49.** Suppose $n(A) = 2$, and $n(B) = 6$.  Find the number of elements in:
(a)  $A \times B, B \times A$,       (b)  $A^2, B^2, A^3, B^3$;       (c)  $A \times A \times B \times A$

## CLASSES OF SETS, PARTITIONS

**4.50.** Let $S = [\{a,b\}, \{c,d,e\}, \{r,s,t\}, \{x,y\}]$.       (a)  Find the elements of $S$.       (b)  Find $n(S)$.

**4.51.** Let $S$ be the collection of sets in Problem 4.50.   Find the subcollection $X$ of $S$ which consists of those sets in $S$ with exactly: (a)  2 elements,       (b)  3 elements,       (c)  4 elements.

**4.52.** Let $A = \{a,b,c,d,e\}$.       (a)  Find the power set $\mathcal{P}(A)$ of $A$.       (b)  Find $n(\mathcal{P}(A))$.

**4.53.** Find the number of elements in the power set of each of the following sets:

(a)  {days of the week}       (c)  {seasons of the year}

(b)  {positive divisors of 12}       (d)  {letters in the word "*yes*"}

**4.54.** Let $S = \{1,2,3,4,5,6\}$.   Determine whether each of the following is a partition of $S$:

(a)  [{1,3,5},  {2,4},  {3,6}],       (d)  [{1},  {3,6},  {2,4,5},  {3,6}]

(b)  [{1,5},  {2},  {3,6}],       (e)  [{1,2,3,4,5,6}]

(c)  [{1,5},  {2},  {4},  {3,6}],       (f)  [{1},  {2},  {3},  {4},  {5},  {6}]

**4.55.** Find all partitions of $S = \{1,2,3\}$.

**4.56.** Let $P_1 = [A_1, A_2, ..., A_m]$ and $P_2 = [B_1, B_2 ..., B_n]$ be partitions of $S$.   Let $P$ be the the collection of sets obtained by intersecting each set in $P_1$ with each set in $P_2$ and deleting the empty set $\emptyset$.   That is:

$$P = [A_i \cap B_j; i = 1, ..., m, j = 1, ..., n] \setminus \emptyset$$

Show that $P$ is also a partition of $S$ (called the *cross partition*.)

**4.57.** Let $S = \{1,2,3, ..., 8,9\}$.   Consider the following partitions of $S$:

$P_1 = [\{1, 2, 3, 4, 5\}, \{6, 7, 8, 9\}]$ and $P_2 = [\{1, 3, 6\}, \{2, 7, 8, 9\}, \{4, 5\}]$
Find the cross partition $P$ of $P_1$ and $P_2$.

## MATHEMATICAL INDUCTION

**4.58.** Prove:   $2 + 4 + 6 + ... + 2n = n(n + 1)$.

**4.59.** Prove:   $1 + 4 + 7 + ... + (3n - 2) = 2n(3n - 1)$.

**4.60.** Prove:   $1^2 + 2^2 + 3^2 + ... + n^2 = \dfrac{n(n + 1)(2n + 1)}{6}$.

**4.61.** Prove: (a)   For $n \geq 3$, we have $2^n \geq n^2$.        (b)   For $n \geq 4$, we have $n! \geq 2^n$.   [Here $n!$ is the product of the integers from 1 to $n$.]

**4.62.** Prove:   $\dfrac{1}{1 \cdot 3} + \dfrac{1}{3 \cdot 5} + \dfrac{1}{5 \cdot 7} + ... + \dfrac{1}{(2n - 1)(2n + 1)} = \dfrac{1}{2n + 1}$.

## AUGUMENTS AND VENN DIAGRAMS

**4.63.** Draw a Venn diagram for the following assumptions:

$S_1$ :   No practical car is expensive.

$S_2$ :   Cars with sunroofs are expensive.

$S_3$ :   All (station) wagons are practical.

Use the Venn diagram to determine the validity of each of the following conclusions:

(a)   No practical car has a sunroof.        (c)   No wagon has a sunroof.

(b)   All practical cars are wagons.        (d)   Cars with sunroofs are not practical.

**4.64.** Draw a Venn diagram for the following assumptions:

$S_1$ :   All poets are poor.

$S_2$ :   In order to be a teacher, one must graduate from college.

$S_3$ :   No college graduate is poor.

Use the Venn diagram to determine the validity of each of the following conclusions:

(a)   Teachers are not poor.        (c)   College graduates do not become poets.

(b)   Poets are not teachers.        (d)   Every poor person becomes a poet.

# Answers to Supplementary Problems

**4.30.**   $B = C = E = F;\ \ A = D = G = H$.

**4.31.**   $A = \{a, e, i, o, u\},$        $B = D = \{l, i, t, e\},$        $C = \{a, b, c, d, e\}$.

**4.32.**   (a)   $C$ and $E$,        (b)   $D$ and $E$,        (c)   $A, B, D$,        (d)   None.

**4.33.** (*a*)   $A \cap B = \{2, 5\}$,   $A \cap C = \{1, 5\}$,        (*b*)   $A \cup B = \{1, 2, 5, 6, 7\}$,   $B \cup C = \{1, 2, 3, 5, 7, 9\}$,
(*c*)   $A^c = \{3, 4, 7, 8, 9\}$,   $C^c = \{2, 4, 6, 8\}$.

**4.34.** (*a*)   $A \backslash B = \{1, 6\}$, $A \backslash C = \{2, 6\}$,        (*b*)   $(A \cup C \backslash B = \{1, 3, 6, 9\}$,        (*c*)   $(A \cup B)^c = \{3, 4, 8, 9\}$,
(*d*)   $(B \cap C) \backslash A = \{7\}$

**4.35.** (*a*)   $A \cap (B \cup D) = \{a, b, d, e\}$,        (*b*)   $B \backslash (C \cup D) = \{a\}$,        (*c*)   $(A \cap D) \cup B = \{a, b, d, e, f, g\}$,
(*d*)   $(A \cup D) \backslash C = \{a, d, f\}$,

**4.37.** $A \cup B = (A^c \cap B^c)^c$

**4.38.** See Fig. 4-10.

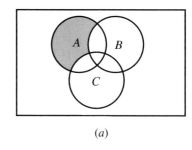  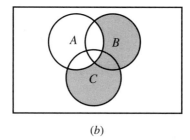  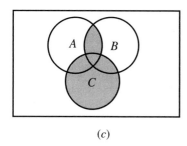

(*a*)                                (*b*)                                (*c*)

**Fig.4-10**

**4.40.** (*a*)   Infinite,        (*b*)   finite,        (*c*)   finite,        (*c*)   infinite.

**4.41.** (*a*)   $n(A \cup B) = 17$,        (*b*)   $n(A^c) = 8$,        (*c*)   $n(B^c) - 11$,        (*d*)   $n(A \backslash B) = 8$,        (*e*)   $n(\emptyset) = 0$.

**4.42.** (*a*)   55,        (*b*)   65,        (*c*)   25,        (*d*)   55

**4.43.** (*a*)   80,        (*b*)   75,        (*c*)   25,        (*d*)   35,        (*e*)   60,        (*f*)   45

**4.44.** (*a*)   See Fig. 4-11.        (*b*)   (*i*)   8,        (*ii*)   10,        (*iii*)   9,        (*iv*)   8,        (*v*)   27,
(*vi*)   11.

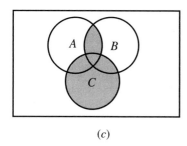

**Fig. 4-11**

**4.45.** (*a*)   $x = 2, y = -3$;        (*b*)   $x = 4, y = -1$.

**4.46.** $x = 2$,   $y = -3$,   $z = 1$

**4.47.** (*a*)   $A \times B = \{(a, 1), (a, 2), (a, 3), (a, 4), (b, 1), (b, 2), (b, 3), (b, 4)\}$
(*b*)   $B \times A = \{(1, a), (2, a), (3, a), (4, a), (1, b), (2, b), (3, b), (4, b)\}$
(*c*)   $A^2 = \{(a, a), (a, b), (b, a), (b, b)\}$

**4.48.** Note $n(C^2) = 2^2 = 4$ and $n(C^4) = 2^4 = 16$.

    (a)   $C^2 = C \times C = \{HH, HT, TH, TT\}$;

    (b)   $C^4 = C \times C \times C \times C = \{HHHH, HHHT, HHTH, HHTT, HTHH, HTHT, HTTH, HTTT, THHH, THHT,$
        $THTH, THTT, TTHH, TTHT, TTTH, TTTT\}$.

**4.49.**   (a)  12, 12,     (b)  4, 36, 8, 216,     (c)  48.

**4.50.**   (a)  $\{a, b\}, \{c, d, e\}, \{r, s, t\}$, and $\{x, y\}$,     (b)  $n(S) = 4$

**4.51.**   (a)  $X = [\{a, b\}, \{x, y\}]$,     (b)  $X = [\{c, d, e\}, \{r, s, t\}]$,     (c)  $X = \emptyset$,

**4.52.** Note $\mathscr{P}(A)$ has $2^5 = 32$ elements; that is, there are 32 subsets of $A$.  Each subset has at most 5 elements, and we
list them in terms of their numbers of elements. Here we write, say, *abd* for $\{a, b, d\}$:
    None (1): $\emptyset$
      One (5):   *a, b, c, d, e*
      Two (10):   *ab, ac, ad, ae, bc, bd, be, cd, ce, de*
      Three (10):   *abc, abd, abe, acd, ace, ade, bcd, bce, bde, cde*
      Four (5):   *abcd, abce, abde, acde, bcde*
      Five (1):   $A = abcde$

**4.53.**   (a)  $2^7 = 128$,     (b)  $2^6 = 64$,     (c)  $2^4 = 16$,     (d)  $2^3 = 8$,

**4.54.**   (a)  and     (b):  no.  Others: yes.

**4.55.** There are five:  $[S]$,  $[\{1, 2\}, \{3\}]$,  $[\{1, 3\}, \{2\}]$,  $[\{1\}, \{2, 3\}]$,  $[\{1\}, \{2\}, \{3\}]$.

**4.57.**   $P = [\{1, 3\}, \{2\}, \{4, 5\}, \{6\}, \{7, 8, 9\}]$

**4.63.** See Fig. 4-12(*a*).     (a)  Yes,     (b)  No,     (c)  Yes,     (d)  Yes

**4.64.** See Fig. 4-12(*b*).     (a)  Yes,     (b)  Yes,     (c)  Yes,     (d)  No

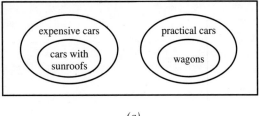

          (*a*)                                       (*b*)

**Fig. 4-12**

# CHAPTER 5

# Techniques of Counting

## 5.1 INTRODUCTION

This chapter develops some techniques for determining, without direct enumeration, the number of possible outcomes of particular event or the number of elements in a set.   Such sophisticated counting is sometimes called *combinatorial analysis*.   It includes the study of permutations and combinations.

## 5.2 BASIC COUNTING PRINCIPLES

There are two basic counting principles used throughout this chapter.   The first one involves addition and the second one involves multiplication.   Also, each principle has a set theoretical interpretation [where $n(A)$ denotes the number of elements in a set $A$].

The first counting principle follows:

---

*Sum Rule Principle*
Suppose some event $E$ can occur in $m$ ways and a second event $F$ can occur in $n$ ways, and suppose both events cannot occur at the same time.   Then $E$ or $F$ can occur in $m + n$ ways.

---

*Sum Rule Principle*
If $A$ and $B$ are disjoint sets, then

$$n(A \cup B) = n(A) + n(B).$$

---

The second counting principle follows

---

*Product Rule Principle:*
Suppose there is an event $E$ which can occur in $m$ ways, and independent of this event, there is a second event $F$ which can occur in $n$ ways.   Then combinations of $E$ and $F$ can occur in $mn$ ways.

---

93

*Product Rule Principle:*
Let $A \times B$ be the cartesian product of sets $A$ and $B$.  Then

$$n(A \times B) = n(A) \cdot n(B).$$

The above principles can be extended to three or more events.   That is, suppose an event $E_1$ can occur in $n_1$ ways, a second event $E_2$ can occur in $n_2$ ways, a third event $E_3$ can occur in $n_3$ ways, and so on.   Then:
[Sum Rule] If no two of the events can occur at the same time, then one of the events can occur in

$$n_1 + n_2 + n_3 + \cdots \text{ ways}$$

[Product Rule] If the events occur one after the other, then all the events can occur in the order indicated in
$$n_1 \cdot n_2 \cdot n_3 \cdots \text{ ways}$$

## EXAMPLE 5.1

(a)   Suppose a restaurant has 3 different appetizers and 4 different entrees.   Then there are

$$n = 3 (4) = 12$$

different ways to order an appetizer and an entree.

(b)   Suppose a college has 3 different history courses, 4 different literature courses, and 2 different science courses (with no prerequisits).

   (i)   The number $n$ of ways a student can choose one of each kind of courses is

$$n = 3 (4) (2) = 24$$

   (ii)   The number $m$ of ways a student can choose just one of the courses is

$$m = 3 + 4 + 2 = 9$$

Here the Sum Rule is used.

## 5.3   MATHEMATICAL FUNCTIONS

We discuss two important mathematical functions frequently used in combinatorics.

### Factorial Function

The product of the positive integers from 1 to $n$ inclusive is denoted by $n!$, read "$n$ factorial".   Namely:

$$n! = 1 \cdot 2 \cdot 3 \cdot \ldots \cdot (n-2)(n-1)n = n(n-1)(n-2) \cdot \ldots \cdot 3 \cdot 2 \cdot 1$$

Accordingly, $1! = 1$ and $n! = n \cdot (n-1)!$.   It is also convenient to define $0! = 1$.

## EXAMPLE 5.2

(a)   $3! = 3 \cdot 2 \cdot 1 = 6, \quad 4! = 4 \cdot 3 \cdot 2 \cdot 1 = 24, \quad 5 = 5 \cdot 4! = 5(24) = 120$

(b)   $\dfrac{12 \cdot 11 \cdot 10}{3 \cdot 2 \cdot 1} = \dfrac{12 \cdot 11 \cdot 10 \cdot 9!}{3 \cdot 2 \cdot 1 \cdot 9!} = \dfrac{12!}{3! \, 9!}$ and, more generally,

$$\frac{n(n-1) \cdots (n-r+1)}{r(r-1) \cdots 3 \cdot 2 \cdot 1} = \frac{n(n-1) \cdots (n-r+1)(n-r)!}{r(r-1) \cdots 3 \cdot 2 \cdot 1 \cdot (n-r)!} = \frac{n!}{r!\,(n-r)!}$$

(c)   For large $n$, one uses Stirling's approximation:

$$n! \approx \sqrt{2\pi n} \; n^n e^{-n}$$

(where $e = 2.718\ldots$).

## Binomial Coefficients

The symbol $\binom{n}{r}$, read "$nCr$" or "$n$ choose $r$," where $r$ and $n$ are positive integers with $r \leq n$, is defined as follows:

$$\binom{n}{r} = \frac{n(n-1)\cdots(n-r+1)}{r(r-1)\cdots 3\cdot 2\cdot 1} \qquad \text{or equivalently} \qquad \binom{n}{r} = \frac{n!}{r!\,(n-r)!}$$

Note that $n - (n - r) = r$. This yields the following important relation.

**Lemma 5.1:** $\binom{n}{n-r} = \binom{n}{r}$ or equivalently, $\binom{n}{a} = \binom{n}{b}$ where $a + b = n$.

Motivated by that fact that $0! = 1$, we define:

$$\binom{n}{0} = \frac{n!}{0!n!} = 1 \qquad \text{and} \qquad \binom{0}{0} = \frac{0!}{0!\,0!} = 1$$

### EXAMPLE 5.3

(a) $\binom{8}{2} = \dfrac{8\cdot 7}{2\cdot 1} = 28; \quad \binom{9}{4} = \dfrac{9\cdot 8\cdot 7\cdot 6}{4\cdot 3\cdot 2\cdot 1} = 126; \quad \binom{12}{5} = \dfrac{12\cdot 11\cdot 10\cdot 9\cdot 8}{5\cdot 4\cdot 3\cdot 2\cdot 1} = 792$

Note that $\binom{n}{r}$ has exactly $r$ factors in both the numerator and the denominator.

(b) Suppose we want to compute $\binom{10}{7}$. There will be 7 factors in both the numerator and the denominator. However, $10 - 7 = 3$. Thus, we use Lemma 5.1 to compute:

$$\binom{10}{7} = \binom{10}{3} = \frac{10\cdot 9\cdot 8}{3\cdot 2\cdot 1} = 120$$

## Binomial Coefficients and Pascal's Triangle

The numbers $\binom{n}{r}$ are called *binomial coefficients*, since they appear as the coefficients in the expansion of $(a + b)^n$. Specifically:

**Theorem (Binomial Theorem) 5.2:** $(a + B)^n = \displaystyle\sum_{k=0}^{n} \binom{n}{r} a^{n-k}b^k$.

The coefficients of the successive powers of $a + b$ can be arranged in a triangular array of numbers, called Pascal's triangle, as pictured in Fig. 5–1. The numbers in Pascal's triangle have the following interesting properties:

(*i*) The first and last number in each row is 1.

(*ii*) Every other number can be obtained by adding the two numbers appearing above it. For example:

$$10 = 4 + 6, \qquad 15 = 5 + 10, \qquad 20 = 10 + 10$$

Since these numbers are binomial coefficients, we state the above property formally.

**Theorem 5.3:** $\binom{n+1}{r} = \binom{n}{r-1} + \binom{n}{r}$.

$$
\begin{array}{ll}
(a+b)^0 = 1 & \qquad\qquad 1 \\
(a+b)^1 = a+b & \qquad\qquad 1 \quad 1 \\
(a+b)^2 = a^2 + 2ab + b^2 & \qquad\qquad 1 \quad 2 \quad 1 \\
(a+b)^3 = a^3 + 3a^2b + 3ab^2 + b^3 & \qquad\qquad 1 \quad 3 \quad 3 \quad 1 \\
(a+b)^4 = a^4 + 4a^3b + 6a^2b^2 + 4ab^3 + b^4 & \qquad\qquad 1 \quad 4 \quad 6 \quad 4 \quad 1 \\
(a+b)^5 = a^5 + 5a^4b + 10a^3b^2 + 10a^2b^3 + 5ab^4 + b^5 & \qquad 1 \quad 5 \quad (10) \quad 10 \quad 5 \quad 1 \\
(a+b)^6 = a^6 + 6a^5b + 15a^4b^2 + 20a^3b^3 + 15a^2b^4 + 6ab^5 + b^6 & \quad 1 \quad 6 \quad (15) \quad (20) \quad 15 \quad 6 \quad 1 \\
\end{array}
$$

**Fig. 5-1** Pascal's triangle.

## 5.4  PERMUTATIONS

Any arrangement of a set of objects in a given order is called a *permutation* of the objects (taken all at a time).   Any arrangement of $r \leq n$ of these objects in a given order is called an "*r* permutation" or "a permutation of the *n* objects taken *r* at a time." Consider, for example, the set of letters $A,B,C,D$.   Then:

   (*i*)   *BDCA, DCBA, ACDB* are permutations of the four letters (taken all at a time).

   (*ii*)   *BAD, ADB, CDB* are permutations of the four letters taken three at a time.

   (*iii*)   *AD, CB, BD* are permutations of the four letters taken two at a time.

We usually are interested in the number of such permutations without listing all of them.   We let

$$P(n, r)$$

denote the number of permutations of *n* objects taken *r* at a time.   The following theorem applies.

**Theorem 5.4:**   $P(n, r) = n (n - 1) (n - 2) \cdots (n - r + 1) = \dfrac{n!}{(n - r)!}$

We emphasize that there are *r* factors in $n(n - 1) (n - 2) \cdots (n - r + 1)$.

**EXAMPLE 5.4**   Find the number *m* of permutations of six objects, say, *A, B, C, D, E, F*, taken three at a time.   In other words, find the number of "three-letter words" using only the given six letters without repetition.

Let us represent the general three-letter word by the following three positions:

$$\underline{\qquad} , \underline{\qquad} , \underline{\qquad}$$

The first letter can be chosen in 6 ways; following this the second letter can be chosen in 5 ways; and, finally, the third letter can be chosen in 4 ways.   Write each number in its appropriate position as follows:

$$\underline{\quad 6 \quad} , \underline{\quad 5 \quad} , \underline{\quad 4 \quad}$$

By the Product Rule there are $m = 6 \cdot 5 \cdot 4 \cdot = 120$ possible three-letter words without repetition from the six letters. Namely, there are 120 permutations of 6 objects taken 3 at a time.   This agrees with the formula in Theorem 5.4:

$$P(6, 3) = 6 \cdot 5 \cdot 4 = 120$$

In fact, Theorem 5.4 is proven in the same way as we did for this particular case.

Consider now the special case of $P(n, r)$ when $r = n$.   We get the following result.

**Corollary 5.5:**   There are *n*! permutations of *n* objects (taken all at a time).

For example, there are $3! = 6$ permutations of the three letters *A, B, C*.   These are

$$ABC, \qquad ACB, \qquad BAC, \qquad BCA, \qquad CAB, \qquad CBA$$

### Permutations with Repetitions (Optional)

Frequently we want to know the number of permutations of a *multiset*, that is, a set of objects where some are alike.   We will let

$$P(n; n_1, n_2, \cdots, n_r)$$

denote the number of permutations of *n* objects of which $n_1$ are alike, $n_2$ are alike, ..., $n_r$ are alike.   The general formula follows.

**Theorem 5.6:**   $P(n; n_1, n_2, \cdots, n_r) = \dfrac{n!}{n_1! n_2! \cdots n_r!}$

**EXAMPLE 5.5**   Find the number $m$ of 7-letter words that can be formed using the letters of the word "BENZENE."

We seek the number of permutations of 7 objects, where 3 are alike, the three $E$'s, and 2 are alike, the two $N$'s.   By Theorem 5.6:

$$m = P(7; 3, 2) = \frac{7!}{3!2!} = \frac{7 \cdot 6 \cdot 5 \cdot 4 \cdot 3 \cdot 2 \cdot 1}{3 \cdot 2 \cdot 1 \cdot 2 \cdot 1} = 420$$

### Ordered Samples

Many problems are concerned with choosing an element from a set $S$, say, with $n$ elements.   When we choose one element after another, say, $r$ times, we call the choice an *ordered sample* of size $r$.   We consider two cases.

(*i*)   *Sampling with replacement.*

Here the element is replaced in the set $S$ before the next element is chosen.   Thus, each time there are $n$ ways to choose the element (repetitions are allowed).   The Product Rule tells us that there are

$$n \cdot n \cdot n \cdots n \cdot n \ (r \text{ factors}) = n^r$$

ordered samples with replacement of size $r$.

(*ii*)   *Sampling without replacement.*

Here the element is not replaced in the set $S$ before the next element is chosen.   Thus, there are no repetitions in the ordered example.   Such a sample is simply an $r$-permutation.   Thus, there are

$$P(n,r) = n \ (n-1) \ (n-2) \cdots (n-r+1) = \frac{n!}{(n-r)!}$$

ordered samples without replacement of size $r$ in a set $S$ with $n$ elements.

**EXAMPLE 5.6**   Three cards are chosen in succession from a deck with 52 cards.   Find the number $m$ of ways this can be done:

(*a*)   with replacement,        (*b*)   without replacement.

(*a*)   Here each card can be chosen in 52 ways.   Thus:

$$m = 52 \ (52) \ (52) = 52^3 = 140,608$$

(*b*)   Since there is no replacement, the first card can be chosen in 52 ways, the second in 51 ways, and the third in 50 ways.   Thus:

$$m = P(52, 3) = 52 \ (51) \ (50) = 132,600$$

## 5.5   COMBINATIONS

Let $S$ be a set with $n$ elements.   A *combination* of the $n$ elements taken $r$ at a time is any selection of $r$ elements where order does not count.   Such a selection is called an *r-combination*; it is simply a subset of $S$ with $r$ elements.   The number of such combinations will be denoted by

$$C(n,r)$$

We note that any $r$-combination of $n$ objects determines $r!$ permutations of the objects in the combination. Thus:

$$P(n,r) = r! \ C(n,r)$$

Accordingly, we obtain the following formula for $C(n,r)$, which we formally state as a theorem.

**Theorem 5.7:**   $C(n,r) = \dfrac{P(n,r)}{r!} = \dfrac{n!}{r! \ (n-r)!}$

The binomial coeficient $\binom{n}{r}$ was defined to be $\dfrac{n!}{r!\,(n-r)!}$ . Thus:

$$C(n,r) = \binom{n}{r}$$

We will use $C(n,r)$ and $\binom{n}{r}$ interchangeably.

**Remark:** The essential difference between a permutation and a combination is that order counts in a permutation but not in a combination.

### EXAMPLE 5.7

(a) Find the number $m$ of committees of 3 that can be chosen from 8 people.

Each committee is essentially a combination of the people taken 3 at a time. Hence:

$$m = C(8,3) = \binom{8}{3} = \frac{8\cdot7\cdot6}{3\cdot2\cdot1} = 56$$

(b) A farm has 6 cows, 5 pigs, and 4 hens. Find the number $m$ of ways a person can buy 3 cows, 2 pigs, and 4 hens from the farm.

The person can choose the cows in $\binom{6}{3}$ ways, the pigs in $\binom{5}{2}$ ways, and the hens in $\binom{8}{4}$ ways. By the Product Rule,

$$m = \binom{6}{3}\binom{5}{2}\binom{8}{4} = \frac{6\cdot5\cdot4}{3\cdot2\cdot1} \cdot \frac{5\cdot4}{2\cdot1} \cdot \frac{8\cdot7\cdot6\cdot5}{4\cdot3\cdot2\cdot1} = 20\cdot10\cdot70 = 14{,}000$$

### 5.6 TREE DIAGRAMS

A *tree diagram* is a device used to enumerate all the possible outcomes of a sequence of events where each event can occur in a finite number of ways. The constuction of tree diagrams is illustrated in the following example.

### EXAMPLE 5.8

(a) Find the product set $A\times B\times C$, where $A = \{1, 2\}$, $B = \{a, b, c\}$, $C = \{x, y\}$.

The tree diagram for $A\times B\times C$ appears in Fig. 5-2(a). Here the tree is constructed from left to right, and the number of branches at each point corresponds to the possible outcomes of the next event. Each endpoint (leaf) of the tree is labeled by the corresponding element of $A\times B\times C$. As expected, $A\times B\times C$ has $n = 2(3)(2) = 12$ elements.

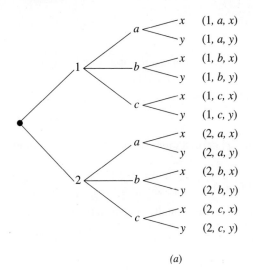

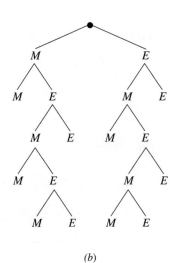

(a)                                                         (b)

**Fig. 5-2**

(b)  Mark and Erik are to play a tennis tournament.   The first person to win two games in a row or who wins a total of three games wins the tournament.   Find the number of ways the tournament can occur.

The tree diagram showing the possible outcomes of the tournament appears in Fig. 5-2(b).   Here the tree is constructed from top-down rather than from left-right.   (That is, the "root" is on the top of the tree.)   Note that there are 10 endpoints, and the endpoints correspond to the following 10 ways the tournament can occur:

$$MM, \; MEMM, \; MEMEM, \; MEMEE, \; MEE, \; EMM, \; EMEMM, \; EMEME, \; EMEE, \; EE$$

The path from the beginning (top) of the tree to the endpoint describes who won which game in the tournament.

# Solved Problems

## FACTORIAL NOTATION, BINOMIAL COEFFICIENTS

**5.1.**  Compute:   (a)   4!, 5!,        (b)   6!, 7!, 8!, 9!

(a)   $4! = 4 \cdot 3 \cdot 2 \cdot 1 = 24,$        $5! = 5 \cdot 4 \cdot 3 \cdot 2 \cdot 1 = 5\,(24) = 120$

(b)   Now use $(n + 1) ! = (n + 1) \, n!$:

$$6! = 5\,(5!) = 6\,(120) = 720, \qquad 8! = 8\,(7!) = 8\,(5040) = 40{,}320$$
$$7! = 7\,(6!) = 7\,(720) = 5040, \qquad 9! = 9\,(8!) = 9\,(40{,}320) = 362{,}880$$

**5.2.**  Compute:   (a)   $\dfrac{11!}{9!}$,        (b)   $\dfrac{6!}{9!}$

(a)   $\dfrac{11!}{9!} = \dfrac{11 \cdot 10 \cdot 9 \cdot 8 \cdot 7 \cdot 6 \cdot 5 \cdot 4 \cdot 3 \cdot 2 \cdot 1}{9 \cdot 8 \cdot 7 \cdot 6 \cdot 5 \cdot 4 \cdot 3 \cdot 2 \cdot 1} = 11 \cdot 10 = 110$

Alternately, this could be solved as follows:

$$\frac{11!}{9!} = \frac{11 \cdot 10 \cdot 9!}{9!} = 11 \cdot 10 = 110$$

(b)   $\dfrac{6!}{9!} = \dfrac{6!}{9 \cdot 8 \cdot 7 \cdot 6!} = \dfrac{1}{9 \cdot 8 \cdot 7} = \dfrac{1}{504}$

**5.3.**  Compute:   (a)   $\dbinom{14}{3}$,        (b)   $\dbinom{11}{4}$

Recall that there are as many factors in the numerator as in the denominator.

(a)   $\dbinom{14}{3} = \dfrac{14 \cdot 13 \cdot 12}{3 \cdot 2 \cdot 1} = 364,$        (b)   $\dbinom{11}{4} = \dfrac{11 \cdot 10 \cdot 9 \cdot 8}{4 \cdot 3 \cdot 2 \cdot 1} = 330$

**5.4.**  Compute:   (a)   $\dbinom{8}{6}$,        (b)   $\dbinom{10}{7}$.

(a)   $\dbinom{8}{6} = \dfrac{8 \cdot 7 \cdot 6 \cdot 5 \cdot 4 \cdot 3}{6 \cdot 5 \cdot 4 \cdot 3 \cdot 2 \cdot 1} = 28$

or, since $8 - 6 = 2$, we can use Lemma 7.1 to obtain

$$\binom{8}{6} = \binom{8}{2} = \frac{8 \cdot 7}{2 \cdot 1} = 28$$

(b)   Since $10 - 7 = 3$, Lemma 7.1 tells us that

$$\binom{10}{7} = \binom{10}{3} = \frac{10 \cdot 9 \cdot 8}{3 \cdot 2 \cdot 1} = 120$$

## COUNTING PRINCIPLES

**5.5.**   Suppose a bookcase shelf has 5 History texts, 3 Sociology texts, 6 Anthropology texts, and 4 Psychology texts.   Find the number $n$ of ways a student can choose:
(a)   one of the texts,          (b)   one of each type of text.

(a)   Here the Sum Rule applies; hence, $n = 5 + 3 + 6 + 4 = 18$.

(b)   Here the Product Rule applies; hence, $n = 5 \cdot 3 \cdot 6 \cdot 4 = 360$.

**5.6.**   A restaurant has a menu with 4 appetizers, 5 entrees, and 2 desserts.   Find the number $n$ of ways a customer can order an appetizer, entree, and desert.

Here the Product Rule applies, since the customer orders one of each.   Thus, $n = 4 \cdot 5 \cdot 2 = 40$.

**5.7.**   A history class contains 8 male students and 6 female students.   Find the number $n$ of ways that the class can elect: (a)  1 class representative,     (b)  2 class representatives, 1 male and 1 female, (c)  1 president and 1 vice president.

(a)   Here the Sum Rule is used; hence, $n = 8 + 6 = 14$.

(b)   Here the Product Rule is used; hence, $n = 8 \cdot 6 = 48$.

(c)   There are 14 ways to elect the president, and then 13 ways to elect the vice president.   Thus, $n = 14 \cdot 13 = 182$.

**5.8.**   Suppose a password consists of four characters, the first two being letters in the (English) alphabet and the last two being digits.   Find the number $n$ of

(a)   passwords,          (b)   passwords beginning with a vowel

(a)   There are 26 ways to choose each of the first two characters, and 10 ways to choose each of the last two characters.   Thus, by the Product Rule:

$$n = 26 \cdot 26 \cdot 10 \cdot 10 = 67,600$$

(b)   Here there are only 5 ways to choose the first character, the others being the same.   Thus:

$$n = 5 \cdot 26 \cdot 10 \cdot 10 = 13,000$$

## PERMUTATIONS, ORDERED SAMPLES

**5.9.**   State the essential diference between permutations and combinations, with examples.

Order counts with permutations, such as words, sitting in a row, and electing a president, vice president, and treasurer.   Order does not count with combinations, such as committees, and teams (without counting positions).   The product rule is usually used with permutations, since the choice for each of the ordered positions may be viewed as a sequence of events.

**5.10.** Find the number $n$ of ways that 4 people can sit in a row with 4 seats.

The four empty seats may be pictured by:

$$\underline{\qquad}, \ \underline{\qquad}, \ \underline{\qquad}, \ \underline{\qquad}.$$

The first seat can be occupied by any one of the 4 people—that is, there are 4 ways to fill the first seat. After the first person sits down, there are three people left, and so there are 3 ways to fill the second seat. Similarly, the third seat can be filled in 2 ways, and the last seat in 1 way. This is pictured by:

$$\underline{\ 4\ }, \ \underline{\ 3\ }, \ \underline{\ 2\ }, \ \underline{\ 1\ }.$$

Thus, by the Product Rule, $n = 4 \cdot 3 \cdot 2 \cdot 1 = 24$.

Alternately, $n$ is the number of permutations of 4 things taken 4 at a time; hence,

$$n = P(4, 4) = 4! = 24$$

**5.11.** Find the number $n$ of distinct permutations that can be formed from all the letters of each word:
(a)  THOSE,          (b)  UNUSUAL,          (c)  SOCIOLOGICAL.

This problem concerns permutations with repetitions.

(a)  $n = 5! = 120$, since there are 5 letters and no repetitions.

(b)  $n = \dfrac{7!}{3!} = 840$, since there are 7 letters of which 3 are $U$ and no other letter is repeated.

(c)  $n = \dfrac{12!}{3!2!2!2!}$, since there are 12 letters of which 3 are O, 2 are C, 2 are I, and 2 are L.  (We leave the answer using factorials, since the number is very large.)

**5.12.** Suppose we are given 4 identical red flags and 2 identical blue flags.  Find the number $n$ of different signals that can be formed by hanging the 6 flags in a vertical line.

This problem concerns permutations with repetitions.  Thus, $n = \dfrac{6!}{4!2!} = 15$, since there are 6 flags, of which 4 are red and 2 are blue.

**5.13.** A class contains 8 students.  Find the number $n$ of samples of size 3:
(a)  with replacement,          (b)  without replacement

(a)  Each student in the ordered sample can be chosen in 8 ways; hence, there are
$$n = 8 \cdot 8 \cdot 8 = 8^3 = 512 \text{ samples of size 3 with replacement}$$

(b)  The first student in the sample can be chosen in 8 ways, the second in 7 ways, and the last in 6 ways. Thus, there are $n = 8 \cdot 7 \cdot 6 = 336$ samples of size 3 without replacement.

**5.14.** Find $n$ if $P(n, 2) = 72$.

$P(n, 2) = n(n - 1) = n^2 - n$.  Thus, we get

$$n^2 - n = 72 \quad \text{or} \quad n^2 - n - 72 = 0 \quad \text{or} \quad (n - 9)(n - 8) = 0$$

Since $n$ must be positive, the only answer is $n = 9$.

## COMBINATIONS

**5.15.** There are 12 students who are elegible to attend the National Student Association annual meeting. Find the number $n$ of ways a delegation of four students can be selected from the 12 elegible students.

This concerns combinations, not permutations, since order does not count in a delegation. There are "12 choose 4" such delegations. That is:

$$n = C(12, 4) = \binom{12}{4} = \frac{12 \cdot 11 \cdot 10 \cdot 9}{4 \cdot 3 \cdot 2 \cdot 1} = 495$$

**5.16.** A student is to answer 8 out of 10 questions on an exam. (*a*) Find the number $n$ of ways the student can choose 8 of the 10 questions. (*b*) Find $n$ if the student must answer the first three questions.

(*a*) The eight questions can be selected "10 chose 8" ways. That is:

$$n = C(10, 8) = \binom{10}{8} = \binom{10}{2} = \frac{10 \cdot 9}{2 \cdot 1} = 45$$

(*b*) After the first three questions are answered, the student must choose the other five questions from the remaining seven questions. Therefore:

$$n = C(7, 5) = \binom{7}{5} = \binom{7}{2} = \frac{7 \cdot 6}{2 \cdot 1} = 21$$

**5.17.** A class contains 10 students with 6 men and 4 women. Find the number $n$ of ways the class can:

(*a*) Select a 4-member committee from the students.

(*b*) Select a 4-member committee with 2 men and 2 women.

(*c*) Elect a president, vice president, and treasurer.

(*a*) This concerns combinations, not permutations, since order does not count in a committee. There are "10 choose 4" such committees. That is:

$$n = C(10, 4) = \binom{10}{4} = \frac{10 \cdot 9 \cdot 8 \cdot 7}{4 \cdot 3 \cdot 2 \cdot 1} = 210$$

(*b*) The 2 men can be chosen from the 6 men in $C(6,2)$ ways, and the 2 women can be chosen from the 4 women in $C(4, 2)$ ways. Thus, by the Product Rule:

$$n = \binom{6}{2}\binom{4}{2} = \frac{6 \cdot 5}{2 \cdot 1} \cdot \frac{4 \cdot 3}{2 \cdot 1} = 15(6) = 90$$

(*c*) This concerns permutations, not combinations, since order does count. Thus,

$$n = P(6, 3) = 6 \cdot 5 \cdot 4 = 120$$

**5.18.** A box contains 8 blue socks and 6 red socks. Find the number of ways two socks can be drawn from the box if: (*a*) They can be any color. (*b*) They must be the same color.

(a)   There are "14 choose 2" ways to select 2 of the 14 socks.   Thus:

$$n = C(14, 2) = \binom{14}{2} = \frac{14 \cdot 13}{2 \cdot 1} = 91$$

(b)   There are $C(8, 2) = 28$ ways to choose 2 of the 8 blue socks, and $C(6, 2) = 15$ ways to choose 2 of the 4 red socks.   By the Sum Rule, $n = 28 + 15 = 43$.

## TREE DIAGRAMS

**5.19.**   Teams $A$ and $B$ play in a tournament.   The first team to win three games wins the tournament. Find the number $n$ of possible ways the tournament can occur.

Construct the appropriate tree diagram in Fig. 5-3(a).   The tournament can occur in 20 ways:

*AAA, AABA, AABBA, AABBB, ABAA, ABABA, ABABB, ABBAA, ABBAB, ABBB,*
*BBB, BBAB, BBAAB, BBAAA, BABB, BABAB, BABAA, BAABB, BAABA, BAAA*

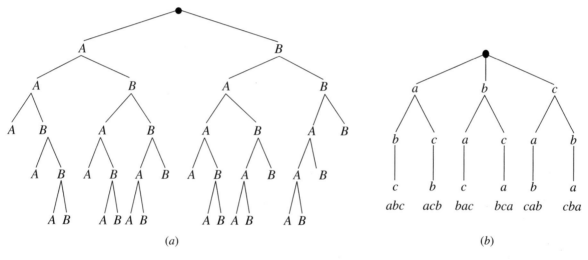

*(a)*                                    *(b)*

**Fig. 5-3**

**5.20.**   Construct the tree diagram that gives the permutations of $\{a, b, c\}$.

The tree diagram appears in Fig. 5-3(b).   There are six permutations, and they are listed on the bottom of the diagram.

## MISCELLANEOUS PROBLEMS (OPTIONAL)

**5.21.**   Find 50!.

Since $n$ is very large, we use Sterling's approximation:

$$n! \sim \sqrt{2\pi n} \; n^n e^{-n} \text{ (where } e \approx 2.718)$$

Thus:

$$50! \sim N = \sqrt{100\pi} \; 50^{50} e^{-50}$$

Evaluating $N$ using a calculator, we get $N = 3.04 \times 10^{64}$ (which has 65 digits).

Alternately, using (base 10) logarithms, we get

$$\log N = \log(\sqrt{100\pi}\ 50^{50}e^{-50})$$

$$= \frac{1}{2}\log 100 + \frac{1}{2}\log \pi + 50\log 50 - 50\log e$$

$$= \frac{1}{2}(2) + \frac{1}{2}(0.4972) + 50(1.6990) - 50(0.4343)$$

$$= 64.4836$$

The antilog yields $N = 3.04 \times 10^{64}$.

**5.22.** Prove Theorem 5.3: $\dbinom{n+1}{r} = \dbinom{n}{r-1} + \dbinom{n}{r}$.

First we have

$$\binom{n}{r-1} + \binom{n}{r} = \frac{n!}{(r-1)!\cdot(n-r+1)!} + \frac{n!}{r!\cdot(n-r)!}.$$

To obtain the same denominator in both fractions, multiply the first fraction by $\dfrac{r}{r}$ and the second fraction by $\dfrac{n-r+1}{n-r+1}$.  This yields

$$\binom{n}{r-1} + \binom{n}{r} = \frac{r\cdot n!}{r\cdot(r-1)!\cdot(n-r+1)!} + \frac{(n-r+1)\cdot n!}{r!\cdot(n-r+1)\cdot(n-r)!}$$

$$= \frac{r\cdot n!}{r!\cdot(n-r+1)!} + \frac{(n-r+1)\cdot n!}{r!\cdot(n-r+1)!}$$

$$= \frac{r\cdot n! + (n-r+1)\cdot n!}{r!\cdot(n-r+1)!} = \frac{[r+(n-r+1)]\cdot n!}{r!\cdot(n-r+1)!}$$

$$= \frac{(n+1)\cdot n!}{r!\cdot(n-r+1)!} = \frac{(n+1)!}{r!\cdot(n-r+1)!} = \binom{n+1}{r}$$

**5.23.** There are 12 students in a class.  Find the number $n$ of ways that the 12 students can take three tests if four students are to take each test.

There are $C(12, 4) = 495$ ways to choose 4 of the 12 students to take the first test.  Following this, there are $C(8, 4) = 70$ ways ways to choose 4 of the remaining 8 students to take the second test.  The remaining students take the third test.  Thus:

$$n = 70\,(495) = 34{,}650$$

**5.24.** Prove Binomial Theorem 5.2: $(a+b)^n = \displaystyle\sum_{r=0}^{n}\binom{n}{r}a^{n-r}b^r$.

The theorem is true for $n = 1$, since

$$\sum_{r=0}^{1}\binom{1}{r}a^{1-r}b^r = \binom{1}{0}a^1b^0 + \binom{1}{1}a^0b^1 = a + b = (a+b)^1$$

We assume the theorem is true for $(a + b)^n$ and prove it is true for $(a + b)^{n+1}$.

$$(a + b)^{n+1} = (a + b)(a + b)^n$$

$$= (a + b)\left[a^n + \binom{n}{1} a^{n-1} b + \cdots + \binom{n}{r-1} a^{n-r+1} b^{r-1}\right.$$

$$\left. + \binom{n}{r} a^{n-r} b^r + \cdots + \binom{n}{1} a b^{n-1} + b^n\right]$$

Now the term in the product which contains $b^r$ is obtained from

$$b\left[\binom{n}{r-1} a^{n-r+1} b^{r-1}\right] + a\left[\binom{n}{r} a^{n-r} b^r\right] = \binom{n}{r-1} a^{n-r+1} b^r + \binom{n}{r} a^{n-r+1} b^r$$

$$= \left[\binom{n}{r-1} + \binom{n}{r}\right] a^{n-r+1} b^r$$

But, by Theorem 5.3, $\begin{pmatrix} n \\ r-1 \end{pmatrix} + \begin{pmatrix} n \\ r \end{pmatrix} = \begin{pmatrix} n+1 \\ r \end{pmatrix}$. Thus, the term containing $b^r$ follows:

$$\binom{n+1}{r} a^{n-r+1} b^r$$

Note that $(a + b)(a + b)^n$ is a polynomial of degree $n + 1$ in $b$. Consequently:

$$(a + b)^{n+1} = (a + b)(a + b)^n = \sum_{r=0}^{n+1} \binom{n+1}{r} a^{n-r+1} b^r$$

which was to be proved.

**5.25.** Let $n$ and $n_1, n_2, \ldots, n_r$ be nonnegative integers such that $n_1 + n_2 + \ldots + n_r = n$. The *multinomial coefficients* are denoted and defined by

$$\begin{pmatrix} n \\ n_1, n_2, \ldots, n_r \end{pmatrix} = \frac{n!}{n_1! n_2! \ldots n_r!}$$

Compute the following multinomial coefficients:

(a) $\begin{pmatrix} 6 \\ 3,2,1 \end{pmatrix}$,      (b) $\begin{pmatrix} 8 \\ 4,2,2,0 \end{pmatrix}$,      (c) $\begin{pmatrix} 10 \\ 5,3,2,2 \end{pmatrix}$.

(a) $\begin{pmatrix} 6 \\ 3, 2, 1 \end{pmatrix} = \frac{6!}{3! \, 2! \, 1!} = \frac{6 \cdot 5 \cdot 4 \cdot 3 \cdot 2 \cdot 1}{3 \cdot 2 \cdot 1 \cdot 2 \cdot 1 \cdot 1} = 60$

(b) $\begin{pmatrix} 8 \\ 4, 2, 2, 0 \end{pmatrix} = \frac{8!}{4! \, 2! \, 2! \, 0!} = \frac{8 \cdot 7 \cdot 6 \cdot 5 \cdot 4 \cdot 3 \cdot 2 \cdot 1}{4 \cdot 3 \cdot 2 \cdot 1 \cdot 2 \cdot 1 \cdot 2 \cdot 1 \cdot 1} = 420$

(c) $\begin{pmatrix} 10 \\ 5, 3, 2, 2 \end{pmatrix}$ has no meaning, since $5 + 3 + 2 + 2 \neq 10$.

# Supplementary Problems

### FACTORIAL NOTATION, BINOMIAL COEFFICIENTS

**5.26.** Find: (a) $10!, 11!, 12!,$      (b) $60!$ [*Hint*: Use Sterling's approximation to $n!$ in Problem 5.21.]

**5.27.** Evaluate: (a) $\frac{16!}{14!}$,      (b) $\frac{14!}{11!}$,      (c) $\frac{8!}{10!}$,      (d) $\frac{10!}{13!}$.

**5.28.** Write in terms of factorials: (a) $24 \cdot 23 \cdot 22 \cdot 21$,      (b) $\frac{1}{12 \cdot 11 \cdot 10}$.

**5.29.** Simplify: (a) $\frac{(n + 1)!}{n!}$,      (b) $\frac{n!}{(n - 2)!}$,      (c) $\frac{(n + 2)!}{(n - 1)!}$.

**5.30.** Evaluate: (a) $\begin{pmatrix} 5 \\ 2 \end{pmatrix}$,      (b) $\begin{pmatrix} 7 \\ 3 \end{pmatrix}$,      (c) $\begin{pmatrix} 14 \\ 2 \end{pmatrix}$,      (d) $\begin{pmatrix} 6 \\ 4 \end{pmatrix}$,      (e) $\begin{pmatrix} 20 \\ 17 \end{pmatrix}$,      (f) $\begin{pmatrix} 18 \\ 15 \end{pmatrix}$.

**5.31.** The eighth row of Pascal's triangle follows:

$$1 \quad 8 \quad 28 \quad 56 \quad 70 \quad 56 \quad 28 \quad 8 \quad 1$$

Find the (a) ninth and (b) tenth rows of the triangle.

**5.32.** Evaluate the following multinomial coeficients (defined in Problem 5.25):

(a) $\begin{pmatrix} 6 \\ 2,\ 3,\ 1 \end{pmatrix}$,　　(b) $\begin{pmatrix} 7 \\ 3,\ 2,\ 2,\ 0 \end{pmatrix}$,　　(c) $\begin{pmatrix} 9 \\ 3,\ 5,\ 1 \end{pmatrix}$,　　(d) $\begin{pmatrix} 8 \\ 4,\ 3,\ 2 \end{pmatrix}$

## COUNTING PRINCIPLES, SUM AND PRODUCT RULES

**5.33.** A store sells clothes for men. It has 3 different kinds of jackets, 7 different kinds of shirts, and 5 different kinds of pants. Find the number of ways a person can buy: (a) one of the items for a present, (b) one of each of the three kinds of clothes for a present.

**5.34.** The desert menu of a restaurant has 4 kinds of cakes, 2 kinds of cookies, and 3 kinds of ice cream. Find the number of ways a person can select:

(a) one of the deserts, (b) one of each of the three kinds of deserts.

**5.35.** A class contains 10 male students and 8 female students. Find the number of ways that the class can elect: (a) a class representative, (b) 2 class representatives, one male and one female, (c) a class president and vice president.

**5.36.** Suppose a pasword consists of four characters where the first character must be a letter of the (English) alphabet, but each of the other characters may be a letter or a digit. Find the number of:

(a) passwords, (b) passwords beginning with one of the five vowels

**5.37.** Suppose a code consists of five characters, two letters followed by three digits Find the number of: (a) codes, (b) codes with distinct letters, (c) codes with the same letters.

## PERMUTATIONS AND COMBINATIONS

**5.38.** Find the number $n$ of ways a judge can award first, second, and third places in a contest with 18 contestants.

**5.39.** A restaurant has 6 different deserts. Find the number $n$ of ways a customer can choose 2 of the deserts.

**5.40.** A store has 8 different mystery books. Find the number $n$ of ways a customer can buy 3 of the books.

**5.41.** A debating team consists of 3 boys and 3 girls. Find the number $n$ of ways they can sit in a row where: (a) there are no restrictions, (b) the boys and girls are each to sit together, (c) just the girls are to sit together.

**5.42.** A box contains 6 blue socks and 4 white socks. Find the number $n$ of ways two socks can be drawn from the box where: (a) there are no restrictions, (b) they are different colors, (c) they are the same color.

**5.43.** Find the number $n$ of ways 5 large books, and 3 small books can be placed on a shelf where: (a) there are no restrictions, (b) all books of the same size are together.

**5.44.** A class contains 9 boys and 3 girls. Find the number of ways a teacher can select a committee of 4 from the class.

**5.45.** Repeat Problem 5.44, but where the committee consists of:

(a) 2 boys and 2 girls, (b) exactly one girl, (c) at least one girl.

**5.46.** A women has 11 close friends.   Find the number $n$ of ways she can invite 5 of them to dinner.

**5.47.** Repeat Problem 5.46, but where:   (*a*)   two of the friends are married to each other and will not attend separately,       (*b*)   two of the friends are not speaking with each other and will not attend together.

**5.48.** A student must answer 10 out of 13 questions on an exam.   Find the number $n$ of choices if there are no restrictions.

**5.49.** Repeat Problem 5.48, but where the student must answer:   (*a*)   the first two questions, (*b*)   the first or second question but not both.

## PERMUTATIONS WITH REPETITIONS, ORDERED SAMPLES

**5.50.** Find the number $n$ of permutations that can be formed from all of the letters of each word: (*a*)   QUEUE,       (*b*)   COMMITTEE,       (*c*)   PROPOSITION,       (*d*)   BASEBALL.

**5.51.** Suppose we are given 4 identical red flags, 2 identical blue flags, and 2 identical green flags.   Find the number $n$ of different signals that can be formed by hanging the 8 flags in a vertical line.

**5.52.** A box contains 12 lightbulbs.   Find the number $n$ of ordered samples of size 3:   (*a*)   with replacement, (*b*)   without replacement.

**5.53.** A class contains 10 students.   Find the number $n$ of ordered samples of size 4:   (*a*)   with replacement, (*b*)   without replacement.

## TREE DIAGRAMS

**5.54.** Teams $A$ and $B$ play in the World Series of baseball, where the team that first wins four games wins the series.   Suppose $A$ wins the first game and that the team that wins the second game also wins the fourth game.   (*a*)   Construct the appropriate tree diagram.       (*b*)   Find and list the number n of ways the series can occur.       (*c*)   How many ways will B win the series?       (*d*)   How many ways will the series last seven games.

# Answers to Supplentary Problems

**5.26.**   (*a*)   3,628,800; 39,916,800; 479,001,600;       (*b*)   $\log(60!) = 81.920$; hence, $60! = 6.59 \times 10^{81}$

**5.27.**   (*a*)   240,       (*b*)   2184,       (*c*)   1/90,       (*d*)   1/1716

**5.28.**   (*a*)   24!/20!,       (*b*)   9!/12!

**5.29.**   (*a*)   $n + 1$,       (*b*)   $n(n-1)$,       (*b*)   $n(n + 1)(n + 2)$

**5.30.**   (*a*)   10,       (*b*)   35,       (*c*)   91,       (*d*)   15,       (*e*)   1140,       (*f*)   816

**5.31.**   (*a*)   1, 9, 36, 84, 126, 126, 84, 36, 9, 1
          (*b*)   1, 10, 45, 120, 210, 252, 210, 120, 45, 10, 1

**5.32.**   (*a*)   60,       (*b*)   210,       (*c*)   504       (*d*)   Not defined.

**5.33.**   (*a*)   15,       (*b*)   105

**5.34.**   (*a*)   9,       (*b*)   24

**5.35.** (*a*)  18,        (*b*)  80,        (*c*)  306

**5.36.** (*a*)  $26(36^3)$,        (*b*)  $5(36^3)$

**5.37.** (*a*)  $26^2 \cdot 10^3 = 676,000$;        (*b*)  $26 \cdot 25 \cdot 10^3 = 650,000$;        (*c*)  $26 \cdot 10^3 = 26,000$;

**5.38.** $n = 18 \cdot 17 \cdot 16 = 4896$

**5.39.** $C(6, 2) = 15$

**5.40.** $C(8, 3) = 56$

**5.41.** (*a*)  $6! = 720$,        (*b*)  $2 \cdot 3! \cdot 3! = 72$,        (*c*)  $4 \cdot 3! \cdot 3! = 144$

**5.42.** (*a*)  $C(10, 2) = 45$,        (*b*)  $6(4) = 24$,        (*c*)  $C(6, 2) + C(4, 2) = 21$  or  $45 - 24 = 21$

**5.43.** (*a*)  $8!$,        (*b*)  $2 \cdot 5! \cdot 3! = 1440$

**5.44.** $C(12, 4) = 495$

**5.45.** (*a*)  $C(9, 2) \cdot C(3, 2) = 108$,        (*b*)  $C(9, 3) \cdot 3 = 252$,
(*c*)  $9 + 108 + 252 = 369$  or  $C(12, 4) - C(9, 4) = 369$

**5.46.** $C(11, 5) = 462$

**5.47.** (*a*)  $126 + 84 = 210$,        (*b*)  $C(9, 5) + 2C(9, 4) = 378$

**5.48.** $C(13, 10) = C(13, 3) = 286$

**5.49.** (*a*)  $C(11, 8) = C(11, 3) = 165$,        (*b*)  $2 \cdot C(11, 9) = 110$

**5.50.** (*a*) 30;        (*b*)  $\dfrac{9!}{2!2!2!} = 45,360$;        (*c*)  $\dfrac{11!}{2!3!2!} = 1,663,200$;        (*d*)  $\dfrac{8!}{2!2!2!} = 5040$

**5.51.** $n = \dfrac{8!}{4!2!2!} = 420$

**5.52.** (*a*)  $12^3 = 1728$,        (*b*)  1320

**5.53.** (*b*)  $10^4 = 10,000$,        (*b*)  $10 \cdot 9 \cdot 8 \cdot 7 = 5040$

**5.54.** (*a*)   See Fig. 5-4.   Note that the tree begins at *A*, the winner of the first game, and that there is only one choice in the fourth game, the winner of the second game.

(*b*)   *n* = 15, as follows:

*AAAA, AABAA, AABABA, AABABBA, AABABBB, ABABAA, ABABABA, ABABABB, ABABBAA, ABABBAB, ABABBB, ABBBAAA, ABBBAAB, ABBBAB, ABBBB*

(*c*)   6,        (*d*)   8

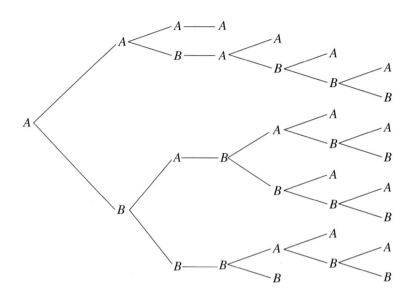

**Fig. 5-4**

# CHAPTER 6

# Probability Theory

## 6.1 INTRODUCTION

Probability theory is a mathematical modeling of the phenomemon of chance or randomness. If a coin is tossed in a random manner, it can land heads or tails, but we do not know which of these will occur in a single toss. However, suppose we let *s* be the number of times heads appears when the coin is tossed *n* times. As *n* increases, the ratio $f = s/n$, called the *relative frequency* of the outcome, becomes more stable. If the coin is perfectly balanced, then we expect that the coin will land heads approximately 50 percent of the time, or in other words, the relative frequence will approach 1/2. Alternately, assuming the coin is perfectly balanced, we can arrive at the value 1/2 deductively. That is, any side of the coin is as likely to occur as the other; hence, the chances of getting a heads is one in two, which means the probability of getting a heads is 1/2. Although the specific outcome on any one toss is unknown, the behavior over the long run is determined. This stable long-run behavior of random phenomena forms the basis of probability theory.

A probabilistic mathematical model of random phenonmena is defined by assigning "probabilities" to all the possible outcomes of an experiment. The reliability of our mathematical model for a given experiment depends upon the closeness of the assigned probabilities to the actual limiting relative frequences. This then gives rise to problems of testing and reliability, which form the subject matter of statistics.

## 6.2 SAMPLE SPACE AND EVENTS

The set *S* of all possible outcomes of an experiment is called the *sample space*. A particular outcome $a \in S$ is called a *sample point*. An *event* A is a set of outcomes, and so A is a subset of the sample space *S*. In particular, the set $\{a\}$ consisting of a single sample point $a \in S$ is called an *elementary event*. Furthermore, the empty set Ø and the sample space *S* are subsets of *S* and so are events; Ø is called the *impossible event* or the *null event*, and *S* is called the *sure event*.

Since an event is a set, we can combine events to form new events using the various set operations:

   (*i*)   $A \cup B$ is the event that occurs iff A occurs *or* B occurs (or both occur).

   (*ii*)  $A \cap B$ is the event that occurs iff A occurs *and* B occurs.

  (*iii*)  $A^c$, the complement of A, also written $\overline{A}$, is the event that occurs iff A does *not* occur.

(As usual in mathematics, iff is short for "if and only if.") Two events A and B are called *mutually exclusive* if they are disjoint, that is, if $A \cap B = \varnothing$. In other words, A and B are mutually exclusive iff they cannot occur simultaneously. Three or more events are mutually exclusive if every two of them are mutually exclusive.

## EXAMPLE 6.1

(*a*)   Experiment: Toss a die and observe the number (of dots) that appears on top.
    The sample space *S* consists of that six possible numbers, namely:

$$S = \{1, 2, 3, 4, 5, 6\}$$

Let *A* be the event that an even number occurs, *B* that an odd number occurs, and *C* that a number greater than 3 occurs. That is, let

$$A = \{2, 4, 6\}, \qquad B = \{1, 3, 5\}, \qquad C = \{4, 5, 6\}$$

Then

    $A \cap C = \{4, 6\}$ is the event that a number that is even *and* greater than 3 occurs.
    $B \cup C = \{1, 3, 4, 5, 6\}$ is the event that a number that is odd *or* greater than 3 occurs.
        $C^c = \{1, 2, 3\}$ is the event that a number that is *not* greater than 3 occurs.
Also, *A* and *B* are mutually exclusive: In other words, an even number and an odd number cannot occur simultaneously.

(*b*)   Experiment: Toss a coin three times and observe the sequence of heads (*H*) and tails (*T*) that appears.
    The sample space *S* consists of the following eight elements:

$$S = \{HHH, HHT, HTH, HTT, THH, THT, TTH, TTT\}$$

Let *A* be the event that two or more heads appear consecutively, and *B* that all three tosses are the same.   That is, let

$$A = \{HHH, HHT, THH\} \qquad \text{and} \qquad B = \{HHH, TTT\}$$

Then $A \cap B = \{HHH\}$ is the elementary event in which only heads appear.   The event that five heads appear is the empty set Ø.

(*c*)   Experiment: Toss a coin until a head appears and then count the number of times the coin is tossed.
    The sample space of this experiment is $S = \{1, 2, 3, \ldots\}$.   Since every positive integer is an element of *S*, the sample space is infinite.

**Remark:**   The sample space *S* in Example 6.1(*c*), as noted, is not finite.   The theory concerning such sample spaces lies beyond the scope of this text.   Thus, unless otherwise stated, all our sample spaces *S* shall be finite.

## 6.3   FINITE PROBABILITY SPACES

The following definition applies.

**Definition**:   Let *S* be a finite sample space, say, $S = \{a_1, a_2, \ldots, a_n\}$.   Suppose there is assigned to each point $a_i \in S$ a real number $p_i$ satisfying the following properties:

    (*i*)   Each $p_i$ is nonnegative; that is, $p_i \geq 0$.
    (*ii*)   The sum of the $p_i$ is 1; that is, $p_1 + p_2 + \ldots + p_n = 1$.

Then *S* is called a *finite probability space*, or *probability model*, and $p_i$ is called the the *probability* of $a_i$.   The *probability* of an event *A*, written *P(A)*, is defined to be the sum of the probabilities of the points in *A*.   For notational convenience, we write $P(a_i)$ for $P(\{a_i\})$.

**EXAMPLE 6.2.**   Experiment: Let three coins be tossed and the number of heads observed.
[Compare with Example 6.1 (*b*).]

The sample space is $S = \{0, 1, 2, 3\}$.   The following assignments on the elements of *S* defines a probability space:

$$P(0) = \frac{1}{8}, \qquad P(1) = \frac{3}{8}, \qquad P(2) = \frac{3}{8}, \qquad P(3) = \frac{1}{8}$$

That is, each probability is nonnegative, and the sum of the probabilities is 1.   Let *A* be the event that at least one head appears, and let *B* be the event that all heads or all tails appear.   That is, let

$$A = \{1, 2, 3\} \quad \text{and} \quad B = \{0, 3\}$$

Then, by definition:

$$P(A) = P(1) + P(2) + P(3) = \frac{3}{8} + \frac{3}{8} + \frac{1}{8} = \frac{7}{8}$$

and

$$P(B) = P(0) + P(3) = \frac{1}{8} + \frac{1}{8} = \frac{1}{4}$$

## Equiprobable Spaces

Frequently, the physical characteristics of an experiment suggest that the various outcomes of the sample space $S$ be assigned equal probabilities. Such a finite probability space $S$ will be called an *equiprobable space*.

Suppose an equiprobable space $S$ has $n$ points. Then the probability of each point must be $1/n$. Moreover, if an event $A$ has $r$ points, then its probability must be $r(1/n) = r/n$. In other words:

$$P(A) = \frac{\text{number of elements in } A}{\text{number of elements in } S} = \frac{n(A)}{n(S)}$$

or

$$P(A) = \frac{\text{number of outcomes favorable to } A}{\text{total number of possible outcomes}}$$

Where $n(A)$ denotes the number of elements in a set $A$.

**Remark:** The above formula for $P(A)$ can only be used with respect to an equiprobable space and cannot be used in general.

The expression "at random" will be used only with respect to an equiprobable space. Moreover, the statement "choose a point at random from a set $S$" means that every point in $S$ has the same probability of being chosen.

**EXAMPLE 6.3**  Let a card be selected from an ordinary deck of 52 playing cards. Let

$$A = \{\text{the card is a spade}\} \quad \text{and} \quad B = \{\text{the card is a face card}\}$$

(A face card is a jack, queen, or king.) Note that $A \cap B$ is the set of spade face cards. We compute $P(A)$, $P(B)$, and $P(A \cap B)$. Since we have an equiprobable space:

$$P(A) = \frac{\text{number of spades}}{\text{number of cards}} = \frac{13}{52} = \frac{1}{4} \qquad P(B) = \frac{\text{number of face cards}}{\text{number of cards}} = \frac{12}{52} = \frac{3}{13}$$

$$P(A \cap B) = \frac{\text{number of spade face cards}}{\text{number of cards}} = \frac{3}{52}$$

## Theorems on Finite Probability Spaces

The following theorem follows directly from the fact that the probability of an event is the sum of the probabilities of its points.

**Theorem 6.1:**  The probability function $P$ defined on the class of all events in a finite probability space $S$ has the following properties:

[$P_1$]  For every event $A$, $0 \leq P(A) \leq 1$.

[$P_2$]  $P(S) = 1$.

[$P_3$]  If events $A$ and $B$ are mutually exclusive, then $P(A \cup B) = P(A) + P(B)$.

The next theorem formalizes our intution that if $p$ is the probability that an event $E$ occurs, then $1 - p$ is the probability that $E$ does not occur.    (That is, if we hit a target $p = 1/3$ of the times, then we miss the target $1 - p = 2/3$ of the times.)

**Theorem 6.2:**    Let $A$ be any event.    Then $P(A^c) = 1 - P(A)$.

The following theorem follows directly from Theorem 6.1.

**Theorem 6.3:**    Let $\emptyset$ be the empty set, and suppose $A$ and $B$ are any events.    Then:

      (*i*)   $P(\emptyset) = 0$.

      (*ii*)   $P(A\backslash B) = P(A) - P(A \cap B)$.

      (*iii*)   If $A \subseteq B$, then $P(A) \leq P(B)$.

Observe that property $[P_3]$ in Theorem 6.1 gives the probability of the union of events in the case that the events are disjoint.    The general formula (proved in Problem 6.16) is called the *addition principle*. Specifically:

**Theorem 6.4    (Addition Principle):**    For any events $A$ and $B$:

$$P(A \cup B) = P(A) + P(B) - P(A \cap B)$$

**EXAMPLE 6.4.**    Suppose a student is selected at random from 100 students, where 30 are taking mathematics, 20 are taking chemistry, and 10 are taking mathematics and chemistry.    Find the probability $p$ that the student is taking mathematics or chemistry.

Let $M = \{$students taking mathematics$\}$ and $C = \{$students taking chemistry$\}$.    Since the space is equiprobable:

$$P(M) = \frac{30}{100} = \frac{3}{10}, P(C) = \frac{20}{100} = \frac{1}{5}, P(M \text{ and } C) = P(M \cap C) = \frac{10}{100} = \frac{1}{10}$$

Thus, by the addition principle (Theorem 6.4):

$$P = P(M \text{ or } C) = P(M \cup C) = P(M) + P(C) - P(M \cap C) = \frac{3}{10} + \frac{1}{5} - \frac{1}{10} = \frac{2}{5}$$

## 6.4   CONDITIONAL PROBABILITY

Suppose $E$ is an event in a sample space $S$ with $P(E) > 0$.    The probability that an event $A$ occurs once $E$ has occured or, specifically, the *conditional probability of A given E*, written $P(A|E)$, is defined as follows:

$$P(A|E) = \frac{P(A \cap E)}{P(E)}$$

As pictured in the Venn diagram in Fig. 6-1, $P(A|E)$ measures, in a certain sense, the relative probability of $A$ with respect to the reduced space $E$.

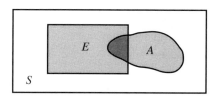

**Fig. 6-1**

Now suppose $S$ is an equiprobable space, and we let $n(A)$ denote the number of elements in the event $A$. Then:

$$P(A \cap E) = \frac{n(A \cap E)}{n(S)}, \quad P(E) = \frac{n(E)}{n(S)}, \text{ and so } P(A|E) = \frac{P(A \cap E)}{P(E)} = \frac{n(A \cap E)}{n(E)}$$

We state this result formally:

**Theorem 6.5:**   Suppose $S$ is an equiprobable space and $A$ and $B$ are events.   Then:

$$P(A|E) = \frac{\text{number of elements in } A \cap E}{\text{number of elements in } E} = \frac{n(A \cap E)}{n(E)}$$

**EXAMPLE 6.5**   A pair of fair dice is tossed.   The sample space S consists of the 36 ordered pairs $(a, b)$, where $a$ and $b$ can be any of the integers from 1 to 6.   (See Problem 6.3.)   Thus, the probability of any point is 1/36.   Find the probability that one of the die is 2 if the sum is 6.   That is, find $P(A|E)$ where

$$E = \{\text{sum is } 6\} \quad \text{and} \quad A = \{2 \text{ appears on at least one die}\}$$

Also find $P(A)$.

Now $E$ consists of five elements, specifically:

$$E = \{(1, 5), (2, 4), (3, 3), (4, 2), (5, 1)\}$$

Two of them, $(2, 4)$ and $(4, 2)$, belong to $A$.   That is:

$$A \cap E = \{ (2, 4), (4, 2) \}$$

By Theorem 6.5, $P(A|E) = 2/5$.

On the other hand, $A$ consists of 11 elements, specifically:

$$A = \{ (2, 1), (2, 2), (2, 3), (2, 4), (2, 5), (2, 6), (1, 2), (3, 2), (4, 2), (5, 2), (6, 2) \}$$

also $S$ consists of 36 elements. Hence, $P(A) = 11/36$.

**Multiplication Theorem for Conditional Probability**

Suppose $A$ and $B$ are events in a sample space $S$ with $P(A) > 0$.   By definition of conditional probability:

$$P(B|A) = \frac{P(A \cap B)}{P(A)}$$

Multiplying both sides by $P(A)$ gives us the following useful result:

**Theorem 6.6   (Multiplication Theorem for Conditional Probability):**

$$P(A \cap B) = P(A) \, P(B|A)$$

The multiplication theorem gives us a formula for the probability that events $A$ and $B$ both occur.   It can easily be extended to three or more events $A_1, A_2, \ldots A_m$.   That is:

$$P(A_1 \cap A_2 \cap \ldots \cap A_m) = P(A_1) \cdot P(A_2|A_1) \cdot \ldots \cdot P(A_m|A_1 \cap A_2 \cap \ldots \cap A_{m-1})$$

**EXAMPLE 6.6**   Suppose a lot contains 12 items of which 4 are defective, so 8 are nondefective.   Three items are drawn at random one after the other.   Find the probability $p$ that all three are nondefective.

The probability that the first item is nondefective is 8/12, since 8 of the 12 items are nondefective.   If the first item is nondefective, then the probability that the second item is nondefective is 7/11, since only 7 of the remaining 11 items are nondefective.   If the first two items are nondefective, then the probability that the third item is nondefective is 6/10, since only 6 of the remaining 10 items are nondefective.   Therefore, by the Multiplication Theorem 6.6,

$$p = \frac{8}{12} \cdot \frac{7}{11} \cdot \frac{6}{10} = \frac{14}{55} \approx 0.25$$

**Stochastic Processes**

A *stochastic process* is a sequence of experiments where each experiment has a finite number of outcomes with given probabilities. A convenient way of describing such a process is by a tree diagram where the Multiplication Theorem 6.2 is used to compute the probability that a given path occurs. We illustrate this in the next example.

**EXAMPLE 6.7**   We are given three boxes as follows:

   Box X has 10 lightbulbs of which 4 are defective.

   Box Y has 6 lightbulbs of which 1 is defective.

   Box Z has 8 lightbulbs of which 3 are defective.

We select a box at random, and then draw a bulb at random. Find the probability $p$ that the bulb is defective.
   Here we perform a sequence of two experiments:

   (*i*)   Select one of three boxes at random.

   (*ii*)   Select a bulb which is either defective ($D$) or nondefective ($N$).

The tree diagram in Fig. 6-2(*a*) describes this process, and it also shows the probability of each edge of the tree. By the multiplication theorem, the probability that any path of the tree occurs is the product of the probabilities of each edge in

the path. For example, the probability of selecting box $X$ and then a defective bulb $D$ is $\dfrac{1}{3} \cdot \dfrac{2}{5} = \dfrac{2}{15}$.

   There are three mutually exclusive paths which lead to a defective bulb $D$. Thus, $p$ is the sum of the probabilities of these paths. Accordingly:

$$p = \frac{1}{3} \cdot \frac{2}{5} + \frac{1}{3} \cdot \frac{1}{6} + \frac{1}{3} \cdot \frac{3}{8} = \frac{113}{360} \approx 0.314$$

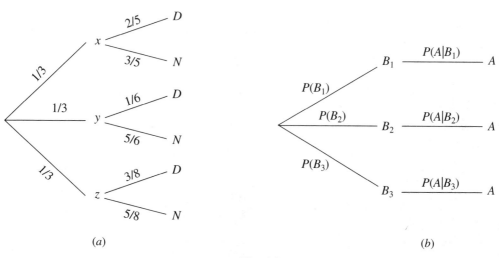

(*a*)                                                                                    (*b*)

**Fig. 6-2**

**Total Probability and Bayes' Formula**

Throughout this subsection, we assume $A$ is an event in a sample space $S$, and that $\{B_1, B_2, ..., B_n\}$ is a partition of $S$. That is, $S$ is the union of the $B$'s and the $B$'s are mutually disjoint. Then:

$$A = A \cap S = A \cap (B_1 \cup B_2 \cup ... \cup B_n) = (A \cap B_1) \cup (A \cap B_2) \cup ... \cup (A \cap B_n)$$

where the $n$ subsets on the right are also mutually disjoint. Therefore:

$$P(A) = P(A \cap B_1) + P(A \cap B_2) + ... + P(A \cap B_n)$$

Accordingly, using the multiplication theorem, we get the following theorem called the *law of total probability*.

**Theorem 6.7:** $P(A) = P(A|B_1) P(B_1) + P(A|B_2) P(B_2) + \dots + P(A|B_n) P(B_n)$

Observe that, for any set $B$, we have

$$P(B|A) = \frac{P(B \cap A)}{P(A)} = \frac{P(A|B) P(B)}{P(A)}$$

Accordingly, Theorem 6.7 gives us the following theorem called *Bayes' formula*.

**Theorem 6.8   (Bayes' Formula):**

$$P(B_i|A) = \frac{P(A|B_i) P(B_i)}{P(A|B_1)P(B_1) + P(A|B_2) P(B_2) + \dots + P(A|B_n) P(B_n)}$$

Frequently, problems involving the law of total probability and Bayes' formula may be viewed as a two-step process.   The first step involves the partition $\{B_1, \dots, B_n\}$, and the second step involves the event $A$.   The stochastic tree for three sets $B_1$, $B_2$, $B_3$ and the event $A$ appears in Fig. 6.2($b$).   Using the tree diagram, we obtain

$$P(A) = P(B_1) P(A|B_1) + P(B_2) P(A|B_2) + P(B_3) P(A|B_3)$$

Suppose, also, we want to find the probability of, say, $B_3$, given $A$,—that is, $P(B_3|A)$.   Using the tree diagram, we get

$$P(B_3|A) = \frac{P(B_3) P(A|B_3)}{P(B_1) P(A|B_1) + P(B_2) P(A|B_2) + P(B_3) P(A|B_3)}$$

$$= \frac{\text{Path to } B_3 \text{ and then to } A}{\text{Sum of paths to } A}$$

Observe that these two equations are simply the total probability law and Bayes' formula for $n = 3$.

**EXAMPLE 6.8**   Consider the data in Example 6.7.   Assuming a defective bulb $D$ is selected, find the probability that it came from box $X$, that is, find $P(X|D)$.

By Example 6.7, $P(X \cap D) = 2/15$ and $P(D) = 113/360$.   Thus:

$$P(X|D) = \frac{P(X \cap D)}{P(D)} = \frac{2/15}{113/360} \approx 0.425$$

Alternately, viewing $\{X, Y, Z\}$ as a partition, Bayes' formula gives us:

$$P(X|D) = \frac{\text{Path to } X \text{ and then to } D}{\text{Sum of paths to } D} = \frac{\frac{1}{3} \cdot \frac{2}{5}}{\frac{1}{3} \cdot \frac{2}{5} + \frac{1}{3} \cdot \frac{1}{6} + \frac{1}{3} \cdot \frac{3}{8}} = \frac{\frac{2}{15}}{\frac{113}{360}} = \frac{48}{113} \approx 0.425$$

## 6.5   INDEPENDENT EVENTS

Events $A$ and $B$ in a probability space $S$ are said to be *independent* if the occurrence of one of them does not influence the occurrence of the other.   More specifically, $B$ is independent of $A$ if $P(B)$ is the same as $P(B|A)$. Now substituting $P(B)$ for $P(B|A)$ in the Multiplication Theorem 6.6 that $P(A \cap B) = P(A) P(B|A)$ yields

$$P(A \cap B) = P(A) P(B)$$

We formally use the above equation as our definition of independence.

**Definition:** Events $A$ and $B$ are *independent* if $P(A \cap B) = P(A)\,P(B)$; otherwise, they are *dependent*.

We emphasize that independence is a symmetric relation.   In particular:

$$P(A \cap B) = P(A)\,P(B) \text{ implies both } P(B|A) = P(B) \text{ and } P(A|B) = P(A)$$

Now suppose $A$ and $B$ are mutually exclusive; hence, $P(A \cap B) = 0$.   In such a case, $A$ and $B$ are independent if and only if $P(A) = 0$ or $P(B) = 0$.

**EXAMPLE 6.9**   A fair coin is tossed three times yielding the equiprobable space

$$S = \{HHH, HHT, HTH, HTT, THH, THT, TTH, TTT\}$$

Consider the events:

$$A = \{\text{first toss is heads}\} = \{HHH, HHT, HTH, FTT\}$$
$$B = \{\text{second toss is heads}\} = \{HHH, HHT, THH, THT\}$$
$$C = \{\text{exactly two heads in a row}\} = \{FFT, THH\}$$

Show that $A$ and $B$ are independent, A and C are independent, but $B$ and $C$ are dependent.
    First of all, we have

$$P(A) = \frac{4}{8} = \frac{1}{2},\, P(B) = \frac{4}{8} = \frac{1}{2},\, P(C) = \frac{2}{8} = \frac{1}{4}$$

Also:

$$P(A \cap B) = P(\{HHT, HHT\}) = \frac{1}{4}, \quad P(A \cap C) = P(\{HHT\}) = \frac{1}{8} \quad P(B \cap C) = P(\{HHT, THHT\}) = \frac{1}{4}$$

Accordingly:

$$P(A)\,P(B) = \frac{1}{2} \cdot \frac{1}{2} = \frac{1}{4} = P(A \cap B), \quad \text{and so } A \text{ and } B \text{ are independent.}$$

$$P(A)\,P(C) = \frac{1}{2} \cdot \frac{1}{4} = \frac{1}{8} = P(A \cap C), \quad \text{and so } A \text{ and } C \text{ are independent.}$$

$$P(B)\,P(C) = \frac{1}{2} \cdot \frac{1}{4} = \frac{1}{8} \neq P(B \cap C), \quad \text{and so } B \text{ and } C \text{ are dependent.}$$

Frequently, we will postulate that two events are independent, or the experiment itself will imply that two events are independent.

**EXAMPLE 6.10**   The probability that $A$ hits a target is $\frac{1}{4}$, and the probability that $B$ hits the target is $\frac{2}{5}$.   Both shoot at the target.   Find the probability that at least one of them hits the target, that is, that $A$ or $B$ (or both) hit the target.

We are given that $P(A) = \frac{1}{4}$ and $P(B) = \frac{2}{5}$, and we want $P(A \cup B)$.   We assume that $A$ hitting the target is independent of $B$ hitting the target, that is, that $P(A \cap B) = P(A)\,P(B)$.   Thus, by the Addition Principle Theorem 6.4:

$$P(A \cup B) = P(A) + P(B) - P(A \cap B) = \frac{1}{4} + \frac{2}{5} - \left[ \frac{1}{4} \cdot \frac{2}{5} \right] = \frac{11}{20}$$

## 6.6   INDEPENDENT REPEATED TRIALS; BINOMIAL DISTRIBUTION

Previously we discussed probability spaces which were associated with an experiment repeated a finite number of times, such as tossing a coin three times.   This concept of repetition is formalized as follows:

**Definition:**   Let $S$ be a finite probability space.   The probability space of *n independent repeated trials* is the probability space $S_n$ consisting of $n$-tuples of elements of $S$ with the probability of an $n$-tuple defined to be the product of the probabilities of its components.   That is:

$$P(s_1, s_2, \ldots, s_n) = P(s_1)\,P(s_2) \ldots P(s_n)$$

**EXAMPLE 6.11** Whenever three horses $A$, $B$, and $C$ race together, their respective probabilities of winning are 1/2, 1/3, and 1/6. That is, $S = \{A, B, C\}$ with $P(A) = 1/2$, $P(B) = 1/3$, and $P(C) = 1/6$. Suppose the horses race twice. Find the sample space $S_2$ of the two repeated trials (races), and the probability of each point in $S_2$.

$S_2$ consists of ordered pairs of elements in $S$. Writing $XY$ for an ordered pair $(X, Y)$:

$$S_2 = \{AA, AB, AC, BA, BB, BC, CA, CB, CC\}$$

The probability of each point in $S_2$ follows:

$$P(AA) = P(A)\,P(A) = \frac{1}{2} \cdot \frac{1}{2} = \frac{1}{4}, \qquad P(BA) = \frac{1}{6}, \qquad P(CA) = \frac{1}{12}$$

$$P(AB) = P(A)\,P(B) = \frac{1}{2} \cdot \frac{1}{3} = \frac{1}{6}, \qquad P(BB) = \frac{1}{9}, \qquad P(CB) = \frac{1}{18}$$

$$P(AC) = P(A)\,P(C) = \frac{1}{2} \cdot \frac{1}{6} = \frac{1}{12}, \qquad P(BC) = \frac{1}{18}, \qquad P(CC) = \frac{1}{36}$$

Thus, the probability that $C$ wins the first race and $A$ wins the second race is $P(CA) = 1/12$.

### Repeated Trials with Two Outcomes; Bernoulli Trials

Now consider an experiment with only two outcomes. Independent repeated trials of such an experiment are called *Bernoulli trials*, named after the Swiss mathematician Jacob Bernoulli (1654–1705). The term *independent trials* means that the outcome of any trial does not depend on the previous outcomes (such as tossing a coin). We will call one of the outcomes *success* and the other outcome *failure*.

Let $p$ denote the probability of success in a Bernoulli trial, and so $q = 1 - p$ is the probability of failure. A *binomial experiment* consists of a fixed number of Bernoulli trials. The notation

$$B(n, p)$$

will be used to denote a binomial experiment with $n$ trials and probability $p$ of success.

Frequently, we are interested in the number of successes in a binomial experiment and not in the order in which they occur. The next theorem (proved in Problem 6.36) applies. We note that

$$\binom{n}{k} = \frac{n\,(n-1)\,\ldots\,(n-k+1)}{k\,(k-1)\,\ldots\,3 \cdot 2 \cdot 1} = \frac{n!}{k!\,(n-k)!}$$

is the binomial coefficient which is discussed in detail in Chapter 5.

**Theorem 6.9:** The probability of exactly $k$ success in a binomial experiment $B(n, p)$ is given by

$$P(k) = P\,(k \text{ successes}) = \binom{n}{k} p^k q^{n-k}$$

The probability of one or more successes is $1 - q^n$.

**EXAMPLE 6.12** A fair coin is tossed 6 times. For this example, we'll call heads a success. This is a binomial experiment with $n = 6$ and $p = q = 1/2$.

(a) The probability that exactly $k = 2$ heads occurs follows:

$$P(2) = \binom{6}{2}\left(\frac{1}{2}\right)^2 \left(\frac{1}{2}\right)^4 = \frac{15}{64}$$

(b) The probability of getting at least four heads, that is, $k = 4$, 5, or 6, follows:

$$P(4) + P(5) + P(6) = \binom{6}{4}\left(\frac{1}{2}\right)^4\left(\frac{1}{2}\right)^2 + \binom{6}{5}\left(\frac{1}{2}\right)^5\left(\frac{1}{2}\right)^2 + \binom{6}{6}\left(\frac{1}{2}\right)^6$$

$$= \frac{15}{64} + \frac{6}{64} + \frac{1}{64} = \frac{11}{32} \approx 0.34$$

(c) The probability of getting no heads (i.e., all failures) is $q^6 = (1/2)^6 = 1/64$, so the probability of one or more heads is
$$1 - q^n = 1 - 1/64 = 63/64 \approx 0.94$$

## 6.7  RANDOM VARIABLES

Let $S$ be a sample space of an experiment.   As noted previously, the outcome of the experiment, or the points in $S$, need not be numbers.   However, we frequently wish to assign a specific number to each outcome of the experiment.   For example, in the tossing of a pair of die, we may want to assign the sum of the two integers to the outcome.   Such an assignment of numerical values is called a *random variable*.   More generally, we have the following definition.

**Definition:**   A random variable $X$ is a rule that assigns a numerical value to each outcome in a sample space $S$.

The *range space* of a random variable $X$, denoted by $R_X$, is the set of numbers assigned by $X$.

**Remark:**   In more formal terminology, $X$ is a function from $S$ to the real numbers **R**, and $\mathbf{R}_X$ is the range of $X$. Also, for some infinite sample spaces $S$, not every function from $S$ to **R** is a random variable.   However, the sample spaces $S$ here are all finite and so every function from $S$ to **R** is a random variable.

### EXAMPLE 6.13

(a)   A pair of fair dice is tossed.   (See Problem 6.3.)   The sample space $S$ consists of the 36 ordered pairs $(a, b)$, where $a$ and $b$ can be any integers between 1 and 6.   That is:

$$S = \{(1, 1), (1, 2), ..., (1, 6), (2, 1), ..., (6, 6)\}$$

Let $X$ assign to each point in $S$ the sum of the numbers and let $Y$ assign to each point in $S$ the maximum of the two numbers.   For example:

$$X(2, 5) = 7, \qquad X(6, 3) = 9, \qquad Y(2, 5) = 5, \qquad Y(6, 3) = 6$$

Then $X$ and $Y$ are random variables on $S$ with respective range spaces

$$R_X = \{2, 3, 4, 5, 6, 7, 8, 9, 10, 11, 12\} \quad \text{and} \quad R_Y = \{1, 2, 3, 4, 5, 6\}$$

(b)   A box contains 12 items of which 3 are defective.   A sample of 3 items is selected from the box.   The sample space $S$ consists of the $\binom{12}{3} = 220$ different samples of size 3.

Let $X$ denote the number of defective items in the sample; then $X$ is a random variable with range space $R_X = \{0, 1, 2, 3\}$

### Probability Distribution of a Random Variable

Let $X$ be a random variable on a finite sample space $S$ with range space $R_X = \{x_1, x_2, ..., x_t\}$.   The $X$ induces an assignment of probabilities on $R_X$ as follows:

$$p_i = P(x_i) = P(X = x_i) = \text{sum of probabilities of points in } S \text{ whose image is } x_i.$$

The set of ordered pairs $(x_1, p_1), (x_2, p_2), ..., (x_t, p_t)$ is usually given by a table as follows: Such a table is called the *distribution* of the random variable $X$.

| $x_i$ | $x_1$ | $x_2$ | $x_3$ | ... | $x_t$ |     (6.1)|
|-------|-------|-------|-------|-----|-------|
| $p_i$ | $p_1$ | $p_2$ | $p_3$ | ... | $p_t$ |

In the case that $S$ is an equiprobable space, we can easily obtain such a distribution as follows:

**Theorem 6.10:**   Let $S$ be an equiprobable space, and let $X$ be a random variable on $S$ with range space

$$R_X = \{x_1, x_2, ..., x_t\}$$

Then

$$p_i = P(x_i) = \frac{\text{number of points in } S \text{ whose image is } x_i}{\text{number of points in } S}$$

## EXAMPLE 6.14

(a)   Let $X$ be the random variable in Example 6.13(a) which assigns the sum to the toss of a pair of die.   Find the distribution of $X$.

Using Theorem 6.10, we obtain the following:

$P(2) = 1/36$, since there is only one outcome $(1, 1)$ whose sum is 2.

$P(3) = 2/36$, since there are two outcomes, $(1, 2)$ and $(2, 1)$, whose sum is 3.

$P(4) = 3/36$, since there are three outcomes, $(1, 3)$, $(2, 2)$, and $(3, 1)$, whose sum is four.

Similarly, $P(5) = 4/36$, $P(6) = 5/36$, ..., $P(12) = 1/36$.   Thus, the distribution of $X$ follows:

| $x_i$ | 2 | 3 | 4 | 5 | 6 | 7 | 8 | 9 | 10 | 11 | 12 |
|-------|---|---|---|---|---|---|---|---|----|----|----|
| $p_i$ | $\dfrac{1}{36}$ | $\dfrac{2}{36}$ | $\dfrac{3}{36}$ | $\dfrac{4}{36}$ | $\dfrac{5}{36}$ | $\dfrac{6}{36}$ | $\dfrac{5}{36}$ | $\dfrac{4}{36}$ | $\dfrac{3}{36}$ | $\dfrac{2}{36}$ | $\dfrac{1}{36}$ |

(b)   Let $X$ be the random variable in Example 6.13(b).   Find the distribution of $X$.

Again use Theorem 6.10.   We obtain the following:

$P(0) = \dfrac{84}{220}$, since there are $\dbinom{9}{3} = 80$ samples of size 3 with no defective items.

$P(1) = \dfrac{108}{220}$, since there are $3 \dbinom{9}{2} = 108$ samples of size 3 with one defective item.

$P(2) = \dfrac{27}{220}$, since there are $9 \dbinom{3}{2} = 27$ samples of size 3 with two defective items.

$P(3) = \dfrac{1}{220}$, since there are is only one sample of size 3 with three defective items.

The distribution of $X$ follows:

| $x_i$ | 0 | 1 | 2 | 3 |
|-------|---|---|---|---|
| $p_i$ | $\dfrac{84}{220}$ | $\dfrac{108}{220}$ | $\dfrac{27}{220}$ | $\dfrac{1}{220}$ |

**Remark:**   Let $X$ is a random variable on a probability space $S = \{a_1, a_2, ..., a_m\}$, and let $f(x)$ be any polynomial.   Then $f(X)$ is the random variable on $S$ defined by

$$f(X)(a_i) = f(X(a_i))$$

That is, $F(X)$ assigns $f(X(a_i))$ to the point $a_i$ in $S$.   Thus, if (11.1) is the distribution of $X$, then $f(X)$ takes on the values $f(x_1), f(x_2), ..., f(x_n)$ with the same corresponding probabilities.   Accordingly, the distribution of $F(X)$ consists of the pairs $(y_k, q_k)$ where the probability $q_k$ of $y_k$ is the sum of the $p_i$'s for which $y_k = f(x_i)$.

### Expectation of a Random Variable

Let $X$ be a random variable on a probability space $S = \{a_1, a_2, ..., a_m\}$.   The *mean* or *expectation* of $X$, denoted by $\mu$, $\mu_X$, or $E(X)$, is defined as follows:

$$\mu = E(X) = X(a_1) P(a_1) + X(a_2) P(a_2) + ... + X(a_m)P(a_m) = \Sigma X(a_i) P(a_i)$$

In particular, if $X$ is given by the distribution (6.1), then the *expectation* of $X$ is as follows:

$$\mu = E(X) = x_1 p_1 + x_2 p_2 + \ldots + x_n p_n = \Sigma x_i p_i$$

(For notational convenience, we have omitted the limits in the summation symbol $\Sigma$.)

## EXAMPLE 6.15

(a)  Suppose a fair coin is tossed six times.   The number of heads which can occur with their respective probabilities are as follows:
Then the mean or expectation or expected number of heads follows:

| $x_i$ | 0 | 1 | 2 | 3 | 4 | 5 | 6 |
|-------|---|---|---|---|---|---|---|
| $p_i$ | $\dfrac{1}{64}$ | $\dfrac{6}{64}$ | $\dfrac{15}{64}$ | $\dfrac{20}{64}$ | $\dfrac{15}{64}$ | $\dfrac{6}{64}$ | $\dfrac{1}{64}$ |

$$\mu = E(X) = 0\left(\frac{1}{64}\right) + 1\left(\frac{6}{64}\right) + 2\left(\frac{15}{64}\right) + 3\left(\frac{20}{64}\right) + 4\left(\frac{15}{64}\right) + 5\left(\frac{6}{64}\right) + 6\left(\frac{1}{64}\right) = 3$$

This agrees with our intuition.   When we toss 6 coins, we expect that 3 should be heads.

(b)  Consider the random variable $X$ in Example 6.13(b) whose distribution appears in Example 6.14(b).   Then the expectation of $X$ or, in other words, the expected number of defective items in a sample of size 3 follows:

$$\mu = E(X) = 0\left(\frac{84}{220}\right) + 1\left(\frac{108}{220}\right) + 2\left(\frac{27}{220}\right) + 3\left(\frac{1}{220}\right) = 0.75$$

(c)  Three horses $A$, $B$, $C$ are in a race, and suppose their respective probabilities of winning are $\dfrac{1}{2}, \dfrac{1}{3}, \dfrac{1}{6}$.   Let $X$ denote the payoff function for the winning horse, and suppose $X$ pays \$2, \$6, or \$9 according as $A$, $B$, or $C$ wins the race.   The expected payoff for the race follows:

$$E(X) = X(A)\ P(A) + X(B)\ P(B) + X(C)\ P(C) = 2\left(\frac{1}{2}\right) + 6\left(\frac{1}{3}\right) + 9\left(\frac{1}{6}\right) = 4.5$$

## Variance and Standard Deviation of a Random Variable

Let $X$ be a random variable with mean $\mu$ and probability distribution $\{(x_i, y_i)\}$ appearing in (6.1).   The *variance* Var($X$) and *standard deviation* $\sigma$ of $X$ are defined by:

$$\text{Var}(X) = (x_1 - \mu)^2 p_1 + (x_2 - \mu)^2 p_2 + \ldots + (x_n - \mu)^2 p_n = \Sigma (x_i - \mu)^2 p_i = E((X - \mu)^2)$$

$$\sigma = \sqrt{\text{Var}(X)}$$

The following formula is usually more convenient for computing Var($X$) than the above:

$$\text{Var}(X) = x_1^2 p_1 + x_2^2 p_2 + \ldots + x_n^2 p_n - \mu^2 = \Sigma x_i^2 p_i - \mu^2 = E(X^2) - \mu^2$$

**Remark:**   According to the above formula, Var($X$) = $\sigma^2$.

Both $\sigma^2$ and $\sigma$ measure the weighted spread of the values $x_i$ about the mean $\mu$; however, $\sigma$ has the same units as $\mu$.

**EXAMPLE 6.16**

(a) Let $X$ denote the number of times heads occurs when a fair coin is tossed six times. The distribution of $X$ appears in Example 6.15(a), where its mean $\mu = 3$ is computed. The variance of $X$ is computed as follows:

$$\text{Var}(X) = (0 - 3)^2 \frac{1}{64} + (1 - 3)^2 \frac{6}{64} + (2 - 3)^2 \frac{15}{64} + \cdots + (6 - 3)\frac{1}{64} = 1.5$$

Alternately:

$$\text{Var}(X) = 0^2 \frac{1}{64} + 1^2 \frac{6}{64} + 2^2 \frac{15}{64} + 3^2 \frac{20}{64} + 4^2 \frac{15}{64} + 5^2 \frac{6}{64} + 6^2 \frac{1}{64} = 1.5$$

Thus, the standard deviation is $\sigma = \sqrt{1.5} \approx 1.225$ (heads).

(b) Consider the random variable $X$ in Example 6.13(b) whose distibution appears in 6.14(b) and whose mean $\mu = 0.75$ is computed in Example 6.15(b). The variance of $X$ is computed as follows:

$$\text{Var}(X) = 0^2 \frac{84}{220} + 1^2 \frac{108}{220} + 2^2 \frac{27}{220} + 3^2 \frac{1}{220} - (.75)^2 = 0.46$$

Thus, the standard deviation of $X$ follows:

$$\sigma = \sqrt{\text{Var}(X)} = \sqrt{.46} = 0.66$$

## Binomial Distribution

Consider a binomial experiment $B(n, p)$. That is, $B(n, p)$ consists of $n$ independent repeated trials with two outcomes, success or failure, and $p$ is the probability of success. The number $X$ of $k$ successes is a random variable with the following distribution:

| $k$ | 0 | 1 | 2 | $\cdots$ | $n$ |
|-----|-----|-----|-----|-----|-----|
| $P(k)$ | $q^n$ | $\binom{n}{1} q^{n-2} p^2$ | $\binom{n}{2} q^{n-2} p^2$ | $\cdots$ | $p^n$ |

The following theorem applies.

**Theorem 6.11:** Consider the binomial distribution $B(n, p)$. Then:

(i)   Expected value $E(X) = \mu = np$.

(ii)  Variance $\text{Var}(X) = \sigma^2 = npq$.

(iii) Standard distribution $\sigma = \sqrt{npq}$.

**EXAMPLE 6.17**

(a) The probability that a man hits a target is $p = 1/5$. He fires 100 times. Find the expected number $\mu$ of times he will hit the target and the standard deviation $\sigma$.

Here $p = 1/5$ and so $q = 4/5$. Hence,

$$\mu = np = 100 \cdot \frac{1}{5} = 20 \quad \text{and} \quad \sigma = \sqrt{npq} = \sqrt{100 \cdot \frac{1}{5} \cdot \frac{4}{5}} = 4$$

(b) Find the expected number $E(X)$ of correct answers obtained by guessing in a true-false test with 25 questions, and find the standard deviation $\sigma$.

Here $p = 1/2$ and so $q = 1/2$. Hence,

$$E(X) = np = 25 \cdot \frac{1}{2} = 12.5 \quad \text{and} \quad \sigma = \sqrt{npq} = \sqrt{25 \cdot \frac{1}{2} \cdot \frac{1}{2}} = 2.5$$

## 6.8   JOINT DISTRIBUTIONS AND INDEPENDENT RANDOM VARIABLES

Independent events were defined in Section 6.5.   Here we define independent random variables.

### Joint Distribution

Suppose $X$ and $Y$ are random variables on a probability space $S$.   If $x$ is a value of $X$ and $y$ of $Y$, let the event $A$ consist of all outcomes in $S$ to which $X$ assigns the value $x$ and $Y$ the value $y$.   Then, by definition,

$$P(x, y) = P(X = x, Y = y) = P(A)$$

The values of $P(x, y)$ for each pair $(x, y)$, usually displayed in a table, form the *joint distribution* of $X$ and $Y$.

**Definition:**   Two random variables $X$ and $Y$ on the same sample space are said to be *independent* if for all $x$ and $y$,

$$P(x, y) = P(X = x)P(Y = y)$$

**EXAMPLE 6.18**   Toss a fair coin twice.   $X = 1$ if the first toss is a head, $X = 0$ otherwise; $Y = 1$ if both tosses are heads, $Y = 0$ otherwise.   (a) Find the joint distribution of $X$ and $Y$.   (b) Determine whether $X$ and $Y$ are independent.

(a)   The possible outcomes are HH, HT, TH, TT, which are equiprobable and correspond to $(x, y) = (1, 1), (1, 0), (0, 0),$ $(0, 0)$, respectively.   Hence, the joint distribution of $X$ and $Y$ is given in Fig. 6-3(a), where the entry in the $i$th row and $j$th column is $P(x_i, y_j)$.

(b)   $P(0, 0) = \frac{1}{2}$ but $P(X = 0) = \frac{1}{2}$ and $P(Y = 0) = \frac{3}{4}$.   Since $\frac{1}{2} \neq \frac{1}{2} \cdot \frac{3}{4}$, $X$ and $Y$ are not independent.

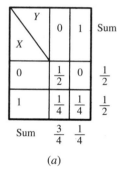

(a)                                          (b)

**Fig. 6-3**

**EXAMPLE 6.19**   Toss a fair coin twice.   $X = 1$ if the first toss is a head, 0 otherwise; $Y = 1$ if the second toss is a head, $Y = 0$ otherwise.   (a) Find the joint distribution of $X$ and $Y$.   (b) Determine whether $X$ and $Y$ are independent.

(a)   Here the equiprobable outcomes HH, HT, TH, TT correspond to $(x, y) = (1, 1), (1, 0), (0, 1), (0, 0)$, respectively, and the joint distribution of $X$ and $Y$ is in Fig. 6-3(b).   $P(x_i, y_j)$ is the entry in the $i$th row and $j$th column.

(b)   Since $P(X = x) = \frac{1}{2}$ for $x = 0$ or 1 and $P(Y = y) = \frac{1}{2}$ for $y = 0$ or 1, it follows that $P(x, y) = P(X = x)P(Y = y)$ for all possible $x$ and $y$.   Hence, $X$ and $Y$ are independent.

## 6.9   NORMAL DISTRIBUTION

### Introduction: Random Variables on Infinite Sample Spaces

Up to now, all sample spaces have been finite and therefore all random variables have assumed only a finite number of values.   There are occasions in which infinite sample spaces arise whose associated random variables can assume an entire interval of values. For example, the range of $X$ may be a time interval $[t_0, t_1]$ or even $(-\infty, \infty)$. When a probability space $S$ is infinite, and a random variable $X$ associates with each outcome $s$ in $S$ a real number $X(s)$, we assume that $P(a \le X \le b)$ is defined for any interval $[a, b]$; that is, all outcomes $s$ in $S$, for which $a \le X(s) \le b$, form an event $A$ in $S$, and $P(A)$ is defined.

### Continuous Random Variables

By definition, a random variable $X$ on an infinite sample space $S$ is *continuous* if there is a nonnegative function $f(x)$ with domain $(-\infty, \infty)$ for which $P(a \le X \le b)$ is equal to the area under the graph of $y = f(x)$ between $a$ and $b$ (see Fig. 6-4). The function $f(x)$ is called the *probability density function* for $X$.

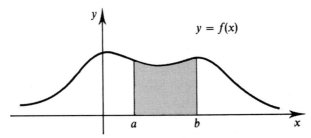

$$P(a \le X \le b) = \text{area of shaded region}$$

**Fig. 6-4**

In calculus, the area under the graph of $f(x)$ between $a$ and $b$ is denoted by $\int_a^b f(x)$. Hence, using the notation of calculus,

$$P(a \le X \le b) = \int_a^b f(x)\, dx$$

The probability is 1 that $X$ assumes a value between $-\infty$ and $\infty$. Therefore,

$$\int_{-\infty}^{\infty} f(x)\, dx = 1$$

The net area* determined by the graph of $y = xf(x)$, assuming it exists, is the *expected value* of $X$, denoted by $E(X)$ or $\mu$; the area under the graph of $y = (x - \mu)^2 f(x)$, assuming it exists, is the *variance* of $X$, denoted by $\text{Var}(X)$. That is, by definition,

$$E(X) = \int_{-\infty}^{\infty} xf(x)dx \quad \text{and} \quad \text{Var}(X) = \int_{-\infty}^{\infty} (x - \mu)^2 f(x)\, dx$$

As in the case of a finite random variable, the *standard deviation* $\sigma$ of $X$ is the nonnegative square root of $\text{Var}(X)$.

### Normal Random Variable

The most important continuous random variable is the *normal* random variable, whose density function has a bell-shaped graph. More precisely, there is a normal random variable $X$ for each pair of parameters $\sigma > 0$ and $\mu$ where the corresponding density function is

$$f(x) = \frac{1}{\sqrt{2\pi}\sigma}\, e^{-(1/2)[(x - \mu)/\sigma]^2}$$

---

* If the graph of a function $y = g(x)$ lies partly above and partly below the $x$ axis, the net area determined by the graph is the area above the $x$ axis minus the area below the $x$ axis.

Figure 6-5($a$) shows how the bell-shaped normal curves change as $\mu$ varies and $\sigma$ remains fixed. Figure 6-5($b$) shows how the curves change as $\sigma$ varies and $\mu$ remains fixed. Note that each curve reaches its highest point at $x = \mu$ and is symmetric about $\mu$. The inflection points, where the direction of the bend of the curve changes, occur for $x = \mu + \sigma$ and $x = \mu - \sigma$. It can be shown that $\mu$ is the *mean*, or *expected value*, of $X$, and $\sigma$ is the *standard deviation* of $X$.

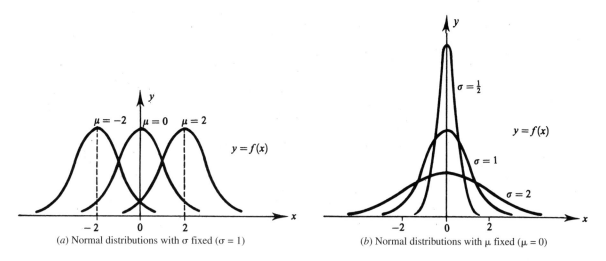

(a) Normal distributions with $\sigma$ fixed ($\sigma = 1$)         (b) Normal distributions with $\mu$ fixed ($\mu = 0$)

**Fig. 6-5**

The probability distribution of a normal random variable $X$ with mean $\mu$ and standard deviation $\sigma$ is denoted by $N(\mu, \sigma^2)$. We say $X$ is normally distributed, or, more precisely, $X$ is $N(\mu, \sigma^2)$.

### Standard Normal Distribution

If $X$ is $N(\mu, \sigma^2)$, then the standardized random variable $Z = (X - \mu)/\sigma$ is $N(0, 1)$. The density function for $Z$ is

$$\phi(z) = \frac{1}{\sqrt{2\pi}}\, e^{-z^2/2}$$

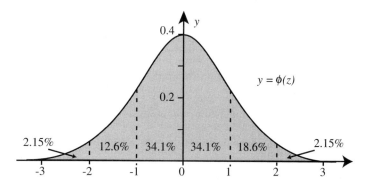

Normal distribution $N(0, 1)$

**Fig. 6-6**

whose graph is shown in Fig. 6-6.   Note that 68.2 percent of the area under the curve occurs for $-1 \leq z \leq 1$, 95.4 percent for $-2 \leq z \leq 2$, and 99.7 percent for $-3 \leq z \leq 3$.   In general, if $X$ is $N(\mu, \sigma^2)$, then 68.2 percent of the area under its density curve occurs for $\mu - \sigma \leq X \leq \mu + \sigma$, 95.4 percent for $\mu - 2\sigma \leq x \leq \mu + 2\sigma$, and 99.7 percent for $\mu - 3\sigma \leq x \leq \mu + 3\sigma$.

### Evaluating Normal Probabilities

To evaluate $P(a \leq X \leq b)$, where $X$ is $N(\mu, \sigma^2)$, we usually change $a$ and $b$ into the standard units

$$z_1 = \frac{a - \mu}{\sigma} \qquad \text{and} \qquad z_2 = \frac{b - \mu}{\sigma}$$

respectively.   Then

$$P(a \leq X \leq b) = P(z_1 \leq Z \leq z_2)$$

which is equal to the area under the standard normal curve between $z_1$ and $z_2$.

The area under portions of the standard normal curve can be determined by means of Appendix B.   Let $\Phi(z)$ denote the area between zero and $z$, for $z \geq 0$.   Then, using the symmetry of the curve, we find, for $z_1 \leq z_2$,

$$P(z_1 \leq Z \leq z_2) = \begin{cases} \Phi(z_2) - \Phi(z_1) & \text{if } z_1 \geq 0, \quad z_2 \geq 0 \\ \Phi(z_2) + \Phi(|z_1|) & \text{if } z_1 < 0, \quad z_2 \geq 0 \\ \Phi(|z_1|) - \Phi(|z_2|) & \text{if } z_1 < 0, \quad z_2 < 0 \end{cases}$$

(see Fig. 6-7).

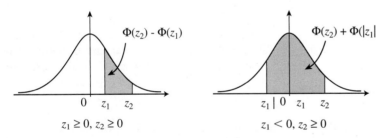
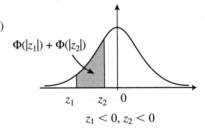

**Fig. 6-7**

**EXAMPLE 6.20**   A random variable $X$ is $N(70, 4)$.   Use Appendix B to find

$$(a)\ P(72 \leq X \leq 75),\ (b)\ P(68 \leq X \leq 74),\ (c)\ P(63 \leq X \leq 68)$$

$X$ has mean $\mu = 70$ and standard deviation $\sigma = \sqrt{4} = 2$.   With reference to Fig. 6-7, we make the following computations:

(a)   $a = 72, b = 75; z_1 = \dfrac{72 - 70}{2} = 1; z_2 = \dfrac{75 - 70}{2} = 2.5$.   Thus,

$$P(72 \leq X \leq 75) = P(1 \leq Z \leq 2.5) = \Phi(2.5) - \Phi(1) = .4938 - .3413 = .1525$$

(b)   $a = 68, b = 74; z_1 = \dfrac{68 - 70}{2} = -1, z_2 = \dfrac{74 - 70}{2} = 2$.   Thus,

$$P(68 \leq X \leq 74) = P(-1 \leq Z \leq 2) = \Phi(2) + \Phi(1) = .4772 + .3413 = .8184$$

(c)   $a = 63, b = 68; z_1 = \dfrac{63 - 70}{2} = -3.5, z_2 = \dfrac{68 - 70}{2} = -1$.   Thus,

$$P(63 \leq X \leq 68) = P(-3.5 \leq Z \leq -1) = \Phi(3.5) - \Phi(1) = .4998 - .3413 = 0.1585$$

**EXAMPLE 6.21**   Prove the following result, which is called the *68-95-99.7 rule*: If $X$ is $N(\mu, \sigma^2)$, then

$$(a)\ P(\mu - \sigma \leq X \leq \mu + \sigma) \approx 0.68,\ (b)\ P(\mu - 2\sigma \leq X \leq \mu + 2\sigma) \approx 0.95,\ (c)\ P(\mu - 3\sigma \leq X \leq \mu + 3\sigma) \approx 0.997$$

In all three cases, we change to standard units and then use Appendix B

(a)   $P(\mu - \sigma \le X \le \mu + \sigma) = P\left(\dfrac{\mu - \sigma - \mu}{\sigma} \le Z \le \dfrac{\mu + \sigma - \mu}{\sigma}\right) = P(-1 \le Z \le 1) = 2\Phi(1) = 2(.3413) \approx 0.68$

(b)   $P(\mu - 2\sigma \le X \le \mu + 2\sigma) = P\left(\dfrac{\mu - 2\sigma - \mu}{\sigma} \le Z \le \dfrac{\mu + 2\sigma - \mu}{\sigma}\right) = P(-2 \le Z \le 2) = 2\Phi(2) = 2(.4772) \approx 0.95$

(c)   $P(\mu - 3\sigma \le X \le \mu + 3\sigma) = P\left(\dfrac{\mu - 3\sigma - \mu}{\sigma} \le Z \le \dfrac{\mu + 3\sigma - \mu}{\sigma}\right) = P(-3 \le Z \le 3) = 2\Phi(3) = 2(.4987) \approx 0.997$

The 68-95-99.7 rule says that in a normally distributed population, 68 percent (approximately) of the population falls within 1 standard deviation of the mean, 95 percent within 2 standard deviations of the mean, and 99.7 percent falls within 3 standard deviations of the mean.

**Remark:**   The normal random variable has, as does any continuous random variable, the peculiar property that $P(X = a) = 0$ for any value $a$.   That is, $P(X = a) = P(a) \le X \le a) = 0$.   For example, suppose the height of American men is (approximately) normally distributed with mean 68 inches and standard deviation 2.5 inches.   Then the probability that an American man is exactly, say, 70 inches tall is zero, even though it is quite possible that some man is, in fact, exactly 70 inches tall.   A complete explanation of this phenomenon involves a precise study of the real number system as a continuum of values, a study that is conducted in advanced mathematics.   For our purposes, rather than ask what is the probability that someone is exactly 70 inches tall, we ask what is the probability that someone is approximately 70 inches tall.   For instance, what is the probability that an American man is between 69.5 inches and 70.5 inches tall? Then, as in Example 6.20 we find that $P(69.5 \le X \le 70.5) = .3413 - .2258 = 0.1155$.   Hence, approximately 11.6 percent of American men are between 69.5 and 70.5 inches tall.

## 6.10   NORMAL APPROXIMATION OF THE BINOMIAL DISTRIBUTION

Corresponding to any binomial distribution $X = B(n, p)$ there is a bar graph where the values $k = 0, 1, 2,$ …, $n$, assumed by $X$, are along the $x$ axis and the probabilities $P(k)$ are along the $y$ axis.   Such a bar graph is called a *probability histogram* (see Section 7.3.) and it can be approximated by the normal distribution $N(\mu, \sigma^2) = N(np, npq)$ when $np > 5$ and $nq > 5$.   For example, Fig. 6-8 shows the histogram of $B(20, 0.7)$ and its approximation $N(14, 4.2)$.   Here $\mu = 14$ and $\sigma^2 = 4.2$ for both distributions.   Accordingly:

> The binomial probability $P(k)$ for $B(n, p)$ can be approximated by the normal probability $P(k - 0.5 \le X \le k + 0.5)$ for $N(np, npq)$, provided $np \ge 5$ and $nq \ge 5$.

A theoretical justification for the approximation of $B(n, p)$ by $N(np, npq)$ is based on the Central Limit Theorem which is discussed in Section 8.2.

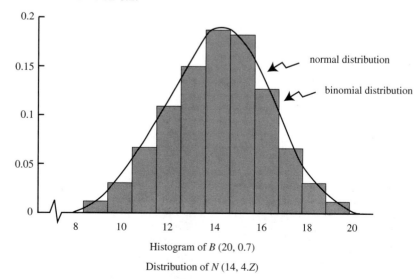

Histogram of $B(20, 0.7)$

Distribution of $N(14, 4.Z)$

**Fig. 6-8**

**EXAMPLE 6.22** Use the normal distribution to approximate the binomial probability $P(60)$, where $N = 100$ and $p = 0.5$.

Here, $\mu = np = 100(.5) = 50$ and $\sigma^2 = npq = 100(.5)(.5) = 25$. If $X$ is $N(50, 25)$, then $BP(60) \approx NP(59.5 \le X \le 60.5)$, where $BP$ stands for binomial probability and $NP$ for normal probability. Proceeding as in Example 6.20, let

$$z_1 = \frac{59.5 - 50}{5} = 1.9 \quad \text{and} \quad z_2 = \frac{60.5 - 50}{5} = 2.1$$

Then

$$BP(60) \approx NP(59.5 \le X \le 60.5) = NP(1.9 \le Z \le 2.1) = .4821 - .4713 = 0.0108$$

We note that the result agrees with the exact value of $BP(60)$ to four decimal places. That is, to four decimal places,

$$BP(60) = \binom{100}{60}(.5)^{60}(.5)^{30} = 0.0108$$

# Solved Problems

## SAMPLE SPACES AND EVENTS

**6.1.** Let $A$ and $B$ be events. Find an expression and exhibit the Venn diagram for the event:
   (*a*) $A$ but not $B$,     (*b*) neither $A$ nor $B$,     (*c*) either $A$ or $B$, but not both

   (*a*)  Since $A$ but not $B$ occurs, shade the area of $A$ outside of $B$, as in Fig. 6-9(*a*). This is the set difference $A\backslash B$ or, equivalently, $A \cap B^c$.

   (*b*)  "Neither $A$ nor $B$" means "not $A$ and not $B$" or $A^c \cap B^c$. By DeMorgan's law, this is also the set $(A \cup B)^c$; hence, shade the area outside of both $A$ and $B$ as in Fig. 6-9(*b*).

   (*c*)  Since $A$ or $B$, but not both, occurs, shade the area of $A$ and of $B$, except where they intersect, as in Fig. 6-9(*c*). The event is equivalent to the occurance of $A$ but not $B$ or $B$ but not $A$. Thus, the event is $(A\backslash B) \cup (B\backslash A)$ or, equivalently, $(A \cap B^c) \cup (B \cap A^c)$.

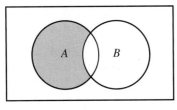     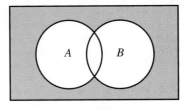     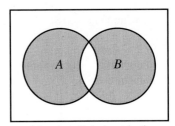

    (*a*)  $A$ but not $B$.          (*b*)  Neither $A$ nor $B$.        (*c*)  $A$ or $B$, but not both.

**Fig. 6-9**

**6.2.** A coin and a die are tossed, yielding the following 12-element sample space $S$:

$$S = \{H1, H2, H3, H4, H5, H6, T1, T2, T3, T4, T5, T6\}$$

   (*a*)  Express explicitly the following events: $A = \{H$ and even number appears$\}$,
   $B = \{$number less than 3 appears$\}$, $C = \{T$ and odd number appears$\}$

(b)   Express explicitly the events: (*i*) *A* or *B*, (*ii*) *B* and *C*, (*iii*) only *B*.

(c)   Which pair of the events *A*, *B*, *C* are mutually exclusive?

(a)   $A = \{H2, H4, H6\}$,   $B = \{H1, H2, T1, T2\}$,   $C = \{T1, T3, T5\}$

(b)   (*i*) $A \cup B = \{H1, H2, H4, H6, T1, T2\}$,   (*ii*) $B \cap C = \{T1\}$,   (*iii*) $B \backslash (A \cup C) = \{H1, T2\}$.

(c)   Only *A* and *C* are mutually exclusive, since $A \cap C = \varnothing$.

**6.3.**   A pair of dice is tossed and the two numbers appearing on the top are recorded.   Describe the sample space *S*, and find the number $n(S)$ of elements in *S*.

There are six possible numbers, 1, 2, ..., 6, on each die.   Hence, $n(S) = 6 \cdot 6 = 36$, and *S* consists of the 36 pairs of numbers from 1 to 6.   Figure 6-10 shows these 36 pairs of numbers in an array where each row has the same first element and each column has the same second element.

$$
\begin{array}{cccccc}
(1, 1), & (1,2), & (1,3), & (1,4), & (1,5), & (1,6) \\[6pt]
(2, 1), & (2,2), & (2,3), & (2,4), & (2,5), & (2,6) \\[6pt]
(3, 1), & (3,2), & (3,3), & (3,4), & (3,5), & (3,6) \\[6pt]
(4, 1), & (4,2), & (4,3), & (4,4), & (4,5), & (4,6) \\[6pt]
(5, 1), & (5,2), & (5,3), & (5,4), & (5,5), & (5,6) \\[6pt]
(6, 1), & (6,2), & (6,3), & (6,4), & (6,5), & (6,6)
\end{array}
$$

**Fig. 6-10**

**6.4.**   Consider the sample space *S* in Problem 6.3.   Find the number of elements in each of the following events:

(a)   $A = \{$two numbers are equal$\}$        (c)   $C = \{$5 appears on first die$\}$

(b)   $B = \{$sum is 11 or more$\}$        (d)   $D = \{$5 appears on at least one die$\}$

Use Fig. 6-10 to help count the number of elements in each event:

(a)   $A = \{(1, 1), (2, 2), ..., (6, 6)\}$, so $n(A) = 6$.

(b)   $B = \{(5, 6), (6, 5), (6, 6)\}$, so $n(B) = 3$.

(c)   $C = \{(5, 1), (5, 2), ..., (5, 6)\}$, so $n(C) = 6$.

(d)   There are six pairs with 5 as the first element, and six pairs with 5 as the second element.   However, (5, 5) appears in both places.   Hence:

$$n(D) = 6 + 6 - 1 = 11$$

Alternately, count the pairs in Fig. 6-10 to get $n(D) = 11$.

**6.5.**   A single card is drawn at random from an ordinary deck *S* of 52 cards.   Describe the sample space *S*, and find the number of elements in each event: $E = \{$red cards$\}$ and $F = \{$face cards$\}$.

The sample space *S* of 52 cards is divided into four 13-element suits, named clubs, diamonds, hearts, spades, and each card is either numbered from 2 to 10 or is a jack (*J*), queen (*Q*), king (*K*), or ace (*A*).

Figure 6-11 shows these four suits.   The red cards are the suits diamonds and hearts; hence $n(E) = 26$.
The face cards are the jacks, queens, and kings.   Hence, $n(F) = 12$.

| Clubs: | A, K, Q, J, 10, 9, 8, 7, 6, 5, 4, 3, 2 |
|---|---|
| Diamonds: | A, K, Q, J, 10, 9, 8, 7, 6, 5, 4, 3, 2 |
| Hearts: | A, K, Q, J, 10, 9, 8, 7, 6, 5, 4, 3, 2 |
| Spades: | A, K, Q, J, 10, 9, 8, 7, 6, 5, 4, 3, 2 |

**Fig. 6-11**

## FINITE EQUIPROBABLE SPACES

**6.6.**  Determine the probability $p$ of each event:

(a)   An even number appears in the toss of a fair die.

(b)   One or more heads appear in the toss of three fair coins.

(c)   A red marble appears in a random drawing of one marble from a box containing

4 white, 3 red, and 5 blue marbles

Each sample space $S$ is an equiprobable space.   Hence, for each event $E$, use

$$P(E) = \frac{\text{number of elements in } E}{\text{number of elements in } S} = \frac{n(E)}{n(S)}$$

(a)   The event can occur in one of three ways, 2, 4, 6, out of 6 cases; hence, $p = 3/6 = 1/2$.

(b)   Assuming the coins are distinguished, there are 8 cases:

*HHH, HHT, HTH, HTT, THH, THT, TTH, TTT*

Only the last case is not favorable; hence, $p = 7/8$.

(c)   There are $4 + 3 + 5 = 12$ marbles of which 3 are red; hence, $p = 3/12 = 1/4$.

**6.7.**  Consider the sample space $S$ in Problem 6.2.   Assume the coin and die are fair; hence, $S$ is an
equiprobable space.   Find: (a) $P(A), P(B), P(C)$,        (b) $P(A \cup B), P(B \cap C), P(B \cap A^c \cap C^c)$

Since $S$ is an equiprobable space, use $P(E) = n(E)/n(S)$.   Here $n(S) = 12$.   So we need only count the
number of elements in the given set.

(a)   $P(A) = 3/12$,   $P(B) = 6/12$,   $P(C) = 3/12$.

(b)   $P(A \cup B) = 8/12$,   $P(B \cap C) = 2/12$,   $P(B \cap A^c \cap C^c) = 3/12$

**6.8.**  A single card is drawn at random from an ordinary deck $S$ of 52 cards.   Find the probability $p$
that the the card is:

(a)   a face card

(b)   a heart

(c)   a face card and a heart

(d)   a face card or a heart

Here $n(S) = 52$, where $S$ is described in Fig. 6-11.

(a)   There are $4(3) = 12$ face cards; hence, $p = 12/52 = 3/13$.

(b)   There are 13 hearts; hence, $p = 13/52 = 1/4$.

(c)   There are three face cards which are hearts; hence, $p = 3/52$.

(d)   Letting $F = \{$face cards$\}$ and $H = \{$hearts$\}$, we have

$$n(F \cup H) = n(F) + n(H) - n(F \cap H) = 12 + 13 - 3 = 22$$

Hence, $p = 22/52 = 11/26$.

**6.9.**   A box contains two white socks and two blue socks.   Two socks are drawn at random.   Find the probability $p$ they are a match (same color).

There are $\binom{4}{2} = 6$ ways to draw two of the socks.   Only two pairs will yield a match.   Thus, $p = 2/6 = 1/3$.

**6.10.**   Five horses are in a race.   Audrey picks two of the horses at random and bets on each of them. Find the probability $p$ that Audrey picked the winner.

There are $\binom{5}{2} = 10$ ways to pick two of the five horses.   Four of the pairs will contain the winner. Thus, $p = 4/10 = 2/5$.

## FINITE PROBABILITY SPACES

**6.11.**   Let $S$ be sample space with four elements, say, $S = \{a_1, a_2, a_3, a_4\}$, and let $P$ be a function on $S$ where

$$P(a_1) = p_1, \qquad P(a_2) = p_2, \qquad P(a_3) = p_3, \qquad P(a_4) = p_4$$

Determine whether each of the following values of $p_1, p_2, p_3, p_4$ define $S$ to be a probability space.

(a)   $p_1 = \dfrac{1}{2}, \quad p_2 = \dfrac{1}{3}, \quad p_3 = \dfrac{1}{4}, \quad p_4 = \dfrac{1}{5}$,

(b)   $p_1 = \dfrac{1}{2}, \quad p_2 = \dfrac{1}{4}, \quad p_3 = -\dfrac{1}{4}, \quad p_4 = \dfrac{1}{2}$,

(c)   $p_1 = \dfrac{1}{2}, \quad p_2 = \dfrac{1}{4}, \quad p_3 = \dfrac{1}{8}, \quad p_4 = \dfrac{1}{8}$,

(d)   $p_1 = \dfrac{1}{2}, \quad p_2 = \dfrac{1}{4}, \quad p_3 = \dfrac{1}{4}, \quad p_4 = 0$.

$S$ is a probability space if the $p_i$'s are nonnegative and add up to one.

(a)   No.   The sum of the $p_i$'s is more than one.

(b)   No.   One of the $p_i$'s is negative.

(c)   Yes.

(d)   Yes.   (We allow 0 to be assigned to an element of $S$.)

**6.12.**   A coin is weighted so that heads is twice as likely to appear as tails.   Find $P(T)$ and $P(H)$.

Let $P(T) = p$; then $P(H) = 2p$.   Now set the sum of the probabilities equal to one.   That is, set $p + 2p = 1$.   Then $p = 1/3$.   Thus, $P(H) = 1/3$ and $P(H) = 2/3$.

**6.13.** Suppose $A$ and $B$ are events with $P(A) = 0.6$, $P(B) = 0.3$, and $P(A \cap B) = 0.2$. Find the probability that: (a) $A$ does not occur. (b) $B$ does not occur. (c) $A$ or $B$ occurs. (d) Neither $A$ nor $B$ occurs.

(a)   $P(\text{not } A) = P(A^c) = 1 - P(A) = 0.4$

(b)   $P(\text{not } B) = P(B^c) = 1 - P(B) = 0.7$

(c)   By the addition principle (Theorem 6.4),

$$P(A \text{ or } B) = P(A \cup B) = P(A) + P(B) - P(A \cap B) = 0.6 + 0.3 - 0.2 = 0.7$$

(d)   Recall [Fig. 6-9(b)] that neither $A$ nor $B$ is the complement of $A \cup B$. Therefore:

$$P(\text{neither } A \text{ nor } B) = P((A \cup B)^c) = 1 - P(A \cup B) = 1 - 0.7 = 0.3$$

**6.14.** Prove Theorem 6.2: $P(A^c) = 1 - P(A)$.

$S = A \cup A^c$ where $A$ and $A^c$ are disjoint. Thus, our result follows from

$$1 = P(S) = P(A \cup A^c) = P(A) + P(A^c)$$

**6.15.** Prove Theorem 6.3: (i) $P(\varnothing) = 0$, (ii) $P(A \backslash B) = P(A) - P(A \cap B)$, (iii) If $A \subseteq B$, then $P(A) \leq P(B)$.

(i)   $\varnothing = S^c$ and $P(S) = 1$. Thus, $P(\varnothing) = 1 - 1 = 0$.

(ii)  As indicated by Fig. 6.12(a), $A = (A \backslash B) \cup (A \cap B)$ where $A \backslash B$ and $A \cap B$ are disjoint. Hence, our result follows from:

$$P(A) = P(A \backslash B) + P(A \cap B)$$

(iii) If $A \subseteq B$, then, as indicated by Fig. 6.12(b), $B = A \cup (B \backslash A)$ where $A$ and $B \backslash A$ are disjoint. Hence:

$$P(B) = P(A) + P(B \backslash A)$$

Since $P(B \backslash A) \geq 0$, we have $P(A) \leq P(B)$.

**6.16.** Prove Theorem 6.4 (addition principle): For any events $A$ and $B$:

$$P(A \cup B) = P(A) + P(B) - P(A \cap B)$$

As indicated by Fig. 6-12(c), $A \cup B = (A \backslash B) \cup B$ where $A \backslash B$ and $B$ are disjoint sets. Thus, using Theorem 6.3(ii):

$$P(A \cup B) = P(A \backslash B) + P(B) = P(A) - P(A \cap B) + P(B) = P(A) + P(B) - P(A \cap B)$$

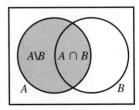

$A$ is shaded

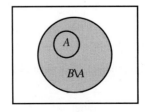

$B$ is shaded

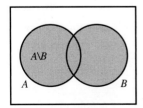

$A \cup B$ is shaded

**Fig. 6-12**

## CONDITIONAL PROBABILITY

**6.17.** Three fair coins—a penny, a nickel, and a dime—are tossed. Find the probability $p$ that they are all heads if: (a) the penny is heads, (b) at least one of the coins is heads.

The sample space has 8 elements:

$S = \{HHH,\ HHT,\ HTH,\ HTT,\ THH,\ THT,\ TTH,\ TTT\}$

(a) If the penny (the first coin) is heads, then the reduced sample space is $A = \{HHH,\ HHT,\ HTH,\ HTT\}$. The coins are all heads in 1 of 4 cases; hence, $p = 1/4$.

(b) Here $B = \{HHH,\ HHT,\ HTH,\ HTT,\ THH,\ THT,\ TTH\}$ is the reduced sample space. Since the coins are all heads in 1 of 7 cases, $p = 1/7$.

**6.18.** A pair of fair dice is thrown. If the two numbers appearing are different, find the probability $p$ that: (a) the sum is six, (b) an ace appears, (c) the sum is 4 or less.

There are 36 ways the pair of dice can be thrown, and six of them—(1, 1), (2, 2), ..., (6, 6)—have the same numbers. Thus, the reduced sample space will consist of $36 - 6 = 30$ elements.

(a) The sum 6 can appear in four ways: (1, 5), (2, 4), (4, 2), (5, 1). [We cannot include (3, 3), since it does not belong to the reduced sample space.] Hence, $p = 4/30 = 2/15$.

(b) An ace can appear in 10 ways: (1, 2), (1, 3), ... (1, 6) and (2, 1), ... , (6, 1). Thus, $p = 10/30 = 1/3$.

(c) The sum of 4 or less can occur in four ways: (1, 2), (2, 1), (1, 3), (3, 1). Hence, $p = 4/30 = 2/15$.

**6.19.** In a certain college town, 25 percent of the students failed mathematics, 15 percent failed chemistry, and 10 percent failed both mathematics and chemistry. A student is selected at random.

(a) If he failed chemistry, what is the probability that he failed mathematics?

(b) If he failed mathematics, what is the probability that he failed chemistry?

(c) What is the probability that he failed mathematics or chemistry?

(d) What is the probability that he failed neither mathematics nor chemistry?

Let $M$ and $C$ be the events that he failed, respectively, mathematics and chemistry.

(a) The probability that the student failed mathematics, given that he failed chemistry, follows:

$$P(M|C) = \frac{P(M \cap C)}{P(C)} = \frac{0.10}{0.15} = \frac{2}{3}$$

(b) The probability that the student failed chemistry, given that he failed mathematics, follows:

$$P(C|M) = \frac{P(M \cap C)}{P(M)} = \frac{0.10}{0.25} = \frac{2}{5}$$

(c) By the addition principle (Theorem 6.4):

$$P(M \cup C) = P(M) + P(C) - P(M \cap C) = 0.25 + 0.15 - 0.10 = 0.30$$

(d) Students who failed neither mathematics nor chemistry form the complement of the set $M \cup C$, that is, form the set $(M \cup C)^c$. Hence:

$$P(M \cup C)^c) = 1 - P(M \cup C) = 1 - 0.30 = 0.70$$

## MULTIPLICATION THEOREM, STOCHASTIC PROCESSES, BAYES' RULE

**6.20.** A class has 12 men and 4 women. Suppose 3 students are selected at random from the class. Find the probability $p$ that they are all men.

The probability that the first student is a man is 12/16, that the second is a man is 11/15, and that the third is a man is 10/14.   By the Multiplication Theorem 6.6,

$$p = \frac{12}{16} \cdot \frac{11}{15} \cdot \frac{10}{14} = \frac{11}{28}$$

**6.21.** Suppose the voters in a certain city view themselves as follows:

45 percent Conservative ($C$), 35 percent Liberal ($L$), and 25 percent Independent ($I$)

The percentage of each group who voted in a particular election follows:

45 percent of Conservatives, 40 percent of Liberals, and 60 percent of Independents.

Suppose a person is randomly selected.

(a)   Find $P(V)$, the probability that the person voted.

(b)   If the person voted, find the probability that the voter was Conservative, that is, find $P(C|V)$.

(a)   By the total probability law,

$$P(V) = P(C)\,P(V|C) + P(L)\,P(V|L) + P(I)\,P(V|I)$$

$$= (0.45)\,(0.45) + (0.35)\,(0.40) + (0.25)\,(0.60) = 0.47$$

(b)   By Bayes' rule:

$$P(C|V) = \frac{P(C)\,P(V|C)}{P(V)} = \frac{(0.40)\,(0.45)}{0.47} = \frac{18}{47} \approx 38.3\%$$

Alternately, we may also consider this problem as a two-step stochastic process with a tree diagram, as in Fig. 6.13(a).

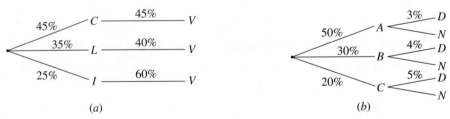

$$(a) \qquad\qquad\qquad\qquad\qquad\qquad (b)$$

**Fig. 6-13**

**6.22.** Three machines—$A$, $B$, $C$—produce, respectively, 50 percent, 30 percent, and 20 percent of the total number of items in a factory.   The percentage of defective output of these machines are, respectively, 3 percent, 4 percent, and 5 percent.   An item is randomly selected.

(a)   Find $P(D)$, the probability the item is defective.

(b)   If the item is defective, find the probability it came from machine $A$, that is, find $P(A|D)$.

(a)   By the total probability law:

$$P(D) = P(A)\,P(D|A) + P(B)\,P(D|B) + P(C)\,P(D|C)$$
$$= (0.50)\,(0.03) + (0.30)\,(0.04) + (0.20)\,(0.05) = 3.7\%$$

(b)   By Bayes' rule:

$$P(A|D) = \frac{P(A)\,P(D|A)}{P(D)} = \frac{(0.50)\,(0.03)}{0.037} \approx 40.5\%$$

Alternately, we may also consider this problem as a two-step stochastic process with a tree diagram, as in Fig. 6-13(b).

## INDEPENDENCE

**6.23.** The probability that $A$ hits a target is $\frac{1}{3}$, and the probability that $B$ hits a target is $\frac{1}{5}$. They both fire at the target. Find the probability that:

(a)  $A$ does not hit the target.        (c)  One of them hits the target.

(b)  Both hit the target.               (d)  Neither hits the target.

We are given $P(A) = \frac{1}{3}$ and $P(B) = \frac{1}{5}$ (and we assume the events are independent).

(a)  $P(\text{not } A) = P(A^c) = 1 - P(A) = 1 - \frac{1}{3} = \frac{2}{3}$.

(b)  Since the events are independent:

$$P(A \text{ and } B) = P(A \cap B) = P(A) \cdot P(B) = \frac{1}{3} \cdot \frac{1}{5} = \frac{1}{15}$$

(c)  By the addition principle (Theorem 6.4):

$$P(A \text{ or } B) = P(A \cup B) = P(A) + P(B) - P(A \cap B) = \frac{1}{3} + \frac{1}{5} - \frac{1}{15} = \frac{7}{15}$$

(d)  We have

$$P(\text{neither } A \text{ nor } B) = P((A \cup B)^c) = 1 - P(A \cup B) = 1 - \frac{7}{15} = \frac{8}{15}$$

**6.24.** Consider the following events for a family with children:

$$E = \{\text{children of both sexes}\} \quad F = \{\text{at most one boy}\}$$

(a)  Show that $E$ and $F$ are independent events if a family has three children.

(b)  Show that $E$ and $F$ are dependent events if a family has only two children.

We assume our sample space $S$ is an equiprobable space.

(a)  Here $S = \{BBB, BBG, BGB, BGG, GBB, GBG, GGB, GGG\}$ and $n(S) = 8$.

$E = \{BBG, BGB, BGG, GBB, GBG, GGB\}$     and so $P(E) = \frac{6}{8} = \frac{3}{4}$

$F = \{BGG, GBG, GGB, GGG\}$     and so $P(F) = \frac{4}{8} = \frac{1}{2}$

$E \cap F = \{BGG, GBG, GGB\}$     and so $P(E \cap F) = \frac{3}{8}$

Since $P(E) \, P(F) = \frac{3}{4} \cdot \frac{1}{2} = \frac{3}{8} = P(E \cap F)$, $E$ and $F$ are independent.

(b)  Here $S = \{BB, BG, GB, GG\}$ and $n(S) = 4$.

$E = \{BG, GB\}$     and so $P(E) = \frac{2}{4} = \frac{1}{2}$

$F = \{BG, GB, GG\}$     and so $P(F) = \frac{3}{4}$

$E \cap F = \{BG, GB\}$     and so $P(E \cap F) = \frac{1}{2}$

Since $P(E) \, P(F) = \frac{1}{2} \cdot \frac{3}{4} = \frac{3}{8} \neq P(E \cap F)$, $E$ and $F$ are dependent.

### REPEATED TRIALS, BINOMIAL DISTRIBUTION

**6.25.** Whenever horses $a$, $b$, $c$, $d$ race together, their respective probabilities of winning are 0.2, 0.5, 0.1, 0.2.   That is, $S = \{a, b, c, d\}$ where $P(a) = 0.2$, $P(b) = 0.5$, $P(c) = 0.1$, and $P(d) = 0.2$. They race three times.

   (a)   Describe and find the number of elements in the product probability space $S_3$.

   (b)   Find the probability that the same horse wins all three races.

   (c)   Find the probability that $a$, $b$, $c$ each win one race.

   (a)   By definition, $S_3 = S \times S \times S = \{(x, y, z) : x, y, z \in S\}$ and $P((x, y, z)) = P(x)\,P(y)\,P(z)$
         Thus, in particular, $S_3$ contains $4^3 = 64$ elements.

   (b)   Writing $xyz$ for $(x, y, z)$, we seek the probability of the event

$$A = \{aaa, bbb, ccc, ddd\}$$

By definition:

$$P(aaa) = (0.2)^3 = 0.008, \qquad P(ccc) = (0.1)^3 = 0.001$$

$$P(bbb) = (0.5)^3 = 0.125, \qquad P(ddd) = (0.2)^3 = 0.008$$

   Thus, $P(A) = 0.0008 + 0.125 + 0.001 + 0.008 = 0.142$.

   (c)   We seek the probability of the event

$$B = \{abc, acb, bac, bca, cab, cba\}$$

Every element in $B$ has the same probability $(0.2)\,(0.5)\,(0.1) = 0.01$.   Hence, $P(B) = 6(0.01) = 0.06$.

**6.26.** The probability that John hits a target is $p = 1/4$.   He fires $n = 6$ times.   Find the probability that he hits the target:   (a)   exactly 2 times,   (b)   more than 4 times,   (c)   at least once.

   This is the binomial experiment $B(6, \frac{1}{4})$ with $n = 6$, $p = \frac{1}{4}$, and $q = 1 - p = \frac{3}{4}$.   By Theorem 6.9:

   (a)   $P(2) = \binom{6}{2} (1/4)^2\,(3/4)^4 = 15\,(3^4)/(4^6) = 1215/4096 \approx 0.297$

   (b)   $P(5) + P(6) = \binom{6}{5} (1/4)^5\,(3/4)^1 + (1/4)^6 = 18/4^6 + 1/4^6 = 19/4^6 = 19/4096 \approx 0.0046$

   (c)   $P(0) = (3/4)^6 = 729/4096$, so $P(X > 0) = 1 - 729/4096 = 3367/4096 \approx 0.82$.

**6.27.** How many dice should be thrown so that there is a better than an even chance of obtaining a six?

   The probability of not obtaining a six on $n$ dice is $\left(\dfrac{5}{6}\right)^n$.

   Hence, we seek the smallest $n$ for which $\left(\dfrac{5}{6}\right)^n$ is less than $\dfrac{1}{2}$.   Compute as follows:

$$\left(\frac{5}{6}\right)^1 = \frac{5}{6}, \qquad \left(\frac{5}{6}\right)^2 = \frac{25}{36}, \qquad \left(\frac{5}{6}\right)^3 = \frac{125}{216}, \qquad \left(\frac{5}{6}\right)^4 = \frac{625}{1296} < \frac{1}{2}$$

   Thus, four dice must be thrown.

**6.28.** A man fires at a target $n = 6$ times and hits it $k = 2$ times.     (a)   List the different ways that this can happen.     (b)   How many ways are there?

(a) List all sequences with two *S*'s (successes) and four *F*'s (failures):

*SSFFFF, SFSFFF, SFFSFF, SFFFSF, SFFFFS, FSSFFF, FSFSFF, FSFFSF,*

*FSFFFS, FFSSFF, FFSFSF, FFSFFS, FFFSSF, FFFSFS, FFFFSS*

(b) There are 15 different ways as indicated by the list. Observe that this is equal to $\binom{6}{2}$, since we are distributing $k = 2$ letters $S$ among the $n = 6$ positions in the sequence.

**6.29.** Prove Theorem 6.9. The probability of exactly $k$ successes in a binomial experiment $B(n, p)$ is given by $P(k) = P(k \text{ successes}) = \binom{n}{k} p^k q^{n-k}$. The probability of one or more successes is $1 - q^n$.

The sample space of the $n$ repeated trials consists of all $n$-tuples ($n$-element sequences) whose components are either $S$ (success) or $F$ (failure). Let $A$ be the event of exactly $k$ successes. Then $A$ consists of all $n$-tuples of which $k$ components are $S$ and $n - k$ components are $F$. The number of such $n$-tuples in the event $A$ is equal to the number of ways that $k$ letters $S$ can be distributed among the $n$ components of an $n$-tuple. (See Problem 6.35 for the special case where $n = 6$ and $k = 2$.) Thus, $A$ consists of $C(n, k) = \binom{n}{k}$ sample points. The probability of each point in $A$ is $p^k q^{n}-\text{k}$. Accordingly:

$$P(k) = P(A) = \binom{n}{k} p^k q^{n-k}$$

In particular, the probability of no successes is

$$P(0) = \binom{n}{0} p^0 q^n = q^n$$

Thus, the probability of one or more successes is $1 - q^n$.

## RANDOM VARIABLES, EXPECTATION

**6.30.** A player tosses two fair coins. He wins \$2 if 2 heads occur and \$1 if 1 head occurs. On the other hand, he loses \$3 if no heads occur. Find the expected value $E$ of the game. Is the game fair? (The game is fair, favorable, or unfavorable to the player accordingly as $E = 0$, $E > 0$, or $E < 0$.)

The sample space is $S = \{HH, HT, TH, TT\}$, and each sample point has probability 1/4. Let $X$ denote the players gain. Then:

$$X(HH) = \$2, \quad X(HT) = X(TH) = \$1, \quad X(TT) = -\$3$$

The distribution of $X$ and its expectation $E = E(X)$ follows:

| $x_i$ | 2 | 1 | $-3$ |
|-------|---|---|------|
| $p_i$ | $\dfrac{1}{4}$ | $\dfrac{2}{4}$ | $\dfrac{1}{4}$ |

$$E = 2\left(\frac{1}{4}\right) + 1\left(\frac{2}{4}\right) - 3\left(\frac{1}{4}\right) = \$0.25$$

Since $E(X) > 0$, the game is favorable to the player.

**6.31.** Two numbers from 1 to 3 are chosen at random with repetitions allowed. Let $X$ denote the sum of the numbers. (a) Find the distribution of $X$. (b) Find the expectation $E(X)$.

(a) There are nine equiprobable pairs making up the sample space $S$. $X$ assumes the values 2, 3, 4, 5, 6 with the following probabilities where we write $ab$ for the pair $(a,b)$:

$$P(2) = P(11) = \frac{1}{9} \qquad P(4) = P(13, 22, 31) = \frac{3}{9} \qquad P(6) = P(33) = \frac{1}{9},$$

$$P(3) = P(12, 21) = \frac{2}{9} \qquad P(5) = P(23, 32) = \frac{2}{9}.$$

Thus, the distribution of X follows:

| $x_i$ | 2 | 3 | 4 | 5 | 6 |
|-------|---|---|---|---|---|
| $p_i$ | $\frac{1}{9}$ | $\frac{2}{9}$ | $\frac{3}{9}$ | $\frac{2}{9}$ | $\frac{1}{9}$ |

(b)   The expectation $E(X)$ is obtained by multiplying each $x$ by its probability and taking the sum:

$$E(X) = 2\left(\frac{1}{9}\right) + 3\left(\frac{2}{9}\right) + 4\left(\frac{3}{9}\right) + 5\left(\frac{2}{9}\right) + 6\left(\frac{1}{9}\right) = \frac{36}{9} = 4$$

## MEAN, VARIANCE, AND STANDARD DEVIATION

**6.32.**   Find the mean $\mu = E(X)$, variance $\sigma^2 = \text{Var}(X)$, and standard deviation $\sigma = \sigma_X$ of each distribution:

(a)

| $x_i$ | 2 | 3 | 11 |
|-------|---|---|----|
| $p_i$ | 1/3 | 1/2 | 1/6 |

(b)

| $x_i$ | 1 | 3 | 4 | 5 |
|-------|---|---|---|---|
| $p_i$ | .4 | .1 | .2 | .3 |

Use the following formulas:

$$\mu = E(X) = x_1 p_1 + x_2 p_2 + \ldots + x_m p_m = \Sigma x_i p_i$$

$$E(X^2) = x_1^2 p_1 + x_2^2 p_2 + \ldots + x_m^2 p_m = \Sigma x_i^2 p_i$$

$$\sigma^2 = \text{Var}(X) = E(X^2) - \mu^2$$

$$\sigma = \sigma_x = \sqrt{\text{Var}(X)}$$

(a)   $\mu = \Sigma x_i p_i = 2\left(\frac{1}{3}\right) + 3\left(\frac{1}{2}\right) + 11\left(\frac{1}{6}\right) = 4$

   $E(X^2) = \Sigma x_i^2 p_i = 2^2\left(\frac{1}{3}\right) + 3^2\left(\frac{1}{2}\right) + 11^2\left(\frac{1}{6}\right) = 26$

   $\sigma^2 = \text{Var}(X) = E(x^2) - \mu^2 = 26 - 4^2 = 10$

   $\sigma = \sqrt{\text{Var}(X)} = \sqrt{10} = 3.2$

(b)   $\mu = \Sigma x_i p_i = 1(.4) + 3(.1) + 4(.2) + 5(.3) = 3$

   $E(X^2) = \Sigma x_i^2 p_i = 1(.4) + 9(.1) + 16(.2) + 25(.3) = 12$

   $\sigma^2 = \text{Var}(X) = E(X^2) - \mu^2 = 12 - 9 = 3$

   $\sigma = \sqrt{\text{Var}(X)} = \sqrt{3} = 1.7$

**6.33.**   The probability that a man hits a target is $p = 0.1$.   He fires $n = 100$ times.   Find the expected number $\mu$ of times he will hit the target, and the standard deviation $\sigma$.

   This is a binomial experiment $B(n, p)$, where $n = 100$, $p = 0.1$, and $q = 1 - p = 0.9$.   Thus, apply Theorem 6.11 to obtain $\mu = np = 100(0.1) = 10$ and $\sigma = \sqrt{npq} = \sqrt{100(0.1)(0.9)} = 3$.

**6.34.** A student takes an 18-question multiple-choice exam, with four choices per question. Suppose one of the choices is obviously incorrect, and the student makes an "educated" guess of the remaining choices. Find the expected number $E(X)$ of correct answers, and the standard deviation $\sigma$.

This is a binomial experiment $B(n, p)$, where $n = 18$, $p = 1/3$, and $q = 1 - p = 2/3$. Hence:

$$E(X) = np = 18\left(\frac{1}{3}\right) = 6 \text{ and } \sigma = \sqrt{npq} = \sqrt{18\left(\frac{1}{3}\right)\left(\frac{2}{3}\right)} = 2$$

## JOINT DISTRIBUTION AND INDEPENDENCE OF RANDOM VARIABLES

**6.35.** Suppose $X$ and $Y$ have the following joint distribution:

| X \ Y | −3 | 2 | 4 | Sum |
|---|---|---|---|---|
| 1 | .1 | .2 | .2 | .5 |
| 3 | .3 | .1 | .1 | .5 |
| Sum | .4 | .3 | .3 | |

(a) Find the distributions of $X$ and $Y$.　(b) Determine whether $X$ and $Y$ are independent.

(a) The sums .5 and .5 at the end of the rows give the distribution for $X$, and the sums .4, .3, .3 at the bottom of the columns give the distribution for $Y$. That is,

| $x_i$ | 1 | 3 |
|---|---|---|
| $P(x_i)$ | .5 | .5 |

Distribution of $X$

| $y_j$ | −3 | 2 | 4 |
|---|---|---|---|
| $P(y_j)$ | .4 | .3 | .3 |

Distribution of $Y$

(b) From the joint distribution, $P(1, -3) = .1$; but $P(X = 1) = .5$ and $P(Y = -3) = .4$. Since $.1 \neq .5(.4)$, $X$ and $Y$ are not independent.

**6.36.** Let $X$ and $Y$ be independent random variables with the following distributions:

| $x_i$ | 1 | 2 |
|---|---|---|
| $P(x_i)$ | .6 | .4 |

Distribution of $X$

| $y_j$ | 5 | 10 | 15 |
|---|---|---|---|
| $P(y_j)$ | .2 | .5 | .3 |

Distribution of $Y$

Find the joint distribution of $X$ and $Y$.

Since $X$ and $Y$ are independent, the joint distribution can be obtained from the distributions of $X$ and $Y$. First construct the joint distribution table with only the $X$ and $Y$ distributions as shown below on the left, and then multiply these entries to obtain the other entries, i.e., set $P(x_i, y_j) = P(x_i)P(y_j)$, as shown below on the right.

| X \ Y | 5 | 10 | 15 | Sum |
|---|---|---|---|---|
| 1 | | | | .6 |
| 2 | | | | .4 |
| Sum | .2 | .5 | .3 | |

| X \ Y | 5 | 10 | 15 | Sum |
|---|---|---|---|---|
| 1 | .12 | .30 | .18 | .6 |
| 2 | .08 | .20 | .12 | .4 |
| Sum | .2 | .5 | .3 | |

**6.37.** Two numbers from 1 to 5 are selected at random (the numbers could be equal). $X = 0$ if the first number is even, and $X = 1$ otherwise; $Y = 1$ if the second number is odd, and $Y = 0$ otherwise.  (*a*) Show that the distributions for $X$ and $Y$ are identical.   (*b*) Find the joint distribution of $X$ and $Y$.   (*c*) Determine if $X$ and $Y$ are independent.

    The equiprobable sample space $S$ consists of all 25 ordered pairs $(a, b)$ of numbers from 1 to 5. Namely,

$$S = \{(1, 1), (1, 2), \ldots, (5, 5)\}$$

(*a*)   There are 10 sample points $(a, b)$ in which the first entry is even, that is, $a = 2$ or 4; $b = 1, 2, 3, 4,$ 5. There are 15 sample points in which $b$ is odd, that is, $b = 1, 3,$ or 5; $a = 1, 2, 3, 4, 5$. Therefore, the distributions for $X$ and $Y$ are as follows:

| $x_i$ | 0 | 1 |
|-------|---|---|
| $P(x_i)$ | $\frac{10}{25}$ | $\frac{15}{25}$ |

Distribution of $X$

| $y_i$ | 0 | 1 |
|-------|---|---|
| $P(y_j)$ | $\frac{10}{25}$ | $\frac{15}{25}$ |

Distribution of $Y$"

    Hence, $X$ and $Y$ are indentically distributed.

(*b*)   For the joint distribution of $X$ and $Y$, we have

$$P(0, 0) = P(a \text{ is even and } b \text{ is even}) = P(\{(2, 2), (2, 4), (4, 2), (4, 4)\}) = \tfrac{4}{25}$$

$$\text{Similarly, } P(0, 1) = \frac{6}{25}, \qquad P(1, 0) = \frac{6}{25}, \qquad P(1, 1) = \frac{9}{25}$$

    Hence, the joint distribution for $X$ and $Y$ is as follows:

| $X \backslash Y$ | 0 | 1 | Sum |
|------------------|---|---|-----|
| 0 | $\frac{4}{25}$ | $\frac{6}{25}$ | $\frac{10}{25}$ |
| 1 | $\frac{6}{25}$ | $\frac{9}{25}$ | $\frac{15}{25}$ |
| Sum | $\frac{10}{25}$ | $\frac{15}{25}$ | |

(*c*)   From the joint distribution,

$$P(0, 0) = \tfrac{4}{25} = \tfrac{10}{25} \cdot \tfrac{10}{25} = P(X = 0)\,P(Y = 0)$$

$$P(0, 1) = \tfrac{6}{25} = \tfrac{10}{25} \cdot \tfrac{15}{25} = P(X = 0)\,P(Y = 1)$$

$$P(1, 0) = \tfrac{6}{25} = \tfrac{15}{25} \cdot \tfrac{10}{25} = P(X = 1)\,P(Y = 0)$$

$$P(1, 1) = \tfrac{9}{25} = \tfrac{15}{25} \cdot \tfrac{15}{25} = P(X = 1)\,P(Y = 1)$$

    Hence, $X$ and $Y$ are independent, even though they are identically distributed.

## NORMAL DISTRIBUTION

**6.38.** The mean and standard deviation on an examination are $\mu = 74$ and $\sigma = 12$, respectively. Find the scores in standard units of students receiving grades: (*a*) 65,   (*b*) 74, (*c*) 86,   (*d*) 92.

(*a*)  $z = \dfrac{x - \mu}{\sigma} = \dfrac{65 - 74}{12} = -0.75$        (*c*)  $z = \dfrac{x - \mu}{\sigma} = \dfrac{86 - 74}{12} = 1.0$

(*b*)  $z = \dfrac{x - \mu}{\sigma} = \dfrac{74 - 74}{12} = 0$        (*d*)  $z = \dfrac{x - \mu}{\sigma} = \dfrac{92 - 74}{12} = 1.5$

**6.39.** Let $Z$ be the random variable with standard normal distribution $\Phi$. Find:

  (a)   $P(0 \leq Z \leq 1.42)$,      (b)   $P(0.73 \leq Z \leq 0)$,      (c)   $P(-1.37 \leq Z \leq 2.01)$

  (a)   $P(0 \leq Z \leq 1.42)$ is equal to the area under the standard normal curve between 0 and 1.42. Thus, using the table in Appendix B, look down the first column until 1.4 is reached, and then continue right to column 2. The entry is .4222. Hence $P(0 \leq Z \leq 1.42) = .4222$. See Fig. 6-14(a).

  (b)   By symmetry, $P(-0.73 \leq Z \leq 0) = P(0 \leq Z \leq 0.73) = .2673$. See Fig. 6.14(b).

  (c)   $P(-1.37 \leq Z \leq 2.01) = P(-1.37 \leq Z \leq 0) + P(0 \leq Z \leq 2.01)$

$$= .4147 + .4778 = 0.8925$$

See Fig. 6.14(c).

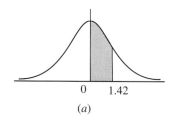
(a)

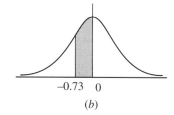
(b)

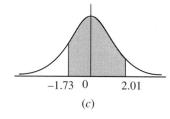
(c)

**Fig. 6-14**

**6.40.** Let $Z$ be the random variable with standard normal distribution $\Phi$. Find:
  (a)   $P(0.65 \leq Z \leq 1.26)$,        (b)   $P(-1.79 \leq Z \leq -0.54)$,        (c)   $P(Z \geq 1.13)$

Use the table in Appendix B and Fig. 6-15.

  (a)   $P(0.65 \leq Z \leq 1.26) = P(0 \leq Z \leq 1.26) - P(0 \leq Z \leq 0.65)$

$$= .3962 - .2422 = 0.1540$$

  (b)   $P(-1.79 \leq Z \leq -0.54) = P(0.54 \leq Z \leq 1.79)$

$$= P(0 \leq Z \leq 1.79) - P(0 \leq Z \leq 0.54)$$

$$= .4633 - .2054 = 0.2579$$

  (c)   $P(Z \geq 1.13) = P(Z \geq 0) - P(0 \leq Z \leq 1.13)$

$$= .5000 - .3708 = 0.1292$$

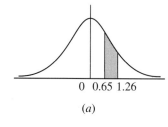
(a)

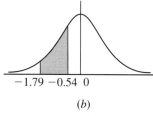
(b)

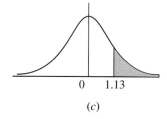
(c)

**Fig. 6-15**

**6.41.** Let $Z$ be the random variable with the standard normal distribution $\Phi$. Determine the value of $z$ if: (a) $P(0 \leq Z \leq z) = .4236$,   (b) $P(Z \leq z) = .7967$,   (c) $P(z \leq Z \leq 2) = .1000$.

  (a)   In the table in Appendix B, the entry .4236 appears to the right of row 1.4 and under column 3. Hence $z = 1.43$. See Fig. 6.16(a).

  (b)   Note first that $z$ must be positive since the probability is greater than 0.5. Thus:

$$P(0 \leq Z \leq z) = P(Z \leq z) - .5 = .7967 - .5000 = 0.2967$$

Thus from Appendix B, we obtain $z = 0.83$. See Fig. 6-16(b).

(c)   $P(0 \le Z \le z) = P(0 \le Z \le 2) - P(z \le Z \le 2)$
      $= .4772 - .1000 = 0.3772$

Thus from Appendix B, we obtain $z = 1.16$.   See Fig. 6-16(c).

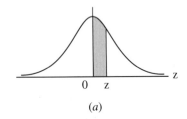 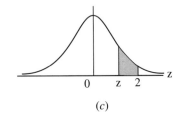

(a)                              (b)                              (c)

**Fig. 6-16**

**6.41.**   Suppose the temperture $T$ during June is normally distributed with mean $\mu = 68°$ and standard
deviation $\sigma = 6°$.   Find the probability that the temperture is between $70°$ and $80°$.

We have:

$$70° \text{ in standard units} = (70 - 68)/6 = 0.33$$
$$80° \text{ in standard units} = (80 - 68)/6 = 2.00$$

Then, using Appendix B and Fig. 6-17(a),

$$p = P(70 \le T \le 80) = P(0.33 \le Z \le 2)$$
$$= P(0 \le Z \le 2) - P(0 \le Z \le 0.33)$$
$$= .4772 - .1293 = 0.3479$$

Here $Z$ is the standardized random variable corresponding to $T$, and so $Z$ has the standard normal
distribution $\varnothing$.

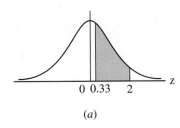 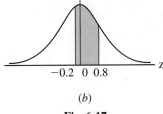 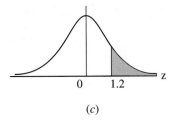

(a)                              (b)                              (c)

**Fig. 6-17**

**6.42.**   Suppose the heights $H$ of 800 students are normally distributed with mean $\mu = 66$ inches and
standard deviation $\sigma = 5$ inches.   Find the number N of students with heights: (a) between 65
and 70 inches, (b) greater than or equal to 6 feet (72 inches).

(a)   We have:

$$65 \text{ inches in standard units} = (65 - 66)/5 = -0.20$$
$$70 \text{ inches in standard units} = (70 - 66)/5 = 0.80$$

Therefore, using Appendix B and Fig. 6-17(b),

$$P(65 \le H \le 70) = P(-0.20 \le Z \le 0.80)$$
$$= .0793 + .2881 = 0.3674$$

Thus $N = 800(.3674) \approx 294$.

(b)   Here, 72 inches in standard units = (72 − 66)/5 = 1.20.   Hence, using Appendix B and Fig. 6-17(c),

$$P(H \geq 72) = P(Z \geq 1.2) = .5000 - .3849 = 0.1151$$

Thus $N = 800(.1151) \approx 92$.

(Here $Z$ is the standardized random variable corresponding to $H$ and so $Z$ has the standard normal distribution Ø.)

## NORMAL APPROXIMATION TO THE BINOMIAL DISTRIBUTION

**6.44.**   Among 10,000 random digits, find the probability $P$ that the digit 3 appears at most 950 times.

Here $\mu = np = 10,000 \cdot \frac{1}{10} = 1000$ and $\sigma = \sqrt{npq} = \sqrt{10,000 \cdot \frac{1}{10} \cdot \frac{9}{10}} = 30$.   Let $X$ denote the number of times the digit 3 appears.   We seek $BP(X \leq 950)$, or, approximately, $NP(X \leq 950.5)$ (see Remark below).   Now

950.5 in standard units = (950.5 − 1000)/30 = −1.65

Therefore, using Appendix B and Fig. 6-18(a),

$$P \approx NP(X \leq 950.5) = NP(Z \leq -1.65) = NP(Z \geq 1.65)$$

$$= .5 - NP(0 \leq Z \leq 1.65) = .5000 - .4505 = 0.0495$$

**Remark:**   Since the binomial normal variable is never negative, $BP(X \leq 950) = BP(0 \leq X \leq 950)$.   Hence, we should write $BP(X \leq 950) \approx NP(-0.5 \leq X \leq 950.5) = NP(-33.5 \leq Z \leq -1.65) = NP(Z \leq -1.65) - NP(Z \leq -33.5)$. However, $NP(-33.5 \leq Z)$ is so small, it can be neglected.

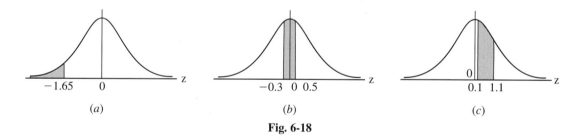

(a)                                        (b)                                        (c)

**Fig. 6-18**

**6.45.**   A fair die is tossed $n = 180$ times.   Find the probability $P$ that the face 6 will appear:

(a)   between 29 and 32 times inclusive,      (b)   between 31 and 35 times inclusive.

Here $\mu = np = 180 \cdot \frac{1}{6} = 30$ and $\sigma = \sqrt{npq} = \sqrt{180 \cdot \frac{1}{6} \cdot \frac{5}{6}} = 5$.   Let $X$ denote the number of times the face 6 appears.

(a)   We seek $BP(29 \leq X \leq 32)$ or, assuming the data is continuous, $NP(28.5 \leq X \leq 32.5)$.   Now

28.5 in standard units = (28.5 − 30)/5 = −0.3

32.5 in standard units = (32.5 − 30)/5 = 0.5

Thus, using Appendix B and Fig. 6-18(b),

$$P \approx NP(28.5 \leq X \leq 32.5) = NP(-0.3 \leq Z \leq 0.5)$$

$$= NP(-0.3 \leq Z \leq 0) + NP(0 \leq Z \leq 0.5)$$

$$= .1179 + .1915 = 0.3094$$

(b)   We seek $BP(31 \leq X \leq 35)$ or, assuming the data is continuous, $NP(30.5 \leq N \leq 35.5)$.   Now

30.5 in standard units = (30.5 − 30)/5 = 0.1

35.5 in standard units = (35.5 − 30)/5 = 1.1

Thus, using Appendix B and Fig. 6-18(c),

$$P \approx NP(30.5 \le X \le 35.5) = NP(0.1 \le Z \le 1.1)$$

$$= NP(0 \le Z \le 1.1) - NP(0 \le Z \le 0.1)$$

$$= .3643 - .0398 = 0.3245$$

# Supplementary Problems

## SAMPLE SPACES AND EVENTS

**6.46.** Let $A$ and $B$ be events. Find an expression and exhibit the Venn diagram for the event that: (a) $A$ or not $B$ occurs, (b) only $A$ occurs.

**6.47.** Let $A$, $B$, and $C$ be events. Find an expression for the event that:  (a)  $A$ and $B$ but not $C$ occurs, (b)  $A$ or $C$, but not $B$,  (c)  none of the events occur.

**6.48.** A penny, a dime, and a die are tossed.

(a)  Describe a suitable sample space $S$, and find $n(S)$.

(b)  Express explicitly the following events:

$$A = \{\text{two heads and an even number}\}, \quad B = \{2 \text{ appears}\},$$

$$C = \{\text{exactly one heads and an odd number}\}$$

(c)  Express explicitly the event: (1) $A$ and $B$, (2) only $B$, (3) $B$ and $C$.

## FINITE EQUIPROBABLE SPACES

**6.49.** Determine the probability of each event:

(a)  An odd number appears in the toss of a fair die.

(b)  One or more heads appear in the toss of four fair coins.

(c)  One or both numbers exceed 4 in the toss of two fair die.

**6.50.** A student is chosen at random to represent a class with five freshman, eight sophomores, three juniors, and two seniors.   Find the probability that the student is:

(a)  a sophomore,  (b)  a junior,  (c)  a junior or a senior.

**6.51.** One card is selected at random from 50 cards numbered 1 to 50.   Find the probability that the number is: (a)  greater than 10,  (b)  divisible by 5,  (c)  greater than 10 and divisible by 5, (d)  greater than 10 or divisible by 5.

**6.52.** Three bolts and three nuts are in a box.   Two parts are chosen at random.   Find the probability that one is a bolt and one is a nut.

**6.53.** A box contains two white socks, two blue socks, and two red socks.   Two socks are drawn at random. Find the probability they are a match (same color).

**6.54.** Of 10 girls in a class, 3 have blue eyes.  Two of the girls are chosen at random.  Find the probability that:

(a)  both have blue eyes,     (b)  at least one has blue eyes,     (c)  neither has blue eyes,
(d)  exactly one has blue eyes.

**6.55.** Of 120 students, 60 are studying French, 50 are studying Spanish, and 20 are studying both French and Spanish.  A student is chosen at random.  Find the probability that the student is studying:
(a)  French or Spanish,     (b)  neither French nor Spanish,     (c)  only French,     (d)  exactly one of the two languages.

## FINITE PROBABILITY SPACES

**6.56.** Let $S = \{a_1, a_2, a_3\}$, and let $P$ be the function on $S$ where $P(a_i) = p_i$.  Determine whether each of the following values of $p_1, p_2, p_3$ define $S$ to be a probability space and, if not, the reason why:

(a)  $p_1 = \dfrac{1}{4}$,  $p_2 = \dfrac{1}{3}$,  $p_3 = \dfrac{1}{2}$          (c)  $p_1 = \dfrac{1}{6}$,  $p_2 = \dfrac{1}{3}$,  $p_3 = \dfrac{1}{2}$

(b)  $p_1 = \dfrac{2}{3}$,  $p_2 = -\dfrac{1}{3}$,  $p_3 = \dfrac{2}{3}$          (d)  $p_1 = 0$,  $p_2 = \dfrac{1}{3}$,  $p_3 = \dfrac{2}{3}$

**6.57.** A coin is weighted so that heads is three times as likely to appear as tails.  Find $P(H)$ and $P(T)$.

**6.58.** Three students $A$, $B$, and $C$ are in a swimming race.  $A$ and $B$ have the same probability of winning, and each is twice as likely to win as $C$.  Find the probability that: (a) $B$ wins, (b) $C$ wins, (c) $B$ or $C$ wins.

**6.59.** Consider the following probability distribution:

| Outcome | 1 | 2 | 3 | 4 | 5 | 6 |
|---------|-----|-----|-----|-----|-----|-----|
| Probability | 0.1 | 0.4 | 0.1 | 0.1 | 0.2 | 0.1 |

For the events $A = \{2, 4, 6\}$,     $B = \{2, 3, 4, 5\}$,     $C = \{1, 2\}$, find:

(a)  $P(A)$,  $P(B)$,  $P(C)$          (b)  $P(A \cap B)$,  $P(A \cup C)$,  $P(B \cap C)$

**6.60.** Suppose $A$ and $B$ are events with $P(A) = .7$, $P(B) = .5$, and $P(A \cap B) = .4$.  Find the probability that:

(a)  $A$ does not occur.          (c)  $A$ but not $B$ occurs.

(b)  $A$ or $B$ occurs.          (d)  Neither $A$ nor $B$ occurs.

## CONDITIONAL PROBABILITY; MULTIPLICATION THEOREM

**6.61.** A fair die is tossed.  Consider events $A = \{2, 4, 6\}$, $B = \{1, 2\}$, $C = \{1, 2, 3, 4\}$.  Find:

(a)  $P(A \text{ and } B)$ and $P(A \text{ or } C)$          (c)  $P(A|C)$ and $P(C|A)$

(b)  $P(A|B)$ and $P(B|A)$          (d)  $P(B|C)$ and $P(C|B)$

Are $A$ and $B$ independent? $A$ and $C$? $B$ and $C$?

**6.62.** A pair of fair die is tossed.  If the number appearing are different, find the probability that:
(a)  The sum is even.     (b)  The sum exceeds nine.

**6.63.** Let $A$ and $B$ be events with $P(A) = .6$, $P(B) = .3$, and $P(A \cap B) = .2$.  Find:
(a)  $P(A \cap B)$,     (b)  $P(A|B)$,     (c)  $P(B|A)$.

**6.64.** In a country club, 60 percent of the members play tennis, 40 percent play golf, and 20 percent play both tennis and golf.   A member is chosen at random.

   (a)   Find the probability he plays tennis or golf.

   (b)   Find the probability he plays neither tennis nor golf.

   (c)   If he plays tennis, find the probability he plays golf.

   (d)   If he plays golf, find the probability he plays tennis.

**6.65.** A women is dealt 3 spades from an ordinary 52-card deck.   (See Fig. 6-11.)   If she is given two more cards, find the probability that both of the cards are also spades.

**6.66.** Two marbles are selected one after the other without replacement from a box containing 3 white mables and 2 red marbles.   Find the probability p that:

   (a)   Both marbles are white.      (c)   The second is white if the first is white.

   (b)   Both marbles are red.        (d)   The second is red if the first is red.

**6.67.** Three students are selected at random one after another without replacement from a class with 10 boys and 5 girls.   Find the probability that:      (a)   all three are boys,      (b)   all three are girls,      (c)   all three are of the same sex.

**6.68.** Refer to previous Problem 6.67.   Find the probability that only the first and third students are of the same sex.

**6.69.** Three cards are drawn at random without replacement from a 52-card deck.   Find the probability that: (a)   all 3 are aces,      (b)   none of the cards are aces.

**6.70.** Refer to previous Problem 6.69.   Find the probability:

   (a)   If the first card is an ace, then the other two are aces.

   (b)   If the first two cards are aces, then the third is an ace.

## STOCHASTIC PROCESSES, BAYES' RULE

**6.71.** Two boxes are given as follows:

   Box $A$ contains 5 red, 3 white, and 8 blue marbles.

   Box $B$ contains 3 red and 5 white marbles.

   A box is selected at random and a marble is randomly chosen from the box.   Find the probability that the marble is: (a)   red,      (b)   white,      (c)   blue.

**6.72.** Refer to the previous Problem 6.62.   Find the probability that box $A$ was chosen if the marble is: (a)   red,      (b)   white,      (c)   blue.

**6.73.** A box contains three coins, two of them are fair and one coin is two-headed.   A coin is selected at random and tossed.   If heads appears, find the probability that the coin is two-headed.

**6.74.** A box contains three coins, two of them fair and one two-headed.   A coin is selected at random and tossed twice.   If heads appears both times, what is the probability that the coin is two-headed?

**6.75.** A city is partitioned into districts *A, B, C*.   Suppose:

   *A* has 20 percent of the registered voters and 50 percent of them are listed as Democrats.

   *B* has 40 percent of the registered voters and 25 percent of them are listed as Democrats.

   *C* has 40 percent of the registered voters and 75 percent of them are listed as Democrats.

   A registered voter is chosen randomly in the city.

   (*a*)   Find the probability that the voter is a listed Democrat.

   (*b*)   If the voter is a listed Democrat, find the probability the voter came from district B.

**6.76.** The undergraduate students at City College are divided into four classes: freshman, sophomore, junior, senior.   Suppose the percentage of students of the college in each class follows:

   Freshman: 30 percent, Sophomores: 25 percent, Juniors: 25 percent, Seniors: 20 percent

Suppose the percentage of women in each of the four classes follows:

   Freshman: 60 percent, Sophomores: 40 percent, Juniors: 40 percent, Seniors: 45 percent

   A student is selected at random.      (*a*)   Find the probability that the student is a woman.      (*b*)   If the student is a woman, what is the probability she is a sophomore?

**6.77.** Refer to previous Problem 6.76.   Suppose one of the classes is randomly chosen first, and then a student is chosen at random from the class.

   (*a*)   Find the probability that the student is a women.

   (*b*)   If the student is a women, what is the probability she is a sophomore.

## INDEPENDENCE

**6.78.** Let *A* and *B* be independent events with $P(A) = 0.3$ and $P(B) = 0.4$.   Find:
   (*a*)   $P(A \cap B)$ and $P(A \cup B)$,      (*b*)   $P(A|B)$ and $P(B|A)$.

**6.79.** Box *A* contains 6 red marbles and 2 blue marbles, and Box *B* contains 2 red and 4 blue.   A marble is drawn at random from each box.   Find the probability *p* that:      (*a*)   both marbles are red,      (*b*)   one is red and one is blue.

**6.80.** The probability that *A* hits a target is 1/4 and that B hits a target is 1/3.   They each fire once at the target. Find the probability that:      (*a*)   they both hit the target,      (*b*)   the target is hit at least once, (*c*)   the target is hit exactly once.

**6.81.** Refer to previous Problem 6.80.   If the target is hit only once, find the pobability that *A* hit the target.

**6.82.** Three fair coins are tossed.   Consider the events:

   *A* = {all heads or all tails}, *B* = {at least two heads}, *C* = {at most two heads}

   Of the pairs (*A, B*), (*A, C*), and (*B, C*), which are independent?

**6.83.** Suppose *A* and *B* are independents.   Show that the following are also independent events:
   (*a*)   *A* and $B^c$,      (*b*)   $A^c$ and *B*,      (*c*)   $A^c$ and $B^c$.

## REPEATED TRIALS; BINOMIAL DISTRIBUTION

**6.84.** Whenever horses *A, B, C* race together, their respective probabilities of winning are .3, .5, and .2.   They race three times.

(a) Find the probability that the same horse wins all three races.

(b) Find the probability that A, B, C each win one race.

**6.85.** The batting average of a baseball player is .300. He comes to bat 4 times. Find the probability that he will get:      (a)   exactly two hits,      (b)   at least one hit.

**6.86.** The probability that Tom scores on a three-point basketball shot is p = .4. He shoots $n = 5$ times. Find the probability that he scores:      (a)   exactly 2 times,      (b)   at least once.

**6.87.** The probability that, in any game, the Hornets will defeat the Rockets is .6. Find the probability that the Hornets will win a best-out-of-three series.

**6.88.** A team wins (W) with probability .5, loses (L) with probability .3, and ties (T) with probability .2. The team plays twice.      (a)   Determine the sample space S and the probability of each elementary event. (b)   Find the probability that the team wins at least once.

**6.89.** A certain type of missile hits its target with probability $p = 1/3$.      (a)   If 3 missiles are fired, find the probability that the target is hit at least once.      (b)   Find the number of missiles that should be fired so that there is at least 90 percent probability of hitting the target (at least once).

## RANDOM VARIABLES

**6.90.** A pair of dice is thrown. Let X denote the minimum of the two numbers which occur. Find the distribution and expectation of X.

**6.91.** A fair coin is tossed four times. Let X denote the longest string of heads. Find the distribution and expectation of X.

**6.92.** A coin, weighted so that $P(H) = 1/3$ and $P(T) = 2/3$, is tossed until a head or five tails occur. Find the expected number E of tosses of the coin.

**6.93.** Find the expected number E of girls in a family with 6 children, assuming sex distributions to be equally probable. Find the probability that E does occur.

**6.94.** A player tosses three fair coins. She wins $5 if three heads occur, $3 if two heads occur, and $1 if one heads occurs. However, she loses $15 if three tails occur. Find the value of the game to the player.

**6.95.** A box contain 10 transistors of which two are defective. A transistor is selected from the box and tested until a nondefective one is chosen. Find the expected number E of transistors to be chosen.

**6.96.** A lottery with 500 tickets gives one prize of $100, three prizes of $50 each, and five prizes of $25 each.

(a)   Find the expected winnings of a ticket.      (b)   If a ticket costs $1, find the expected value of the game.

## MEAN, VARIANCE, AND STANDARD DEVIATION

**6.97.** Find the mean $\mu$, variance $\sigma^2$, and standard deviation of each distribution:

(a)

| $x_i$ | 2 | 3 | 8 |
|-------|---|---|---|
| $p_i$ | $\frac{1}{4}$ | $\frac{1}{2}$ | $\frac{1}{4}$ |

(b)

| $x_i$ | −1 | 0 | 1 | 2 | 3 |
|-------|----|---|---|---|---|
| $p_i$ | .3 | .1 | .1 | .3 | .2 |

**6.98.** A pair of dice is thrown.   Let $X$ denote the minimum of the two numbers which occur.   Find the mean $\mu$, variance $\sigma^2$, and standard deviation $\sigma$ of $X$.

**6.99.** Five fair coins are tossed.   Let $X$ denote the number of heads which occur.   (*a*)   Find the distribution of $X$.   (*b*)   Find the mean $\mu$, variance $\sigma^2$, and standard deviation $\sigma$ of $X$.

**6.100.** Team $A$ has probability $p = .8$ of winning each time it plays.   Let $X$ denote the number of times $A$ will win in $n = 100$ games.   Find the mean $\mu$, variance $\sigma^2$, and standard deviation $\sigma$ of $X$.

**6.101.** Let $X$ be a binomially distributed random variable $B(n, p)$ with $E(X) = 2$ and $\text{Var}(X) = 4/3$.   Find $n$ and $p$.

## JOINT DISTRIBUTION AND INDEPENDENCE OF RANDOM VARIABLES

**6.102.** Suppose $X$ and $Y$ are independent random variables with the following respective distributions:

| $x_i$ | 1 | 2 |
|---|---|---|
| $P(x_i)$ | .7 | .3 |

| $y_j$ | $-2$ | 5 | 8 |
|---|---|---|---|
| $P(y_i)$ | .3 | .5 | .2 |

Find the joint distribution of $X$ and $Y$.

**6.103.** Consider the joint distribution of $X$ and $Y$ in Fig. 6-19(*a*).

(*a*)   Find the distribution of $X$ and of $Y$.      (*b*)   Determine whether $X$ and $Y$ are independent.

**6.104.** Consider the joint distribution of $X$ and $Y$ in Fig. 6-19(*b*).   (*a*)   Find the distribution of $X$ and $Y$.   (*b*)   Determine whether $X$ and $Y$ are independent.

**Remark:**   It is always possible to find the distributions of $X$ and $Y$ from the joint distribution of $X$ and $Y$; but, in general, it is not possible to find the joint distribution from the individual distributions of $X$ and $Y$: Some other information, such as knowing that $X$ and $Y$ are independent, is needed to obtain the joint distribution from the individual distributions.

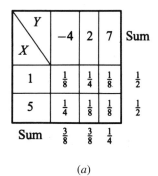

| $X$ \ $Y$ | $-4$ | 2 | 7 | Sum |
|---|---|---|---|---|
| 1 | $\frac{1}{8}$ | $\frac{1}{4}$ | $\frac{1}{8}$ | $\frac{1}{2}$ |
| 5 | $\frac{1}{4}$ | $\frac{1}{8}$ | $\frac{1}{8}$ | $\frac{1}{2}$ |
| Sum | $\frac{3}{8}$ | $\frac{3}{8}$ | $\frac{1}{4}$ | |

(*a*)

| $X$ \ $Y$ | 2 | 3 | 4 | Sum |
|---|---|---|---|---|
| 1 | .06 | .15 | .09 | .30 |
| 2 | .14 | .35 | .21 | .70 |
| Sum | .20 | .50 | .30 | |

(*b*)

**Fig. 6-19**

## NORMAL DISTRIBUTION

**6.105.** Let $Z$ be the random variable with the standard normal distribution $\phi$.   Find:

(*a*)   $P(-0.81 \le Z \le 1.13)$,      (*b*)   $P(0.53 \le Z \le 2.03)$,      (*c*)   $P(Z \le 0.73)$,

**6.106.** Let $X$ be normally distributed with mean $\mu = 8$ and standard deviation $\sigma = 4$.   Find:

(*a*)   $P(5 \le X \le 10)$,      (*b*)   $P(10 \le X \le 15)$,      (*c*)   $P(X \ge 15)$,      (*d*)   $P(X \le 5)$.

**6.107.** Suppose the weights of 2000 male students are normally distributed with mean 155 pounds and standard deviation 20 pounds. Find the number of students with weights:

  (a) less than or equal to 100 pounds,  (c) between 150 and 175 pounds,

  (b) between 120 and 130 pounds,  (d) greater than or equal to 200 pounds.

**6.108.** Suppose the diameters of bolts manufactured by a company are normally distributed with mean 0.25 inch and standard deviation 0.02 inch. A bolt is considered defective if its diameter is $\leq 0.20$ inch or $\geq 0.28$ inch. Find the percentage of defective bolts manufactured by the company.

**6.109.** Suppose the scores on an examination are normally distributed with mean $\mu = 76$ and standard deviation $\sigma = 15$. The top 15 percent of the students receive A's and the bottom 10 percent receive F's. Find (a) the minimum score to receive an A,  (b) the minimum score to pass (not to receive an F).

## NORMAL APPROXIMATION TO THE BINOMIAL DISTRIBUTION

**6.110.** A fair coin is tossed 400 times. Find the probability that the number of heads which occur differs from 200 by:  (a) more than 10,  (b) more than 25.

**6.111.** A fair die is tossed 720 times. Find the probability that the face 6 will occur:
  (a) between 100 and 125 times inclusive,  (b) more than 150 times.

**6.112.** Among 625 random digits, find the probability that the digit 7 appears:
  (a) between 50 and 60 times inclusive,  (b) between 60 and 70 times inclusive.

**6.113.** Assume that 4 percent of the population over 65 years old have Alzheimer's disease. In a random sample of 9600 people over 65, what is the probability that fewer than 400 of them have the disease?

# Answers to Supplementary Problems

**6.46.** (a) $A \cup B^c$,  (b) $A \cap B^c$

**6.47.** (a) $A \cap B \cap C^c$,  (b) $(A \cup C) \cap B$,  (c) $(A \cup B \cup B)^c = A^c \cap B^c \cap C^c$

**6.48.** (a) $n(S) = 24$,  $S = \{H, T\} \times \{H, T\} \times \{1, 2, \ldots, 6\}$
  (b) $A = \{HH2, HH4, HH6\}$,  $B = \{HH2, HT2, TH2, TT2\}$,  $C = \{HT1, HT3, HT5, TH1, TH3, TH5\}$
  (c) (1) $HH2$,  (2) $HT2, TH2, TT2$,  (3) $\emptyset$

**6.49.** (a) 3/6,  (b) 15/16,  (c) 20/36

**6.50.** (a) 8/18,  (b) 3/18,  (c) 5/18

**6.51.** (a) 40/50,  (b) 10/50,  (c) 8/50,  (d) 42/50

**6.52.** 3/5

**6.53.** 1/5

**6.54.** (a) 1/15,  (b) 8/15,  (c) 7/15,  (d) 7/15

**6.55.** (*a*)  3/4,          (*b*)  1/4,          (*c*)  1/3,          (*d*)  7/12

**6.56.** (*c*)  and          (*d*)

**6.57.** $P(H) = 3/4, P(T) = 1/4$

**6.58.** (*a*)  2/5,          (*b*)  1/5,          (*c*)  3/5

**6.59.** (*a*)  0.6, 0.8, 0.5;     (*b*)  0.5, 0.7, 0.4

**6.60.** (*a*)  .3,          (*b*)  .8,          (*c*)  .3,          (*d*)  .2

**6.61.** (*a*)  1/6, 5/6,     (*b*)  1/2, 1/3,          (*c*)  1/2, 2/3,          (*d*)  1/2, 1          (*e*)  yes, yes, no

**6.62.** (*a*)  12/30,          (*b*)  4/30

**6.63.** (*a*)  .7,          (*b*)  2/3,          (*c*)  1/3

**6.64.** (*a*)  80 percent,          (*b*)  20 percent,          (*c*)  1/3,          (*d*)  1/2

**6.65.** 190/2352 ≈ 8.08 percent

**6.66.** (*a*)  3/10,          (*b*)  1/10,          (*c*)  1/2,          (*d*)  1/4

**6.67.** (*a*)  24/91,          (*b*)  2/91,          (*c*)  26/91

**6.68.** 5/21

**6.69.** (*a*)  11/32, 13/32, 8/32,          (*b*)  5/11, 3/13, 1

**6.70.** 1/2

**6.71.** 2/3

**6.72.** (*a*)  50 percent,          (*b*)  20 percent

**6.73.** (*a*)  50 percent,          (*b*)  1/3

**6.74.** (*a*)  65 percent,          (*b*)  10/47 ≈ 21.3 percent

**6.75.** (*a*)  46.25 percent,          (*b*)  21.6 percent

**6.76.** (*a*)  27.1 percent,          (*b*)  47.5 percent,          (*c*)  25.6 percent

**6.77.** (*a*)  2/9,          (*b*)  4/9,          (*c*)  3/9

**6.78.** (*a*)  .12, .58;          (*b*)  .3, .4

**6.79.** (*a*)  1/4,          (*b*)  5/12

**6.80.** (*a*)  1/12,          (*b*)  1/2,          (*c*)  5/12

**6.81.** 2/5

**6.82.** Only *A* and *B* are independent.

**6.84.** (a)  .16,        (b)  .18

**6.85.** (a)  $6 (.3)^2 (.7)^2 = .2646$       (b)  $1 - (.7)^4 = .7599$

**6.86.** (a)  $10 (.4)^2 (.6)^3 = .2646$      (b)  $1 - (.6)^5 = .7599$

**6.87.** .576

**6.88.** (b)  $P(WW, WT, TW) = 0.55$

**6.89.** (a)  $1 - (2/3)^3 = 19/27$,     (b)  five times

**6.90.**

| $x_i$ | 1 | 2 | 3 | 4 | 5 | 6 |
|-------|---|---|---|---|---|---|
| $p_i$ | $\dfrac{11}{36}$ | $\dfrac{9}{36}$ | $\dfrac{7}{36}$ | $\dfrac{5}{36}$ | $\dfrac{3}{36}$ | $\dfrac{1}{36}$ |

$E = 91/36 \approx 2.5$

**6.91.**

| $x_i$ | 0 | 1 | 2 | 3 | 4 |
|-------|---|---|---|---|---|
| $p_i$ | $\dfrac{1}{16}$ | $\dfrac{7}{16}$ | $\dfrac{5}{16}$ | $\dfrac{2}{16}$ | $\dfrac{1}{16}$ |

$E = 27/16 \approx 1.7$

**6.92.** $211/81 \approx 2.6$

**6.93.** 3,  5/16

**6.94.** .25

**6.95.** $11/9 \approx 1.2$

**6.96.** (a)  .75,        (b)  $-.25$

**6.97.** (a)  $\mu = 4$,  $\sigma^2 = 5.5$,  $\sigma = 2.3$     (b)  $\mu = 1$,  $\sigma^2 = 2.4$,  $\sigma = 1.5$

**6.98.** $\mu = 91/36 \approx 2.5$,  $\sigma^2 = 1.49$,  $\sigma = 1.40$,

**6.99.** (a)

| $x_i$ | 0 | 1 | 2 | 3 | 4 | 5 |
|-------|---|---|---|---|---|---|
| $p_i$ | $\dfrac{1}{32}$ | $\dfrac{5}{32}$ | $\dfrac{10}{32}$ | $\dfrac{10}{32}$ | $\dfrac{5}{32}$ | $\dfrac{1}{32}$ |

(b)  $\mu = 2.5$,  $\sigma^2 = 1.25$,  $\sigma = 1.12$

**6.100.** $\mu = 80$,  $\sigma^2 = 16$,  $\sigma = 4$

**6.101.** $n = 6$,  $p = 1/3$

**6.102.**

| Y X | −2 | 5 | 8 | Sum |
|---|---|---|---|---|
| 1 | .21 | .35 | .14 | .7 |
| 2 | .09 | .15 | .06 | .3 |
| Sum | .3 | .5 | .2 | |

**6.103** (a)

| $x_i$ | 1 | 5 |
|---|---|---|
| $p_i$ | $\frac{1}{2}$ | $\frac{1}{2}$ |

| $y_i$ | −4 | 2 | 7 |
|---|---|---|---|
| $p_i$ | $\frac{3}{8}$ | $\frac{3}{8}$ | $\frac{1}{4}$ |

(b)   X and Y are not independent.

**6.104** (a)

| $x_i$ | 1 | 2 |
|---|---|---|
| $p_i$ | .3 | .7 |

| $y_i$ | 2 | 3 | 4 |
|---|---|---|---|
| $p_i$ | .2 | .5 | .3 |

(b)   X and Y are independent.

**6.105.** (a)   .2910 + .3708 = .6618,      (b)   .4788 − .2019 = .2769,      (c)   .5000 + .2673 = .7673,

**6.106.** (a)   .4649,      (b)   .2684,      (c)   .0401,      (d)   .2266

**6.107.** (a)   6,      (b)   131,      (c)   880,      (d)   24

**6.108.** 7.3 percent

**6.109.** (a)   92,      (b)   57

**6.110.** (a)   .2938,      (b)   .0108

**6.111.** (a)   .6886,      (b)   .0011

**6.112.** (a)   .3518,      (b)   .5131

**6.113.** .8051

# Descriptive Statistics

## 7.1 INTRODUCTION; THE NATURE OF STATISTICS

*Statistics* means, on the one hand, lists of numerical values, for example, the salaries of the employees of a company, or the number of children per family in a city. Statistics as a science, on the other hand, is that branch of mathematics which organizes, analyzes, and interprets such raw data. Statistical methods are applicable to any area of human endeavor where numerical data are collected for some type of decision-making process.

In probability theory, we draw conclusions about samples of a population based on our knowledge of the population. In statistics, the inferences go the other way. That is, on the basis of information obtained from samples of a population, we attempt to draw conclusions about the population. For example, suppose a box contains six coins—four dimes and two quarters. If two coins are drawn at random from the box, then, using probability theory, we can determine the likelihood of drawing one dime and one quarter, or two dimes, or two quarters. On the other hand, suppose we do not know the breakdown of the six coins in the box, but are permitted to take a fixed number of two-coin samples in order to estimate the number of each kind. How many samples should we take in order to make an estimate, and how confident can we be in our estimate? Or suppose we have a box containing a very large number of dimes and quarters and we are allowed to take only one sample of coins in order to estimate the proportion of each kind. How large a sample should we take, and how close to the correct proportions will our estimate be? These questions are addressed by inferential statistics.

This chapter covers topics related to gathering and analyzing data, collectively called *descriptive statistics*. Chapter 8 covers the interpretation of data, or *inferential statistics*.

## 7.2 GATHERING DATA; RANDOM SAMPLES

In collecting sample data to draw conclusions about a population, it is important to obtain *random samples*. For a sample to be random, every member of the population must have the same chance of being selected as every other member. For example, if it is desired to conduct a poll to determine the proportion of all voters that favor a particular presidential candidate, then a sample of voters limited to one part of the country would not be a random sample. A sample that is not random is called a *biased sample*. For example, a household telephone survey to determine user preference of telephone service would be biased against many working people if it were conducted between 8 A.M. and 4 P.M.

Table 7-1 is a table of random numbers which can be used to obtain random samples of a given population. We first number each member of the population and then use the table to select a random sample as illustrated in Example 7.1.

### Table 7-1  Random Numbers

| | | | | | | | | | |
|---|---|---|---|---|---|---|---|---|---|
| 1 | 99546 | 63411 | 20034 | 02618 | 79807 | 01009 | 95189 | 83326 | 22097 |
| 2 | 84733 | 36948 | 14382 | 00783 | 87869 | 93515 | 87791 | 10811 | 14624 |
| 3 | 00626 | 33066 | 54898 | 61799 | 85558 | 03143 | 97708 | 42465 | 27830 |
| 4 | 88265 | 27521 | 42947 | 12179 | 01355 | 05258 | 98060 | 72237 | 93157 |
| 5 | 01256 | 55621 | 42111 | 82917 | 30763 | 51501 | 97220 | 77719 | 02881 |
| 6 | 70136 | 83781 | 14840 | 61812 | 31884 | 20508 | 09542 | 98466 | 34426 |
| 7 | 72453 | 28176 | 30174 | 50175 | 24927 | 64264 | 94618 | 39774 | 92521 |
| 8 | 98295 | 04279 | 09441 | 11385 | 07700 | 69654 | 33219 | 98540 | 88797 |
| 9 | 63262 | 86753 | 31242 | 84457 | 08573 | 71471 | 99717 | 76920 | 19809 |
| 10 | 20280 | 39836 | 38516 | 11703 | 22360 | 24039 | 33013 | 85309 | 48462 |
| 11 | 37361 | 42098 | 58728 | 65589 | 60633 | 49280 | 07718 | 07854 | 01697 |
| 12 | 35786 | 01243 | 68100 | 69599 | 15528 | 70108 | 89045 | 88222 | 47576 |
| 13 | 37091 | 30273 | 11757 | 63719 | 45059 | 32614 | 98905 | 57709 | 69774 |
| 14 | 40231 | 54406 | 74051 | 63783 | 00799 | 92951 | 08635 | 67423 | 78599 |
| 15 | 79802 | 14914 | 55220 | 86804 | 33769 | 62398 | 21873 | 73553 | 62173 |
| 16 | 94818 | 88110 | 63044 | 12430 | 30539 | 45003 | 08631 | 46658 | 00473 |
| 17 | 28603 | 25359 | 81688 | 52098 | 98168 | 17201 | 49197 | 10165 | 40419 |
| 18 | 81510 | 22910 | 11530 | 62789 | 69608 | 71740 | 36363 | 80684 | 18276 |
| 19 | 77343 | 26792 | 46384 | 00147 | 92517 | 92617 | 62437 | 62242 | 33352 |
| 20 | 99178 | 45469 | 17379 | 80485 | 20974 | 86761 | 28558 | 25708 | 41937 |
| 21 | 71698 | 86975 | 46813 | 36965 | 47720 | 07540 | 21291 | 77145 | 09478 |
| 22 | 60745 | 36139 | 61004 | 63473 | 36143 | 13745 | 04142 | 66654 | 37149 |
| 23 | 01253 | 24079 | 59775 | 14630 | 27713 | 86094 | 01111 | 45088 | 92064 |
| 24 | 11257 | 83588 | 97487 | 25534 | 28476 | 72567 | 26825 | 24654 | 29773 |
| 25 | 10081 | 81319 | 73091 | 04949 | 22155 | 58424 | 59393 | 05569 | 81966 |

**EXAMPLE 7.1**  Select a random sample of eight people from the following list of 25 students:

| | | | | | | | | | |
|---|---|---|---|---|---|---|---|---|---|
| 00 | Aaron | 05 | Consuela | 10 | Gregory | 15 | Lauren | 20 | Sabina |
| 01 | Alice | 06 | Dawn | 11 | Heather | 16 | Nicholas | 21 | Theresa |
| 02 | Alva | 07 | Dexter | 12 | Jenifer | 17 | Patrick | 22 | Thomas |
| 03 | Barry | 08 | Earle | 13 | Joel | 18 | Regina | 23 | Wendy |
| 04 | Charles | 09 | Gail | 14 | Kristi | 19 | Robert | 24 | William |

We first number the students from 00 to 24 as indicated.  Then, starting from line 10 in Table 7-1 (any place in the table will do), we partition the numbers into groups of two until we have eight numbers in the range from 00 to 24:

$$\underline{20} / 28 / \underline{03} / 98 / 36 / 38 / 51 / 61 / \underline{17} / 03 / \underline{22} / 36 /$$

$$\underline{02} / 40 / 39 / 33 / \underline{01} / 38 / 53 / \underline{09} / 48 / 46 / \underline{23}$$

Hence, Sabina, Barry, Patrick, Thomas, Alva, Alice, Gail, and Wendy are chosen.  Note that the spaces in the table, which make it easier to read, are ignored in the numbering.  Also, the number 03 appears twice in the list, but it only counts once since we want eight *different* people.  Since there were not enough numbers in the range from 00 to 24 in line 10, we went on to line 11, but we could have gone to any other line in Table 7-1.    There is no need to start at the beginning of a line, and we could proceed from one number to another by going through the columns rather than the rows, or in a random fashion.    Proceeding as we did makes it easy to check the selections.

## 7.3   DISPLAYING DATA; FREQUENCY HISTOGRAMS

After raw data have been gathered, they are systematically organized and analyzed before inferences are made.    This phase of descriptive statistics is both graphical and numerical.    Graphs and numerical summaries enable us to tell at a glance basic statistical properties of the data.

One of the first things one usually does with a large list of numerical data is to form some type of *frequency table*, which shows the number of times an individual item occurs or the number of items that fall within a given interval.    These *frequency distributions* can then be pictured as *histograms*.    We illustrate the technique with two examples.

**EXAMPLE 7.2**   An apartment house has 45 apartments, with the following numbers of tenants:

| | | | | | | | | | | | | | | |
|---|---|---|---|---|---|---|---|---|---|---|---|---|---|---|
| 2 | 1 | 3 | 5 | 2 | 2 | 2 | 1 | 4 | 2 | 6 | 2 | 4 | 3 | 1 |
| 2 | 4 | 3 | 1 | 4 | 4 | 2 | 4 | 4 | 2 | 2 | 3 | 1 | 4 | 2 |
| 3 | 1 | 5 | 2 | 4 | 1 | 3 | 2 | 4 | 4 | 2 | 5 | 1 | 3 | 4 |

Observe that the only numbers which appear in the list are 1, 2, 3, 4, 5, and 6.    The frequency distribution of these numbers appears in column 3 of Fig. 7-1.    Column 2 is the tally count.    The last column gives the *cumulative frequency*, which is obtained by adding the frequencies row by row beginning with the top row.    This column gives the number of tenant numbers not exceeding the given number.    For instance, there are 29 apartments with three or fewer tenants.

| Number of people | Tally | Frequency | Cumulative frequency |
|---|---|---|---|
| 1 | #### /// | 8 | 8 |
| 2 | #### #### //// | 14 | 22 |
| 3 | #### // | 7 | 29 |
| 4 | #### #### // | 12 | 41 |
| 5 | /// | 3 | 44 |
| 6 | / | 1 | 45 |
| | SUM | 45 | |

**Fig. 7-1**

Figure 7-2 is the histogram for the frequency distribution in Fig. 7-1.    A histogram is simply a bar graph where the height of the bar gives the number of times that the given number appears in the list.    Similarly, the cumulative frequency distribution could be presented as a histogram; the heights of the bars would be 8, 22, 29, ... , 45.

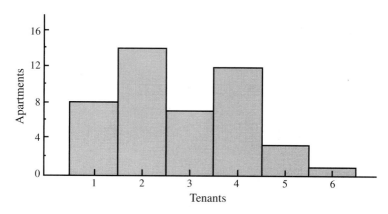

**Fig. 7-2**

**EXAMPLE 7.3**  Suppose the 6:00 P.M. temperatures (in degrees Fahrenheit) for a 35-day period are as follows:

| 72 | 78 | 86 | 93 | 106 | 107 | 98 | 82 | 81 | 77 | 87 | 82 |
| 91 | 95 | 92 | 83 | 76  | 78  | 73 | 81 | 86 | 92 | 93 | 84 |
| 107| 99 | 94 | 86 | 81  | 77  | 73 | 76 | 80 | 88 | 91 |    |

Rather than find the frequency of each individual data item, it is more useful to construct a frequency table which counts the number of times the observed temperature falls in a given class, i.e., an interval with certain limits.  This is done in Fig. 7-3.

The numbers 70, 75, 80, … are called the *class boundaries* or *class limits*.  If a data item falls on a class boundary, it is usually assigned to the higher class; e.g., the number 95° was placed in the 95–100 class.  Sometimes a frequency table

| Class boundaries, °F | Class value, °F | Tally | Frequency | Cumulative frequency |
|---|---|---|---|---|
| 70–75 | 72.5 | /// | 3 | 3 |
| 75–80 | 77.5 | ⅂⅂⅂⅂ / | 6 | 9 |
| 80–85 | 82.5 | ⅂⅂⅂⅂ /// | 8 | 17 |
| 85–90 | 87.5 | ⅂⅂⅂⅂ | 5 | 22 |
| 90–95 | 92.5 | ⅂⅂⅂⅂ // | 7 | 29 |
| 95–100 | 97.5 | /// | 3 | 32 |
| 100–105 | 102.5 | | 0 | 32 |
| 105–110 | 107.5 | /// | 3 | 35 |
| | | SUM | 35 | |

**Fig. 7-3**

also lists each *class value*, i.e., the midpoint of the class interval which serves as an approximation to the values in the interval.   The histogram corresponding to Fig. 7-3 appears in Fig. 7-4.

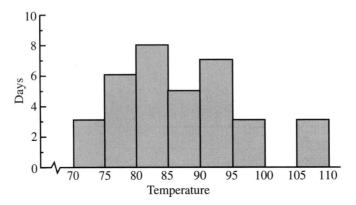

**Fig. 7-4**

The entries forming a class can be denoted in interval notation, using brackets and/or parentheses.   A bracket means the corresponding class boundary is included in the class, and a parenthesis indicates that the boundary is not included in the class.   For instance, [70, 80) contains all numbers between 70 and 80, including 70 but not 80.   Also, there is no fixed rule for the number of classes that should be formed from the data.   The fewer the number of classes, the less specific is the information displayed by the histogram.   On the other hand, a large number of classes defeats the purpose of grouping the data.

| Class | Class value | Tally | Frequency | Cumulative frequency |
|-------|-------|-------|-------|-------|
| [50, 55) | 52.5 | // | 2 | 2 |
| [55, 60) | 57.5 | // | 2 | 4 |
| [60, 65) | 62.5 | // | 2 | 6 |
| [65, 70) | 67.5 | //// | 4 | 10 |
| [70, 75) | 72.5 | ### | 5 | 15 |
| [75, 80) | 77.5 | ### // | 7 | 22 |
| [80, 85) | 82.5 | // | 2 | 24 |
| [85, 90) | 87.5 | ### / | 6 | 30 |
| [90, 95) | 92.5 | /// | 3 | 33 |
| [95, 100] | 97.5 | // | 2 | 35 |
|  |  | SUM | 35 |  |

**Fig. 7-5**

**EXAMPLE 7.4** Find a frequency distribution and its corresponding frequency histogram by partitioning the following 35 test scores into: (a) ten, (b) five, (c) two classes.

| | | | | | | |
|---|---|---|---|---|---|---|
| 75 | 65 | 73 | 54 | 86 | 93 | 77 |
| 67 | 86 | 50 | 72 | 75 | 68 | 95 |
| 84 | 58 | 85 | 75 | 77 | 90 | 62 |
| 88 | 74 | 55 | 87 | 70 | 60 | 83 |
| 71 | 91 | 66 | 76 | 79 | 89 | 97 |

(a) The scores are between 50 and 100, so we use 5 units for the class width. We obtain the frequency distribution in Fig. 7-5, where the interval notation is used to denote the classes. Figure 7-6 is the corresponding histogram.

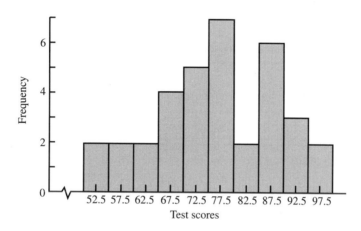

**Fig. 7-6**

(b) The frequency distribution is given in Fig. 7-7 and the corresponding histogram in Fig. 7-8.

| Class | Class value | Tally | Frequency | Cumulative frequency |
|---|---|---|---|---|
| [50, 60) | 55 | //// | 4 | 4 |
| [60, 70) | 65 | ⧵⧵⧵ / | 6 | 10 |
| [70, 80) | 75 | ⧵⧵⧵ ⧵⧵⧵ // | 12 | 22 |
| [80, 90) | 85 | ⧵⧵⧵ /// | 8 | 30 |
| [90, 100] | 95 | ⧵⧵⧵ | 5 | 35 |
| | | SUM | 35 | |

**Fig. 7-7**

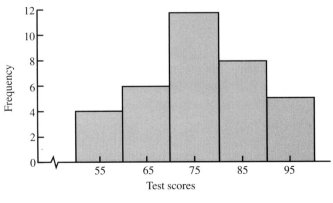

**Fig. 7-8**

(c)  The frequency distribution is given in Fig. 7-9 and the corresponding histogram in Fig. 7-10.

| Class | Class value | Tally | Frequency | Cumulative frequency |
|-------|-------------|-------|-----------|----------------------|
| [50, 75) | 62.5 | ### ### ### | 15 | 15 |
| [75, 100) | 87.5 | ### ### ### ### | 20 | 35 |
| | | SUM | 35 | |

**Fig. 7-9**

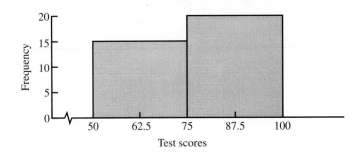

**Fig. 7-10**

## 7.4  MEASURES OF CENTRAL TENDENCY; SAMPLE MEAN AND MEDIAN

In addition to graphical descriptions of data, there are numerical descriptions.  Numbers such as the mean and median give, in some sense, the central or middle values of the data.  Other numbers, such as variance and quartiles, measure the dispersion or spread of the data about the mean and median, respectively.  We study numerical measures of central tendency in this section and measures of dispersion in Sec. 7.5.

The data, for the most part, are assumed to form a random sample of a larger population which is a probability space.  To distinguish between the two classes, we will use the terms (notation) *sample mean* $(\bar{x})$, *sample variance* $(s^2)$, *population mean* $(\mu)$, and *population variance* $(\sigma^2)$, respectively.

**Mean**

Suppose a sample consists of the eight numbers

$$7, \qquad 11, \qquad 11, \qquad 8, \qquad 12, \qquad 7, \qquad 6, \qquad 6$$

The sample mean $\bar{x}$ is defined to be the sum of the values divided by the number of values; that is,

$$\bar{x} = \frac{7 + 11 + 11 + 8 + 12 + 7 + 6 + 6}{8} = \frac{68}{8} = 8.5$$

In general, if $x_1, x_2, \ldots, x_n$ are $n$ numerical values, then the *sample mean* is

$$\bar{x} = \frac{x_1 + x_2 + \cdots + x_n}{n} = \frac{\sum x_i}{n} \qquad\qquad (7.1)$$

Now suppose that the data are organized into a frequency table; let there be $k$ *distinct* numerical values $x_1$, $x_2, \ldots, x_k$, occurring with respective frequencies $f_1, f_2, \ldots, f_k$. Then the product $f_1 x_1$ gives the sum of the $x_1$'s, $f_2 x_2$ gives the sum of the $x_2$'s, and so on. Also:

$$f_1 + f_2 + \cdots + f_k = n$$

the total number of data items. Hence, formula $(7.1)$ can be rewritten as

$$\bar{x} = \frac{f_1 x_1 + f_2 x_2 + \cdots + f_k x_k}{f_1 + f_2 + \cdots + f_k} = \frac{\sum f_i x_i}{\sum f_i} \qquad\qquad (7.2)$$

Conversely, formula $(7.2)$ reduces to formula $(7.1)$ in the special case $k = n$ and all $f_i = 1$.

For data organized into classes, $(7.2)$ is applied with $f_i$ as the number of data items in the $i$th class and $x_i$ as the $i$th class value.

## EXAMPLE 7.5

($a$)  Consider the data of Example 7.2 of which the frequency distribution is given in Fig. 7-1. The mean is

$$\bar{x} = \frac{8(1) + 14(2) + 7(3) + 12(4) + 3(5) + 1(6)}{45} = \frac{126}{45} = 2.8$$

In other words, there is an average of 2.8 people living in an apartment.

($b$)  Consider the data of Example 7.3, of which the frequency distribution is given in Fig. 7-3. Using the class values as approximations to the original values, we obtain

$$\bar{x} = \frac{3(72.5) + 6(77.5) + 8(82.5) + 5(87.5) + 7(92.5) + 3(97.5) + 0(102.5) + 3(107.5)}{35} = \frac{3042.5}{35} \approx 86.9$$

i.e., the mean 6:00 P.M. temperature is approximately 86.9 degrees Fahrenheit.

**Median**

Consider a collection of $n$ data values which are sorted in increasing order. The *median* of the data is the "middle value." That is, if $n$ is odd, then the median is the $[(n + 1)/2]$th term; but if $n$ is even, then the median is the average of the $(n/2)$th and $[(n/2) + 1]$th terms. For example, consider the following two lists of sorted numbers:

$$\text{List A: 11, 11, 16, 17, 25}$$

$$\text{List B: 1, 4, 8, 8, 10, 16, 16, 19}$$

List A has five terms; its median is 16, the middle or third term. List B has eight terms; its median is 9, the average of the fourth term, 8, and the fifth term, 10. For any collection of data values (sorted or not), we note that just as many of the numbers are less than or equal to the median as are greater than or equal to the median. The cumulative frequency distribution can be used to find the median of an arbitrary set of data.

**EXAMPLE 7.6**

($a$)  Consider the data in Fig. 7-1.  There are $n = 45$ values.  The cumulative frequency column tells us that the median is 3, the 23rd value.

($b$)  Consider the data in Fig. 7-3.  The median is 87.5, the approximate 18th value.

Although the mean and median each locate, in some sense, the center of the data, the mean is sensitive to the *magnitude* of the values on either side of it, whereas the median is sensitive only to the *number* of values on either side of it.

**EXAMPLE 7.7**  The owner of a small company has 15 employees.  Five employees earn \$25,000 per year, seven earn \$30,000, three earn \$40,000, and the owner's annual salary is \$153,000.  ($a$)  Find the mean and median salaries of all 16 persons in the company.  ($b$)  Find the mean and median salaries if the owner's salary is increased by \$80,000.

($a$)  The mean salary is

$$\bar{x} = \frac{5 \cdot 25{,}000 + 7 \cdot 30{,}000 + 3 \cdot 40{,}000 + 153{,}000}{16}$$

$$= \frac{608{,}000}{16} = \$38{,}000$$

Since there are 16 persons, the median is the average of the eighth $\left(\frac{16}{2}\right)$ and ninth $\left(\frac{16}{2} + 1\right)$ salaries when the salaries are arranged in increasing order from left to right.  The eighth and ninth salaries are each \$30,000.  Therefore, the median is

$$M = \$30{,}000$$

($b$)  The new mean salary is

$$\bar{x} = \frac{608{,}000 + 80{,}000}{16} = \frac{688{,}000}{16} = \$43{,}000$$

The median $M$ is still \$30,000, the average of the eighth and ninth salaries, which did not change.  Hence, the mean moves in the direction of the increased salary, but the median does not change.

## 7.5  MEASURES OF DISPERSION; SAMPLE VARIANCE AND STANDARD DEVIATION

Consider the following two samples of numerical values:

$$A: 12, 10, 9, 9, 10$$

$$B: 5, 10, 16, 15, 4$$

For both A and B, the sample mean is $\bar{x} = 10$.  However, observe that the values in A are clustered more closely about the mean than the values in B.  To distinguish between A and B in this regard, we define a measure of the dispersion or spread of the values about the mean, called the *sample variance*, and its square root, called the *sample standard deviation*.

Let $\bar{x}$ be the sample mean of the $n$ values $x_1, x_2, \ldots, x_n$.  The difference $x_i - \bar{x}$ is called the *deviation* of the data value about the mean $\bar{x}$; it is positive or negative according as $x_i$ is greater or less than $\bar{x}$.  To avoid canceling of positive and negative deviations, we square the deviation obtaining $(x_i - \bar{x})^2$.  Then the sample variance $s^2$ is defined by

$$s^2 = \frac{(x_1 - \bar{x})^2 + (x_2 - \bar{x})^2 + \cdots + (x_n - \bar{x})^2}{n - 1} \tag{7.3}$$

$$= \frac{\Sigma (x_i - \bar{x})^2}{n - 1}$$

The sample standard deviation $s$ is the nonnegative square root of the sample variance:

$$s = \sqrt{s^2} \tag{7.4}$$

Since each squared deviation is nonnegative, so is $s^2$.   Moreover, $s^2$ is zero precisely when each data value $x_i$ is equal to $\bar{x}$.   The more spread out the data values are, the larger the sample variance and standard deviation will be.

**EXAMPLE 7.8**   In A above, the sample variance and standard deviation are

$$s^2 = \frac{(12 - 10)^2 + (10 - 10)^2 + (9 - 10)^2 + (9 - 10)^2 + (10 - 10)^2}{4}$$

$$= \frac{6}{4} = 1.5$$

and

$$s = \sqrt{1.5} \approx 1.22$$

In B, we have

$$s^2 = \frac{(5 - 10)^2 + (10 - 10)^2 + (16 - 10)^2 + (15 - 10)^2 + (4 - 10)^2}{4}$$

$$= \frac{122}{4} = 30.5$$

and

$$s = \sqrt{30.5} \approx 5.52$$

Note that B, which exhibits more dispersion than A, has a much larger variance and standard deviation than A.

**Remark:**   It may seem more natural to divide by $n$ than by $n - 1$ in formula (7.3), and some statisticians do define $s^2$ this way.   However, we are primarily interested in using the sample variance $s^2$ to estimate the population variance $\sigma^2$ (as defined in Sec. 6.7) when the data are approximately normally distributed (see Sec. 8.3), and in this case the probability that $s^2$ is equal to $\sigma^2$ is higher with $n - 1$ than with $n$ in the denominator.

A formula equivalent to (7.3) is

$$s^2 = \frac{\Sigma x_i^2 - (\Sigma x_i)^2/n}{n - 1} \tag{7.5}$$

Although formula (7.5) may look more complicated than formula (7.3), it is actually more convenient than formula (7.3) for computing $s^2$ when the data are given in tabular form.

**EXAMPLE 7.9**   Use formula (7.5) to find the sample variance for the values 3, 5, 8, 9, 10, 12, 13, 15, and 20.

We first construct the following table:

| | | | | | | | | | | Sum |
|---|---|---|---|---|---|---|---|---|---|---|
| $x_i$ | 3 | 5 | 8 | 9 | 10 | 12 | 13 | 15 | 20 | 95 |
| $x_i^2$ | 9 | 25 | 64 | 81 | 100 | 144 | 169 | 225 | 400 | 1217 |

Then, by formula (7.5), where $n = 9$,

$$s^2 = \frac{1217 - (95)^2/9}{8} \approx \frac{1217 - 1002.7778}{8} \approx 26.78$$

For $n$ data items organized into a frequency distribution consisting of $k$ distinct values $x_1, x_2, \ldots, x_k$ with respective frequencies $f_1, f_2, \ldots, f_k$, the product $f_i (x_i - \bar{x})^2$ gives the sum of the squares of the deviations of each $x_i$ from $\bar{x}$.   Also, $f_1 + f_2 + \cdots + f_k = n$.   Hence, we can rewrite formulas (7.3) and (7.5) as

$$s^2 = \frac{f_1(x_1 - \bar{x})^2 + f_2(x_2 - \bar{x}^2) + \cdots + f_k(x_k - \bar{x})^2}{(f_1 + f_2 + \cdots + f_k) - 1} = \frac{\Sigma f_i(x_i - \bar{x})^2}{(\Sigma f_i) - 1} \tag{7.6}$$

and

$$s^2 = \frac{\Sigma f_i x_i^2 - (\Sigma f_i x_i)^2 / \Sigma f_i}{(\Sigma f_i) - 1} \tag{7.7}$$

**EXAMPLE 16.10**  For the data in Example 7.2, Fig. 7-1 is modified into Fig. 7-11 by the addition of columns for $x_i^2$ and $f_i x_i^2$.  We then obtain, using formula (7.7),

$$s^2 = \frac{430 - (126)^2/45}{44} \approx 1.75 \qquad \text{and} \qquad s \approx 1.32$$

| Number of people, $x_i$ | Frequency, $f_i$ | $f_i x_i$ | $x_i^2$ | $f_i x_i^2$ |
|:---:|:---:|:---:|:---:|:---:|
| 1 | 8 | 8 | 1 | 8 |
| 2 | 14 | 28 | 4 | 56 |
| 3 | 7 | 21 | 9 | 63 |
| 4 | 12 | 48 | 16 | 192 |
| 5 | 3 | 15 | 25 | 75 |
| 6 | 1 | 6 | 36 | 36 |
| Sums | 45 | 126 | | 430 |

**Fig. 7-11**

If the data are organized into classes, we use the $i$th class value for $x_i$ in formula (7.7).

**EXAMPLE 7.11**  Three hundred incoming students take a mathematics exam consisting of 75 multiple-choice questions. If the distribution of the scores on the exam is

| Test scores | 5–15 | 15–25 | 25–35 | 35–45 | 45–55 | 55–65 | 65–75 |
|:---|:---:|:---:|:---:|:---:|:---:|:---:|:---:|
| Number of students | 2 | 0 | 8 | 36 | 110 | 78 | 66 |

find the sample varaince $s^2$ and the standard deviation $s$ of the distribution.
    We first enter the data in Fig. 7-12.  Then, by formula (7.7),

$$s^2 = \frac{944,200 - (16,500)^2/300}{299} \approx 122.74 \qquad \text{and} \qquad s \approx 11.08$$

| Class limits | Class value, $x_i$ | Frequency, $f_i$ | $f_i x_i$ | $x_i^2$ | $f_i x_i^2$ |
|---|---|---|---|---|---|
| 5–15 | 10 | 2 | 20 | 100 | 200 |
| 15–25 | 20 | 0 | 0 | 400 | 0 |
| 25–35 | 30 | 8 | 240 | 400 | 7,200 |
| 35–45 | 40 | 36 | 1,440 | 1600 | 57,600 |
| 45–55 | 50 | 110 | 5,500 | 2500 | 275,000 |
| 55–65 | 60 | 78 | 4,680 | 3600 | 280,800 |
| 65–75 | 70 | 66 | 4,620 | 4900 | 323,400 |
| Sums |  | 300 | 16,500 |  | 944,200 |

**Fig. 7-12**

## Standard Units

The standard deviation is a measure of the deviation of the data from the mean. In many distributions, most of the data will be within 1 standard deviation of the mean and almost all of the data will be within 2 standard deviations of the mean. For instance, if the data are a sufficiently large sample from a normal population, then about 68 percent of the values are in the interval $[\bar{x} - s, \bar{x} + s]$ and about 95 percent are in $[\bar{x} - 2s, \bar{x} + 2s]$ (see Example 6.21).

Standard units are a convenient way to describe data values in terms of their respective number of standard deviations from the mean. For example, suppose a sample has mean $\bar{x} = 70$ and standard deviation $s = 10$. Then a data value of 90 is 20 units or 2 standard deviations to the right of the mean, and a data value of 55 is 15 or 1.5 standard deviations to the left of the mean. In terms of standard units

$$z = \frac{x - \bar{x}}{s} = \frac{x - 70}{10}$$

the mean value 70 changes to zero, and the values 90 and 55 in standard units become 2 and $-1.5$, respectively.

**EXAMPLE 7.12**  A student got 85 in a test whose scores had mean 79 and standard deviation 8. In a second test, where the scores had mean 70 and standard deviation 5, the student got 74. In which test did the student get the higher standard score?

The first standard score is

$$z = \frac{85 - 79}{8} = \frac{6}{8} = 0.75$$

and the second is

$$z = \frac{74 - 70}{4} = \frac{4}{5} = 0.8$$

Hence, the second standard score is higher.

## 7.6  MEASURES OF POSITION; QUARTILES AND PERCENTILES

We have discussed numerical measures of central tendency and of dispersion for a sample of data values, and now we consider numerical measures of position within the values when they are arranged in increasing order.

### Quartiles

The median $M$ of $n$ data values arranged in increasing order has been defined as a number for which at most half the values are less than $M$ and at most half are greater than $M$.  Here, "half" means $n/2$ if $n$ is even and $(n - 1)/2$ if $n$ is odd.  The *lower quartile, $Q_L$*, is defined as the median of the first half of the values, and the *upper quartile, $Q_U$*, is the median of the second half.  Hence, about one-quarter of the data values are less than $Q_L$ and three-quarters are greater than $Q_L$.  Similarly, about three-quarters are less than $Q_U$, and one-quarter are greater than $Q_u$.  The *middle quartile,* is defined to be the median $M$.

**EXAMPLE 7.13**  Find $Q_L$, $M$, and $Q_U$ for the data

$$2 \qquad 5 \qquad 3 \qquad 4 \qquad 7 \qquad 0 \qquad 11 \qquad 2 \qquad 3 \qquad 8$$

We first arrange the values in increasing order:

$$0 \qquad 2 \qquad 2 \qquad 3 \qquad 3 \qquad 4 \qquad 5 \qquad 7 \qquad 8 \qquad 11$$

Since $n = 10$, the median, $M$, is the average of the fifth and sixth value:

$$M = \frac{3 + 4}{2} = 3.5$$

$Q_L$ is the median of the values 0, 2, 2, 3, 3 and hence, $Q_L = 2$.
$Q_U$ is the median of the values 4, 5, 7, 8, 11 and hence, $Q_U = 7$.

### Percentiles

Suppose $n$ data values are arranged in increasing order.  A *kth percentile, $P_k$*, is a number for which at most $k$ percent of the values are less than $P_k$ and at most $(100 - k)$ percent are greater than $P_k$.  To define $P_k$, first compute $kn/100$ and break it into its integer part $I$ and decimal part $D$.  That is:

$$\frac{kn}{100} = I + D$$

If $D \neq 0$, then $P_k =$ the $(I + 1)$th value.

If $D = 0$, then $P_k = \dfrac{I\text{th value} + (I + 1)\text{th value}}{2}$.

**EXAMPLE 7.14**  Given 50 data values arranged in increasing order, find (*a*) $P_{35}$ and (*b*) $P_{30}$.

(*a*)  $n = 50, k = 35$.  Thus:

$$\frac{kn}{100} = \frac{35 \cdot 50}{100} = \frac{35}{2} = 17.5 = 17 + 0.5$$

Here, $I = 17$ and $D = 0.5$.  Since $D \neq 0$, $P_{35} =$ the 18th value.

(*b*)  $n = 50, k = 30$.  Thus:

$$\frac{kn}{100} = \frac{30 \cdot 50}{100} = \frac{30}{2} = 15 = 15 + 0$$

Here, $I = 15$ and $D = 0$.  Since $D = 0$:

$$P_{30} = \frac{15\text{th value} + 16\text{th value}}{2}$$

**EXAMPLE 7.15**   Use the results of Example 7.14 to find $P_{35}$ and $P_{30}$ for the 50 values below:

| 10 | 20 | 35 | 44 | 55 | 64 | 75 | 81 | 87 | 99  |
|----|----|----|----|----|----|----|----|----|-----|
| 11 | 22 | 36 | 48 | 56 | 68 | 76 | 82 | 89 | 101 |
| 13 | 23 | 38 | 49 | 57 | 69 | 76 | 83 | 90 | 102 |
| 15 | 23 | 41 | 50 | 60 | 70 | 78 | 83 | 94 | 105 |
| 18 | 30 | 44 | 50 | 63 | 73 | 80 | 85 | 96 | 107 |

By Example 7.14, $P_{35}$ = the 18th value = 49, and

$$P_{30} = \frac{\text{15th value} + \text{16th value}}{2} = \frac{44 + 44}{2} = 44$$

**EXAMPLE 7.16**   Find (a) $P_{25}$, (b) $P_{50}$, and (c) $P_{75}$ for the data in Example 7.15.   Compare these values with $Q_L$, $M$, and $Q_U$, respectively.

(a)   $n = 50, k = 25$.   Thus:

$$\frac{kn}{100} = \frac{25 \cdot 50}{100} = \frac{25}{2} = 12.5 = 12 + 0.5$$

Since $D = 0.5 \neq 0$, $P_{25}$ = the 13th value = 38.   $Q_L$ is the median of the first 25 values, which is the 13th value, or 38. Hence, $Q_L = P_{25}$.

(b)   $n = 50, k = 50$.   Thus:

$$\frac{kn}{100} = \frac{50 \cdot 50}{100} = 25 = 25 + 0$$

Since $D = 0$, $P_{50} = \dfrac{\text{25th value} + \text{26th value}}{2} = \dfrac{63 + 64}{2} = 63.5$.   $M$ is the median of the 50 values, which is the same as $P_{50}$.

(c)   $n = 50, k = 75$.   Thus:

$$\frac{kn}{100} = \frac{75 \cdot 50}{100} = 37.5 = 37 + 0.5$$

Here $D = 0.5 \neq 0$.   Hence, $P_{75}$ = the 38th value = 83.   $Q_U$ is the median of the last 25 values, which is the 13th of these, or 83.   Hence, $Q_U = P_{75}$.

As illustrated in Example 7.16, quartiles and percentiles are related by the equations

$$Q_L = P_{25} \qquad M = P_{50} \qquad \text{and} \qquad Q_U = P_{75}$$

## 7.7  BIVARIATE DATA, SCATTERPLOTS, AND LINEAR REGRESSION

Quite often in statistics it is desired to determine the relationship, if any, between two variables, for example, between age and weight, weight and height, years of education and salary, amount of daily exercise and cholesterol level, etc.   As with data for a single variable, we can describe bivariate data both graphically and numerically.   In both cases we will be primarily concerned with determining whether there is a *linear* relationship between the two variables under consideration.

It should be kept in mind that a statistical relationship between two variables does not necessarily imply there is a *causal* relationship between them.   For example, a strong relationship between weight and height does not imply that either variable causes the other.

**Scatterplots**

Consider the following data which relate $x$, the respective number of branches that 10 different banks have in a given metropolitan area, with $y$, the corresponding market share of total deposits held by the banks:

| $x$ | 198 | 186 | 116 | 89 | 120 | 109 | 28 | 58 | 34 | 31 |
|-----|------|------|------|------|------|------|------|------|------|------|
| $y$ | 22.7 | 16.6 | 15.9 | 12.5 | 10.2 | 6.8 | 6.8 | 4.0 | 2.7 | 2.8 |

If each point $(x, y)$ of the data is plotted in an $x$, $y$ coordinate plane, the *scatterplot* shown in Fig. 7-13 is obtained.

The scatterplot in Fig. 7-13 indicates that, roughly speaking, the market share increases as the number of branches increases.    We say that $x$ and $y$ have a *positive correlation*.

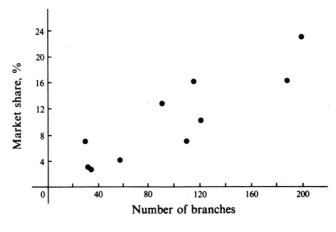

**Fig. 7-13**

On the other hand, when the data below, which relate average daily temperature $x$, in degrees Fahrenheit, and daily natural gas consumption $y$, in cubic feet, are plotted in Fig. 7-14 we see that $y$ tends to decrease as $x$ increases.    Here, $x$ and $y$ have a *negative correlation*.

| $x$, ° F | 50 | 45 | 40 | 38 | 32 | 40 | 55 |
|-----------|-----|-----|-----|-----|-----|-----|-----|
| $y$, ft$^3$ | 2.5 | 5.0 | 6.2 | 7.4 | 8.3 | 4.7 | 1.8 |

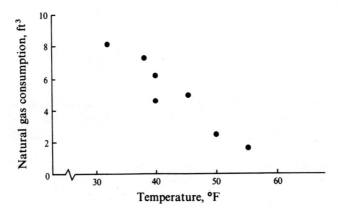

**Fig. 7-14**

Finally, when the data items $(x, y)$ below, which relate daily temperature $x$ over a 10-day period to the Dow Jones stock average $y$, are plotted in Fig. 7-15, there is no apparent relationship between $x$ and $y$:

| | | | | |
|---|---|---|---|---|
| (63, 3385) | (72, 3330) | (76, 3325) | (70, 3320) | (71, 3330) |
| (65, 3325) | (70, 3280) | (74, 3280) | (68, 3300) | (61, 3265) |

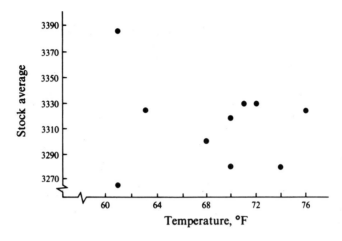

**Fig. 7-15**

## Sample Correlation Coefficient

Scatterplots indicate graphically whether there is a linear relationship between two variables $x$ and $y$. A numeric indicator of a linear relationship is the *sample correlation coefficient* $r$ of $x$ and $y$, which is defined as follows:

$$r = \frac{\Sigma (x_i - \bar{x}) (y_i - \bar{y})}{\sqrt{\Sigma (x_i - \bar{x})^2 \, \Sigma (y_i - \bar{y})^2}} \tag{7.8}$$

We assume that the denominator in formula $(7.8)$ is not zero. It can then be shown that the sample correlation coefficient has the following properties:

(1) $-1 \le r \le 1$.

(2) $r$ is positive if $y$ tends to increase as $x$ increases; $r$ is negative if $y$ tends to decrease as $x$ increases.

(3) The stronger the linear relationship between $x$ and $y$, the closer $r$ is to 1 or $-1$; the weaker the linear relationship is, the closer $r$ is to zero.

Formula $(7.8)$ can be written in more compact form as

$$r = \frac{s_{xy}}{s_x s_y} \tag{7.9}$$

where $s_x$ and $s_y$ are the sample standard deviations of $x$ and $y$, respectively [see formulas $(7.3)$ and $(7.4)$], and where

$$s_{xy} = \frac{\Sigma (x_i - \bar{x}) (y_i - \bar{y})}{n - 1} \tag{7.10}$$

which is called the *sample covariance* of $x$ and $y$. Also, for computing $r$, a more convenient formula is

$$r = \frac{\Sigma x_i y_i - (\Sigma x_i) (\Sigma y_i)/n}{\sqrt{\Sigma x_i^2 - (\Sigma x_i)^2/n} \; \sqrt{\Sigma y_i^2 - (\Sigma y_i)^2/n}} \tag{7.11}$$

**EXAMPLE 7.17** Compute $r$ for the data corresponding to (a) Fig. 7-13, (b) Fig. 7-14, and (c) Fig. 7-15. In all three cases, we first construct a table of values from the data and then apply formula (7.11).

(a)

| $x_i$ | $y_i$ | $x_i^2$ | $y_i^2$ | $x_iy_i$ |
|---|---|---|---|---|
| 198 | 22.7 | 39,204 | 515.29 | 4494.6 |
| 186 | 16.6 | 34,596 | 275.56 | 3087.6 |
| 116 | 15.9 | 13,456 | 252.81 | 1844.4 |
| 89 | 12.5 | 7,921 | 156.25 | 1112.5 |
| 120 | 10.2 | 14,400 | 104.04 | 1224.0 |
| 109 | 6.8 | 11,881 | 46.24 | 741.2 |
| 28 | 6.8 | 784 | 46.24 | 190.4 |
| 58 | 4.0 | 3,364 | 16.00 | 232.0 |
| 34 | 2.7 | 1,156 | 7.29 | 91.8 |
| 31 | 2.8 | 961 | 7.84 | 86.8 |
| **Sums** 969 | 101.0 | 127,723 | 1427.56 | 13,105.3 |

$$r = \frac{13,105.3 - (969)(101)/10}{\sqrt{127,723 - (969)^2/10}\ \sqrt{1427.56 - (101)^2/10}} \approx .8938$$

Note that $r$ is close to 1, which is to be expected since the scatterplot in Fig. 7-13 indicates a strong positive linear relationship between $x$ and $y$.

(b)

| $x_i$ | $y_i$ | $x_i^2$ | $y_i^2$ | $x_iy_i$ |
|---|---|---|---|---|
| 50 | 2.5 | 2,500 | 6.25 | 125.0 |
| 45 | 5.0 | 2,025 | 25.00 | 225.0 |
| 40 | 6.2 | 1,600 | 38.44 | 248.0 |
| 38 | 7.4 | 1,444 | 54.76 | 281.2 |
| 32 | 8.3 | 1,024 | 68.89 | 265.6 |
| 40 | 4.7 | 1,600 | 22.09 | 188.0 |
| 55 | 1.8 | 3,025 | 3.24 | 99.0 |
| **Sums** 300 | 35.9 | 13,218 | 218.67 | 1431.8 |

$$r = \frac{1431.8 - (300)(35.9)/7}{\sqrt{13,218 - (300)^2/7}\ \sqrt{218.67 - (35.9)^2/7}} \approx -.9562$$

Here, $r$ is close to $-1$, and the scatterplot in Fig. 7-14 shows a strong negative linear relationship between $x$ and $y$.

(c)

| $x_i$ | $y_i$ | $x_i^2$ | $y_i^2$ | $x_i y_i$ |
|---|---|---|---|---|
| 63 | 3,385 | 3969 | 11,458,225 | 213,255 |
| 72 | 3,330 | 5184 | 11,088,900 | 239,760 |
| 76 | 3,325 | 5776 | 11,055,625 | 252,700 |
| 70 | 3,320 | 4900 | 11,022,400 | 232,400 |
| 71 | 3,330 | 5041 | 11,088,900 | 236,430 |
| 65 | 3,325 | 4225 | 11,055,625 | 216,125 |
| 70 | 3,280 | 4900 | 10,758,400 | 229,600 |
| 74 | 3,280 | 5476 | 10,758,400 | 242,720 |
| 68 | 3,300 | 4624 | 10,890,000 | 224,400 |
| 61 | 3,265 | 3721 | 10,660,225 | 199,165 |
| **Sums** 690 | 33,140 | 47816 | 109,836,700 | 2,286,555 |

$$r = \frac{2{,}286{,}555 - (690)(33{,}140)/10}{\sqrt{47{,}816 - (690)^2/10}\ \sqrt{109{,}836{,}700 - (33{,}140)^2/10}} \approx -.0706$$

Here, $r$ is close to zero, and the scatterplot in Fig. 7-15 indicates no linear relationship.

### Line of Best Fit

If a scatterplot of data points $(x_i, y_i)$ indicates that there is a linear relationship between $x$ and $y$, then the next step is to find a line that, in some sense, fits the data. In Fig. 7-16, a nonvertical line $L: y = a + bx$, is drawn through a scatterplot. For each data point $(x_i, y_i)$, let $y_i^* = a + bx_i$; that is, $y_i^*$ is the $y$ value of the point on $L$ corresponding to $x_i$. The difference $d_i = y_i - y_i^*$ is positive if $(x_i, y_i)$ is above line $L$, negative if $(x_i, y_i)$ is below $L$, and zero if $(x_i, y_i)$ is on $L$. The sum

$$\Sigma\, d_i^2 = d_1^2 + d_2^2 + \cdots + d_n^2$$

is called the *squares error* of $L$. (The $d_i$'s are squared so that negative values do not cancel positive values when added.)

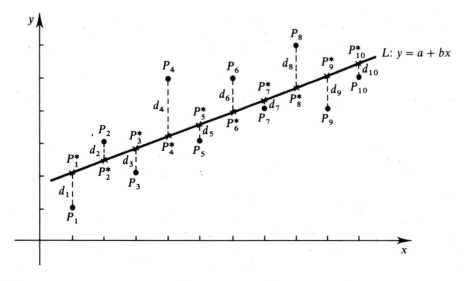

**Fig. 7-16** $P_i$ is the data point $(x_i, y_i)$ and $P_i^*$ is the point $(x_i, y_i^*)$ on $L$, where $y_i^* = a + bx_i$ $(i = 1, 2, \ldots, 10)$.

The *line of best fit*, also called the *least-squares line* or the *regression line*, is by definition the line whose squares error is as small as possible.   It can be shown that there is a unique line of best fit, and its equation is

$$y = a + bx \qquad\qquad (7.12)$$

where the *slope b* and *y intercept a* are given by

$$b = \frac{rs_y}{s_x} \qquad \text{and} \qquad a = \bar{y} - b\bar{x} \qquad\qquad (7.13)$$

The second equation in (7.13) says that the point $(\bar{x}, \bar{y})$ lies on the regression line $L$ [because $\bar{y} = (\bar{y} - b\bar{x}) + b\bar{x} = a + b\bar{x}$], and the first equation says that the point $(\bar{x} + s_x, \bar{y} + rs_y)$ is also on $L$ (see Fig. 7-17).

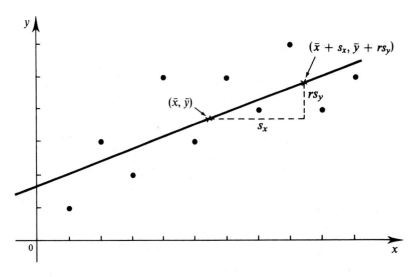

**Fig. 7-17**

**EXAMPLE 7.18**   Use the computations in Example 7.17 to find the line of best fit for the scatterplot in (*a*) Fig. 7-13 and (*b*) Fig. 7-14.   In each case, graph the line of best fit through the scatterplot.

(*a*)   From Example 7.17(*a*), $r = .8938$, $\bar{x} = 969/10 = 96.9$, $\bar{y} = 101/10 = 10.1$, and, using formulas (7.4) and (7.5):

$$s_x = \sqrt{\frac{127{,}723 - (969)^2/10}{9}} = 61.3070$$

and

$$s_y = \sqrt{\frac{1427.56 - (101)^2/10}{9}} = 6.7285$$

Substituting these values in formulas (7.13), we get

$$b = \frac{(.8938)(6.7285)}{61.3070} = 0.0981$$

and

$$a = 10.1 - (0.0981)(96.9) = 0.5941$$

Hence, the line $L$ of best fit is

$$y = 0.5941 + 0.0981x$$

To graph $L$, we need plot only two points lying on $L$ and then draw the line through these points.   Since $(0, a)$ and $(\bar{x}, \bar{y})$ are always on the line of best fit, we plot $(0, 0.5941)$ and $(96.9, 10.1)$ (approximately), and then draw $L$, as shown in Fig. 7-18(*a*).

(b)  From Example 7.17(b), $r = -.9562$, $\bar{x} = 300/7 = 42.8571$, $\bar{y} = 35.9/7 = 5.1286$, and by formulas (7.4) and (7.5):

$$s_x = \sqrt{\frac{13{,}218 - (300)^2/7}{6}} = 7.7552$$

and

$$s_y = \sqrt{\frac{218.67 - (35.9)^2/7}{6}} = 2.3998$$

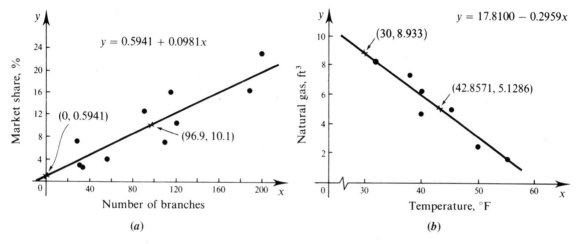

**Fig. 7-18**

Substituting in formulas (7.13) gives

$$b = \frac{(-0.9562)(2.3998)}{7.7552} = -0.2959$$

and

$$a = 5.1286 - (-0.2959)(42.8571) = 17.8100$$

Therefore, the line $L$ of best fit is

$$y = 17.8100 - 0.2959x$$

The graph of $L$, obtained by plotting (30, 8.933) and (42.8571, 5.1286) (approximately) and drawing the line through these points, is shown in Fig. 7-18(b).

# Solved Problems

## RANDOM SAMPLES

**7.1.** A psychology professor wishes to interview 10 of the 50 students in her class to obtain their opinions about the course content and its presentation. She asks for 10 volunteers for the survey. Why do these 10 not form a random sample?

Some students are more likely to volunteer than others, which means that not every student is as likely to be chosen as every other student. Hence, the sample is biased. A biased sample of this type is called a *voluntary-response sample*.

**7.2.** A pharmaceutical company wishes to test a new drug for relieving depression on 30 people suffering from the malady. However, there is a tendency, called the *placebo* effect, for patients to respond favorably to any type of drug, even if it contains no active ingredients. How can the test be conducted in such a way as to nullify the bias caused by the placebo effect?

From a group of 60 people suffering from depression, 30 are chosen at random to be given the drug. The remaining 30, which form the *control group*, are given an inactive drug. No person in either group knows which drug he or she is receiving. The placebo effect applies equally to both groups and is thereby nullified.

**7.3.** Use the table of random numbers (Table 7-1) starting at line (*a*) 7, (*b*) 15, and (*c*) 22 to find a random sample of seven different numbers and the corresponding names from the following list of United States presidents:

| | | | | | |
|---|---|---|---|---|---|
| 01 | George Washington | 02 | John Adams | 03 | Thomas Jefferson |
| 04 | James Madison | 05 | James Monroe | 06 | John Quincy Adams |
| 07 | Andrew Jackson | 08 | Martin Van Buren | 09 | William Harrison |
| 10 | John Tyler | 11 | James Polk | 12 | Zachary Taylor |
| 13 | Millard Fillmore | 14 | Franklin Pierce | 15 | James Buchanan |
| 16 | Abraham Lincoln | 17 | Andrew Johnson | 18 | Ulysses Grant |
| 19 | Rutherford Hayes | 20 | James Garfield | 21 | Chester Arthur |
| 22 | Grover Cleveland | 23 | Benjamin Harrison | 24 | Grover Cleveland |
| 25 | William McKinley | 26 | Theodore Roosevelt | 27 | Willian Taft |
| 28 | Woodrow Wilson | 29 | Warren Harding | 30 | Calvin Coolidge |
| 31 | Herbert Hoover | 32 | Franklin Roosevelt | 33 | Harry Truman |
| 34 | Dwight Eisenhower | 35 | John Kennedy | 36 | Lyndon Johnson |
| 37 | Richard Nixon | 38 | Gerald Ford | 39 | Jimmy Carter |
| 40 | Ronald Reagan | 41 | George Bush | 42 | Bill Clinton |

Since the list contains only two-digit numbers, we break the random numbers in the table up into groups of two, starting at the designated place, until five different numbers in the range 01 to 42 are found.

(*a*) Starting at line 7, we get

72  45  <u>32</u>  81  76  <u>30</u>  <u>17</u>  45  <u>01</u>  75  <u>24</u>  92  76
<u>42</u>  64  94  61  83  97  74  92  52  <u>19</u>

which results in Franklin Roosevelt, Calvin Coolidge, Andrew Johnson, George Washington, Grover Cleveland, Bill Clinton, and Rutherford Hayes.

(*b*) Starting at line 15, we get

79  80  <u>21</u>  49  <u>14</u>  55  <u>22</u>  <u>08</u>  68  <u>04</u>  <u>33</u>  76  96
<u>23</u>

which results in Chester Arthur, Franklin Pierce, Grover Cleveland, Martin Van Buren, James Madison, Harry Truman, and Benjamin Harrison.

(*c*) Starting at line 22, we get

60  74  53  61  <u>39</u>  61  00  46  <u>34</u>  73  <u>36</u>  <u>14</u>  <u>31</u>
<u>37</u>  45  <u>04</u>

which results in Jimmy Carter, Dwight Eisenhower, Lyndon Johnson, Franklin Pierce, Herbert Hoover, Richard Nixon, and James Madison.

Note that, although numbers ranging from 01 to 42 were chosen at random, the corresponding names are not completely random, since Grover Cleveland, who served as the 22nd and 24th president, is twice as likely to be chosen as any other president.

## HISTOGRAMS

**7.4.** Display in a histogram the following scores on an exam with 20 questions:

| x (Correct answers) | 9 | 10 | 12 | 13 | 14 | 15 | 16 | 17 | 18 | 19 | 20 |
|---|---|---|---|---|---|---|---|---|---|---|---|
| f (Students) | 1 | 2 | 1 | 2 | 7 | 2 | 1 | 7 | 2 | 6 | 4 |

The histogram is shown in Fig. 7-19.

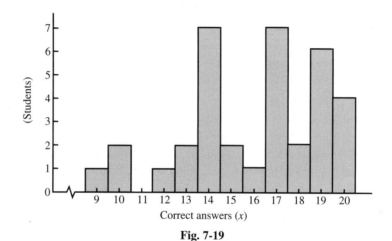

**Fig. 7-19**

**7.5.** For the following data, construct a frequency (*f*) and cummulative frequency (*cf*) distribution. Display the frequency distribution in a histogram.

| 3 | 5 | 3 | 4 | 4 | 7 | 6 | 5 | 2 | 4 |
|---|---|---|---|---|---|---|---|---|---|
| 2 | 5 | 5 | 6 | 4 | 3 | 5 | 4 | 5 | 5 |

The distribution chart is shown below.   The histogram is shown in Fig. 7-20.

| x | Tally | f | cf |
|---|---|---|---|
| 2 | // | 2 | 2 |
| 3 | /// | 3 | 5 |
| 4 | ##// | 5 | 10 |
| 5 | ## // | 7 | 17 |
| 6 | // | 2 | 19 |
| 7 | / | 1 | 20 |

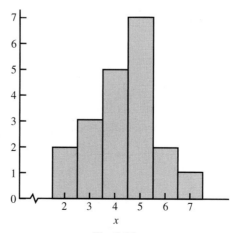

**Fig. 7-20**

**7.6.** Construct a histogram for the frequency distribution appearing below on the left.

The histogram is shown in Fig. 7-21.

| Class boundaries | Frequency |
|:---:|:---:|
| 20–25 | 5 |
| 25–30 | 20 |
| 30–35 | 25 |
| 35–40 | 15 |
| 40–45 | 10 |

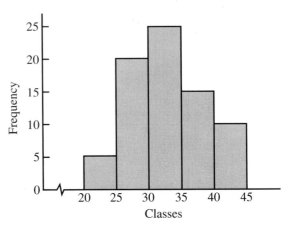

**Fig. 7-21**

**7.7.** The following scores were obtained in a statistics exam:

| 74 | 80 | 65 | 85 | 95 | 72 | 76 | 72 | 93 | 84 |
|---|---|---|---|---|---|---|---|---|---|
| 75 | 75 | 60 | 74 | 75 | 63 | 78 | 87 | 90 | 70 |

Classify the data into the four classes 60–70, 70–80, 80–90, and 90–100, and display the results in a histogram.   (If a number falls on a class boundary, put it in the class to the right of the number.)

The classification of the data is shown in the table below.   The histogram is shown in Fig. 7-22.

| Class | Tally | Frequency |
|:---:|:---:|:---:|
| 60–70 | /// | 3 |
| 70–80 | #### #### | 10 |
| 80–90 | //// | 4 |
| 90–100 | /// | 3 |

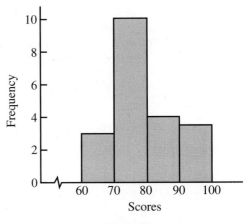

**Fig. 7-22**

**7.8.** The yearly rainfall, measured to the nearest tenth of a centimeter, for a 30-year period is as follows:

| 42.3 | 35.7 | 47.6 | 31.2 | 28.3 | 37.0 | 41.3 | 32.4 | 41.3 | 29.3 |
|---|---|---|---|---|---|---|---|---|---|
| 34.3 | 35.2 | 43.0 | 36.3 | 35.7 | 41.5 | 43.2 | 30.7 | 38.4 | 46.5 |
| 43.2 | 31.7 | 36.8 | 43.6 | 45.2 | 32.8 | 30.7 | 36.2 | 34.7 | 35.3 |

Classify the data into the 10 classes [28, 30), [30, 32), [32, 34), ..., [44, 46), [46, 48), and display the results in a histogram.    Identify each class by its class value.

The classification of the data is shown in the table below.    The histogram is shown in Fig. 7-23.

| Class limits, cm | Class value, $x_i$ | Tally | Frequency, $f_i$ |
|---|---|---|---|
| 28–30 | 29 | // | 2 |
| 30–32 | 31 | //// | 4 |
| 32–34 | 33 | // | 2 |
| 34–36 | 35 | //// / | 6 |
| 36–38 | 37 | //// | 4 |
| 38–40 | 39 | / | 1 |
| 40–42 | 41 | /// | 3 |
| 42–44 | 43 | //// | 5 |
| 44–46 | 45 | / | 1 |
| 46–48 | 47 | // | 2 |
| | | Sums | 30 |

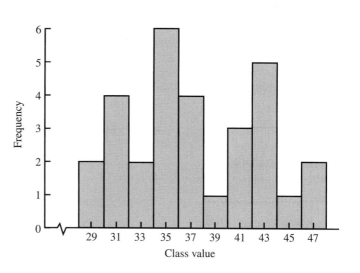

**Fig. 7-23**

## MEAN, MEDIAN, VARIANCE, AND STANDARD DEVIATION

In Problems 7.9 to 7.12, find the sample mean $\bar{x}$, median $M$, variance $s^2$, and standard deviation $s$ for the indicated data.

**7.9.**    The numbers 4, 6, 6, 7, 9, 10.    Use formula (7.3) for $s^2$.

There are $n = 6$ numbers.    Hence:

$$\bar{x} = \frac{4 + 6 + 6 + 7 + 9 + 10}{6} = \frac{42}{6} = 7$$

The median is the average of the third and fourth numbers:

$$M = \frac{6 + 7}{2} = 6.5$$

By formula (7.3):

$$s^2 = \frac{(4-7)^2 + (6-7)^2 + (6-7)^2 + (7-7)^2 + (9-7)^2 + (10-7)^2}{5}$$

$$= \frac{9 + 1 + 1 + 0 + 4 + 9}{5} = \frac{24}{5} = 4.8$$

$$s = \sqrt{4.8} \approx 2.19$$

**7.10.** The numbers 8, 7, 12, 5, 6, 7, 4.   Use formula (7.5) for $s^2$.

There are $n = 7$ numbers.   Hence:

$$\bar{x} = \frac{8 + 7 + 12 + 5 + 6 + 7 + 4}{7} = \frac{49}{7} = 7$$

To find the median, first arrange the numbers in increasing order:

$$4 \quad\quad 5 \quad\quad 6 \quad\quad 7 \quad\quad 7 \quad\quad 8 \quad\quad 12$$

The median is the fourth number: $M = 7$.
To apply formula (7.5) for $s^2$, we first construct the following table from the given data.

| | | | | | | | | Sum |
|---|---|---|---|---|---|---|---|---|
| $x$ | 8 | 7 | 12 | 5 | 6 | 7 | 4 | 49 |
| $x^2$ | 64 | 49 | 144 | 25 | 36 | 49 | 16 | 383 |

Then, by formula (7.5),

$$s^2 = \frac{383 - (49)^2/7}{6} \approx 6.67$$

$$s = \sqrt{s^2} \approx 2.58$$

**7.11.** The number $x$ of correct answers on an exam as tabulated in Problem 7.4.   Use formula (7.2) for $\bar{x}$ and (7.7) for $s^2$.

First we complete the following table:

| $x_i$ | $f_i$ | $f_i x_i$ | $x_i^2$ | $f_i x_i^2$ |
|---|---|---|---|---|
| 9 | 1 | 9 | 81 | 81 |
| 10 | 2 | 20 | 100 | 200 |
| 12 | 1 | 12 | 144 | 144 |
| 13 | 2 | 26 | 169 | 338 |
| 14 | 7 | 98 | 196 | 1372 |
| 15 | 2 | 30 | 225 | 450 |
| 16 | 1 | 16 | 256 | 256 |
| 17 | 7 | 119 | 289 | 2023 |
| 18 | 2 | 36 | 324 | 648 |
| 19 | 6 | 154 | 361 | 2166 |
| 20 | 4 | 80 | 400 | 1600 |
| Sums | 35 | 560 | | 9278 |

Then, by formula (7.2),

$$\bar{x} = \frac{\Sigma f_i x_i}{\Sigma f_i} = \frac{560}{35} = 16$$

The 35 scores $x_i$ (including repetitions) are arranged in increasing order in the table above.   The median is the 18th score: $M = 17$.

Using formula (7.7) for $s_2$, we get

$$s^2 = \frac{\Sigma f_i x_i^2 - (\Sigma f_i x_i)^2 / \Sigma f_i}{(\Sigma f_i) - 1} = \frac{9278 - (560)^2/35}{34} \approx 9.35$$

$$s = \sqrt{s^2} \approx 3.06$$

**7.12.** The scores obtained in a statistics exam as tabulated in Problem 7.7. Let $x_i$ equal the class value of the $i$th class, and use formula (7.2) for $\bar{x}$, formula (7.7) for $s^2$.

With reference to Problem 17.7, we first complete the following table:

| Class limits | Class value, $x_i$ | $f_i$ | $f_i x_i$ | $x_i^2$ | $f_i x_i^2$ |
|---|---|---|---|---|---|
| 60–70 | 65 | 3 | 195 | 4225 | 12,675 |
| 70–80 | 75 | 10 | 750 | 5625 | 56,250 |
| 80–90 | 85 | 4 | 340 | 7225 | 28,900 |
| 90–100 | 95 | 3 | 285 | 9025 | 27,075 |
| Sums | | 20 | 1570 | | 124,900 |

By formula (7.2),

$$\bar{x} = \frac{1570}{20} = 78.5$$

The median is the average of the 10th and 11th class values: $M = \dfrac{75 + 75}{2} = 75$. Using formula (7.7) for $s^2$, we get

$$s^2 = \frac{124,900 - (1570)^2/20}{19} \approx 87.11$$

$$s \approx 9.33$$

**7.13.** Express the data in Problem 7.9 in terms of standard units.

The $x$ values in Problem 7.9 are 4, 6, 6, 7, 9, and 10, which have mean $\bar{x} = 7$ and standard deviation $s = 2.19$. The formula for standard units is

$$z = \frac{x - \bar{x}}{s}$$

Hence, $z_1 = (4 - 7)/2.19 = -1.37$, $z_2 = z_3 = (6 - 7)/2.19 = -0.46$, $z_4 = (7 - 7)/2.19 = 0$, $z_5 = (9 - 7)/2.19 = 0.91$, and $z_6 = (10 - 7)/2.19 = 1.37$.

## QUARTILES AND PERCENTILES

**7.14.** Find the lower quartile $Q_L$, middle quartile $M$, and upper quartile $Q_U$ for the following data:

2   7   4   4   6   1   8   15   12   7   3   16   1   2   11   5   15   4

First arrange the data in numerical order:

$$1 \quad 1 \quad 2 \quad 2 \quad 3 \quad 4 \quad 4 \quad 4 \quad 5 \quad 6 \quad 7 \quad 7 \quad 8 \quad 11 \quad 12 \quad 15 \quad 15 \quad 16$$

$M$ is the median $\tilde{x}$, and since there are 18 values, $M$ is the average of the 9th and 10th values:

$$M = \frac{5 + 6}{2} = 5.5$$

$Q_L$ is the median of the values to the left of $M$.   There are nine of these, so $Q_L$ is the fifth one: $Q_L = 3$.

$Q_U$ is the median of the values to the right of $\tilde{x}$.   There are also nine of these, so $Q_U$ is the fifth one: $Q_U = 11$.

**7.15.** The *five-number summary* of a collection of data points consists of the lowest value $L$, the quartiles $Q_L$, $M$, $Q_U$, and the highest value $H$.   Find the five-number summary for the data in Problem 7.14.

$$L = 1 \qquad Q_L = 3 \qquad M = 5.5 \qquad Q_U = 11 \qquad H = 16$$

**7.16.** Find the percentiles (a)   $P_{21}$,   (b)   $P_{40}$, and   (c)   $P_{75}$ for the following data:

| 5 | 10 | 21 | 32 | 41 | 65 | 81 | 90 |
| 6 | 12 | 22 | 34 | 48 | 75 | 84 | 91 |
| 7 | 15 | 25 | 34 | 51 | 76 | 88 | 92 |
| 7 | 15 | 27 | 35 | 56 | 78 | 88 | 93 |
| 9 | 20 | 28 | 40 | 57 | 80 | 89 | 97 |

There are 40 data points, and they are arranged in numerical order.   To determine the $k$th percentile, we first break up $kn/100$ into its integer and decimal part.

(a)   $n = 40, k = 21$.   Thus:

$$\frac{k \cdot n}{100} = \frac{21 \cdot 40}{100} = 8.4 = 8 + 0.4$$

The integer part is 8 and the decimal part is 0.4.   Hence:

$$P_{21} = \text{9th value} = 15$$

(b)   $n = 40, k = 40$.   Thus:

$$\frac{k \cdot n}{100} = \frac{40 \cdot 40}{100} = 16 = 16 + 0$$

Here, the integer part is 16 and the decimal part is zero.   Hence:

$$P_{40} = \frac{\text{16th value} + \text{17th value}}{2} = \frac{32 + 34}{2} = 33$$

(c)   $n = 40, k = 75$.   Thus:

$$\frac{k \cdot n}{100} = \frac{75 \cdot 40}{100} = 30 = 30 + 0$$

The integer part is 30 and the decimal part is zero, so

$$P_{75} = \frac{30\text{th value} + 31\text{st value}}{2} = \frac{80 + 81}{2} = 80.5$$

**7.17.** Verify (a) $Q_L = P_{25}$, (b) $M = P_{50}$, and (c) $Q_U = P_{75}$ for the 40 data points in Problem 7.16.

(a)  $Q_L$ is the median of the first 20 data points, which is the average of the 10th and 11th values:

$$Q_L = \frac{20 + 21}{2} = 20.5$$

For $P_{25}$ we first compute $(25 \cdot 40)/100 = 10 = 10 + 0$.  Hence, $P_{25}$ is also the average of the 10th and 11th values.

(b)  $Q_M$ is the median of all 40 data points, which is the average of the 20th and 21st values:

$$M = \frac{40 + 41}{2} = 40.5$$

For $P_{50}$ we first compute $(50 \cdot 40)/100 = 20 = 20 + 0$.  Hence, $P_{50}$ is also the average of the 20th and 21st values.

(c)  $Q_U$ is the median of the last 20 values, or the average of the 30th and 31st values:

$$Q_U = \frac{80 + 81}{2} = 80.5$$

which is the value of $P_{75}$ determined in Problem 7.16.

## OTHER GRAPHICAL AND NUMERICAL DESCRIPTIONS OF SINGLE VARIABLE DATA

### Dotplots and Stem-and-Leaf Displays

A *dotplot* of a list of numerical data is similar to a histogram, but in a dotplot there is no vertical scale for the frequency of a data value.  The frequency is denoted by tallies in the form of dots.  A *stem-and-leaf display* of numerical data sorts the values first by one or more high-order digits (*stem*) and then by the remaining low-order digits (*leaves*).

**7.18.** Construct a dotplot for the following class values of exam scores:

| 65 | 70 | 60 | 65 | 75 | 80 | 70 | 70 | 75 | 85 |
|----|----|----|----|----|----|----|----|----|----|
| 95 | 65 | 90 | 90 | 75 | 60 | 75 | 80 | 90 | 80 |

We mark off a scale from 60 to 95 on a horizontal axis, and then record each occurrence of a given value by a dot above the tick mark for the value, as shown in Fig. 7-24.

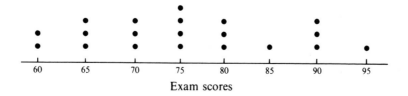

Exam scores

**Fig. 7-24**

**7.19.** Construct a stem-and-leaf display for the following exam scores:

| 63 | 68 | 59 | 66 | 76 | 82 | 70 | 71 | 74 | 85 |
|----|----|----|----|----|----|----|----|----|----|
| 97 | 65 | 89 | 90 | 77 | 61 | 75 | 79 | 92 | 82 |

We use the tens digit for the stem and the units digit for the leaf.

| Stem | Leaf |
|------|------|
| 5 | 9 |
| 6 | 3 8 5 6 1 |
| 7 | 6 7 0 5 1 9 4 |
| 8 | 9 2 5 2 |
| 9 | 7 0 2 |

## Mode and Midrange

The *mode* of a list of numerical data is the value that appears most often, assuming there is only one such value. The *midrange* is the average of the lowest and highest data values.

**7.20.** Find the mode and midrange for the numerical data in (a) Problem 7.18 and (b) Problem 7.19.

(a) Mode = 75, midrange = (60 + 95)/2 = 77.5

(b) Mode = 82, midrange = (59 + 97)/2 = 78

## BIVARIATE DATA

**7.21.** For the following table of values, (a) plot the data in a scatterplot, (b) compute the correlation coefficient $r$, (c) find the least-squares line $L: y = a + bx$, and (d) graph $L$ on the scatterplot in part (a):

| $x_i$ | 4 | 2 | 10 | 5 | 8 |
|-------|---|---|----|----|----|
| $y_t$ | 8 | 12 | 4 | 10 | 2 |

(a) and (d) The scatterplot with $L$ is shown in Fig. 7-25.

(b) We first complete the following table:

| $x_i$ | $y_i$ | $x_i^2$ | $y_i^2$ | $x_i y_i$ |
|-------|-------|---------|---------|-----------|
| 4 | 8 | 16 | 64 | 32 |
| 2 | 12 | 4 | 144 | 24 |
| 10 | 4 | 100 | 16 | 40 |
| 5 | 10 | 25 | 100 | 50 |
| 8 | 2 | 64 | 4 | 16 |
| Sums 29 | 36 | 209 | 328 | 162 |

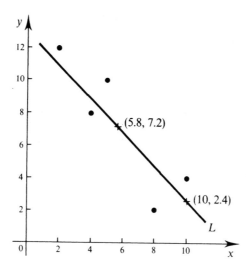

**Fig. 7-25**

Then, by formula (*7.11*), where $n = 5$,

$$r = \frac{162 - [(29)(36)]/5}{\sqrt{209 - (29)^2/5}\ \sqrt{328 - (36)^2/5}}$$

$$= \frac{-46.8}{\sqrt{40.8}\ \sqrt{68.8}} = -.8833$$

(*c*)   We first compute the standard deviations $s_x$ and $s_y$ of $x$ and $y$, respectively.   By formulas (*7.4*) and (*7.5*), we have

$$s_x = \sqrt{\frac{209 - (29)^2/5}{4}} = 3.1937$$

$$s_y = \sqrt{\frac{328 - (36)^2/5}{4}} = 4.1473$$

Substituting $r$, $s_x$, and $s_y$ into formula (*7.13*) for the slope $b$ of the least-squares line $L$ gives

$$b = \frac{(-0.8833)(4.1473)}{3.1937} = -1.1470$$

To determine the $y$ intercept $a$ of $L$, we first compute

$$\bar{x} = \frac{29}{5} = 5.8 \qquad \text{and} \qquad \bar{y} = \frac{36}{5} = 7.2$$

Then, by formula (*7.13*),

$$a = 7.2 - (-1.1470)(5.8) = 13.8526$$

Hence, the equation of $L$ is

$$y = 13.8526 - 1.1470x$$

(*d*)   To graph $L$, we plot two points on it and draw the line through them, as shown in the scatterplot in part (*a*).   One of the two points is $(5.8, 7.2) = (\bar{x}, \bar{y})$, which is on any least-squares lines; the other point is $(10, 2.3826)$, which is obtained by substituting $x = 10$ in the regression equation and solving for $y$.

**7.22.** Use the equation of the least-squares line $L$ in Problem 7.21 to compute the predicted value of $y$ for $x = 4, 2, 10, 5,$ and 8, and compare these $y$ values with the actual $y$ values on the scatterplot.

By substituting the given values of $x$ in the equation $y = 13.8526 - 1.1470x$, and rounding off to the nearest tenth, we get the predicted values shown in the table below:

| $x_i$ | 4 | 2 | 10 | 5 | 8 |
|---|---|---|---|---|---|
| Predicted $y_i$ | 9.3 | 11.6 | 2.4 | 8.1 | 4.7 |
| Actual $y_i$ | 8 | 12 | 4 | 10 | 2 |

**7.23.** Repeat Problem 7.21 for the following table of values:

| $x_i$ | 8 | 12 | 4 | 10 | 2 |
|---|---|---|---|---|---|
| $y_i$ | 4 | 2 | 10 | 5 | 8 |

We first note that the table here is obtained from that in the previous problem by interchanging the values of $x$ and $y$.

(a) and (d)   The scatterplot with $L$ is shown in Fig. 7-26.

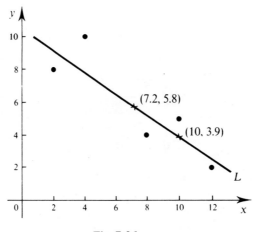

**Fig. 7-26**

(b)   Since the respective values of $x$ and $y$ here are interchanged with the $x$ and $y$ values in Problem 7.21, the correlation coefficient $r$ remains the same:

$$r = -.8833$$

(c)   The standard deviations of $x$ and $y$, respectively, are interchanged with those in Problem 7.21:

$$s_x = 4.1473 \qquad \text{and} \qquad s_y = 3.1937$$

Also, the means $\bar{x}$ and $\bar{y}$ are interchanged:

$$\bar{x} = 7.2 \qquad \text{and} \qquad \bar{y} = 5.8$$

The slope $b$ and $y$ intercept $a$ of the least-squares line $L$: $y = a + bx$, as given by formula (7.13), are

$$b = \frac{(-.8833)(3.1937)}{4.1473} = -0.6802$$

$$a = 5.8 - (-0.6802)(7.2) = 10.6974$$

Hence, the equation of $L$ is

$$y = 10.6974 - 0.6802x$$

Note that least-squares equation here is *not* the inverse of the equation of $L$ in Problem 7.21. That is, the equation of $L$ in this problem is not obtained by interchanging $x$ and $y$ in the equation of $L$ in Problem 7.21.

(d)  The graph of $L$ shown in the scatterplot in part (a) is the line through $(7.2, 5.8) = (\bar{x}, \bar{y})$ and $(10, 3.8954)$, where the last value of $y$ is obtained by substituting $x = 10$ in the equation of $L$.

**7.24.**  Compute the sample covariance $s_{xy}$ of $x$ and $y$ in Problems 7.21 and 7.23.

By formula (7.10):

$$s_{xy} = \frac{\Sigma(x_i - \bar{x})(y_i - \bar{y})}{n - 1}$$

Since the data in Problem 7.23 are obtained by interchanging $x$ and $y$ in Problem 7.21, the formula above tells us that the covariance will be the same in each problem. Using the data in Problem 7.21 we get

$$s_{xy} = [(4 - 5.8)(8 - 7.2) + (2 - 5.8)(12 - 7.2)$$
$$+ (10 - 5.8)(4 - 7.2) + (5 - 5.8)(10 - 7.2)$$
$$+ (8 - 5.8)(2 - 7.2)]/4$$
$$= [(-1.8)(.8) + (-3.8)(4.8) + (4.2)(-3.2)$$
$$+ (-.8)(2.8) + (2.2)(-5.2)]/4$$
$$= [-1.44 - 18.24 - 13.44 - 2.24 - 11.44]/4$$
$$= -46.8/4 = -11.7$$

Note that the variances $s_x$ and $s_y$ are always nonnegative but the covariance $s_{xy}$ can be negative. A negative covariance indicates that $y$ tends to decrease as $x$ increases.

# Supplementary Problems

## RANDOM SAMPLES

**7.25.**  A machine that operates daily from 8 A.M. to 4 P.M. fills bottles with 1500 aspirin tablets. Each day, the first five bottles filled by the machine are checked to see that the tablet count is correct. Explain why these five bottles form a biased sample. How can a random sample of five bottles be obtained?

**7.26.** Use Table 7-1, starting at row 1, to find a random sample of five National Hockey League teams from the following list:

| | | | |
|---|---|---|---|
| (01) | Pittsburg | (13) | Dallas |
| (02) | New York Rangers | (14) | Toronto |
| (03) | New York Islanders | (15) | Detroit |
| (04) | New Jersey | (16) | Tampa Bay |
| (05) | Philadelphia | (17) | Chicago |
| (06) | Washington | (18) | St. Louis |
| (07) | Boston | (19) | Calgary |
| (08) | Montreal | (20) | Los Angeles |
| (09) | Buffalo | (21) | Vancouver |
| (10) | Quebec | (22) | Winnipeg |
| (11) | Hartford | (23) | Edmonton |
| (12) | Ottawa | (24) | San Jose |

## HISTOGRAMS, DOTPLOTS, AND STEM-AND-LEAF DISPLAYS

**7.27.** The following distribution gives the numbers of hours of overtime during one month for the employees of a company:

| Overtime, h | 0 | 1 | 2 | 3 | 4 | 5 | 6 | 7 | 8 | 9 | 10 |
|---|---|---|---|---|---|---|---|---|---|---|---|
| Employees | 10 | 2 | 4 | 2 | 6 | 4 | 2 | 4 | 6 | 2 | 8 |

Display the data in a histogram.

**7.28.** During a 30-day period, the daily number of station wagons rented by an automobile rental agency was as follows:

| | | | | | | | | | | | | | | |
|---|---|---|---|---|---|---|---|---|---|---|---|---|---|---|
| 7 | 10 | 6 | 7 | 9 | 4 | 7 | 9 | 9 | 8 | 5 | 5 | 7 | 8 | 4 |
| 6 | 9 | 7 | 12 | 7 | 9 | 10 | 4 | 7 | 5 | 9 | 8 | 9 | 5 | 7 |

(a) Construct a frequency distribution for the data.

(b) Display the frequency distribution in a histogram.

**7.29.** The weekly wages of a group of unskilled workers follow:

| Weekly wages, $ | 140–160 | 160–180 | 180–200 | 200–220 | 220–240 | 240–260 | 260–280 |
|---|---|---|---|---|---|---|---|
| Number of workers | 18 | 24 | 32 | 20 | 8 | 6 | 2 |

Display the data in a histogram.

**7.30.** The amounts of 45 personal loans from a loan company follow:

| $700 | $450 | $725 | $1125 | $675 | $1650 | $750 | $400 | $1050 |
|------|------|------|-------|------|-------|------|------|-------|
| $500 | $750 | $850 | $1250 | $725 | $475 | $925 | $1050 | $925 |
| $850 | $625 | $900 | $1750 | $700 | $825 | $550 | $925 | $850 |
| $475 | $750 | $550 | $725 | $575 | $575 | $1450 | $700 | $450 |
| $700 | $1650 | $925 | $500 | $675 | $1300 | $1125 | $775 | $850 |

(a) Group the data into $200-classes, beginning with $400, and construct a frequency distribution for the grouped data.

(b) Display the frequency distribution in a histogram.

**7.31.** Construct a dotplot (see Problem 7.18) for the data in (a) Problem 7.27 and (b) Problem 7.28.

**7.32.** The following data are weights of the men (M) and women (W) in an exercise class.

| 122 | (W) | 117 | (W) | 117 | (W) | 167 | (M) | 114 | (W) |
|-----|-----|-----|-----|-----|-----|-----|-----|-----|-----|
| 195 | (M) | 145 | (M) | 158 | (M) | 158 | (M) | 190 | (M) |
| 110 | (W) | 134 | (W) | 165 | (M) | 104 | (W) | 132 | (W) |
| 107 | (W) | 105 | (W) | 181 | (M) | 142 | (W) | 123 | (W) |
| 155 | (M) | 155 | (M) | 172 | (M) | 149 | (M) | 120 | (W) |
| 140 | (W) | 163 | (M) | 125 | (W) | 130 | (W) | 150 | (M) |
| 187 | (M) | 147 | (M) | 118 | (W) | 159 | (M) | 160 | (M) |
| 115 | (W) | 175 | (M) | 125 | (W) | 177 | (M) | 121 | (W) |

(a) Construct a stem-and-leaf display of the data (see Problem 7.19) with the tens and hundreds digits as the stem and the units digit as the leaf.

(b) Construct a stem-and-leaf display of the data as in part (a), but put the leaves for the mens' weights to the right of the stem and the leaves for the womens' weights to the left of the stem.

## MEAN, MEDIAN, MODE, MIDRANGE, VARIANCE, AND STANDARD DEVIATION

**7.33.** The prices of a pound of coffee in seven stores are $5.58, $6.18, $5.84, $5.75, $5.67, $5.95, $5.62. Find (a) the mean price and (b) the median price.

**7.34.** For a given week, the average daily temperature in degrees Fahrenheit was 35°, 33°, 30°, 36°, 40°, 37°, 38°. Find (a) the mean temperature and (b) the median temperature.

**7.35.** During a given month, 10 salespeople in an automobile dealership sold 13, 17, 10, 18, 17, 9, 17, 13, 15, and 14 cars, respectively. Find (a) the mean, (b) the median, (c) the mode, and (d) the midrange. (See Problem 7.20.

**7.36.** Find the mean, median, mode, and midrange for the data in (a) Problem 7.27 and (b) Problem 7.28.

**7.37.** Use the class value to find the mean, median, mode, and midrange for the data in (a) Problem 7.29 and (b) Problem 7.30.

**7.38.** Find the variance and standard deviation for the data in (a) Problem 7.27 and (b) Problem 7.28.

**7.39.** Use the class value to find the variance and standard deviation for the data in (a) Problem 7.29 and (b) Problem 7.30.

## QUARTILES AND PERCENTILES

**7.40.** Find the quartiles $Q_L$, $M$, $Q_U$ for the following data: 15, 17, 17, 20, 21, 21, 25, 27, 30, 31, 35.

**7.41.** Find the five-number summary for the data in Problem 7.40.

**7.42.** Find the five-number summary for the data in Problem 7.28.

**7.43.** Find $P_{40}$, $P_{50}$, and $P_{85}$ for the following test scores:

| | | | | | | |
|----|----|----|----|----|----|----|
| 55 | 60 | 68 | 73 | 76 | 84 | 88 |
| 57 | 62 | 70 | 75 | 77 | 84 | 90 |
| 58 | 64 | 71 | 75 | 79 | 85 | 91 |
| 58 | 66 | 71 | 76 | 80 | 87 | 93 |
| 58 | 66 | 72 | 76 | 82 | 88 | 95 |

**7.44.** With reference to the data in Problem 7.32, find $P_{60}$, $P_{75}$, and $P_{93}$ for (a) the men's weights, (b) the women's weights, and (c) the men's and women's weights combined.

## BIVARIATE DATA

**7.45.** The following table lists one person's oxygen utilization in units of liters per minute for times of $t$ minutes into an exercise routine and $t$ minutes following the routine:

| $t$, min | liters/min during exercise | liters/min following exercise |
|----------|----------------------------|-------------------------------|
| 0 | 0.2 | 3.0 |
| 4 | 0.4 | 1.0 |
| 12 | 0.9 | 0.5 |
| 16 | 1.2 | 0.4 |
| 26 | 3.0 | 0.2 |

Let $x$ = the oxygen rate during exercise and $y$ = the rate after exercise. Find (a) the covariance $s_{xy}$ and (b) the correlation coefficient $r$.

**7.46.** For the data in Problem 7.45, (a) plot $x$ against $y$ in a scatterplot, (b) find the equation of the line $y = a + bx$ of best fit, and (c) graph the line of best fit on the scatterplot in (a).

**7.47.** The following table lists average male weight in pounds and height in inches for ages ranging from 1 to 21:

| Age | Weight | Height |
|-----|--------|--------|
| 1   | 20     | 28     |
| 3   | 30     | 36     |
| 6   | 45     | 44     |
| 10  | 60     | 50     |
| 13  | 95     | 60     |
| 16  | 140    | 66     |
| 21  | 155    | 70     |

Find the correlation coefficient for  (*a*) age and weight,  (*b*) age and height,  (*c*) weight and height.

**7.48.** For the data in Problem 7.47, let $x$ = weight, $y$ = height, and (*a*) plot $x$ against $y$ in a scatterplot, (*b*) find the equation of the line of best fit, and (*c*) graph the line of best fit on the scatterplot in (*a*).

**7.49.** Repeat parts (*a*), (*b*), and (*c*) of Problem 7.48, letting $x$ = height and $y$ = weight.

# Answers to Supplementary Problems

**7.25.** In a random sample, every bottle filled throughout the day should have the same chance of being checked as every other bottle.   A random sample could be obtained by using a table of random digits each day to select five bottle numbers between 1 and the total number of bottles filled per day.

**7.26.** Hartford, Los Angeles, New York Islanders, St. Louis, Quebec.

**7.27.** The histogram is shown in Fig. 7-27.

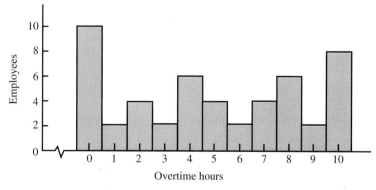

**Fig. 7-27**

**7.28.**  The frequency distribution is shown in part (*a*); the histogram for part (*b*) is shown in Fig. 7-28.

(*a*)

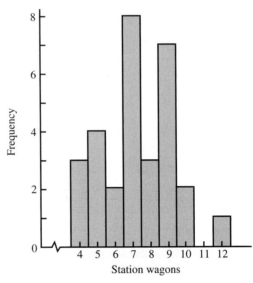

| Station wagons | Frequency |
|:---:|:---:|
| 4 | 3 |
| 5 | 4 |
| 6 | 2 |
| 7 | 8 |
| 8 | 3 |
| 9 | 7 |
| 10 | 2 |
| 11 | 0 |
| 12 | 1 |

**Fig. 7-28**

**7.29.**  The histogram is shown in Fig. 7-29.

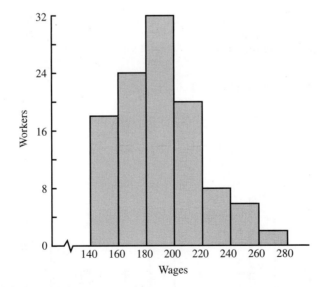

**Fig. 7-29**

**7.30.**  (*a*)

| Amount ÷ $100 | 4–6 | 6–8 | 8–10 | 10–12 | 12–14 | 14–16 | 16–18 |
|:---|:---:|:---:|:---:|:---:|:---:|:---:|:---:|
| Number of loans | 11 | 14 | 10 | 4 | 2 | 1 | 3 |

**7.30.** (*b*) The histogram is shown in Fig. 7-30.

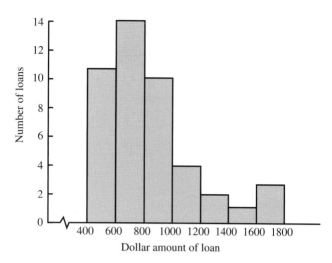

**Fig. 7-30**

**7.31.** The dotplot for part (*a*) is shown in Fig. 7-31(*a*); the dotplot for part (*b*) is shown in Fig. 7-31(*b*).

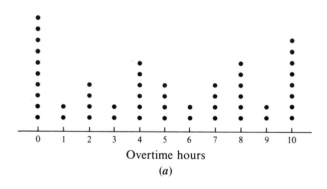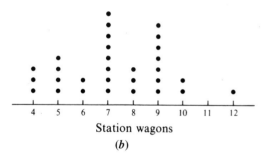

**Fig. 7-31**

**7.32.** (*a*)

| 10 | 7 5 4 |
|----|-------|
| 11 | 0 5 7 7 8 5 4 |
| 12 | 2 5 3 0 1 |
| 13 | 4 0 2 |
| 14 | 0 5 7 2 9 |
| 15 | 5 5 8 8 9 0 |
| 16 | 3 5 7 0 |
| 17 | 5 2 7 |
| 18 | 7 1 |
| 19 | 5 0 |

| Women | | Men |
|-------|----|-----|
| 4 5 7 | 10 | |
| 4 5 8 7 7 5 0 | 11 | |
| 1 0 3 5 2 | 12 | |
| 2 0 4 | 13 | |
| 2 0 | 14 | 5 7 9 |
| | 15 | 5 5 8 8 9 0 |
| | 16 | 3 5 7 0 |
| | 17 | 5 2 7 |
| | 18 | 7 1 |
| | 19 | 5 0 |

**7.33.**  (a)  $5.80,        (b)  $5.75

**7.34.**  (a)  35.67°,       (b)  36.5°

**7.35.**  (a)  14.3,        (b)  14.5,        (c)  17,        (d)  13

**7.36.**  (a)  $\bar{x} = 4.92$ hours,   $M = 5$ hours,   mode $= 0$ hours, midrange $= 5$ hours;
(b)  $\bar{x} = 7.3$,   $M = 7$,   mode $= 7$,   midrange $= 8$

**7.37.**  (a)  $\bar{x} = \$190.36$, $M = \$190$, mode $= \$190$, midrange $= \$210$;
(b)  $\bar{x} = \$842.22$, $M = \$700$, mode $= \$700$, midrange $= \$1100$

**7.38.**  (a)  $s^2 = 12.97$ hours squared, $s = 3.60$ hours;        (b)  $s^2 = 4.00$, $s = 2.00$

**7.39.**  (a)  $s^2 = 858.58$ dollars squared, $s = \$29.30$;        (b)  $s^2 = 112{,}040.40$ dollars squared, $s = \$334.72$

**7.40.**  $Q_L = 17, M = 21, Q_U = 30$

**7.41.**  $L = 15, Q_L = 17, M = 21, Q_U = 30, H = 35$

**7.42.**  $L = 4, Q_L = 6, M = 7, Q_U = 9, H = 12$

**7.43.**  $P_{40} = 71.5, P_{50} = 75, P_{85} = 88$

**7.44.**  (a)  $P_{60} = 166, P_{75} = 176, P_{93} = 190$;        (b)  $P_{60} = 121.5, P_{75} = 127.5, P_{93} = 140$;
(c)  $P_{60} = 152.5, P_{75} = 161.5, P_{93} = 187$

**7.45.**  (a)  $s_{xy} = -.82$,        (b)  $r = -.64$

**7.46.**  (a) and (c)   The scatterplot is shown in Fig. 7-32.        (b)  $y = 1.78 - 0.66x$.

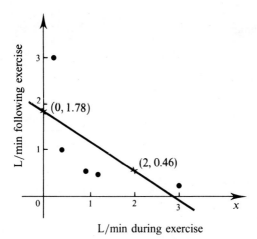

**Fig. 7-32**

**7.47.**  (a)  $r = .98$,        (b)  $r = .98$,        (c)  $r = .97$.

**7.48.** (*a*) and (*c*)   The scatterplot is shown in Fig. 7-33.          (*b*)   $y = 28.55 + 0.28x$.

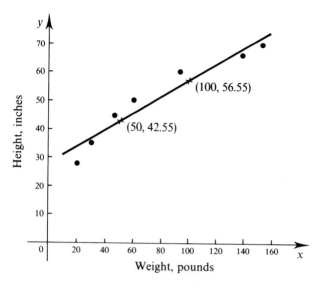

**Fig. 7-33**

**7.49.** (*a*) and (*c*)   The scatterplot is shown in Fig. 7-34.          (*b*)   $y = -88.98 + 3.30x$.

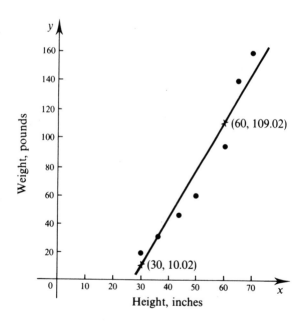

**Fig. 7-34**

# Inferential Statistics

## 8.1  SAMPLING DISTRIBUTIONS

The object of inferential statistics is to draw conclusions about a given population based on an analysis of random samples of the population.  For example, we may want to predict the winner of a presidential election, in which all eligible voters form the population, by polling a random sample of eligible voters.  If we select two random samples of the same size, we may not get the same proportion of voters favoring a given candidate in each sample.  Therefore, before drawing a conclusion about all eligible voters, it is important to understand the variability that can be expected in random samples.  This variability is determined by means of *sampling distributions*.

**EXAMPLE 8.1**    A population consists of the set $S = \{2, 6, 10\}$, taken as an equiprobable space, and the sample space $S_2$ consists of all pairs $(a, b)$, including repetitions, of numbers in $S$.   The sample mean $\overline{X}_2$, which associates with each pair the average $\overline{x} = (a + b)/2$, is a random variable on $S_2$, and its probability distribution is a sampling distribution. Determine the mean $\overline{\mu}$ and standard deviation $\overline{\sigma}$ of $\overline{X}_2$ and compare these with the mean $\mu$ and standard deviation $\sigma$ of the population $S$.

Table 8-1 lists the members of $S_2$ in the first column and the corresponding sample means $\overline{x}$ in the second column.   Table 8-2 is the probability distribution for $\overline{X}_2$.

<table>
<tr><td colspan="2" align="center">**Table 8-1**</td></tr>
<tr><td align="center">$(a, b)$</td><td align="center">$\overline{x}$</td></tr>
<tr><td align="center">$(2, 2)$</td><td align="center">2</td></tr>
<tr><td align="center">$(2, 6)$</td><td align="center">4</td></tr>
<tr><td align="center">$(2, 10)$</td><td align="center">6</td></tr>
<tr><td align="center">$(6, 2)$</td><td align="center">4</td></tr>
<tr><td align="center">$(6, 6)$</td><td align="center">6</td></tr>
<tr><td align="center">$(6, 10)$</td><td align="center">8</td></tr>
<tr><td align="center">$(10, 2)$</td><td align="center">6</td></tr>
<tr><td align="center">$(10, 6)$</td><td align="center">8</td></tr>
<tr><td align="center">$(10, 10)$</td><td align="center">10</td></tr>
</table>

| **Table 8-2** | |
| :---: | :---: |
| $\overline{x}$ | $P(\overline{x})$ |
| 2 | $\frac{1}{9}$ |
| 4 | $\frac{2}{9}$ |
| 6 | $\frac{3}{9}$ |
| 8 | $\frac{2}{9}$ |
| 10 | $\frac{1}{9}$ |

From Table 8-2 we get

$$\overline{\mu} = E(\overline{X}_2) = 2 \cdot \frac{1}{9} + 4 \cdot \frac{2}{9} + 6 \cdot \frac{3}{9} + 8 \cdot \frac{2}{9} + 10 \cdot \frac{1}{9} = \frac{54}{9} = 6$$

and

$$\overline{\sigma} = \sqrt{(\Sigma \overline{x}^2 P(\overline{x})) - (\overline{\mu})^2}$$

$$= \sqrt{4 \cdot \frac{1}{9} + 16 \cdot \frac{2}{9} + 36 \cdot \frac{3}{9} + 64 \cdot \frac{2}{9} + 100 \cdot \frac{1}{9} - 36}$$

$$= \sqrt{\frac{48}{9}} = \sqrt{\frac{16}{3}} = \frac{4}{\sqrt{3}} \approx 2.3$$

The mean and standard deviation of the population $S$ are

$$\mu = 2 \cdot \frac{1}{3} + 6 \cdot \frac{1}{3} + 10 \cdot \frac{1}{3} = 6$$

and

$$\sigma = \sqrt{4 \cdot \frac{1}{3} + 36 \cdot \frac{1}{3} + 100 \cdot \frac{1}{3} - 36} = \sqrt{\frac{32}{3}} = 4\sqrt{\frac{2}{3}}$$

Comparing the two means and standard deviations, we see that

$$\overline{\mu} = \mu \quad \text{and} \quad \overline{\sigma} = \frac{\sigma}{\sqrt{2}}$$

Hence, the mean of the sampling distribution of sample means is equal to the mean of the original population, and the standard deviation of the sampling distribution of sample means is equal to standard deviation of the original population divided by the square root of 2 (which is the sample size).

The results of Example 8.1 can be generalized to Theorem 8.1.

**Theorem 4.1:**   Suppose $S$ is a numerical population with mean $\mu$ and standard deviation $\sigma$, and let the sample space $S_n$ consist of all random samples of size $n$ ($n$-tuples) of elements in $S$.   Then the mean $\overline{x}$ of each sample is a random variable $\overline{X}_n$ on $S_n$ with mean $\overline{\mu} = \mu$ and standard deviation $\overline{\sigma} = \sigma/\sqrt{n}$

## Terminology

The random variable $\overline{X}_n$ in Theorem 8.1 is called the *sample mean* (see remark below), and its probability distribution is called a *sampling distribution*.   In general, the probability distribution of *any* random variable on the sample space $S_n$ is called a sampling distribution.   In Sec. 8.3 we will consider the probability distribution of a random variable $\overline{S}^2_n$ on $S_n$, called the *sample variance*.

## Applications of Theorem 8.1

In Example 8.1, the population $S$ has only three elements, and the samples are of size 2.   If we were applying the theorem to a population survey, then most likely $S$ would have many more than three elements and the sample size would be larger than 2.   However, even if $S$ is small, the sample size can still be large because we are allowing repetitions in the sample.   For example, let $S = \{1, 0\}$ be the possible outcomes in a single toss of a coin, 1 for heads and zero for tails.   If we toss the coin 10 times, then the sample space $S_{10}$ consists of $2^{10} = 1024$ 10-tuples of 1s and 0s, and the value of the sample mean $\overline{X}_{10}$ on a 10-tuple $t$ is

$$\overline{x} = \frac{\text{the number of 1s in } t}{10}$$

The probability distribution for $\overline{X}_{10}$ (see Problem 8.5), assuming the coin is fair, is given in Table 8-3.

**Table 8-3**

| $\bar{x}$ | 0 | .1 | .2 | .3 | .4 | .5 | .6 | .7 | .8 | .9 | 1 |
|---|---|---|---|---|---|---|---|---|---|---|---|
| $P(\bar{x})$ | .001 | .010 | .004 | .117 | .205 | .246 | .205 | .117 | .044 | .010 | .001 |

**EXAMPLE 8.2**   An American roulette wheel has 38 pockets, 18 red, 18 black, and two green.   If a $1 bet is placed on red or black, then the player wins $1 if the ball lands in a pocket of the same color; otherwise, the player loses $1.   Suppose 10,000 $1 roulette bets are placed each day in a casino.   What is the expected value and the standard deviation of the casino's average daily roulette winnings per game on these bets?

Here $S = \{1, -1\}$, where 1 represents a $1 win for the casino, $-1$ represents a $1 loss for the casino in any one game, and $S_{10,000}$ consists of all 10,000-tuples of 1s and $-1$s.   The value of the sample mean $\bar{X}_{10,000}$ for a sample $t$ (10,000-tuple) is

$$\bar{x} = \frac{(\#1\text{s in } t) - (\#-1\text{s in } t)}{10,000}$$

$$= \text{net casino winnings per game for the sample } t$$

On any one play, the probability that the casino wins is $\frac{20}{38}$ and the probability of losing is $\frac{18}{38}$.   Hence, the casino's expected winnings on any one play is

$$\mu = E = 1(\tfrac{20}{38}) + (-1)(\tfrac{18}{38}) = \tfrac{2}{38} \approx 0.05$$

and the standard deviation is

$$\sigma = \sqrt{1^2 \tfrac{20}{38} + (-1)^2 \tfrac{18}{38} - (\tfrac{2}{38})^2} = \sqrt{\tfrac{1440}{1444}} \approx 1$$

By Theorem 8.1, the sample mean $\bar{X}_{10,000}$ has expected value $\bar{\mu} = .05$ and standard deviation

$$\bar{\sigma} = \frac{\sigma}{\sqrt{10,000}} \approx \frac{1}{100} = 0.01$$

Hence, the casino's expected average winnings per game in 10,000 games is the same as the expected winnings in any one game, namely $0.05, or 5 cents.   On the other hand, there is much less variability in $\bar{X}_{10,000}$ than in the winnings for a single play.   In any one play, the casino either wins or loses $1, but over 10,000 plays, it is highly unlikely that the casino will lose any money.   We will see just how unlikely in Example 8.3.

**Remark 1.**   In Section 6.6 we defined the space $S_n$ of $n$ independent trials of an experiment as the collection of all $n$-tuples of possible (numerical) outcomes of the experiment.   Here we are calling each $n$-tuple $t$ a sample of size $n$.

**Remark 2.**   Both $S$ and $S_n$ are sample spaces in the sense of probability.   However, to avoid confusion in this context, we refer to $S$ as the *population* (or *population space*) and $S_n$ as the *sample space*.

## Summary I

*(Numerical) Population:* $S = \{x_1, x_2, \ldots, x_k\}$; $P(x_i) = p_i$
*Population Mean:* $\mu = \Sigma x_i p_i$
*Population Standard Deviation:* $\sigma = \sqrt{(\Sigma x_i^2 p_i) - \mu^2}$
*Sample Space of Random Samples of Size $n$:*

$$S_n = \{t = (x_1, x_2, \ldots, x_n) \mid x_i \in S\}; P(t) = P(x_1) P(x_2) \ldots P(x_n)$$

($S$ has $k$ elements, and $S_n$ has $k^n$ elements, each an $n$-tuple.)

***Random Variables on*** $S_n$:

$$X_i(t) = x_i \qquad (i = 1, 2, \ldots, n)$$

$$\overline{X}_n = \frac{X_1 + X_2 + \cdots + X_n}{n}$$

The $X_i$'s are independent, each having mean $\mu$ and standard deviation $\sigma$, and $\overline{X}_n$ is called the *sample mean*. The value of $\overline{X}_n$ on a sample $t$ is

$$\overline{x} = \frac{x_1 + x_2 + \cdots + x_n}{n}$$

which will be used to estimate $\mu$ (see Sec. 8.3).

***Mean and Standard Deviation of*** $\overline{X}_n$:

$$\overline{\mu} = E(\overline{X}_n) = \mu \qquad \overline{\sigma} = \frac{\sigma}{\sqrt{n}}$$

These equations show why the value $\overline{x}$ of $\overline{X}_n$ on a sample $t$ is used to estimate $\mu$. That is, the expected value of $\overline{X}_n$ is $\mu$, and the larger $n$ is, the less variability there is in the values of $\overline{X}_n$.

## 8.2 THE CENTRAL LIMIT THEOREM

Theorem 8.1 expresses the mean and standard deviation of the sample mean $\overline{X}_n$ in terms of the mean and standard deviation of the population $S$. It can also be shown that if the elements of $S$ are normally distributed, then so is $\overline{X}_n$. Theorem 8.2, which is one of the most important results in probability theory, states that even if $S$ is not normally distributed, the sample mean $\overline{X}_n$ tends to become normal as $n$ gets large.

**Theorem 8.2 (Central Limit Theorem):** Suppose $S$ is a numerical population with mean $\mu$ and standard deviation $\sigma$, and let $S_n$ consist of all random samples of size $n$ of elements in $S$. For large values of $n$, the sample mean $\overline{X}_n$ on $S_n$ is approximately normally distributed with mean $\overline{\mu} = \mu$ and standard deviation $\overline{\sigma} = \sigma/\sqrt{n}$.

The sample size $n$ at which $\overline{X}_n$ becomes approximately normal depends on the population $S$, but a rule of thumb is that $\overline{X}_n$ is approximately normal for $n \geq 30$.

**EXAMPLE 8.3** With reference to Example 8.2, use the central limit theorem to (*a*) approximate the probability that the casino's average daily winnings on the \$1 bets will be negative, that is, that the casino will lose money on any given day, and (*b*) find the probability that the average winnings over a 10-day period are at least 4 cents per game, that is, find $P(\overline{X}_{100,000} \geq 0.04)$.

From Example 8.2, we have $\mu = 0.05 = \overline{\mu}$, $\sigma = 1$, and $\overline{\sigma} = 0.01$.

(*a*) We wish to find $P(\overline{X}_{10,000} < 0)$. To use the standard normal tables, we transform $\overline{X}_{10,000}$ into the standardized normal variable $Z$ with mean zero and standard deviation 1:

$$Z = \frac{\overline{X}_{10,000} - \overline{\mu}}{\overline{\sigma}} = \frac{\overline{X}_{10,000} - 0.05}{.01}$$

Then

$$P(\overline{X}_{10,000} < 0) = P\left(Z < \frac{0 - 0.05}{0.01} = -5\right) = \Phi(-5) = .0000003.$$

Hence, the casino is almost certain to win money each day on the \$1 roulette games.

(b)   The mean of $\overline{X}_{100,000}$ is the same as the mean of $\overline{X}_{10,000}$, namely, 0.05, but the standard deviation of $\overline{X}_{100,000}$ is

$$\overline{\sigma} = \frac{\sigma}{\sqrt{100,000}} = \frac{1}{\sqrt{100,000}} \approx 0.003$$

Then

$$P(\overline{X}_{100,000} \geq 0.04) = P(0Z \geq \frac{0.04 - .05}{.003} \approx -3.330)$$

$$= .5 + \Phi(3.33) = 0.9996$$

Hence, the casino is almost certain to win an average of at least 4 cents per game on the $1 roulette bets over a 10-day period.

### Alternative Form of the Central Limit Theorem

If we consider the $n$-tuples $t = (x_1, x_2, \ldots, x_n)$ of the sample space $S_n$ as $n$ independent trials, then the value $x_i$ of the $i$th trial is a random variable $X_i$ ($i = 1, 2, \ldots, n$), and the random variables $X_1, X_2, \ldots, X_n$ are independent with mean $\mu$ and standard deviation $\sigma$ (see Remark 1 at the end of Sec. 8.1).   The sum

$$Y_n = X_1 + X_2 + \cdots + X_n$$

and the sample mean

$$\overline{X}_n = \frac{X_1 + X_2 + \cdots + X_n}{n}$$

are related by the equation $Y_n = n\overline{X}_n$.   The central limit theorem says:

> For large values of $n$, the sum $Y_n = X_1 + X_2 + \ldots + X_n$ is approximately normally distributed with mean $\tilde{\mu} = n\mu$ and standard deviation $\tilde{\sigma} = n \cdot \sigma/\sqrt{n} = \sqrt{n}\,\sigma$

The central limit theorem is often stated in terms of random variable $Y_n$ rather than $\overline{X}_n$.

**EXAMPLE 8.4 (Normal Approximation of the Binomial)**   A binomial experiment $B(n,p)$ consists of $n$ independent Bernoulli trials, each with mean $\mu = p$ and standard deviation $\sigma = \sqrt{pq}$, where $q = 1 - p$.   The binomial random variable $Y_n$, which gives the number of successes in $n$ Bernoulli trials, is equal to the sum

$$Y_n = X_1 + X_2 + \cdots + X_n$$

where $X_i = 1$ if the $i$th trial is a success ($i = 1, 2, \ldots, n$) and zero otherwise.   By the alternative form of the central limit theorem, for large values of $n$, the sum $Y_n$ is approximately normally distributed with mean $\tilde{\mu} = np$ and standard deviation $\tilde{\sigma} = \sqrt{npq}$.   Hence, the normal approximation of the binomial which was stated in Sec. 6.10 is justified by the central limit theorem.

### 8.3   CONFIDENCE INTERVALS FOR POPULATION MEANS

#### Introduction

Suppose $S$ is a numerical population with mean $\mu$, which is unknown.   From a random sample of size $n$, the value $\overline{x}$ of the sample mean $\overline{X}_n$ can be used to estimate $\mu$ at the 95 percent confidence level as follows.   First choose a value $E$ for which

$$P(\mu - E \leq \overline{X}_n \leq \mu + E) = .95$$

Equivalently, $P(\overline{X}_n - E \leq \mu \leq \overline{X}_n + E) = .95$ (see Problem 8.10).   Then, by definition, the interval $[\overline{x} - E, \overline{x} + E]$ is called a *95 percent confidence interval* for $\mu$ with $E$ as the *margin of error* This means that the probability is .95 that a random sample will result in an interval $[\overline{x} - E, \overline{x} + E]$ that contains $\mu$.   In other words, as $\overline{x}$ ranges through all possible values of $\overline{X}_n$, 95 percent of the intervals $[\overline{x} - E, \overline{x} + E]$ contain $\mu$ (see Fig. 8-1).

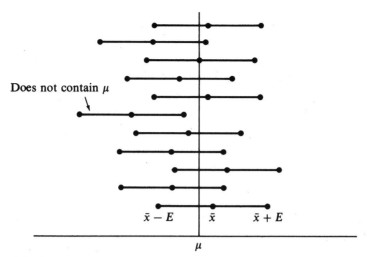

**Fig. 8-1**  Ninety-five percent of all intervals $[\bar{x} - E, \bar{x} + E]$ contain $\mu$.

In general, if .95 is replaced by $1 - \alpha$, where $0 < \alpha < 1$, then the corresponding interval $[\bar{x} - E, \bar{x} + E]$ is called a $100(1 - \alpha)$ percent confidence interval for $\mu$, or, simply, a $(1 - \alpha)$ confidence interval; $\alpha$ is called the *significance level* and is equal to the probability that the interval obtained will *not* contain $\mu$.  That is:

$$\alpha = 1 - P(\overline{X}_n - E \le \mu \le \overline{X}_n + E)$$

In this section we consider $(1 - \alpha)$ confidence intervals for $\mu$ in the following cases:

(1)  When $\sigma$ is known

(2)  When $\sigma$ is unknown

(3)  When $\mu = p$, the binomial proportion

If not stated explicitly, we will assume that either $\overline{X}_n$ is normally distributed or that $n$ is large enough so that (by the central limit theorem) $\overline{X}_n$ is approximately normally distributed.  If $\overline{X}_n$ is only approximately normal, then the confidence intervals obtained are also approximate, but we will still refer to them as confidence intervals.

**Confidence Intervals for $\mu$ When $\sigma$ is Known**

**EXAMPLE 8.5**  A statistician, using data from every employee in a very large corporation, computes the mean and standard deviation of the employees' salaries.  Because of a computer failure, the data are lost, but the statistician remembers that the standard deviation was $10,000.  She then decides to estimate the mean salary for the corporation by computing the mean salary of a random sample of employees.  How large a sample must be taken to find a 95 percent confidence interval for the mean salary with a margin of error equal to $1000?

Let $\mu$ be the mean salary.  We wish to determine the smallest integer $n$ for which

$$P(\mu - 1000 \le \overline{X}_n \le \mu + 1000) = .95$$

First switch from $\mu - 1000$ and $\mu + 1000$ to the standard units

$$z_1 = \frac{\mu - 1000 - \mu}{\sigma/\sqrt{n}} = \frac{-1000}{10,000/\sqrt{n}} = \frac{-\sqrt{n}}{10}$$

and

$$z_2 = \frac{\mu + 1000 - \mu}{\sigma/\sqrt{n}} = \frac{1000}{10,000/\sqrt{n}} = \frac{\sqrt{n}}{10}$$

We then want the smallest integer $n$ for which the standardized random variable $Z$ satisfies

$$P\left(\frac{-\sqrt{n}}{10} \le Z \le \frac{\sqrt{n}}{10}\right) = .95 \qquad \text{or} \qquad 2\Phi\left(\frac{\sqrt{n}}{10}\right) = .95 \qquad \text{or} \qquad \Phi\left(\frac{\sqrt{n}}{10}\right) = .475$$

(see Fig. 8-2).

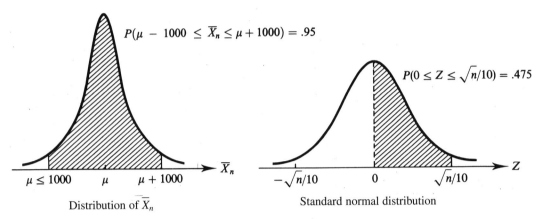

$$P(\mu - 1000 \leq \overline{X}_n \leq \mu + 1000) = .95$$

$$P(0 \leq Z \leq \sqrt{n}/10) = .475$$

Distribution of $\overline{X}_n$                  Standard normal distribution

**Fig. 8-2**

It is assumed that $n$ is large enough that the central limit theorem applies. Then $Z$ is approximately normal with mean zero and standard deviation 1. From Appendix B:

$$\frac{\sqrt{n}}{10} = 1.96 \qquad \text{or} \qquad \sqrt{n} = 19.6 \qquad \text{or} \qquad n = 385$$

[rounding $(19.6)^2 = 384.16$ up to an integer]. Hence, if the mean salary $\overline{x}$ of a random sample of 385 employees is computed, the interval $[\overline{x} - 1000, \overline{x} + 1000]$ will be a 95 percent confidence interval for the mean salary of all the employees.

**EXAMPLE 8.6** Suppose the statistician in Example 8.5 computes the mean salary $\overline{x}$ from a random sample of 900 employees. What will the confidence level $1 - \alpha$ be for the corresponding confidence interval $[\overline{x} - 1000, \overline{x} + 1000]$?
    The confidence level $1 - \alpha$ satisfies the equation

$$P(\mu - 1000 \leq \overline{X}_n \leq \mu + 1000) = 1 - \alpha$$

which, as shown in Example 8.5, becomes, in standard units,

$$P\left(\frac{-\sqrt{n}}{10} \leq Z \leq \frac{\sqrt{n}}{10}\right) = 1 - \alpha \qquad \text{or} \qquad 2\Phi\left(\frac{\sqrt{n}}{10}\right) = 1 - \alpha$$

Substituting $n = 900$, we get $2\Phi(3) = 1 - \alpha$, and from Appendix B, $2\Phi(3) = .997$. Hence, 99.7 percent of the intervals $[\overline{x} - 1000, \overline{x} + 1000]$ obtained from a random sample of 900 employees will contain the true mean salary $\mu$.

### Generalization

    We can generalize the results of Examples 8.5 and 8.6. First note that the standard units $z_1$ and $z_2$ in Example 8.5 satisfy $z_1 = -z_2$. The value $z_2$ is usually denoted by $z_{\alpha/2}$ because $\alpha/2$ is the area under the standard normal curve to the right of $z_{\alpha/2}$ (see Fig. 8-3). The generalization, which is illustrated in Fig. 8-3, can now be stated as follows:

**Theorem 8.3:** Suppose $S$ is a population with unknown mean $\mu$ and known standard deviation $\sigma$. Let $\overline{x}$ be the value of the sample mean $\overline{X}_n$ obtained in a random sample of size $n$, where $n$ is large enough so that the distribution of $\overline{X}_n$ is approximately normal (as a rule, $n \geq 30$). Also, let

$$E = \frac{z_{\alpha/2} \cdot \sigma}{\sqrt{n}}$$

where $z_{\alpha/2}$ is the standard normal unit satisfying

$$2\Phi(z_{\alpha/2}) = 1 - \alpha \qquad \text{or} \qquad \Phi(z_{\alpha/2}) = \frac{1 - \alpha}{2}$$

Then $[\overline{x} - E, \overline{x} + E]$ is a $(1 - \alpha)$ confidence interval for $\mu$ with margin of error $E$.

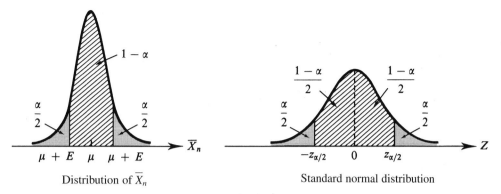

Distribution of $\overline{X}_n$                                    Standard normal distribution

**Fig. 8-3**

## Confidence Intervals for $\mu$ When $\sigma$ Is Unknown

If the standard deviation $\sigma$ of the population is not known, then $\sigma$ can be estimated from the data obtained in a random sample of the population. It can be shown that the random variable called the *sample variance*, which is defined by

$$\overline{S}_n^2 = \frac{\Sigma(X_i - \overline{X}_n)^2}{n - 1}$$

satisfies $E(\overline{S}_n^2) = \sigma^2$. (It may seem more natural to use $n$ in place of $n - 1$ in the definition of $\overline{S}_n^2$, and some statisticians do this, but the resulting random variable does not have $\sigma^2$ for its expected value.) Hence, $\overline{S}_n = \sqrt{\overline{S}_n^2}$ can be used to estimate $\sigma$. We will assume that, for large values of $n$, the standardized random variable

$$Z = \frac{\overline{X}_n - \mu}{\overline{S}_n/\sqrt{n}}$$

is approximately normal with mean 0 and standard deviation 1. (For a normal population and any positive value of $n$, $Z$ has a student's $t$ distribution with $n - 1$ degrees of freedom, but we do not treat $t$ distributions in this text.)

Therefore, if $\sigma$ is not known, Theorem 8.3 can be modified as follows:

Suppose $S$ is a population with unknown mean $\mu$ and unknown standard deviation $\sigma$. Let $\bar{x} = \sum x_i/n$ and $\bar{s}^2 = \sum (x_i - \bar{x})^2/(n - 1)$ be the values of the sample mean and sample variance, respectively, in a random sample of size $n \geq 30$. Also let

$$E = \frac{z_{\alpha/2} \cdot \bar{s}}{\sqrt{n}}$$

where $z_{\alpha/2}$ is the standard normal unit satisfying

$$2\Phi(z_{\alpha/2}) = 1 - \alpha \qquad \text{or} \qquad \Phi(z_{\alpha/2}) = \frac{1 - \alpha}{2}$$

Then $[\bar{x} - E, \bar{x} + E]$ is a $(1 - \alpha)$ confidence interval for $\mu$ with margin of error $E$.

**EXAMPLE 8.7** In a random sample of 400 calculus students at a state college, it is found that the average numerical grade is 72 with a standard deviation of 10. Assuming the grades are approximately normally distributed, find a 95 percent confidence interval for the true average grade of all of the calculus students at the college.

We set $\bar{x} = 72$, $\bar{s} = 10$, $1 - \alpha = .95$, and $2\Phi(z_{\alpha/2}) = .95$, or $\Phi(z_{\alpha/2}) = .475$. From Appendix B, $z_{\alpha/2} = 1.96$. Therefore, the margin of error is

$$E = \frac{1.96 \cdot 10}{\sqrt{400}} = .98 \approx 1$$

and a 95 percent confidence interval is $[72 - 1, 72 + 1] = [71, 73]$.

### Confidence Intervals for the Binomial Proportion $p$

The object of many surveys is to determine the proportion of a population that fits into one of two categories. For example, a surveyor may want to determine the proportion $p$ of TV viewers that watch the Monday night football game. In such a case, we may partition the viewing population into category 1 (do watch the game) and category 0 (do not watch the game), with $P(1) = p$ and $P(0) = 1 - p$. That is, the population $S$ is $B(1, p)$ with $\mu = p$ and $\sigma = \sqrt{p(1 - p)}$.

In a random sample of $n$ viewers, let $\bar{p}$ denote the proportion of viewers that watch the game; that is, $\bar{p}$ is the value of the sample mean $\bar{X}_n$ for that sample. Since the population mean $\mu = p$ is not known, neither is the population standard deviation $\sigma = \sqrt{p(1 - p)}$. We will estimate $\sigma$ by $\sqrt{\bar{p}(1 - \bar{p})}$. Then, when $n$ is sufficiently large, an approximate $(1 - \alpha)$ confidence interval for $p$ with margin of error $E$ is $[\bar{p} - E, \bar{p} + E]$, where

$$E = \frac{z_{\alpha/2} \cdot \sqrt{\bar{p}(1 - \bar{p})}}{\sqrt{n}} \qquad \text{and} \qquad 2\Phi(z_{\alpha/2}) = 1 - \alpha$$

**EXAMPLE 8.8** In a poll of 400 randomly selected voters conducted before the 1992 presidential election, the voters were asked to choose between George Bush and Bill Clinton; 220 favored Clinton and 180 favored Bush. Find (a) a 95 percent confidence interval for the proportion of all voters that favored Clinton at the time of the poll, and (b) a 90 percent confidence interval for the proportion of all voters that favored Bush at the time of the poll.

Let $p$ be the proportion of all voters that favored Clinton and $q = 1 - p$ the proportion that favored Bush (assuming one or the other must be favored). As described above, the voting population $S$ can be modeled as a Bernoulli distribution with mean $\mu = p$ and standard deviation $\sigma = \sqrt{pq}$. That is, $S = \{1, 0\}$, where $P(1) = P(\text{Clinton}) = p$ and $P(0) = P(\text{Bush}) = q$.

(a) The proportion of the 400 voters that favored Clinton (i.e., the sample mean) is $\bar{p} = 220/400 = .55$. The 95 percent confidence interval for $p$ is $[.55 - E, .55 + E]$, where $E$ is the margin of error. To compute $E$ from the formulas above, we first solve the equation $2\Phi(z_{\alpha/2}) = .95$, or $\Phi(z_{\alpha/2}) = .475$, for $z_{\alpha/2}$. From Appendix B, $z_{\alpha/2} = 1.96$. Then

$$E = \frac{1.96\sqrt{.55(1 - .55)}}{\sqrt{400}} \approx .05$$

The 95 percent confidence interval for $p$ is $[.55 - .05, .55 + .05] = [.5, .6]$. We say that 55 percent (.55) of the voters favored Clinton with a margin of error equal to 5 percent (.05).

(b) The proportion of the 400 voters favoring Bush is $\bar{q} = 180/400 = .45$. To find $E$ we first solve $2\Phi(z_{\alpha/2}) = .9$, or $\Phi(z_{\alpha/2}) = .45$, for $z_{\alpha/2}$, obtaining (from Appendix B) $z_{\alpha/2} = 1.64$. Then

$$E = \frac{1.64\sqrt{.45(1 - .45)}}{\sqrt{400}} \approx .04$$

The 90 percent confidence interval for $q$ is $[.45 - .04, .45 + .04] = [.41, .49]$.

For reference, Table 8-4 lists the $z$ scores for 90, 95, and 99 percent confidence intervals for the population mean $\mu$.

**Table 8-4**

| $1 - \alpha$ | $z_{\alpha/2}$ |
|---|---|
| .90 | 1.64 |
| .95 | 1.96 |
| .99 | 2.58 |

### Summary II

The results of this section can be summarized as follows. Suppose:

(1) $S$ is a population with mean $\mu$, which is unknown, and standard deviation $\sigma$, which may or may not be known.

(2)  $\bar{x}$ is the mean of a random sample of size $n \geq 30$, and $\bar{s}$ is the sample standard deviation.

(3)  $\alpha$ is a number greater than zero and less than 1, and the standard normal unit $z_{\alpha/2}$ satisfies $2\Phi(z_{\alpha/2}) = 1 - \alpha$.

Then a $(1 - \alpha)$ confidence interval for $\mu$ with margin of error $E$ is $[\bar{x} - E, \bar{x} + E]$ if $\sigma$ is known and approximately $[\bar{x} - E, \bar{x} + E]$ if $\sigma$ is not known, where $E = (z_{\alpha/2} \cdot \sigma)/\sqrt{n}$ if the value of $\sigma$ is known, and $E = (z_{\alpha/2} \cdot \bar{s})/\sqrt{n}$ if the value of $\sigma$ is not known.

In the case of a confidence interval for a proportion $p$ of a population, based on a proportion $\bar{p}$ of a sample of size $n$, let $\bar{x} = \bar{p}$ and $\bar{s} = \sqrt{\bar{p}(1 - \bar{p})}$ in the formula for $E$ above.

### Terminology: Parameters and Statistics

The mean $\mu$ and variance $\sigma^2$ of a population are called *parameters*, and the sample mean $\bar{x}$ and sample variance $\bar{s}^2$ of a random sample are called *statistics*.  In general, any quantity associated with a population is called a *parameter*, and any quantity computed from a sample of the population is called a *statistic*.  Statistics are used to estimate parameters.

A random variable is called a statistic if it does not explicitly depend on any unknown parameter of the population.  For example, the sample mean $\bar{X}_n = \Sigma X_i/n$ is a statistic, and the sample variance $\bar{s}_n^2 = \Sigma (X_i - \bar{X}_n^2)/(n - 1)$ is a statistic.  A random-variable statistic $X$ whose value on a random sample is used to estimate a parameter of the population is called an *unbiased estimator* if $E(X)$ is equal to the parameter.  Otherwise, $X$ is called a *biased estimator*.  $\bar{X}_n$ and $\bar{S}_n^2$ are unbiased estimators of $\mu$ and $\sigma^2$, respectively.  If the denominator $n - 1$ is replaced by $n$ in the definition of $\bar{S}_n^2$, the resulting statistic is a biased estimator of $\sigma^2$.

## 8.4  CHI-SQUARE TEST FOR GOODNESS OF FIT

### The Chi-Square Distribution

Because of the central limit theorem, the normal distribution plays a major role in finding confidence intervals for the mean of a population.  Another continuous probability distribution that plays an important role in inferential statistics is the chi-square distribution.  As illustrated in Fig. 8-4, there is a chi-square distribution for each positive number $k$, which is called the number of *degrees of freedom* of the distribution.  The chi-square random variable with $k$ degrees of freedom is often denoted by $\chi^2(k)$.  [It can be shown that if $Z$ is the standard normal random variable, then $Z^2$ is $\chi^2(1)$.]  Note that $\chi^2(k)$ assumes only nonnegative values.  Also, as $k$ increases, the $\chi^2(k)$ curves become less skewed to the right and more symmetric about the value, $\chi^2 = k - 2$.

Table 8-5 gives, for $k = 1, 2, \ldots, 10$, the value $c$ of $\chi^2(k)$ for which the area to the right of $c$ is equal to .05. That is, $P(\chi^2(k) \geq c) = .05$; $c$ is called the 5-percent *critical level* (see Fig. 8-5).

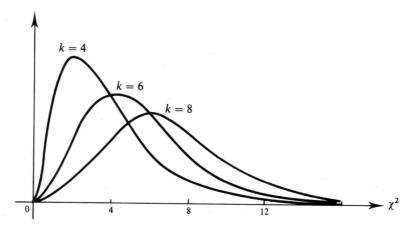

**Fig. 8-4**   For each choice of $k$, the probability that the random variable $\chi^2(k)$ lies between two values $a$ and $b$ $(0 < a < b)$ is the area under the corresponding curve above the interval $[a, b]$.

**Table 8-5\***

| k | 1 | 2 | 3 | 4 | 5 | 6 | 7 | 8 | 9 | 10 |
|---|---|---|---|---|---|---|---|---|---|---|
| c | 3.84 | 5.99 | 7.81 | 9.49 | 11.1 | 12.6 | 14.1 | 15.5 | 16.9 | 18.3 |

\* $k$ = degrees of freedom; $c$ = 5 percent critical level; $P(\chi^2(k) \geq c) = .05$.

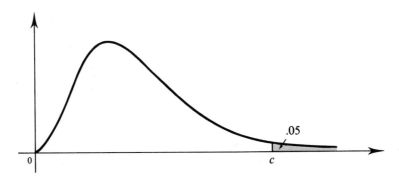

**Fig. 8-5**   $P(\chi^2(k) \geq c) = .05$.

### The Chi-Square Goodness-of-Fit Test

The chi-square distribution can be used to determine how well experimental data match expected values in a probability model. For example, if we toss a fair coin 10 times, the expected number of heads is 5, as is the expected number of tails. However, we could get more or fewer heads than tails in 10 tosses. It would not be very surprising to get 6 heads and 4 tails (probability $\approx .2$). It is even possible to get 10 heads with a fair coin, but the probability of 10 straight heads is only about .001, so we might begin to doubt that the coin is fair. Due to chance, we expect some variation in the data, but a great deal of variation would make us suspect that the model is not very accurate. Where do we draw the line? The chi-square test, which is based on Theorem 8.4, addresses this question.

**Theorem 8.4 (Basis for the Chi-Square Test):** In a probability model, let $a_1, a_2, \ldots, a_m$ be the possible outcomes of an experiment, with corresponding probabilities $p_1, p_2 \ldots, p_m$. For each performance of $n$ independent trials of the experiment, $np_i$ is the expected number of occurrences of $a_i$, and let $f_i$ be the actual number of occurrences of $a_i$ ($f_1 + f_2 + \cdots + f_m = n$). Then, for large values of $n$, the random variable

$$\chi^2 = \frac{(f_1 - np_1)^2}{np_1} + \frac{(f_2 - np_2)^2}{np_2} + \cdots + \frac{(f_m - np_m)^2}{np_m}$$

is approximately $\chi^2(m-1)$.

If $\chi^2 = 0$, then the experimental data exactly match the expected values, which supports the hypothesis that the probability model accurately represents the actual experiment; the larger $\chi^2$ is, the less likely it is that the model represents the experiment.

Just how large $n$ should be for a good approximation depends on the probability model, but a rule of thumb is that $np_i \geq 5$ for $i = 1, 2, \ldots, m$. If this condition is met, we compute $\chi^2$ and then apply the following criterion, which is called the *chi-square test at the 5 percent significance level*:

> If $\chi^2$ is greater than the 5 percent critical level for $m-1$ degrees of freedom, reject the model; otherwise, do not reject the model.

**EXAMPLE 8.9**　A die is tossed 60 times, and the frequency of each face is as indicated in the chart:

| $a_i$ (Face) | 1 | 2 | 3 | 4 | 5 | 6 |
|---|---|---|---|---|---|---|
| $f_i$ (Frequency) | 15 | 11 | 13 | 6 | 8 | 7 |

Assume the die is fair and apply the chi-square test at the 5 percent significance level to either reject or not reject the assumption.

If the die is fair, $np_i = 60(\frac{1}{6}) = 10$ for $i = 1, 2, ..., 6$.　Then

$$\chi^2 = \frac{(15-10)^2}{10} + \frac{(11-10)^2}{10} + \frac{(13-10)^2}{10} + \frac{(6-10)^2}{10} + \frac{(8-10)^2}{10} + \frac{(7-10)^2}{10}$$

$$= 6.4$$

From Table 8-5, the critical level $c$ at $6 - 1 = 5$ degrees of freedom is 11.1.　Since $\chi^2 = 6.4 < 11.1 = c$, we do not reject the fair die model.

**EXAMPLE 8.10**　A bag is supposed to contain 20 percent red beans and 80 percent white beans by number.　A random sample of 50 beans is taken from the bag.　The sample contains 16 red and 34 white beans.　Apply the chi-square test at the 5 percent significance level to either reject or not reject the hypothesis that the contents are as advertised.

If the contents are 20 percent red and 80 percent white, then $p_1 = P(\text{red}) = .2$, $p_2 = P(\text{white}) = .8$, $np_1 = 50(.2) = 10$, $np_2 = 50(.8) = 40$, and

$$\chi^2 = \frac{(16-10)^2}{10} + \frac{(34-40)^2}{40} = 4.5$$

From Table 8-5, the critical level $c$ at $2 - 1 = 1$ degree of freedom is 3.84.　Since $X^2 = 4.5 > 3.84$, we reject the hypothesis that there are 20 percent red and 80 percent white beans.

# Solved Problems

## SAMPLING DISTRIBUTIONS

**8.1.**　Find all samples of size $n = 3$ for the population $S = \{0, 1\}$.

$S_3 = \{(0, 0, 0), (0, 0, 1), (0, 1, 0), (0, 1, 1), (1, 0, 0), (1, 0, 1), (1, 1, 0), (1, 1, 1)\}$

**8.2.**　If a population has seven elements, how many elements are in the sample space $S_5$?

Each element in $S_5$ is a 5-tuple $(x_1, x_2, x_3, x_4, x_5)$ of elements in $S$.　Since $S$ has seven elements, there are

$$7 \cdot 7 \cdot 7 \cdot 7 \cdot 7 = 7^5 = 16{,}807$$

5-tuples in $S_5$.

**8.3.**　Given that the population $S = \{0, 1\}$ in Problem 8.1 is an equiprobable space, find the probability distribution of the sample mean $\overline{X}_3$.

The first of the following two tables gives the value $\bar{x} = (a + b + c)/3$ of $\overline{X}_3$ for each triple $(a, b, c)$ in $S_3$. The second table is the probability distribution of $\overline{X}_3$, where

$$P(\bar{x}) = \frac{\text{frequency of } \bar{x}}{8}$$

| $(a, b, c)$ | $\bar{x}$ |
|---|---|
| $(0, 0, 0)$ | $0$ |
| $(0, 0, 1)$ | $\frac{1}{3}$ |
| $(0, 1, 0)$ | $\frac{1}{3}$ |
| $(0, 1, 1)$ | $\frac{2}{3}$ |
| $(1, 0, 0)$ | $\frac{1}{3}$ |
| $(1, 0, 1)$ | $\frac{2}{3}$ |
| $(1, 1, 0)$ | $\frac{2}{3}$ |
| $(1, 1, 1)$ | $1$ |

| $\bar{x}$ | $P(\bar{x})$ |
|---|---|
| $0$ | $\frac{1}{8}$ |
| $\frac{1}{3}$ | $\frac{3}{8}$ |
| $\frac{2}{3}$ | $\frac{3}{8}$ |
| $1$ | $\frac{1}{8}$ |

**8.4.** Find the sample mean $\bar{\mu}$ and standard deviation $\bar{\sigma}$ of the random variable $\overline{X}_3$ in Problem 8.3, and compare these values to the population mean $\mu$ and standard deviation $\sigma$.

$$\bar{\mu} = E(\overline{X}_3) = 0 \cdot \tfrac{1}{8} + \tfrac{1}{3} \cdot \tfrac{3}{8} + \tfrac{2}{3} \cdot \tfrac{3}{8} + 1 \cdot \tfrac{1}{8} = \tfrac{4}{8} = \tfrac{1}{2}$$

$$\bar{\sigma} = \sqrt{(\Sigma \bar{x}^2 P(\bar{x}) - \bar{\mu}^2)}$$

$$= \sqrt{0 \cdot \tfrac{1}{8} + \tfrac{1}{9} \cdot \tfrac{3}{8} + \tfrac{4}{9} \cdot \tfrac{3}{8} + 1 \cdot \tfrac{1}{8} - \tfrac{1}{4}} = \sqrt{\tfrac{1}{12}} = \tfrac{1}{2\sqrt{3}}$$

Also, since the population $S = \{0, 1\}$ is an equiprobable space,

$$\mu = 0 \cdot \frac{1}{2} + 1 \cdot \frac{1}{2} = \frac{1}{2}$$

and

$$\sigma = \sqrt{\sigma = 0 \cdot \frac{1}{2} + 1 \cdot \frac{1}{2} - \frac{1}{4}} = \frac{1}{2}$$

Hence, we have

$$\bar{\mu} = \mu \quad \text{and} \quad \bar{\sigma} = \frac{\sigma}{\sqrt{3}}$$

which agrees with Theorem 8.1, where $n = 3$.

**8.5.** Let $S = \{1, 0\}$ be the possible outcomes of a single toss of a fair coin, 1 for heads and 0 for tails. If the coin is tossed 10 times, the sample space $S_{10}$ consists of $2^{10} = 1024$ 10-tuples of 1s and 0s, and the value $\bar{x}$ of the sample mean $\overline{X}_{10}$ on a 10-tuple $t$ is

$$\bar{x} = \frac{\text{number of 1s in } t}{10}$$

Find the probability distribution for $\overline{X}_{10}$.

First note that $\overline{X}_{10}$ can take on the values 0, .1, .2, .3, ..., 1. Note also that a single toss of the coin is a Bernoulli trial with $p$ = probability of a head = $\frac{1}{2}$, and $q$ = probability of a tail = $\frac{1}{2}$; 10 tosses are a binomial experiment $B(10, \frac{1}{2})$ (see Sec. 6.6). Now let $X$ = the number of heads in 10 tosses. Then $\overline{X}_{10} = X/10$, or $X = 10X$, and $P(X_{10} = \overline{x}) = P(X = 10\overline{x})$ where $10\overline{x} = 0, 1, 2, 3, ..., 10$. By substituting into the binomial probability formula

$$P(X = k) = \frac{n!}{k!\,(n-k)!}\,p^k q^{n-k} \qquad k = 0, 1, 2, ..., 10$$

we get the following probability distribution for $\overline{X}_{10}$:

| $\overline{x}$ | 0 | .1 | .2 | .3 | .4 | .5 | .6 | .7 | .8 | .9 | 1 |
|---|---|---|---|---|---|---|---|---|---|---|---|
| $P(\overline{x})$ | .001 | .010 | .044 | .177 | .205 | .246 | .205 | .117 | .044 | .010 | .001 |

**8.6.** Find the sample mean $\overline{\mu}$ and standard deviation $\overline{\sigma}$ of the random variable $\overline{X}_{10}$ in Problem 8.5 and verify Theorem 8.1 in this case.

From the probability distribution for $\overline{X}_{10}$ in Problem 8.5, we get

$$\overline{\mu} = E(\overline{X}_{10}) = 0(.001) + .1(.010) + .2(.044) + .3(.117)$$
$$+ .4(.205) + .5(.246) + .6(.205) + .7(.117)$$
$$+ .8(.044) + .9(.010) + 1(.001)$$
$$= .5$$
$$\overline{\sigma}^2 = \Sigma \overline{x}^2 P(\overline{x}) - \overline{\mu}^2$$
$$= 0(.001) + .01(.010) + .04(.044) + .09(.117)$$
$$+ .16(.205) + .25\,(.246) + .36(.205) + .49(.117)$$
$$+ .64(.044) + .81(.010) + 1(.001) - .25$$
$$= .025$$
$$\overline{\sigma} = \sqrt{.025}$$

Also, since the population $S = \{1, 0\}$ is an equiprobable space, we get, as in Problem 8.4, $\mu = .5$ and $\sigma = .5$. Hence, $\mu = .5 = \overline{\mu}$ and $\sigma/\sqrt{10} = .5/\sqrt{10} = \sqrt{.25/10} = \sqrt{.025} = \overline{\sigma}$, as stated in Theorem 8.1.

## THE CENTRAL LIMIT THEOREM

**8.7.** The daily number in a state lottery is a number between 000 and 999. A person buys a lottery ticket for \$1, and if the three digits on the ticket exactly match the daily number, the person wins \$500. If the numbers do not match, the state wins the \$1 cost of the ticket.

(a) What is the mean and standard deviation of the state's income on any one lottery ticket?

(b) If 1 million \$1 lottery tickets are purchased over a period of time; what is the mean and standard deviation of the state's average income per ticket?

(c) Use the central limit theorem to determine the probability that the state's average income per ticket for 1 million tickets will be less than \$0.45.

(a) Let $X$ be the state's income per ticket, positive for a state win, negative for a loss. If the lottery ticket does not match the daily number, $X = \$1$; in the case of a match, $X = -\$499$, that is, \$1 for the cost of the ticket minus $500 paid out to the winning ticket. Since there is only one winning number out of the 1000 numbers from 000 to 999:

$$P(X = 1) = \frac{999}{1000} \quad \text{and} \quad P(X = -499) = \frac{1}{1000}$$

Therefore, the mean of the state's income for one ticket is

$$\mu = E(X) = 1 \cdot \frac{999}{1000} + (-499)\frac{1}{1000} = \frac{500}{1000} = \$0.5$$

The standard deviation is

$$\sigma = \sqrt{1^2 \cdot \frac{999}{1000} + (-499)^2 \frac{1}{1000} - (.5)^2} = \$15.80$$

(b) By Theorem 8.1, the mean $\overline{\mu}$ and standard deviation $\overline{\sigma}$ of the state's average income $\overline{X}_{1,000,000}$ for 1 million $1 tickets is

$$\overline{\mu} = \mu = \$0.5 \quad \text{and} \quad \overline{\sigma} = \frac{\sigma}{\sqrt{1,000,000}} = \frac{15.80}{1000} = \$0.0158$$

(c) By the central limit theorem, $\overline{X}_{10,000}$ is approximately normally distributed with mean $\overline{\mu} = \$5$ and standard deviation $\overline{\sigma} = \$0.0158$. Switching to standard units $Z = (\overline{X}_{1,000,000} - .5)/0.0158$, we get

$$P(\overline{X}_{1,000,000} < .45) = P\left(Z < \frac{.45 - .5}{.0158} = -3.16\right)$$
$$= .5 - \Phi(3.16)$$
$$= .5 - .4992$$
$$= .0008$$

Hence, it is extremely unlikely that the state will average less than $0.45 per ticket for 1 million tickets.

**8.8.** With reference to Problem 8.7, if a person buys a $1 lottery ticket 360 days a year for 10 years, what is the probability that the person's average winnings per ticket will be negative, i.e., that the person will have a net loss after 10 years?

Since the mean and standard deviation of the state's income per ticket are $0.5 and $15.80, respectively, it follows that the mean and standard deviation of a player's winnings per ticket are $\mu = -\$0.5$ and $\sigma = \$15.80$, respectively.

In 10 years, or 3600 plays, the average winnings per ticket, $\overline{X}_{3600}$, has, by Theorem 8.1, mean $\overline{\mu} = -\$0.5$, and standard deviation $\overline{\sigma} = 15.80/\sqrt{3600} = \$0.2633$. Then:

$$P(\overline{X}_{3600} < 0) = P\left(Z < \frac{0 - (-.5)}{.2633} = 1.90\right) = .5 + \Phi(1.90) = .5 + .4713 = .9713$$

Hence, it is virtually certain that a person will have a net loss over a 10-year period.

**8.9.** A fair coin is tossed 10,000 times. Use the central limit theorem to approximate the probability that the number of heads obtained is between (a) 4900 and 5100, (b) 4850 and 5150.

The result of the $i$th toss of the coin (1 for a head, zero for a tail) is a Bernoulli random variable $X_i$ with mean $\mu = 1(.5)$ and standard deviation $\sigma = \sqrt{1(.5)\,(.5)} = .5$. By the alternative form of the central limit theorem, the number of heads in 10,000 tosses,

$$Y_{10,000} = X_1 + X_2 + \cdots + X_{10,000}$$

is approximately normal with mean $\mu = 10,000(.5) = 5000$ and standard deviation
$$\hat{\sigma} = \sqrt{10,000\,(.5)(.5)} = 50$$

(a)  Since 4900 is 2 standard deviations to the left of the mean 5000, and 5100 is 2 standard deviations to the right of the mean, it follows by the 68-95-99.7 rule (see Example 6.21) that the probability of $Y_{10,000}$ falling between 4900 and 5100 is approximately .95.

(b)  Since 4850 is 3 standard deviations to the left of the mean, and 5150 is 3 standard deviations to the right, it follows from the 68–95–99.7 rule that the probability of $Y_{10,000}$ falling between 4850 and 5150 is approximately .997.

## CONFIDENCE INTERVALS FOR POPULATION MEANS

**8.10.**  Show that $P(\mu - E \le \overline{X}_n \le \mu + E) = .95$ is equivalent to $P(\overline{X}_n - E \le \mu \le \overline{X}_n + E) = .95$.

We show that the inequalities inside the parentheses for the two probabilities are equivalent by reducing the first to the second in a series of reversible steps. Starting with

$$\mu - E \le \overline{X}_n \le \mu + E$$

add $-\mu + (-\overline{X}_n)$ to both sides of each inequality to obtain

$$-\overline{X}_n - E \le -\mu \le -\overline{X}_n + E$$

Multiplying through by $-1$ reverses the inequalities. Hence:

$$\overline{X}_n + E \ge \mu \ge \overline{X}_n - E$$

which can be rewritten as

$$\overline{X}_n - E \le \mu \le \overline{X}_n + E$$

**8.11.**  For each of the following probabilities in the form $P(\mu - E \le \overline{X}_n \le \mu + E) = 1 - \alpha$, find the mean $\mu$, the margin of error $E$, and the significance level $\alpha$:       (a)   $P(70 \le \overline{X}_n \le 90) = .95$; (b)   $P(-5 \le \overline{X}_n \le 10) = .9$;       (c)   $P(-15 \le \overline{X}_n \le -10) = .98$.

(a)  To find $\mu$ and $E$, we solve the system of equations

$$\mu - E = 70$$
$$\mu + E = 90$$

Adding the equations gives $2\mu = 160$, or $\mu = 80$. Substituting $\mu = 80$ in the second equation gives $80 + E = 90$, or $E = 10$. To find $\alpha$, we set $.95 = 1 - \alpha$, which gives $\alpha = .05$.

(b)  Proceeding as in part (a), we obtain $\mu = 2.5$, $E = 7.5$, and $\alpha = .1$.

(c)  Here the method of part (a) gives $\mu = -12.5$, $E = 2.5$, and $\alpha = .02$.

**8.12.**  For each of the following probabilities and sample means $\overline{x}$, find the corresponding 95 percent confidence interval:       (a)   $P(\overline{X}_n - 3 \le \mu \le \overline{X}_n + 3) = .95$, $\overline{x} = 47$; (b)   $P(\overline{X}_n - .1 \le \mu \le \overline{X}_n + .1) = .95$, $\overline{x} = 7.4$.

(a)  $[\overline{x} - E, \overline{x} + E] = [47 - 3, 47 + 3] = [44, 50]$

(b)  $[\overline{x} - E, \overline{x} + E] = [7.4 - .1, 7.4 + .1] = [7.3, 7.5]$

**8.13.**  The heights of American men and women are each approximately normally distributed with a standard deviation of 2.5 inches.   Find the sample size needed in each case to find a 95 percent confidence interval for the mean height with margin of error equal to 1 inch.

We use the formula $E = (z_{\alpha/2} \cdot \sigma)/ \sqrt{n}$ from Theorem 8.3.   Since $1 - \alpha = .95$, we get, from Table 8-4, $z_{\alpha/2} = 1.96$ (note that the 68-95-99.7 rule gives $z \approx 2$).   Substituting in the formula above for $E$ gives

$$1 = \frac{1.96 \cdot 2.5}{\sqrt{n}} \qquad \text{or} \qquad \sqrt{n} = 1.96 \cdot 2.5 = 4.9$$

Hence, $n = (4.9)^2 \approx 24$.

**8.14.**  With reference to Problem 8.13, suppose the heights in inches of (*a*) 24 men and (*b*) 24 women, each selected at random, are as follows:

(*a*)  | 71 | 66 | 63 | 70 | 74 | 68 | 72 | 70 | 76 | 66 | 69 | 68 |
|---|---|---|---|---|---|---|---|---|---|---|---|
| 69 | 71 | 67 | 69 | 70 | 73 | 68 | 64 | 70 | 69 | 67 | 73 |

(*b*)  | 62 | 63 | 59 | 66 | 60 | 64 | 65 | 64 | 62 | 68 | 61 | 63 |
|---|---|---|---|---|---|---|---|---|---|---|---|
| 66 | 64 | 63 | 64 | 61 | 67 | 62 | 63 | 65 | 69 | 61 | 62 |

Use these to construct in each case a 95 percent confidence interval for the mean height with margin of error 1 inch.

(*a*)   The value of the sample mean $\bar{x}$ is 69.3.   The 95 percent confidence interval for $\mu$ is [68.3, 70.3].

(*b*)   Here, $\bar{x} = 63.5$, and the 95 percent confidence interval for $\mu$ is [62.5, 64.5].

**8.15.**  IQ tests administered to 10,000 people resulted in an average score $\bar{x} = 100.1$.   Assuming that IQ scores are approximately normally distributed with standard deviation $\sigma = 10$, find the corresponding 99 percent confidence interval for the mean IQ.

We use the formulas in Theorem 8.3.   Since $1 - \alpha = .99$, we get $z_{\alpha/2} = 2.58$ from Table 8-4.   The margin of error is

$$E - \frac{2.58 \cdot 10}{\sqrt{10,000}} = \frac{25.8}{100} = .258$$

Hence, the corresponding 99 percent confidence interval is
$$[100.1 - .256, 100.1 + .258] = [99.844, 100.358] \text{ or, approximately, } [99.8, 100.4]$$

**8.16.**  A sample of size $n = 100$ is taken from a population that is normally distributed with a standard deviation $\sigma = 5$.   The sample mean is $\bar{x} = 75$.   What is the corresponding confidence interval for the population mean $\mu$ having a margin of error $E = 1.5$? What is the confidence level $1 - \alpha$?

The confidence interval is $[75 - 1.5, 75 + 1.5] = [73.5, 76.5]$.   To find $1 - \alpha$, we first substitute in the formula $E = (z_{\alpha/2} \cdot \sigma)/\sqrt{n}$, getting $1.5 = (z_{\alpha/2} \cdot 5)/\sqrt{100} = z_{\alpha/2}/2$, or $z_{\alpha/2} = 3$.   Then, from Table 15.3, we find that $\Phi(3) = .4987$.   Finally, substituting in the formula $2\Phi(z_{\alpha/2}) = 1 - \alpha$, we get $2(.4987) = .9974 = 1 - \alpha$.   Hence, [73.5, 76.5] is a 99.74 percent confidence interval.

## WHEN σ IS NOT KNOWN

**8.17.** Assuming that the standard deviation of the height of American men is not known, use the data in Problem 8.14(*a*) to find a 95 percent confidence interval for the mean height $\mu$. Compare this with the 95 percent confidence interval obtained in Problem 8.14(*a*).

From Problem 8.14(*a*), $n = 25$, $\bar{x} = 69.3$, and from Table 8-4, $z_{\alpha/2} = 1.96$. To find the margin of error $E$, we must first compute the sample standard deviation $\bar{s}$. Using the 24 values of $x_i$ in Problem 8.14(*a*), we get

$$\bar{s} = \sqrt{\frac{\Sigma(x_i - 69.3)^2}{23}} \approx 3.06$$

Then, $E = (z_{\alpha/2} \cdot \bar{s})/\sqrt{24} \approx [(1.96)(3.06)]/\sqrt{24} \approx 1.2$, and the 95 percent confidence interval for $\mu$ is $[69.3 - 1.2, 69.3 + 1.2] = [68.1, 70.5]$, compared to $[68.3, 70.3]$ obtained in Problem 8.14(*a*).

**8.18.** Given $n = 400$ and $\sigma \leq 10$, find the maximum margin of error $E$ at the 95 percent confidence level.

From Table 8-4, $z_{\alpha/2} = 1.96$. Then

$$E = \frac{1.96\sigma}{\sqrt{400}} \leq \frac{(1.96)(10)}{20} = .98$$

**8.19.** If $n = 100$, what is the maximum standard deviation $\sigma$ for which the margin of error $E$ is no more than 3 at the 95 percent confidence level?

From Table 8-4, $z_{\alpha/2} = 1.96$. Then

$$E = \frac{1.96\sigma}{\sqrt{100}} \leq 3 \qquad \text{implies} \qquad \sigma \leq \frac{3(10)}{1.96} \approx 15.3$$

## CONFIDENCE INTERVALS FOR THE BINOMIAL PROPORTION *p*

**8.20.** One week after Bill Clinton was elected the 42nd U.S. President, 1000 people were polled and asked what they felt the top priority of the new administration should be. The results were the following:

(*a*)  Create jobs              50 percent

(*b*)  Cut the deficit          18 percent

(*c*)  Reform health care       14 percent

(*d*)  Improve education         8 percent

(*e*)  Other                    10 percent

Find 95 percent confidence intervals for categories (*a*) and (*b*).

(*a*)   The sample proportion $\bar{p}$ is .5, and from Table 8-4, $z_{\alpha/2} = 1.96$.   The margin of error is

$$E = \frac{z_{\alpha/2}\sqrt{\bar{p}(1-\bar{p})}}{\sqrt{n}} = \frac{1.96\sqrt{.5(1-.5)}}{\sqrt{1000}} \approx .03$$

The 95 percent confidence interval for the proportion *p* of the people in the United States whose top priority is creating jobs is [.5 − .03, 5 + .03] = [.47, .53], or [47%, 53%].

(*b*)   $\bar{p} = .18$, $z_{\alpha/2} = 1.96$, and $E = 1.96\sqrt{.18(.82)}/\sqrt{1000} \approx .02$.   The 95 percent confidence interval for the proportion of people whose top priority is to cut the deficit is
$$[.18 - .02, .18 + .02] = [.16, .20], \text{ or } [16\%, 20\%]$$

**8.21.**   Find 90 percent confidence intervals for categories (*c*) and (*d*) in Problem 8.20.

(*c*)   Here, $\bar{p} = .14$, and from Table 8-4, $z_{\alpha/2} = 2.58$.   The margin of error is $E = 2.58\sqrt{.14(.86)}/\sqrt{1000}$ $\approx .03$.   The 99 percent confidence interval for the proportion of people in the United States whose top priority is to reform health care is [.14 − .03, .14 + .03] = [.11, .17], or [11%, 17%].

(*d*)   $\bar{p} = .08$, $z_{\alpha/2} = 2.58$, and $E = [2.58\sqrt{.08(.92)}]/\sqrt{1000} \approx .02$.   The 99 percent confidence interval for the proportion of people whose top priority is to improve education is
$$[.08 - .02, .08 + .02] = [.06, .10], \text{ or } [6\%, 10\%]$$

**8.22.**   It can be shown that if $0 < p < 1$, then $0 < p(1-p) < .25$.   Use this to show that a sample of size 1500 will give a margin of error less than 3 percent for the binomial proportion at the 95 percent confidence level.

$$z_{\alpha/2} = 1.96$$

and   $$E = \frac{1.96\sqrt{p(1-p)}}{\sqrt{1500}} < \frac{1.96\sqrt{.25}}{\sqrt{1500}} \approx .0253 = 2.53\% < 3\%$$

**8.23.**   The monthly unemployment rates released by the U.S. Bureau of Labor Statistics are based on polls of 60,000 families.   Find the maximum margin of error for unemployment rates at the 90 percent confidence level.

From Table 8-4, $z_{\alpha/2} = 1.64$, and from Problem 8.22, $0 < \bar{p}(1-\bar{p}) < .25$.   Hence, the margin of error *E* satisfies

$$E = \frac{1.64\sqrt{\bar{p}(1-\bar{p})}}{\sqrt{60,000}} < \frac{1.64\sqrt{.25}}{\sqrt{60,000}} \approx .0034 \qquad \text{or} \qquad .34\%$$

**8.24.**   What must the sample size be in order to have a margin of error at most 2 percent for the binomial proportion at the confidence level   (*a*) 90 percent,   (*b*) 95 percent, and   (*c*) 99 percent?

If $\bar{p} > 0$ is the sample proportion, then, from Problem 8.22, $0 < \bar{p}(1-\bar{p}) < .25$.   We want

$$E = \frac{z_{\alpha/2}\sqrt{\bar{p}(1-\bar{p})}}{\sqrt{n}} < \frac{z_{\alpha/2}\sqrt{.25}}{\sqrt{n}} \leq .02$$

or

$$\sqrt{n} \geq \frac{z_{\alpha/2}(.5)}{.02} = 25z_{\alpha/2} \qquad \text{or} \qquad n \geq 625\,(z_{\alpha/2})^2$$

(a)   From Table 8-4, $z_{\alpha/2} = 1.64$;   $n \geq 625(1.64)^2 = 1681$.

(b)   $z_{\alpha/2} = 1.96$;   $n \geq 625(1.96)^2 = 2401$.

(c)   $z_{\alpha/2} = 2.58$;   $n \geq 625(2.58)^2 = 4160.25$.

## CHI-SQUARE TEST

**8.25.**   A coin is tossed 100 times, resulting in 60 heads (H) and 40 tails (T).   Assume the coin is fair and apply the chi-square test at the 5 percent significance level to either reject or not reject the hypothesis of fairness.

By assumption, $P(H) = .5 = P(T)$, so $nP(H) = 100(.5) = 50 = nP(T)$.   Therefore,

$$\chi^2 = \frac{(60-50)^2}{50} + \frac{(40-50)^2}{50} = 4$$

Here, $m = 2$, so there is $m - 1 = 1$ degree of freedom, for which the critical level is $c = 3.84$ by Table 8-5.   Since $\chi^2 = 4 > 3.84$, we reject the hypothesis that the coin is fair.

**8.26.**   Suppose a coin is tossed 100 times, resulting in $y$ heads.   For what value of $y$ will the hypothesis that the coin is fair not be rejected on the basis of a chi-square test at the 5 percent significance level?

If $y =$ the number of heads, then $100 - y =$ the number of tails.   For the hypothesis of fairness not to be rejected at the 5 percent significance level, we must have (see Problem 8.25)

$$\chi^2 = \frac{(y-50)^2}{50} + \frac{(100-y-50)^2}{50} \leq 3.84$$

which simplifies to

$$\frac{(y-50)^2}{50} + \frac{(50-y)^2}{50} \leq 3.84 \qquad \text{or} \qquad \frac{2(y-50)^2}{50} \leq 3.84$$

Simplifying further

$$(y-50)^2 \leq 25(3.84) \qquad \text{or} \qquad |y - 50| \leq 5\sqrt{3.84} \approx 9.80 < 10$$

Hence, $y$ must satisfy $|y - 50| < 10$, which is equivalent to $-10 < y - 50 < 10$, or $40 < y < 60$. Therefore, if there are more than 40 but fewer than 60 heads in 100 tosses, the hypothesis of fairness will not be rejected.

**8.27.**   A random digit generator on a calculator gave the following results out of 100 digits generated:

| Digit | 0 | 1 | 2 | 3 | 4 | 5 | 6 | 7 | 8 | 9 |
|---|---|---|---|---|---|---|---|---|---|---|
| Frequency | 11 | 11 | 9 | 8 | 8 | 11 | 9 | 11 | 13 | 9 |

Test the hypothesis that the digits are random by a chi-square test at the 5 percent significnace level.

If the digits are random, then the probability that an $i$ will occur, for $i = 0, 1, 2, \ldots, 9$, is $p_i = .1$. Therefore, $np_i = 100( \cdot 1) = 10$. Note that four of the digits occurred 11 times, three occurred 9 times, two occurred 8 times, and one occurred 13 times. Hence:

$$\chi^2 = \frac{4(11 - 10)^2}{10} + \frac{3(9 - 10)^2}{10} + \frac{2(8 - 10)^2}{10} + \frac{(13 - 10)^2}{10}$$

$$= \frac{4 + 3 + 8 + 9}{10} = 2.4$$

There are $10 - 1 = 9$ degrees of freedom for which the critical level, by Table 8-5, is 16.9. Since $2.4 < 16.9$, we do not reject the hypothesis that the digits are random.

**8.28.** The standard normal random variable $Z$, with mean zero and standard deviation 1, has a probability distribution, in terms of interval classes of length 1, as shown in the first two columns of the following table. The third column shows the class frequencies of 100 $z$ scores chosen at random from some population. Use the data given in the rest of the table to apply a chi-square test at the 5 percent significance level to the hypothesis that the $z$ scores are a sample from a standard normal population.

| $z_i$ | $p_i$ | $f_i$ | $100p_i$ | $f_i - 100p_i$ | $\dfrac{(f_i - 100p_i)^2}{100p_i}$ |
|---|---|---|---|---|---|
| $(-\infty, -2.5)$ | .0062 | 1 | 0.62 | 0.38 | 0.23 |
| $[-2.5, -1.5)$ | .0606 | 6 | 6.06 | -0.06 | 0.00 |
| $[-1.5, -0.5)$ | .2417 | 15 | 24.17 | -9.17 | 3.48 |
| $[-0.5, 0.5)$ | .3830 | 45 | 38.30 | 6.70 | 1.17 |
| $[0.5, 1.5)$ | .2417 | 25 | 24.17 | 0.83 | 0.03 |
| $[1.5, 2.5)$ | .0606 | 8 | 6.06 | 1.94 | 0.62 |
| $[2.5, \infty)$ | .0062 | 0 | 0.62 | -0.62 | 0.62 |

The sum of the values in the last column gives $\chi^2 = 6.15$. There are $m = 7$ classes, so the number of degrees of freedom is $7 - 1 = 6$. From Table 8-5, the critical value for 6 degrees of freedom is 12.6. Since $6.15 < 12.6$, we do not reject the hypothesis that the $z$ scores are from a normal population.

**8.29.** Use the class frequency distribution of Problem 8.28 to apply a chi-square test at the 5 percent significance level to the hypothesis that the following 50 test scores are approximate normally distributed:

| | | | | |
|---|---|---|---|---|
| 30 | 66 | 71 | 78 | 88 |
| 40 | 66 | 72 | 78 | 89 |
| 42 | 67 | 72 | 80 | 90 |
| 52 | 67 | 73 | 80 | 90 |
| 55 | 68 | 74 | 82 | 92 |
| 60 | 68 | 74 | 83 | 93 |
| 60 | 68 | 75 | 84 | 93 |
| 62 | 70 | 76 | 84 | 94 |
| 64 | 70 | 76 | 85 | 95 |
| 65 | 70 | 78 | 86 | 97 |

First, we compute the sample mean and standard deviation of the scores to be $\bar{x} = 73.84$ and $S = 14.40$, respectively.   Next, we convert the $X$ scores to standard $z$ scores $z = (x - \bar{x})/s$, as follows:

| | | | | |
|---|---|---|---|---|
| −3.04 | −0.54 | −0.20 | 0.29 | 0.98 |
| −2.35 | −0.54 | −0.13 | 0.29 | 1.05 |
| −2.21 | −0.48 | −0.13 | 0.43 | 1.12 |
| −1.52 | −0.48 | −0.06 | 0.43 | 1.12 |
| −1.31 | −0.41 | 0.01 | 0.57 | 1.26 |
| −0.96 | −0.41 | 0.01 | 0.64 | 1.33 |
| −0.96 | −0.41 | 0.08 | 0.71 | 1.33 |
| −0.82 | −0.27 | 0.15 | 0.71 | 1.40 |
| −0.68 | −0.27 | 0.15 | 0.78 | 1.47 |
| −0.61 | −0.27 | 0.29 | 0.84 | 1.61 |

As in Problem 8.28, the $z$ scores are used to complete the following table:

| $z_i$ | $p_i$ | $f_i$ | $50p_i$ | $f_i - 50p_i$ | $\dfrac{(f_i - 50p_i)^2}{50p_i}$ |
|---|---|---|---|---|---|
| $(-\infty, -2.5)$ | .0062 | 1 | 0.310 | 0.690 | 1.54 |
| $[-2.5, -1.5)$ | .0606 | 3 | 3.030 | −0.030 | 0.00 |
| $[-1.5, -0.5)$ | .2417 | 8 | 12.085 | −4.085 | 1.38 |
| $[-0.5, 0.5)$ | .3830 | 22 | 19.150 | 2.850 | 0.42 |
| $[0.5, 1.5)$ | .2417 | 15 | 12.085 | 2.915 | 0.70 |
| $[1.5, 2.5)$ | .0606 | 1 | 3.030 | −2.030 | 1.36 |
| $[2.5, \infty)$ | .0062 | 0 | 0.310 | −0.310 | 0.31 |

The sum of the terms in the last column is $\chi^2 = 5.71$, which is less than the critical value $c = 12.6$ for 6 degrees of freedom (see Problem 8.28).   Hence, we do not reject the hypothesis that the test scores are approximately normally distributed.

# Supplementary Problems

## SAMPLING DISTRIBUTIONS

**8.30.**   Find all samples of size $n = 2$ for the population $S = \{1, 2, 3, 4\}$.

**8.31.**   Assuming the population $S$ in the Problem 8.30 is an equiprobable space, find the probability distribution for the sample mean $\bar{X}_2$ on the sample space $S_2$.

**8.32.**   Compute $\bar{\mu}$ and $\bar{\sigma}$ for the sample mean $\bar{X}_2$ in Problem 8.31.

**8.33.** Suppose that a numerical population $S$ has five elements, mean $\mu$, and standard deviation $\sigma$. How many elements does the sample space $S_3$ have? What are the mean $\bar{\mu}$ and standard $\bar{\sigma}$ of the random variable $\bar{X}_3$?

**8.34.** Suppose that a population $S$ has standard deviation 10. How large must $n$ be for the sample mean $\bar{X}_n$ to have standard deviation 1?

## CONFIDENCE INTERVALS

**8.35.** An approximately normal population has standard deviation 100. How large must a sample be to find a 95 percent confidence interval for the population mean with margin of error at most (*a*) $E = 10$ and (*b*) $E = 1$?

**8.36.** Suppose $\bar{x} = 75$ for a sample of size 100 of an approximately normal population with $\sigma = 25$. Find a 90 percent confidence interval for $\mu$.

**8.37.** A sample of size 50 produces a margin of error $E = 8$, at a 95 percent confidence level, for a population mean. What is the standard deviation of the population?

**8.38.** Using the sample data in Problem 8.14, find a 90 percent confidence interval for the heights of: (*a*) American men and (*b*) American women. (Use $\sigma = 2.5$ inches in each case.)

**8.39.** Suppose the pulse rates of a random sample of 20 males under the age of 30 were as follows:

| 60 | 75 | 72 | 58 | 64 | 80 | 60 | 72 | 56 | 65 |
|----|----|----|----|----|----|----|----|----|----|
| 72 | 60 | 73 | 65 | 62 | 78 | 82 | 70 | 68 | 60 |

Use these data to find a 95 percent confidence interval for the mean pulse rate of males under 30.

**8.40.** Suppose 75 percent of a random sample of 36 children 6 years old say they believe in Santa Claus. Find a 90 percent confidence interval for the percent of 6-year-olds that believe in Santa Claus.

**8.41.** A marketing research firm wishes to conduct a poll in a certain region to determine the proportion of residents that favor the construction of a new shopping mall in the region. Determine the sample size needed to be 90 percent confident that the sample proportion will be within .05 of the true proportion.

## CHI-SQUARE TEST

**8.42.** Over the years, the grades in a certain college professor's class are typically as follows: 10 percent A's, 20 percent B's, 50 percent C's, 15 percent D's, and 5 percent F's. The grades for her current class of 100 are 16 A's, 28 B's, 46 C's, 10 D's, and 0 F's. Test the hypothesis that the current class is typical by a chi-square test at the 5 percent significance level.

**8.43.** It is estimated that the political preference in a certain community is as follows: 50 percent Democrat, 25 percent Republican, 15 percent Independent, and 10 percent other. A random sample of 200 people gave the results 90 Democrat, 65 Republican, 25 Independent, and 20 other. Test the hypothesis that the estimate is correct by a chi-square test at the 5 percent significance level.

# Answers to Supplementary Problems

**8.30.**  $S_2 = \{(1, 1), (1, 2), (1, 3), (1, 4), (2, 1), (2, 2), (2, 3), (2, 4), (3, 1), (3, 2), (3, 3), (3, 4), (4, 1), (4, 2), (4, 3), (4, 4)\}$

**8.31.**

| $\bar{x}$ | 1 | 1.5 | 2 | 2.5 | 3 | 3.5 | 4 |
|---|---|---|---|---|---|---|---|
| $P(\bar{x})$ | $\dfrac{1}{16}$ | $\dfrac{2}{16}$ | $\dfrac{3}{16}$ | $\dfrac{4}{16}$ | $\dfrac{3}{16}$ | $\dfrac{2}{16}$ | $\dfrac{1}{16}$ |

**8.32.**  $\bar{\mu} = 2.5, \bar{\sigma} \approx .79$

**8.33.**  $S_3$ has $5^3 = 125$ elements, $\bar{\mu} = \mu, \bar{\sigma} = \sigma/\sqrt{5}$.

**8.34.**  100

**8.35.**  (a)  385,    (b)  38,416

**8.36.**  [70.9, 79.1]

**8.37.**  Approximately 28.86

**8.38.**  (a)  [68.5, 70.1],    (b)  [62.7, 64.3]

**8.39.**  [64.2, 71]

**8.40.**  [63.2%, 86.8%]

**8.41.**  Approximately 270

**8.42.**  $\chi^2 = 13.79, k = 4, c = 9.49$; since $13.79 > 9.49$, reject the hypothesis that the class is typical.

**8.43.**  $\chi^2 = 6.33, k = 3, c = 7.81$; since $6.33 \leq 7.81$, do not reject the estimate.

# CHAPTER 9

# Graphs and Networks

## 9.1 INTRODUCTION

Graphs, directed graphs, networks, and tree graphs appear in many applications of of mathematics. We treat these topics in this chapter. First we give some basic definitions.

### Graphs, Vertices, and Edges

The term *graph* has several meanings in mathematics. Here we define a graph $G$ to consist of two things:

    (*i*)    A finite collection $V$ of elements called *vertices* or *points* of $G$.

    (*ii*)    A finite collection $E$ of edges of $G$ where each edge e links a pair of vertices, called the endpoints of $e$, or links a vertex to itself.

Graphs are pictured by diagrams in the plane in a natural way. Specifically, each vertex $v$ in $V$ is represented by a dot (or small circle), and each edge $e$ is represented by a curve which connects its endpoints.

### EXAMPLE 9.1

(*a*)    The graph in Fig. 9-1(*a*) consists of four vertices $A$, $B$, $C$, and $D$ and five edges $e_1$, $e_2$, $e_3$, $e_4$, and $e_5$ linking vertices $A$ and $B$, $B$ and $C$, $C$ and $D$, $A$, and $C$, and $B$ and $D$, respectively. These edges could also be denoted by $AB$, $BC$, $CD$, $AC$, and $BD$, respectively. Note that the point of intersection of the two edges $e_4$ and $e_5$ is *not* a vertex.

(*b*)    The graph in Fig. 9-1(*b*) consists of four vertices and seven edges. The two edges $e_4$ and $e_5$ linking $A$ to $C$ are called *multiple edges*. The edge $e_7$ linking vertex $D$ to itself is called a *loop*. Graphs without multiple edges or loops are called *simple graphs*.

(*c*)    The graph in Fig. 9-1(*c*) consists of eight vertices $A$, $B$, $C$, $D$, $J$, $K$, $L$, $M$ and eight edges.

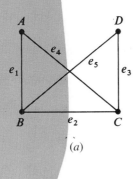

(*a*)

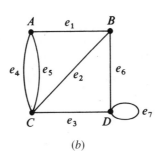

(*b*)

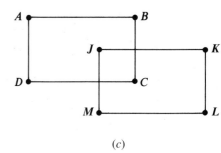

(*c*)

**Fig. 9-1**

## Paths and Connected Graphs

A sequence of edges $A_iA_{i+1}$, $i = 1, 2, ..., n - 1$, is called a *path* from $A_1$ to $A_n$, or a path linking $A_1$ to $A_n$. A graph is *connected* if for every two of its vertices there is a path linking them. Graphs in Fig. 9-1($a$) and ($b$) are connected, but the graph in Fig. 9-1($c$) is not connected, since none of the vertices $A$, $B$, $C$, $D$ can be linked by a path to any of the vertices $J$, $K$, $L$, $M$.

## 9.2   EULER CIRCUITS

### The Königsberg Bridge Problem

The eighteenth-century East Prussian town of Königsberg included two islands and seven bridges shown in Fig. 9-2($a$). As a common Sunday pastime, the citizens would stroll over all seven bridges, which led to the following question: *Beginning and ending at the same point, can a person walk across each of the seven bridges exactly once?*

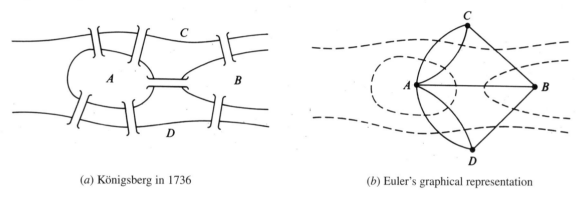

(a) Königsberg in 1736                             (b) Euler's graphical representation

**Fig. 9-2**

The Swiss mathematician Leonhard Euler (1707–1783) proved in 1736 that such a walk is impossible. He represented the islands and the two sides of the river by vertices and the bridges by edges, obtaining the graph in Fig. 9-2($b$). Euler not only proved that the Königsberg walk was impossible; he also showed what conditions must be satisfied by a graph in order that such a problem have a solution. To facilitate the statement of Euler's theorem, we first give some definitions.

### Degree of a Vertex

The *degree* (or *valence*) of a vertex is the number of edges in the graph that have the vertex as an endpoint. In Fig. 9-3($a$) the vertices $P_1$, $P_2$, $P_3$, $P_4$, $P_5$, and $P_6$ have degrees 1, 3, 2, 3, 3, and 0, respectively.

In computing the degree, a loop is counted as two edges. For example, in Fig. 9-3($b$), vertices $P_1$, $P_2$, $P_3$, $P_4$, and $P_5$ have degrees 4, 3, 2, 3, and 4, respectively.

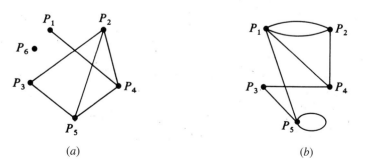

(a)                                             (b)

**Fig. 9-3**

### Euler Circuits and Eulerian Graphs

A path that begins and ends at the same vertex is called a *closed path*, and a closed path that includes every edge of a graph exactly once is called an *Euler circuit*.

For example, in Fig. 9-4(a), starting at $A$, the path $e_1 e_2 e_5$ is a closed path but not an Euler circuit because not every edge in the graph is traversed. The path $e_1 e_2 e_5 e_4 e_3 e_5$ is a closed path in which every edge is traversed, but it is not an Euler circuit because edge $e_5$ is traversed more than once. In Fig. 9-4(b), starting at $A$, the closed path $e_1 e_2 e_5 \ e_4 e_3 e_6$ is an Euler circuit.

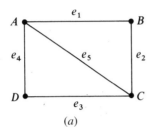 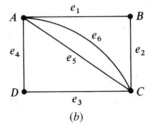

| | |
|---|---|
| (a) | (b) |

**Fig. 9-4**

A graph that has an Euler circuit is called an *Eulerian graph*. In these terms, the Königsberg bridge problem becomes: *Is the Königsberg bridge graph an Eulerian graph?*
Euler's answer is as follows.

**Theorem 9.1:**   A graph is Eulerian if and only if it is connected, and every vertex has an even degree.

Note that every vertex of the Königsberg graph in Fig. 9-2(b) has odd degree, so there is no Euler circuit.

**EXAMPLE 9.2**   Determine which of the graphs in Fig. 9-5 are Eulerian.

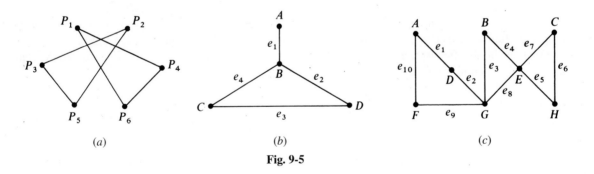

| | | |
|---|---|---|
| (a) | (b) | (c) |

**Fig. 9-5**

The graph in Fig. 9-5(a) is not connected, so it is not Eulerian, and that in Fig. 9-5(b) is not Eulerian because vertex $A$ has odd degree. The graph in Fig. 9-5(c) is Eulerian.

Theorem 9.1 tells us the necessary and sufficient conditions for a graph to have an Euler circuit; it does not tell us how to find one. A systematic procedure for finding an Euler circuit is given by the following algorithm:

**Fleury's Algorithm:**   To find an Euler circuit in an Eulerian graph $G$, start at any vertex. Then at each stage go from one vertex to another along an edge $e$ that has not already been used and which satisfies (a) $e$ is the only choice, or (b) the removal of $e$ *does not disconnect the part* $G'$ *of* $G$ not yet traversed (a vertex $v$ is in $G'$ if any edge linked to $v$ is in $G'$).

In applying the alorithm, it is helpful to number the edges as they are chosen, and it is important to keep track of the vertices that are in the part $G'$ not yet traversed.

**EXAMPLE 9.3**   Apply Fleury's algorithm to the Eulerian graph in Fig. 9-5($c$).

One possibility is to start at vertex $A$ and go along edges

$$e_1 e_2 e_3 e_4 e_5 \; e_6 e_7 e_8 e_9 e_{10}$$

as labeled in the figure.   There are other Euler circuits starting and ending at $A$.   For instance,

$$e_1 e_2 e_8 e_7 e_6 e_5 e_4 e_3 e_9 e_{10} \quad \text{and} \quad e_{10} e_9 e_8 e_5 e_6 e_7 e_4 e_3 e_2 e_1$$

are also Euler circuits that begin and end at $A$.

### Traversable Graphs

A graph that has a path, not necessarily closed, which includes every edge exactly once is called a *travers-able* (or *semi-Eulerian*) graph.   In particular, every Eulerian graph is traversable.   The graph in Fig. 9-1(a) is not Eulerian but is transversable, since $e_1 e_4 e_2 e_5 \; e_3$ covers each edge exactly once, beginning at $B$ and ending at $C$.

The following result can be deduced from Theorem 9.1:

**Theorem 9.2:**   A graph is traversable if and only if it is connected and has either zero or two vertices of odd degree.

For example, we have seen that the graph in Fig. 9-1($a$) is traversable: Vertices $B$ and $C$ have degree 3, and all other vertices have even degrees.   The graph in Fig. 9-5($b$) is also traversable: $A$ has degree 1, $B$ degree 3, and $C$ and $D$ have degree 2.   Every Eulerian graph has zero vertices of odd degree and is traversable.

Note that the graph in Fig. 9-2($b$) is not traversable, since it has four vertices of odd degree.   This means that there is no way to cross each of the seven Königsberg bridges in Fig. 9-2($a$) exactly once even if we allow the ending point to be different from the starting point.

## 9.3   THE LETTER CARRIER PROBLEM

Suppose a connected graph has one or more vertices with an odd degree and therefore is not Eulerian. Then every closed path that includes all of the edges must traverse at least one edge more than once.   [For example, in Fig. 9-5($b$), the closed path $e_1 e_2 e_3 e_4 e_1$ traverses edge $e_1$ twice.] Suppose also that each edge is assigned a length or weight.   Then the *letter carrier problem* is as follows: *Find a closed path that traverses each edge and whose length (total weight) is as small as possible.*

If each edge has the same length or weight, the letter carrier problem becomes: *Find a closed path that traverses each edge and whose total number of edges is as small as possible.*

There are systematic procedures for solving either version of the letter carrier problem.   Of the two, the second is the less difficult, and we illustrate a method for dealing with it.

### Eulerizing a Graph

Consider the connected graph in Fig. 9-6($a$).   It is not Eulerian, since vertices $B$ and $D$ have odd degree. However, if we add a new edge from $B$ to $D$, as indicated by the broken line in Fig. 9-6($b$), then all the vertices now have even degree.   We call the graph in Fig. 9-6($b$) an *Eulerized* version of the graph shown in Fig. 9-6($a$).

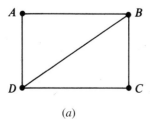

(a)

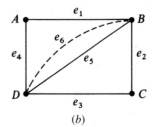

(b)

**Fig. 9-6**

The path $e_1e_2e_3e_5e_6\,e_4$ in Fig. 9-6(b) is an Euler circuit.   It corresponds to the path *ABCDBDA* in Fig. 9-6(a).   That is, in Fig. 9-6(a) the edge between *B* and *D* is traversed twice, once in each direction.   Since only one edge has been traversed more than once, it is clear that the path *ABCDBDA* is a solution of the letter carrier problem in this simple case.

As another example, consider the graph in Fig. 9-7(a).   Here, vertices *B*, *D*, *E*, and *F* have odd degree. The graph in Fig. 9-7(b) is an Eulerized version of the one in Fig. 9-7(a).   Using Fleury's algorithm, the path $e_1e_2e_3e_7\,e_8e_4e_{11}e_5e_9\,e_{10}e_6$ is an Euler circuit in Fig. 9-7(b).   It corresponds to the path *ABCFBEFEDBDA* in Fig. 9-7(a).

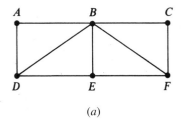
(a)

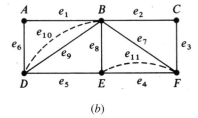
(b)

**Fig. 9-7**

In the Eulerization process we wish to add as few edges as necessary to change a connected non-Eulerian graph into an Eulerian graph.   Also, we add edges only between vertices already connected by an edge in the original graph.   This latter restriction ensures that traversing a new edge in the Eulerized graph corresponds to tracing or retracing an edge of the original graph.

## 9.4   HAMILTONIAN CIRCUITS

Previously, the emphasis was on traversing edges; here we concentrate on visiting vertices.   *Hamiltonian circuit*—named after the nineteenth-century Irish mathematician William Hamilton (1805–1865)—is a closed path that visits every vertex of a graph exactly once.   A graph that has a Hamiltonian circuit is called a *Hamiltonian graph*.   Note that an Eulerian circuit traverses every edge exactly once but may repeat vertices, while a Hamiltonian circuit visits each vertex exactly once but may skip edges.   The circuit *ABCFEDA* in Fig. 9-8(a) is a Hamiltonian circuit that is not an Euler circuit, and *ABCEDBFEA* in Fig. 9-8(b) is an Euler circuit that is not a Hamiltonian circuit.

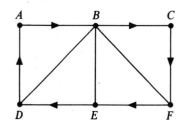
(a)   Hamiltonian and non-Eulerian

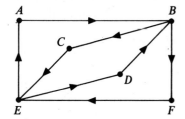
(b)   Eulerian and non-Hamiltonian

**Fig. 9-8**

Although it is clear that only connected graphs can have Hamiltonian circuits, there is no theorem that gives both necessary and sufficient conditions for a graph to be Hamiltonian.   We do have the following sufficient condition, which is due to G. A. Dirac.

**Theorem 9.3 (Dirac's Theorem):**     A simple, connected graph is Hamiltonian if the number of vertices is at least three and at most twice the degree of each vertex.   (Recall that a graph is simple if it has no multiple edges or loops.)

**EXAMPLE 9.4**   Apply Theorem 9.3 if possible, to the graphs in Fig. 9-9.

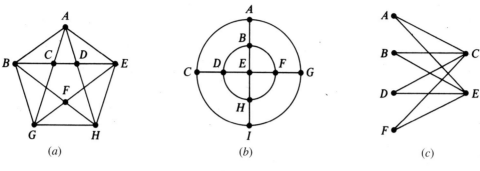

**Fig. 9-9**

First note that all three graphs are simple and connected.

(a)   There are eight vertices, each with degree 4.   Since $3 \leq 8 \leq 2 \cdot 4$, it follows from Dirac's theorem that the graph is Hamiltonian.   The path *ABCDHGFEA* is a Hamiltonian circuit.

(b)   There are nine vertices.   Since the degree of *A* is 3 and $9 < 3$, Theorem 9.3 does not apply.   However, the graph is Hamiltonian since the path *ACIGFHDEBA* is a Hamiltonian circuit.

(c)   There are six vertices.   Since the degree of *A* is 3 and $6 < 3$, Theorem 9.8 does not apply.   This graph is not Hamiltonian.   Any closed path through all six vertices, whether it starts on the left or on the right, must repeat one of the vertices *C* or *E* in returning to the starting point.

## 9.5   COMPLETE GRAPHS

A graph is *complete* if it is simple and every two of its vertices have an edge connecting them.   For example, the graph in Fig. 9-10(*a*) is complete and those in Figs. 9-10(*b*) and 9-10(*c*) are not. Note that since a complete graph is simple, it has no multiple edges or loops.   Also, a complete graph is connected.

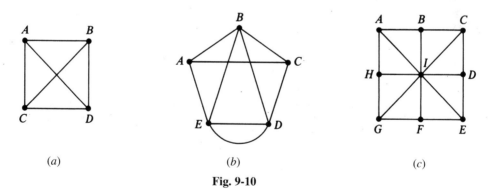

**Fig. 9-10**

A complete graph with at least two vertices is Hamiltonian.   A proof of this is given by the following algorithm which can be used to find a Hamiltonian circuit in any complete graph with at least two vertices:

**Algorithm:**

1.   Start at any vertex.

2.   Proceed from one vertex to another not already visited by going along an edge not already used until all vertices except the starting one have been visited.

3.   Return to the starting vertex.

It can be also shown that a complete graph with *n* vertices has $n(n - 1)/2$ edges (see Problem 9.22).   For example, the graph in Fig. 9-10(*a*) has four vertices and $4(4 - 1)/2 = 6$ edges.

### Counting Hamiltonian Circuits

It is conventional to consider two Hamiltonian circuits to be equivalent if they are made up of the same edges, regardless of their starting points or the directions traveled along an edge.   For example, with reference to Fig. 9-10(a), the Hamiltonian circuits *ABCDA*, *ADCBA*, and *BCDAB* are all made up of edges *AB, BC, CD*, and *DA* and are therefore equivalent.   In counting the number of Hamiltonian circuits in a graph, equivalent circuits count as a single one.

Using the equivalency convention above, it can be shown (see Problem 9.23) that the number of distinct Hamiltonian circuits in a complete graph with $n \geq 3$ vertices is $(n - 1)!/2$.   For example, the graph in Fig. 9-10(a) has $(4 - 1)!/2 = 6/2 = 3$ Hamiltonian circuits: *ABCDA*, *ACDBA*, and *ADBCA*.

**EXAMPLE 9.5**   Find the number of edges and Hamiltonian circuits of a complete graph with 15 edges.

It has $15(14)/2 = 105$ edges and $14!/2 = 43{,}589{,}145{,}600$ Hamiltonian circuits.

**EXAMPLE 9.6**   Draw complete graphs with (a) three vertices, (b) five vertices, (c) six vertices, and determine the number of edges and Hamiltonian circuits in each graph.

In each case we first position the vertices equally spaced around the perimeter of a circle (undrawn).   Then, starting with any vertex, connect it to each of the remaining vertices by a straight line.   Repeat the process at each vertex, as needed, until each pair of vertices is connected by a line.   The results are shown in Fig. 9-11 The respective numbers of edges and Hamiltonian circuits are as follows:

(a)   Edges: $3 \cdot 2/2 = 3$; circuits: $(3 - 1)!/2 = 1$

(b)   Edges: $5 \cdot 4/2 = 10$; circuits: $(5 - 1)!/2 = 4!/2 = 24/2 = 24/2 = 12$

(c)   Edges: $6 \cdot 5/2 = 15$; circuits: $(6 - 1)!/2 = 5!/2 = 120/2 = 60$

 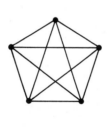 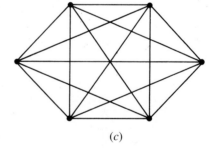

| (a) | (b) | (c) |

**Fig. 9-11**

### 9.6   TRAVELING SALESPERSON PROBLEM

A graph in which each edge is assigned a weight, such as the graph in Fig. 9-12 is called a *weighted graph*. For example, a weighted graph could depict the routes flown by an airline in which the vertices represent cities, and the weight assigned to each edge is the distance between the two cities that the edge connects.

The *traveling salesperson problem* is to find a Hamiltonian circuit of minimum weight in a complete, weighted graph.   (The weight of a path is the sum of the weights of the edges making up the path.)   Since equivalent paths have the same edges, equivalent paths have the same weight.

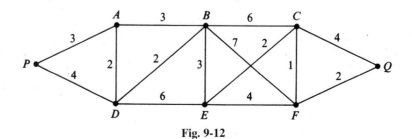

**Fig. 9-12**

**EXAMPLE 9.7**   Solve the traveling salesperson problem for the complete, weighted graph in Fig. 9-13.

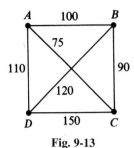

**Fig. 9-13**

Figure 9-13 is Fig. 9-10($a$) with weights assigned to the edges.   Since there are four vertices in the graph, there are $3!/2 = 3$ Hamiltonian circuits.   These circuits, along with their weights, are as follows:

$$ABCDA: \qquad 100 + 90 + 150 + 110 = 450$$

$$ACDBA: \qquad 75 + 150 + 120 + 100 = 445$$

$$ADBCA: \qquad 110 + 120 + 90 + 75 = 395$$

Hence, circuit *ADBCA* has the minimum weight.

In Example 9-7 we were able to solve the problem by finding all possible Hamiltonian circuits and computing the weight of each one.   However, for a graph with many vertices, this approach would be impractical.  For instance, in Example 9-5 we determined that a complete graph with 15 vertices has over 43.5 billion Hamiltonian circuits.   Hence, for circuits with many vertices, a strategy of some kind is needed to solve the traveling salesperson problem.   No general solution of the problem has yet been found, but there are many algorithms for dealing with it.   We discuss one of the simplest here.

**Nearest-Neighbor Algorithm**

The nearest-neighbor algorithm, starting at a given vertex, chooses the edge to the next possible vertex that has the least weight, that is, in terms of distance, the closest vertex.   This strategy is continued at each successive vertex until a Hamiltonian circuit is completed.

**EXAMPLE 9.8**   Apply the nearest-neighbor algorithm to the weighted graph in Fig. 9-13 starting at ($a$) A, ($b$) B, ($c$) C, ($d$) D.

($a$)   Starting at $A$, the closest vertex is $C$; from $C$, the closer of $B$ and $D$ is $B$, and from $B$ there is no choice but go to $D$; from $D$, there is no choice but to return to $A$.   We get the weighted circuit.

$$ACBDA: \qquad 75 + 90 + 120 + 110 = 395$$

which, as shown in Example 9.7, is the circuit of minimum weight (*ACBDA* is equivalent to *ADBCA* in Example 9.7).

($b$)   Starting at $B$, the closest vertex is $C$, and from $C$, the closer of $A$ and $D$ is $A$.   From $A$ we go to $D$ and then back to $B$.   The weighted circuit is

$$BCADB: \qquad 90 + 75 + 110 + 120 = 395$$

which is the circuit of minimum weight.   Note that *BCADA* is equivalent to the circuit *ADBCA* in Example 9.7.

($c$)   Starting at $C$, the nearest-neighbor algorithm gives the weighted circuit

$$CABDC: \qquad 75 + 100 + 120 + 150 = 445$$

which is not a circuit of minimal weight.

($d$)   Starting at $D$, we get the weighted circuit.

$$DACBD: \qquad 110 + 75 + 90 + 120 = 395$$

which is equivalent to the circuit *ADBCA* of minimal weight.

The idea behind the nearest-neighbor algorithm is to minimize the total weight by minimizing the weight at each step.    Although this may seem reasonable, part (c) of Example 9.8 shows that there are times when the algorithm does not give a circuit of minimum weight.

## 9.7   DIRECTED GRAPHS

Previously, when considering Euler and Hamiltonian circuits, we were not concerned with the direction of the circuits.    However, in practical applications, the edges of a graph may represent city streets or flight paths along which traffic is constrained to go in a particular direction.    Then any Euler or Hamiltonian circuit on such a graph would have to be consistent with the direction assigned to each edge.    In general, a graph in which each edge is assigned a direction is called a *directed graph* or *digraph*.    Examples of directed graphs are given in Fig. 9-14.

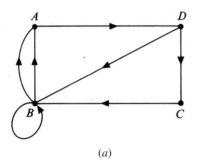    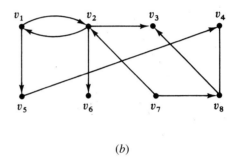

(a)                                                                  (b)

**Fig. 9-14**

The directed graph in Fig. 9-15 is also a *weighted graph*.    The numbers assigned to each edge represent the percentage of a state's population that emigrates each year from one state to another in the direction of the edge.    Hence, 10 percent of the New York population moves to California each year, while 14 percent of the California population moves to New York.

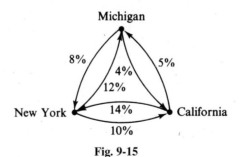

**Fig. 9-15**

The map in Fig. 9-16(a) shows the location of three art galleries, A, B, and C, in a neighborhood with only one-way streets.    The weights on the digraph in Fig. 9-16(b) indicate the least number of blocks you must travel to get from one gallery to another.

In Figs. 9-15 and 9-16, weights were assigned to the edges of the corresponding digraphs.    In Fig. 9-17, weights have been assigned to the vertices.    Each vertex may indicate a basic task to be performed in an overall process represented by the graph.    The weight assigned to each vertex is the number of time units required to perform the corresponding task.    The directions indicate the order in which the tasks must be performed.    For example, the weighted digraph may represent tasks that must be performed in assembling an automobile.

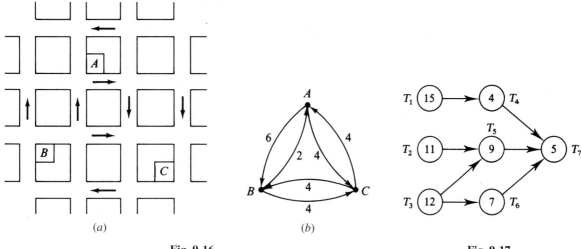

Fig. 9-16                                    Fig. 9-17

If we wanted to reduce the overall time required to complete a process, such as the one represented Fig. 9-17, we would have to shorten the time required for the longest (in time units) series of tasks in the process.   In terms of the graph representing the process, the longest path is called the *critical path*.   In Fig. 9-17, there are four paths to be considered:

$$T_1 T_4 T_5 : \qquad 15 + 4 + 5 = 24$$

$$T_2 T_5 T_7 : \qquad 11 + 9 + 5 = 25$$

$$T_3 T_5 T_7 : \qquad 12 + 9 + 5 = 26$$

$$T_3 T_6 T_7 : \qquad 12 + 7 + 5 + 24$$

The critical path is $T_3 T_5 T_7$, which equals 26 time units.   If task $T_3$ were reduced from 12 to 11 time units, then there would be two critical paths, $T_2 T_5 T_7$, and $T_3 T_5 T_7$, in the new graph, each equal to 25 time units.

## 9.8   TREES

In graph theory a *tree* is defined as a connected graph containing no closed paths.   Examples of trees are shown in Fig. 9-18.

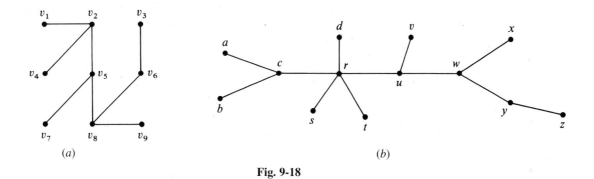

Fig. 9-18

Some other definitions of trees equivalent to the one above are given in Theorem 9.4.

**Theorem 9.4**   Let $G$ be a graph with $n > 1$ vertices.   Then the following statements are equivalent:

   (*i*)   $G$ is a tree.
  (*ii*)   $G$ contains no closed paths and has $n - 1$ edges.
 (*iii*)   $G$ is connected and has $n - 1$ edges.

With reference to Theorem 9.4, note that the tree in Fig. 9-18(a) has nine vertices and eight edges; that in Fig. 9-18(b) has 13 vertices and 12 edges.

## 9.9 SPANNING TREES

A subgraph $T$ of a connected graph $G$ is called a *spaning tree of G* if $T$ is a tree and includes all the vertices of $G$.   Figure 9-19 shows a connected graph $G$ and spanning trees $T_1$, $T_2$, and $T_3$ of $G$.

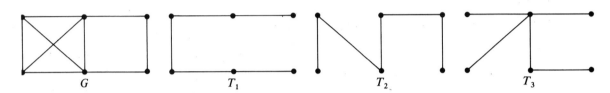

**Fig. 9-19**

### Minimal Spanning Trees

Suppose $G$ is a connected, weighted graph.   That is, each edge of $G$ is assigned a nonnegative number called the *weight of the edge*.   Then any spanning tree $T$ of $G$ has a total weight obtained by adding the weights of the edges in $T$.   A *minimal spanning tree of G* is a spanning tree of $G$ whose total weight is as small as possible.   As an application, $G$ may represent a communications network where the vertices are cities, the edges are lines of communication, and the weight of each edge is the cost of communicating between the two cities linked by the edge.   A minimal spanning tree would enable all cities to communicate at lowest possible overall cost.

Algorithms 9.1 and 9.2 enable us to find a minimal spanning tree of a connected, weighted graph with $n$ vertices:

### Algorithm 9.1:

1.  Arrange the edges of $G$ in the order of decreasing weights.
2.  Proceeding sequentially, delete each edge that does not disconnect the graph until $n-1$ edges remain.

### Algorithm 9.2 (Kruskal's Algorithm):

1.  Arrange the edges of $G$ in the order of increasing weights.
2.  Proceeding sequentially, add each edge that does not result in a closed path until $n-1$ edges are added.

**EXAMPLE 9.9** Apply Algorithm 9.1 to the graph $Q$ in Fig. 9-20(a).

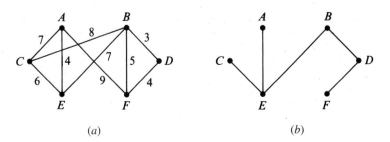

$(a)$ $(b)$

**Fig. 9-20**

Graph $Q$ has six vertices; hence, any spanning tree of $Q$ will have five edges.   By Algorithm 9.1, the edges are ordered by decreasing lengths and are successively deleted (without disconnecting $Q$) until five edges remain.   This yields the following data:

| Edges | AF | BC | AC | BE | CE | BF | AE | DF | BD |
|---|---|---|---|---|---|---|---|---|---|
| Length | 9 | 8 | 7 | 7 | 6 | 5 | 4 | 4 | 3 |
| Delete? | Yes | Yes | Yes | No | No | Yes | | | |

Thus, the minimal spanning tree of $Q$ contains the edges

$$BE \qquad CE \qquad AE \qquad DF \qquad BD$$

This spanning tree has length 24, and it is shown in Fig. 9-20($b$)

**EXAMPLE 9.10**   Apply Algorithm 9.2 to the graph $Q$ in Fig. 9-20($a$)

Again, any spanning tree of $Q$ will have five edges.   By Algorithm 9.2, the edges are ordered by increasing lengths and are successively added (without forming any cycles) until five edges are included.   This yields the following data:

| Edges | BD | AE | DF | BF | CE | AC | BE | BC | AF |
|---|---|---|---|---|---|---|---|---|---|
| Length | 3 | 4 | 4 | 5 | 6 | 7 | 7 | 8 | 9 |
| Add? | Yes | Yes | Yes | No | Yes | No | Yes | | |

The minimal spanning tree of $Q$ therefore contains the edges

$$BD \qquad AE \qquad DF \qquad CE \qquad BE$$

This spanning tree is the same as the one obtained in Example 9.9, where Algorithm 9.1 was used.
   The weight of a minimal spanning tree is uniquely determined, but the minimal spanning tree itself is not.   Different minimal spanning trees can occur when two or more edges have the same weight.   In such cases, the arrangement of the edges in step 1 of Algorithm 9.1 or 9.2 is not unique, and different arrangements can result in different minimal spanning trees (see Problems 9.31 and 9.32).

# Solved Problems

**GRAPHS**

**9.1.**   Describe each of the graphs in Fig. 9-21.

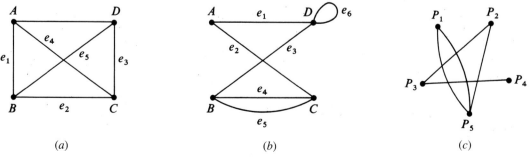

(a)                                         (b)                                         (c)

**Fig. 9-21**

(a) The graph has four vertices $A$, $B$, $C$, and $D$, and six edges $e_1 = AB$ (or $BA$), $e_2 = BC$ (or $CB$), $e_3 = CD$ (or $DC$), $e_4 = AC$ (or $CA$), $e_5 = BD$ (or $DB$), and $e_6 = AD$ (or $DA$). (No direction is specified along the edges. Hence, the notation $AB$ or $BA$ here means only that edge $e_1$ links vertices $A$ and $B$.) Since there are no multiple edges or loops, it is a simple graph.

(b) The graph has four vertices $A$, $B$, $C$, $D$, and six edges $e_1 = AD$, $e_2 = AC$, $e_3 = BD$, $e_4 = BC$, $e_5 = BC$, and $e_6 = DD$. The graph in Fig. 9-21($b$) has both a multiple edge and a loop; it is not a simple graph. [Note that although $e_4$ and $e_5$ are different edges, they are both denoted by $BC$. If necessary, we could be more specific by using notation such as $(BC)_1$ and $(BC)_2$.]

(c) The graph has five vertices $P_1$, $P_2$, $P_3$, $P_4$, $P_5$ and five edges $P_1P_5$, $P_1P_5$, $P_2P_3$, $P_2P_5$, and $P_3P_4$. Since it has a multiple edge, it is not a simple graph.

**9.2.** Draw graphs with the given vertices and edges:

(a) vertices $A$, $B$, $C$, $D$; edges $AB$, $AD$, $AC$, $CD$

(b) vertices $a$, $b$, $c$, $d$, $e$; edges $ab$, $ac$, $bc$, $de$

(c) vertices $P_1$, $P_2$, $P_3$, $P_4$, $P_5$; edges $P_2P_4$, $P_2P_3$, $P_3P_5$, $P_4P_5$

(d) vertices $P_1$, $P_2$, $P_3$, $P_4$, $P_5$; edges $P_1P_1$, $P_2P_3$, $P_2P_4$, $P_2P_3$, $P_1P_4$, $P_4P_5$

The graphs are drawn in Fig. 9-22

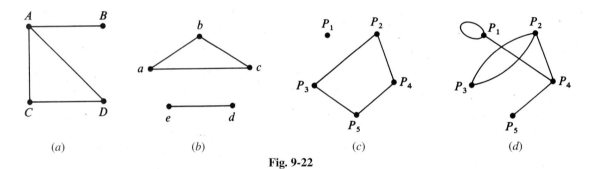

$(a)$                          $(b)$                          $(c)$                          $(d)$

**Fig. 9-22**

**9.3.** Find the degree of each vertex in Problem 9.2.

($a$):  $A, 3$;   $B, 1$;   $C, 2$;   $D, 2$

($b$):  $a, 2$;   $b, 2$;   $c, 2$;   $d, 1$;   $e, 1$

($c$):  $P_1, 0$;   $P_2, P_3, P_4, P_5, 2$

($d$):  $P_1, 3$;   $P_2, 3$; $P_3, 2$;   $P_4, 3$;   $P_5, 1$

**9.4.** Each edge is counted twice in counting the degrees of the vertices of a graph. We then get the following theorem:

**Theorem 9.5:**  The sum of the degrees of the vertices of a graph is equal to twice the number of edges.

Verify the theorem for the graphs in Problem 9.2.

(a) The total number of edges is 4, and from Problem 9.3, the sum of the degrees of the vertices is $3 + 1 + 2 + 2 = 8$.

(b) The total number of edges is 4, and from Problem 9.3, the sum of the degrees of the vertices is $3 \cdot 2 + 2 \cdot 1 = 8$.

(c) The total number of edges is 4, and from Problem 9.3, the sum of the degrees of the vertices is $4 \cdot 2 = 8$.

(d) The total number of edges is 6, and from Problem 9.3, the sum of the degrees of the vertices is $3 + 3 + 2 + 3 + 1 = 12$.

**9.5.** Consider the following paths in the graph shown in Fig. 9-23: (*a*) $e_1 e_4 e_6 e_5$, (*b*) $e_2 e_5 e_3 e_4 e_6 e_3 e_1$. Convert each sequence of edges into a corresponding sequence of vertices.

      We list the initial vertex of the first edge followed by the terminal (end) vertex of each edge in the sequence to obtain (*a*) *ABZYX*, (*b*) *AXYBZYBA*.

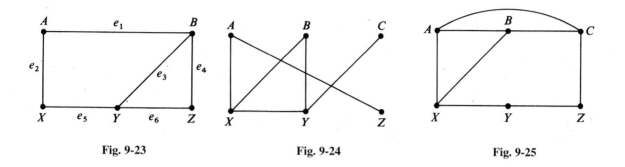

Fig. 9-23                  Fig. 9-24                  Fig. 9-25

**9.6.** Let *G* be the graph in Fig. 9-24. Determine whether or not each of the following sequences of (directionless) edges forms a path: (*a*) *AX, XB, CY, YX*; (*b*) *XB, BY, YC*; (*c*) *BY, XY, AX*

      A sequence of edges forms a path if successive edges have a common vertex.

(*a*)  No.  Edges *XB* and *CY* have no common vertex.

(*b*)  Yes.  The path is *XBYC*.

(*c*)  Yes.  The path is *BYXA*.

**9.7.** Find all paths that contain no repeated edges: (*a*)  from *A* to *Z* in Fig. 9-23;
(*b*)  from *A* to *C* in Fig. 9-24;    (*c*)  from *A* to *Z* in Fig. 9-25.

(*a*)  There are four such paths:     *ABZ,*     *ABYZ,*     *AXYZ,*     *AXYBZ.*

(*b*)  There are only two such paths:     *AXYC,*     *AXBYC.*

(*c*)  There are eight such paths:     *ACZ,*     *ABCZ,*     *AXYZ,*     *ABXYZ,*     *AXBCZ,*
                                     *AXBACZ,*     *ACBAXYZ,*     *ABCAXYZ.*

**9.8.** Determine whether or not each of the graphs in Fig. 9-26 is connected.

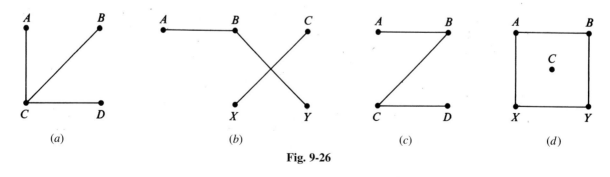

(*a*)                (*b*)              (*c*)               (*d*)

Fig. 9-26

(*a*)  Yes.  There is a path between any two vertices of the graph.

(*b*)  No.  Here *A, B,* and *Y* are connected, and *C* and *X* are connected, but there is no path from *A, B,* or *Y* to either *C* or *X*.

(*c*)  Yes.  There is a path between any two vertices of the graph.

(*d*)  No.  There is no path from *C* to any other vertex of the graph.

**9.9.**   Determine whether or not each of the graphs in Fig. 9-27 is connected.

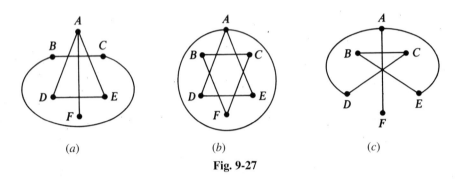

**Fig. 9-27**

(a)   No.   None of the vertices *A, D, E, F* can be linked to any of the vertices *B, C*.

(b)   No.   None of the vertices *A, D, E* can be linked to any of the vertices *B, C, F*.

(c)   Yes.   Any vertex can be linked to any other vertex by a sequence of edges.

## EULER CIRCUITS

**9.10.**   Determine which of the graphs in Fig. 9-28 are Eulerian or traversable.

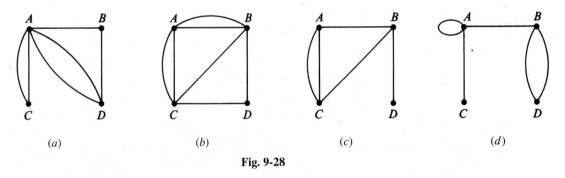

**Fig. 9-28**

(a)   Traversable, since exactly two of its vertices, *A* and *D*, are of odd degree.      Not Eulerian.

(b)   Both Eulerian and traversable, since all of its vertices are of even degree.

(c)   Neither Eulerian nor traversable, since all four vertices are of odd degree.

(d)   Traversable, since exactly two of its vertices, *B* and *C*, are of odd degree.      Not Eulerian.

**9.11.**   Determine which of the graphs in Fig. 9-29 are Eulerian or traversable.

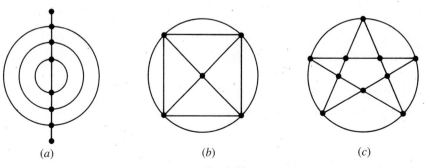

**Fig. 9-29**

(a)   Traversable, since the top and bottom vertices have degree 1 and the other six vertices have degree 4. Not Eulerian.

(b)   Neither Eulerian nor traversable, since there are four odd vertices.

(c)   Both Eulerian and traversable, since all 10 vertices have even degree.

**9.12.**   Find an Euler circuit:   (a) in Fig. 9-28(b);   (b) in Fig. 9-29(c).

(a)   An Euler circuit *ABDCBACA* is indicated by the arrows in Fig. 9-30(a).

Any vertex in the circuit can be chosen as the starting and ending point.

(b)   An Euler circuit *IFCA-DGJ-HFB-CDE-GHI-BAEJI* beginning and ending at *I* is indicated by the arrows in Fig. 9-30(b).   Any vertex in the circuit can be chosen as the starting and ending point.

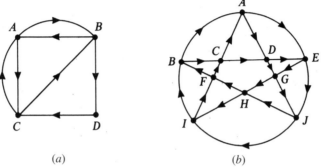

(a)                                   (b)

**Fig. 9-30**

**9.13.**   Find a traversable path for the graph in Fig. 9-31(a).

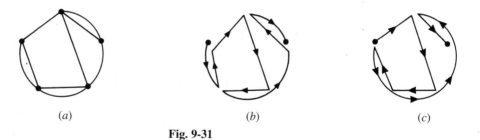

(a)                          (b)                          (c)

**Fig. 9-31**

There are many possible solutions, but all of them will start at one of the odd vertices and end at the other.   Figures 9-31(b) and 9-31(c) give two possible solutions.

**9.14.**   Eulerize the graph in Fig. 9-32(a).   Find an Euler circuit on the Eulerized graph and indicate the closed path on the original graph that corresponds to the Euler circuit.

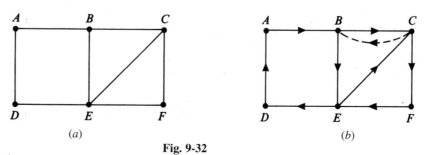

(a)                                             (b)

**Fig. 9-32**

The graph in Fig. 9-32(*b*) is an Eulerized version of that shown in Fig. 9-32(*a*). The Euler circuit *ABCFECBEDA* in Fig. 9-32(*b*) corresponds to the closed path *ABCFECBEDA* on the original graph in which edge *BC* is traversed twice, once in each direction.

## HAMILTONIAN CIRCUITS; COMPLETE GRAPHS

**9.15.** Classify each of the graphs in Fig. 9-33 as Eulerian only, Hamiltonian only, both, or neither.

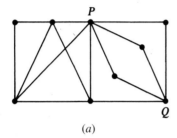

(*a*)                                        (*b*)

**Fig. 9-33**

(*a*) Eulerian only. The graph is Eulerian, since all of its vertices have even degree. However, any closed path that includes all of the vertices will have to visit *P* or *Q* more than once. Hence, the graph is not Hamiltonian.

(*b*) Hamiltonian only. The graph is not Eulerian, since vertex *A* (also *F*) has odd degree. However, the closed path *ABFDECA* is a Hamiltonian circuit. Note that Dirac's theorem (Theorem 9.3) also tells us that the graph is Hamiltonian. That is, the graph is simple, connected, and there are six vertices; since the smallest degree of any vertex is 3, the hypothesis of Dirac's theorem is satisfied.

**9.16.** Find the number of edges and Hamiltonian circuits in a complete graph with (*a*) seven vertices, (*b*) 11 vertices.

We compute $n(n-1)/2$ for the number of edges, and $(n-1)!/2$ for the number of Hamiltonian circuits:

(*a*) Edges: $7 \cdot 6/2 = 21$; Hamiltonian circuits: $6!/2 = 360$

(*b*) Edges: $11 \cdot 10/2 = 55$; Hamiltonian circuits: $10!/2 = 1,814,400$

**9.17.** For what positive integers *n* is a complete graph with *n* vertices both Eulerian and Hamiltonian?

A complete graph with *n* vertices is Hamiltonian for any integer $n \geq 2$. This follows from the algorithm for finding a Hamiltonian circuit given in Sec. 9.5. Also, if $n \geq 2$, each of the *n* vertices is linked by an edge to the $n-1$ remaining vertices; hence, each vertex has degree $n-1$. It follows that a complete graph with *n* vertices will be Eulerian whenever $n-1$ is even, that is, whenever *n* is odd. Therefore, a complete graph with *n* vertices will be both Eulerian and Hamiltonian whenever *n* is an odd integer greater than or equal to 3.

**9.18.** Find all 12 Hamiltonian circuits in a complete graph with five vertices.

First note that 12 is the correct number, since $4!/2 = 12$ (see also Example 9.6). The graph is shown in Fig. 9-34. We list each circuit and the edges that make up the circuit in the following table:

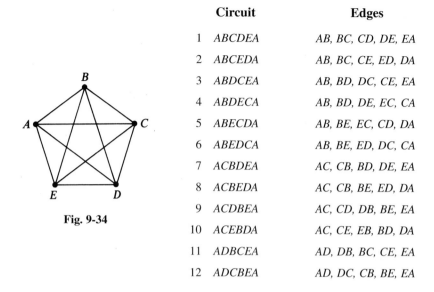

| | Circuit | Edges |
|---|---|---|
| 1 | ABCDEA | AB, BC, CD, DE, EA |
| 2 | ABCEDA | AB, BC, CE, ED, DA |
| 3 | ABDCEA | AB, BD, DC, CE, EA |
| 4 | ABDECA | AB, BD, DE, EC, CA |
| 5 | ABECDA | AB, BE, EC, CD, DA |
| 6 | ABEDCA | AB, BE, ED, DC, CA |
| 7 | ACBDEA | AC, CB, BD, DE, EA |
| 8 | ACBEDA | AC, CB, BE, ED, DA |
| 9 | ACDBEA | AC, CD, DB, BE, EA |
| 10 | ACEBDA | AC, CE, EB, BD, DA |
| 11 | ADBCEA | AD, DB, BC, CE, EA |
| 12 | ADCBEA | AD, DC, CB, BE, EA |

Fig. 9-34

## TRAVELING SALESPERSON PROBLEM

**9.19.** Find the Hamiltonian circuit of minimal weight in the complete weighted graph in Fig. 9-35.

The 12 Hamiltonian circuits are given in the previous problem. Their weights are as follows:

| | Circuits | Weights |
|---|---|---|
| 1 | ABCDEA | 100 + 125 + 300 + 75 + 175 = 775 |
| 2 | ABCEDA | 100 + 125 + 275 + 75 + 150 = 725 |
| 3 | ABDCEA | 100 + 250 + 300 + 275 + 175 = 1100 |
| 4 | ABDECA | 100 + 250 + 75 + 275 + 200 = 900 |
| 5 | ABECDA | 100 + 225 + 275 + 300 + 150 = 1050 |
| 6 | ABEDCA | 100 + 225 + 75 + 300 + 200 = 900 |
| 7 | ACBDEA | 200 + 125 + 250 + 75 + 175 = 825 |
| 8 | ACBEDA | 200 + 125 + 225 + 75 + 150 = 775 |
| 9 | ACDBEA | 200 + 300 + 250 + 225 + 175 = 1150 |
| 10 | ACEBDA | 200 + 275 + 225 + 250 + 150 = 1100 |
| 11 | ADBCEA | 150 + 250 + 125 + 275 + 175 = 975 |
| 12 | ADCBEA | 150 + 300 + 125 + 225 + 175 = 975 |

Fig. 9-35

Hence, the minimum weight is 725, and the only circuit with that weight is *ABCEDA*.

**9.20.** Apply the nearest-neighbor algorithm to the weighted graph in Problem 9.19 starting at (*a*) *A*, (*b*) *B*, (*c*) *C*, (*d*) *D*. For each circuit obtained, determine which of the 12 circuits in Problem 9.18 is equivalent to it.

(*a*) Starting at *A*, the closest (in terms of weight) vertex is *B*. From *B*, the closest vertex is *C*. From *C* we go to *E*, then to *D*, and back to *A*. Hence, the circuit is *ABCEDA*, which has weight 725. Therefore, the nearest-neighbor algorithm, starting at *A*, gives the circuit of minimal weight.

(*b*) Starting at *B*, the nearest-neighbor algorithm gives the circuit *BADECB*, which has weight 725 and is equivalent to *ABCEDA* in Problem 9.19, the circuit of minimal weight.

(c)   Starting at $C$, we get the circuit $CBADEC$, which also has weight 725 and is equivalent to $ABCEDA$ above.

(d)   Starting at $D$, we get $DEABCD$, which has weight 775.   This circuit is equivalent to $ABCDEA$ in Problem 9.19.

Hence, in three out of these four cases, the nearest-neighbor algorithm gives the circuit of minimal weight.

**9.21.**   *Ordered-edges algorithm.*   As shown in Example 9.8 and Problem 9.20, the circuit obtained by the nearest-neighbor algorithm depends on the starting point.   Another algorithm for attempting to find a Hamiltonian circuit of minimal weight, but which does not depend on the starting point, is the *ordered-edges algorithm.*   To apply this algorithm, we first arrange the edges in the order of increasing weight.   Then starting with the first on the list, we proceed through the list selecting any edge that (1) does not form a closed path unless all of the vertices are included in it, and (2) does not result in three edges meeting at a single vertex.   We stop when a Hamiltonian circuit has been obtained.   Apply the ordered-edges algorithm to the weighted graph in Fig. 9-35.

In the order of increasing weight, the edges are $DE$, 75;   $AB$, 100;   $BC$, 125;   $AD$, 150;   $AE$, 175;   $AC$, 200;   $BE$, 225;   $BD$, 250;   $CE$, 275;   $CE$, 300.

With reference to Fig. 9-35, as we go through the list, we obtain the partial paths shown in Fig. 9-36.

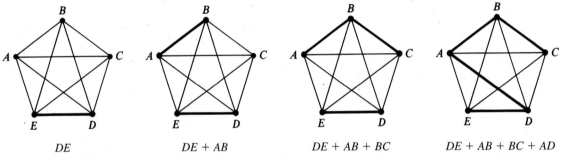

$DE$                    $DE + AB$                    $DE + AB + BC$                    $DE + AB + BC + AD$

**Fig. 9-36**

The next edge on the list is $AE$, but we reject this edge, since accepting it would result in a closed path $ADEA$ that does not include $C$.   The next edge on the list is $AC$, but this is also rejected because the closed path $ABCA$ that does not include $E$ or $D$ would result.   The next edge, $BE$, is also rejected because three edges would meet at $B$.   Similarly, $BD$ is rejected.   The next edge is $CE$, which is accepted and results in the Hamiltonian circuit $ABCEDA$ of weight 725 indicated by the dark line in Fig. 9-37.

Hence, the ordered-edges algorithm gives the circuit of minimal weight.   Note that as the circuit is being formed, the edges need not be connected.

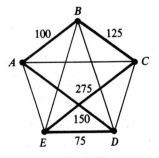

**Fig. 9-37**

**9.22.**   Prove that a complete graph with $n \geq 1$ vertices has $n(n-1)/2$ edges.

First note that a graph with one vertex is complete by default (i.e., an edge is required only between every *two* vertices), and such a graph has $1(1-1)/2 = 0$ edges.

Now consider a graph with $n \geq 2$ vertices. By a basic counting principle, there are a total of $n(n-1)$ pairs of vertices. That is, the first vertex can be chosen in $n$ ways, and with each of these choices, the second vertex can be chosen in $(n-1)$ ways, which results in $n(n-1)$ choices for the first and second vertices. Since very two pairs with the same entries, say $(A, B)$ and $(B, A)$, determine one edge, the graph has a total of $n(n-1)/2$ edges.

**9.23.**   Prove that the number of distinct Hamiltonian circuits in a complete graph with $n \geq 3$ vertices is $(n-1)!/2$.

The counting convention for Hamiltonian circuits enables us to designate any vertex in a given circuit to be the starting point. From the starting point we can go to any one of $n-1$ vertices, and from there to any one of $n-2$ vertices, and so on until arriving at the last vertex and then returning to the starting point. By the basic counting principle discussed in Problem 9.22, there are a total of $(n-1)(n-2)\cdots 1 = (n-1)!$ circuits that can be formed with the given starting point. Any two such circuits, in which one is in the opposite direction to the other, determine the same Hamiltonian circuit. For $n \geq 3$ vertices, every circuit with the given starting point can be paired with one in the opposite direction. Hence, there are a total of $(n-1)!/2$ Hamiltonian circuits.

## DIGRAPHS

**9.24.**   Consider the weighted digraph in Fig. 9-15. (*a*) What percent of the population of Michigan moves to New York each year? (*b*) What percent of the population of California moves to either New York or Michigan each year? (*c*) To which state does 10 percent of the population of New York move each year?

Using the information contained in the digraph, we have: (*a*) 8 percent of the population of Michigan moves to New York each year; (*b*) since 14 percent of the population of California moves to New York and 5 percent moves to Michigan, a total of 19 percent moves to either of these states each year; (*c*) 10 percent of the population of New York moves to California each year.

**9.25.**   Consider the three galleries in Fig. 9-16(*a*). Beginning at any one gallery, say, gallery $A$, there are only two possible circuits that would include all three galleries and return you to where you started: $A$ to $B$ to $C$ to $A$, or $A$ to $C$ to $B$ to $A$. Which circuit is the shortest?

Referring to the weighted digraph in Fig. 9-16(*b*), add the numbers of blocks in each circuit. Thus, the shortest circuit is $A$ to $C$ to $B$ to $A$. Specifically, this circuit consists of only 10 blocks, whereas the other circuit requires 14 blocks.

**9.26.**   The number associated with each vertex in the digraph in Fig. 9-38 represents the time units required to complete a task indicated by the vertex. Find the time-length of each path starting at either $T_1$ or $T_2$ and ending at either $T_7$ or $T_8$. What is the critical path (the path of maximum time-length)?

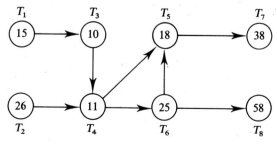

**Fig. 9-38**

The possible paths and their time-lengths are as follows:

$$\begin{array}{ll}
T_1T_3T_4T_5T_7: & 15 + 10 + 11 + 18 + 38 = 92 \\
T_1T_3T_4T_6T_8: & 15 + 10 + 11 + 25 + 58 = 119 \\
T_1T_3T_4T_6T_5T_7: & 15 + 10 + 11 + 25 + 18 + 38 = 117 \\
T_2T_4T_5T_7: & 26 + 11 + 18 + 38 = 93 \\
T_2T_4T_6T_8: & 26 + 11 + 25 + 58 = 120 \\
T_2T_4T_6T_5T_7: & 26 + 11 + 25 + 18 + 38 = 118
\end{array}$$

Hence, the critical path is $T_2T_4T_6T_8$.

**9.27.** Find the critical path (see Problem 9.26) from $T_1$ to $T_8$ in Fig. 9-39(a).

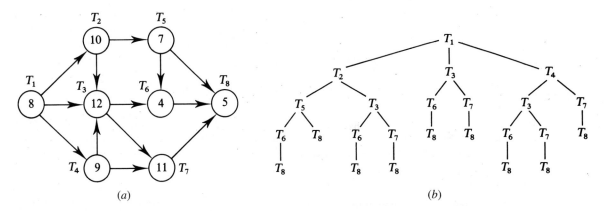

(a)                              (b)

**Fig. 9-39**

With the aid of the tree diagram in Fig. 9-39(b), we see that all possible paths and their time-lengths are as follows:

$$\begin{array}{ll}
T_1T_2T_5T_6T_8: & 8 + 10 + 7 + 4 + 5 = 34 \\
T_1T_2T_5T_8: & 8 + 10 + 7 + 5 = 30 \\
T_1T_2T_3T_6T_8: & 8 + 10 + 12 + 4 + 5 = 39 \\
T_1T_2T_3T_7T_8: & 8 + 10 + 12 + 11 + 5 = 46 \\
T_1T_3T_6T_8: & 8 + 12 + 4 + 5 = 29 \\
T_1T_3T_7T_8: & 8 + 12 + 11 + 5 = 36 \\
T_1T_4T_3T_6T_8: & 8 + 9 + 12 + 4 + 5 = 38 \\
T_1T_4T_3T_7T_8: & 8 + 9 + 12 + 11 + 5 = 45 \\
T_1T_4T_3T_7T_8: & 8 + 9 + 11 + 5 = 33
\end{array}$$

Hence, the critical path is $T_1T_2T_3T_7T_8$.

## SPANNING TREES

**9.28.** Find all spanning trees of the graph $G$ shown in Fig. 9-40.

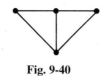

**Fig. 9-40**

There are eight such spanning trees, as shown in Fig. 9-41. Each spanning tree must have $4 - 1 = 3$ edges, since $G$ has four vertices. Thus, each tree can be obtained by deleting two of the five edges of $G$. This can be done in 10 ways, except that two of the ways lead to disconnected graphs. Hence, the above eight spanning trees are all the spanning trees of $G$.

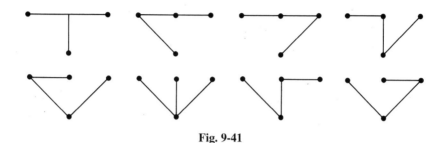

**Fig. 9-41**

**9.29.** Consider a finite connected graph $G$. Must all the spanning trees $T$ of $G$ have the same number of edges?

> Yes. In fact, if $G$ has $n$ vertices, then any spanning tree $T$ of $G$ must have $n - 1$ edges.

## MINIMAL SPANNING TREES

**9.30.** The weighted graph $G$ in Fig. 9-42 has three spanning trees. (a) Find the spanning trees of $G$ and their weights. (b) Which is the minimal spanning tree of $G$?

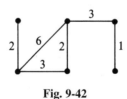

**Fig. 9-42**

(a) The three spanning trees are shown in Fig. 9-43. The weight of each spanning tree is the sum of the weights of its edges. Thus, the weights of $T_1$, $T_2$, and $T_3$ are, respectively, 14, 11, and 15.

(b) $T_2$ has the smallest weight, 11, and is therefore the minimal spanning tree.

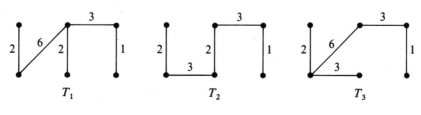

**Fig. 9-43**

**9.31.** Apply Algorithm 9.1 to the graph $Q$ in Fig. 9-44($a$).

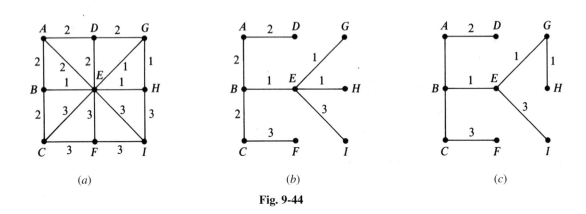

(a)             (b)             (c)

**Fig. 9-44**

Graph $Q$ has nine vertices; hence, any spanning tree will have eight edges. We first order the edges by decreasing weights and then apply step 2 in Algorithm 9.1:

| Edges | HI | FI | EI | EF | CF | CE | DG | DE | BC | AE | AD | AB | GH | EH | EG | BE |
|---|---|---|---|---|---|---|---|---|---|---|---|---|---|---|---|---|
| Weights | 3 | 3 | 3 | 3 | 3 | 3 | 2 | 2 | 2 | 1 | 1 | 1 | 1 | 1 | 1 | 1 |
| Delete? | Yes | Yes | No | Yes | No | Yes | Yes | Yes | No | Yes | No | No | Yes | No | No | No |

Therefore, the minimal spanning tree has edges

$$EI \qquad CF \qquad BC \qquad AD \qquad AB \qquad EH \qquad EG \qquad BE$$

which has weight 15 and is shown in Fig. 9-44($b$) Note that if $GH$ and $EH$, which both have weight 1, are interchanged in the above arrangement of edges, the minimal spanning tree in Fig. 9-44($c$) would result.

**9.32.** Apply Algorithm 9.2 to the graph in Fig. 9-45($a$).

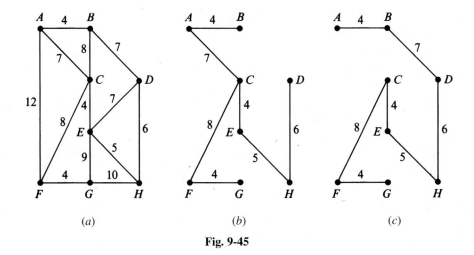

(a)             (b)             (c)

**Fig. 9-45**

Graph $Q$ has eight vertices, so any spanning tree will have seven edges.   We first order the edges by increasing weights and then apply step 2 of Algorithm 9.2:

| Edges | AB | CE | FG | EH | DH | AC | BD | DE | BC | CF | EG | GH | AF |
|-------|----|----|----|----|----|----|----|----|----|----|----|----|----|
| Weights | 4 | 4 | 4 | 5 | 6 | 7 | 7 | 7 | 8 | 8 | 9 | 10 | 12 |
| Add? | Yes | Yes | Yes | Yes | Yes | Yes | No | No | No | Yes | No | No | No |

This produces the spanning tree shown in Fig. 9-45($b$) with edges

$$AB \qquad CE \qquad FG \qquad EH \qquad DH \qquad AC \qquad CF$$

Note that either edge $AC$ or $BD$ could have been added, since both have weight 7 and neither would have produced a cycle.   Thus, a second minimal spanning tree, shown in Fig. 9-45($c$), has edges

$$AB \qquad CE \qquad FG \qquad EH \qquad DH \qquad BD \qquad CF$$

# Supplementary Problems

## GRAPHS

**9.33.** Describe each of the graphs in Fig. 9-46.

**9.34.** Find the degree of each vertex in Fig. 9-46.

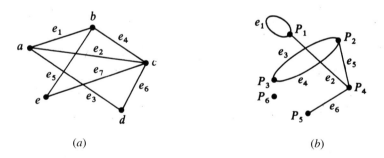

(a)                                                                (b)

**Fig. 9-46**

**9.35.** Draw graphs with the given vertices and edges: ($a$)   vertices $A, B, C, D, E, F$; edges $AD, AE, BD, CD, CF,$ $DE, DF, EF, EF$;   ($b$)   vertices $P_1, P_2, P_3, P_4, P_5$; edges $P_1, P_2, P_1 P_2, P_1 P_4, P_1 P_5, P_2 P_4,$ $P_3 P_4, P_3 P_5, P_5 P_5$.

**9.36.** Verify Theorem 9.5 (see Problem 9.4) for the graphs in Fig. 9-46.

**9.37.** Consider the following paths shown in Fig. 9-47: ($a$) $e_1 e_5 e_8 e_9 e_{10}$,   ($b$) $e_7 e_{10} e_{11} e_8 e_5\ e_1 e_2 e_6$.   Convert each sequence of edges into a sequence of vertices.

**9.38.** Let $G$ be the graph in Fig. 9-47, Find all paths from $A$ to $H$ that contain no repeated edges and never move to the left (i.e., west, northwest, southwest).

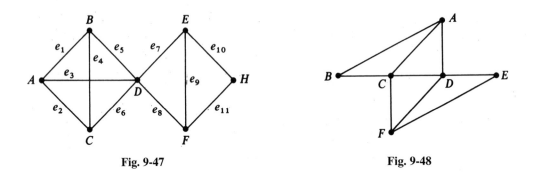

Fig. 9-47                                        Fig. 9-48

**9.39.** Let $G$ be the graph in Fig. 9-48.   Determine whether or not each of the following sequences of (direction-less) edges forms a path: (a) $AB;\ BC,\ DC,\ DE;$      (b)   $AC,\ CF,\ DE;$      (c)   $AB,\ AD,\ DE,\ FE.$

**9.40.** Determine whether or not each of the graphs in Fig. 9-49 is connected.

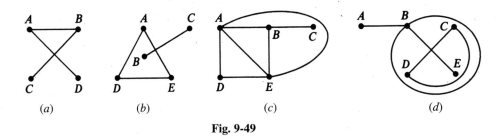

(a)             (b)                  (c)                     (d)

Fig. 9-49

## EULER CIRCUITS

**9.41.** Determine which of the graphs in Fig. 9-50 are Eulerian or traversable.   Explain your answer.

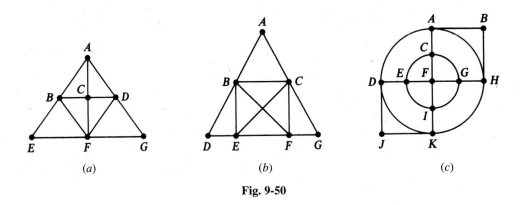

(a)                       (b)                       (c)

Fig. 9-50

**9.42.** Find an Euler circuit in Fig. 9-50(c).

**9.43.** Find a traversable path from $A$ to $F$ in Fig. 9-50(a) and from $B$ to $C$ in Fig. 9-50(b).

**9.44.** Eulerize the graph in Fig. 9-51(*a*).   Find an Euler circuit on the Eulerized graph and indicate the closed path on the original graph that corresponds to the Euler circuit.

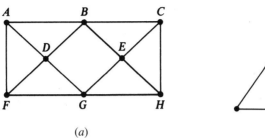

(*a*)                                                              (*b*)

**Fig. 9-51**

## HAMILTONIAN CIRCUITS

**9.45.** Classify the graph in Fig. 9-51(*b*) as Eulerian only, Hamiltonian only, both, or neither.

**9.46.** Construct a graph with five vertices that is Hamiltonian but not Eulerian.

**9.47.** Find all Hamiltonian circuits for each of the graphs in Fig. 9-52.

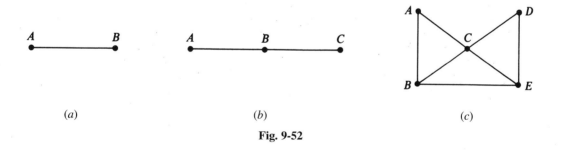

(*a*)                                         (*b*)                                     (*c*)

**Fig. 9-52**

**9.48.** Find all Hamiltonian circuits for the graph in Fig. 9-12.

## TRAVELING SALESPERSON PROBLEM

**9.49.** Solve the traveling salesperson problem (i.e., find the Hamiltonian circuit of least weight) for the graph in Fig. 9-12.

**9.50.** Find all Hamiltonian circuits for the graph in Fig. 9-53(*a*).

**9.51.** Solve the traveling salesperson problem for the graph in Fig. 9-53(*a*).

**9.52.** Apply the nearest-neighbor algorithm to the graph in Fig. 9-53(*a*), starting at: (*a*) *A*,   (*b*) *B*,   (*c*) *C*.

**9.53.** Apply the ordered-edges algorithm (see Problem 9.21) to the graph in Fig. 9-53(*a*).

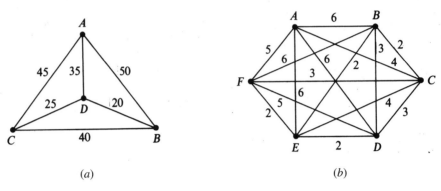

(*a*)                                                                              (*b*)

**Fig. 9-53**

**9.54.** Apply the nearest-neighbor algorithm to the graph in Fig. 9-53(*b*), starting at *A*.

**9.55.** Apply the ordered-edges algorithm to the graph in Fig. 9-53(*b*).

## DIGRAPHS

**9.56.** Suppose Friendly Airways has nine daily flights with their corresponding flight numbers as follows:

| 103 | Atlanta to Houston | 203 | Boston to Denver | 305 | Chicago to Miami |
|-----|-------------------|-----|------------------|-----|------------------|
| 106 | Houston to Atlanta | 204 | Denver to Boston | 308 | Miami to Boston |
| 201 | Boston to Chicago | 301 | Denver to Reno | 401 | Reno to Chicago |

Describe the data by means of a weighted digraph.

**9.57.** Consider the flight information in Problem 9.56. Identify other data that might also be assigned to the: (*a*) edges, (*b*) vertices.

**9.58.** Find a critical path (see Problem 9.26) for the digraph in Fig. 9-54.

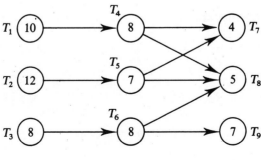

**Fig. 9-54**

**9.59.** Find a critical path for the digraph in Fig. 9-55

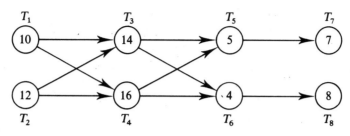

**Fig. 9-55**

## TREES

**9.60.** Find all spanning trees of the graph $H$ shown in Fig. 9-56($a$).

**9.61.** Find two distinct minimal spanning trees of the labeled graph $G$ in Fig. 9-56($b$).

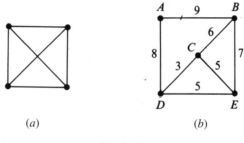

($a$)          ($b$)

**Fig. 9-56**

**9.62.** Apply Algorithm 9.2 to the graph in Fig. 9-44($a$).

**9.63.** Apply Algorithm 9.1 to the graph in Fig. 9-45($a$).

**9.64.** Consider the graph in Fig. 9-57. Apply ($a$) Algorithm 9.1, ($b$) Algorithm 9.2.

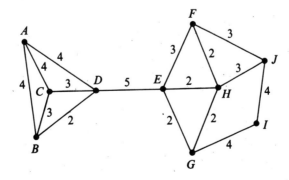

**Fig. 9-57**

# Answers to Supplementary Problems

**9.33.** (a) The graph has five vertices $a$, $b$, $c$, $d$, and $e$, and seven edges, $e_1 = ab$, $e_2 = ac$, $e_3 = ad$, $e_4 = bc$, $e_5 = be$, $e_6 = cd$, and $e_7 = ce$. It is a simple graph.

(b) The graph has six vertices $P_1$, $P_2$, $P_3$, $P_4$, $P_5$, and $P_6$ (isolated), and six edges $e_1 = P_1 P_1$, $e_2 = P_1P_4$, $e_3 = P_2 P_3$, $e_4 = P_2 P_3$, $e_5 = P_2 P_4$, and $e_6 = P_4 P_5$. There is one loop and a multiple edge. The graph is not simple.

**9.34.** (a) $a, 3$; $b, 3$; $c, 4$; $d, 2$; $e, 2$; (b) $P_1, 3$; $P_2, 3$; $P_3, 2$; $P_4, 3$; $P_5, 1$; $P_6, 0$.

**9.35.** The graphs are drawn in Fig. 9-58.

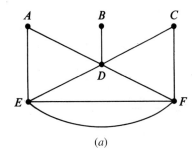

(a)  (b)

**Fig. 9-58**

**9.36.** (a) The total number of edges is seven; the sum of the degrees of the vertices (see previous problem) is $3 + 3 + 4 + 2 + 2 = 14$.

(b) The total number of edges is six; the sum of the degrees of the vertices is $3 + 3 + 2 + 3 + 1 = 12$.

**9.37.** (a) *ABDFEH*, (b) *DEHFDBACD*

**9.38.** *ABDEH, ABDEFH, ABDFH, ABDFEH; ADEH, ADEFH, ADFH, ADFEH; ACDEH, ACDEFH, ACDFH, ACDFEH; ABCDEH, ABCDEFH, ABCDFH, ABCDFEH; ACBDEH, ACBDEFH, ACBDFH, ACBDFEH.*

**9.39.** (a) Yes: *ABCDE*. (b) No. *CF* and *DE* have no vertex in common. (c) Yes: *BADEF*.

**9.40.** (a) Yes. (b) No, there is no path from $A$, $D$, or $E$ to $B$ or $C$. (c) Yes. (d) No, there is no path from $A$, $B$, or $E$ to $D$ or $C$.

**9.41.** (a) Traversable, since $A$ and $F$ have odd degree and the other vertices have even degree. Not Eulerian.

(b) Traversable, since $B$ and $C$ have odd degree and the other vertices have even degree. Not Eulerian.

(c) Both Eulerian and traversable, since all vertices have even degree.

**9.42.** *ABHG-FECG-IEDA-HKJD-KIFCA*

**9.43.** (a) *ABCD-ACFB-EFGDF*, (b) *BACG-FCEF-BDEBC*

**9.44.** The Eulerized graph is shown in Fig. 9-59. The Euler circuit *ABCH-CEHG-EBDG-FDAFA* on the graph in Fig. 9-59 corresponds to the same sequence of vertices on the original graph in Fig. 9-51($a$) except that, in Fig. 9-51$a$ the edges *CH* and *AF* are traversed twice, once in each direction.

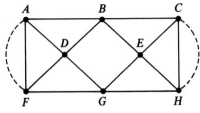

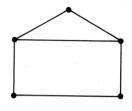

Fig. 9-59                                               Fig. 9-60

**9.45.**   Eulerian only.

**9.46.**   One possibility is the graph in Fig. 9-60.

**9.47.**   (*a*)   *ABA* (equivalent to *BAB*).        (*b*)   There are none.        (*c*)   All Hamiltonian circuits are equivalent to *ACDEBA*.

**9.48.**   *PABCQFEDP,   PABFQCEDP.*

**9.49.**   *PABCQFEDP* is the Hamiltonian circuit of minimal weight, 30.

**9.50.**   *ABCDA,   ABDCA,   ADBCA.*

**9.51.**   *ABDCA* and *ADBCA* each have minimum weight, 140.

**9.52.**   The nearest-neighbor algorithm, starting at *A*, gives *ADBCA*.

**9.53.**   The ordered-edges algorithm gives *ABDCA*.

**9.54.**   The nearest-neighbor algorithm, starting at *A*, gives either *ACBEDFA*, with weight 20, or *ACBEFDA*, with weight 21.

**9.55.**   The ordered-edges algorithm gives the circuit formed from the edges *BC, BE, DE, CF, AD, AF*, i.e., *ADEBCFA*.

**9.56.**   The data are described by the graph in Fig. 9-61 (where the flight numbers have been omitted for notational convenience).

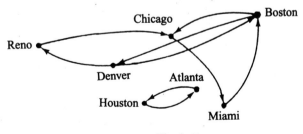

Fig. 9-61

**9.57.**   (*a*)   The flights (edges) usually contain the price, time, type of aircraft, etc.
            (*b*)   The cities (vertices) may contain the name of their airport, hotels at the airport, etc.

**9.58.**   The critical path is $T_2T_5T_8$, which has weight 24.

**9.59.**   There are two critical paths, $T_2T_4T_5T_7$ and $T_2T_4T_6T_8$, each of weight 40.

**9.60.** There are 12 spanning trees as shown in Fig. 9-62.

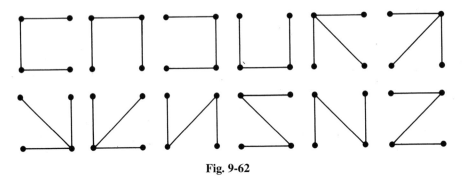

**Fig. 9-62**

**9.61.** Two minimal spanning trees are shown in Fig. 9-63.

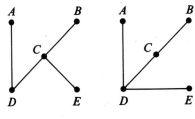

**Fig. 9-63**

**9.62.** Ordering the edges as follows and applying step 2 of Algorithm 9.2 gives the graph in Figure 9-44(*c*).

| Edges | BE | EG | GH | EH | AB | AD | AE | BC | DE | DG | CE | CF | EF | EI | FI | HI |
|-------|----|----|----|----|----|----|----|----|----|----|----|----|----|----|----|----|
| Weights | 1 | 1 | 1 | 1 | 1 | 1 | 1 | 2 | 2 | 2 | 3 | 3 | 3 | 3 | 3 | 3 |
| Add? | Yes | Yes | Yes | No | Yes | Yes | No | Yes | No | No | No | Yes | No | Yes | No | No |

**9.63.** Ordering the edges as follows and applying step 2 of Algorithm 9.1 gives the graph in Figure 9-45(*c*).

| Edges | AF | GH | EG | CF | BC | DE | BD | AC | DH | EH | FG | CE | AB |
|-------|----|----|----|----|----|----|----|----|----|----|----|----|----|
| Weights | 12 | 10 | 9 | 8 | 8 | 7 | 7 | 7 | 6 | 5 | 4 | 4 | 4 |
| Delete? | Yes | Yes | Yes | No | Yes | Yes | Yes | No | No | No | No | No | No |

**9.64.** Ordering the edges as follows and applying step 2 of Algorithm 9.1 gives the minimal spanning tree in Fig. 9-64:

| Edges | DE | IJ | GI | AD | AC | AB | HJ | FJ | EF | CD | BC | GH | FH | EH | EG | BD |
|-------|----|----|----|----|----|----|----|----|----|----|----|----|----|----|----|----|
| Weights | 5 | 4 | 4 | 4 | 4 | 4 | 3 | 3 | 3 | 3 | 3 | 3 | 2 | 2 | 2 | 2 |
| Delete? | No | Yes | No | Yes | Yes | No | Yes | No | Yes | Yes | No | Yes | No | No | No | No |

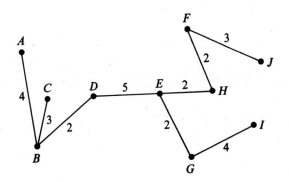

**Fig. 9-64**

**9.65.** Ordering the edges as follows and applying step 2 of Algorithm 9.2 gives the minimal spanning tree in Fig. 9-64:

| Edges | BD | EG | EH | FH | GH | BC | CD | EF | FJ | HJ | AB | AC | AD | GI | IJ | DE |
|---|---|---|---|---|---|---|---|---|---|---|---|---|---|---|---|---|
| Weights | 2 | 2 | 2 | 2 | 2 | 3 | 3 | 3 | 3 | 3 | 4 | 4 | 4 | 4 | 4 | 5 |
| Add? | Yes | Yes | Yes | Yes | No | Yes | No | No | Yes | No | Yes | No | No | Yes | No | Yes |

# CHAPTER 10

# Voting Systems

## 10.1 INTRODUCTION

This chapter deals with some of the methods employed to consolidate the individual preferences expressed by members of a group into one unified preference for the group as a whole. It is convenient to present these methods in terms of elections where the goal is to select one candidate out of a set of candidates on the basis of ballots cast by a group of voters. Several voting systems with different types of ballots and methods of reaching the goal are considered below, along with some of the desirable and undesirable consequences of each system.

## 10.2 ELECTIONS WITH TWO CANDIDATES

### Majority System

Suppose that the goal is to choose between two candidates running for an office and voters are required to submit their preferences on a ballot. The most common voting system employed in this situation is the familiar *majority system*, where the candidate with the most votes is declared the winner.

**Remark:** The majority system may lead to a tie when the total number of voters is even. A tie may occur in this system even when the number of voters is odd due to some of the votes being declared invalid. Ties are also not uncommon with the other systems we will consider in this chapter. Ties are usually broken using methods agreed upon prior to the election—such as by flipping a coin—but we shall not include any discussion of these methods in this chapter.

It is easy to verify that the majority rule has the following desirable properties:

(1) The candidates are treated in an equitable manner—that is, if *all* the voters were to change their preference from their original choice to the other candidate, then the loser of the original election would become the new winner.

(2) The voters are treated equally in the sense that if any two voters were to exchange their completed ballots prior to submission, the outcome of the election would remain the same.

(3) (*Monotonicity*) If one or more of the voters who voted for the loser originally were to change their preference to the original winner, then the outcome of the new election would be the same.

An important result in voting theory states that in two-candidate elections involving an odd number of voters, among all voting systems that never result in ties, the majority system is the only one that satisfies all of the above three properties.

## 10.3   SINGLE-VOTE PLURALITY SYSTEM WITH THREE OR MORE CANDIDATES

Suppose that the goal is to elect one out of three or more candidates running for an office and that each voter is required to vote for one of the candidates.   According to the *plurality* method, the winner is that candidate with the most votes.

Clearly, this method is simply a straightforward extension of the majority system.   But the winner under plurality may not have the approval of a majority (more than one-half) of the voters.   It is, nevertheless, true that *if* a candidate receives a majority of the votes, that candidate would be the winner according to the single-vote plurality system.   In other words, this system satisfies the fairness criterion defined below.

**Definition:**   A voting system is said to satisfy the *majority fairness criterion* if whenever a candidate receives a majority of the votes, that candidate will be chosen as the winner by the system.

In addition to the majority criterion, the single-vote plurality system satisfies the three desirable properties mentioned above in connection with the majority system with two candidates.   These properties, of course, have to be properly modified to reflect the fact that we now have three or more candidates.   Assuming there are three candidates, $A$, $B$, and $C$, of whom $A$ is the winner, the three properties satisfied by the single-vote plurality system are as follows:

(1)   If all the voters who voted for either $A$ or $B$ were to switch their preference between $A$ and $B$, then $B$ would become the new winner.   Similarly, if all the voters switched between $A$ and $C$, $C$ would become the winner, but if they switched between $B$ and $C$, $A$ would remain the winner.

(2)   If any two voters were to exchange their completed ballots prior to submission, the outcome of the election would remain the same.

(3)   (*Monotonicity fairness criterion*) If one or more voters who voted for either $B$ or $C$ in the original election were to change their choice to $A$, then $A$ would still be the winner of the new election.

The first two of the above three properties are satisfied by all the voting systems discussed in this chapter, so we shall not discuss them here any further.   Monotonicity, however, is of much more interest, since some of the voting systems we study do not have this property and it is not always straightforward to determine if a given system satisfies it.

## 10.4   VOTING SYSTEMS WITH PREFERENCE LIST BALLOTS AND MORE THAN TWO CANDIDATES

Most of the voting systems involving three or more candidates employ ballots consisting of the different rank orderings of the candidates.   For example, if the candidates are $A$, $B$, $C$, $D$, each voter has to vote for one out of the 24 (= 4!) possible rank orderings or permutations of the four candidates.   These ballots may be denoted by $<A, B, C, D>$, $<A, B, D, C>$, $<A, C, B, D>$,..., $<D, C, B, A>$.   (The ballot $<C, D, A, B>$, for instance, indicates that for the voter candidate $C$ is the first preference, $D$ is the second preference, $A$ is the third preference, and $B$ is the fourth preference.) These rank orderings are referred to as *preference lists*.

**EXAMPLE 10.1**   Suppose that there are three candidates, $A$, $B$, $C$, and 13 voters in an election and that the ballots are cast as follows:

1. $<A, B, C>$; 2. $<A, C, B>$;   3. $<C, B, A>$;   4. $<A, C, B>$;   5. $<B, C, A>$;   6. $<A, C, B>$; 7. $<A, B, C>$;
8. $<A, B, C>$;   9. $<C, B, A>$;   10. $<B, C, A>$;   11. $<A, B, C>$;   12. $<C, B, A>$;   13. $<A, B, C>$.

The results of the election may then be summarized in a table as follows.   This table is known as the *preference schedule* of the election.

| Number of Voters | 5 | 3 | 2 | 3 |
|---|---|---|---|---|
| 1st preference | $A$ | $A$ | $B$ | $C$ |
| 2nd preference | $B$ | $C$ | $C$ | $B$ |
| 3rd preference | $C$ | $B$ | $A$ | $A$ |

This preference schedule tells us immediately that the preference lists submitted by the voters are $<A, B, C>$, $<A, C, B>$, $<B, C, A>$, and $<C, B, A>$, with respective numbers of votes 5, 3, 2, and 3.

### The Plurality Method

In the plurality system with preference lists, the candidate receiving the largest number of first-place votes is declared the winner. For instance, in the election described in Example 10.1, candidate $A$ would be the winner according to the plurality system.

**EXAMPLE 10.2** The results of an election with 4 candidates and 30 voters are tallied in the preference schedule below.

| Number of Voters | 8 | 5 | 4 | 6 | 7 |
|---|---|---|---|---|---|
| 1$^{st}$ preference | $A$ | $B$ | $C$ | $C$ | $D$ |
| 2$^{nd}$ preference | $B$ | $C$ | $A$ | $B$ | $B$ |
| 3$^{rd}$ preference | $C$ | $D$ | $B$ | $D$ | $C$ |
| 4$^{th}$ preference | $D$ | $A$ | $D$ | $A$ | $A$ |

We see that $C$ is the winner of this election according to the plurality system, since the number of first-place votes for $C$ is 10, as opposed to 8 for $A$, 5 for $B$, and 7 for $D$.

Note that the winner in the above example doesn't have majority support, whereas the plurality winner in Example 10.1 does. It can be easily seen that whenever there is a candidate with a majority of first-place preferences, that candidate would be the winner in the plurality system. In other words, the plurality system with preference lists satisfies the following fairness criterion.

**Definition:** A voting system with preference lists is said to satisfy the *majority fairness criterion* if whenever there is a candidate with a majority of first-place votes, that candidate will be the winner of the election according to that system.

The fairness criterion of *monotonicity*, introduced earlier, may be defined as follows in the context of voting systems with preference list ballots.

**Definition:** A voting system is said to satisfy the *monotonicity fairness criterion* if the winner of any election under the system remains the winner if any of the original ballots are modified in favor of the winner without changing the relative positions of the other candidates within each ballot (that is, if the winner's rank is higher in any modified preference list than in the original list but the relative positions of the other candidates are the same in both lists.)

**EXAMPLE 10.3** Consider the election data given in Example 10.2. Suppose now that two of the seven voters who submitted the preference list $<D, B, C, A>$ change their minds and submit the list $<D, C, B, A>$ instead and that one voter switches from $<B, C, D, A>$ to $<C, B, D, A>$. All changes in preference lists are thus in favor of the original winner $C$ without in any way changing the original relative ordering among $A$, $B$, and $D$. The preference schedule for the new election is given below. It can be seen that $C$ is now ranked in first place by 11 of the 30 voters, and therefore $C$ is still the winner of the election under the plurality system.

| Number of Voters | 8 | 4 | 5 | 6 | 5 | 2 |
|---|---|---|---|---|---|---|
| 1$^{st}$ preference | $A$ | $B$ | $C$ | $C$ | $D$ | $D$ |
| 2$^{nd}$ preference | $B$ | $C$ | $A$ | $B$ | $B$ | $C$ |
| 3$^{rd}$ preference | $C$ | $D$ | $B$ | $D$ | $C$ | $B$ |
| 4$^{th}$ preference | $D$ | $A$ | $D$ | $A$ | $A$ | $A$ |

In general, when a preference list is modified only in favor of the original winner without changing the relative positions of the losers, no new preference list can be created with any of the losers in first place. On the other hand, the modification could possibly result in the original winner moving up to first place on a given ballot from an original ranking below first place on that ballot.    We can therefore conclude that *the plurality system with preference lists always satisfies the criterion of monotonicity.*

One of the drawbacks of the plurality system with preference lists becomes apparent when we examine the preference schedule of Example 10.2 from the perspective of candidate *B*.    It is true that *B* is ranked first by only 5 of the 30 voters and is actually dead last when it comes to the number of first place votes.    It is, nevertheless, also the case that *B* would be the winner in a head-to-head matchup (under the majority rule) with any of the other three candidates: *B* is preferred over *A, C,* and *D,* respectively, in 18, 20, and 23 ballots! It is therefore unfair to *B* that *C* has been declared the winner by the plurality system.    This leads us to another criterion by which the fairness of a voting system may be judged.

**Definition:**    A *Condorcet winner* in an election is a candidate who defeats every other candidate in a head-to-head matchup using the majority rule.

**Definition:**    A voting system is said to satisfy the *Condorcet fairness criterion* if, whenever a Condorcet winner emerges, this winner must also be the winner of the election under the system.

As we have just seen, the preference schedule in Example 10.1 shows that *the plurality method may violate the Condorcet criterion.*    The following example provides another instance of this violation.

**EXAMPLE 10.4**    Consider the preference schedule in Example 10.2.    To see if a Condorcet winner exists for this election, we have to determine the winner in each of the six head-to-head matchups, between: *A* and *B; A* and *C; A* and *D; B* and *D; C* and *D*.    The matchup between *A* and *B* is accomplished by removing *C* and *D* from the schedule.    This results in the following collapsed schedule, which shows that *B* beats *A* by 18 to 12.

| Number of Voters | 12 | 18 |
|---|---|---|
| 1ˢᵗ preference | A | B |
| 2ⁿᵈ preference | B | A |

It can be similarly established that *B* also beats *C* and *D*.    Now there is no need to determine the winner in the remaining three matchups, since *B* has already emerged as the Condorcet winner of the election by defeating each of the other three candidates.    The plurality winner of the election, however, is *C*.    Thus, the Condorcet criterion is violated.

**EXAMPLE 10.5**    Consider the following preference schedule.    There is no Condorcet winner in this case, since every candidate loses to at least one other candidate in a head-to-head matchup (*A* is defeated by *C, B* is defeated by *A, C* is defeated by *D,* and *D* is defeated by *B*).

| Number of Voters | 2 | 1 | 1 | 1 | 1 | 1 |
|---|---|---|---|---|---|---|
| 1ˢᵗ preference | A | A | B | C | C | D |
| 2ⁿᵈ preference | B | D | C | A | B | B |
| 3ʳᵈ preference | D | C | D | B | D | C |
| 4ᵗʰ preference | C | B | A | D | A | A |

Another drawback of the plurality system with preference lists becomes apparent when we reexamine the preference schedule from Example 10.3, reproduced below.

| Number of Voters | 8 | 4 | 5 | 6 | 5 | 2 |
|---|---|---|---|---|---|---|
| 1ˢᵗ preference | A | B | C | C | D | D |
| 2ⁿᵈ preference | B | C | A | B | B | C |
| 3ʳᵈ preference | C | D | B | D | C | B |
| 4ᵗʰ preference | D | A | D | A | A | A |

As pointed out earlier, $C$ is the plurality winner of this election.   But suppose that for some reason, before the results are announced, $A$ decides to withdraw from the election.   The original preference schedule, collapsed as a result of this change, would be as follows:

| Number of Voters | 12 | 11 | 5 | 2 |
|---|---|---|---|---|
| 1st preference | $B$ | $C$ | $D$ | $D$ |
| 2nd preference | $C$ | $B$ | $B$ | $C$ |
| 3rd preference | $D$ | $D$ | $C$ | $B$ |

The plurality winner of this modified schedule obviously is $B$ and we see that the original winner, $C$, has been edged out simply because a loser dropped out of the election!

The same sort of reversal between $C$ and $B$ could happen here if, for instance, the 8 voters who originally chose the preference list $<A, B, C, D>$ were to change their minds about the two losers, namely, $A$ and $B$, and changed their ballots to $<B, A, C, D>$.   The resulting schedule would then be as follows, and the new winner would once again be $B$.

| Number of Voters | 8 | 4 | 5 | 6 | 5 | 2 |
|---|---|---|---|---|---|---|
| 1st preference | $B$ | $B$ | $C$ | $C$ | $D$ | $D$ |
| 2nd preference | $A$ | $C$ | $A$ | $B$ | $B$ | $C$ |
| 3rd preference | $C$ | $D$ | $B$ | $D$ | $C$ | $B$ |
| 4th preference | $D$ | $A$ | $D$ | $A$ | $A$ | $A$ |

What is unreasonable about the above two situations is that in both instances one of the original losers (namely, $B$) has become the new winner without any modifications to the ballots with respect to the relative preference between the original winner (namely, $C$) and the new winner ($B$), but only with respect to candidates who are irrelevant to the reversal.

The fairness criterion that has been violated in this way is known as the *independence of irrelevant alternatives (IIA) criterion*, defined below.

**Definition:**   A voting system is said to satisfy the *independence of irrelevant alternatives criterion* if the only way an original loser under the system could become a winner is through a modification to at least one ballot that results in the reversal of the relative position of the original winner and the new winner.

We have thus shown that *the plurality system may violate the IIA criterion.*

**Remark:**   It is instructive to see some of the possible modifications to a ballot that do not reverse the relative position of the original and the new winner.   Suppose that $A$ is the original winner and $B$ is the new winner (after one or more preference lists were modified).   Then each of the following preference lists would be a modification of the original list $<C, A, B, D>$ that is obtained *without* changing the ranking of $A$ and $B$ relative to each other in the original list: (*a*) $<C, A, D, B>$—this is obtained by switching $B$ and $D$;   (*b*) $< D, A, B, C>$, obtained by switching $C$ and $D$; (*c*) $<A, B, C, D>$, obtained by moving $C$ below $B$ but above $D$;   (*d*) $<A, C, B, D>$, obtained by placing $C$ between $A$ and $B$; and (*e*) $<A, B>$, obtained by dropping $C$ and $D$ from the election.

### The Top-Two Runoff Method

As its name implies, in the *top-two runoff method*, all but the two candidates with the highest first-place votes are dropped from the preference schedule and the candidate with the most first-place votes in the modified schedule is declared the winner.   This method is also known as the *single runoff method*.

**EXAMPLE 10.6**   Let us apply the top-two runoff method to the preference schedule from Example 10.2.   Candidates $C$ (10 first-place votes) and $A$ (8 first-place votes) have the two highest first-place votes, so we remove $B$ and $D$ from the preference schedule.   This gives us the following modified schedule.   The winner of the election by the top-two runoff method is therefore $C$.   Note that $C$ is also the winner in the plurality system but, as the next example shows, this need not always be the case.

| Number of Voters | 8 | 22 |
|---|---|---|
| 1st preference | A | C |
| 2nd preference | C | A |

**EXAMPLE 10.7**   For the preference schedule below, the winner by the plurality method is $A$, but $B$ is the winner according to the top-two runoff method.

| Number of Voters | 7 | 6 | 5 | 3 |
|---|---|---|---|---|
| 1st preference | A | B | C | D |
| 2nd preference | B | A | B | C |
| 3rd preference | C | C | A | A |
| 4th preference | D | D | D | B |

It is not difficult to establish that if in an election there is a candidate with a majority of first-place preferences, then that candidate would be the winner by the top-two runoff method. In other words, *the top-two runoff method satisfies the majority criterion.* The result follows from the fact that a majority winner would defeat *any* of the other candidates in a head-to-head matchup.

The top-two runoff method may, however, violate all three of the monotonicity, Condorcet, and IIA criteria. In the preference schedule of Example 10.6 (see also Example 10.1), $B$ is a Condorcet winner but $C$ is the winner by the top-two runoff method, thus providing an instance where the top-two runoff method violates the Condorcet criterion. The same preference schedule provides an instance where the IIA criterion is violated by the top-two runoff method. To see this, suppose that the 8 voters who submitted the preference list $<A, B, C, D>$ change their preference to $<B, A, C, D>$—a change that does not cause a reversal of rank between $C$ (the original winner) and any of the original losers. The resulting preference schedule is given below. It can be verified that $B$ has now become the winner by the top-two runoff method.

| Number of Voters | 8 | 5 | 4 | 6 | 7 |
|---|---|---|---|---|---|
| 1st preference | B | B | C | C | D |
| 2nd preference | A | C | A | B | B |
| 3rd preference | C | D | B | D | C |
| 4th preference | D | A | D | A | A |

Finally, the following example shows that the *top-two runoff method violates the monotonicity criterion.*

**EXAMPLE 10.8**   For the schedule below, the winner by the top-two runoff method is $A$. Suppose now that the four voters who submitted the list $<B, A, C>$ all change their ballot to $<A, B, C>$.

| Number of Voters | 12 | 4 | 10 | 11 |
|---|---|---|---|---|
| 1st preference | A | B | B | C |
| 2nd preference | B | A | C | A |
| 3rd preference | C | C | A | B |

This change does not affect the relative position of $B$ and $C$ but has moved the winner up in the rank order. The modified schedule, given below, yields $C$ as the new winner by the top-two runoff method.

| Number of Voters | 16 | 10 | 11 |
|---|---|---|---|
| 1st preference | A | B | C |
| 2nd preference | B | C | A |
| 3rd preference | C | A | B |

## The Sequential Runoff Method

This method is somewhat similar to the top-two runoff method. According to this method, the candidate receiving the least number of first-place preferences is first eliminated. This process is then repeated with the resulting collapsed preference schedule until only two candidates remain, at which point the one with a majority of first-place preferences is declared the winner. The sequential runoff method is also known as the *elimination method*.

It can be seen that if, at any stage of the elimination process, there is a candidate with a majority of first-place preferences, then the process could be stopped, since this candidate would ultimately be the winner by the sequential runoff method.

**EXAMPLE 10.9**   Consider the following preference schedule discussed in Examples 10.2 and 10.6.

| Number of Voters | 8 | 5 | 4 | 6 | 7 |
|---|---|---|---|---|---|
| 1$^{st}$ preference | A | B | C | C | D |
| 2$^{nd}$ preference | B | C | A | B | B |
| 3$^{rd}$ preference | C | D | B | D | C |
| 4$^{th}$ preference | D | A | D | A | A |

Clearly, none the four candidates has a majority (16 or more) of first-place preferences. The candidate receiving the least number of first place votes, namely *B*, is therefore removed from the preference schedule. This leads to the following collapsed schedule for the remaining three candidates. Candidate *D* has the least number of first-place votes in this schedule and is removed next.

| Number of Voters | 8 | 11 | 4 | 7 |
|---|---|---|---|---|
| 1$^{st}$ preference | A | C | C | D |
| 2$^{nd}$ preference | C | D | A | C |
| 3$^{rd}$ preference | D | A | D | A |

We are then left with the following final schedule showing *C* as the winner.

| Number of Voters | 8 | 22 |
|---|---|---|
| 1$^{st}$ preference | A | C |
| 2$^{nd}$ preference | C | A |

With respect to the various fairness criteria, the behavior of the sequential runoff method is very similar to that of the top-two runoff method. As we have just seen, the sequential runoff method satisfies the majority criterion. Using the same reasoning as in the case of the top-two runoff method, we can see that the preference schedule of Example 10.6 is an instance where the *Condorcet and IIA criteria are both violated by the sequential runoff method*. The preference schedule of Example 10.7 shows that the *monotonicity criterion may also be violated by the sequential runoff method*.

## The Method of Pairwise Comparisons

In this method each candidate is matched head-to-head with every other candidate. The candidate that wins the largest number of these matches is declared the winner of the election.

**EXAMPLE 10.10**   Consider the following preference schedule. Since there are five candidates, the number of head-to-head matches to be examined is 10. In the matchup between *A* and *B*, *A* is preferred to *B* in 4 out of the 5 ballots, so *A* beats *B*. It can be seen that the number of matches won by *A* is 3, while *B*, *C*, and *D* have two wins each and *D* has one win (*A* beats *B*, *C* and *D*; *B* beats *D* and *E*; *C* beats *B* and *E*; and *E* beats *A*). Therefore, *A* is the winner according to the method of pairwise comparisons.

| Number of Voters | 1 | 1 | 1 | 1 | 1 |
|---|---|---|---|---|---|
| 1st preference | A | A | B | C | D |
| 2nd preference | B | D | E | E | E |
| 3rd preference | D | C | A | A | A |
| 4th preference | C | B | D | B | C |
| 5th preference | E | E | C | D | B |

It can be shown using straightforward reasoning that the method of pairwise comparisons satisfies the majority, Condorcet, and monotonicity criteria.   But we can show that *the pairwise comparisons method may violate the IIA criterion*.   The preference schedule from Example 10.10 provides an instance where this happens; if in that election candidates *B, C,* and *D* (all non-winners) drop out, then *E* becomes the winner.

### The Method of Borda Counts

In this method, candidates are assigned weights on each ballot according to their placement in the preference list.   With four candidates, for instance, the weight given to a candidate given first preference is 4; the weight for a candidate given second preference is 3; and so on.   For the ballot $<C, B, D, A>$, for example, the candidates *A, B, C,* and *D* would receive weights of 1, 3, 4, and 2, respectively.   The weighting method with any number of candidates is similar.   With five candidates, for example, the candidate with first preference on a ballot would receive a weight of 5 for that ballot, and the candidate in fourth preference would receive a weight of 2.   The *Borda count* for any candidate is then defined as the sum of that candidate's weights on all the ballots.   According to the method of Borda counts, the candidate with the highest Borda count in an election is declared the winner.

**EXAMPLE 10.11**   Consider the following preference schedule.

| Number of Voters | 5 | 4 |
|---|---|---|
| 1st preference | A | B |
| 2nd preference | B | C |
| 3rd preference | C | A |

Each of the five preference lists $<A, B, C>$ assigns a weight of 3 to *A*, 2 to *B*, and 1 to *C*.   Each of the five preference lists $<B, C, A>$ assigns a weight of 3 to *B*, 2 to *C*, and 1 to *A*.   Totaling these weights over the nine ballots, we arrive at the Borda count for *A* as $(5 \times 3) + (4 \times 1) = 19$.   Similarly, the counts for *B* and *C* may be shown to be 22 and 13, respectively.   Candidate *B* is therefore the winner of the election according to the method of Borda counts.

As with the other methods we have studied thus far, the Borda counts method may also violate some of the fairness criteria while satisfying others.   The preference schedule of Example 10.11 shows immediately that *the method of Borda counts violates the majority, Condorcet, and IIA criteria*.   These results follow, respectively, from the facts that in this election *(i)* A is the majority winner, *(ii)* A is the Condorcet winner, and *(iii)* A wins by the Borda method if *C* were to drop out.

The monotonicity criterion, however, is always satisfied by the method of Borda counts.   This follows from the observation that any modification to a preference list that moves the Borda winner up in rank without changing the relative ordering of the other candidates would result in an increase in the Borda count for the winner but would either decrease or leave unchanged the count for each non-winner.   For example, if the *C* is the Borda winner in an election and one of the ballots—say, $<B, A, C, D>$—is modified to $<B, C, A, D>$, then the Borda count for *C* would go up by 1, the count for *A* would go down by 1, and the counts for *B* and *D* would remain the same as before the modification.

### Arrow's Impossibility Theorem

The following table summarizes the performance of the various voting systems studied in this chapter with respect to the fairness criteria we have introduced.   It is at once clear from this table that none of the systems we have seen thus far satisfies all four fairness criteria.

**VOTING SYSTEMS**

| FAIRNESS CRITERION | Plurality | Top-Two Runoff | Sequential Runoff | Pairwise Comparisons | Borda Counts |
|---|---|---|---|---|---|
| Majority | S | S | S | S | V |
| Monotonicity | S | V | V | S | S |
| Condorcet | V | V | V | S | V |
| IIA | V | V | V | V | V |

\* S means always "satisfies" and V means may "violate" the given fairness criterion

The following result, from Kenneth Arrow, states that it is futile to search for such a perfect system.

**Arrow's Impossibility Theorem:**   It is impossible to devise a voting system that satisfies all four of the majority, monotonicity, condorcet, and independence of irrelevant alternatives criteria in all cases.

# Solved Problems

## PREFERENCE LISTS AND PREFERENCE SCHEDULES

**10.1.**   The preference lists submitted in a five-candidate election are given below.   Construct the corresponding preference schedule.

| <B, C, E, D, A> | <C, B, D, A, E> | <A, E, C, D, B> | <B, C, E, D, A> | <C, B, D, A, E> |
|---|---|---|---|---|
| <C, B, D, A, E> | <C, B, D, A, E> | <B, C, E, D, A> | <C, B, D, A, E> | <E, D, B, A, C> |
| <A, E, C, D, B> | <A, E, C, D, B> | <C, B, D, A, E> | <C, B, D, A, E> | <B, C, E, D, A> |

Note that the distinct preference lists involved here are <A, E, C, D, B>, <B, C, E, D, A>, <C, B, D, A, E>, and <E, D, B, A, C>.   The preference schedule is

| Number of Voters | 3 | 4 | 7 | 1 |
|---|---|---|---|---|
| 1$^{st}$ preference | A | B | C | E |
| 2$^{nd}$ preference | E | C | B | D |
| 3$^{rd}$ preference | C | E | D | B |
| 4$^{th}$ preference | D | D | A | A |
| 5$^{th}$ preference | B | A | E | C |

**10.2.**   For the preference schedule below, find the modified preference schedule under each of the following changes: (*a*) candidate *C* drops out of the election; (*b*) two out of the 5 voters who submitted <C, B, D, A> switched their rank orderings for *B* and *D*; (*c*) all three of the voters who turned in the ballot <B, D, C, A> moved *A* up to first preference while keeping the relative positions of the other candidates unchanged.

| Number of Voters | 4 | 3 | 5 | 2 | 6 |
|---|---|---|---|---|---|
| 1st preference | A | B | C | C | D |
| 2nd preference | B | D | B | D | C |
| 3rd preference | D | C | D | B | B |
| 4th preference | C | A | A | A | A |

(a) The modified schedule when C drops out is

| Number of Voters | 4 | 8 | 8 |
|---|---|---|---|
| 1st preference | A | B | D |
| 2nd preference | B | D | B |
| 3rd preference | D | A | A |

(b) The modified schedule is

| Number of Voters | 4 | 3 | 3 | 4 | 6 |
|---|---|---|---|---|---|
| 1st preference | A | B | C | C | D |
| 2nd preference | B | D | B | D | C |
| 3rd preference | D | C | D | B | B |
| 4th preference | C | A | A | A | A |

(c) When A is moved up to first preference without any change to the order of the other candidates, the list <B, D, C, A> becomes <A, B, D, C>. The modified schedule would therefore be

| Number of Voters | 7 | 5 | 2 | 6 |
|---|---|---|---|---|
| 1st preference | A | C | C | D |
| 2nd preference | B | B | D | C |
| 3rd preference | D | D | B | B |
| 4th preference | C | A | A | A |

## THE VOTING METHODS

**10.3.** For the preference schedule in Problem 10.2, find the winner according to the (a) plurality method, (b) top-two runoff method, (c) sequential runoff method, (d) Borda counts method.

(a) Candidate C has the most first preference votes (7) and is therefore the winner by the plurality method.

(b) Candidates C and D have the two highest first preference votes. A runoff between them would be based on the following schedule

| Number of Voters | 7 | 13 |
|---|---|---|
| 1st preference | C | D |
| 2nd preference | D | C |

D is therefore the winner by the top-two runoff method.

(c) B has the least number of first preference votes and is therefore the first candidate to be dropped. This gives us

| Number of Voters | 4 | 7 | 9 |
|---|---|---|---|
| 1st preference | A | C | D |
| 2nd preference | D | D | C |
| 3rd preference | C | A | A |

The next candidate to be dropped is *A*.   This leads to

| Number of Voters | 13 | 7 |
|---|---|---|
| 1st preference | D | C |
| 2nd preference | C | D |

*D* is therefore the winner by the top-two runoff method.

(d)   The Borda counts for candidate *A* is $(4 \times 4) + (3 \times 1) + (5 \times 1) + (2 \times 1) + (6 \times 1) = 32$.   The Borda counts for *B, C, D* are obtained similarly and are, respectively, 55, 56, and 57.   The winner by the method of Borda counts is therefore *D*.

**10.4**   For the preference schedule below, show that the winner is the same according to all five methods used with preference lists.

| Number of Voters | 12 | 11 | 10 | 8 |
|---|---|---|---|---|
| 1st preference | A | A | C | D |
| 2nd preference | D | B | B | C |
| 3rd preference | C | C | D | A |
| 4th preference | B | D | A | B |

Note that *A* has scored a majority of first preference votes.   This is enough to show that *A* would obviously be the winner by the plurality, Condorcet, top-two runoff, sequential runoff, and pairwise comparisons methods.   The Borda counts winner is therefore the only one left to be determined.   The Borda counts for *A, B, C, D* are, respectively, 118, 83, 110, and 99.   *A* is therefore also the winner by the method of Borda counts.

## THE PLURALITY METHOD AND THE FAIRNESS CRITERIA

**10.5**   Consider the following preference schedule from Example 10.7. (a) Find the plurality winner, (b) Show that the plurality method violates the Condorcet fairness criterion, and (c) Show that the plurality method violates the IIA fairness criterion by studying the consequence of *C* dropping out of the election.

| Number of Voters | 7 | 6 | 5 | 3 |
|---|---|---|---|---|
| 1st preference | A | B | C | D |
| 2nd preference | B | A | B | C |
| 3rd preference | C | C | A | A |
| 4th preference | D | D | D | B |

The plurality winner clearly is *A*.   If *C* drops out of the election, then the above schedule becomes

| Number of Voters | 7 | 11 | 3 |
|---|---|---|---|
| 1st preference | A | B | D |
| 2nd preference | B | A | A |
| 3rd preference | D | D | B |

The new plurality winner, from this revised schedule, is *B*.    Since the only change we have effected in the original schedule is to remove the "irrelevant" candidate *C* (i.e., a candidate other than the original or new winner), the relative ranking of *A* and *B* remains intact.    This shows that the plurality method violates the IIA criterion in this instance.

**10.6**    In the preference schedule below, show that the plurality method violates the IIA fairness criterion by studying the consequence of candidate *D* dropping out of the election.

| Number of Voters | 12 | 11 | 10 | 8 |
|---|---|---|---|---|
| 1st preference | A | B | C | D |
| 2nd preference | D | A | B | C |
| 3rd preference | C | C | D | A |
| 4th preference | B | D | A | B |

The winner of the election by the plurality method is *A*.    Suppose now that candidate *D* drops out of the election.    The revised schedule would then be

| Number of Voters | 12 | 11 | 10 | 8 |
|---|---|---|---|---|
| 1st preference | A | B | C | C |
| 2nd preference | C | A | B | A |
| 3rd preference | B | C | A | B |

and the new plurality winner is *C*.    We can therefore conclude that the IIA fairness criterion is violated in this instance.

## THE TOP-TWO RUNOFF METHOD AND THE FAIRNESS CRITERIA

**10.7**    Show that in the preference schedule of Problem 10.4 the top-two runoff method satisfies the Condorcet fairness criterion.

To show that any given method violates the Condorcet criterion, we have to show an instance where a Condorcet winner exists but is different from the winner according to that method.    In Problem 10.4 the Condorcet winner exists and it is candidate *A*.    But the winner by the top-two runoff method is also *A*. Therefore, the Condorcet criterion is satisfied in this instance, although this is not always the case with the top-two runoff method.

**10.8**    Use the preference schedule below to show that the top-two runoff method may violate the IIA criterion by studying the consequence of candidates *B* and *D* dropping out of the election.

| Number of Voters | 3 | 3 | 2 | 1 |
|---|---|---|---|---|
| 1st preference | A | B | C | D |
| 2nd preference | B | C | D | C |
| 3rd preference | C | A | A | A |
| 4th preference | D | D | B | B |

Let us first determine the original winner of the election by the top-two runoff method.    The top two candidates are *A* and *B*.    Dropping the other two candidates leads us to the schedule

| Number of Voters | 6 | 3 |
|---|---|---|
| 1st preference | A | B |
| 2nd preference | B | A |

and *A* is the winner by the top-two runoff method.

To show violation of the IIA criterion, let us study the consequence of candidates $B$ and $D$ dropping out of the election. This changes the original schedule with four candidates to the following

| Number of Voters | 3 | 6 |
|---|---|---|
| 1ˢᵗ preference | A | C |
| 2ⁿᵈ preference | C | A |

and candidate $C$ emerges as the new winner by the top-two runoff method. We have thus changed the winner of the election by dropping two irrelevant candidates, thereby showing that the top-two runoff method violates the IIA criterion in this instance.

## THE SEQUENTIAL RUNOFF METHOD AND THE FAIRNESS CRITERIA

**10.9**  Consider the preference schedule in Example 10.7 (*a*) Show that the winner of this election by the sequential runoff method is $A$. (*b*) Use this schedule to show that the sequential runoff method may violate the IIA criterion by studying the consequence of candidates $C$ and $D$ dropping out of the election. (*c*) Show that the sequential runoff method violates the Condorcet criterion in this instance.

(*a*)  The preference schedule from Example 10.7 is reproduced below.

| Number of Voters | 7 | 6 | 5 | 3 |
|---|---|---|---|---|
| 1ˢᵗ preference | A | B | C | D |
| 2ⁿᵈ preference | B | A | B | C |
| 3ʳᵈ preference | C | C | A | A |
| 4ᵗʰ preference | D | D | D | B |

Since candidate $D$ has the least number of first place votes, we drop $D$ from the schedule first. This leads us to the modified schedule

| Number of Voters | 7 | 6 | 5 | 3 |
|---|---|---|---|---|
| 1ˢᵗ preference | A | B | C | C |
| 2ⁿᵈ preference | B | A | B | A |
| 3ʳᵈ preference | C | C | A | B |

The next candidate to be dropped is $B$. This leads to the schedule

| Number of Voters | 13 | 8 |
|---|---|---|
| 1ˢᵗ preference | A | C |
| 2ⁿᵈ preference | C | A |

Candidate $A$ is therefore the winner by the sequential runoff method.

(*b*)  To show violation of the IIA criterion, suppose that $C$ and $D$, two original non-winners, drop out of the election. This results in the following modified schedule

| Number of Voters | 10 | 11 |
|---|---|---|
| 1ˢᵗ preference | A | B |
| 2ⁿᵈ preference | B | A |

and the new winner by the sequential runoff method is $B$.

(*c*)  To show violation of the Condorcet fairness criterion, note that $B$ beats $A$, $C$, and $D$ and is therefore a Condorcet winner. But we have shown in part (*a*) that the winner by the sequential runoff method is $A$.

**10.10**  Use the following preference schedule to show that the sequential runoff method may violate the monotonicity criterion.  (*Hint*: Modify the four preference lists $<B, C, A>$.)

| Number of Voters | 8 | 7 | 4 | 10 |
|---|---|---|---|---|
| 1$^{st}$ preference | A | B | B | C |
| 2$^{nd}$ preference | C | A | C | B |
| 3$^{rd}$ preference | B | C | A | A |

We first find the winner by the sequential runoff method.  Candidate $A$ has the least number of 1$^{st}$ preference votes.  So $A$ is dropped first.  This gives us the collapsed schedule below.  $C$ is therefore the winner by the sequential runoff method.

| Number of Voters | 11 | 18 |
|---|---|---|
| 1$^{st}$ preference | B | C |
| 2$^{nd}$ preference | C | A |

Suppose now that the four voters who originally voted for the preference list $<B, C, A>$ switch to $<C, B, A>$.  This doesn't change the relative ranking of $A$ and $B$ with respect to each other but moves the winner ($C$) up in rank.  This gives us the following modified schedule:

| Number of Voters | 8 | 7 | 14 |
|---|---|---|---|
| 1$^{st}$ preference | A | B | C |
| 2$^{nd}$ preference | C | A | B |
| 3$^{rd}$ preference | B | C | A |

The candidate scoring the least number of 1$^{st}$ preference votes in this schedule is $B$; dropping $B$ from the election now leads to the schedule

| Number of Voters | 15 | 14 |
|---|---|---|
| 1$^{st}$ preference | A | C |
| 2$^{nd}$ preference | C | A |

Candidate $A$ (one of the original non-winners) comes out as the winner by the method of sequential runoff; this clearly is in violation of the monotonicity fairness criterion.

## THE PAIRWISE COMPARISONS METHOD AND THE FAIRNESS CRITERIA

**10.11**  Show that the following preference schedule provides an instance where the pairwise comparisons method violates the IIA criterion.

| Number of Voters | 15 | 2 | 5 | 8 | 12 |
|---|---|---|---|---|---|
| 1$^{st}$ preference | A | B | B | C | D |
| 2$^{nd}$ preference | E | D | C | B | E |
| 3$^{rd}$ preference | B | A | A | A | B |
| 4$^{th}$ preference | C | E | D | D | C |
| 5$^{th}$ preference | D | C | E | E | A |

Let us first determine the winner of the election by the method of pairwise comparisons.  The following results may be directly verified: $A$ beats $D$ and $E$; $B$ beats $A$, $C$, and $D$; $C$ beats $A$ and $D$; $D$ beats $E$; and $E$ beats $B$ and $C$.  Candidate $B$ with the largest number of wins in pairwise comparisons is therefore the winner by the method of pairwise comparisons.

Suppose now that *A* and *D* drop out of the election. The original preference schedule would then be collapsed to the following schedule:

| Number of Voters | 27 | 2 | 5 | 8 |
|---|---|---|---|---|
| 1st preference | E | B | B | C |
| 2nd preference | B | E | C | B |
| 3rd preference | C | C | E | E |

It can be readily seen that in this schedule *E* beats *B* and *C*, *B* beats *C*, and *C* beats no one. Candidate *E* is therefore the new winner by the method of pairwise comparisons. This shows that the pairwise comparisons method violates the IIA criterion in this example.

## THE BORDA COUNTS METHOD AND THE FAIRNESS CRITERIA

**10.12** Does the following preference schedule provide an instance of the fact that the Borda counts method may violate the Condorcet fairness criterion?

| Number of Voters | 4 | 1 | 1 |
|---|---|---|---|
| 1st preference | A | B | C |
| 2nd preference | B | C | A |
| 3rd preference | C | A | B |

The Borda count for *A* is $(4 \times 3) + (1 \times 1) + (1 \times 2) = 15$. The Borda counts for *B* and *C* are, respectively, 12 and 9, so the winner by the Borda counts method is *A*. But the Condorcet winner in this schedule is also *A*, since *A* beats both *B* (5 to 1) and *C* (4 to 2). This schedule therefore does not provide an instance where the Condorcet winner exists but is different from the Borda counts winner.

**10.13** Show that the following preference schedule provides an instance where the Borda counts method violates the IIA fairness criterion. (*Hint*: What would happen if *C* drops out?)

| Number of Voters | 4 | 3 | 1 |
|---|---|---|---|
| 1st preference | A | B | C |
| 2nd preference | B | C | A |
| 3rd preference | C | A | B |

The Borda counts for *A, B, C* are, respectively 17, 18, and 13, so the winner of the Borda counts method is *B*. Suppose now that *C* drops out of the election. Then the collapsed schedule is

| Number of Voters | 5 | 3 |
|---|---|---|
| 1st preference | A | B |
| 2nd preference | B | A |

and the Borda counts winner is *A*. This shows that the Borda counts method violates the IIA criterion in this instance.

# Supplementary Problems

## PREFERENCE LISTS AND PREFERENCE SCHEDULES

**10.14**   The preference lists submitted in a 5-candidate election are given below.   Construct the corresponding preference schedule.

| | | | | |
|---|---|---|---|---|
| <B, C, E, D, A> | <C, B, D, A, E> | <A, E, C, D, B> | <B, C, E, D, A> | <C, B, D, A, E> |
| <C, B, D, A, E> | <C, E, D, A, B> | <B, C, E, D, A> | <C, B, D, A, E> | <E, D, B, A, C> |
| <A, E, C, D, B> | <A, C, E, D, B> | <C, B, D, A, E> | <C, E, D, A, B> | <B, C, E, D, A> |

**10.15**   For the preference schedule below, find the modified preference schedule under each of the following changes: (*a*) candidate *C* drops out of the election; (*b*) 3 out of the 5 voters who submitted <*C, B, D, A*> switched their rank orderings for *A* and *B*; (*c*) 2 out of the 3 voters who turned in the ballot <*B, D, C, A*> moved *C* up to second preference while keeping the relative positions of the other candidates unchanged.

| Number of Voters | 4 | 3 | 5 | 2 | 6 |
|---|---|---|---|---|---|
| 1$^{st}$ preference | A | B | C | C | D |
| 2$^{nd}$ preference | B | D | B | D | C |
| 3$^{rd}$ preference | D | C | D | B | B |
| 4$^{th}$ preference | C | A | A | A | A |

## THE VOTING METHODS

**10.16**   For the following preference schedule, find the winner according to the (*a*) plurality method, (*b*) the top-two runoff method, (*c*) sequential runoff method, (*d*) Borda counts method.

| Number of Voters | 4 | 3 | 1 |
|---|---|---|---|
| 1$^{st}$ preference | A | B | C |
| 2$^{nd}$ preference | B | C | A |
| 3$^{rd}$ preference | C | A | B |

**10.17.**   For the following preference schedule, find the winner according to the (*a*) plurality method, (*b*) the top-two runoff method, (*c*) sequential runoff method, (*d*) pairwise comparisons method, (*e*) Borda counts method.

| Number of Voters | 13 | 11 | 10 | 9 |
|---|---|---|---|---|
| 1$^{st}$ preference | A | B | C | D |
| 2$^{nd}$ preference | D | A | B | C |
| 3$^{rd}$ preference | C | C | D | A |
| 4$^{th}$ preference | B | D | A | B |

## THE PLURALITY METHOD AND THE FAIRNESS CRITERIA

**10.18.** Consider the following preference schedule. (*a*) Find the plurality winner; (*b*) Show that the plurality method violates the Condorcet fairness criterion; (*c*) Show that the plurality method violates the IIA fairness criterion by studying the consequence of candidate *D* dropping out of the election.

| Number of Voters | 7 | 5 | 4 | 2 |
|---|---|---|---|---|
| 1st preference | A | B | D | D |
| 2nd preference | B | D | B | C |
| 3rd preference | C | C | C | B |
| 4th preference | D | A | A | A |

## THE TOP-TWO RUNOFF METHOD AND THE FAIRNESS CRITERIA

**10.19.** Show that the preference schedule in Problem 10.18 provides an instance where the top-two runoff method violates the Condorcet fairness criterion.

**10.20.** Show that the preference schedule in Problem 10.18 provides an instance where the top-two runoff method violates the IIA fairness criterion.

## THE SEQUENTIAL RUNOFF METHOD AND THE FAIRNESS CRITERIA

**10.21.** Show that the preference schedule in Problem 10.18 provides an instance where the sequential runoff method violates the Condorcet fairness criterion.

**10.22.** Show that the preference schedule in Problem 10.18 provides an instance where the sequential runoff method violates the IIA fairness criterion.   (*Hint*: Find the winner if *A* drops out of the election.)

## THE PAIRWISE COMPARISONS METHOD AND THE FAIRNESS CRITERIA

**10.23.** Show that the preference schedule below provides an instance where the pairwise comparisons method violates the IIA fairness criterion.

| Number of Voters | 2 | 10 | 8 | 4 | 8 | 15 |
|---|---|---|---|---|---|---|
| 1st preference | A | B | C | D | E | E |
| 2nd preference | C | D | A | E | B | C |
| 3rd preference | B | E | D | B | A | B |
| 4th preference | D | A | E | A | C | A |
| 5th preference | E | C | B | C | D | D |

## THE BORDA COUNTS METHOD AND THE FAIRNESS CRITERIA

**10.24.** Does the following preference schedule provide an instance of the fact that the Borda counts method may violate (*a*) the Condorcet fairness criterion? (*b*) the majority criterion?

| Number of Voters | 4 | 2 | 1 |
|---|---|---|---|
| 1st preference | A | B | C |
| 2nd preference | B | C | A |
| 3rd preference | C | A | B |

**10.25.** Show that the following preference schedule provides an instance of the fact that the Borda counts method may violate the IIA criterion.

| Number of Voters | 4 | 2 | 3 |
|---|---|---|---|
| 1st preference | A | B | C |
| 2nd preference | B | C | A |
| 3rd preference | C | A | B |

# Answers to Supplementary Problems

**10.14.**

| Number of Voters | 1 | 2 | 4 | 5 | 2 | 1 |
|---|---|---|---|---|---|---|
| 1st preference | A | A | B | C | C | E |
| 2nd preference | C | E | C | B | E | D |
| 3rd preference | E | C | E | D | D | B |
| 4th preference | D | D | D | A | A | A |
| 5th preference | B | B | A | E | B | C |

**10.15.** (a)

| Number of Voters | 4 | 8 | 8 |
|---|---|---|---|
| 1st preference | A | B | D |
| 2nd preference | B | D | B |
| 3rd preference | D | A | A |

(b)

| Number of Voters | 4 | 3 | 3 | 2 | 2 | 6 |
|---|---|---|---|---|---|---|
| 1st preference | A | B | C | C | C | D |
| 2nd preference | B | D | A | B | D | C |
| 3rd preference | D | C | D | D | B | B |
| 4th preference | C | A | B | A | A | A |

(c)

| Number of Voters | 4 | 2 | 1 | 5 | 2 | 6 |
|---|---|---|---|---|---|---|
| 1st preference | A | B | B | C | C | D |
| 2nd preference | B | C | D | B | D | C |
| 3rd preference | D | D | C | D | B | B |
| 4th preference | C | A | A | A | A | A |

**10.16.**   (a)  A        (b)  A       (c)  A       (d)  B

**10.17.**   (a)  A        (b)  A       (c)  A       (d)  A       (e)  C

**10.18.**   (a)  A        (b)  The winner by the pairwise method is B but the plurality winner is A.
(c)  If D drops out, B becomes the plurality winner, whereas A was the original plurality winner.

**10.19.** Candidate D is the winner by the top-two runoff method, but B is the winner by the method of pairwise comparisons.

**10.20.** Candidate $D$ is the winner by the top-two runoff method, but if $A$ drops out of the election, then $B$ becomes the winner by the top-two runoff method.

**10.21.** Candidate $D$ is the winner by the sequential runoff method, but $B$ is the winner by the method of pairwise comparisons.

**10.22.** Candidate $D$ is the winner by the sequential runoff method, but if $A$ drops out, then $B$ becomes the winner by the sequential runoff method.

**10.23.** Candidate $E$ is the winner by the method of pairwise comparisons. If $A$, $B$, and $C$ drop out of the race, then $D$ becomes the winner.

**10.24.** The Borda winner is $A$. The majority winner is $A$. The Condorcet (pairwise) winner is $A$. So this schedule does not provide an opportunity to show that the Borda method may violate the Condorcet and majority criteria.

**10.25.** The original Borda winner is $A$. The Borda winner if $B$ drops out is $C$. This shows that the Borda counts method may violate the IIA criterion.

# CHAPTER 11

# Geometry

## 11.1 INTRODUCTION

We use geometry to describe the physical world around us. In more technical language, *geometry* is the study of the properties, measurement, and relationships of points, lines, curves, angles, surfaces, and solids in space. The subject can be partitioned into two parts: plane geometry, which deals with objects lying in two dimensions, and solid geometry, which deals with three-dimensional objects (see Fig. 11-1).

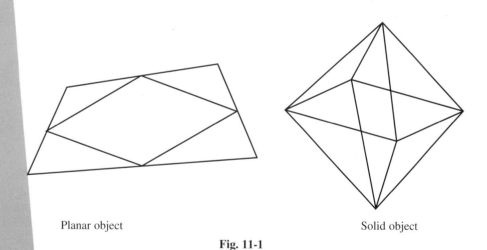

Planar object                    Solid object

**Fig. 11-1**

## 11.2 BASIC OBJECTS OF PLANE GEOMETRY

In order to study geometry, or to use geometry to describe our physical world, we have to familiarize ourselves with the names of some basic objects. The most basic geometric object is a *point*, and all other geometric objects—lines, curves, angles, surfaces, solids, and space itself—are collections of points. We conceive of a point as a specific position in space. Points can be illustrated by dots, for example, made by a pen or a sharp pencil, but if such a mark were examined under a microscope, we would see that it is composed of many smaller marks, and each of these is composed of smaller marks, and so on. In spite of the impossibility of constructing an actual point physically, we have no difficulty in visualizing a point in our mind's eye.

A *line* is a continuous collection of points extending indefinitely in a specific direction and in the opposite direction. Two points determine a line; that is, given two points, there is one and only one line containing the two points. If $P$ and $Q$ are two points, then the line containing them will be denoted by $\overleftrightarrow{PQ}$ (see Fig. 11-2).

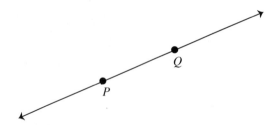

**Fig. 11-2**   The line through points $P$ and $Q$ is denoted by $\overleftrightarrow{PQ}$

**QUESTION**   How many lines are determined by one point? By three points?

**Answer**   There are an infinite number of lines passing through a single point.   Several such lines passing through point
$P$ are shown in Fig. 11-3($a$).   In the case of three points, say, $P_1$, $P_2$, $P_3$, if they do not all lie on a single line,
then they determine three lines, namely, $\overleftrightarrow{P_1P_2}$, $\overleftrightarrow{P_1P_3}$, and $\overleftrightarrow{P_2P_3}$, as shown in Fig. 11-3($b$).

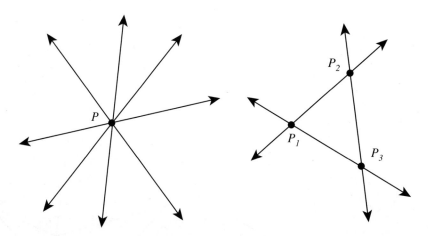

($a$)   An infinite number of lines pass through point $P$.        ($b$)   Three lines are determined by points $P_1$, $P_2$, and $P_3$.

**Fig. 11-3**

A *ray* or *half-line* is a continuous collection of points starting at a given point, called an endpoint, and
extending indefinitely in a specific direction.   A ray, starting at point $P$ and passing through point $Q$ will be
denoted by $\overrightarrow{PQ}$.

A *line segment* is a portion of a line lying between two points, called endpoints of the segment.   A line
segment joining points $P$ and $Q$ will be denoted by $\overline{PQ}$.

These four basic geometric objects are illustrated in Fig. 11-4.

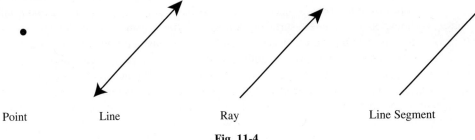

Point              Line              Ray              Line Segment

**Fig. 11-4**

*Parallel lines* are distinct lines that correspond to the same direction but do not intersect, that is, have no points in common [Fig. 11-5(*a*)].    A *plane* can be described as a collection of all parallel lines with the property that any line that intersects two of the lines in the collection intersects all of them.    We think of a plane as a flat surface [Fig. 11-5(*b*)].

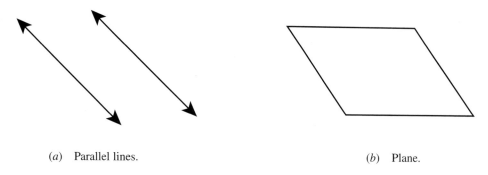

(*a*)   Parallel lines.                                                            (*b*)   Plane.

**Fig. 11-5**

A point has no length, breadth, or depth; a line has infinite length but no breadth or depth; and a plane has infinite length and breadth, but no depth.    Since all physical objects have all three properties—length, breadth, and depth—points, lines, and planes do not actually exist in a physical sense but are abstract geometric objects.

A *curve* is a continuous collection of points joining two fixed points (endpoints).    A *closed curve* is a curve in which the endpoints are the same.

A *circle* is a closed curve lying in a plane and consisting of all points at a fixed distance from a given point. The fixed distance is called the *radius* of the circle, and the given point is called the *center* of the circle.    An *arc* is a portion of a circle lying between two points on the circle.    Some basic curves are illustrated in Fig. 11-6.

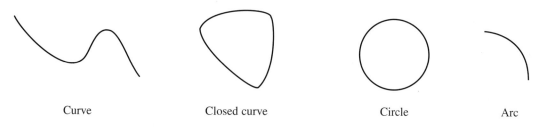

Curve                           Closed curve                         Circle                       Arc

**Fig. 11-6**

A *disc* is a circle including the planar region interior to the circle; in this sense, the circle is the boundary of the disc.    However, sometimes the word "circle" itself refers to the whole disc in which case the boundary is called the *circumference* of the circle.    You can usually tell from context what meaning of circle is being used.

An *angle* is an arc of a circle.    The center of the circle is called the *vertex* of the angle, and the radial line segments from the center to endpoints of the arc are called the *sides* of the angle.    We often think of an angle as a rotation from one of the sides to the other.    The starting side is then called the *initial side*, and the ending side is called the *terminal side* of the angle.    In this interpretation, we adopt the convention that the rotation from the initial to the terminal side is counterclockwise.    We also sometimes think of an angle as the space between the two sides.    Three representations of angles are shown in Fig. 11-7.

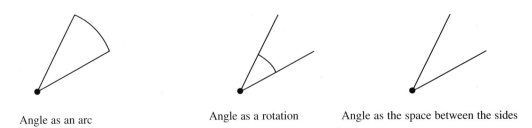

Angle as an arc          Angle as a rotation          Angle as the space between the sides

**Fig. 11-7**

## 11.3   ANGLE MEASUREMENT

In assigning a measure to angles we think of an angle as a rotation in which the unit of measurement is called a *degree*.   One complete counterclockwise rotation in which the terminal side coincides with the initial side, constitutes 360 degrees, denoted by 360° (see Fig. 11-8).

A *right angle* is 90°, which corresponds to a quarter rotation (see Fig. 11-8).   A *straight angle* is 180°, which corresponds to a half rotation (see Fig. 11-8).

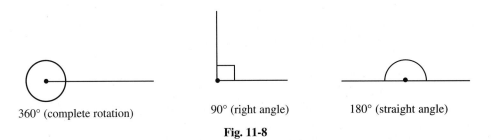

360° (complete rotation)          90° (right angle)          180° (straight angle)

**Fig. 11-8**

**EXAMPLE 11.1**   Give the degree measure of the following angles:

(a)   $\dfrac{1}{8}$ rotation          (b)   $\dfrac{2}{5}$ rotation          (c)   $\dfrac{3}{4}$ rotation

In all cases we multiply the fraction defining the rotation by 360° to obtain the degree measure of the angle.

(a)   $\dfrac{1}{8}$ 360° = 45°

45°

(b)   $\dfrac{2}{5}$ 360° = 144°

144°

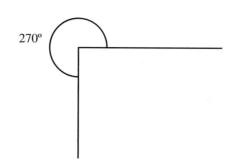

(c)  $\dfrac{3}{4}$ 360° = 270°

**EXAMPLE 11.2**   Convert the following degree measures into a fraction of a rotation:

(a)  30°        (b)  72°        (c)  145°

In all cases we divide the angle by 360° to obtain the corresponding fraction of a rotation.

(a)  $\dfrac{30°}{360°} = \dfrac{1}{12}$

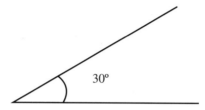

(b)  $\dfrac{72°}{360°} = \dfrac{1}{5}$

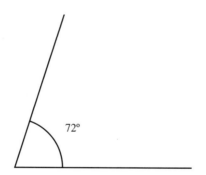

(c)  $\dfrac{145°}{360°} = \dfrac{29}{72}$

*Supplementary angles* are any two angles whose sum is 180°. *Complementary angles* are any two angles whose sum is 90°. Two intersecting lines are *perpendicular* if their angle of intersection is 90° (see Fig. 11-9).

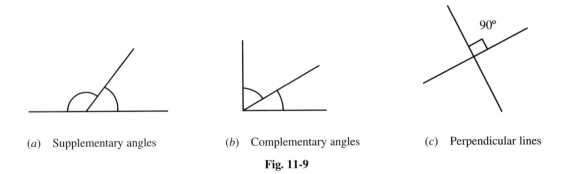

(a)   Supplementary angles        (b)   Complementary angles        (c)   Perpendicular lines

**Fig. 11-9**

A *plane*, which was defined above in terms of parallel lines, can also be defined as the collection of all lines through a given point and perpendicular to a given line (see Fig. 11-10).

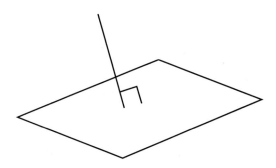

**Fig. 11-10**   Plane

## 11.4   PLANAR FIGURES

A *triangle* is a planar figure formed by the line segments connecting three points that are not on a common line.   The line segments are called the *sides* of the triangle.   The three points are called the *vertices* of the triangle.   A triangle has three interior angles, one at each vertex, as well as three sides (see Fig. 11-11).

A *quadrilateral* is a closed planar figure with four sides (see Fig. 11-11).   A *polygon* is any closed planar figure with three or more line segments as sides (see Fig. 11-11).   A polygon with *n* sides also has *n* vertices and *n* interior angles, one at each vertex.   When we refer to the angle of a polygon at a vertex, we mean the interior angle.   If the measure of such an angle is $x°$, then the corresponding exterior angle has measure $(360 - x)°$.   A polygon whose sides are of equal length is called a *regular* polygon.

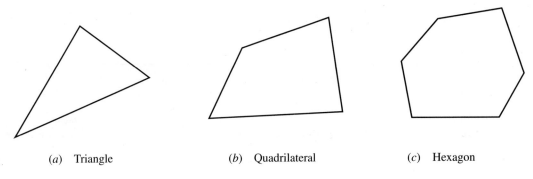

(a)   Triangle              (b)   Quadrilateral              (c)   Hexagon

**Fig. 11-11**

### Types of Triangles

An *equilateral* triangle is a triangle whose three sides have the same length. An *isosceles* triangle is a triangle in which two of its sides have the same length.   We call the vertex angle formed by the two equal sides the apex angle.   A *right triangle* is a triangle in which one of its angles is 90°.   The side opposite the 90° angle is called the *hypotenuse*. (See Fig. 11-12.)

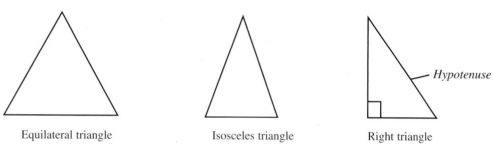

    Equilateral triangle          Isosceles triangle          Right triangle

**Fig. 11-12**

### Types of Quadrilaterals

A **rectangle** is a quadrilateral whose four angles are right angles.   A **square** is a rectangle whose four sides are equal.   A **parallelogram** is a quadrilateral whose opposite sides are parallel.   A **trapezoid** is a quadrilateral with exactly two parallel sides.   See Fig. 11-13.

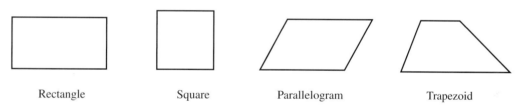

    Rectangle          Square          Parallelogram          Trapezoid

**Fig. 11-13**

Since each of the four angles of a rectangle is 90°, their sum is 360°.   If two opposite vertices of a rectangle are connected, two identical right triangles are formed, so the sum of the angles in each right triangle is 180°. We will show in Section 11.5 that the sum of the angles of *any* triangle is 180°.

**EXAMPLE 11.3**   Use the fact that the sum of the angles of triangle is 180° to prove that the sum of the angles of a parallelogram and of a trapezoid is 360°.

By connecting two opposite vertices in either a parallelogram or a trapezoid (see Fig. 11-13), two triangles are formed. The sum of the three angles of each triangle is 180°, so the sum of all six angles is 360°, and this sum is equal to the sum of the four angles of the parallelogram or trapezoid.

### Congruence and Similarity

Two geometric objects are *congruent* if they have the same shape and size—that is, if they are identical except for position.   For example, two line segments are congruent if they have the same length, and two triangles are congruent if they have the same angles and if sides opposite corresponding angles have the same length.

Two geometric objects are *similar* if they have the same shape and are proportional in size.   For example, any two line segments are similar, and two triangles are similar if their angles are equal and corresponding sides (sides opposite equal angles) are proportional.   In Fig. 11-14, triangle *ABC* is similar to triangle *DEF* with *scale factor* $\frac{1}{2}$, meaning that angles $A,B,C$ are equal to angles $D,E,F$, respectively, and $\overline{DE} = \frac{1}{2}\overline{AB}$,

$\overline{EF} = \frac{1}{2}\overline{BC}$, and $\overline{DF} = \frac{1}{2}\overline{AC}$.   Note that two triangles are congruent if they are similar with scale factor 1.

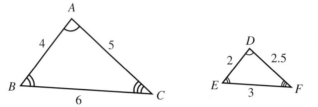

**Fig. 11-14**   Triangle *DEF* is similar to triangle *ABC* with scale factor $\frac{1}{2}$.

It can be shown that if the angles of one triangle are equal, respectively, to the angles of another triangle, then their corresponding sides are proportional, so the triangles are similar.   Also, since the sum of the angles of any triangle is 180°, it follows that if two of the angles of one triangle are equal, respectively, to two angles of another triangle, they will have three angles in common.   We can then state the following criterion for similarity.

**Angle-Angle (AA) Similarity Criterion**

Two triangles are similar if two angles of one of them are equal, respectively, to two angles of the other (see Fig. 11-15).

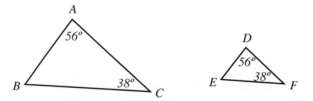

**Fig. 11-15**   Triangles *ABC* and *DEF* are similar by the AA criterion.

It can also be shown that if the sides of one triangle are proportional to the sides of another triangle, then their respective angles will be equal.   We can therefore state the following criterion for similarity.

**Side-Side-Side (SSS) Similarity Criterion**

Two triangles are similar if the sides of one of them are proportional to the sides of the other.   In Fig. 11-16, triangles *DEF* and *ABC* have their sides in the proportion $\dfrac{\overline{DE}}{\overline{AB}} = \dfrac{\overline{EF}}{\overline{BC}} = \dfrac{\overline{DF}}{\overline{AC}} = \dfrac{1}{2}$.   Note that two triangles are congruent by the SSS criterion if they are similar by the SSS criterion with common ratio 1.

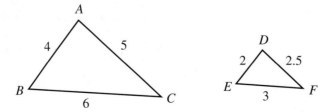

**Fig. 11-16**   Triangles *ABC* and *DEF* are similar by the SSS criterion.

It can also be shown that if two sides of one triangle are proportional to two sides of another triangle, and the corresponding included angles are equal, then all three sides are proportional, and all three angles are equal. Therefore, a third criterion for similarity is as follows.

### Side-Angle-Side (SAS) Similarity Criterion

Two triangles are similar if two sides of one of them are proportional to two sides of the other and the corresponding included angles are equal.    In Fig. 11-17, triangles *ABC* and *DEF* have two corresponding sides satisfying the proportion $\dfrac{DE}{AB} = \dfrac{DF}{AC} = \dfrac{1}{2}$, and the included angle of each pair is 56°.

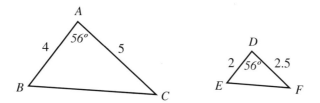

**Fig. 11-17**    Triangles *ABC* and *DEF* are similar by the SAS criterion.

### 11.5   EUCLID'S POSTULATES: THE DEVELOPMENT OF PLANE GEOMETRY

Plane geometry was first formalized in a text by Euclid (circa 300 B.C.) called "The Elements" consisting of 13 chapters (called "books").    Properties related to lines, angles, and polygons were derived from basic logical principles and the following five postulates, along with some implicit assumptions related to the postulates.

E1    It is possible to draw a line segment from any point to any other point.

E2    It is possible to extend a line segment continuously.

E3    It is possible to construct a circle with any center and radius.

E4    All right angles are equal.

E5    Through a point not on a given line, there is exactly one line parallel to the given line.

Constructions in Euclidean geometry are carried out with a straightedge (a ruler without a measurement scale) and a compass (see Fig. 11-18), as illustrated in the following example.

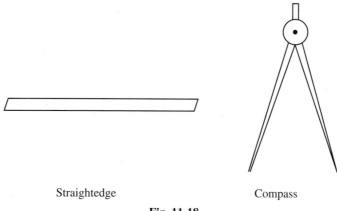

Straightedge                              Compass

**Fig. 11-18**

**EXAMPLE 11.4**    Construct an equilateral triangle with a given line segment as one of its sides.

Using a compass, first construct a circular arc with one end of the given line segment as center and the length of the line segment as radius [Fig. 11-19(*a*)].    Then construct a circular arc of the same radius having the other end of the given line segment as vertex [Fig. 11-19(*b*)]. Using a straightedge, draw the line segments from each end of the given line segment to the point of intersection of the two arcs [Fig. 11-19(*c*)]. The resulting triangle is equilateral.

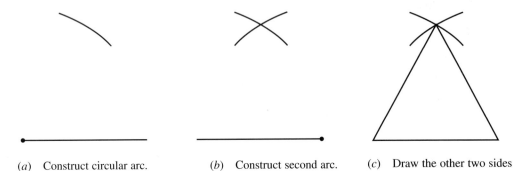

(*a*)   Construct circular arc.          (*b*)   Construct second arc.          (*c*)   Draw the other two sides
                                                                                              of the triangle.

**Fig. 11-19**

The following example illustrates the use of Euclid's postulates to derive a basic property of triangles.

**EXAMPLE 11.5**   The sum of the angles of any triangle is 180°.

**Proof:** Let a triangle with angles *A*, *B*, and *C* be given as shown in Fig. 11-20(*a*). Through the vertex of angle *B*, construct a line parallel to the side opposite *B* [see Fig. 11-20(*b*)]. The fifth postulate guarantees the existence of this parallel line. With reference to Fig. 11-20(*c*), angle *D* is equal to angle *A*, and angle *E* is equal to angle *C* (otherwise, the parallel line and the line obtained by extending the side opposite *B* would intersect). But angles *D*, *B*, and *E* combine to make a straight angle. That is, $D + B + E = 180°$. Therefore, $A + B + C = 180°$.

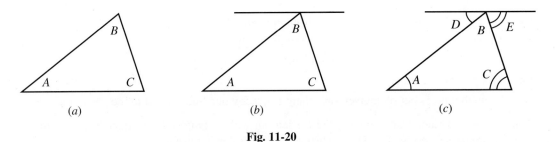

(*a*)                          (*b*)                          (*c*)

**Fig. 11-20**

## 11.6   PYTHAGOREAN THEOREM

The first major result in mathematics was the *Pythagorean theorem*, discovered around 500 B.C. The theorem states that the square of the length of the hypotenuse of any right triangle is equal to the sum of the squares of the lengths of the other two sides (see Fig. 11-21).

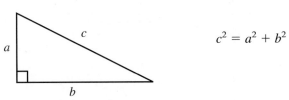

$$c^2 = a^2 + b^2$$

**Fig. 11-21**

**EXAMPLE 11.6**   Find the length of the hypotenuse of each of the following right triangles:

(*a*)   $a = 3, b = 4$                     (*b*)   $a = 5, b = 8$

(*a*)   $c^2 = 3^2 + 4^2 = 25$;           $c = \sqrt{25} = 5$

(*b*)   $c^2 = 5^2 + 8^2 = 89$;           $c = \sqrt{89} \approx 9.434$

**EXAMPLE 11.7**   The length of the hypotenuse of a right triangle is 25, and one side has length 7.   What is the length of the remaining side?

$$25^2 = 7^2 + b^2, \ b^2 = 25^2 - 7^2 = 576, \ b = \sqrt{576} = 24$$

### Proof of the Pythagorean Theorem

There are many proofs of the Pythagorean theorem.   The proof in Euclid's Elements is fairly complicated because it has only a limited number of geometric assumptions.   Here we give a proof that is based on the formulas for the area of a square and of a triangle, as well as some basic algebra.

We consider a right triangle with sides $a$ and $b$ and hypotenuse $c$ as in Fig. 11-21.   Now in Fig. 11-22, the area of the large square on the left with side $a + b$ is the sum of the areas of two rectangles, each with sides $a$ and $b$, and two squares, one with side $a$ and one with side $b$.   The total area is $2ab + a^2 + b^2$.   In Fig. 11-22 on the right, the same large square with side $a + b$ is partitioned into four right triangles of sides $a$ and $b$ and one square of side $c$.   Here the total area is $4(\frac{1}{2}ab) + c^2 = 2ab + c^2$.   We then have the equation $2ab + a^2 + b^2 = 2ab + c^2$, from which we can conclude that $a^2 + b^2 = c^2$.

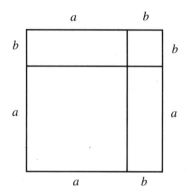

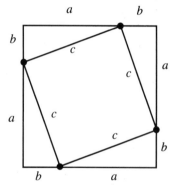

Area of large square $= 2ab + a^2 + b^2$          Area of large square $= 4(ab/2) + c^2 = 2ab + c^2$

**Fig. 11-22**

## 11.7   NON-EUCLIDEAN GEOMETRY

Geometry, based on Euclid's postulates and developed over centuries, provides us with a fixed or static model of objects in the space around us—that is, a model of position, shape, and form without regard to motion. Isaac Newton's laws of motion, derived in the seventeenth century, provide us with a dynamic model of our solar system.   Although both Euclidean geometry and Newtonian physics explain phenomena in our solar system fairly well, in the nineteenth century, mathematicians developed non-Euclidean geometries, and early in the twentieth century, Albert Einstein's theory of relativity provided a non-Newtonian and non-Euclidean dynamic model that extends our understanding of natural phenomena beyond our solar system.

Although the term non-Euclidean can apply to any geometry based on axioms other than Euclid's postulates, two especially important examples are *spherical geometry* and *hyperbolic geometry*.   In both of these, the first four postulates of Euclid hold, but the fifth (called the parallel postulate) is replaced, respectively, by

S5:   Through a point not on a given line, there are no lines parallel to the given line.

H5:   Through a point not on a given line, there are an infinite number of lines parallel to the given line.

### Spherical Geometry

As the name implies, the underlying space in spherical geometry is the surface of a sphere.   Points are the usual (Euclidean) points on the surface, and lines are great circles—that is, circles that are formed by the intersection of the surface of the sphere with planes that pass through the center of the sphere.   Equivalently, a great circle on a sphere is one whose radius is equal to the radius of the sphere.   Spherical geometry satisfies the Euclidean postulates E1 to E4, but any two lines intersect in two points (see Fig. 11-23), so there are no parallel lines.    Also, in spherical geometry, the sum of the angles of a triangle is greater than 180° (see Fig. 11-24), and the sum is different for noncongruent triangles.

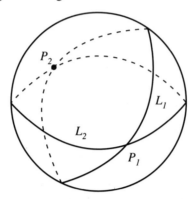

**Fig. 11-23**    Line $L_1$ intersects line $L_2$ in points $P_1$ and $P_2$.

**Fig. 11-24**    A traingle in spherical geometry.

### Example of a Hyperbolic Geometry

Consider a geometry in which the underlying space of points is the upper half of the coordinate plane $H$, that is, all points $(x, y)$ in the plane for which $y > 0$.    A line in this geometry consists of a Euclidean semicir- cle in $H$ whose center is on the $x$ axis or a ray in $H$ perpendicular to the $x$ axis.    Several such lines are shown in Fig. 11-25.    This geometry satisfies the Euclidean postulates E1 to E4, but through a point outside a given line, there are an infinite number of lines through the point and parallel to (i.e., do not intersect) the given line. In Fig. 11-25, $P$ is a point outside of line $L$, and $L_1$ and $L_2$ are two of the infinite number of lines through $P$ parallel to $L$.    In hyperbolic geometry, the sum of the angles of a triangle is less than 180° (see Fig. 11-26). and the sum is different for noncongruent triangles

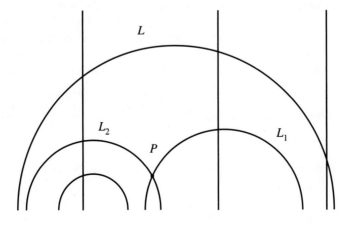

**Fig. 11-25**

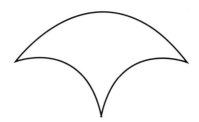

**Fig. 11-26**    A triangle in hyperbolic geometry.

## 11.8   UNITS OF MEASUREMENT AND FORMULAS FOR REFERENCE

We use the notions of length, area, and volume to measure the extent or capacity of one-, two-, and three-dimensional objects, respectively.   Linear units, such as inches or centimeters, are used in measuring the length of a line segment or curve.   Square units, such as square yards or square meters, are used in measuring the area of a surface; and cubic units, such as cubic inches or cubic centimeters, are used for measuring the volume of a solid.

The linear unit determines all three measures—length, area, and volume.   For example, if we choose an inch as our basic unit of length, then by definition, 1 square inch is the area a square whose sides are each 1 inch, and 1 cubic inch is the volume of a cube whose edges are each 1 inch (see Fig. 11-27).   The area of any surface is then equal to the number of 1-inch squares that the surface contains.   Sometimes this area can be determined algebraically, as in the case of a rectangle, where the area is equal to length times width, and sometimes more general methods, such as those provided by calculus, are needed.   Similarly, the volume of a solid is equal to the number of 1-inch cubes the solid contains.

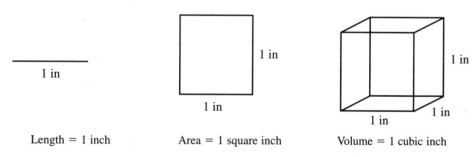

Length = 1 inch                  Area = 1 square inch              Volume = 1 cubic inch

**Fig. 11-27**

### Formulas from Plane Geometry

The following formulas give the perimeter (length of the boundary) and area of basic planar figures. For a *rectangle* with sides of lengths $a$ and $b$, see Fig. 11-28.

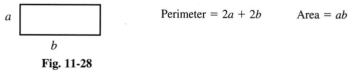

Perimeter = $2a + 2b$          Area = $ab$

**Fig. 11-28**

For a *square* with sides of length $a$, see Fig. 11-29.

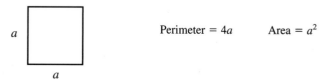

Perimeter = $4a$          Area = $a^2$

**Fig. 11-29**

For a *parallelogram* with sides of length $a$ and $b$ and height $h$, see Fig. 11-30.

Perimeter $= 2a + 2b$        Area $= bh$

**Fig. 11-30**

For a *trapezoid* with parallel sides of length $a$ and $b$, height $h$, and slant heights $c$ and $d$, see Fig. 11-31.

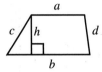

Perimeter $= a + b + c + d$,        Area $= h(a + b)/2$

**Fig. 11-31**

For a *triangle* with height $h$, base $b$, and remaining sides $a$, $c$ (Fig. 11-32).

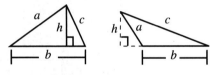

Perimeter $= a + b + c$,        Area $= \dfrac{1}{2}bh$,

Area $= \sqrt{s(s - a)(s - b)(s - c)}$, where

$$s = \frac{1}{2}(a + b + c)$$

**Fig. 11-32**

For a *circle* with radius $r$ (Fig. 11-33).

Circumference $= 2\pi r$
Area $= \pi r^2$

**Fig. 11-33**

## Formulas from Solid Geometry

All of the figures in plane geometry lie in two dimensions.   In solid geometry we consider three-dimensional objects.   Idealizations of common solids are illustrated in Fig. 11-34.

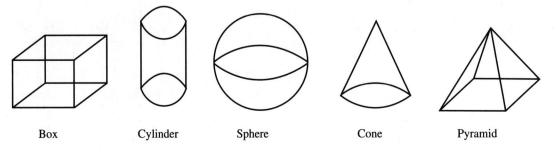

Box          Cylinder          Sphere          Cone          Pyramid

**Fig. 11-34**

Formulas for the volume and surface area of the three-dimensional objects in Fig. 11-34 are given in the following.

For a *box* (rectangular parallelepiped) with sides of length *a, b*, and *c*, see Fig. 11-35.

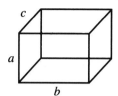

Volume = $abc$

Surface area = $2(ab + ac + bc)$

**Fig. 11-35**

For a *cylinder* of height *h* and radius of base *r*, see Fig. 11-36.

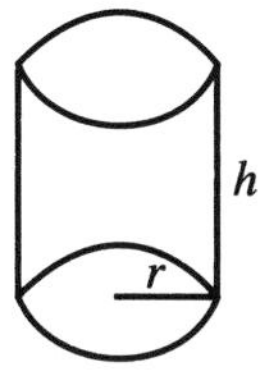

Volume = $\pi r^2 h$

Lateral surface area = $2\pi rh$

**Fig. 11-36**

For a *sphere* of radius *r*, see Fig. 11-37.

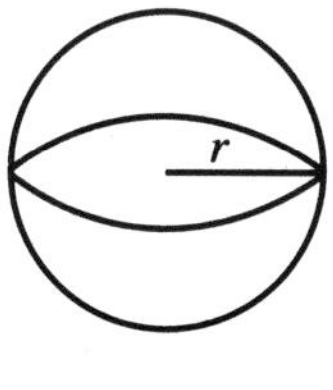

Volume = $\dfrac{4}{3}\pi r^3$

Surface area = $4\pi r^2$

**Fig. 11-37**

For a *cone* of height *h* and radius of base *r*, see Fig. 11-38.

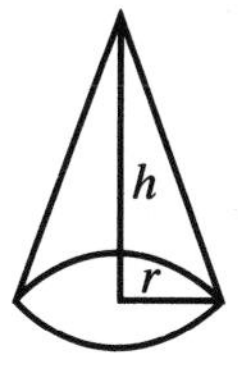

Volume = $\dfrac{1}{3}\pi r^2 h$

Surface area = $\pi r \sqrt{r^2 + h^2}$

**Fig. 11-38**

For a *pyramid* of height *h* and square base of side *b*, see Fig. 11-39.

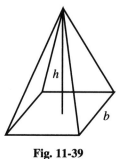

Volume = $\dfrac{1}{3}b^2 h$

Surface area = $b\sqrt{b^2 + 4h^2}$

**Fig. 11-39**

# Solved Problems

## BASIC OBJECTS

**11.1.** Define *point* and *line*.

Technically, point and line are undefined geometric objects. However, we can think of a point as a position in space and a line as a continuous set of points extending indefinitely in a specific direction and in its opposite direction.

**11.2.** Given that two distinct points determine a line, how many lines are determined by four points, no three of which lie on a single line.

Let the points be denoted by $P_1, P_2, P_3, P_4$. The lines determined by the four points are $\overleftrightarrow{P_1P_2}$, $\overleftrightarrow{P_1P_3}$, $\overleftrightarrow{P_1P_4}$, $\overleftrightarrow{P_2P_3}$, $\overleftrightarrow{P_2P_4}$, $\overleftrightarrow{P_3P_4}$, six lines in all, as shown in Fig. 11-40.

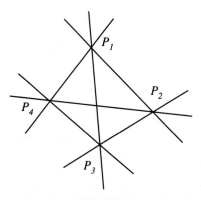

**Fig. 11-40**

**11.3.** Generalize Problem 11.2 to find the number of lines determined by $n$ points, no three of which lie on a single line.

Let the points be denoted by $P_1, P_2, P_3, \ldots, P_n$. Then the lines determined are $\overleftrightarrow{P_1P_2}$, $\overleftrightarrow{P_1P_3}$, $\ldots$, $\overleftrightarrow{P_1P_n}$ $(n - 1$ lines), $\overleftrightarrow{P_2P_3}$, $\overleftrightarrow{P_2P_4}$, $\ldots$, $\overleftrightarrow{P_2P_n}$ $(n - 2$ lines), $\overleftrightarrow{P_3P_4}$, $\overleftrightarrow{P_3P_5}$, $\ldots$, $\overleftrightarrow{P_3P_n}$ $(n - 3$ lines), $\ldots$, $\overleftrightarrow{P_{n-2}P_{n-1}}$, $\overleftrightarrow{P_{n-2}P_n}$ $(2$ lines), $\overleftrightarrow{P_{n-1}P_n}$ $(1$ line). The total number of lines is

$$1 + 2 + \ldots + (n - 3) + (n - 2) + (n - 1) = \frac{(n - 1)n}{2}$$

**11.4.** Given that three points not on a single line determine a plane, how many planes are determined by four points not on a single plane?

Let the points be denoted by $P_1, P_2, P_3, P_4$. If three of them were on a line, then together with the remaining point, the four would lie on a plane. Therefore, no three of them lie on a line. The planes determined are $P_1P_2P_3$, $P_1P_2P_4$, $P_1P_3P_4$, $P_2P_3P_4$, four in all. These planes form the faces of a tetrahedron, as shown in Fig. 11-41.

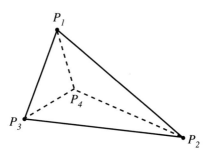

**Fig. 11-41**

## ANGLE MEASUREMENT

**11.5.** Give the degree measure of each of the following angles:

(a) $\dfrac{1}{3}$ rotation  (b) $\dfrac{5}{16}$ rotation  (c) 1.5 rotations

To convert from rotation measure to degree measure, we multiply each the rotation measures by 360°. We get  (a) $\dfrac{1}{3}360° = 120°$,  (b) $\dfrac{5}{16}360° = 112.5°$,  (c) $(1.5)360° = 540°$.

**11.6.** Give the rotation measure of each of the following degree measures:

(a) 60°  (b) 630°  (c) 760°

To convert from degree measure to rotation measure, we divide by 360°:

(a) $\dfrac{60°}{360°} = \dfrac{1}{6}$ rotation  (b) $\dfrac{630°}{360°} = 1.75$ rotations  (c) $\dfrac{760°}{360°} = 2\dfrac{1}{9}$ rotations

**11.7.** Find the complements of each of the following angles:

(a) 32°  (b) 45°  (c) 75°

The complementary angles are  (a) $90° - 32° = 58°$,  (b) 45°,  (c) 15°.

**11.8.** Find the supplements of each of the following angles:

(a) 32°  (b) 45°  (c) 75°

The supplementary angles are  (a) $180° - 32° = 148°$,  (b) 135°,  (c) 105°.

**11.9.** Suppose two rays from the same point form a line. Find the angle between the rays' degrees.

The angle between them is 180°.

**11.10.** Suppose two rays from the same point are perpendicular. Find the angle between them.

The angle between them is either 90° or 270°, depending on which ray is designated as the initial side.

**11.11.** When two lines intersect, as in Fig. 11-42, four angles are formed. The angles in the adjacent pairs $(A, B)$, $(A, D)$, $(B, C)$, and $(C, D)$ are supplementary. The nonadjacent angles $A$ and $C$ are called *vertical angles*, as are the nonadjacent angles $B$ and $D$. Show that vertical angles are equal.

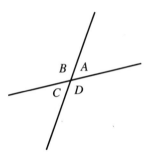

**Fig. 11-42**

$A + B = 180° = B + C$. Therefore, $A = C$. Similarly, $B + C = 180° = C + D$. Therefore, $B = D$.

**11.12.** A line that intersects two or more other lines is called a *transversal*. When a transversal $T$ intersects two lines $L_1$, $L_2$, as illustrated in Fig. 11-43, eight angles are formed. The angles in the pairs $(A, E)$, $(B, F)$, $(C, G)$, and $(D, H)$ are called *corresponding angles*. Prove that if the angles in any one pair of corresponding angles are equal, then the angles in every pair of corresponding angles are equal.

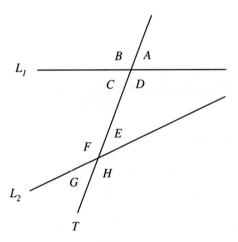

$A$ and $E$ are corresponding angles.
$B$ and $F$ are corresponding angles.
$C$ and $G$ are corresponding angles.
$D$ and $H$ are corresponding angles.

**Fig. 11-43**

Suppose that the corresponding angles $A$ and $E$ are equal. Then since $A + B = 180° = E + F$, it follows that $B = F$. Also, since the vertical angles $A$ and $C$ are equal, as are $E$ and $G$, it follows that $C = G$. Finally, since $A + D = 180° = E + H$, it follows that $D = H$. The same type of argument can be used starting with any pair of equal corresponding angles.

**11.13.** When a transversal $T$ intersects two lines $L_1$, $L_2$, as illustrated in Fig. 11.44, the angles $C$, $D$, $E$, and $F$ between the lines are called *interior angles*, and the angles $A$, $B$, $G$, and $H$ outside the lines are called *exterior angles*. Angles $A$ and $G$ are called *alternate exterior angles*, as are $B$

and *H*.    Similarly, *C* and *E* are called *alternate interior angles*, as are *D* and *F*.    Prove that if the angles in any one pair of alternate interior or alternate exterior angles are equal, then the angles in all pairs of alternate interior and alternate exterior angles are equal.

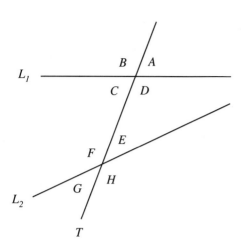

*A* and *G* are alternate exterior angles.
*B* and *H* are alternate exterior angles.
*C* and *E* are alternate interior angles.
*D* and *F* are alternate interior angles.

**Fig. 11-44**

Suppose that the alternate exterior angles *A* and *G* are equal.    Then, since $A + B = 180° = G + H$, it follows that the alternate exterior angles *B* and *H* are equal.    Also, the vertical angles *A* and *C* are equal, as are *E* and *G*.    Since $A = G$, it follows that the alternate interior angles *C* and *E* are equal.    Then, since $C + D = 180° = E + F$ it follows that the alternate interior angles *D* and *F* are equal.    A similar argument can be made, starting with any pair of equal alternate interior or exterior angles.

**11.14.**    Prove that if the angles of any one pair of corresponding angles are equal, then the angles in every pair of alternate interior and alternate exterior angles are equal.

With reference to the figures in Problems 11.12 and 11.13, suppose that the corresponding angles *A* and *E* are equal.    Then, since the vertical angles *E* and *G* are equal, the alternate exterior angles *A* and *G* are equal.    Therefore, by Problem 11.13, the angles in all pairs of alternate exterior and alternate interior angles are equal.    The same type of argument can be used starting with any pair of equal corresponding angles.

**11.15.**    Prove that if the angles in any one pair of alternate exterior or interior angles are equal, then the angles in every pair of corresponding angles are equal.

With reference to the figures in Problems 11.12 and 11.13, suppose the alternate exterior angles *A* and *G* are equal.    Then, since the vertical angles *E* and *G* are equal it follows that the corresponding angles *A* and *E* are equal.    Therefore, by Problem 11.12, the angles in every pair of corresponding angles are equal.    The same type of argument can be used starting with any pair of equal alternate exterior or interior angles.

**11.16.**    It can be shown that lines $L_1$, $L_2$ are parallel if and only if the angles in any pair of corresponding angles are equal.    Based on Problems 11.12 to 11.15, give an equivalent statement relating parallel lines and alternate angles.    (See Fig. 11-45.)

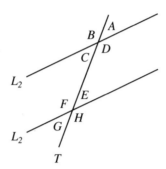

**Fig. 11-45**

Lines $L_1$, $L_2$ are parallel if and only if the angles in any pair of alternate interior or alternate exterior angles are equal.

## PLANAR FIGURES; CONGRUENCE AND SIMILARITY

**11.17.** Prove that the two non-right angles in a right triangle are complementary.

The sum of the angles of any triangle is 180°, and since right angle $B$ in Fig. 11-46 is 90°, the sum of the non-right angles $A$ and $C$ must be 90°.

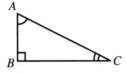

**Fig. 11-46**

**11.18.** Prove that the angles in an equilateral triangle are equal.

Let $ABC$ be the equilateral triangle shown in Fig. 11-47. By the SSS, triangle $ABC$ is congruent to triangle $BCA$, which in turn is congruent to triangle $CAB$. Therefore, the corresponding angles $B$, $C$, and $A$ are equal.

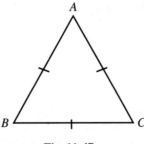

**Fig. 11-47**

**11.19.** Prove that the angles in an equilateral triangle are equal to 60°.

By Problem 11-18, the angles in an equilateral triangle are equal. Since the sum of the angles of any triangle is 180°, each angle must be equal to 60°.

**11.20.** A polygon is said to be *convex* if the line segment connecting any two points in the polygon lies inside the polygon. Show that the sum of the vertex angles of a convex polygon with 7 sides is $5 \cdot 180°$.

As illustrated in the 7-sided convex polygon in Fig. 11-48, choose a point $P$ inside the polygon, and connect $P$ to each vertex, forming 7 triangles. The sum of the angles of the 7 triangles is $7 \cdot 180°$. All 7 triangles meet at point $P$, and the sum of the angles at $P$ is $360°$. By subtracting $360°$ from $7 \cdot 180°$, we get the sum of the vertex angles of the polygon, and $7 \cdot 180° - 360° = 5 \cdot 180°$.

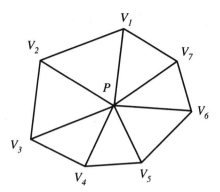

**Fig. 11-48**

**11.21.** Generalize the result of Problem 11.20 to show that the sum of the angles of a convex polygon with $n$ sides is equal to $(n - 2) \cdot 180°$.

If the procedure in Problem 11.20 is performed on an $n$=sided convex polygon, we find that the sum of the vertex angles of the polygon is $n \cdot 180° - 360° = n \cdot 180° - 2 \cdot 180° = (n - 2) \cdot 180°$.

**11.22** Prove that the angles opposite equal sides of an isosceles triangle are equal.

Let $ABC$ be an isosceles triangle as shown in Fig. 11-49. Bisect the apex angle $A$ by a line segment that intersects the base of the triangle at $P$. By SAS, triangle $BAP$ is congruent to triangle $CAP$. Therefore, angle $B$ is equal to angle $C$.

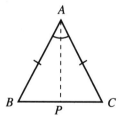

**Fig. 11-49**

**11.23** A *median* of a triangle is a line segment joining a vertex of the triangle with the midpoint of the opposite side. Prove that a median from the apex angle of an isosceles triangle is perpendicular to the opposite side.

With reference to Problem 11.22 and its figure, since triangle $BAP$ is congruent to triangle $CAP$, segment $BP$ has the same length as segment $CP$. Therefore, the angle bisector $AP$ is also the median from the apex angle $A$ to its opposite side. Since angle $BPA$ is equal to angle $CPA$, and their sum is $180°$, it follows that each is $90°$.

**11.24** Prove that the median from the apex angle of an isosceles triangle bisects that angle.

As was shown in Problem 11.23, the median from the apex angle $A$ and the bisector of $A$ are the same segment.

**11.25**  Prove that line segments from opposite ends of a diameter of a circle to another point on the circumference of the circle form a right angle at that point (Thale's theorem).

In Fig. 11-50, *C* is the center of a circle, *AB* is a diameter, and *P* is a point on the circumference. Segments *AC*, *BC*, and *CP* are equal in length to the radius of the circle, so triangles *ACP* and *BCP* are isosceles triangles.   Therefore, angle *CAP* equals angle *CPA*, and angle *CBP* equals angle *CPB*.   Also, since the sum of the angles of triangle *ABP* is 180°, we have

$$2\angle CPA + 2\angle CPB = 180°$$

$$\angle CPA + \angle CPB = 90°$$

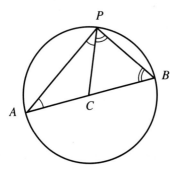

**Fig. 11-50**

**11.26**  Use *Ceva's theorem*, illustrated in Fig. 11-51, to prove that the medians of a triangle intersect in a point.

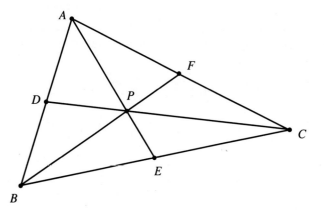

Ceva's theorem (Giovanni Ceva 1648–1734)
Segments *AE, BF, CD* meet at a point *P* if and only if
$$\frac{AD}{BD} \cdot \frac{BE}{CE} \cdot \frac{CF}{AF} = 1.$$

**Fig. 11-51**

Suppose line segments *AE, BF,* and *CD* are the medians of triangle *ABC* in the above figure.   Then $BE = CE$, $AF = CF$, and $AD = BD$.   Therefore, $\dfrac{AD}{BD} \cdot \dfrac{BE}{CE} \cdot \dfrac{CF}{AF} = 1\cdot1\cdot1 = 1$.   Hence, by Ceva's theorem, the medians intersect in a point.

**11.27**  Prove that the lines that bisect the vertex angles of a triangle intersect in a point.

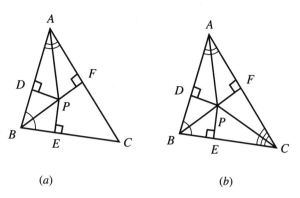

**Fig. 11-52**

Let *ABC* be the triangle illustrated in Fig. 11-52(*a*). The bisectors of angles *A* and *B* intersect in a point *P*. From *P* construct segments *PD, PE,* and *PF* perpendicular to sides *AB, BC,* and *AC,* respectively. Then triangles *APF* and *APD* have two and therefore three equal angles, and side *AP* in common, so they are congruent. Similarly, triangles *BPD* and *BPE* are congruent. Therefore, *PD = PE = PF*. Then right triangles *CEP* and *CFP* have equal sides *EP* and *FP,* and hypotenuse *CP* in common. Therefore, sides *CE* and *CF* are equal, so the triangles *CEP* and *CFP* are congruent. Therefore, segment *CP* bisects angle *C,* and all three angle bisectors meet in the single point *P,* as shown in Fig. 11-52(*b*).

**11.28.** In Problem 11.27, the point *P* of intersection of the vertex angle bisectors is called the *incenter* of triangle *ABC*. Show that *P* is the center of a circle contained in the triangle whose circumference is tangent to the sides of the triangle.

In Problem 11.27, the segments *PD, PE,* and *PF* are equal and perpendicular to the sides of triangle *ABC*. The circle with center *P* and radius *PD* shown in Fig. 11-53 is therefore tangent to the sides of triangle *ABC*. This circle is called the *inscribed circle* of triangle *ABC*.

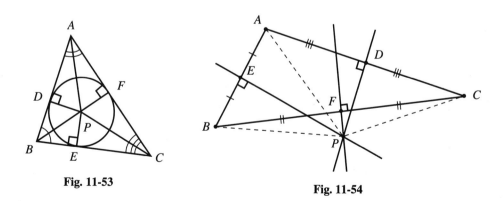

**Fig. 11-53**

**Fig. 11-54**

**11.29** The perpendicular bisectors of the sides of triangle *ABC* in Fig. 11-54 meet at point *P*. Show that *P* is equidistant from the vertices of the triangle.

Triangles *AEP* and *BEP* are congruent, so *PA = PB*. Similarly, triangles *ADP* and *CDP* are congruent, so *PA = PC*. Hence, *P* is equidistant from the vertices of triangle *ABC*. *P* is called the *circumcenter* of triangle *ABC*.

**11.30.** Show that it is possible to construct a circle whose circumference passes through the vertices of a given triangle.

With reference to the figure in Problem 11.29, the circle with center $P$ and radius $AP$ passes through the vertices of triangle $ABC$, as shown in Fig. 11-55. This circle is called the *circumscribed circle* of triangle $ABC$.

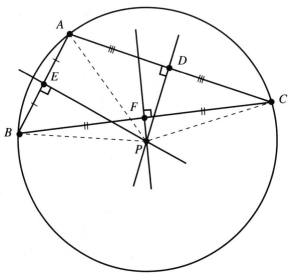

**Fig. 11-55**

**11.31.** Show that a line segment joining the midpoints of two sides of a triangle is parallel to the third side and half its length.

In Fig. 11-56, line segment $\overline{DE}$ joins the midpoints of sides $AB$ and $AC$ of triangle $ABC$. By SAS, triangle $DAE$ is similar to triangle $BAC$ with scale factor $\frac{1}{2}$. Therefore, side $DE$ is half the length of side $BC$. Also, angle $ADE$ is equal to angle $ABC$, so side $DE$ is parallel to side $BC$.

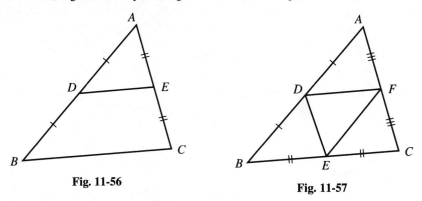

**Fig. 11-56**                    **Fig. 11-57**

**11.32.** Show the triangle formed by joining the midpoints of the sides of a given triangle is similar to the given triangle.

In Fig. 11-57, triangle $EDF$ is obtained by joining the midpoints of the sides of triangle $ABC$. By SAS, triangle $DBE$ is similar to triangle $ABC$ with a scale factor of $\frac{1}{2}$. Therefore, $\overline{DE} = \frac{1}{2}\,\overline{AC}$. Triangles $FEC$ and $ADF$ are also similar by SAS to triangle $ABC$ with scale factor $\frac{1}{2}$, so $\overline{EF} = \frac{1}{2}\overline{AB}$ and $\overline{DF} = \frac{1}{2}\overline{BC}$. By SSS, triangle $EFD$ is similar to triangle $ABC$ with a scale factor of $\frac{1}{2}$. Triangle $EFD$ is called the *medial triangle* of triangle $ABC$.

**11.33.** Show that the four inner triangles formed by joining the midpoints of the sides of a given triangle are congruent.

With reference to Problem 11.32 and the figure there, it was shown that $\overline{DE} = \frac{1}{2}\overline{AC}$, $\overline{EF} = \frac{1}{2}\overline{AB}$, and $\overline{DF} = \frac{1}{2}\overline{BC}$. Therefore, by SSS, all four inner triangles are congruent.

**11.34.** Show that if the midpoints of a quadrilateral are joined by line segments, then the resulting quadrilateral is a parallelogram.

Let *ABCD* be a quadrilateral as shown in Fig. 11-58, and let *PQRS* be the quadrilateral obtained by joining the midpoints of *ABCD*. By Problem 11.31, line segment *PS* is parallel to diagonal *BD* and half its length. Similarly, *QR* is parallel to *BD* and half its length. Therefore, *PS* and *QR* are parallel and have the same length. Therefore, *PQRS* is a parallelogram. The result is true for both convex quadrilaterals, as in the figure, and for non-convex quadrilaterals.

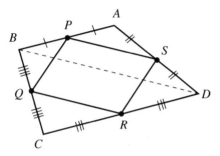

**Fig. 11-58**

## CONSTRUCTIONS WITH STRAIGHTEDGE AND COMPASS

**11.35.** Bisect a given angle.

Let angle *A* be given as shown in Fig. 11-59. With the vertex of *A* as center, draw arcs of equal radius, intersecting the sides of *A* in points *B* and *C*, respectively. Now with *B* and then *C* as center, draw two arcs of equal radius intersecting at some point *D*. The line through the vertex of *A* and point *D* bisects angle *A*.

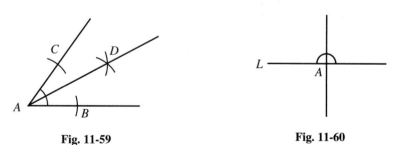

**Fig. 11-59**                                   **Fig. 11-60**

**11.36.** Construct a line perpendicular to a given line through a given point on the line.

Let line *L* be as shown in Fig. 11-60, and let *A* be the given point on the line. *L* defines a 180° angle with vertex *A*, and the bisector of this angle, as constructed in Problem 11.35, defines a line perpendicular to *L* at *A*.

**11.37.** Construct a line perpendicular to a given line through a given point not on the line.

Let line *L* be as shown in Fig. 11-61, and let *P* be a point not on *L*. With *P* as center, draw two arcs of equal radius, intersecting *L* at points *A* and *B*, respectively. Now with *A* and then *B* as center, draw two arcs of equal radius intersecting at some point $Q$.  The line through $P$ and $Q$ is perpendicular to $L$.

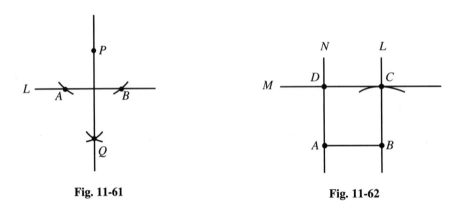

Fig. 11-61                                                    Fig. 11-62

**11.38.**  Construct a square with a given line segment as a side.

Let $AB$ be the given line segment as in Fig. 11-62.  With $B$ as center, construct a circular arc of radius $AB$.  Through $B$, construct line $L$ perpendicular to $AB$ as in Problem 11.36.  Let $C$ be the intersection of the arc and the perpendicular line.  Through $C$, construct line $M$ perpendicular to $L$ as in Problem 11.36, and through $A$, construct line $N$ perpendicular to $M$ as in Problem 11.37.  Let $D$ be the intersection of $M$ and $N$.  Then $ABCD$ is a square with $AB$ as a side.

**11.39.**  Construct a regular octagon inscribed in a circle of a given radius.

Let $AB$ be the given radius as shown in Fig. 11-63.  Extend $AB$ to line $L$.  Through $B$, draw a line $M$ perpendicular to $L$.  Through $B$, draw a circle of radius $AB$, intersecting line $L$ at $A$ and $C$, and line $M$ at $D$ and $E$.  Then $AECD$ is a square inscribed in the circle.  Let $F$, $G$, $H$, $I$, be the points of intersection of the circle with the bisectors of angles $ABD$, $ABE$, $CBE$, $CBD$, respectively.  Then $AGEHCIDF$ is a regular octagon inscribed in the circle.

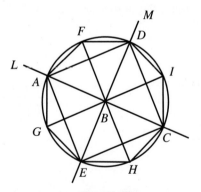

Fig. 11-63

**11.40.**  Explain how to inscribe a regular polygon with $2^n$ sides, where $n$ is any positive integer greater than or equal to 2, in a circle of a given radius.

In Problem 11.39, a square ($2^2$ sides) was inscribed in a circle of a given radius, and then a regular octagon ($2^3$ sides) was inscribed in the circle by bisecting the angles of the square.  If the angles of the octagon are bisected, we get an inscribed regular polygon with $2^4$ sides.  Continuing in this way, we can get a regular inscribed polygon with $2^n$ sides for any positive integer $n$ greater than 1.

**11.41.** Construct a regular hexagon inscribed in a given circle.

Let $C$ be the center of the given circle, and let $P$ be any point on the circle, as shown in Fig. 11-64. With $P$ as center, draw a circular arc of radius $CP$, intersecting the circle at $Q$. By SSS, triangle $CPQ$ is equilateral and therefore each of its angles is 60°. Now, with $Q$ as center, draw another circular arc of radius $CP$, intersecting the circle at $R$. Then triangle $CQR$ is also equilateral. Repeat the process. The resulting polygon $PQRSTU$ is a regular hexagon.

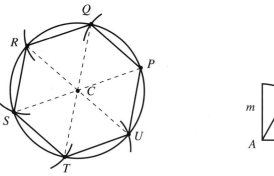

**Fig. 11-64**

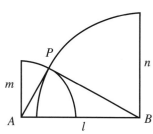

**Fig. 11-65**

**11.42.** Show that line segments of lengths $l$, $m$, and $n$, respectively, form the sides of a (unique) triangle if and only if the length of the longest side is less than the sum of the lengths of the other two sides.

Let $AB$ be the longest segment and suppose its length is $l$, as shown in Fig. 11-65. With $A$ as center, draw a circular arc of radius $m$, and with $B$ as center, draw a circular arc of radius $n$. The arcs will intersect in a point $P$ not on $AB$, forming a triangle $APB$ if and only if $l < m + n$.

# Supplementary Problems

**11.43.** Three points not on a straight line determine a triangle. How many triangles are determined by four points, no three of which lie on a straight line?

**11.44.** How many triangles are determined by $n$ points ($n \geq 3$), no three of which lie on a straight line?

**11.45.** Prove that three points not on a straight line lie on a circle. *Hint:* Let the points be labeled $A$, $B$, $C$, as shown in Fig. 11-66. Draw line $L$, the perpendicular bisector of $AB$, and draw line $M$, the perpendicular bisector of $BC$. Let $P$ be the point of intersection of $L$ and $M$. Show that the line segments $PA$, $PB$, and $PC$ all have the same length. Use this result to prove that $A$, $B$, and $C$ lie on a circle

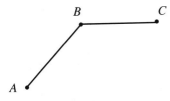

**Fig. 11-66**

**11.46.** Prove that the circle determined in Problem 11.45 is unique. That is, there is only one circle through three non-collinear points.
*Hint:* In how many points can two circles intersect?

**11.47.** Let *ABCD* be a quadrilateral inscribed in a circle, as shown in Fig. 11-67.   Show that the sum of opposite angles of the quadrilateral is 180°, i.e., $A + C = 180°$ and $B + D = 180°$.   *Hint:* Connect the center *P* of the circle to the vertices *A, B, C, D*, forming four isosceles triangles.   Now use the fact that the sum of the angles of a triangle is 180°.

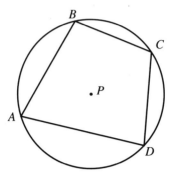

**Fig. 11-67**

**11.48.** Let two circles having centers *P* and *Q*, respectively, and equal radii intersect in points *A* and *B*, as shown in Fig. 11-68.   Show that the quadrilateral *PAQB* is a rhombus, i.e., an equilateral parallelogram.

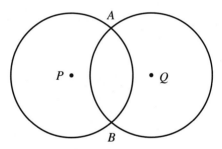

**Fig. 11-68**

**11.49.** In Problem 11.48, what must the length of the segment *PQ* be in order for the rhombus to be a square?

**11.50.** Prove that the sum of the exterior angles *A, B, C, D, E* of the pentagon shown in Fig. 11-69 is 360°.   *Hint:* see Problem 11.21.

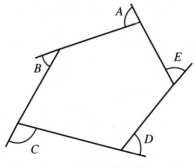

**Fig. 11-69**

**11.51.** Generalize Problem 11.50 to show that the sum of the exterior angles of any convex polygon is 360°.

**11.52.** Prove that the measure of each exterior angle of a regular pentagon is (five sides of equal length) is 72°.

**11.53.** Generalize Problem 11.52 to prove that the measure of each exterior angle of a regular *n*-gon is $\left(\dfrac{360}{n}\right)°$.

**11.54.** Prove that the measure of each interior angle of a regular pentagon 108°.

**11.55.** Generalize Problem 11.54 to prove that the measure of each interior angle of a regular $n$-gon is $\left(\dfrac{n-2}{n}\right)180°$.

**11.56.** Two circles with centers $P$ and $Q$, respectively, intersect in points $A$ and $B$, as shown in Fig. 11-70.   Show that the line segments $AB$ and $PQ$ intersect at right angles.

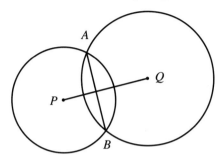

**Fig. 11-70**

**11.57.** Use the fact that area of a rectangle is equal to length $\times$ width to prove that the area of a parallelogram with base $b$ and height $h$, as shown in Fig. 11-71, is equal to $bh$.

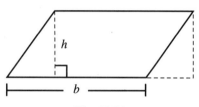

**Fig. 11-71**

**11.58.** Use the fact that the area of a rectangle is equal to length $\times$ width to prove that the area of a right triangle, with base $b$ and height $h$, is equal to $\dfrac{1}{2}bh$.

**11.59.** Use the fact that the area of a right triangle is equal to $\dfrac{1}{2}$ base $\times$ height to prove that the area of the triangle in Fig. 11-72 is $\dfrac{1}{2}bh$.

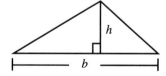

**Fig. 11-72**

**11.60.** In Fig. 11-73 are three copies of triangle $ABC$.   Use the result of Problem 11.59 to prove that the area of $ABC$ is given by each of the formulas $\dfrac{1}{2}AB \cdot h_1, \dfrac{1}{2}BC \cdot h_2, \dfrac{1}{2}AC \cdot h_3$.

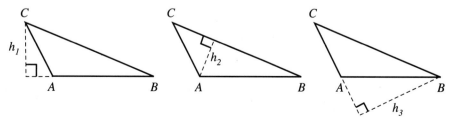

**Fig. 11-73**

**11.61.** Based on the result of Problem 11.60, what can you conclude about the area of a triangle?

**11.62.** With reference to Fig. 11-74, prove that the area of a trapezoid is equal to (the average length of the parallel sides) × height, i.e., $\frac{1}{2}(a + b)h$.

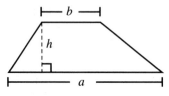

**Fig. 11-74**

**11.63.** Devise a strategy for finding the area of the pentagon in Fig. 11-75.

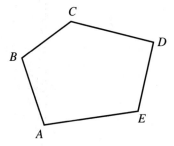

**Fig. 11-75**

**11.64.** Generalize Problem 11.63 to devise a strategy for computing the area of any convex polygon with $n$ sides.

**11.65.** A polygon is called star-shaped if there is a point $P$ in its interior that can be connected to each of its vertices by a line segment lying in the interior of the polygon. Devise a strategy for finding the area of the eight-sided star shaped polygon show in Fig. 11-76.

**Fig. 11-76**

**11.66.** Devise a strategy for finding the area of any $n$ sided star-shaped polygon.

**11.67.** *Area of a Circle.* In almost all ancient cultures it was discovered that the ratio of the circumference of a circle to its diameter was the same value, regardless of the size of the circle. We denote this ratio by the Greek letter $\pi$, and it is now known that $\pi$ is an irrational number approximately equal to 3.14159. Hence, if $C$ is the circumference of a circle, and $r$ is the radius, or half the diameter, then $C = 2\pi r$. Suppose a circle of radius $r$ is divided into a number of very thin circular rings, and these rings are straightened into approximate rectangles and stacked in a triangle as shown in Fig. 11-77.   Use Fig. 11-77 to arrive at the formula $\pi r^2$ for the area of the circle.

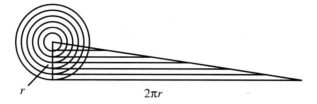

**Fig. 11-77**

**11.68.**   *Area of a Circle.*   Suppose a circle of radius $r$ is divided into a very large number of circular sectors, and these sectors are placed next to each other as approximate triangles shown in Fig. 11-78.   Use Fig. 11-78 to arrive at the formula $\pi r^2$ for the area of the circle.

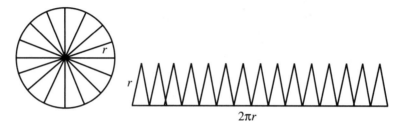

**Fig. 11-78**

**11.69.**   *Volume of a Cone.*   Suppose that a cone of height $h$ whose base is a circle of radius $r$ is subdivided into $n$ conical sections, each of thickness $h/n$.   Assuming that $n$ is a very large number, we can approximate the $k$th conical section, counting from the top, as a flat cylinder with height $h/n$ whose base is a circle of radius $kr/n$.

The sum of the volumes of the cylinders is $\sum_{k=1}^{n} \pi \left(\dfrac{kr}{n}\right)^2 \dfrac{h}{n}$.   Use the equation $\sum_{k=1}^{n} k^2 = \dfrac{n(n+1)(2n+1)}{n}$

to arrive at the formula (first discovered by Archimedes) $\frac{1}{3}\pi r^2 h$ for the volume of the cone.

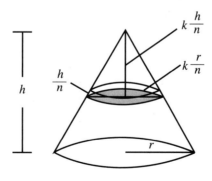

**Fig. 11-79**

**11.70.**   Bonaventura Cavalieri (1598–1647), a student of Galileo, discovered that if two solids have equal cross-sectional areas for every intersecting plane parallel to their bases, as shown in Fig. 11-80, then the two solids have equal volumes.   Think of each solid as being (approximately) a stack of very thin cylindrical sections.   Use the fact that the volume of a cylinder is equal to the area of its base times its height to arrive at Cavalieri's theorem.

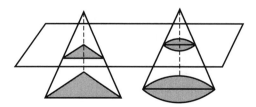

**Fig. 11-80**

**11.71.** *Volume of a Sphere.*   Figure 11-81 shows a hemisphere of radius $r$ next to a cylinder of height $r$ whose base is a circle of radius $r$.   An inverted cone of height $r$ whose base is a circle of radius $r$ has been removed from the cylinder.   Show that for each height $h$, where $0 < h < r$, the area of the cross-sectional circle of radius $\sqrt{r^2 - h^2}$ in the sphere is equal to the area of the circular ring of inner radius $h$ and outer radius $r$ in the cylinder with the cone removed.   By Cavalieri's theorem (Problem 11.70), the hemisphere and the cylinder with the cone removed have the same volume.   Using the formulas for the volume of a cylinder and a cone, deduce that the volume of a sphere of radius $r$ is $\dfrac{4}{3}\pi r^3$.

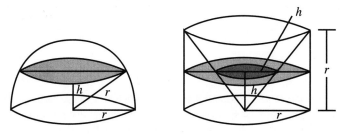

**Fig. 11-81**

# Answers to Supplementary Problems

**11.43.**   four

**11.44.**   $\dbinom{n}{3} = \dfrac{n!}{3!(n-3)!}$

**11.49.**   $\sqrt{2}r$, where $r$ is the common radius of the two circles.

**11.61.**   The area of a triangle is $\dfrac{1}{2}bh$, where $b$ is the length of any side of the triangle, and $h$ is the length of the perpendicular segment from that side to the opposite vertex.

**11.63.**   From a point inside the pentagon, draw segments to each vertex, forming five disjoint triangles and use the formula $A = \sqrt{s(s-a)(s-b)(s-c)}$ to compute the area of each triangle.   The area of the pentagon is the sum of these areas.

**11.64.**   From a point inside the convex $n$-gon, draw segments to each vertex forming $n$ disjoint triangles, and proceed as in Problem 11.63.

**11.65.**   Similar to 11.63.

**11.66.**   Similar to 11.64.

**CHAPTER 12**

# Linear Inequalities and Linear Programming

## 12.1. INTRODUCTION

Linear programming is a method for making an optimum choice where several choices are possible. We restrict ourselves to finding the maximum or minimal value of a function of the form

$$f = Ax + By$$

at various points in the $xy$ plane. First we need to discuss linear inequalities in the plane.

## 12.2. LINEAR INEQUALITIES IN THE PLANE

This section considers linear inequalities of the form

$$ax + by \leq c \qquad \text{or} \qquad ax + by \geq c \qquad (12.1)$$

where $a$ and $b$ are not both zero. The solution of such an inequality consists of all points in the plane $\mathbf{R}^2$ that satisfy the given inequality.

Now suppose $L$ is the line $ax + by = c$. Then one can show that $L$ divides the plane into two *half-planes* such that the points on one of the sides of $L$ satisfy $ax + by < c$ and the points on the other side of $L$ satisfy $ax + by > c$. Accordingly, one can graph the solution of the inequality *(12.1)* as follows:

**Step 1.** Graph the line $L$: $ax + by = c$ (see Chap. 1).

**Step 2.** Choose a *test* point $P(x_0, y_0)$ *not on* $L$ and substitute the point in the inequality, i.e., let $x = x_0$ and $y = y_0$ in the inequality. [If $c \neq 0$, choose the origin $(0, 0)$ as the test point.]

    *(a)* Suppose the test point $P$ is a solution of the inequality; that is, the derived statement is true. Then shade the side of $L$ containing $P$.

(b) Suppose the test point $P$ is not a solution of the inequality; that is, the derived statement is not true. Then shade the other side of $L$; that is, shade the side of $L$ that does not contain $P$.

The graph of the solution is then the shaded part of the plane together with its boundary.

**EXAMPLE 12.1**  Solve (graph) the inequality: $2x + 3y \leq 6$.

First graph the line $L$: $2x + 3y = 6$, as in Fig. 12-1(*a*). The origin 0(0, 0) is not on $L$, so choose it as the test point. Substitute (0, 0) into the inequality to obtain

$$2(0) + 3(0) \leq 6 \qquad \text{or} \qquad 0 + 0 \leq 6 \qquad \text{or} \qquad 0 \leq 6$$

This statement is true; that is, the test point (0, 0) does satisfy the inequality. Thus, shade the side of $L$ containing the test point (0, 0) as in Fig. 12-1(*b*). The solution consists of the shaded region and its boundary.

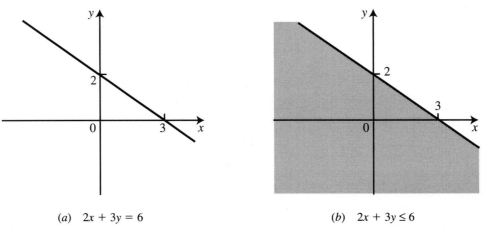

(a)  $2x + 3y = 6$                               (b)  $2x + 3y \leq 6$

**Fig. 12-1**

## 12.3  SYSTEMS OF LINEAR INEQUALITIES AND CORNER POINTS

Consider now a system of two or more linear inequalities of the form $ax + by \leq c$ or $ax + by \geq c$. The solution of the system is a region $R$ in the plane which is common to each of the individual solutions. This region $R$ can be determined as follows:

> For each inequality in the system, "cross out" the region of the plane *not satisfied* by the inequality. After this procedure has been followed for each inequality, the region $R$ remaining with its boundary is the solution of the system.

We will indicate that an area is discarded or crossed out by drawing lines in the area perpendicular to the boundary line. We will also indicate the solution of the system, represented by the remaining region $R$ with its boundary, by shading the region $R$.

**EXAMPLE 12.2**  Graph the solution of the system:  $\begin{cases} 3x + y \leq 12 \\ 2x + 3y \leq 15 \\ x \geq 0, y \geq 0 \end{cases}$

The solution of the system appears in Fig. 12-2. Observe that we first cross out, for each inequality in the system, that part of the plane that does not satisfy the inequality. The remaining region, shaded in Fig. 12-2, including its boundary line segments, constitutes the solution of the system. Note that the last two inequalities, $x \geq 0$ and $y \geq 0$, which were written on one line for notational convenience, restrict the solution to the first quadrant.

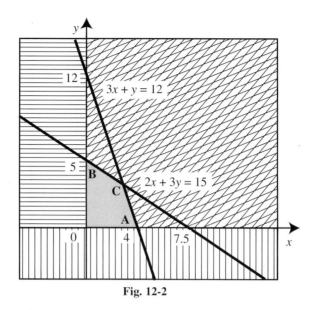

**Fig. 12-2**

### Corner Points

Consider the solution region $R$ of any system of linear inequalities. Since $R$ is the intersection of half-planes, its boundary will consist of lines, half-lines, and line segments. (We will refer to any of them simply as *boundary lines*.) A point $P$ on the boundary of $R$ is called a *corner point* of $R$ if $P$ is the intersection of two such boundary lines. These corner points play an important role in this subject matter. Any particular corner point $P$ can be obtained as follows:

> Find the equations of the boundary lines that determine the corner point $P$. Then solve the system consisting of these linear equations.

If a corner point $P$ lies on an axis, then it can be easily obtained as the $x$ or $y$ intercept of some line.

**EXAMPLE 12.3.** Consider the solution region $R$ in Fig. 12-2. There are four corner points. One is the origin $0(0,0)$, a second is the point $A(4, 0)$, which is the x intercept of $3x + y = 12$, and a third is $B(5,0)$, which is the y intercept of $2x + 3y = 15$. The fourth point $C$ is the intersection of the nonaxis boundary lines,

$$3x + y = 12 \qquad \text{and} \qquad 2x + 3y = 15$$

Solving the $2 \times 2$ system yields $x = 3$, $y = 3$. Thus, $C(3, 3)$ is the fourth corner point of the system.

### 12.4 APPLICATIONS OF SYSTEMS OF LINEAR INEQUALITIES

The next examples illustrate some applications of systems of linear inequalities.

**EXAMPLE 12.4.** A clock company manufactures two types of clocks, say, A and B. Each type A clock costs the company \$25 in parts and requires 5 hours of labor. Each type B clock costs \$40 in parts but requires only 4 hours of labor. Suppose \$2000 is available for parts, and 320 hours for labor. Find the combinations of A and B clocks that can be produced.

**Table 12-1**  Product-Resource Chart

| Resources | Products | | Resources available |
| --- | --- | --- | --- |
| | Type A clocks ($x$) | Type B Clocks ($y$) | |
| Parts | \$25 per clock | \$40 per clock | \$2000 |
| Labor | 5 hours per clock | 4 hours per clock | 320 hours |

First summarize the given data in a *product-resource* (PR) chart, say, as shown in Table 12-1, where we let $x$ = number of A clocks produced and $y$ = number of B clocks produced. Then the following inequalities must be satisfied:

$25x + 40y \leq 2000$: The total amount spent on *parts* for $x$ type A and $y$ type B clocks cannot exceed $2000.

$5x + 4y \leq 320$: The total hours of *labor* in making $x$ type A and $y$ type B clocks cannot exceed 320.

$x \geq 0, y \geq 0$: The number of each type of clock cannot be negative.

Proceeding as in previous examples, we obtain the solution of the system as the shaded region $R$ in Fig. 12-3(*a*). Thus, any pair of integers $(x, y)$ in $R$ represents a combination of type A and type B clocks that can be manufactured within the given *constraints*, that is, the given linear inequalities. This solution set $R$ is called the *feasible region* for the system of inequalities, and any point in $R$ is called a *feasible solution*.

Observe that $R$ has four corner points, the origin $0(0, 0)$; the point $A(64, 0)$, which is the $x$ intercept of $5x + 4y = 320$; the point $B(0, 50)$, which is the $y$ intercept of $25x + 40y = 2000$; and the point $C(48, 20)$, which is the intersection of the two nonaxis boundary lines. These four corner points are also feasible solutions of the system.

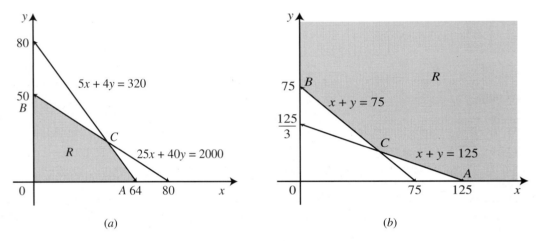

Fig. 12-3

**EXAMPLE 12.5**  A construction company buys lumber in 8-foot and 14-foot board lengths. Each 8-foot board is cut into one 5-foot and one 3-foot length, and each 14-foot board is cut into one 5-foot and three 3-foot lengths. Suppose the company requires at least seventy-five 5-foot lengths and one hundred and twenty-five 3-foot lengths to complete a project. Find the number of combinations of 8-foot boards and 14-foot boards that will be sufficient for the project.

Table 12-2   Product-Resource Chart

|  | Products | |
|---|---|---|
| Resources | 5-foot lengths | 3-foot lengths |
| 8-foot boards ($x$) | 1 per board | 1 per board |
| 14-foot boards ($y$) | 1 per board | 3 per board |
| Products needed | 75 | 125 |

Again, first organize the given in a PR chart, say, as in Table 12-2, where we let $x$ = number of required 8-foot boards and $y$ = number of required 14-foot boards. Then the following inequalities must be satisfied:

$x + y \geq 75$: The total number of 5-*foot lengths* cut from $x$ 8-foot and $y$ 14-foot boards must be at least 75.

$x + 3y \geq 125$: The total number of 3-*foot lengths* cut from $x$ 8-foot and $y$ 14-foot boards must be at least 125.

$x \geq 0, y \geq 0$: The number of 8-foot and 14-foot boards cannot be negative.

The solution of the above system, called the *feasible region*, is the shaded area $R$ in Fig. 12-3(*b*). Any pair $(x, y)$ of integers in $R$ is a feasible solution, that is, a combination of 8-foot boards and 14-foot boards that will be sufficient for the job.

Note that the feasible region $R$ has three corner points: the point $A(125, 0)$, which is the $x$ intercept of $x + 3y = 125$; the point $B(0, 75)$, which is the $y$ intercept of $x + y = 75$; and the point $C(50, 25)$, which is the intersection of the two nonaxis boundary lines.   These three corner points are also feasible solutions of the system.

## 12.5   A MAXIMUM LINEAR PROGRAMMING PROBLEM

Suppose that the clock company in Example 12.4 makes $10 profit on each type A clock and $12 on each type B clock.   Then the company would want to know which combinations of types A and B clocks provide the *most profit*.   The profit $P$ obtained for $x$ type A clocks and $y$ type B clocks is

$$P = 10x + 12y$$

We call $P$ the *objective function*, and the object is to find the production points $(x, y)$ in the feasible region $R$ shown in Fig. 12-3($a$) that make $P$ a maximum.

Now the graph of $P = 10x + 12y$, for each value of $P$, is a line $L_p$ in the $xy$ plane.   Also, different values of $P$ correspond to parallel lines.   (All the lines have slopes $m = \frac{5}{6}$.)   This fact is pictured in Fig. 12-4($a$).   Furthermore, as $P$ becomes larger, the line $L_p$ becomes farther away from the origin.   Accordingly:

> The maximum profit will occur on the line $P = 10x + 12y$ $\left(\text{with slope } m = -\frac{5}{6}\right)$ that is farthest from the origin but still touches the feasible region $R$.   In particular, the maximum profit will occur at a corner point of $R$.

As indicated in Fig. 12-4($b$), the line of maximum profit is the line that passes through the corner point $(48, 20)$.   In particular:

$$P = P(48, 20) = 10(48) + 12(20) = 480 + 240 = 720$$

so the maximum profit is $720, which is achieved by selling 48 type A and 20 type B clocks.

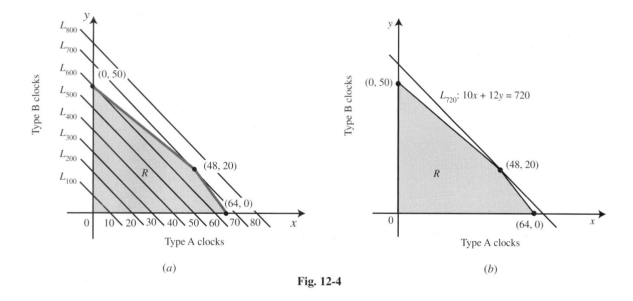

Fig. 12-4

## 12.6   A MINIMUM LINEAR PROGRAMMING PROBLEM

The objective in Example 12.5 is not to maximize profits but to *minimize costs*.   For instance, suppose the company pays $0.50 per foot for each board.   Then the cost $C$ in dollars for $x$ 8-foot and $y$ 14-foot boards is given by

$$C = 4x + 7y$$

Here $C$ is called the *objective function*, and now we want to find the minimum value of $C$ for all possible combinations $(x, y)$ of 8-foot and 14-foot boards in the feasible region $R$ in Fig. 12-3(b).

Now the graph of the cost equation $C = 4x + 7y$, for each value of $C$, is a line $L_C$ in the $xy$ plane. Also, different values of $C$ correspond to parallel lines. $\left(\text{All the lines have slope } m = -\frac{4}{7}.\right)$ This fact is pictured in Fig. 12-5(a). Furthermore, as $C$ becomes smaller, the line $L_C$ becomes closer to the origin. Accordingly:

---

The minimum cost will occur on the line $C = 4x + 7y \left(\text{with slope } m = -\frac{4}{7}\right)$ that is closest to the origin but still touches the feasible region $R$. In particular, the minimum cost will occur at a corner point of $R$.

---

As shown in Fig. 12-5(b), the line of minimum cost is the line that passes through the corner point (50, 25). In particular:

$$C = C(50, 25) = 4(50) + 7(25) = 200 + 175 = 375$$

so the minimum cost is $375, which is achieved by buying fifty 8-foot and twenty-five 14-foot boards.

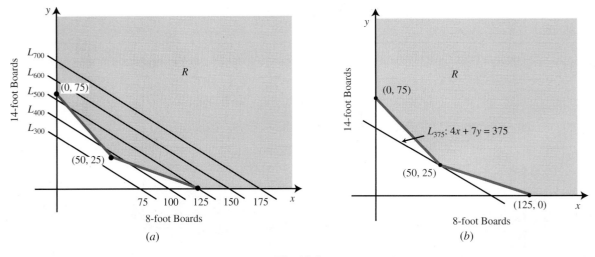

**Fig. 12-5**

# Solved Problems

### SYSTEMS OF LINEAR INEQUALITIES AND APPLICATIONS

**12.1.** A company packages and sells 16-ounce containers of mixed nuts. Brand A contains 12 ounces of peanuts and 4 ounces of cashews. Brand B contains 8 ounces of peanuts and 8 ounces of cashews. Suppose 120 pounds of peanuts and 96 pounds of cashews are available. (Recall that 1 pound equals 16 ounces.) Find the number of containers of each brand that can be packaged.

First organize the given data in a product-resource chart, say as in Table 12-3, where we let $x =$ number of brand A packages and $y =$ number of brand B packages. Note that there are $(120)(16) = 1920$ ounces of peanuts and $(96)(16) = 1536$ ounces of cashews available.

**Table 12-3**

| Resources | Products | | Resources available |
|---|---|---|---|
| | Brand A ($x$) | Brand B ($y$) | |
| Peanuts | 12 ounces per pound | 8 ounces per pound | 120 pounds = 1920 ounces |
| Cashews | 4 ounces per pound | 8 ounces per pound | 96 pounds  = 1536 ounces |

Then, as indicated by the table, the following inequalities must be satisfied:

$$12x + 8y \le 1920$$
$$4x + 8y \le 1536$$
$$x \ge 0, y \ge 0$$

The solution, or feasible region, of the above system of inequalities is the shaded region $R$ appearing in Fig. 12-6.   Thus, any pair $(x, y)$ of integers in $R$ is a combination of brand A and brand B containers that can be packaged.   Note, also, that there are four corner points, the origin $0(0, 0)$, $A(160, 0)$, $B(0, 192)$, and $C(48, 168)$, the intersection of the nonaxis boundary lines.

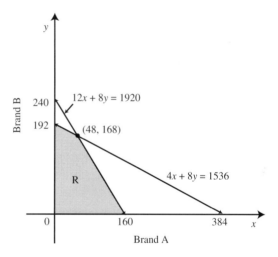

**Fig. 12-6**

**12.2.**   A garden requires at least 10, 12, and 12 units of chemicals A, B, and C, respectively.   A jar of liquid fertilizer contains 5, 2, and 1 units of A, B, and C, respectively.   A bag of granular fertilizer contains 1, 2, and 4 units of A, B, and C, respectively.   Find the combinations of jars and bags that will meet the requirements of the garden.

Form a PR chart, say, as in Table 12-4, where we let $x$ = number of jars and $y$ = number of bags.

**Table 12-4**

| Resources | Products (chemicals) | | |
|---|---|---|---|
| | A | B | C |
| Liquid fertilizer ($x$ jars) | 5 units per jar | 2 units per jar | 1 unit per jar |
| Granular fertilizer ($y$ bags) | 1 unit per bag | 2 units per bag | 4 units per bag |
| Units needed | 10 | 12 | 12 |

Then the requirements of the garden lead to the following inequalities:

$$5x + y \geq 10$$
$$2x + 2y \geq 12$$
$$x + 4y \geq 12$$
$$x \geq 0, y \geq 0$$

The feasible region $R$ for the above system is the shaded region in Fig. 12-7.   Any pair $(x, y)$ of integers in $R$ is a possible combination of jars and bags that can meet the requirements of the garden.   There are four corner points, $A(12, 0)$, $B(0, 10)$, $C(1, 5)$, and $D(4, 2)$.

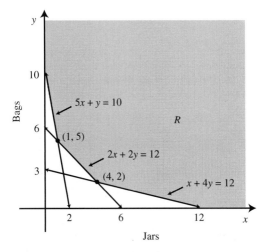

**Fig. 12-7**

## LINEAR PROGRAMMING PROBLEMS

**12.3.**   Consider Problem 12.1.   Find the number of containers of brand A and brand B that the company should package and sell in order to maximize its profit $P$ when the profit on each individual container is as follows:

(a)   \$0.75 on brand A and \$1.00 on brand B
(b)   \$1.00 on brand A and \$0.25 on brand B

The feasible region $R$ appears in Fig. 12-6.   The corner points are $(0, 192)$, $(48, 168)$, $(160, 0)$, and the origin $(0, 0)$.   We need evaluate the profit function $P$ only at three corner points [excluding $(0, 0)$, which will give the value 0].

(a)   Here $P(x, y) = 0.75x + y$.   Hence:

$$P(0, 192) = 0.75(0) + 192 = 0 + 192 = 192$$
$$P(48, 168) = 36 + 168 = 204, \qquad P(160, 0) = 120 + 0 = 120$$

Thus, the company should package and sell 48 containers of brand A and 168 containers of brand B for a maximum profit of $P = \$204$.

(b)   Here $P(x, y) = x + 0.25y$.   Hence:

$$P(0, 192) = 0 + 0.25(192) = 0 + 48 = 48$$
$$P(48, 168) = 48 + 42 = 90, \qquad P(160, 0) = 160 + 0 = 160$$

Thus, the company should package and sell 160 containers of brand A and zero containers of brand B for a maximum profit of $P = \$160$.

**12.4.** A truck rental company has two types of trucks. Type A has 20 cubic meters of refrigerated space and 40 cubic meters of nonrefrigerated space, and type B has 30 cubic meters of refrigerated space and also 30 cubic meters of nonrefrigerated space. A food plant must ship 900 cubic meters of refrigerated food and 1200 cubic meters of nonrefrigerated food. Suppose truck A rents for $0.90 per mile and B for $1.20. Find the number of trucks of each type that the plant should rent so as to minimize cost.

Consider truck types A and B as the resources and the refrigerated and nonrefrigerated space as the products. Then construct a PR chart, say, as in Table 12-5, where we let $x$ = number of type A trucks, and $y$ = number of type B trucks.

**Table 12-5**

| Space | Resources | | Products needed |
| --- | --- | --- | --- |
| | Type A ($x$) | Type B ($y$) | |
| Refrigerated | 20 cubic meters | 30 cubic meters | 900 cubic meters |
| Nonrefrigerated | 40 cubic meters | 30 cubic meters | 1200 cubic meters |

Table 12-5 indicates that the following inequalities must be satisfied:

$$20x + 30y \geq 900$$
$$40x + 30y \geq 1200$$
$$x \geq 0, \ y \geq 0$$

Graphing the system of inequalities yields the shaded region in Fig. 12-8. There are three corner points: $P(0, 40)$, which is the $y$ intercept of $40x + 30y = 1200$; $R(45, 0)$, which is the $x$ intercept of $20x + 30y = 900$; and $Q(15, 20)$, which is the intersection of the two nonaxis lines.

The cost function is $C = C(x, y) = 0.90x + 1.20y$. Evaluating the cost function $C$ at the corner points yields

$$C(0, 40) = 0.90(0) + 1.20(40) = 0 + 48.00 = 48.00$$
$$C(15, 20) = 0.90(15) + 1.20(20) = 13.50 + 24.00 = 37.50$$
$$C(45, 0) = 0.90(45) + 1.20(0) = 40.50 + 0 = 40.50$$

Thus, the company should rent 15 type A trucks and 20 type B trucks for a minimum cost of $37.50 per mile.

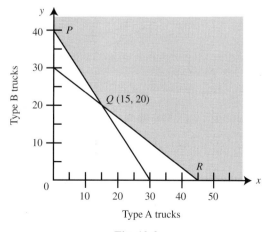

**Fig. 12-8**

**12.5.** A tailor has the following materials available: 16 square yards of cotton, 11 square yards of silk, and 15 square yards of wool. A suit requires 2 square yards of cotton, 1 square yard of silk, and 1 square yard of wool. A gown requires 1 square yard of cotton, 2 square yards of silk, and 3 square yards of wool. Suppose the profit P is $30 on a suit and $50 on a gown. Find the maximum profit that can be made and the corresponding number of suits and gowns that yield the maximum profit.

Summarize the data in a PR chart, say as in Table 12-6, where we let
$$x = \text{number of suits} \quad \text{and} \quad y = \text{number of gowns}$$

**Table 12-6**

| Resources | Products | | Resources available |
|---|---|---|---|
| | Suits ($x$) | Gowns ($y$) | |
| Cotton | 2 square yards | 1 square yard | 16 square yards |
| Silk | 1 square yard | 2 square yards | 11 square yards |
| Wool | 1 square yard | 3 square yards | 15 square yards |

Then the available amounts of cotton, silk, and wool lead to the following inequalities:

$$2x + y \le 16$$
$$x + 2y \le 11$$
$$x + 3y \le 15$$
$$x \ge 0,\, y \ge 0$$

The feasible region $R$ for the above system is the shaded region in Fig. 12-9. Note that there are five corner points, the origin $0(0, 0)$, $A(8, 0)$, $B(0, 5)$, $C(3, 4)$ and $D(7, 2)$. The profit $P$ in dollars for selling $x$ suits and $y$ gowns is given by

$$P = P(x, y) = 30x + 50y$$

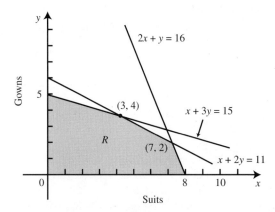

**Fig. 12-9**

Evaluate the profit function $P$ at the four corner points [other than $(0, 0)$]:

$$P(0, 5) = 30(0) + 50(5) = 0 + 250 = 250$$
$$P(3, 4) = 30(3) + 50(4) = 90 + 200 = 290$$
$$P(7, 2) = 30(7) + 50(2) = 210 + 100 = 310$$
$$P(8, 0) = 30(8) + 50(0) = 240 + 0 = 240$$

Accordingly, the maximum profit is $310, which is obtained by selling 7 suits and 2 gowns.


# Supplementary Problems


**12.6.** A manufacturer makes two kinds of sweaters, wool and cotton. It costs $10 to make a wool sweater and $8 to make a cotton sweater. The company can only make at most 240 sweaters per week, and budgets no more than $2000. Suppose there is a profit of $12 on each wool sweater but only $10 on each cotton sweater. How many of each type of sweater should be made to maximize profit?

**12.7.** A toy manufacturer makes dolls and teddy bears. Each doll costs $5 and sells for $10, and each bear costs $3 and sells for $7. Suppose at most 280 of the toys can be made each week, and costs cannot exceed $1200. How many of each type of toy should be made to maximize profit?

**12.8.** A kennel houses dogs and cats. It costs $3 to feed and maintain a dog each day, and $2 for each cat. The kennel limits its daily costs to $60 and has room for only 25 animals. If it charges $5 per day for a dog and $3.50 for a cat, how many of each type of animal should be housed to maximize profit?

**12.9.** An oil company has two processing plants, plant A and plant B. Plant A processes 100 barrels of high-grade and 40 barrels of low-grade oil each day. Plant B processes 50 barrels of high-grade and 30 barrels of low-grade oil each day. The daily cost is $10,000 to operate plant A, and $6,000 to operate plant B. Suppose the company receives an order for 1000 barrels of high-grade and 480 barrels of low-grade oil. Find the number of days each plant should operate to fill the order and minimize the cost.

**12.10.** The United Nations needs to evacuate 2400 people by air and wants to minimize its cost. It can lease at most 14 planes, which come in two types. Type A seats 200 people and type B seats 150 people. Find the number of airplanes of each type that should be leased if (a) type A rents for $10,000 and type B for $6,000, (b) type A rents for $10,000, but type B for $8,000.

**12.11.** A furniture factory receives a daily shipment of 50 boards of oak and 60 boards of maple, which they use to make cabinets and tables. Each cabinet uses two oak boards and two maple boards, and yields a profit of $80. Each table uses two oak boards and three maple boards, and yields a profit of $100. How many cabinets and tables should the factory make daily to maximize profit?

**12.12.** Suppose that 8, 12, and 9 units of proteins, carbohydrates, and fats, respectively, are the minimum weekly requirements for a person. Food A contains 2, 6, and 1 units of proteins, carbohydrates, and fats, respectively, per pound; food B contains 1, 1, and 3 units, respectively, per pound. Find the number of each food type that should be made to minimize cost while meeting requirements if (a) food A costs $3.40 per pound and B costs $1.60 per pound; (b) food A costs $3.00 per pound and B costs $1.60 per pound.

**12.13.**    A baker has 150, 90, and 150 units of ingredients A, B, C, respectively.   A loaf of bread requires 1, 1, and 2 units of A, B, C, respectively; a cake requires 5, 2, and 1 units of A, B, C, respectively.   Find the number of each that should be baked in order to maximize gross income if: (*a*) A loaf of bread sells for $1.40, and a cake for $3.20. (*b*) A loaf of bread sells for $1.80, and a cake for $3.20.

**12.14.**    A manufacturer has 240, 370, and 180 pounds of wool, plastic, and steel, respectively.   Product A requires 1, 3, and 2 pounds of wool, plastic, and steel, respectively; product B requires 3, 4, and 1 pound, respectively.   Find the number of each product that should be made in order to maximize gross income if: (*a*) product A sells for $40, and B for $60; (*b*) product A sells for $40, and B for $50.

**12.15.**    An oil company requires 9000, 12,000, and 26,000 barrels of high-, medium-, and low-grade oil, respectively.   It owns two oil refineries, A and B.   Refinery A produces 100, 300, and 400 barrels of high-, medium-, and low-grade oil, respectively, per day; refining B produces 200, 100, and 300 barrels, respectively.   Find the number of days that each refinery should run in order to meet the requirments and minimize costs if: (*a*) Each refinery costs $20,000 per day to operate. (*b*) A costs $30,000 per day to operate, and B costs $20,000.

# Answers to Supplementary Problems

**12.6.**    40 wool and 200 cotton for $2480

**12.7.**    180 dolls and 100 bears for $1300

**12.8.**    10 dogs and 15 cats for $42.50

**12.9.**    6 days plant A and 8 days plant B for $108,000

**12.10.**    (*a*)   6 type A and 8 type B,              (*b*)   10 type A

**12.11.**    15 cabinets and 10 tables for $2200

**12.12.**    (*a*)   1 of food A and 6 of food B for $13,     (*b*)   3 of A and 2 of B for $12.20

**12.13.**    (*a*)   50 loaves and 20 cakes for $134,      (*b*)   70 loaves and 10 cakes for $158

**12.14.**    (*a*)   30 of A and 70 of B for $5400,       (*b*)   70 of A and 40 of B for $4800

**12.15.**    (*a*)   A for 50 days and B for 20 days,      (*b*)   A for 20 days and B for 60 days

# APPENDIX A

# Tables

**Table A-1** $(1 + i)^n$

| | | | $i$ | | | |
|---|---|---|---|---|---|---|
| $n$: | 0.01 (1%) | 0.015 (1½%) | 0.02 (2%) | 0.025 (2½%) | 0.03 (3%) | 0.035 (3½%) |
| 1 | 1.01000 | 1.01500 | 1.02000 | 1.02500 | 1.03000 | 1.03500 |
| 2 | 1.02010 | 1.03022 | 1.04040 | 1.05062 | 1.06090 | 1.07122 |
| 3 | 1.03030 | 1.04568 | 1.06121 | 1.07689 | 1.09273 | 1.10872 |
| 4 | 1.04060 | 1.06136 | 1.08243 | 1.10381 | 1.12551 | 1.14752 |
| 5 | 1.05101 | 1.07728 | 1.10408 | 1.13141 | 1.15927 | 1.18769 |
| 6 | 1.06152 | 1.09344 | 1.12616 | 1.15969 | 1.19405 | 1.22926 |
| 7 | 1.07214 | 1.10984 | 1.12869 | 1.18869 | 1.22987 | 1.27228 |
| 8 | 1.08286 | 1.12649 | 1.17166 | 1.21840 | 1.26677 | 1.31681 |
| 9 | 1.09369 | 1.14339 | 1.19509 | 1.24886 | 1.30477 | 1.36290 |
| 10 | 1.10462 | 1.16054 | 1.21899 | 1.28008 | 1.34392 | 1.41060 |
| 11 | 1.11567 | 1.17795 | 1.24337 | 1.31209 | 1.38423 | 1.45997 |
| 12 | 1.12683 | 1.19562 | 1.26824 | 1.34489 | 1.42576 | 1.51107 |
| 13 | 1.13809 | 1.21355 | 1.29361 | 1.37851 | 1.46853 | 1.56396 |
| 14 | 1.14947 | 1.23176 | 1.31948 | 1.41297 | 1.51259 | 1.61869 |
| 15 | 1.16097 | 1.25023 | 1.34587 | 1.44830 | 1.55797 | 1.67535 |
| 16 | 1.17258 | 1.26899 | 1.37279 | 1.48451 | 1.60471 | 1.73399 |
| 17 | 1.18430 | 1.28802 | 1.40024 | 1.52162 | 1.65285 | 1.79468 |
| 18 | 1.19615 | 1.30734 | 1.42825 | 1.55966 | 1.70243 | 1.85749 |
| 19 | 1.20811 | 1.32695 | 1.45681 | 1.59865 | 1.75351 | 1.92250 |
| 20 | 1.22019 | 1.34686 | 1.48595 | 1.63862 | 1.80611 | 1.98979 |
| 21 | 1.23239 | 1.36706 | 1.51567 | 1.67958 | 1.86029 | 2.05943 |
| 22 | 1.24472 | 1.38756 | 1.54598 | 1.72157 | 1.91610 | 2.13151 |
| 23 | 1.25716 | 1.40838 | 1.57690 | 1.76461 | 1.97359 | 2.20611 |
| 24 | 1.26973 | 1.42950 | 1.60844 | 1.80873 | 2.03279 | 2.28333 |
| 25 | 1.28243 | 1.45095 | 1.64061 | 1.85394 | 2.09378 | 2.36324 |
| 26 | 1.29526 | 1.47271 | 1.67342 | 1.90029 | 2.15659 | 2.44596 |
| 27 | 1.30821 | 1.49480 | 1.70689 | 1.94780 | 2.22129 | 2.53157 |
| 28 | 1.32129 | 1.51722 | 1.74102 | 1.99650 | 2.28793 | 2.62017 |
| 29 | 1.33450 | 1.53998 | 1.77584 | 2.04641 | 2.35657 | 2.71188 |
| 30 | 1.34785 | 1.56308 | 1.81136 | 2.09757 | 2.42726 | 2.80679 |
| 31 | 1.36133 | 1.58653 | 1.84759 | 2.15001 | 2.50008 | 2.90503 |
| 32 | 1.37494 | 1.61032 | 1.88454 | 2.20376 | 2.57508 | 3.00671 |
| 33 | 1.38869 | 1.63448 | 1.92223 | 2.25885 | 2.65234 | 3.11194 |
| 34 | 1.40258 | 1.65900 | 1.96068 | 2.31532 | 2.73191 | 3.22086 |
| 35 | 1.41660 | 1.68388 | 1.99989 | 2.37321 | 2.81386 | 3.33359 |
| 36 | 1.43077 | 1.70914 | 2.03989 | 2.43254 | 2.89828 | 3.45027 |
| 37 | 1.44508 | 1.73478 | 2.08069 | 2.49335 | 2.98523 | 3.57103 |
| 38 | 1.45953 | 1.76080 | 2.12230 | 2.55568 | 3.07478 | 3.69601 |
| 39 | 1.47412 | 1.78721 | 2.16474 | 2.61957 | 3.16703 | 3.82537 |
| 40 | 1.48886 | 1.81402 | 2.20804 | 2.68506 | 3.26204 | 3.95926 |
| 41 | 1.50375 | 1.84123 | 2.25220 | 2.75219 | 3.35990 | 4.09783 |
| 42 | 1.51879 | 1.86885 | 2.29724 | 2.82100 | 3.46070 | 4.24126 |
| 43 | 1.53398 | 1.89688 | 2.34319 | 2.89152 | 3.56452 | 4.38970 |
| 44 | 1.54932 | 1.92533 | 2.39005 | 2.96381 | 3.67145 | 4.54334 |
| 45 | 1.56481 | 1.95421 | 2.43785 | 3.03790 | 3.78160 | 4.70236 |
| 46 | 1.58046 | 1.98353 | 2.48661 | 3.11385 | 3.89504 | 4.86694 |
| 47 | 1.59626 | 2.01328 | 2.53634 | 3.19170 | 4.01190 | 5.03728 |
| 48 | 1.61223 | 2.04348 | 2.58707 | 3.27149 | 4.13225 | 5.21359 |
| 49 | 1.62835 | 2.07413 | 2.63881 | 3.35328 | 4.25622 | 5.39606 |
| 50 | 1.64463 | 2.10524 | 2.69159 | 3.43711 | 4.38391 | 5.58493 |
| 51 | 1.66108 | 2.13682 | 2.74542 | 3.52304 | 4.51542 | 5.78040 |
| 52 | 1.67769 | 2.16887 | 2.80033 | 3.61111 | 4.65089 | 5.98271 |
| 53 | 1.69447 | 2.20141 | 2.85633 | 3.70139 | 4.79041 | 6.19211 |
| 54 | 1.71141 | 2.23443 | 2.91346 | 3.79392 | 4.93412 | 6.40883 |
| 55 | 1.72852 | 2.26794 | 2.97173 | 3.88877 | 5.08215 | 6.63314 |
| 56 | 1.74581 | 2.30196 | 3.03117 | 3.98599 | 5.23461 | 6.86530 |
| 57 | 1.76327 | 2.33649 | 3.09179 | 4.08564 | 5.39165 | 7.10559 |
| 58 | 1.78090 | 2.37154 | 3.15362 | 4.18778 | 5.55340 | 7.35428 |
| 59 | 1.79871 | 2.40711 | 3.21670 | 4.29248 | 5.72000 | 7.61168 |
| 60 | 1.81670 | 2.44322 | 3.28103 | 4.39979 | 5.89160 | 7.87809 |

**Table A-1**　　$(1 + i)^n$ **(Continued)**

| n: | 0.04 (4%) | 0.045 (4½%) | 0.05 (5%) | 0.06 (6%) | 0.07 (7%) | 0.08 (8%) |
|---|---|---|---|---|---|---|
| 1 | 1.04000 | 1.04500 | 1.05000 | 1.06000 | 1.07000 | 1.08000 |
| 2 | 1.08160 | 1.09202 | 1.10250 | 1.12360 | 1.14490 | 1.16640 |
| 3 | 1.12486 | 1.14117 | 1.15762 | 1.19102 | 1.22504 | 1.25971 |
| 4 | 1.16986 | 1.19252 | 1.21551 | 1.26248 | 1.31080 | 1.36049 |
| 5 | 1.21665 | 1.24618 | 1.27628 | 1.33823 | 1.40255 | 1.46933 |
| 6 | 1.26532 | 1.30226 | 1.34010 | 1.41852 | 1.50073 | 1.58687 |
| 7 | 1.31593 | 1.36086 | 1.40710 | 1.50363 | 1.60578 | 1.71382 |
| 8 | 1.36857 | 1.42210 | 1.47746 | 1.59385 | 1.71819 | 1.85093 |
| 9 | 1.42331 | 1.48610 | 1.55133 | 1.68948 | 1.83846 | 1.99900 |
| 10 | 1.48024 | 1.55297 | 1.62889 | 1.79085 | 1.96715 | 2.15892 |
| 11 | 1.53945 | 1.62285 | 1.71034 | 1.89830 | 2.10485 | 2.33164 |
| 12 | 1.60101 | 1.69588 | 1.79586 | 2.01220 | 2.25219 | 2.51817 |
| 13 | 1.66507 | 1.77220 | 1.88565 | 2.13293 | 2.40985 | 2.71962 |
| 14 | 1.73168 | 1.85194 | 1.97993 | 2.26090 | 2.57853 | 2.93719 |
| 15 | 1.80094 | 1.93528 | 2.07893 | 2.39656 | 2.75903 | 3.17217 |
| 16 | 1.87298 | 2.02237 | 2.18287 | 2.54035 | 2.95216 | 3.42594 |
| 17 | 1.94790 | 2.11338 | 2.29202 | 2.69277 | 3.15882 | 3.70002 |
| 18 | 2.02582 | 2.20848 | 2.40662 | 2.85434 | 3.37993 | 3.99602 |
| 19 | 2.10685 | 2.30786 | 2.52695 | 3.02560 | 3.61653 | 4.31570 |
| 20 | 2.19112 | 2.41171 | 2.65330 | 3.20714 | 3.86968 | 4.66096 |
| 21 | 2.27877 | 2.52024 | 2.78596 | 3.39956 | 4.14056 | 5.03383 |
| 22 | 2.36992 | 2.63365 | 2.92526 | 3.60354 | 4.43040 | 5.43654 |
| 23 | 2.46472 | 2.75217 | 3.07152 | 3.81975 | 4.74053 | 5.87146 |
| 24 | 2.56330 | 2.87601 | 3.22510 | 4.04893 | 5.07237 | 6.34118 |
| 25 | 2.66584 | 3.00543 | 3.38635 | 4.29187 | 5.42743 | 6.84848 |
| 26 | 2.77247 | 3.14068 | 3.55567 | 4.54938 | 5.80735 | 7.39635 |
| 27 | 2.88337 | 3.28201 | 3.73346 | 4.82235 | 6.21387 | 7.98806 |
| 28 | 2.99870 | 3.42970 | 3.92013 | 5.11169 | 6.64884 | 8.62711 |
| 29 | 3.11865 | 3.58404 | 4.11614 | 5.41839 | 7.11426 | 9.31727 |
| 30 | 3.24340 | 3.74532 | 4.32194 | 5.74349 | 7.61226 | 10.06266 |
| 31 | 3.37313 | 3.91386 | 4.53804 | 6.08810 | 8.14511 | 10.86767 |
| 32 | 3.50806 | 4.08998 | 4.76494 | 6.45339 | 8.71527 | 11.73708 |
| 33 | 3.64838 | 4.27403 | 5.00319 | 6.84059 | 9.32534 | 12.67605 |
| 34 | 3.79432 | 4.46636 | 5.25335 | 7.25103 | 9.97811 | 13.69013 |
| 35 | 3.94609 | 4.66735 | 5.51602 | 7.68609 | 10.67658 | 14.78534 |
| 36 | 4.10393 | 4.87738 | 5.79182 | 8.14725 | 11.42394 | 15.96817 |
| 37 | 4.26809 | 5.09686 | 6.08141 | 8.63609 | 12.22362 | 17.24563 |
| 38 | 4.43881 | 5.32622 | 6.38548 | 9.15425 | 13.07927 | 18.62528 |
| 39 | 4.61637 | 5.56590 | 6.70475 | 9.70351 | 13.99482 | 20.11530 |
| 40 | 4.80102 | 5.81636 | 7.03999 | 10.28572 | 14.97446 | 21.72452 |
| 41 | 4.99306 | 6.07810 | 7.39199 | 10.90286 | 16.02267 | 23.46248 |
| 42 | 5.19278 | 6.35162 | 7.76159 | 11.55703 | 17.14426 | 25.33948 |
| 43 | 5.40050 | 6.63744 | 8.14967 | 12.25045 | 18.34435 | 27.36664 |
| 44 | 5.61652 | 6.93612 | 8.55715 | 12.98548 | 19.62846 | 29.55597 |
| 45 | 5.84118 | 7.24825 | 8.98501 | 13.76461 | 21.00245 | 31.92045 |
| 46 | 6.07482 | 7.57442 | 9.43426 | 14.59049 | 22.47262 | 34.47409 |
| 47 | 6.31782 | 7.91527 | 9.90597 | 15.46592 | 24.04571 | 37.23201 |
| 48 | 6.57053 | 8.27146 | 10.40127 | 16.39387 | 25.72891 | 40.21057 |
| 49 | 6.83335 | 8.64367 | 10.92133 | 17.37750 | 27.52993 | 43.42742 |
| 50 | 7.10668 | 9.03264 | 11.46740 | 18.42015 | 29.45703 | 46.90161 |
| 51 | 7.39095 | 9.43910 | 12.04077 | 19.52536 | 31.51902 | 50.65374 |
| 52 | 7.68659 | 9.86386 | 12.64281 | 20.69689 | 33.72535 | 54.70604 |
| 53 | 7.99405 | 10.30774 | 13.27495 | 21.93870 | 36.08612 | 59.08252 |
| 54 | 8.31381 | 10.77159 | 13.93870 | 23.25502 | 38.61215 | 63.80913 |
| 55 | 8.64637 | 11.25631 | 14.63563 | 24.65032 | 41.31500 | 68.91386 |
| 56 | 8.99222 | 11.76284 | 15.36741 | 26.12934 | 44.20705 | 74.42696 |
| 57 | 9.35191 | 12.29217 | 16.13578 | 27.69710 | 47.30155 | 80.38112 |
| 58 | 9.72599 | 12.84532 | 16.94257 | 29.35893 | 50.61265 | 86.81161 |
| 59 | 10.11503 | 13.42336 | 17.78970 | 31.12046 | 54.15554 | 93.75654 |
| 60 | 10.51963 | 14.02741 | 18.67919 | 32.98769 | 57.94643 | 101.25706 |

*Source*: Hummel, P. and Seebeck, Jr., C., *Mathematics of Finance*, 2d ed., McGraw-Hill, New York, 1971, chap. 11, pp. T.0 to T.1. Reproduced with permission.

**Table A-2** $(1 + i)^{-n}$

| | | | $i$ | | | |
|---|---|---|---|---|---|---|
| $n$: | 0.01 (1%) | 0.015 ($1\frac{1}{2}$%) | 0.02 (2%) | 0.025 ($2\frac{1}{2}$%) | 0.03 (3%) | 0.035 ($3\frac{1}{2}$%) |
| 1 | 0.99010 | 0.98522 | 0.98039 | 0.97561 | 0.97087 | 0.96618 |
| 2 | 0.98030 | 0.97066 | 0.96117 | 0.95181 | 0.94260 | 0.93351 |
| 3 | 0.97059 | 0.95632 | 0.94232 | 0.92860 | 0.91514 | 0.90194 |
| 4 | 0.96098 | 0.94218 | 0.92385 | 0.90595 | 0.88849 | 0.87144 |
| 5 | 0.95147 | 0.92826 | 0.90573 | 0.88385 | 0.86261 | 0.84197 |
| 6 | 0.94205 | 0.91454 | 0.88797 | 0.86230 | 0.83748 | 0.81350 |
| 7 | 0.93272 | 0.90103 | 0.87056 | 0.84127 | 0.81309 | 0.78599 |
| 8 | 0.92348 | 0.88771 | 0.85349 | 0.82075 | 0.78941 | 0.75941 |
| 9 | 0.91434 | 0.87459 | 0.83676 | 0.80073 | 0.76642 | 0.73373 |
| 10 | 0.90529 | 0.86167 | 0.82035 | 0.78120 | 0.74409 | 0.70892 |
| 11 | 0.89632 | 0.84893 | 0.80426 | 0.76214 | 0.72242 | 0.68495 |
| 12 | 0.88745 | 0.83639 | 0.78849 | 0.74356 | 0.70138 | 0.66178 |
| 13 | 0.87866 | 0.82403 | 0.77303 | 0.72542 | 0.68095 | 0.63940 |
| 14 | 0.86996 | 0.81185 | 0.75788 | 0.70773 | 0.66112 | 0.61778 |
| 15 | 0.86135 | 0.79985 | 0.74301 | 0.69047 | 0.64186 | 0.59689 |
| 16 | 0.85282 | 0.78803 | 0.72845 | 0.67362 | 0.62317 | 0.57671 |
| 17 | 0.84438 | 0.77639 | 0.71416 | 0.65720 | 0.60502 | 0.55720 |
| 18 | 0.83602 | 0.76491 | 0.70016 | 0.64117 | 0.58739 | 0.53836 |
| 19 | 0.82774 | 0.75361 | 0.68643 | 0.62553 | 0.57029 | 0.52016 |
| 20 | 0.81954 | 0.74247 | 0.67297 | 0.61027 | 0.55368 | 0.50257 |
| 21 | 0.81143 | 0.73150 | 0.65978 | 0.59539 | 0.53755 | 0.48557 |
| 22 | 0.80340 | 0.72069 | 0.64684 | 0.58086 | 0.52189 | 0.46915 |
| 23 | 0.79544 | 0.71004 | 0.63416 | 0.56670 | 0.50669 | 0.45329 |
| 24 | 0.78757 | 0.69954 | 0.62172 | 0.55288 | 0.49193 | 0.43796 |
| 25 | 0.77977 | 0.68921 | 0.60953 | 0.53939 | 0.47761 | 0.42315 |
| 26 | 0.77205 | 0.67902 | 0.59758 | 0.52623 | 0.46369 | 0.40884 |
| 27 | 0.76440 | 0.66899 | 0.58586 | 0.51340 | 0.45019 | 0.39501 |
| 28 | 0.75684 | 0.65910 | 0.57437 | 0.50088 | 0.43708 | 0.38165 |
| 29 | 0.74934 | 0.64936 | 0.56311 | 0.48866 | 0.42435 | 0.36875 |
| 30 | 0.74192 | 0.63976 | 0.55207 | 0.47674 | 0.41199 | 0.35628 |
| 31 | 0.73458 | 0.63031 | 0.54125 | 0.46511 | 0.39999 | 0.34423 |
| 32 | 0.72730 | 0.62099 | 0.53063 | 0.45377 | 0.38834 | 0.33259 |
| 33 | 0.72010 | 0.61182 | 0.52023 | 0.44270 | 0.37703 | 0.32134 |
| 34 | 0.71297 | 0.60277 | 0.51003 | 0.43191 | 0.36604 | 0.31048 |
| 35 | 0.70591 | 0.59387 | 0.50003 | 0.42137 | 0.35538 | 0.29998 |
| 36 | 0.69892 | 0.58509 | 0.49022 | 0.41109 | 0.34503 | 0.28983 |
| 37 | 0.69200 | 0.57644 | 0.48061 | 0.40107 | 0.33498 | 0.28003 |
| 38 | 0.68515 | 0.56792 | 0.47119 | 0.39128 | 0.32523 | 0.27056 |
| 39 | 0.67837 | 0.55953 | 0.46195 | 0.38174 | 0.31575 | 0.26141 |
| 40 | 0.67165 | 0.55126 | 0.45289 | 0.37243 | 0.30656 | 0.25257 |
| 41 | 0.66500 | 0.54312 | 0.44401 | 0.36335 | 0.29763 | 0.24403 |
| 42 | 0.65842 | 0.53509 | 0.43530 | 0.35448 | 0.28896 | 0.23578 |
| 43 | 0.65190 | 0.52718 | 0.42677 | 0.34584 | 0.28054 | 0.22781 |
| 44 | 0.64545 | 0.51939 | 0.41840 | 0.33740 | 0.27237 | 0.22010 |
| 45 | 0.63905 | 0.51171 | 0.41020 | 0.32917 | 0.26444 | 0.21266 |
| 46 | 0.63273 | 0.50415 | 0.40215 | 0.32115 | 0.25674 | 0.20547 |
| 47 | 0.62646 | 0.49670 | 0.39427 | 0.31331 | 0.24926 | 0.19852 |
| 48 | 0.62026 | 0.48936 | 0.38654 | 0.30567 | 0.24200 | 0.19181 |
| 49 | 0.61412 | 0.48213 | 0.37896 | 0.29822 | 0.23495 | 0.18532 |
| 50 | 0.60804 | 0.47500 | 0.37153 | 0.29094 | 0.22811 | 0.17905 |
| 51 | 0.60202 | 0.46798 | 0.36424 | 0.28385 | 0.22146 | 0.17300 |
| 52 | 0.59606 | 0.46107 | 0.35710 | 0.27692 | 0.21501 | 0.16715 |
| 53 | 0.59016 | 0.45426 | 0.35010 | 0.27017 | 0.20875 | 0.16150 |
| 54 | 0.58431 | 0.44754 | 0.34323 | 0.26358 | 0.20267 | 0.15603 |
| 55 | 0.57853 | 0.44093 | 0.33650 | 0.25715 | 0.19677 | 0.15076 |
| 56 | 0.57280 | 0.43441 | 0.32991 | 0.25088 | 0.19104 | 0.14566 |
| 57 | 0.56713 | 0.42799 | 0.32344 | 0.24476 | 0.18547 | 0.14073 |
| 58 | 0.56151 | 0.42167 | 0.31710 | 0.23879 | 0.18007 | 0.13598 |
| 59 | 0.55595 | 0.41544 | 0.31088 | 0.23297 | 0.17483 | 0.13138 |
| 60 | 0.55045 | 0.40930 | 0.30478 | 0.22728 | 0.16973 | 0.12693 |

**Table A-2**   $(1 + i)^{-n}$  **(Continued)**

|        |                   |                   | $i$               |                   |                   |                   |
|--------|-------------------|-------------------|-------------------|-------------------|-------------------|-------------------|
| $n$:   | 0.04 (4%)         | 0.045 ($4\frac{1}{2}$%) | 0.05 (5%)   | 0.06 (6%)         | 0.07 (7%)         | 0.08 (8%)         |
| 1      | 0.96154           | 0.95694           | 0.95238           | 0.94340           | 0.93458           | 0.92593           |
| 2      | 0.92456           | 0.91573           | 0.90703           | 0.89000           | 0.87344           | 0.85734           |
| 3      | 0.88900           | 0.87630           | 0.86384           | 0.83962           | 0.81630           | 0.79383           |
| 4      | 0.85480           | 0.83856           | 0.82270           | 0.79209           | 0.76290           | 0.73503           |
| 5      | 0.82193           | 0.80245           | 0.78353           | 0.74726           | 0.71299           | 0.68058           |
| 6      | 0.79031           | 0.76790           | 0.74622           | 0.70496           | 0.66634           | 0.63017           |
| 7      | 0.75992           | 0.73483           | 0.71068           | 0.66506           | 0.62275           | 0.58349           |
| 8      | 0.73069           | 0.70319           | 0.67684           | 0.62741           | 0.58201           | 0.54027           |
| 9      | 0.70259           | 0.67290           | 0.64461           | 0.59190           | 0.54393           | 0.50025           |
| 10     | 0.67556           | 0.64393           | 0.61391           | 0.55839           | 0.50835           | 0.46319           |
| 11     | 0.64958           | 0.61620           | 0.58468           | 0.52679           | 0.47509           | 0.42888           |
| 12     | 0.62460           | 0.58966           | 0.55684           | 0.49697           | 0.44401           | 0.39711           |
| 13     | 0.60057           | 0.56427           | 0.53032           | 0.46884           | 0.41496           | 0.36770           |
| 14     | 0.57748           | 0.53997           | 0.50507           | 0.44230           | 0.38782           | 0.34046           |
| 15     | 0.55526           | 0.51672           | 0.48102           | 0.41727           | 0.36245           | 0.31524           |
| 16     | 0.53391           | 0.49447           | 0.45811           | 0.39365           | 0.33873           | 0.29189           |
| 17     | 0.51337           | 0.47318           | 0.43630           | 0.37136           | 0.31657           | 0.27027           |
| 18     | 0.49363           | 0.45280           | 0.41552           | 0.35034           | 0.29586           | 0.25025           |
| 19     | 0.47464           | 0.43330           | 0.39573           | 0.33051           | 0.27651           | 0.23171           |
| 20     | 0.45639           | 0.41464           | 0.37689           | 0.31180           | 0.25842           | 0.21455           |
| 21     | 0.43883           | 0.39679           | 0.35894           | 0.29416           | 0.24151           | 0.19866           |
| 22     | 0.42196           | 0.37970           | 0.34185           | 0.27751           | 0.22571           | 0.18394           |
| 23     | 0.40573           | 0.36335           | 0.32557           | 0.26180           | 0.21095           | 0.17032           |
| 24     | 0.39012           | 0.34770           | 0.31007           | 0.24698           | 0.19715           | 0.15770           |
| 25     | 0.37512           | 0.33273           | 0.29530           | 0.23300           | 0.18425           | 0.14602           |
| 26     | 0.36069           | 0.31840           | 0.28124           | 0.21981           | 0.17220           | 0.13520           |
| 27     | 0.34682           | 0.30469           | 0.26785           | 0.20737           | 0.16093           | 0.12519           |
| 28     | 0.33348           | 0.29157           | 0.25509           | 0.19563           | 0.15040           | 0.11591           |
| 29     | 0.32065           | 0.27902           | 0.24295           | 0.18456           | 0.14056           | 0.10733           |
| 30     | 0.30832           | 0.26700           | 0.23138           | 0.17411           | 0.13137           | 0.09938           |
| 31     | 0.29646           | 0.25550           | 0.22036           | 0.16425           | 0.12277           | 0.09202           |
| 32     | 0.28506           | 0.24450           | 0.20987           | 0.15496           | 0.11474           | 0.08520           |
| 33     | 0.27409           | 0.23397           | 0.19987           | 0.14619           | 0.10723           | 0.07889           |
| 34     | 0.26355           | 0.22390           | 0.19035           | 0.13791           | 0.10022           | 0.07305           |
| 35     | 0.25342           | 0.21425           | 0.18129           | 0.13011           | 0.09366           | 0.06763           |
| 36     | 0.24367           | 0.20503           | 0.17266           | 0.12274           | 0.08754           | 0.06262           |
| 37     | 0.23430           | 0.19620           | 0.16444           | 0.11579           | 0.08181           | 0.05799           |
| 38     | 0.22529           | 0.18775           | 0.15661           | 0.10924           | 0.07646           | 0.05369           |
| 39     | 0.21662           | 0.17967           | 0.14915           | 0.10306           | 0.07146           | 0.04971           |
| 40     | 0.20829           | 0.17193           | 0.14205           | 0.09722           | 0.06678           | 0.04603           |
| 41     | 0.20028           | 0.16453           | 0.13528           | 0.09172           | 0.06241           | 0.04262           |
| 42     | 0.19257           | 0.15744           | 0.12884           | 0.08653           | 0.05833           | 0.03946           |
| 43     | 0.18517           | 0.15066           | 0.12270           | 0.08163           | 0.05451           | 0.03654           |
| 44     | 0.17805           | 0.14417           | 0.11686           | 0.07701           | 0.05095           | 0.03383           |
| 45     | 0.17120           | 0.13796           | 0.11130           | 0.07265           | 0.04761           | 0.03133           |
| 46     | 0.15461           | 0.13202           | 0.10600           | 0.06854           | 0.04450           | 0.02901           |
| 47     | 0.15828           | 0.12634           | 0.10095           | 0.06466           | 0.04159           | 0.02686           |
| 48     | 0.15219           | 0.12090           | 0.09614           | 0.06100           | 0.03837           | 0.02487           |
| 49     | 0.14634           | 0.11569           | 0.09156           | 0.05755           | 0.03632           | 0.02303           |
| 50     | 0.14071           | 0.11071           | 0.08720           | 0.05429           | 0.03395           | 0.02132           |
| 51     | 0.13530           | 0.10594           | 0.08305           | 0.05122           | 0.03173           | 0.01974           |
| 52     | 0.13010           | 0.10138           | 0.07910           | 0.04832           | 0.02965           | 0.01828           |
| 53     | 0.12509           | 0.09701           | 0.07533           | 0.04558           | 0.02771           | 0.01693           |
| 54     | 0.12028           | 0.09284           | 0.07174           | 0.04300           | 0.02590           | 0.01567           |
| 55     | 0.11566           | 0.08884           | 0.06833           | 0.04057           | 0.02420           | 0.01451           |
| 56     | 0.11121           | 0.08501           | 0.06507           | 0.03827           | 0.02262           | 0.01344           |
| 57     | 0.10693           | 0.08135           | 0.06197           | 0.03610           | 0.02114           | 0.01244           |
| 58     | 0.10282           | 0.07785           | 0.05902           | 0.03406           | 0.01976           | 0.01152           |
| 59     | 0.09886           | 0.07450           | 0.05621           | 0.03213           | 0.01847           | 0.01067           |
| 60     | 0.09506           | 0.07129           | 0.05354           | 0.03031           | 0.01726           | 0.00988           |

*Source*: Hummel, P. and Seebeck, Jr., C., *Mathematics of Finance*, 2d ed., McGraw-Hill, New York, 1971, chap. 11, pp. T.4 to T.5. Reproduced with permission.

**TABLE A-3   Exponential Functions**

| x | $e^x$ | $e^{-x}$ | x | $e^x$ | $e^{-x}$ |
|------|--------|----------|------|--------|----------|
| 0.00 | 1.0000 | 1.0000 | 1.5 | 4.4817 | 0.2231 |
| 0.01 | 1.0101 | 0.9901 | 1.6 | 4.9530 | 0.2019 |
| 0.02 | 1.0202 | 0.9802 | 1.7 | 5.4739 | 0.1827 |
| 0.03 | 1.0305 | 0.9705 | 1.8 | 6.0496 | 0.1653 |
| 0.04 | 1.0408 | 0.9608 | 1.9 | 6.6859 | 0.1496 |
| 0.05 | 1.0513 | 0.9512 | 2.0 | 7.3891 | 0.1353 |
| 0.06 | 1.0618 | 0.9418 | 2.1 | 8.1662 | 0.1225 |
| 0.07 | 1.0725 | 0.9324 | 2.2 | 9.0250 | 0.1108 |
| 0.08 | 1.0833 | 0.9231 | 2.3 | 9.9742 | 0.1003 |
| 0.09 | 1.0942 | 0.9139 | 2.4 | 11.023 | 0.0907 |
| 0.10 | 1.1052 | 0.9048 | 2.5 | 12.182 | 0.0821 |
| 0.11 | 1.1163 | 0.8958 | 2.6 | 13.464 | 0.0743 |
| 0.12 | 1.1275 | 0.8869 | 2.7 | 14.880 | 0.0672 |
| 0.13 | 1.1388 | 0.8781 | 2.8 | 16.445 | 0.0608 |
| 0.14 | 1.1503 | 0.8694 | 2.9 | 18.174 | 0.0550 |
| 0.15 | 1.1618 | 0.8607 | 3.0 | 20.086 | 0.0498 |
| 0.16 | 1.1735 | 0.8521 | 3.1 | 22.198 | 0.0450 |
| 0.17 | 1.1853 | 0.8437 | 3.2 | 24.533 | 0.0408 |
| 0.18 | 1.1972 | 0.8353 | 3.3 | 27.113 | 0.0369 |
| 0.19 | 1.2092 | 0.8270 | 3.4 | 29.964 | 0.0334 |
| 0.20 | 1.2214 | 0.8187 | 3.5 | 33.115 | 0.0302 |
| 0.21 | 1.2337 | 0.8106 | 3.6 | 36.598 | 0.0273 |
| 0.22 | 1.2461 | 0.8025 | 3.7 | 40.447 | 0.0247 |
| 0.23 | 1.2586 | 0.7945 | 3.8 | 44.701 | 0.0224 |
| 0.24 | 1.2712 | 0.7866 | 3.9 | 49.402 | 0.0202 |
| 0.25 | 1.2840 | 0.7788 | 4.0 | 54.598 | 0.0183 |
| 0.30 | 1.3499 | 0.7408 | 4.1 | 60.340 | 0.0166 |
| 0.35 | 1.4191 | 0.7047 | 4.2 | 66.686 | 0.0150 |
| 0.40 | 1.4918 | 0.6703 | 4.3 | 73.700 | 0.0136 |
| 0.45 | 1.5683 | 0.6376 | 4.4 | 81.451 | 0.0123 |
| 0.50 | 1.6487 | 0.6065 | 4.5 | 90.017 | 0.0111 |
| 0.55 | 1.7333 | 0.5769 | 4.6 | 99.484 | 0.0101 |
| 0.60 | 1.8221 | 0.5488 | 4.7 | 109.95 | 0.0091 |
| 0.65 | 1.9155 | 0.5220 | 4.8 | 121.51 | 0.0082 |
| 0.70 | 2.0138 | 0.4966 | 4.9 | 134.29 | 0.0074 |
| 0.75 | 2.1170 | 0.4724 | 5.0 | 148.41 | 0.0067 |
| 0.80 | 2.2255 | 0.4493 | 5.5 | 244.69 | 0.0041 |
| 0.85 | 2.3396 | 0.4274 | 6.0 | 403.43 | 0.0025 |
| 0.90 | 2.4596 | 0.4066 | 6.5 | 665.14 | 0.0015 |
| 0.95 | 2.5857 | 0.3867 | 7.0 | 1096.6 | 0.0009 |
| 1.0 | 2.7183 | 0.3679 | 7.5 | 1808.0 | 0.0006 |
| 1.1 | 3.0042 | 0.3329 | 8.0 | 2981.0 | 0.0003 |
| 1.2 | 3.3201 | 0.3012 | 8.5 | 4914.8 | 0.0002 |
| 1.3 | 3.6693 | 0.2725 | 9.0 | 8103.1 | 0.0001 |
| 1.4 | 4.0552 | 0.2466 | 10.0 | 22026 | 0.00005 |

*Source*: Schiller, J. J. and Wurster, M. A., *College Algebra and Trigonometry: Basics through Precalculus*, 2d ed., Kendall/Hunt, Dubuque, Iowa © 1988. Copyright by John J. Schiller and Marie A. Wurster.

**Table A-4** $s_{\overline{n}|i} = \dfrac{(1+i)^n - 1}{i}$

| $n$: | 0.01 (1%) | 0.015 ($1\frac{1}{2}$%) | 0.02 (2%) | 0.025 ($2\frac{1}{2}$%) | 0.03 (3%) | 0.035 ($3\frac{1}{2}$%) |
|---|---|---|---|---|---|---|
| 1 | 1.00000 | 1.00000 | 1.00000 | 1.00000 | 1.00000 | 1.00000 |
| 2 | 2.01000 | 2.01500 | 2.02000 | 2.02500 | 2.03000 | 2.03500 |
| 3 | 3.03010 | 3.04522 | 3.06040 | 3.07562 | 3.09090 | 3.10622 |
| 4 | 4.06040 | 4.09090 | 4.12161 | 4.15252 | 4.18363 | 4.21494 |
| 5 | 5.10101 | 5.15227 | 5.20404 | 5.25633 | 5.30914 | 5.36247 |
| 6 | 6.15202 | 6.22955 | 6.30812 | 6.38774 | 6.46841 | 6.55015 |
| 7 | 7.21354 | 7.32299 | 7.43428 | 7.54743 | 7.66246 | 7.77941 |
| 8 | 8.28567 | 8.43284 | 8.58297 | 8.73612 | 8.89234 | 9.05169 |
| 9 | 9.36853 | 9.55933 | 9.75463 | 9.95452 | 10.15911 | 10.36850 |
| 10 | 10.46221 | 10.70272 | 10.94972 | 11.20338 | 11.46388 | 11.73139 |
| 11 | 11.56683 | 11.86326 | 12.16872 | 12.48347 | 12.80780 | 13.14199 |
| 12 | 12.68250 | 13.04121 | 13.41209 | 13.79555 | 14.19203 | 14.60196 |
| 13 | 13.80933 | 14.23683 | 14.68033 | 15.14044 | 15.61779 | 16.11303 |
| 14 | 14.94742 | 15.45038 | 15.97394 | 16.51895 | 17.08632 | 17.67699 |
| 15 | 16.09690 | 16.68214 | 17.29342 | 17.93193 | 18.59891 | 19.29568 |
| 16 | 17.25786 | 17.93237 | 18.63929 | 18.38022 | 20.15688 | 20.97103 |
| 17 | 18.43044 | 19.20136 | 20.01207 | 20.86473 | 21.76159 | 22.70502 |
| 18 | 19.61475 | 20.48938 | 21.41231 | 22.38635 | 23.41444 | 24.49969 |
| 19 | 20.81090 | 21.79672 | 22.84056 | 23.94601 | 25.11687 | 26.35718 |
| 20 | 22.01900 | 23.12367 | 24.29737 | 25.54466 | 26.87037 | 28.27968 |
| 21 | 23.23919 | 24.47052 | 25.78332 | 27.18327 | 28.67649 | 30.26947 |
| 22 | 24.47159 | 25.83758 | 27.29898 | 28.86286 | 30.53678 | 32.32890 |
| 23 | 25.71630 | 27.22514 | 28.84496 | 30.58443 | 32.45288 | 34.46041 |
| 24 | 26.97346 | 28.63352 | 30.42186 | 32.34904 | 34.42647 | 36.66653 |
| 25 | 28.24320 | 30.06302 | 32.03030 | 34.15776 | 36.45926 | 38.94986 |
| 26 | 29.52563 | 31.51397 | 33.67091 | 36.01171 | 38.55304 | 41.31310 |
| 27 | 30.82089 | 32.98668 | 35.34432 | 37.91200 | 40.70963 | 43.75906 |
| 28 | 32.12910 | 34.48148 | 37.05121 | 39.85980 | 42.93092 | 46.29063 |
| 29 | 33.45039 | 35.99870 | 38.79223 | 41.85630 | 45.21885 | 48.91080 |
| 30 | 34.78489 | 37.53868 | 40.56808 | 43.90270 | 47.57542 | 51.62268 |
| 31 | 36.13274 | 39.10176 | 42.37944 | 46.00027 | 50.00268 | 54.42947 |
| 32 | 37.49407 | 40.68829 | 44.22703 | 48.15028 | 52.50276 | 57.33450 |
| 33 | 38.86901 | 42.29861 | 46.11157 | 50.35403 | 55.07784 | 60.34121 |
| 34 | 40.25770 | 43.93309 | 48.03380 | 52.61289 | 57.73018 | 63.45315 |
| 35 | 41.66028 | 45.59209 | 49.99448 | 54.92821 | 60.46208 | 66.67401 |
| 36 | 43.07688 | 47.27597 | 51.99437 | 57.30141 | 63.27594 | 70.00760 |
| 37 | 44.50765 | 48.98511 | 54.03425 | 59.73395 | 66.17422 | 73.45787 |
| 38 | 45.95272 | 50.71989 | 56.11494 | 62.22730 | 69.15945 | 77.02889 |
| 39 | 47.41225 | 52.48068 | 58.23724 | 64.78298 | 72.23423 | 80.72491 |
| 40 | 48.88637 | 54.26789 | 60.40198 | 67.40255 | 75.40126 | 84.55028 |
| 41 | 50.37524 | 56.08191 | 62.61002 | 70.08762 | 78.66330 | 88.50954 |
| 42 | 51.87899 | 57.92314 | 64.86222 | 72.83981 | 82.02320 | 92.60737 |
| 43 | 53.39778 | 59.79199 | 67.15947 | 75.66080 | 85.48389 | 96.84863 |
| 44 | 54.93176 | 61.68887 | 69.50266 | 78.55232 | 89.04841 | 101.23833 |
| 45 | 56.48107 | 63.61420 | 71.89271 | 81.51613 | 92.71986 | 105.78167 |
| 46 | 58.04589 | 65.56841 | 74.33056 | 84.55403 | 96.50146 | 110.48403 |
| 47 | 59.62634 | 67.55194 | 76.81718 | 87.66789 | 100.39650 | 115.35097 |
| 48 | 61.22261 | 69.56522 | 79.35352 | 90.85958 | 104.40840 | 120.38826 |
| 49 | 62.83483 | 71.60870 | 81.94059 | 94.13107 | 108.54065 | 125.60185 |
| 50 | 64.46318 | 73.68283 | 84.57940 | 97.48435 | 112.79687 | 130.99791 |
| 51 | 66.10781 | 75.78807 | 87.27099 | 100.92146 | 117.18077 | 136.58284 |
| 52 | 67.76889 | 77.92489 | 90.01641 | 104.44449 | 121.69620 | 142.36324 |
| 53 | 69.44658 | 80.09376 | 92.81674 | 108.05561 | 126.34708 | 148.34595 |
| 54 | 71.14105 | 82.29517 | 95.67307 | 111.75700 | 131.13749 | 154.53806 |
| 55 | 72.85246 | 84.52960 | 98.58653 | 115.55092 | 136.07162 | 160.94689 |
| 56 | 74.58098 | 86.79754 | 101.55826 | 119.43969 | 141.15377 | 167.58003 |
| 57 | 76.32679 | 89.09951 | 104.58943 | 123.42569 | 146.38838 | 174.44533 |
| 58 | 78.09006 | 91.43600 | 107.68122 | 127.51133 | 151.78003 | 181.55092 |
| 59 | 79.87096 | 93.80754 | 110.83484 | 131.69911 | 151.33343 | 188.90520 |
| 60 | 81.66967 | 96.21465 | 114.05154 | 135.99159 | 163.05344 | 196.51688 |

**Table A-4** $s_{\overline{n}|i}$ **(Continued)**

| | | | $i$ | | | |
|---|---|---|---|---|---|---|
| $n$: | 0.04 (4%) | 0.045 ($4\frac{1}{2}$%) | 0.05 (5%) | 0.06 (6%) | 0.07 (7%) | 0.08 (8%) |
| 1 | 1.00000 | 1.00000 | 1.00000 | 1.00000 | 1.00000 | 1.00000 |
| 2 | 2.04000 | 2.04500 | 2.05000 | 2.06000 | 2.07000 | 2.08000 |
| 3 | 3.12160 | 3.13702 | 3.15250 | 3.18360 | 3.21490 | 3.24640 |
| 4 | 4.24646 | 4.27819 | 4.31012 | 4.37462 | 4.43994 | 4.50611 |
| 5 | 5.41632 | 5.47071 | 5.52563 | 5.63709 | 5.75074 | 5.86660 |
| 6 | 6.63298 | 6.71689 | 6.80191 | 6.97532 | 7.15329 | 7.33593 |
| 7 | 7.89829 | 8.01915 | 8.14201 | 8,39384 | 8.65402 | 8.92280 |
| 8 | 9.21423 | 9.38001 | 9.54911 | 9.89747 | 10.25980 | 10.63663 |
| 9 | 10.58280 | 10.80211 | 11.02656 | 11.49132 | 11.97799 | 12.48756 |
| 10 | 12.00611 | 12.28821 | 12.57789 | 13.18079 | 13.81645 | 14.48656 |
| 11 | 13.48635 | 13.84118 | 14.20679 | 14.97164 | 15.78360 | 16.64549 |
| 12 | 15.02581 | 15.46403 | 15.91713 | 16.86994 | 17.88845 | 18.97713 |
| 13 | 16.62684 | 17.15991 | 17.71298 | 18.88214 | 20.14064 | 21.49530 |
| 14 | 18.29191 | 18.93211 | 19.59863 | 21.01507 | 22.55049 | 24.21492 |
| 15 | 20.02359 | 20.78405 | 21.57856 | 23.27597 | 25.12902 | 27.15211 |
| 16 | 21.82453 | 22.71934 | 23.65749 | 25.67253 | 27.88805 | 30.32428 |
| 17 | 23.69751 | 24.74171 | 25.84037 | 28.21288 | 30.84022 | 33.75023 |
| 18 | 25.64541 | 26.85508 | 28.13238 | 30.90565 | 33.99903 | 37.45024 |
| 19 | 27.67123 | 29.06356 | 30.53900 | 33.75999 | 37.37896 | 41.44626 |
| 20 | 29.77808 | 31.37142 | 33.06595 | 36.78559 | 40.99549 | 45.76196 |
| 21 | 31.96920 | 33.78314 | 35.71925 | 39.99273 | 44.86518 | 50.42292 |
| 22 | 34.24797 | 36.30338 | 38.50521 | 43.39229 | 49.00574 | 55.45676 |
| 23 | 36.61789 | 38.93703 | 41.43048 | 46.99583 | 53.43614 | 60.89330 |
| 24 | 39.08260 | 41.68920 | 44.50200 | 50.81558 | 58.17667 | 66.76476 |
| 25 | 41.64591 | 44.56521 | 47.72710 | 54.86451 | 63.24904 | 73.10594 |
| 26 | 44.31174 | 47.57064 | 51.11345 | 59.15638 | 68.67647 | 79.95442 |
| 27 | 47.08421 | 50.71132 | 54.66913 | 63.70577 | 74.48382 | 87.35077 |
| 28 | 49.96758 | 53.99333 | 58.40258 | 68.52811 | 80.69769 | 95.33883 |
| 29 | 52.96629 | 57.42303 | 62.32271 | 73.63980 | 87.34653 | 103.96594 |
| 30 | 56.08494 | 61.00707 | 66.43885 | 79.05819 | 94.46079 | 113.28321 |
| 31 | 59.32834 | 64.75239 | 70.76079 | 84.80168 | 102.07304 | 123.34587 |
| 32 | 62.70147 | 68.66625 | 75.29883 | 90.88978 | 110.21815 | 134.21354 |
| 33 | 66.20954 | 72.75623 | 80.06377 | 97.34316 | 118.93343 | 145.95062 |
| 34 | 69.85791 | 77.03026 | 85.06696 | 104.18375 | 128.25876 | 158.62667 |
| 35 | 73.65222 | 81.49662 | 90.32031 | 111.43478 | 138.23688 | 172.31680 |
| 36 | 77.59831 | 86.16397 | 95.83632 | 119.12087 | 148.91346 | 187.10215 |
| 37 | 81.70225 | 91.04134 | 101.62814 | 127.26812 | 160.33740 | 203.07032 |
| 38 | 85.97034 | 96.13820 | 107.70955 | 135.90421 | 172.56102 | 220.31595 |
| 39 | 90.40915 | 101.46442 | 114.09502 | 145.05846 | 185.64029 | 238.94122 |
| 40 | 95.02552 | 107.03032 | 120.79977 | 154.76197 | 199.63511 | 259.05652 |
| 41 | 99.82654 | 112.84669 | 127.83976 | 165.04768 | 214.60957 | 280.78104 |
| 42 | 104.81960 | 118.92479 | 135.23175 | 175.95054 | 230.63224 | 304.24352 |
| 43 | 110.01238 | 125.27640 | 142.99334 | 187.50758 | 247.77650 | 329.58301 |
| 44 | 115.41288 | 131.91384 | 151.14301 | 199.75803 | 266.12085 | 356.94965 |
| 45 | 121.02939 | 138.84997 | 159.70016 | 212.74351 | 285.74931 | 386.50562 |
| 46 | 126.87057 | 146.09821 | 168.68516 | 226.50812 | 306.75176 | 418.42607 |
| 47 | 132.94539 | 153.67263 | 178.11942 | 241.09861 | 329.22439 | 452.90015 |
| 48 | 139.26321 | 161.58790 | 188.02539 | 256.56453 | 353.27009 | 490.13216 |
| 49 | 145.83373 | 169.85936 | 198.42666 | 272.95840 | 378.99900 | 530.34274 |
| 50 | 152.66708 | 178.50303 | 209.34800 | 290.33590 | 406.52893 | 573.77016 |
| 51 | 159.77377 | 187.53566 | 220.81540 | 308.75606 | 435.98595 | 620.67177 |
| 52 | 167.16472 | 196.97477 | 232.85617 | 328.28142 | 467.50497 | 671.32551 |
| 53 | 174.85131 | 206.83863 | 245.49897 | 348.97831 | 501.23032 | 726.03155 |
| 54 | 182.84536 | 217.14637 | 258.77392 | 370.91701 | 537.31644 | 785.11408 |
| 55 | 191.15917 | 227.91796 | 272.71262 | 394.17203 | 575.92859 | 848.92320 |
| 56 | 199.80554 | 239.17427 | 287.34825 | 418.82235 | 617.24359 | 917.83706 |
| 57 | 208.79776 | 250.93711 | 302.71566 | 444.95169 | 661.45065 | 992.26402 |
| 58 | 218.14967 | 263.22928 | 318.85144 | 472.64879 | 708.75219 | 1072.64514 |
| 59 | 227.87566 | 276.07460 | 335.79402 | 502.00772 | 759.36484 | 1159.45676 |
| 60 | 237.99069 | 289.49795 | 353.58372 | 533.12818 | 813.52038 | 1253.21330 |

**Table A-5** $\dfrac{1}{s_{\overline{n}|i}}$

| | | | $i$ | | | |
|---|---|---|---|---|---|---|
| $n$: | 0.01 (1%) | 0.015 (1½%) | 0.02 (2%) | 0.025 (2½%) | 0.03 (3%) | 0.035 (3½%) |
| 1 | 1.00000 | 1.00000 | 1.00000 | 1.00000 | 1.00000 | 1.00000 |
| 2 | 0.49751 | 0.49628 | 0.49505 | 0.49383 | 0.49261 | 0.49140 |
| 3 | 0.33002 | 0.32838 | 0.32675 | 0.32514 | 0.32353 | 0.32193 |
| 4 | 0.24628 | 0.24444 | 0.24262 | 0.24082 | 0.23903 | 0.23725 |
| 5 | 0.19604 | 0.19409 | 0.19216 | 0.19025 | 0.18835 | 0.18648 |
| 6 | 0.16255 | 0.16053 | 0.15853 | 0.15655 | 0.15460 | 0.15267 |
| 7 | 0.13863 | 0.13656 | 0.13451 | 0.13250 | 0.13051 | 0.12854 |
| 8 | 0.12069 | 0.11858 | 0.11651 | 0.11447 | 0.11246 | 0.11048 |
| 9 | 0.10674 | 0.10461 | 0.10252 | 0.10046 | 0.09843 | 0.09645 |
| 10 | 0.09558 | 0.09343 | 0.09133 | 0.08926 | 0.08723 | 0.08524 |
| 11 | 0.08645 | 0.08429 | 0.08218 | 0.08011 | 0.07808 | 0.07609 |
| 12 | 0.07885 | 0.07668 | 0.07456 | 0.07249 | 0.07046 | 0.06848 |
| 13 | 0.07241 | 0.07024 | 0.06812 | 0.06605 | 0.06403 | 0.06206 |
| 14 | 0.06690 | 0.06472 | 0.06260 | 0.06054 | 0.05853 | 0.05657 |
| 15 | 0.06212 | 0.05994 | 0.05783 | 0.05577 | 0.05377 | 0.05183 |
| 16 | 0.05794 | 0.05577 | 0.05365 | 0.05160 | 0.04961 | 0.04768 |
| 17 | 0.05426 | 0.05208 | 0.04997 | 0.04793 | 0.04595 | 0.04404 |
| 18 | 0.05098 | 0.04881 | 0.04670 | 0.04467 | 0.04271 | 0.04082 |
| 19 | 0.04805 | 0.04588 | 0.04378 | 0.04176 | 0.03981 | 0.03794 |
| 20 | 0.04542 | 0.04325 | 0.04116 | 0.03915 | 0.03722 | 0.03536 |
| 21 | 0.04303 | 0.04087 | 0.03878 | 0.03679 | 0.03487 | 0.03304 |
| 22 | 0.04086 | 0.03870 | 0.03663 | 0.03465 | 0.03275 | 0.03093 |
| 23 | 0.03889 | 0.03673 | 0.03467 | 0.03270 | 0.03081 | 0.02902 |
| 24 | 0.03707 | 0.03492 | 0.03287 | 0.03091 | 0.02905 | 0.02727 |
| 25 | 0.03541 | 0.03326 | 0.03122 | 0.02928 | 0.02743 | 0.02567 |
| 26 | 0.03387 | 0.03173 | 0.02970 | 0.02777 | 0.02594 | 0.02421 |
| 27 | 0.03245 | 0.03032 | 0.02829 | 0.02638 | 0.02456 | 0.02285 |
| 28 | 0.03112 | 0.02900 | 0.02699 | 0.02509 | 0.02329 | 0.02160 |
| 29 | 0.02990 | 0.02778 | 0.02578 | 0.02389 | 0.02211 | 0.02045 |
| 30 | 0.02875 | 0.02664 | 0.02465 | 0.02278 | 0.02102 | 0.01937 |
| 31 | 0.02768 | 0.02557 | 0.02360 | 0.02174 | 0.02000 | 0.01837 |
| 32 | 0.02667 | 0.02458 | 0.02261 | 0.02077 | 0.01905 | 0.01744 |
| 33 | 0.02573 | 0.02364 | 0.02169 | 0.01986 | 0.01816 | 0.01657 |
| 34 | 0.02484 | 0.02276 | 0.02082 | 0.01901 | 0.01732 | 0.01576 |
| 35 | 0.02400 | 0.02193 | 0.02000 | 0.01821 | 0.01654 | 0.01500 |
| 36 | 0.02321 | 0.02115 | 0.01923 | 0.01745 | 0.01580 | 0.01428 |
| 37 | 0.02247 | 0.02041 | 0.01851 | 0.01674 | 0.01511 | 0.01361 |
| 38 | 0.02176 | 0.01972 | 0.01782 | 0.01607 | 0.01446 | 0.01298 |
| 39 | 0.02109 | 0.01905 | 0.01717 | 0.01544 | 0.01384 | 0.01239 |
| 40 | 0.02046 | 0.01843 | 0.01656 | 0.01484 | 0.01326 | 0.01183 |
| 41 | 0.01985 | 0.01783 | 0.01597 | 0.01427 | 0.01271 | 0.01130 |
| 42 | 0.01928 | 0.01726 | 0.01542 | 0.01373 | 0.01219 | 0.01080 |
| 43 | 0.01873 | 0.01672 | 0.01489 | 0.01322 | 0.01170 | 0.01033 |
| 44 | 0.01820 | 0.01621 | 0.01439 | 0.01273 | 0.01123 | 0.00988 |
| 45 | 0.01771 | 0.01572 | 0.01391 | 0.01227 | 0.01079 | 0.00945 |
| 46 | 0.01723 | 0.01525 | 0.01345 | 0.01183 | 0.01036 | 0.00905 |
| 47 | 0.01677 | 0.01480 | 0.01302 | 0.01141 | 0.00996 | 0.00867 |
| 48 | 0.01633 | 0.01437 | 0.01260 | 0.01101 | 0.00958 | 0.00831 |
| 49 | 0.01591 | 0.01396 | 0.01220 | 0.01062 | 0.00921 | 0.00796 |
| 50 | 0.01551 | 0.01357 | 0.01182 | 0.01026 | 0.00887 | 0.00763 |
| 51 | 0.01513 | 0.01319 | 0.01146 | 0.00991 | 0.00853 | 0.00732 |
| 52 | 0.01476 | 0.01283 | 0.01111 | 0.00957 | 0.00822 | 0.00702 |
| 53 | 0.01440 | 0.01249 | 0.01077 | 0.00925 | 0.00791 | 0.00674 |
| 54 | 0.01406 | 0.01215 | 0.01045 | 0.00895 | 0.00763 | 0.00647 |
| 55 | 0.01373 | 0.01183 | 0.01014 | 0.00865 | 0.00735 | 0.00621 |
| 56 | 0.01341 | 0.01152 | 0.00985 | 0.00837 | 0.00708 | 0.00597 |
| 57 | 0.01310 | 0.01122 | 0.00956 | 0.00810 | 0.00683 | 0.00573 |
| 58 | 0.01281 | 0.01094 | 0.00929 | 0.00784 | 0.00659 | 0.00551 |
| 59 | 0.01252 | 0.01066 | 0.00902 | 0.00759 | 0.00636 | 0.00529 |
| 60 | 0.01224 | 0.01039 | 0.00877 | 0.00735 | 0.00613 | 0.00509 |

**Table A-5** $\dfrac{1}{s_{\overline{n}|i}}$ **(Continued)**

| | | | $i$ | | | |
|---|---|---|---|---|---|---|
| $n$: | 0.04 (4%) | 0.045 (4½%) | 0.05 (5%) | 0.06 (6%) | 0.07 (7%) | 0.08 (8%) |
| 1 | 1.00000 | 1.00000 | 1.00000 | 1.00000 | 1.00000 | 1.00000 |
| 2 | 0.49020 | 0.48900 | 0.48780 | 0.48544 | 0.48309 | 0.48077 |
| 3 | 0.32035 | 0.31877 | 0.31721 | 0.31411 | 0.31105 | 0.30803 |
| 4 | 0.23549 | 0.23374 | 0.23201 | 0.22859 | 0.22523 | 0.22192 |
| 5 | 0.18463 | 0.18279 | 0.18097 | 0.17740 | 0.17389 | 0.17046 |
| 6 | 0.15076 | 0.14888 | 0.14702 | 0.14336 | 0.13980 | 0.13632 |
| 7 | 0.12661 | 0.12470 | 0.12282 | 0.11914 | 0.11555 | 0.11207 |
| 8 | 0.10853 | 0.10661 | 0.10472 | 0.10104 | 0.09747 | 0.09401 |
| 9 | 0.09449 | 0.09257 | 0.09069 | 0.08702 | 0.08349 | 0.08008 |
| 10 | 0.08329 | 0.08138 | 0.07950 | 0.07587 | 0.07238 | 0.06903 |
| 11 | 0.07415 | 0.07225 | 0.07039 | 0.06679 | 0.06336 | 0.06008 |
| 12 | 0.06655 | 0.06467 | 0.06283 | 0.05928 | 0.05590 | 0.05270 |
| 13 | 0.06014 | 0.05828 | 0.05646 | 0.05296 | 0.04965 | 0.04652 |
| 14 | 0.05467 | 0.05282 | 0.05102 | 0.04758 | 0.04434 | 0.04130 |
| 15 | 0.04994 | 0.04811 | 0.04634 | 0.04296 | 0.03979 | 0.03683 |
| 16 | 0.04582 | 0.04402 | 0.04227 | 0.03895 | 0.03586 | 0.03298 |
| 17 | 0.04220 | 0.04042 | 0.03870 | 0.03544 | 0.03243 | 0.02963 |
| 18 | 0.03899 | 0.03724 | 0.03555 | 0.03236 | 0.02941 | 0.02670 |
| 19 | 0.03614 | 0.03441 | 0.03275 | 0.02962 | 0.02675 | 0.02413 |
| 20 | 0.03358 | 0.03188 | 0.03024 | 0.02718 | 0.02439 | 0.02185 |
| 21 | 0.03128 | 0.02960 | 0.02800 | 0.02500 | 0.02229 | 0.01983 |
| 22 | 0.02920 | 0.02755 | 0.02597 | 0.02305 | 0.02041 | 0.01803 |
| 23 | 0.02731 | 0.02568 | 0.02414 | 0.02128 | 0.01871 | 0.01642 |
| 24 | 0.02559 | 0.02399 | 0.02247 | 0.01968 | 0.01719 | 0.01498 |
| 25 | 0.02401 | 0.02244 | 0.02095 | 0.01823 | 0.01581 | 0.01368 |
| 26 | 0.02257 | 0.02102 | 0.01956 | 0.01690 | 0.01456 | 0.01251 |
| 27 | 0.02124 | 0.01972 | 0.01829 | 0.01570 | 0.01343 | 0.01145 |
| 28 | 0.02001 | 0.01852 | 0.01712 | 0.01459 | 0.01239 | 0.01049 |
| 29 | 0.01888 | 0.01741 | 0.01605 | 0.01358 | 0.01145 | 0.00962 |
| 30 | 0.01783 | 0.01639 | 0.01505 | 0.01265 | 0.01059 | 0.00883 |
| 31 | 0.01686 | 0.01544 | 0.01413 | 0.01179 | 0.00980 | 0.00811 |
| 32 | 0.01595 | 0.01456 | 0.01328 | 0.01100 | 0.00907 | 0.00745 |
| 33 | 0.01510 | 0.01374 | 0.01249 | 0.01027 | 0.00841 | 0.00685 |
| 34 | 0.01431 | 0.01298 | 0.01176 | 0.00960 | 0.00780 | 0.00630 |
| 35 | 0.01358 | 0.01227 | 0.01107 | 0.00897 | 0.00723 | 0.00580 |
| 36 | 0.01289 | 0.01161 | 0.01043 | 0.00839 | 0.00672 | 0.00534 |
| 37 | 0.01224 | 0.01098 | 0.00984 | 0.00786 | 0.00624 | 0.00492 |
| 38 | 0.01163 | 0.01040 | 0.00928 | 0.00736 | 0.00580 | 0.00454 |
| 39 | 0.01106 | 0.00986 | 0.00876 | 0.00689 | 0.00539 | 0.00419 |
| 40 | 0.01052 | 0.00934 | 0.00828 | 0.00646 | 0.00501 | 0.00386 |
| 41 | 0.01002 | 0.00886 | 0.00782 | 0.00606 | 0.00466 | 0.00356 |
| 42 | 0.00954 | 0.00841 | 0.00739 | 0.00568 | 0.00434 | 0.00329 |
| 43 | 0.00909 | 0.00798 | 0.00699 | 0.00533 | 0.00404 | 0.00303 |
| 44 | 0.00866 | 0.00758 | 0.00662 | 0.00501 | 0.00376 | 0.00280 |
| 45 | 0.00826 | 0.00720 | 0.00626 | 0.00470 | 0.00350 | 0.00259 |
| 46 | 0.00788 | 0.00684 | 0.00593 | 0.00441 | 0.00326 | 0.00239 |
| 47 | 0.00752 | 0.00651 | 0.00561 | 0.00415 | 0.00304 | 0.00221 |
| 48 | 0.00718 | 0.00619 | 0.00532 | 0.00390 | 0.00283 | 0.00204 |
| 49 | 0.00686 | 0.00589 | 0.00504 | 0.00366 | 0.00264 | 0.00189 |
| 50 | 0.00655 | 0.00560 | 0.00478 | 0.00344 | 0.00246 | 0.00174 |
| 51 | 0.00626 | 0.00533 | 0.00453 | 0.00324 | 0.00229 | 0.00161 |
| 52 | 0.00598 | 0.00508 | 0.00429 | 0.00305 | 0.00214 | 0.00149 |
| 53 | 0.00572 | 0.00483 | 0.00407 | 0.00287 | 0.00200 | 0.00138 |
| 54 | 0.00547 | 0.00461 | 0.00386 | 0.00270 | 0.00186 | 0.00127 |
| 55 | 0.00523 | 0.00439 | 0.00367 | 0.00254 | 0.00174 | 0.00118 |
| 56 | 0.00500 | 0.00418 | 0.00348 | 0.00239 | 0.00162 | 0.00109 |
| 57 | 0.00479 | 0.00399 | 0.00330 | 0.00225 | 0.00151 | 0.00101 |
| 58 | 0.00458 | 0.00380 | 0.00314 | 0.00212 | 0.00141 | 0.00093 |
| 59 | 0.00439 | 0.00362 | 0.00298 | 0.00199 | 0.00132 | 0.00086 |
| 60 | 0.00420 | 0.00345 | 0.00283 | 0.00188 | 0.00123 | 0.00080 |

**Table A-6** $\quad a_{\overline{n}|i} = \dfrac{1 - (1+i)^{-n}}{i}$

| | | | | $i$ | | |
|---|---|---|---|---|---|---|
| $n$: | 0.01 (1%) | 0.015 ($1\frac{1}{2}$%) | 0.02 (2%) | 0.025 ($2\frac{1}{2}$%) | 0.03 (3%) | 0.035 ($3\frac{1}{2}$%) |
| 1 | 0.99010 | 0.98522 | 0.98039 | 0.97561 | 0.97087 | 0.96618 |
| 2 | 1.97040 | 1.95588 | 1.94156 | 1.92742 | 1.91347 | 1.89969 |
| 3 | 2.94099 | 2.91220 | 2.88388 | 2.85602 | 2.82861 | 2.80164 |
| 4 | 3.90197 | 3.85438 | 3.80773 | 3.76197 | 3.71710 | 3.67308 |
| 5 | 4.85343 | 4.78264 | 4.71346 | 4.64583 | 4.57971 | 4.51505 |
| 6 | 5.79548 | 5.69719 | 5.60143 | 5.50813 | 5.41719 | 5.32855 |
| 7 | 6.72819 | 6.59821 | 6.47199 | 6.34939 | 6.23028 | 6.11454 |
| 8 | 7.65168 | 7.48593 | 7.32548 | 7.17014 | 7.01969 | 6.87396 |
| 9 | 8.56602 | 8.36052 | 8.16224 | 7.97087 | 7.78611 | 7.60769 |
| 10 | 9.47130 | 9.22218 | 8.98259 | 8.75206 | 8.53020 | 8.31661 |
| 11 | 10.36763 | 10.07112 | 9.78685 | 9.51421 | 9.25262 | 9.00155 |
| 12 | 11.25508 | 10.90751 | 10.57534 | 10.25776 | 9.95400 | 9.66333 |
| 13 | 12.13374 | 11.73153 | 11.34837 | 10.98318 | 10.63496 | 10.30274 |
| 14 | 13.00370 | 12.54338 | 12.10625 | 11.69091 | 11.29607 | 10.92052 |
| 15 | 13.86505 | 13.34323 | 12.84926 | 12.38138 | 11.93794 | 11.51741 |
| 16 | 14.71787 | 14.13126 | 13.57771 | 13.05500 | 12.56110 | 12.09412 |
| 17 | 15.56225 | 14.90765 | 14.29187 | 13.71220 | 13.16612 | 12.65132 |
| 18 | 16.39827 | 15.67256 | 14.99203 | 14.35336 | 13.75351 | 13.18968 |
| 19 | 17.22601 | 16.42617 | 15.67846 | 14.97889 | 14.32380 | 13.70984 |
| 20 | 18.04555 | 17.16864 | 16.35143 | 15.58916 | 14.87747 | 14.21240 |
| 21 | 18.85698 | 17.90014 | 17.01121 | 16.18455 | 15.41502 | 14.69797 |
| 22 | 19.66038 | 18.62082 | 17.65805 | 16.76541 | 15.93692 | 15.16712 |
| 23 | 20.45582 | 19.33086 | 18.29220 | 17.33211 | 16.44361 | 15.62041 |
| 24 | 21.24339 | 20.03041 | 18.91393 | 17.88499 | 16.93554 | 16.05837 |
| 25 | 22.02316 | 20.71961 | 19.52346 | 18.42438 | 17.41315 | 16.48151 |
| 26 | 22.79520 | 21.39863 | 20.12104 | 18.95061 | 17.87684 | 16.89035 |
| 27 | 23.55961 | 22.06562 | 20.70690 | 19.46401 | 18.32703 | 17.28536 |
| 28 | 24.31644 | 22.72672 | 21.28127 | 19.96489 | 18.76411 | 17.66702 |
| 29 | 25.06579 | 23.37608 | 21.84438 | 20.45355 | 19.18845 | 18.03577 |
| 30 | 25.80771 | 24.01584 | 22.39646 | 20.93029 | 19.60044 | 18.39205 |
| 31 | 26.54229 | 24.64615 | 22.93770 | 21.39541 | 20.00043 | 18.73628 |
| 32 | 27.26959 | 25.26714 | 23.46833 | 21.84918 | 20.38877 | 19.06887 |
| 33 | 27.98969 | 25.87895 | 23.98856 | 22.29188 | 20.76579 | 19.39021 |
| 34 | 28.70267 | 26.48173 | 24.49859 | 22.72379 | 21.13184 | 19.70068 |
| 35 | 29.40858 | 27.07559 | 24.99862 | 23.14516 | 21.48722 | 20.00066 |
| 36 | 30.10751 | 27.66068 | 25.48884 | 23.55625 | 21.83225 | 20.29049 |
| 37 | 30.79951 | 28.23713 | 25.96945 | 23.95732 | 22.16724 | 20.57053 |
| 38 | 31.48466 | 28.80505 | 26.44064 | 24.34860 | 22.49246 | 20.84109 |
| 39 | 32.16303 | 29.36458 | 26.90259 | 24.73034 | 22.80822 | 21.10250 |
| 40 | 32.83469 | 29.91585 | 27.35548 | 25.10278 | 23.11477 | 21.35507 |
| 41 | 33.49969 | 30.45896 | 27.79949 | 25.46612 | 23.41240 | 21.59910 |
| 42 | 34.15811 | 30.99405 | 28.23479 | 25.82061 | 23.70136 | 21.83486 |
| 43 | 34.81001 | 31.52123 | 28.66156 | 26.16645 | 23.98190 | 22.06269 |
| 44 | 35.45545 | 32.04062 | 29.07996 | 26.50385 | 24.25427 | 22.28279 |
| 45 | 36.09451 | 32.55234 | 29.49016 | 26.83302 | 24.51871 | 22.49545 |
| 46 | 36.72724 | 33.05649 | 29.89231 | 27.15417 | 24.77545 | 22.70092 |
| 47 | 37.35370 | 33.55319 | 30.28658 | 27.46748 | 25.02471 | 22.89944 |
| 48 | 37.97396 | 34.04255 | 30.67312 | 27.77315 | 25.26671 | 23.09124 |
| 49 | 38.58808 | 34.52468 | 31.05208 | 28.07137 | 25.50166 | 23.27656 |
| 50 | 39.19612 | 34.99969 | 31.42361 | 28.36231 | 25.72976 | 23.45562 |
| 51 | 39.79814 | 35.46767 | 31.78785 | 28.64616 | 25.95123 | 23.62862 |
| 52 | 40.39419 | 35.92874 | 32.14495 | 28.92308 | 26.16624 | 23.79576 |
| 53 | 40.98435 | 36.38300 | 32.49505 | 29.19325 | 26.37499 | 23.95726 |
| 54 | 41.56866 | 36.83054 | 32.83828 | 29.45683 | 26.57766 | 24.11330 |
| 55 | 42.14719 | 37.27147 | 33.17479 | 29.71398 | 26.77443 | 24.26405 |
| 56 | 42.71999 | 37.70588 | 33.50469 | 29.96486 | 26.96546 | 24.40971 |
| 57 | 43.28712 | 38.13387 | 33.82813 | 30.20962 | 27.15094 | 24.55045 |
| 58 | 43.84863 | 38.55554 | 34.14523 | 30.44841 | 27.33101 | 24.68642 |
| 59 | 44.40459 | 38.97097 | 34.45610 | 30.68137 | 27.50583 | 24.81780 |
| 60 | 44.95504 | 39.38027 | 34.76089 | 30.90866 | 27.67556 | 24.94473 |

**Table A-6**  $a_{\overline{n}|i}$ **(Continued)**

| | | | $i$ | | | |
|---|---|---|---|---|---|---|
| $n$: | 0.04 (4%) | 0.045 (4½%) | 0.05 (5%) | 0.06 (6%) | 0.07 (7%) | 0.08 (8%) |
| 1 | 0.96154 | 0.95694 | 0.95238 | 0.94340 | 0.93458 | 0.92593 |
| 2 | 1.88609 | 1.87267 | 1.85941 | 1.83339 | 1.80802 | 1.78326 |
| 3 | 2.77509 | 2.74896 | 2.72325 | 2.67301 | 2.62432 | 2.57710 |
| 4 | 3.62990 | 3.58753 | 3.54595 | 3.46511 | 3.38721 | 3.31213 |
| 5 | 4.45182 | 4.38998 | 4.32948 | 4.21236 | 4.10020 | 3.99271 |
| 6 | 5.24214 | 5.15787 | 5.07569 | 4.91732 | 4.76654 | 4.62288 |
| 7 | 6.00205 | 5.89270 | 5.78637 | 5.58238 | 5.38929 | 5.20637 |
| 8 | 6.73274 | 6.59589 | 6.46321 | 6.20979 | 5.97130 | 5.74664 |
| 9 | 7.43533 | 7.26879 | 7.10782 | 6.80169 | 6.51523 | 6.24689 |
| 10 | 8.11090 | 7.91272 | 7.72173 | 7.36009 | 7.02358 | 6.71008 |
| 11 | 8.76048 | 8.52892 | 8.30641 | 7.88687 | 7.49867 | 7.13896 |
| 12 | 9.38507 | 9.11858 | 8.86325 | 8.38384 | 7.94269 | 7.53608 |
| 13 | 9.98565 | 9.68285 | 9.39357 | 8.85268 | 8.35765 | 7.90378 |
| 14 | 10.56312 | 10.22283 | 9.89864 | 9.29498 | 8.74547 | 8.24424 |
| 15 | 11.11839 | 10.73955 | 10.37966 | 9.71225 | 9.10791 | 8.55948 |
| 16 | 11.65230 | 11.23402 | 10.83777 | 10.10590 | 9.44665 | 8.85137 |
| 17 | 12.16567 | 11.70719 | 11.27407 | 10.47726 | 9.76322 | 9.12164 |
| 18 | 12.65930 | 12.15999 | 11.68959 | 10.82760 | 10.05909 | 9.37189 |
| 19 | 13.13394 | 12.59329 | 12.08532 | 11.15812 | 10.33560 | 9.60360 |
| 20 | 13.59033 | 13.00794 | 12.46221 | 11.46992 | 10.59401 | 9.81815 |
| 21 | 14.02916 | 13.40472 | 12.82115 | 11.76408 | 10.83553 | 10.01680 |
| 22 | 14.45112 | 13.78442 | 13.16300 | 12.04158 | 11.06124 | 10.20074 |
| 23 | 14.85684 | 14.14777 | 13.48857 | 12.30338 | 11.27219 | 10.37106 |
| 24 | 15.24696 | 14.49548 | 13.79864 | 12.55036 | 11.46933 | 10.52876 |
| 25 | 15.62208 | 14.82821 | 14.09394 | 12.78336 | 11.65358 | 10.67478 |
| 26 | 15.98277 | 15.14661 | 14.37519 | 13.00317 | 11.82578 | 10.80998 |
| 27 | 16.32959 | 15.45130 | 14.64303 | 13.21053 | 11.98671 | 10.93516 |
| 28 | 16.66306 | 15.74287 | 14.89813 | 13.40616 | 12.13711 | 11.05108 |
| 29 | 16.98371 | 16.02189 | 15.14107 | 13.59072 | 12.27767 | 11.15841 |
| 30 | 17.29203 | 16.28889 | 15.37245 | 13.76483 | 12.40904 | 11.25778 |
| 31 | 17.58849 | 16.54439 | 15.59281 | 13.92909 | 12.53181 | 11.34980 |
| 32 | 17.87355 | 16.78889 | 15.80268 | 14.08404 | 12.64656 | 11.43500 |
| 33 | 18.14765 | 17.02286 | 16.00255 | 14.23023 | 12.75379 | 11.51389 |
| 34 | 18.41120 | 17.24676 | 16.19290 | 14.36814 | 12.85401 | 11.58693 |
| 35 | 18.66461 | 17.46101 | 16.37419 | 14.49825 | 12.94767 | 11.65457 |
| 36 | 18.90828 | 17.66604 | 16.54685 | 14.62099 | 13.03521 | 11.71719 |
| 37 | 19.14258 | 17.86224 | 16.71129 | 14.73678 | 13.11702 | 11.77518 |
| 38 | 19.36786 | 18.04999 | 16.86789 | 14.84602 | 13.19347 | 11.82887 |
| 39 | 19.58448 | 18.22966 | 17.01704 | 14.94907 | 13.26493 | 11.87858 |
| 40 | 19.79277 | 18.40158 | 17.15909 | 15.04630 | 13.33171 | 11.92461 |
| 41 | 19.99305 | 18.56611 | 17.29437 | 15.13802 | 13.39412 | 11.96723 |
| 42 | 20.18563 | 18.72355 | 17.42321 | 15.22454 | 13.45245 | 12.00670 |
| 43 | 20.37079 | 18.87421 | 17.54591 | 15.30617 | 13.50696 | 12.04324 |
| 44 | 20.54884 | 19.01838 | 17.66277 | 15.38318 | 13.55791 | 12.07707 |
| 45 | 20.72004 | 19.15635 | 17.77407 | 15.45583 | 13.60552 | 12.10840 |
| 46 | 20.88465 | 19.28837 | 17.88007 | 15.52437 | 13.65002 | 12.13741 |
| 47 | 21.04294 | 19.41471 | 17.98102 | 15.58903 | 13.69161 | 12.16427 |
| 48 | 21.19513 | 19.53561 | 18.07716 | 15.65003 | 13.73047 | 12.18914 |
| 49 | 21.34147 | 19.65130 | 18.16872 | 15.70757 | 13.76680 | 12.21216 |
| 50 | 21.48218 | 19.76201 | 18.25593 | 15.76186 | 13.80075 | 12.23348 |
| 51 | 21.61749 | 19.86795 | 18.33898 | 15.81308 | 13.83247 | 12.25323 |
| 52 | 21.74758 | 19.96933 | 18.41807 | 15.86139 | 13.86212 | 12.27151 |
| 53 | 21.87267 | 20.06634 | 18.49340 | 15.90697 | 13.88984 | 12.28843 |
| 54 | 21.99296 | 20.15918 | 18.56615 | 15.94998 | 13.91573 | 12.30410 |
| 55 | 22.10861 | 20.24802 | 18.63347 | 15.99054 | 13.93994 | 12.31861 |
| 56 | 22.21982 | 20.33303 | 18.69854 | 16.02881 | 13.96256 | 12.33205 |
| 57 | 22.32675 | 20.41439 | 18.76052 | 16.06492 | 13.98370 | 12.34449 |
| 58 | 22.42957 | 20.49224 | 18.81954 | 16.09898 | 14.00346 | 12.35601 |
| 59 | 22.52843 | 20.56673 | 18.87575 | 16.12111 | 14.02192 | 12.36668 |
| 60 | 22.62349 | 20.63802 | 18.92929 | 16.16143 | 14.03918 | 12.37655 |

*Source*: Hummel, P. and Seebeck, Jr., C., *Mathematics of Finance*, 2d ed., McGraw-Hill, New York, 1971, chap. 11, pp. T.16 to T.17. Reproduced with permission.

**Table A-7**  $\dfrac{1}{a_{\overline{n}|i}}$

| | | | $i$ | | | |
|---|---|---|---|---|---|---|
| $n$: | 0.01 (1%) | 0.015 ($1\frac{1}{2}$%) | 0.02 (2%) | 0.025 ($2\frac{1}{2}$%) | 0.03 (3%) | 0.035 ($3\frac{1}{2}$%) |
| 1 | 1.01000 | 1.01500 | 1.02000 | 1.02500 | 1.03000 | 1.03500 |
| 2 | 0.50751 | 0.51128 | 0.51505 | 0.51883 | 0.52261 | 0.52640 |
| 3 | 0.34002 | 0.34338 | 0.34675 | 0.35014 | 0.35353 | 0.35693 |
| 4 | 0.25628 | 0.25944 | 0.26262 | 0.26582 | 0.26903 | 0.27225 |
| 5 | 0.20604 | 0.20909 | 0.21216 | 0.21525 | 0.21835 | 0.22148 |
| 6 | 0.17255 | 0.17553 | 0.17853 | 0.18155 | 0.18460 | 0.18767 |
| 7 | 0.14863 | 0.15156 | 0.15451 | 0.15750 | 0.16051 | 0.16354 |
| 8 | 0.13069 | 0.13358 | 0.13651 | 0.13947 | 0.14246 | 0.14548 |
| 9 | 0.11674 | 0.11961 | 0.12252 | 0.12546 | 0.12843 | 0.13145 |
| 10 | 0.10558 | 0.10843 | 0.11133 | 0.11426 | 0.11723 | 0.12024 |
| 11 | 0.09645 | 0.09929 | 0.10218 | 0.10511 | 0.10808 | 0.11109 |
| 12 | 0.08885 | 0.09168 | 0.09456 | 0.09749 | 0.10046 | 0.10348 |
| 13 | 0.08241 | 0.08524 | 0.08812 | 0.09105 | 0.09403 | 0.09706 |
| 14 | 0.07690 | 0.07972 | 0.08260 | 0.08554 | 0.08853 | 0.09157 |
| 15 | 0.07212 | 0.07494 | 0.07783 | 0.08077 | 0.08377 | 0.08683 |
| 16 | 0.06794 | 0.07077 | 0.07365 | 0.07660 | 0.07961 | 0.08268 |
| 17 | 0.06426 | 0.06708 | 0.06997 | 0.07293 | 0.07595 | 0.07904 |
| 18 | 0.06098 | 0.06381 | 0.06670 | 0.06967 | 0.07271 | 0.07582 |
| 19 | 0.05805 | 0.06088 | 0.06378 | 0.06676 | 0.06981 | 0.07294 |
| 20 | 0.05542 | 0.05825 | 0.06116 | 0.06415 | 0.06722 | 0.07036 |
| 21 | 0.05303 | 0.05587 | 0.05878 | 0.06179 | 0.06487 | 0.06804 |
| 22 | 0.05086 | 0.05370 | 0.05663 | 0.05965 | 0.06275 | 0.06593 |
| 23 | 0.04889 | 0.05173 | 0.05467 | 0.05770 | 0.06081 | 0.06402 |
| 24 | 0.04707 | 0.04992 | 0.05287 | 0.05591 | 0.05905 | 0.06227 |
| 25 | 0.04541 | 0.04826 | 0.05122 | 0.05428 | 0.05743 | 0.06067 |
| 26 | 0.04387 | 0.04673 | 0.04970 | 0.05277 | 0.05594 | 0.05921 |
| 27 | 0.04245 | 0.04532 | 0.04829 | 0.05138 | 0.05456 | 0.05785 |
| 28 | 0.04112 | 0.04400 | 0.04699 | 0.05009 | 0.05329 | 0.05660 |
| 29 | 0.03990 | 0.04278 | 0.04578 | 0.04889 | 0.05211 | 0.05545 |
| 30 | 0.03875 | 0.04164 | 0.04465 | 0.04778 | 0.05102 | 0.05437 |
| 31 | 0.03768 | 0.04057 | 0.04360 | 0.04674 | 0.05000 | 0.05337 |
| 32 | 0.03667 | 0.03958 | 0.04261 | 0.04577 | 0.04905 | 0.05244 |
| 33 | 0.03573 | 0.03864 | 0.04169 | 0.04486 | 0.04816 | 0.05157 |
| 34 | 0.03484 | 0.03776 | 0.04082 | 0.04401 | 0.04732 | 0.05076 |
| 35 | 0.03400 | 0.03693 | 0.04000 | 0.04321 | 0.04654 | 0.05000 |
| 36 | 0.03321 | 0.03615 | 0.03923 | 0.04245 | 0.04580 | 0.04928 |
| 37 | 0.03247 | 0.03541 | 0.03851 | 0.04174 | 0.04511 | 0.04861 |
| 38 | 0.03176 | 0.03472 | 0.03782 | 0.04107 | 0.04446 | 0.04798 |
| 39 | 0.03109 | 0.03405 | 0.03717 | 0.04044 | 0.04384 | 0.04739 |
| 40 | 0.03046 | 0.03343 | 0.03656 | 0.03984 | 0.04326 | 0.04683 |
| 41 | 0.02985 | 0.03283 | 0.03597 | 0.03927 | 0.04271 | 0.04630 |
| 42 | 0.02928 | 0.03226 | 0.03542 | 0.03873 | 0.04219 | 0.04580 |
| 43 | 0.02873 | 0.03172 | 0.03489 | 0.03822 | 0.04170 | 0.04533 |
| 44 | 0.02820 | 0.03121 | 0.03439 | 0.03773 | 0.04123 | 0.04488 |
| 45 | 0.02771 | 0.03072 | 0.03391 | 0.03727 | 0.04079 | 0.04445 |
| 46 | 0.02723 | 0.03025 | 0.03345 | 0.03683 | 0.04036 | 0.04405 |
| 47 | 0.02677 | 0.02980 | 0.03302 | 0.03641 | 0.03996 | 0.04367 |
| 48 | 0.02633 | 0.02937 | 0.03260 | 0.03601 | 0.03958 | 0.04331 |
| 49 | 0.02591 | 0.02896 | 0.03220 | 0.03562 | 0.03921 | 0.04296 |
| 50 | 0.02551 | 0.02857 | 0.03182 | 0.03526 | 0.03887 | 0.04263 |
| 51 | 0.02513 | 0.02819 | 0.03146 | 0.03491 | 0.03853 | 0.04232 |
| 52 | 0.02476 | 0.02783 | 0.03111 | 0.03457 | 0.03822 | 0.04202 |
| 53 | 0.02440 | 0.02749 | 0.03077 | 0.03425 | 0.03791 | 0.04174 |
| 54 | 0.02406 | 0.02715 | 0.03045 | 0.03395 | 0.03763 | 0.04147 |
| 55 | 0.02373 | 0.02683 | 0.03014 | 0.03365 | 0.03735 | 0.04121 |
| 56 | 0.02341 | 0.02652 | 0.02985 | 0.03337 | 0.03708 | 0.04097 |
| 57 | 0.02310 | 0.02622 | 0.02956 | 0.03310 | 0.03683 | 0.04073 |
| 58 | 0.02281 | 0.02594 | 0.02929 | 0.03284 | 0.03659 | 0.04051 |
| 59 | 0.02252 | 0.02566 | 0.02902 | 0.03259 | 0.03636 | 0.04029 |
| 60 | 0.02224 | 0.02539 | 0.02877 | 0.03235 | 0.03613 | 0.04009 |

**Table A-7** $\dfrac{1}{a_{\overline{n}|i}}$ **(Continued)**

| | | | $i$ | | | |
|---|---|---|---|---|---|---|
| $n$: | 0.04 (4%) | 0.045 (4½%) | 0.05 (5%) | 0.06 (6%) | 0.07 (7%) | 0.08 (8%) |
| 1 | 1.04000 | 1.04500 | 1.05000 | 1.06000 | 1.07000 | 1.08000 |
| 2 | 0.53020 | 0.53400 | 0.53780 | 0.54544 | 0.55309 | 0.56077 |
| 3 | 0.36035 | 0.36377 | 0.36721 | 0.37411 | 0.38105 | 0.38803 |
| 4 | 0.27549 | 0.27874 | 0.28201 | 0.28859 | 0.29523 | 0.30192 |
| 5 | 0.22463 | 0.22779 | 0.23097 | 0.23740 | 0.24389 | 0.25046 |
| 6 | 0.19076 | 0.19388 | 0.19702 | 0.20336 | 0.20980 | 0.21632 |
| 7 | 0.16661 | 0.16970 | 0.17282 | 0.17914 | 0.18555 | 0.19207 |
| 8 | 0.14853 | 0.15161 | 0.15472 | 0.16104 | 0.16747 | 0.17401 |
| 9 | 0.13449 | 0.13757 | 0.14069 | 0.14702 | 0.15349 | 0.16008 |
| 10 | 0.12329 | 0.12638 | 0.12950 | 0.13587 | 0.14238 | 0.14903 |
| 11 | 0.11415 | 0.11725 | 0.12039 | 0.12679 | 0.13336 | 0.14008 |
| 12 | 0.10655 | 0.10967 | 0.11283 | 0.11928 | 0.12590 | 0.13270 |
| 13 | 0.10014 | 0.10328 | 0.10646 | 0.11296 | 0.11965 | 0.12652 |
| 14 | 0.09467 | 0.09782 | 0.10102 | 0.10758 | 0.11434 | 0.12130 |
| 15 | 0.08994 | 0.09311 | 0.09634 | 0.10296 | 0.10979 | 0.11683 |
| 16 | 0.08582 | 0.08902 | 0.09227 | 0.09895 | 0.10586 | 0.11298 |
| 17 | 0.08220 | 0.08542 | 0.08870 | 0.09544 | 0.10243 | 0.10963 |
| 18 | 0.07899 | 0.08224 | 0.08555 | 0.09236 | 0.09941 | 0.10670 |
| 19 | 0.07614 | 0.07941 | 0.08275 | 0.08962 | 0.09675 | 0.10413 |
| 20 | 0.07358 | 0.07688 | 0.08024 | 0.08718 | 0.09439 | 0.10185 |
| 21 | 0.07128 | 0.07460 | 0.07800 | 0.08500 | 0.09229 | 0.09983 |
| 22 | 0.06920 | 0.07255 | 0.07597 | 0.08305 | 0.09041 | 0.09803 |
| 23 | 0.06731 | 0.07068 | 0.07414 | 0.08128 | 0.08871 | 0.09642 |
| 24 | 0.06559 | 0.06899 | 0.07247 | 0.07968 | 0.08719 | 0.09498 |
| 25 | 0.06401 | 0.06744 | 0.07095 | 0.07823 | 0.08581 | 0.09368 |
| 26 | 0.06257 | 0.06602 | 0.06956 | 0.07690 | 0.08456 | 0.09251 |
| 27 | 0.06124 | 0.06472 | 0.06829 | 0.07570 | 0.08343 | 0.09145 |
| 28 | 0.06001 | 0.06352 | 0.06712 | 0.07459 | 0.08239 | 0.09049 |
| 29 | 0.05888 | 0.06241 | 0.06605 | 0.07358 | 0.08145 | 0.08962 |
| 30 | 0.05783 | 0.06139 | 0.06505 | 0.07265 | 0.08059 | 0.08883 |
| 31 | 0.05686 | 0.06044 | 0.06413 | 0.07179 | 0.07980 | 0.08811 |
| 32 | 0.05595 | 0.05956 | 0.06328 | 0.07100 | 0.07907 | 0.08745 |
| 33 | 0.05510 | 0.05874 | 0.06249 | 0.07027 | 0.07841 | 0.08685 |
| 34 | 0.05431 | 0.05798 | 0.06176 | 0.06960 | 0.07780 | 0.08630 |
| 35 | 0.05358 | 0.05727 | 0.06107 | 0.06897 | 0.07723 | 0.08580 |
| 36 | 0.05289 | 0.05661 | 0.06043 | 0.06839 | 0.07672 | 0.08534 |
| 37 | 0.05224 | 0.05598 | 0.05984 | 0.06786 | 0.07624 | 0.08492 |
| 38 | 0.05163 | 0.05540 | 0.05928 | 0.06736 | 0.07580 | 0.08454 |
| 39 | 0.05106 | 0.05486 | 0.05876 | 0.06689 | 0.07539 | 0.08419 |
| 40 | 0.05052 | 0.05434 | 0.05828 | 0.06646 | 0.07501 | 0.08386 |
| 41 | 0.05002 | 0.05386 | 0.05782 | 0.06606 | 0.07466 | 0.08356 |
| 42 | 0.04954 | 0.05341 | 0.05739 | 0.06568 | 0.07434 | 0.08329 |
| 43 | 0.04909 | 0.05298 | 0.05699 | 0.06533 | 0.07404 | 0.08303 |
| 44 | 0.04866 | 0.05258 | 0.05662 | 0.06501 | 0.07376 | 0.08280 |
| 45 | 0.04826 | 0.05220 | 0.05626 | 0.06470 | 0.07350 | 0.08259 |
| 46 | 0.04788 | 0.05184 | 0.05593 | 0.06441 | 0.07326 | 0.08239 |
| 47 | 0.04752 | 0.05151 | 0.05561 | 0.06415 | 0.07304 | 0.08221 |
| 48 | 0.04718 | 0.05119 | 0.05532 | 0.06390 | 0.07283 | 0.08204 |
| 49 | 0.04686 | 0.05089 | 0.05504 | 0.06366 | 0.07264 | 0.08189 |
| 50 | 0.04655 | 0.05060 | 0.05478 | 0.06344 | 0.07246 | 0.08174 |
| 51 | 0.04626 | 0.05033 | 0.05453 | 0.06324 | 0.07229 | 0.08161 |
| 52 | 0.04598 | 0.05008 | 0.05429 | 0.06305 | 0.07214 | 0.08149 |
| 53 | 0.04572 | 0.04983 | 0.05407 | 0.06287 | 0.07200 | 0.08138 |
| 54 | 0.04547 | 0.04961 | 0.05386 | 0.06270 | 0.07186 | 0.08127 |
| 55 | 0.04523 | 0.04939 | 0.05367 | 0.06254 | 0.07174 | 0.08118 |
| 56 | 0.04500 | 0.04918 | 0.05348 | 0.06239 | 0.07162 | 0.08109 |
| 57 | 0.04479 | 0.04899 | 0.05330 | 0.06225 | 0.07151 | 0.08101 |
| 58 | 0.04458 | 0.04880 | 0.05314 | 0.06212 | 0.07141 | 0.08093 |
| 59 | 0.04439 | 0.04862 | 0.05298 | 0.06199 | 0.07132 | 0.08086 |
| 60 | 0.04420 | 0.04845 | 0.05283 | 0.06188 | 0.07123 | 0.08080 |

*Source*: Hummel, P. and Seebeck, Jr., C., *Mathematics of Finance*, 2d ed., McGraw-Hill, New York, 1971, chap. 11, pp. T.20 to T.21. Reproduced with permission.

# Standard Normal Curve Areas

## STANDARD NORMAL CURVE AREAS

This table gives areas $\Phi(z)$ under the standard normal distribution $\phi$ between 0 and $z \geq 0$ in steps of 0.01.

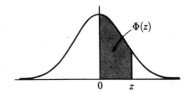

| z | 0 | 1 | 2 | 3 | 4 | 5 | 6 | 7 | 8 | 9 |
|---|---|---|---|---|---|---|---|---|---|---|
| 0.0 | .0000 | .0040 | .0080 | .0120 | .0160 | .0199 | .0239 | .0279 | .0319 | .0359 |
| 0.1 | .0398 | .0438 | .0478 | .0517 | .0557 | .0596 | .0636 | .0675 | .0714 | .0754 |
| 0.2 | .0793 | .0832 | .0871 | .0910 | .0948 | .0987 | .1026 | .1064 | .1103 | .1141 |
| 0.3 | .1179 | .1217 | .1255 | .1293 | .1331 | .1368 | .1406 | .1443 | .1480 | .1517 |
| 0.4 | .1554 | .1591 | .1628 | .1664 | .1700 | .1736 | .1772 | .1808 | .1844 | .1879 |
| 0.5 | .1915 | .1950 | .1985 | .2019 | .2054 | .2088 | .2123 | .2157 | .2190 | .2224 |
| 0.6 | .2258 | .2291 | .2324 | .2357 | .2389 | .2422 | .2454 | .2486 | .2518 | .2549 |
| 0.7 | .2580 | .2612 | .2642 | .2673 | .2704 | .2734 | .2764 | .2794 | .2823 | .2852 |
| 0.8 | .2881 | .2910 | .2939 | .2967 | .2996 | .3023 | .3051 | .3078 | .3106 | .3133 |
| 0.9 | .3159 | .3186 | .3212 | .3238 | .3264 | .3289 | .3315 | .3340 | .3365 | .3389 |
| 1.0 | .3413 | .3438 | .3461 | .3485 | .3508 | .3531 | .3554 | .3577 | .3599 | .3621 |
| 1.1 | .3643 | .3665 | .3686 | .3708 | .3729 | .3749 | .3770 | .3790 | .3810 | .3830 |
| 1.2 | .3849 | .3869 | .3888 | .3907 | .3925 | .3944 | .3962 | .3980 | .3997 | .4015 |
| 1.3 | .4032 | .4049 | .4066 | .4082 | .4099 | .4115 | .4131 | .4147 | .4162 | .4177 |
| 1.4 | .4192 | .4207 | .4222 | .4236 | .4251 | .4265 | .4279 | .4292 | .4306 | .4319 |
| 1.5 | .4332 | .4345 | .4357 | .4370 | .4382 | .4394 | .4406 | .4418 | .4429 | .4441 |
| 1.6 | .4452 | .4463 | .4474 | .4484 | .4495 | .4505 | .4515 | .4525 | .4535 | .4545 |
| 1.7 | .4554 | .4564 | .4573 | .4582 | .4591 | .4599 | .4608 | .4616 | .4625 | .4633 |
| 1.8 | .4641 | .4649 | .4656 | .4664 | .4671 | .4678 | .4686 | .4693 | .4699 | .4706 |
| 1.9 | .4713 | .4719 | .4726 | .4732 | .4738 | .4744 | .4750 | .4756 | .4761 | .4767 |
| 2.0 | .4772 | .4778 | .4783 | .4788 | .4793 | .4798 | .4803 | .4808 | .4812 | .4817 |
| 2.1 | .4821 | .4826 | .4830 | .4834 | .4838 | .4842 | .4846 | .4850 | .4854 | .4857 |
| 2.2 | .4861 | .4864 | .4868 | .4871 | .4875 | .4878 | .4881 | .4884 | .4887 | .4890 |
| 2.3 | .4893 | .4896 | .4898 | .4901 | .4904 | .4906 | .4909 | .4911 | .4913 | .4916 |
| 2.4 | .4918 | .4920 | .4922 | .4925 | .4927 | .4929 | .4931 | .4932 | .4934 | .4936 |
| 2.5 | .4938 | .4940 | .4941 | .4943 | .4945 | .4946 | .4948 | .4949 | .4951 | .4952 |
| 2.6 | .4953 | .4955 | .4956 | .4957 | .4959 | .4960 | .4961 | .4962 | .4963 | .4964 |
| 2.7 | .4965 | .4966 | .4967 | .4968 | .4969 | .4970 | .4971 | .4972 | .4973 | .4974 |
| 2.8 | .4974 | .4975 | .4976 | .4977 | .4977 | .4978 | .4979 | .4979 | .4980 | .4981 |
| 2.9 | .4981 | .4982 | .4982 | .4983 | .4984 | .4984 | .4985 | .4985 | .4986 | .4986 |
| 3.0 | .4987 | .4987 | .4987 | .4988 | .4988 | .4989 | .4989 | .4989 | .4990 | .4990 |
| 3.1 | .4990 | .4991 | .4991 | .4991 | .4992 | .4992 | .4992 | .4992 | .4993 | .4993 |
| 3.2 | .4993 | .4993 | .4994 | .4994 | .4994 | .4994 | .4994 | .4995 | .4995 | .4995 |
| 3.3 | .4995 | .4995 | .4995 | .4996 | .4996 | .4996 | .4996 | .4996 | .4996 | .4997 |
| 3.4 | .4997 | .4997 | .4997 | .4997 | .4997 | .4997 | .4997 | .4997 | .4997 | .4998 |
| 3.5 | .4998 | .4998 | .4998 | .4998 | .4998 | .4998 | .4998 | .4998 | .4998 | .4998 |
| 3.6 | .4998 | .4998 | .4999 | .4999 | .4999 | .4999 | .4999 | .4999 | .4999 | .4999 |
| 3.7 | .4999 | .4999 | .4999 | .4999 | .4999 | .4999 | .4999 | .4999 | .4999 | .4999 |
| 3.8 | .4999 | .4999 | .4999 | .4999 | .4999 | .4999 | .4999 | .4999 | .4999 | .4999 |
| 3.9 | .5000 | .5000 | .5000 | .5000 | .5000 | .5000 | .5000 | .5000 | .5000 | .5000 |

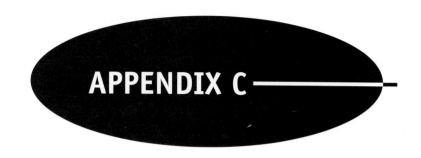

# Apportionment

## C.1  INTRODUCTION

Apportionment is the process of distributing a number of items of equal value among several groups on the basis of the group sizes. The most common example of this is the apportionment of congressional seats to states in the U.S. in proportion to the population of each state, and it was in this context that the apportionment methods presented in this appendix–the Hamilton, Jefferson, Webster, and Hill-Huntington methods–were all originally developed. We describe the steps involved in the implementation of each method and discuss its desirable properties and drawbacks.

## C.2  THE HAMILTON METHOD AND THE QUOTA CRITERION

The Hamilton method was the first to be introduced to apportion congressional seats to the states. While it is the only method, among the four we have included in this appendix, that satisfies a basic principle of fairness known as the quota criterion, the Hamilton method may sometimes lead to paradoxical results.

**EXAMPLE C.1**  Twenty teaching assistants have to be distributed among three large sections of a math course in proportion to the number of students in each as shown in Table C-1.

**Table C-1**

| Section | A | B | C | Totals |
|---|---|---|---|---|
| Number of students | 240 | 150 | 210 | 600 |
| **Final apportionment** | **8** | **5** | **7** | **20** |

Since section $A$'s share of the total number of students is 40 percent, it is reasonable to expect that forty percent of the 20 available teaching assistants should be allocated to section $A$. Similarly, 25 percent of the teaching assistants should be assigned to section $B$ and 35 percent to section $C$. This reasoning would lead to the final apportionment given on the third row of Table C-1.

A slightly different but equivalent way of arriving at this solution is to look at the "number of students per teaching assistant," which is 600/20 = 30, and conclude that since section $A$ has 240 students, its fair share of teaching assistants is 240/30 = 8. Similarly, sections $B$ and $C$ deserve, respectively, 150/30 = 5 and 210/30 = 7 teaching assistants.

The number of students per teaching assistant that we have calculated here is commonly known as the *standard divisor*. In the context of a general apportionment problem, the standard divisor is defined by

$$\text{Standard divisor} = \frac{\text{Total of the group sizes}}{\text{Number of items to be distributed}}$$

The number of items allocated to any individual group is then given by

$$\text{Number of items allocated to a group} = \frac{\text{Size of the group}}{\text{Standard divisor}}$$

It is known as the *standard quota* for that group.

The apportionment problem presented in Example C.1 is rather straightforward due to the fact that the standard quotas here all turn out to be whole numbers. This, however, is rarely the case. By making a minor modification in Example C.1 we arrive at the following situation that is more typical of the kinds of apportionment problems encountered in practice.

**EXAMPLE C.2** Suppose that the number of teaching assistants available in Example C.1 is 21 instead of 20. What is the final apportionment in that case?

Following the same reasoning as in Example C.1, we see that the standard divisor now is $600/21 = 28.57$ and the standard quota for sections $A$, $B$, and $C$ based on this standard divisor are, respectively, $240/28.57 = 8.40$, $150/28.57 = 5.25$, and $210/28.57 = 7.35$. These are given on the third row of Table C-2.

**Table C-2**   (21 items; 3 groups; Hamilton method)

| Section | A | B | C | Totals |
|---|---|---|---|---|
| **Number of Students** | **240** | **150** | **210** | **600** |
| Standard quota: divisor $600/21 = 28.57$ | 8.40 | 5.25 | 7.35 | 21.00 |
| Lower quota | 8 | 5 | 7 | 20 |
| Fractional remainder | 0.40 | 0.25 | 0.35 | 1.00 |
| **Final Hamilton apportionment** | **9** | **5** | **7** | **21** |

We can conclude from these standard quotas that sections $A$, $B$, and $C$, respectively, should receive a minimum of 8, 5, and 7 teaching assistants. These minimums, arrived at by rounding the standard quotas *down*, are known as the *lower standard quotas* or simply *lower quotas*. Note that if a standard quota is a whole number, then the corresponding lower quota would equal the standard quota. Since the lower quotas add up to only 20 in our example, we are faced with an excess of one item and the problem of deciding which of the three groups deserves it the most. The central problem in the area of apportionment essentially is to find a fair way of distributing the excess or left over items once the groups have been allotted their lower quotas.

**Remark:** If in Example C.2 we round the standard quotas *up*, we arrive at the apportionment of 9, 6, and 8, respectively to sections $A$, $B$, and $C$, which add up to more than the available number of teaching assistants. In general, the quotas obtained by rounding *up* the standard quotas are known as the *upper standard quotas* or simply *upper quotas*. If a standard quota is a whole number, then the corresponding upper quota is defined as the standard quota plus 1.

One of the first suggested solutions to the apportionment problem is due to Alexander Hamilton. In the Hamilton method, we first allocate to each group its lower quota. If any items are left over, then we calculate for each group the difference, the standard quota for the group minus its lower quota, known as its *fractional remainder*. The groups are next ranked in descending order of their fractional remainders; and the excess items are then distributed, one-at-a-time, to the groups, starting with the group with the largest fractional remainder.

If we apply the Hamilton method to the problem in Example C.2, we arrive at the fractional remainders shown on the fifth row of Table C-2. Arranging these remainders in descending order we see that any left over teaching assistants should be assigned one-at-a-time to the three sections in the order $A$, $C$, $B$. Since there is only one teaching assistant remaining after the distribution of the lower quotas, section $A$ receives one more and we arrive at the final apportionment shown in Table C-2.

**EXAMPLE C.3**   Apply the Hamilton method to form a committee of 15 students proportionally representing the groups of freshmen, sophomores, juniors, and seniors if the number of students in each group is as in Table C-3.

**Table C-3**   (15 items; 4 groups; Hamilton method)

| Group | Freshman | Junior | Sophomore | Senior | Totals |
|---|---|---|---|---|---|
| **Number of Students** | **258** | **222** | **212** | **185** | **877** |
| Standard quota: divisor 877/15 = 58.47 | 4.41 | 3.80 | 3.63 | 3.16 | 15.00 |
| Lower quota | 4 | 3 | 3 | 3 | 13 |
| Fractional remainder | 0.41 | 0.80 | 0.63 | 0.16 | 2.00 |
| **Final Hamilton apportionment** | **4** | **4** | **4** | **3** | **15** |

The standard divisor in this problem is 877/15 = 58.47.   Dividing each entry in the second row of Table C-3 by 58.47 we get the corresponding standard quotas of row 3.   The lower quotas, given in row 4, add up to 13, leaving 2 committee members to be assigned to the groups.   Ranking the fractional remainders we see that the first of the remaining two committee members must be a junior and the second a sophomore.   This leads to the final apportionment by the Hamilton method given in the last row of Table C-3.

It is not difficult to see that the sum of the standard quotas can never exceed the sum of the lower quotas by more than the number of groups.   Consequently, the final apportionment to any group by the Hamilton method must be either the group's lower quota or its upper quota.   Apportionment methods that have this desirable property are said to satisfy the *quota criterion*.   The Hamilton method thus always satisfies the quota criterion.

## C.3   THE HAMILTON METHOD AND THE POPULATION, ALABAMA, AND NEW STATES PARADOXES

We now present some examples to show that although the Hamilton method satisfies the quota criterion, it may sometimes lead to paradoxical outcomes when there is a change in one or more of the following: the sizes of the groups, the number of items to be apportioned, and the number of groups.

### The Population Paradox

We say that the *population paradox* occurs whenever a reapportionment of items necessitated by a change in group sizes results in a group losing one or more items to another with relatively lower proportional growth.

**EXAMPLE C.4**   One hundred items are to be apportioned among three groups with sizes as shown in Table C-4.   The Hamilton method yields the final apportionment shown on the last row of Table C-4.

**Table C-4**   (100 items, 3 groups, Hamilton method)

| Group | A | B | C | Totals |
|---|---|---|---|---|
| **Size** | **657,000** | **237,000** | **106,000** | **1,000,000** |
| Standard quota: divisor 1,000,000/100 = 10,000 | 65.7 | 23.7 | 10.6 | 100.0 |
| Lower quota | 65 | 23 | 10 | 98 |
| Fractional remainder | 0.7 | 0.7 | 0.6 | 2.0 |
| **Final Hamilton apportionment** | **66** | **24** | **10** | **100** |

Suppose now that all three groups undergo a change in their sizes as shown in Table C-5, with groups *A* and *B* experiencing an increase while group *C* has a decrease in size. The Hamilton method applied to this new situation yields the apportionment shown in the row before the last row of Table C-5. The original apportionment, obtained from Table C-4, is given on the last row of Table C-5.

**Table C-5**    (100 items, 3 groups, Hamilton method)

| Group | A | B | C | Totals |
|---|---|---|---|---|
| **Size** | **660,000** | **245,100** | **104,900** | **1,010,000** |
| Standard quota: divisor 1,010,000/100 = 10,100 | 65.35 | 24.27 | 10.39 | 100.01 |
| Lower quota | 65 | 24 | 10 | 99 |
| Fractional remainder | 0.35 | 0.27 | 0.39 | 1.01 |
| **Final Hamilton apportionment** | **65** | **24** | **11** | **100** |
| Original Hamilton apportionment | 66 | 24 | 10 | 100 |

Comparing the last two rows of Table C-5 we can see that the result is clearly paradoxical in that group *A* with an increase in size has ended up losing an item to group *C* that has actually gone down in size.

## The Alabama Paradox

The *Alabama paradox* is said to occur whenever an increase in the number of items to be apportioned results in the new apportionment to one of the groups being lower than its original apportionment.

**Remark:** The Alabama paradox owes its name to the historical fact that it was discovered in 1981 and that by the Hamilton method, Alabama would have received 8 seats on the House of Representatives if the House had 299 seats whereas it would have received only 7 seats with a House size of 300.

Suppose that the original situation is as in Table C-5, but the number of items to be apportioned increases to 101 from 100. The Hamilton method applied to the new situation is presented in Table C-6. The original apportionment, corresponding to the situation with 100 items (see Table C-5), is given on the last row of Table C-6.

**Table C-6**    (101 items, 3 groups, Hamilton method)

| Group | A | B | C | Totals |
|---|---|---|---|---|
| **Size** | **660,000** | **245,100** | **104,900** | **1,010,000** |
| Standard quota: divisor 1,010,000/101 = 10,000 | 66.00 | 24.51 | 10.49 | 101.00 |
| Lower quota | 66 | 24 | 10 | 100 |
| Fractional remainder | 0.00 | 0.51 | 0.49 | 1.00 |
| **Final Hamilton apportionment** | **66** | **25** | **10** | **101** |
| Original Hamilton apportionment | 65 | 24 | 11 | 100 |

The new apportionment provides an instance of the Alabama paradox since the revised apportionment to group *C* is lower than its original apportionment (see Table C-5).

### The New-States Paradox

The *new-states paradox* is said to occur when the introduction of an additional group along with a reasonable number of additional items to be apportioned results in an unfair shift in the original apportionment.

To see how the Hamilton method may sometimes lead to the new-states paradox, let us start with the situation presented in Table C-5. If we then add an additional group of size 58,000 and six extra items, we are faced with the problem of apportioning 106 items to four groups. Hamilton's method applied to this problem yields the final apportionment shown in Table C-7. The last row of this table gives the apportionment obtained in Table C-5 for 100 items and 3 groups with a total group size of 1,010,000.

Clearly, we have an instance of the new-states paradox here since the introduction of group *D* and a reasonable number of extra items has resulted in group *C* giving up one of its original items to group *A*.

**Table C-7**  (106 items, 4 groups, Hamilton method)

| Group | A | B | C | D | Totals |
|---|---|---|---|---|---|
| **Size** | **660,000** | **245,100** | **104,900** | **58,000** | **1,068,000** |
| Standard quota: divisor 1,068,000/106 = 10,075.47 | 65.51 | 24.33 | 10.41 | 5.76 | 106.01 |
| Lower quota | 65 | 24 | 10 | 5 | 104 |
| Fractional remainder | 0.51 | 0.33 | 0.41 | 0.76 | 2.01 |
| **Final Hamilton apportionment** | **66** | **24** | **10** | **6** | **106** |
| Original Hamilton apportionment | 65 | 24 | 11 | — | 100 |

## C.4  APPORTIONMENT METHODS THAT AVOID PARADOXES

Several modifications of the Hamilton method have been suggested to eliminate the occurrence of these paradoxical results. The three most important of these–the Jefferson, Webster, and Hill-Huntington methods are presented below. These differ from the Hamilton method in that they sometimes use modified divisors in addition to the standard divisor and employ different rounding procedures to arrive at the final apportionment. It can be shown that the population, Alabama, and new-states paradoxes cannot occur with any of these three methods.

### The Jefferson Method

In the Jefferson method, we first calculate the standard divisor and the standard quotas as in the Hamilton method. If the lower quotas add up to the total number of items to be apportioned, then these become the final apportionment by the Jefferson method. If, on the other hand, the sum of the lower quotas is strictly less than the number of items to be apportioned, then we choose a number less than the standard divisor, known as a *modified divisor*, and calculate the corresponding modified quota for each group using the formula

$$\text{Modified quota} = \frac{\text{Group size}}{\text{Modified divisor}}$$

These modified quotas rounded down are known as the *lower modified quotas*. If the lower modified quotas add up to the number of items to be apportioned, we are done and these become the final apportionment by the Jefferson method. If the sum of the lower modified quotas is less than the number of items to be apportioned, we choose a second modified divisor smaller than the first and repeat the process. If, on the other hand, the sum is more than the number of items, we choose a second modified divisor larger than the first and repeat the steps of getting modified quotas and lower modified quotas. We thus continue the process, choosing modified divisors by trial and error depending upon the results from the previous stage, until we arrive at lower modified quotas that add up to the number of items to be apportioned. The lower modified quotas at the last stage become the final apportionment according to the Jefferson method.

**EXAMPLE C.5**   Consider the situation treated in Example C.2. We have 21 items to be apportioned and we see from Table C-8 that the lower quotas add up to only 20. The standard divisor is 28.57 so let us try 26 as the modified divisor. Note that we are trying a modified divisor smaller than the standard divisor. The modified quotas corresponding to this modified divisor are given on the fifth row of Table C-8. Since the modified lower quotas add up to 22 we repeat the process by choosing now the modified divisor 26.5 (larger than 26.) The resulting lower modified quotas add up to 21 and they are therefore the final apportionment by the Jefferson method shown on the last row of Table C-8.

**Table C-8**   (21 items, 3 groups, Jefferson method)

| Section | A | B | C | Totals |
|---|---|---|---|---|
| **Number of Students** | **240** | **150** | **210** | **600** |
| Standard quota: divisor $600/21 = 28.57$ | 8.40 | 5.25 | 7.35 | 21.00 |
| Lower quota | 8 | 5 | 7 | 20 |
| Modified quota: divisor 26 | 9.23 | 5.77 | 8.08 | 23.08 |
| Lower modified quota: Jefferson | 9 | 5 | 8 | 22 |
| Modified quota: divisor 26.5 | 9.06 | 5.66 | 7.92 | 22.64 |
| Lower modified quota: Jefferson | 9 | 5 | 7 | 21 |
| **Final Jefferson apportionment** | **9** | **5** | **7** | **21** |

The trial-and-error process involved in the Jefferson method naturally leads to the question of the uniqueness of the final Jefferson apportionment. For instance, in the above example if we start with 28 as the first modified divisor (instead of 26) and follow a different sequence of modified divisors to a set of lower modified quotas that add up to 21 (the number of items to be apportioned), would we arrive at the same final Jefferson apportionment? Does the final result depend on the sequence of modified divisors employed? Fortunately, it can be shown that no matter what path of modified divisors is followed, the final Jefferson apportionment would always be the same.

The question of uniqueness is also relevant to the Webster and Hill-Huntington methods, presented below. They also use a trial-and-error process of finding a modified divisor that gives a set of rounded quotas adding up to the number of items to be apportioned. Nevertheless, as with the Jefferson method, the final apportionments for both of these methods are independent of the sequence of modified divisors employed.

**The Webster Method**

The steps involved in the Webster method are very similar to those in the Jefferson method except for the way the modified quotas are rounded off. In the Webster method, the standard quotas and modified quotas are *rounded to the nearest integer* rather than always being rounded down as in the Hamilton and Jefferson methods. In other words, a standard or modified quota would be rounded down if its fractional part is less than 0.5 and rounded up otherwise. For example, the numbers 11.2, 0.7, and 3.5 would be rounded off, respectively, to 11, 1, and 4.

**EXAMPLE C.6**  Let us apply the Webster method to the apportionment problem of Example C.2. We see from Table C-8 that the standard quotas for this problem are 8.40, 5.25, and 7.35. When these are rounded off using the Webster method we get the rounded quotas 8, 5, and 7, with a total below 21, the number of items to be apportioned. This calls for a modified divisor less than the standard divisor, 28.57. It is clear from Table C-9 that the modified divisors 26 and 26.5 are both too small since they lead to rounded quotas with total above 21. Trial and error leads to the modified divisor 28.2 that happens to give rounded quotas with a sum of 21 (see Table C-9.) Note that the trial-and-error process involved here is similar to the one in the Jefferson method.

**Table C-9**   (21 items, 3 groups, Webster method)

| Section | A | B | C | Totals |
|---|---|---|---|---|
| **Number of Students** | **240** | **150** | **210** | **600** |
| Standard quota: divisor 600/21 = 28.57 | 8.40 | 5.25 | 7.35 | 21.00 |
| Rounded standard quota: Webster | 8 | 5 | 7 | 20 |
| Modified quota: divisor 26 | 9.23 | 5.77 | 8.08 | 23.08 |
| Rounded modified quota: Webster | 9 | 6 | 8 | 23 |
| Modified quota: divisor 26.5 | 9.06 | 5.66 | 7.92 | 22.64 |
| Rounded modified quota: Webster | 9 | 6 | 8 | 23 |
| Modified quota: divisor 28.2 | 8.51 | 5.32 | 7.45 | 21.28 |
| Rounded modified quota: Webster | 9 | 5 | 7 | 21 |
| **Final Webster apportionment** | **9** | **5** | **7** | **21** |

### The Hill-Huntington Method

The Hill-Huntington method is also very similar to the Jefferson method except for the way the standard and modified quotas are rounded. The rounding scheme used here involves the concept of the geometric mean of two nonnegative numbers, $a$ and $b$, which is defined as the square root of their product, $\sqrt{a \cdot b}$. Specifically, given a standard or modified quota, the Hill-Huntington method compares it to the geometric mean of its lower and upper quotas and rounds the quota down if it is less than this geometric mean and rounds the quota up otherwise.

**EXAMPLE C.7**  Let us apply the Hill-Huntington method to the apportionment problem of Example C.2. The details are presented in Table C-10. We start with the standard quotas and round each quota by comparing it to an appropriate geometric mean. To see how the quotas are rounded off, consider the standard quota, 8.40, for group $A$. The geometric mean of the corresponding lower modified quota, 8, and the upper modified quota, 9, is $\sqrt{8 \times 9} = 8.49$ (given on the fourth row of Table C-10 under group $A$). Since the standard quota 8.40 is less than 8.49, the rounded standard quota by the Hill-Huntington method would be 8 (obtained by rounding down 8.40). Since the three rounded standard quotas add up to only 20 (less than 21) we have tried the modified divisor 28 (less than the standard divisor, 28.7). Note that the modified quota for group $C$ corresponding to 28 (see the sixth row of Table C-10 under group $C$) is rounded up to 8 since 7.50 is greater than 7.48. It can be seen that the modified divisor 28 has turned out to be too small (the rounded modified quotas add up to 22, which is larger than 21, the number of items to be apportioned). Our next, and final, trial is with the larger modified divisor 28.2.

**Table C-10**  (21 items, 3 groups, Hill-Huntington method)

| Section | A | B | C | Totals |
|---|---|---|---|---|
| **Number of Students** | **240** | **150** | **210** | **600** |
| Standard quota: divisor 600/21 = 28.57 | 8.40 | 5.25 | 7.35 | 21.00 |
| Geometric mean | 8.49 | 5.48 | 7.48 | — |
| Rounded standard quota: Hill-Huntington | 8 | 5 | 7 | 20 |
| Modified quota: divisor 28 | 8.57 | 5.36 | 7.50 | 21.43 |
| Geometric mean | 8.49 | 5.48 | 7.48 | — |
| Rounded modified quota: Hill-Huntington | 9 | 5 | 8 | 22 |
| Modified quota: divisor 28.2 | 8.51 | 5.31 | 7.45 | 21.27 |
| Geometric mean | 8.49 | 5.48 | 7.48 | — |
| Rounded modified quota: Hill-Huntington | 9 | 5 | 7 | 21 |
| **Final Hill-Huntington apportionment** | **9** | **5** | **7** | **21** |

## C.5   THE JEFFERSON, WEBSTER, HILL-HUNTINGTON METHODS AND THE QUOTA CRITERION

As mentioned earlier, the Jefferson, Webster, and Hill-Huntington methods were all motivated by the fact that the Hamilton method led to various paradoxical results.   It can indeed be shown that they do avoid the Alabama, population, and new-states paradoxes.   Unfortunately, however, as the following example shows, all three of these methods may sometimes violate the quota criterion!

**EXAMPLE C.8**   Suppose that 100 items have to be apportioned among four groups with sizes as shown in Table C-11($a$). Tables C-11($b$), C-11($c$), and C-11($d$) summarize the solution to the apportionment problem using, respectively, the Jefferson, Webster, and Hill-Huntington method.   Recall that an apportionment method would be in violation of the quota criterion if the allocation to any group under the method is other than the lower or upper quota for that group.   In the current situation, it follows from the lower and upper quotas derived in Table C-11($a$) that a method would be in violation of the quota criterion if its allocation to group $A$ is neither 95 nor 96.   We see from the results that this turns out to be the case with the Jefferson (final apportionment to group $A$: 97), Webster (final apportionment to group $A$: 94), and Hill-Huntington (final apportionment to group $A$: 94) methods.

**Table C-11($a$)**  (100 items, 4 groups, Hamilton method)

| Group | A | B | C | D | Totals |
|---|---|---|---|---|---|
| **Size** | **855** | **16** | **15** | **14** | **900** |
| Standard quota: divisor 900/100 = 9.00 | 95.00 | 1.78 | 1.67 | 1.56 | 100.01 |
| **Lower quota** | **95** | **1** | **1** | **1** | **98** |
| **Upper quota** | **96** | **2** | **2** | **2** | **102** |

**Table C-11($b$)**   (100 items, 4 groups, Jefferson method)

| Group | A | B | C | D | Totals |
|---|---|---|---|---|---|
| **Size** | **855** | **16** | **15** | **14** | **900** |
| Standard quota: divisor 900/100 = 9.00 | 95.00 | 1.78 | 1.67 | 1.56 | 100.01 |
| Lower quota | 95 | 1 | 1 | 1 | 98 |
| Modified quota: divisor 8.8 | 97.16 | 1.82 | 1.70 | 1.59 | 102.27 |
| Lower modified quota: Jefferson | 97 | 1 | 1 | 1 | 100 |
| **Final Jefferson apportionment** | **97** | **1** | **1** | **1** | **100** |

**Table C-11($c$)**   (100 items, 4 groups, Webster method)

| Group | A | B | C | D | Totals |
|---|---|---|---|---|---|
| **Size** | **855** | **16** | **15** | **14** | **900** |
| Standard quota: divisor 900/100 = 9.00 | 95.00 | 1.78 | 1.67 | 1.56 | 100.01 |
| Rounded standard quota: Webster | 95 | 2 | 2 | 2 | 101 |
| Modified quota: divisor 9.1 | 93.96 | 1.76 | 1.65 | 1.54 | 98.91 |
| Rounded modified quota: Webster | 94 | 2 | 2 | 2 | 100 |
| **Final Webster apportionment** | **94** | **2** | **2** | **2** | **100** |

**Table C-11($d$)**   (100 items, 4 groups, Hill-Huntington method)

| Group | A | B | C | D | Totals |
|---|---|---|---|---|---|
| **Size** | **855** | **16** | **15** | **14** | **900** |
| Standard quota: divisor 900/100 = 9.00 | 95.00 | 1.78 | 1.67 | 1.56 | 100.01 |
| Geometric mean | 95.50 | 1.41 | 1.41 | 1.41 | — |
| Modified quota: divisor 9.1 | 93.96 | 1.76 | 1.65 | 1.54 | 98.91 |
| Geometric mean | 93.50 | 1.41 | 1.41 | 1.41 | — |
| Rounded modified quota: Hill-Huntington | 94 | 2 | 2 | 2 | 100 |
| **Final Hill-Huntington apportionment** | **94** | **2** | **2** | **2** | **100** |

## C.6   THE BALINSKI-YOUNG IMPOSSIBILITY THEOREM

We have seen that the Hamilton method satisfies the quota criterion but produces several paradoxical results.   The other three methods, on the other hand, are free of these paradoxes but at times violate the quota criterion.   Undoubtedly, it would be most desirable to have a method that both satisfies the quota criterion and is free of all paradoxes.   But, as the following result by Michael Balinski and H. Peyton Young cautions, all attempts to produce such a flawless method are doomed to fail.

**The Balinski-Young Impossibility Theorem:**   It is mathematically impossible to devise an apportionment method that avoids all paradoxical results and yet obeys the quota criterion.

# Solved Problems

## STANDARD DIVISOR, QUOTAS, FRACTIONAL REMAINDERS

**C.1.**   Suppose $n = 100$ items are to be apportioned among the groups $A$, $B$, and $C$ with respective sizes 1540, 2130, and 5210.          (a)   Find the standard divisor $d$.          (b)   For the groups $A$, $B$, $C$, find ($i$) standard quotas, ($ii$) lower and upper quotas, ($iii$) fractional remainders.

($a$) Standard divisor $= \dfrac{\text{Total of the group sizes}}{\text{Number of items to be distributed}} = \dfrac{1540 + 2130 + 5210}{100} = \dfrac{8880}{100} = 88.8$.

($b$)   ($i$) Standard quota = Group size/standard divisor.   Thus: for $A$: 1540/88.8 = 17.34; for $B$: 2130/88.8 = 23.99; for $C$: 5210/88.8 = 58.67.

($ii$) Recall that the lower quota for a group is obtained by rounding *down* its standard quota and its upper quota by rounding *up* its standard quota.   Thus:
Lower quota: for $A = 17$, for $B = 23$, for $C = 58$
Upper quota: for $A = 18$, for $B = 24$, for $C = 59$

($iii$) The fractional remainder for any group is defined as its standard quota minus its lower quota (that is, the fraction part of its standard quota).   Therefore, for $A = 0.34$, for $B = 0.99$, for $C = 0.67$.

**C.2.**   Suppose $n = 35$ items are to be apportioned among the groups $A$, $B$, $C$, and $D$ with respective sizes 385, 473, 215, and 544.          (a)   Find the standard divisor $d$.          (b)   For the groups $A$, $B$, $C$, $D$, find ($i$) standard quotas, ($ii$) lower and upper quotas, ($iii$) fractional remainders.

($a$) Standard divisor $= \dfrac{385 + 473 + 215 + 544}{35} = 46.20$.

($b$)   ($i$) Standard quotas = Group size/standard divisor.   Thus: for $A = 385/46.2 = 8.33$, for $B = 10.24$; for $C = 4.65$; for $D = 11.77$.

($ii$) Recall that the lower quota for a group is obtained by rounding *down* its standard quota and its upper quota by rounding *up* its standard quota.   Thus:

Lower quota: for $A = 8$, for $B = 10$, for $C = 4$, for $D = 11$
Upper quota: for $A = 9$, for $B = 11$, for $C = 5$, for $D = 12$

($iii$) The fractional remainder for any group is defined as its standard quota minus its lower quota (that is, the fraction part of its standard quota).   Therefore, for $A = 0.33$, for $B = 0.24$, for $C = 0.65$, for $D = 0.77$.

## HAMILTON AND JEFFERSON METHODS

**C.3.**   Use the Hamilton method to find the apportionments for the groups in          (a)   Problem C.1, (b)   Problem C.2.

(a)  The sum of the lower quotas is 98 and there are 100 items to be apportioned.  The 2 extra items are given to the two groups with the largest fractional remainders, $B$ and $C$.  Hence the apportionment: $A = 17$, $B = 24$, $C = 59$.

(b)  The sum of the lower quotas is 33 and there are 35 items to be apportioned.  The 2 extra items are given to the two groups with the largest fractional remainders, $C$ and $D$.  Hence $A = 8$, $B = 10$, $C = 5$, $D = 12$.

**C.4.**  Find the apportionments for the groups in Problem C.1 by the Jefferson method.

The results are presented in the table below.  Since the lower quotas add up to only 98, the modified divisor 88 (less than the standard divisor, 88.8) was tried.

(100 items, 3 groups, Jefferson method)

| Group | $A$ | $B$ | $C$ | Totals |
|---|---|---|---|---|
| **Size** | **1540** | **2130** | **5210** | **8880** |
| Standard quota: divisor 8880/100 = 88.8 | 17.34 | 23.99 | 58.67 | 100.00 |
| Lower quota | 17 | 23 | 58 | 98 |
| Modified quota: divisor 88 | 17.50 | 24.20 | 59.20 | 100.90 |
| Lower modified quota: Jefferson | 17 | 24 | 59 | 100 |
| **Final Jefferson apportionment** | **17** | **24** | **59** | **100** |

**C.5.**  Find the apportionments for the groups in Problem C.2 by the Jefferson method.

The results are presented below.  Note the trial and error process involved in the selection of successive modified divisors.  Since the lower quotas add up to less than the number of items to be apportioned (35), we try a modified divisor (43) less than the standard divisor (46.20).  But the lower modified quotas with this divisor add up to more than 35, so we next try a modified divisor (43.5) slightly larger than 43.  As can be seen below, this was not the last step in our trial-and-error process.

(35 items, 4 groups, Jefferson method)

| Group | $A$ | $B$ | $C$ | $D$ | Totals |
|---|---|---|---|---|---|
| **Size** | **385** | **473** | **215** | **544** | **1617** |
| Standard quota: divisor 1617/35 = 46.20 | 8.33 | 10.24 | 4.65 | 11.77 | 34.99 |
| Lower quota | 8 | 10 | 4 | 11 | 33 |
| Modified quota: divisor 43 | 8.95 | 11.00 | 5.00 | 12.65 | 37.60 |
| Lower modified quota: Jefferson | 8 | 11 | 5 | 12 | 36 |
| Modified quota: divisor 43.5 | 8.85 | 10.87 | 4.94 | 12.51 | 37.17 |
| Lower modified quota: Jefferson | 8 | 10 | 4 | 12 | 34 |
| Modified quota: divisor 43.03125 | 8.95 | 10.99 | 5.00 | 12.65 | 37.59 |
| Lower modified quota: Jefferson | 8 | 11 | 4 | 12 | 35 |
| **Final Jefferson apportionment** | **8** | **10** | **5** | **12** | **35** |

## WEBSTER AND HILL-HUNTINGTON METHODS

**C.6.** Find the apportionments for the groups in Problem C.1 by the Webster method.

The results are presented below. There was no need to try a modified divisor in this case since the standard quotas rounded by the Webster method (i.e., rounded, in the conventional manner, to the closest integer) add up to the total number of items to be apportioned.

(100 items, 3 groups, Webster method)

| Group | A | B | C | Totals |
|---|---|---|---|---|
| **Size** | **1540** | **2130** | **5210** | **8880** |
| Standard quota: divisor 8880/100 = 88.80 | 17.34 | 23.99 | 58.67 | 100.00 |
| Rounded quota: Webster | 17 | 24 | 59 | 100 |
| **Final Webster apportionment** | **17** | **24** | **59** | **100** |

**C.7.** Find the apportionments for the groups in Problem C.2 by the Webster method.

The results are presented below. There was no need to try a modified divisor in this case since the standard quotas rounded by the Webster method (i.e., rounded, in the conventional manner, to the closest integer) add up to the total number of items to be apportioned.

(35 items, 4 groups, Webster method)

| Group | A | B | C | D | Totals |
|---|---|---|---|---|---|
| **Size** | **385** | **473** | **215** | **544** | **1617** |
| Standard quota: divisor 1617/35 = 46.20 | 8.33 | 10.24 | 4.65 | 11.77 | 34.99 |
| Rounded quota: Webster | 8 | 10 | 5 | 12 | 35 |
| **Final Webster apportionment** | **8** | **10** | **5** | **12** | **35** |

**C.8.** Find the apportionments for the groups in Problem C.1 by the Hill-Huntington method.

The results are presented below. There was no need to try a modified divisor since the standard quotas rounded by the Hill-Huntington method (i.e., rounded using the geometric mean of the lower and upper standard or modified quotas) add up to the total number of items to be apportioned.

(100 items, 3 groups, Hill-Huntington method)

| Group | A | B | C | Totals |
|---|---|---|---|---|
| **Size** | **1540** | **2130** | **5210** | **8880** |
| Standard quota: divisor 8880/100 = 88.8 | 17.34 | 23.99 | 58.67 | 100.00 |
| Geometric mean | 17.49 | 23.49 | 58.50 | — |
| Rounded quota: Hill-Huntington | 17 | 24 | 59 | 100 |
| **Final Hill-Huntington apportionment** | **17** | **24** | **59** | **100** |

**C.9.** Find the apportionments for the groups in Problem C.2 by the Hill-Huntington method.

The results are presented below. There was no need to try a modified divisor in this case since the standard quotas rounded by the Hill-Huntington method (i.e., rounded using the geometric mean of the lower and upper standard or modified quotas) add up to the total number of items to be apportioned.

(35 items, 4 groups, Hill-Huntington method)

| Group | A | B | C | D | Totals |
|---|---|---|---|---|---|
| **Size** | **385** | **473** | **215** | **544** | **1617** |
| Standard quota: divisor 1617/35 = 46.20 | 8.33 | 10.24 | 4.65 | 11.77 | 34.99 |
| Geometric mean | 8.49 | 10.49 | 4.47 | 11.49 | — |
| Rounded quota: Hill-Huntington | 8 | 10 | 5 | 12 | 35 |
| **Final Hill-Huntington apportionment** | **8** | **10** | **5** | **12** | **35** |

# Supplementary Problems

**C.10.** Thirteen seats on the governing board of a condominium association are to be apportioned among the three buildings in the condominium complex. The numbers of units and occupants in the buildings are given in the following table.

| Building | Number of occupied units | Total number of occupants |
|---|---|---|
| A | 104 | 440 |
| B | 256 | 625 |
| C | 630 | 712 |

Use the Hamilton method to apportion the seats to the three buildings:

(a) on the basis of the number of occupied units in each building,  (b) on the basis of the number of occupants in each building.

**C.11.** Using the Jefferson method find a suitable modified divisor and the apportionment for the groups in:
(a) Problem C.10(a),  (b) Problem C.10(b).

**C.12.** Using the Webster method find a suitable modified divisor and the apportionment for the groups in:
(a) Problem C.10(a),  (b) Problem C.10(b).

**C.13.** Using the Hill-Huntington method find a suitable modified divisor and the apportionment for the groups in:  (a) Problem C.10(a),  (b) Problem C.10(b).

**C.14.** Suppose 100 items are to be apportioned among groups A, B, C, and D with respective sizes 8785, 126, 125, and 124.  (a) Solve this apportionment problem using the methods of (i) Jefferson, (ii) Webster, (iii) Hill-Huntington.  (b) Verify that the quota criterion is violated by all three methods.

**POPULATION, ALABAMA, AND NEW-STATES PARADOXES**

**C.15.**   In Problem C.10(*a*), suppose that in one year's time the number of occupied units increases to 1034 and each of the three buildings undergoes a change as follows:

        *A*: 120 occupied units ($+15.4\%$), B: 236 occupied units ($-7.8\%$), *C*: 678 occupied units ($+7.6\%$)

Suppose that the governing board stays at 13.        (*a*)   Find the new apportionment using the Hamilton method.        (*b*)   Why is this an example of the population paradox?

**C.16.**   In Problem C.10(*a*), suppose size of the governing board has been increased by 1 to 14.        (*a*)   Find the new apportionment using the Hamilton method.        (*b*)   Why is this an example of the Alabama paradox?

**C.17.**   In Problem C.10(*a*), suppose that building *D*, with 300 occupied units, has been added to the condominium complex and the size of the governing board has been increased from 13 to 17.        (*a*)   Find the new apportionment using the Hamilton method.        (*b*)   Why is this an example of the new-states paradox?

# Answers to Supplementary Problems

**C.10.**   Hamilton:        (*a*)   2, 3, 8, 13;        (*b*) 3, 5, 5, 13

**C.11.**   Jefferson:        (*a*)   divisor = 66: 1, 3, 9, 13;        (*b*)   divisor = 125: 3, 5, 5, 13

**C.12.**   Webster:        (*a*)   divisor = 74: 1, 3, 9, 13;        (*b*)   divisor 136.69: 3, 5, 5, 13

**C.13.**   Hill-Huntington:        (*a*)   divisor = 74: 1, 3, 9, 13;        (*b*)   divisor = 136.69: 3, 5, 5, 13

**C.14.**   (*a*)   All three yield the apportionment 97, 1, 1, 1.        (*b*)   For *A*, lower quota = 95 and upper quota = 96. Thus 97 items for *A* violates the quota criterion.

**C.15.**   (*a*)   1, 3, 9.        (*b*)   *A* lost one member while *C* gained one member and *B* remained the same even though *A* had a larger percent gain than *C* and *B* had a loss in occupied units.

**C.16.**   (*a*)   1, 4, 9.        (*b*)   *B* lost one member even though the number of members increased.

**C.17.**   (*a*)   1, 4, 8, 4.        (*b*)   Building *A* has lost one representative on the board to *B*.

# INDEX